Institutional Investors

Institutional Investors

E. Philip Davis and Benn Steil

The MIT Press
Cambridge, Massachusetts
London, England

This book was set in Palatino in '3B2' by Asco Typesetters, Hong Kong.
Printed and bound in the United States of America.

Library of Congress Cataloging-in-Publication Data

Davis, E. P.
    Institutional investors / E. Philip Davis and Benn Steil.
      p. cm.
    Includes bibliographical references and index.
    ISBN 0-262-04192-8
    1. Institutional investments. I. Steil, Benn. II. Title.
HG4521 .D14   2001
332.67'154—dc21

                               2001030280

Contents

Tables

Acknowledgments

Funding for the project, administered by the Royal Institute of International Affairs (RIIA), was provided by the following:

- Bridge Trading Technologies
- Instinet Corporation
- State Street Bank and Trust Company

The authors are grateful for their support and encouragement.

The authors thank K. Begley, F. Betson, G. Bishop, J. Bisignano, D. Blake, H. Blommestein, P. Booth, H. Bradley, R. Brealey, P. Bull, G. Clark, O. de Bandt, J. Dermine, I. Domowitz, M. Edey, F. Edwards, P. Fortune, R. Holzmann, P. Horne, E. Jackson, R. Kopcke, J. Lomax, J. Lund, H. Picton, D. Plihon, J. Priesemann, A. Rajan, H. Reisen, D. Rule, K. de Ryck, S. Salo, G. Schinasi, H. Stark, G. Tamburi, and A. Wojnilower for comments, advice, and invaluable assistance. They also thank Phuong Anh Le for research support.

The views expressed in the text are entirely those of the authors.

About the Authors

E. Philip Davis is Professor of Economics and Finance at Brunel University in West London and also a Research Associate of the LSE Financial Markets Group, Associate Fellow of the Royal Institute of International Affairs, and Research Fellow of the Pensions Institute at Birkbeck College, London. Davis was previously employed at the Bank of England and the European Central Bank. E-mail: e_philip_davis@msn.com, website: www.geocities.com/e_philip_davis

Benn Steil is Senior Fellow and Linda J. Wachner Chair in Foreign Economic Policy at the Council on Foreign Relations in New York. Much of the research for this book was carried out while he was Director of the International Economics Programme at the Royal Institute of International Affairs (RIIA) in London. He is currently also the Editor of *International Finance* (Blackwell Publishers), a member of the European Shadow Financial Regulatory Committee, and a member of the Advisory Board of the European Capital Markets Institute. E-mail: bsteil@cfr.org, website: www.foreignrelations.org/public/resource.cgi?pers!1637

Introduction and Executive Summary

Institutional investors are a permanent feature of the financial landscape, and their growth will continue at a similar, and perhaps faster pace. The factors that underpin their development are far from transitory and in many cases have only just started having an impact. The behavioral characteristics of institutional investors, therefore, will be an increasingly important determinant of domestic and international financial market conditions, and the implications for financial market stability warrant serious consideration.

Bank for International Settlements, Annual Report (1998), p. 95.

Undoubtedly, one of the most important developments in financial markets in recent years has been the institutionalization of saving associated with the growth of pension funds, life insurance companies, and mutual funds. This has entailed an increasing proportion of household saving being managed by professional portfolio managers instead of being directly invested in the securities markets on the one hand or held in the form of bank deposits on the other.

Two aspects of institutionalization are covered in this book: institutional investment and asset management (also called fund management[1]). Institutional investors may be defined as specialized financial institutions that manage savings collectively on behalf of small investors toward a specific objective in terms of acceptable risk, return maximization, and maturity of claims. Asset management defines the process whereby assets collected by institutional investors are actually invested in the capital markets. Whereas conceptually these aspects are often bundled together, in fact the asset

---

1. We use the terms "asset management" and "fund management" interchangeably in the text. Other expressions that are often used broadly for the same function include "investment management," "money management," and "portfolio management."

manager may or may not be a part of the institutional investor in a legal sense. In effect, asset management may be either internal or external to the institution itself.

Given the twin separations between beneficiary and institutional investor and between institutional investor and asset manager, important principal-agent issues may arise. Self-interested behavior of agents (such as asset managers) may not always be fully in line with the interests of those bearing the risks (such as the corporate sponsors or ultimate beneficiaries). These agency problems give rise in turn to some of the distinctive effects of institutional investors on capital markets. For example, throughout the book, the underlying presumption is that institutional investors operate in efficient capital markets, and indeed their activities may improve market efficiency. However, we also highlight some of the literature on capital market inefficiencies and financial instability more generally, and we seek to probe the possible relationship of the behavior of institutional investors—including that linked to principal-agent issues—to such phenomena.

Much of the analysis focuses on the Anglo-Saxon countries (notably the United States and the United Kingdom) because institutional investor growth has been most marked there, because regulation is less restrictive, and because most academic research has focused on these markets. In a sense, these countries may prove models for the rest of the world. Whereas in the Anglo-Saxon countries the markets for the various types of institutional saving are rather mature, in Continental Europe and to a lesser extent in Japan there is considerable scope for further development of institutional investment. Both areas are still dominated by pay-as-you-go social security, which will ultimately prove unviable. Moreover, Continental Europe is undergoing the structural break of Monetary Union, which by reducing barriers to entry and increasing the integration of markets is providing fertile ground for further development of institutional investors.[2] Emerging market economies also have considerable scope for developing institutional investor sectors, as the example of Chile has shown.

The first three parts of the book, comprising chapters 1–6, trace the origin, nature, and implications of the changes summarized by the term "institutionalization," drawing on the experience of the major

---

2. See Davis (1998d, 1998g, 1999a, 1999b).

industrial countries. These changes are considered to be among the key influences on the evolution of financial structure and behavior in recent years. Given that future growth of institutional investors is virtually inevitable in the light of the aging of the population, the resulting effects are likely to become even more marked in future years. The fourth part of the book, comprising chapters 7 and 8, examines the interrelationship between institutional trading and evolving market structures, focusing in particular on equities.

The text is complemented by a glossary.

In the first chapter, we probe reasons for the **development of institutional investors**. We present data to characterize the growth and size of institutional investors. Then we assess reasons for their growth. Was expansion due to supply-side factors that improved the competitiveness of institutional investors, or were demand factors, which increase the need of the household sector for institutional saving, more prominent? Which was most crucial? Key points raised include the following:

• Institutional investors have grown strongly in the past decades, with their claims being valued at 100% of G-7 gross domestic product (GDP). They also account for 30% of financial intermediation and 30% of household sector assets. These figures are much higher in countries such as the United States and the United Kingdom, where institutional assets are almost twice GDP. Convergence of the rest of the G-7 on these levels would accordingly entail massive further expansion of institutional investment.

• The evolution of financial systems is appropriately analyzed not only in terms of the traditional view of a shift from banking through markets to a securitized phase, but also in terms of the functions of the financial system. These are functions that the financial system is always called on to fulfill, regardless of its institutional form. They thus provide a set of constant features underlying both long-term developments and more recent trends. Evolution of institutional forms and of financial structure such as the growth of institutional investors may be seen as a form of adaptation and improvement in the ways these functions are fulfilled, under pressure from competitive forces.

• In this context, the phenomenon of institutionalization to date can be traced to various supply and demand factors, often linked directly to a better performance of the functions of the financial system by institutional investors, which have made saving via such institutions attractive to households. These include in particular supply-side factors such as ease of diversification, improved corporate control, deregulation, ability to take advantage of technological developments, and enhanced competition. Some demand-side elements also help to explain institutional growth, notably demographic developments, growing wealth, and the difficulties of social security pensions.

• A key factor in a forward-looking sense will be demographic change linked to difficulties of social security pension systems, which will undoubtedly lead to a vast expansion of institutional investing in the future. In particular, in many countries (notably in Continental Europe), future demographic pressures on pay-as-you go social security are likely to lead governments to seek to stimulate further growth of private pensions as a substitute for social security.

The second chapter looks at the **performance of asset managers**. It first outlines the broad influences on portfolio management behavior, both in general and for particular types of institutions, before assessing performance successively at a micro level (how well do managers perform relative to each other and compared to passive indexation?) and at a macro level (what influences can be detected affecting average portfolios, and what was their effect on performance?):

• Portfolio management involves a number of tasks, the most crucial of which are asset allocation (portfolio allocation across instruments) and security selection (choice of specific instruments within a given category). There are a large number of elements in common for all types of asset management, but specialized considerations—based on the nature of liabilities—also apply. The contrasting nature of liabilities may prompt investment behavior that not only differs sharply between institutions but also may appear contrary to the predictions of a paradigm assuming simple optimization of a trade-off between risk and return.

• Results of academic studies of both mutual funds and pension funds in the United States and the United Kingdom show that active security selection tends to be value deducting, although there may be positive returns to asset allocation. The implication is that use of index funds is optimal. Internal management—whereby the institutional investor also conducts asset management—is also found to be superior to external. More generally, the results support the argument that principal-agent problems are important in asset management (since internal managers are subject to closer monitoring).

• Analysis of asset holdings and returns to pension fund sectors show that a myriad of influences can be identified affecting portfolios. The outcomes differ markedly across countries in terms of rates of return and risk in a way that is dependent on both these factors affecting asset allocation and the returns on assets themselves. Conclusions concerning optimality of strategies cannot, however, be simply derived from data on returns and risks, given the additional liability-based constraints (such as the need to hedge against shortfall risk) affecting some sectors.

The third and fourth chapters examine the **industrial structure and dynamics of asset management**. The third chapter assesses what sort of industry asset management is. In this context, we present a framework for assessing the nature of competition for financial institutions, in the light of which we characterize the nature of competition for asset managers. Detailed examinations of pricing behavior and the industrial structure of the industry are undertaken, with a particular focus on the United States, the United Kingdom, and Continental Europe. Reasons for the quite marked differences are suggested:

• Asset management sectors differ sharply between the major Organization for Economic Cooperation and Development (OECD) countries. There is a notable divide between the Anglo-Saxon countries on the one hand and Continental Europe on the other, in terms of the scope of competition. This is reflected in higher fees and a lesser focus on performance in the latter. There are also marked contrasts between the United States and the United Kingdom in terms of active wholesale asset management. In the former, specialist managers are dominant, whereas in the latter, it is the balanced managers who have up until now tended to predominate. The retail (mutual fund) and generic (nondiscretionary wholesale) sectors in the United States and the United Kingdom are much more comparable.

• The generic management sectors in the United States and the United Kingdom, as well as balanced wholesale management in the

United Kingdom, resemble contestable markets: Large firms predominate because of economies of scale, but potential competition
and low sunk costs limit fees to a competitive level. Specialized
wholesale management in the United States and retail asset management in the United States and the United Kingdom are better
characterized as monopolistic competition, with rather few economies of scale or entry barriers and a proliferation of firms with differentiated products.

• Continental systems are typically oligopolies, partly as a consequence of regulatory factors but also because of structural entry
barriers entailing significant sunk costs of entry to the market (e.g.,
owing to control of channels of distribution by incumbent banks).
Market power means that the firms concerned obtain higher profits
than they would in a free market. Companies sponsoring pension
funds on the one hand and consumers on the other are unlikely to
remain content with such structures, given the shortfall in performance. Successful penetration of the market by foreign entrants that
appears to be underway in Japan may be a forerunner of similar
trends in Continental European countries that are currently dominated by local banks.

In the fourth chapter, **influences on the future of asset management** are analyzed in terms of both industry analyses and the results
of a questionnaire that was sent to global asset managers.

• Whereas prospects for institutional asset management are favorable, a number of analysts anticipate marked structural change.
Indeed, a global merger wave is already underway. There are harbingers of potentially major shifts in the organization and behavior
of the industry in the United States and the United Kingdom, under
pressure from factors such as the shift to defined contribution pensions. There may be a marked impact of European Monetary Union
on European sectors. There is potential for globalization of the
industry, but owing to the numerous entry barriers to foreign markets and diseconomies of scale in giant firms, this outcome is by no
means certain.

• Responses to a questionnaire sent to chief investment officers
showed that the key elements of competition in asset management
are returns relative to competitors and relationships with customers
and advisers. Perceived entry barriers in both domestic and foreign

markets include existing firms' distribution channels, relationships, and reputations; foreign entry is seen as a tougher hurdle than entry to other domestic sectors. Marked further consolidation and globalization of the industry are foreseen. Benefits of size accrue mainly by way of reputation, benefits of lower operating costs being offset by costs of the market impact of large trades. The future is seen as being strongly influenced by further mergers, advantages of large firms, and increased participation of commercial and investment banks in asset management.

In the fifth and sixth chapters, we trace the implications of the growth of institutional investors and asset management for the broader economy. In chapter 5, we assess **implications for capital markets and for banks**, addressing among other things the issue as to whether growth of institutional investors may directly or indirectly lead to financial instability.

• Institutional-investor development has had a major impact on capital market size, microstructure, and innovation. Institutionalization by this route makes a contribution to the broader efficiency of the economy by ensuring that the functions of the financial system are carried out in an effective manner.

• The banking sector has experienced heightened competition on both the asset and liability sides of the balance sheet, owing to the growth of institutional investors. Loss of traditional business has at times been followed by increases in balance sheet risk on the part of banks, leading to banking crises. We note, however, that heightened risk taking is not the only feasible response, and many banks have taken the more profitable and sustainable route of shifting to non-interest-earning activities. These include offering services such as custody and passive asset management to institutional investors themselves.

• An increase in average capital market volatility is not detectable with institutionalization; indeed, there is evidence of increased market efficiency. Institutions have matched assets and liabilities that are usually market-to-market and are generally well diversified. Accordingly, their development should help to improve financial stability relative to a system dominated by banks. On the other hand, institutionalization does seem to be linked to a rise in volatility for stocks held by institutions. Moreover, one-way selling of assets by institutions occurs occasionally, usually following a longer wave of buying and price increases. In liquid markets, this may lead to sharp price fluctuations; in less liquid markets, liquidity failure may be the consequence. Such patterns may be linked in turn to sporadic herding behavior by institutions, induced by the types of incentives that portfolio managers face.

In chapter 6, we consider the **effects of growth of institutional investors for the nonfinancial sectors**, notably in terms of saving behavior, international capital flows, and corporate governance. In this context, we also focus on implications for policy-makers—fiscal authorities, regulators, and central banks of the development of institutional investors:

• It appears that institutional investors have had an impact on the portfolio behavior of the household sector, entailing increasing holdings of longer-term instruments, although they have probably had less of an effect on saving itself. One can also identify a sea change in the pattern and locus of international portfolio flows, as banking flows have given way to portfolio flows undertaken by institutional investors.

• In corporate finance, major changes are in prospect as institutions impact on bank-based systems of corporate governance. It is suggested that European and Japanese financial systems are likely to shift to an Anglo-Saxon paradigm under pressure from institutionalization, although the process will be slow.

• On balance, these effects are favorable, as they tend in the direction of greater economic efficiency at a national and, for international investment, a global level. Some questions arise in regard to some countries, for example in relation to the lack of institutional investment in small firms. For instance, this is an important aspect of a U.K. government investigation into institutional investors (Myners, 2000). The effect of "corporate governance activity" on returns is also disputed.

• As regards public policy, institutionalization may make fiscal deficits easier to finance, and institutions are also vigilant against "excesses" of fiscal expansionism that generate default risk. Monetary policy makers benefit from this vigilance but also need to revise their own views of how markets work and about indicator properties of yields. Regulatory policy must learn to cope with the potential for instability generated by an institutionalized financial system while also ensuring by appropriate regulation that the benefits of institutions for financial stability are safeguarded and consumer protection is maintained.

In chapter 7, we examine the rapidly changing **trading environment** in which institutional investors transact securitized products—in particular, equities. Widespread automation of the trading process over the course of the past decade has had a significant impact on the natural industrial structure of the securities trading industry. Applying a combination of network economics and contestability theory, we explain why and how automation is changing the industry, focusing in particular on the pricing of trading services, changing competitive strategies, trading system architecture, cross-border access, exchange alliances and mergers, exchange governance, and the cost of institutional trading. We illustrate the impact of trading automation on institutional trading costs through a study of five years of trading data from a large U.S. mutual fund operator. We document significant cost savings from the use of non-intermediated electronic trading vehicles, which directly affect the performance of the operator's funds.

In chapter 8, we examine **institutional trading** in much greater depth. After discussing the significance of trading costs to investment returns, we analyze in detail the components of such costs and how they are measured. We then consider the impact of both the portfolio management function (investment style) and the trading function (order handling) on the cost of trading, highlighting the impact of a number of common market practices that limit the incentive for cost minimization in fund management firms. Fiduciary problems and regulatory implications are discussed. We then examine how trading costs are affected by different market structures, such as auction and dealer markets, and we highlight the causes of the proliferation of electronic communications networks in the United States. We conclude with an analysis of how institutional trading is likely to change in the coming years, drawing out the implications for public policy.

I

The Development and
Performance of
Institutional Investors

1   The Development of Institutional Investors

1.1   Size of Institutions and Financial Systems
1.2   Characteristics of Institutions and Their Role in the Financial Sector
1.3   Institutional Investors and the Functions of the Financial Sector
1.4   Institutions and Financial Development
1.5   Supply and Demand Factors Underlying the Growth of Institutional Investors

Introduction

This chapter illustrates and analyzes the growth and development of institutional investors: pension funds, insurance companies, and mutual funds. It first provides an overview of the size and growth of institutional investors in the major Organization for Economic Cooperation and Development (OECD) countries. We then consider the differing features of various types of institution and the functions they fulfill in the financial sector, as well as their role in financial development. Using these sections as background, we seek to assess the main causes of growth for institutional sectors. We consider first the supply side: the improved ability of institutional investors to fulfill the various functions of the financial system. We then assess the demand side: the household sector's increased demand for the functions of the financial system that institutional investors fulfill. Both are considered to play an important role in the growth of institutional investment.

1.1   Size of Institutions and Financial Systems

This section provides data for the G-7 countries that illustrate the growth of institutional investors, drawn largely from **national flow-**

of-funds balance sheets. Summary averages are also provided for the G-7, the Anglo-Saxon countries (Canada, the United Kingdom, and the United States), and Europe and Japan (France, Germany, Italy, and Japan). Data are shown for the years 1970, 1980, 1990, 1995, 1997, and 1998. This format is retained for other tables in the rest of the book. The tables seek to offer a baseline set of information regarding the process of institutionalization over the past three decades. They provide an indication, first, of the actual scale of the changes over 1970–1998 and, second, of the degree to which they were apparent for the different countries. In practice, the broad directions of change are remarkably common, both for financial systems that are traditionally seen as bank dominated (Europe and Japan) and for those that are seen as market dominated (Anglo-Saxon), although institutionalization has gone farther in the latter than in the former.

Notes of caution should be sounded in using and interpreting national flow-of-funds data, as there is no guarantee of harmonization in terms of sectors, valuation methods etc. (See Davis, 1986, for a discussion of some of the more obvious discrepancies.) But they do allow a broad picture of developments to be drawn, particularly for one country over time.

1.1.1   Summary Ratios and Institutional Investment

As Goldsmith (1985) suggested, various summary ratios may be constructed showing the stage of financial development that has been attained by an economy (see also section 1.4). Typically, these use the aggregate of financial claims held or liabilities owed by the conventional sectors of the economy under the System of National Accounts: the household, corporate, public, banking, nonbank financial, foreign, and central banking sectors. These data are provided in the above-mentioned flow-of-funds balance sheets for the G-7 countries.

A first summary indicator of financial structure is the so-called **size indicator**, which shows the sum of claims or liabilities as a ratio to gross domestic product (GDP). The data show that the overall size of the financial superstructure has tended to grow sharply over time in all of the G-7 (table 1.1). Ratios of total financial assets to GDP have risen from around four times GDP in 1970 to eight times GDP in 1998. This illustrates the process of financial deepening that typi-

Table 1.1
Size Indicator of Financial Structure (Total Financial Claims as a Proportion of GDP)

	1970	1980	1990	1995	1997	1998	Change 1970–1998
United Kingdom	4.73	4.85	8.86	8.85	9.79	10.20	5.47
United Kingdom excluding Euromarkets	4.73	4.20	7.92	7.99	8.82	9.25	4.52
United States	4.05	4.06	5.91	6.80	7.64	8.59	4.53
Germany	2.89	3.58	4.69	5.28	6.10	6.58	3.69
Japan	3.79	5.06	8.53	8.28	8.46	8.85	5.06
Canada	4.67	5.06	5.78	6.48	6.94	7.34	2.67
France	4.41	4.78	6.92	7.29	8.60	9.19	4.78
Italy	3.35	3.93	4.27	4.84	5.33	5.59	2.23
G-7	**3.99**	**4.38**	**6.29**	**6.71**	**7.41**	**7.91**	**3.93**
Anglo-Saxon	**4.48**	**4.44**	**6.54**	**7.09**	**7.80**	**8.39**	**3.91**
Europe and Japan	**3.61**	**4.34**	**6.10**	**6.43**	**7.12**	**7.55**	**3.94**

Notes: G-7, Anglo-Saxon, and Europe and Japan summary figures are based on simple averages. Anglo-Saxon countries are the United States, the United Kingdom, and Canada; Europe and Japan comprise France, Germany, Italy, and Japan.
Sources: Drawn from national flow-of-funds balance sheet data. Source for the U.S.: Board of Governors of the Federal Reserve System (Flow of Funds Accounts for the United States); for the U.K.: Office of National Statistics (Financial Statistics); for Germany: Deutsche Bundesbank (Deutsche Bundesbank Monthly Review); for Japan: Bank of Japan (Bank of Japan Economic Statistics Monthly); for Canada: Statistics Canada (National Balance Sheet Tables); for France: Banque de France (Tableaux d'Opérations Financières); for Italy: Banca d'Italia (Statistical Supplement to the Monthly Bulletin). GDP data are from IMF (International Financial Statistics).

fies countries as they grow in terms of wealth and income, as has been the case both for the Anglo-Saxon countries and for Europe and Japan. The data indicate that growth of institutional investors has occurred in the context of rapid overall growth in financing in the economies of major industrial countries. One implication is that considerable growth in the absolute size of institutional investors could have taken place even if their share of overall financing had stayed constant.

There are some quite sizable differences in the overall scope of financing, with Germany and Italy in particular showing a lower ratio of financing to GDP. However, this may relate partly to measurement differences. An important point in relation to the United Kingdom is that the presence of an "offshore" international banking sector in the City of London tends to boost indicators of financing quite considerably; hence for comparability purposes, we prefer to

Table 1.2
Financial Intermediation Ratios (Intermediated Claims as a Proportion of the Total)

	1970	1980	1990	1995	1997	1998	Change 1970–1998
United Kingdom	0.32	0.42	0.47	0.58	0.58	0.58	0.26
United Kingdom excluding Euromarkets	0.32	0.34	0.40	0.54	0.53	0.54	0.22
United States	0.33	0.37	0.34	0.38	0.38	0.44	0.11
Germany	0.44	0.45	0.43	0.46	0.47	0.47	0.04
Japan	0.39	0.42	0.42	0.46	0.45	0.45	0.06
Canada	0.29	0.34	0.37	0.40	0.41	0.40	0.10
France	0.34	0.62	0.41	0.43	0.42	0.41	0.06
Italy	0.36	0.32	0.31	0.31	0.32	0.35	−0.01
G-7	**0.35**	**0.41**	**0.38**	**0.43**	**0.43**	**0.44**	**0.08**
Anglo-Saxon	**0.31**	**0.35**	**0.37**	**0.44**	**0.44**	**0.46**	**0.14**
Europe and Japan	**0.38**	**0.45**	**0.39**	**0.42**	**0.41**	**0.42**	**0.04**

Source: National flow-of-funds balance sheet data; for detailed sources, see table 1.1.

present the United Kingdom with and without foreign currency bank assets and liabilities ("euromarkets").

A second ratio of interest is the **financial intermediation ratio**. This shows the proportion of the total of financial claims in an economy that are held by financial intermediaries such as banks and institutional investors instead of being nonintermediated or "direct" claims between nonfinancial sectors (such as household sector holdings of corporate equity or government bonds). The overall degree of financial intermediation has risen in most countries. In other words, direct claims of the nonfinancial sector on itself have tended to decline in importance relative to intermediated claims (table 1.2). Whereas in 1970 intermediation accounted for 35% of G-7 claims, by 1998 it was 44%. The process of financial deepening has thus been accompanied by an increase in the relative size of the financial sector. In 1998, the financial intermediary sector accounted for a larger proportion of total financing in the Anglo-Saxon countries than in Europe and Japan,[1] despite the fact that securities markets (which facilitate growth of direct claims) are also larger in the Anglo-Saxon countries.

The **institutional intermediation ratio** shows the extent to which institutional investors' share of intermediation has also increased.

---

1. Data for Italy and France may, however, be distorted by a change in the treatment of items such as equity in noncorporate business in the 1980s.

Table 1.3
Bank and Institutional Intermediation Ratios (Proportion of Intermediated Claims Held by Banks and Institutional Investors)

		1970	1980	1990	1995	1997	1998	Change 1970–1998
United	Bank	0.58	0.64	0.55	0.47	0.46	0.46	−0.12
Kingdom	Institutional	0.28	0.26	0.32	0.38	0.39	0.40	0.12
United States	Bank	0.58	0.58	0.42	0.30	0.26	0.21	−0.37
	Institutional	0.31	0.31	0.40	0.48	0.52	0.46	0.15
Germany	Bank	0.84	0.86	0.83	0.78	0.75	0.74	−0.10
	Institutional	0.10	0.12	0.17	0.21	0.22	0.23	0.13
Japan	Bank	0.45	0.36	0.38	0.34	0.34	0.32	−0.12
	Institutional	0.10	0.10	0.16	0.19	0.19	0.19	0.09
Canada	Bank	0.45	0.55	0.44	0.49	0.46	0.42	−0.02
	Institutional	0.23	0.19	0.25	0.30	0.33	0.36	0.13
France	Bank	0.94	0.68	0.82	0.74	0.72	0.66	−0.28
	Institutional	0.05	0.04	0.19	0.24	0.26	0.29	0.24
Italy	Bank	0.98	0.98	0.95	0.91	0.91	0.92	−0.06
	Institutional	0.06	0.05	0.11	0.09	0.09	0.10	0.04
G-7	Bank	**0.69**	**0.66**	**0.63**	**0.58**	**0.56**	**0.53**	**−0.15**
	Institutional	**0.16**	**0.15**	**0.23**	**0.27**	**0.29**	**0.29**	**0.13**
Anglo-Saxon	Bank	**0.53**	**0.59**	**0.47**	**0.42**	**0.39**	**0.36**	**−0.17**
	Institutional	**0.28**	**0.25**	**0.32**	**0.39**	**0.42**	**0.41**	**0.13**
Europe and	Bank	**0.80**	**0.72**	**0.74**	**0.70**	**0.68**	**0.66**	**−0.14**
Japan	Institutional	**0.08**	**0.08**	**0.16**	**0.18**	**0.19**	**0.20**	**0.13**

Source: National flow-of-funds balance sheet data; for detailed sources, see table 1.1.

(The institutional sectors that are included in the flow-of-funds data are generally pension funds, insurance companies, and mutual funds.) The result is clear: The share of banks in financial intermediation has tended to decline, even in the traditionally bank-dominated economies (table 1.3). In contrast, the share of financial intermediation undertaken by institutional investors has risen sharply in each of the G-7 countries, albeit attaining a higher level in the Anglo-Saxon countries.[2] On average, the share of intermediation undertaken by institutional investors in 1998 was 29% in the G-7, 41% in the Anglo-Saxon countries, and 20% for Europe and Japan. But in each case, there is an increase of around 13 percentage points in their share of intermediated claims since 1970.

---

2. Note that the data do not sum to 1.0, as there are financial intermediaries other than banks and institutional investors.

Table 1.4
Institutional Investor Claims of the Household Sector as a Proportion of GDP

	1970	1980	1990	1995	1997	1998	Change 1970–1998
United Kingdom	0.42	0.37	1.02	1.62	1.85	1.99	1.57
United States	0.41	0.47	0.79	1.22	1.52	1.74	1.33
Germany	0.12	0.20	0.33	0.51	0.64	0.71	0.59
Japan	0.15	0.21	0.58	0.74	0.73	0.76	0.61
Canada	0.32	0.32	0.52	0.78	0.95	1.05	0.73
France	0.07	0.12	0.52	0.78	0.95	1.09	1.02
Italy	0.07	0.06	0.15	0.14	0.16	0.20	0.13
G-7	**0.23**	**0.25**	**0.56**	**0.83**	**0.97**	**1.08**	**0.85**
Anglo-Saxon	**0.39**	**0.39**	**0.78**	**1.21**	**1.44**	**1.59**	**1.21**
Europe and Japan	**0.11**	**0.15**	**0.40**	**0.54**	**0.62**	**0.69**	**0.59**

Source: National flow-of-funds balance sheet data; for detailed sources, see table 1.1.

The **size of institutional investors** has correspondingly risen relative to GDP much more than has that of banks. A rough estimate,[3] based on the ratio of institutional assets held by the household sector to GDP, is shown in table 1.4. For the G-7 as a whole, the value of institutional claims held by the household sector has increased from the equivalent of 23% to 108% of GDP. The growth has been most dramatic in the Anglo-Saxon countries, where the size of institutional investors has risen from the equivalent of 39%[4] to 159% of GDP. In Europe and Japan, growth has still been marked, from around 11% of GDP to 69%. The United States and the United Kingdom are shown to be in the vanguard of institutionalization, with ratios in 1998 being over 170% of GDP. Besides the long-term comparison with 1970, it is instructive to compare the size of the institutional investor sectors in 1990 with that in 1998. The growth even over this relatively short period is dramatic, with the G-7 average ratio rising from 56% to 107%, while the United States has seen institutional investments held on behalf of households grow from 79% of GDP to 174%.

Concerning **relative growth** of insurance companies, mutual funds, and pension funds (table 1.5), over the long term, pension funds have grown faster than the other types of institutional investor,

---

3. This measure underestimates the total size of the institutional sector, since their claims are also held by sectors other than households, including on behalf of other institutional investors.
4. According to Lakonishok et al. (1992a), the U.S. ratio in 1950 was 21%.

Table 1.5
Average Annual Growth of Institutional Sectors, 1990–1998 (Growth of Assets in Domestic Currency)

	Insurance Companies	Pension Funds	Mutual Funds
United Kingdom	16	11	18
United States	9	14	20
Germany	9	5	15
Japan	5	9	−2
Canada	7	11	31
France	19*	0*	8
Italy	9*	3*	40

*1990–1995 only.
Sources: OECD (1997), National flow-of-funds balance sheets, FEFSI.

reflecting growth in coverage and maturity of pension systems, as well as ongoing population aging (Davis 1995a). However, in recent years, it is mutual funds that have undergone the most rapid growth, partly reflecting their own growing importance as a repository of retirement funds. Over the period from 1990 to 1998, average growth of institutional assets in the G-7 has been 8–13%. Over 1990 to 1998, in the United States, mutual funds grew by 20%, pension funds by 14%, and life insurance companies by 9% (see table 1.5). Over the same period, U.K. mutual fund assets rose by 18% per annum, pension funds by 11%, and insurance companies by 16%. In this context, one may add that the growth in assets only partly reflects new inflows of funds to the sectors concerned. A significant proportion links rather to reinvestment of earnings and capital gains, net of withdrawals, and redemptions. Indeed, in many countries, pension contributions in recent years have been zero or even negative as a consequence of the overfunding of defined benefit pension funds that enabled sponsoring companies to take contribution holidays.

1.1.2 Estimates of the Size of Institutional Investors

We sought to derive an estimate of the **value of institutional assets** by simply summing data (largely from the flow of funds) at 1998 exchange rates (table 1.6). These data show that the value of pension funds in the G-7 at that date was $9.5 trillion, mutual funds $7.2 trillion, and life insurance $7.2 trillion. The value of institutional assets for the G-7 at the end of 1998 is indicated to be $24 trillion, of

Table 1.6
Institutional Investment, 1998

	Life Insurance		Pension Funds		Mutual Funds		Total	
	($ billion)	% of GDP	($ billion)	% of GDP	($ billion)	% of GDP	($ billion)	% of GDP
United Kingdom	1294	93	1163	83	284	20	2742	197
United States	2770	33	7110	84	5087	60	14,967	176
Germany	531	24	72	3	195	9	798	35
Japan	1666	39	688	16	372	9	2727	63
Canada	141	24	277	47	197	34	615	105
France	658	43	91	6	624	41	1373	90
Italy	151	12	77	6	436	35	664	54
G-7	7212		9479		7195		23,886	

Sources: National flow-of-funds balance sheets, FEFSI, Investment and Pensions Europe (1999a). Discrepancies with the estimates from table 1.4 result from (1) different sources and sectoral definitions for some data and (2) the inclusion of institutional assets in table 1.6 that are held by sectors other than households.

which $15 trillion are accounted for by U.S. institutional investors.[5] For comparison, we estimate, using the same data sources, that the value of the G-7 equity markets in 1998 were $30 trillion, and the bond markets were $25 trillion.

Other estimates confirm these impressions drawn from flow-of-funds balance sheets. According to OECD estimates (OECD 1997), total institutional assets of OECD countries (including non-G-7 countries) were 38% of GDP in 1981 ($3.2 trillion), 90% in 1991 ($16.3 trillion), and 106.5% in 1995 ($24.3 trillion). It may be added that other institutional assets (charities, nonfinancial firms Treasury operations, etc.) were estimated at $3.8 trillion for the G-7 in 1995.

Another estimate, by British Invisibles (1997), again concurs with the above orders of magnitude. They consider that total global funds under management in 1995 were $22 trillion, with global pension funds being $8.2 trillion, insurance companies $7 trillion, mutual funds $5.3 trillion, and private client funds $1.5 trillion. Walter (1999) estimates that the total value of global institutional assets is $30 trillion if one includes $7.5 trillion in offshore client accounts. Intersec suggest that world pension assets were $11 trillion in 1998 and projected them to be $15 trillion in 2003. At this point, income from asset management would become the principal source of income of a wide range of financial institutions, including banks (see chapter 5). Overseas assets of institutions were $1.5 trillion in 1998 and were expected to be $2.5 trillion in 2003.

BIS (1998) show that total institutional assets for the G-10 countries in 1996 were over $20 trillion and more than 100% of GDP on average. The respective volumes for each sector were $6.3 trillion for life insurance, $1.7 trillion for non–life insurance, $5.3 trillion for mutual funds, and $7.1 trillion for pension funds. As shown in table 1.7, the United States accounted for over 50% of the total, Japan for 14%, and the United Kingdom for 9%. In this context, the size of insurance companies tends to be larger in countries where the growth of pension funds has been less marked, thus indicating that individuals seek to raise saving via life insurance when the scope for pension saving is limited. The BIS also suggested that the low level of institutional development in Continental Europe indicated considerable scope for further growth there (see tables 1.3 and 1.4).

---

5. Discrepancies with the estimates from table 1.4 result from (1) different sources and sectoral definitions for some data and (2) the inclusion in table 1.6 of institutional assets that are held by sectors other than households.

Table 1.7
Institutional Investors, 1996 (Percent of Global Total)

	Life Insurers	Non–Life Insurers	Mutual Funds	Pension Funds	Total Identified
United States	35.9	47.0	66.8	67.1	55.7
Japan	26.8	16.0	7.9	6.2	13.8
Germany	7.6	12.9	2.5	0.9	4.4
France	7.1	7.9	10.0	0.0	5.5
Italy	0.9	2.4	2.4	0.6	1.3
United Kingdom	11.0	5.7	3.5	12.7	9.2
Canada	2.2	2.0	2.9	3.4	2.8
Spain	1.7	0.0	2.6	0.0	1.2
Netherlands	3.4	1.8	1.3	5.1	3.3
Switzerland	1.9	2.6	0.0	2.7	1.7
Sweden	1.5	1.7	0.0	1.3	1.1
Total of above	100.0	100.0	100.0	100.0	100.0

Source: BIS (1998).

1.2 Characteristics of Institutions and Their Role in the Financial Sector

Institutional investors may be **defined** as specialized financial institutions that manage savings collectively on behalf of small investors toward a specific objective in terms of acceptable risk, return maximization, and maturity of claims. In this section, we trace the essential characteristics of institutional investors, the functions that they fulfill, and their place in the pattern of financial development. This forms a background to the more detailed analysis later in this chapter of the reasons for their growth, as well as for the assessment in later chapters of the performance and industrial organization of institutional sectors and the effects of growing institutionalization on the wider economy.

1.2.1 General Features Common to All Institutional Investors

Institutional investors, in common with other financial institutions, provide a form of **risk pooling** for small investors, thus providing a better trade-off of risk and return than is generally possible via direct holdings. This entails, on the asset side, putting a premium on **diversification**, both by holding a spread of domestic securities (which may be both debt and equity) and by international investment.

Institutions also prefer **liquidity** and hence use large and liquid capital markets, trading standard or "commoditized" instruments, so as to be able to adjust holdings in pursuit of objectives in response to new information. Any holdings of illiquid assets such as property typically account for a relatively small share of the portfolio.

A backup for the approach to investment is the ability to absorb and process **information**, which is superior to that of individual investors in the capital market. On the other hand, unlike banks, institutional investors rely on public information rather than private, which links strongly to their desire for liquidity.

Most institutions have **matched assets and liabilities in terms of maturity**, unlike banks, which tends to minimize the risk of runs. Moreover, in many cases, they have **long-term liabilities**, facilitating the holding of high-risk and high-return instruments. There is, however, a question as to the stability of money market mutual funds, as, like banks, they offer redemption of liabilities at par.[6]

The **size** of institutions has a number of important implications. There may be **economies of scale**, which result in lower average costs for investors. These may arise from, inter alia, the ability to **transact in large volumes**, which typically leads to a lowering of commission charges. Investors share the costly services of expert investment managers and thereby save in advisory fees. Size also enables them to invest in **large indivisible investments** (although there is a tension with desire for diversification).

Considerable **countervailing power** also results from size, which may be used to reduce transactions costs and custodial fees. This countervailing power also gives rise to the ability to ensure fair treatment by capital market intermediaries on the one hand and, on the other, to give potential for improved control over companies in which they invest, thus reducing the incidence of adverse incentive problems.

Further characteristics arise from the process of **asset management**, a service involving management of an investment portfolio on behalf of a client. Such asset management may be undertaken by the institutional investor itself (internal management) or by a separate institution such as a specialist fund manager, a life insurer, or the

---

6. See section 5.3.6. Other types of open-end mutual fund may face attenuated difficulties of a similar kind, since whereas they guarantee that redemption may occur at end-of-day net asset value, cash receipts from securities sales take several days to arise.

asset management arm or subsidiary of an investment bank or commercial bank (external management). There is fierce competition for positions as asset managers among these many and varied financial institutions. As we discuss further in chapter 2, fund management can be broken down into two stages: asset allocation between broad asset categories and security selection of individual assets within those categories.

There are offsetting forces in the asset management relationship. On the one hand, it gives rise to an essentially **fiduciary** relationship to the ultimate investor, which often entails a degree of caution in the portfolio strategy and a desire to limit risks incurred. On the other hand, such delegation raises **principal-agent problems**, as unless the fund manager is perfectly monitored and/or a foolproof contract is drawn up, the fund manager may act in his or her own interests (e.g., in generating excessive commission income)—or, particularly in Europe and Japan, in the interests of related financial institutions—and contrary to those of the liability holders. However, the various means that are used (particularly in Anglo-Saxon countries) to counteract such problems mean that fund management gives rise in turn to a potential for **herding behavior**, as we discuss in chapter 5. This may arise notably from the desire of managers to show that they are of good quality, for example in the context of short mandates, owing to the pressures exerted by performance measurement, or fear of takeover (for life insurers or closed-end funds).

1.2.2 The Main Types of Institutional Investor

The discussion above should, of course, not be taken to imply that institutional investors are homogeneous. They differ generally in terms of the contractual relations between the owners of the assets and the asset managers, that is, the rules determining the distribution of risk and return, as well as in the definition of their liabilities. The main types of institutional investors that we cover in this book are pension funds, life insurance companies, and forms of mutual funds.[7] The main differences stem from liabilities.

---

7. Note that we omit from consideration trading desks of financial institutions and corporate treasury operations. These tend to have smaller asset holdings, have less of a buy-and-hold strategy, are generally leveraged, and have different incentives. Arguably, such an omission is justified institutionally but not in terms of their effect on market dynamics (see chapter 5).

Pension funds collect, pool, and invest funds contributed by sponsors and beneficiaries to provide for the future pension entitlements of beneficiaries (Davis 1995a, 2000a). They thus provide means for individuals to accumulate saving over their working life so as to finance their consumption needs in retirement. Pension funds are typically sponsored by employers, such as companies, public corporations, or industry or trade groups, although personal pensions (generally contracts between individuals and life insurance companies) are also common. Pension funds may be internally or externally managed. In the Anglo-Saxon countries, they are generally organized in the form of a trust,[8] while elsewhere, structures such as foundations or captive insurance companies are employed. Returns to members of pension plans backed by such funds may be purely dependent on the market (defined contribution funds) or may be overlaid by a guarantee of the rate of return by the sponsor (defined benefit funds). The latter have insurance features that are absent in the former (Bodie 1990b). These include guarantees with respect to replacement ratios (pensions as a proportion of income at retirement) subject to the risk of bankruptcy of the sponsor, as well as potential for risk sharing between older and younger beneficiaries.

Defined contribution plans have tended to grow in recent years as employers have sought to minimize the risk of their obligations while employees desired funds that are readily transferable between employers. For both defined benefit and defined contribution funds, the liability tends to be set in real terms, as the objective of asset management is to attain a high replacement ratio at retirement (pension as a proportion of final salary), which is itself determined by the growth rate of average earnings.

In assessing **insurance companies** as institutional investors, we focus throughout this book on life business and abstract from that to property and casualty insurance. The latter, while having significant financial assets to back potential claims,[9] does not constitute a form

---

8. Trust law was originally a means of ensuring that endowments for widows and orphans were correctly managed. Trustees have fiduciary duties to hold the assets in trust for members, act impartially, keep accounts, check that funding is in place, and seek expert advice when necessary. Under common law, in doing so, they must "act in the best interests of the beneficiaries." Clark (2000a) assesses some of the difficulties and conflicts that arise in this form of organization, which may affect investment.
9. For example, in the United Kingdom, the assets of non–life insurers are comparable to those of mutual funds.

of household saving in the manner of life insurance, pension funds, and mutual funds. The characteristics of the property and casualty sector are highly uncertain cash flows that depend on major disasters and court cases as well as the law of large numbers. Their portfolios tend to include more short-term assets and also equities than do life insurers' portfolios.

Life insurance companies, like pension funds, are long-term institutional investors with a large share of tradable assets in their portfolios. They historically provided insurance for dependents against the risk of death at a given time in the future but are increasingly offering long-term saving vehicles for pensions, to repay loans for house purchase, and the like. Whereas life insurance companies' liabilities have traditionally tended to be nominal, that is, offering a guaranteed return that is fixed in money terms, an increasing proportion of policies are now "variable" and either lack such guarantees, or may have option features, with, for example, variable returns but a guaranteed floor. There are increasingly close links with pension funds and pension provision, as life companies offer annuities for guaranteeing pension benefits as well as guaranteed investment contracts (GICs) purchased by pension funds. They often also provide defined contribution pensions directly, they may act as external asset managers for pension funds or may offer insurance to defined benefit funds on behalf of small employers[10].

In the case of (occupational) pension funds and life insurers, the pattern of investments (e.g., the bond/equity split) is driven by the preferences of the sponsors, where the latter are typically distinct from the ultimate beneficiaries of the assets in the household sector. Nevertheless, in doing so, they will take into account the nature of liabilities and regulations, which may in turn affect portfolio distributions.

Mutual funds are simply vehicles for the pooling of assets for investment purposes. In this context, they seek to offer an enhanced risk return profile and greater liquidity to individual investors by exploiting synergies from pooling assets of many individuals, economizing in particular on transactions costs and management costs while offering low minimum holdings. They hence differ from the long-term institutions by offering short-term liquidity on pools of

---

10. For a discussion of life insurers' investments see chapter 2, also Dickinson (1998) and Davis (2000c).

funds, albeit at rates that depend on current market prices, either via direct redemption of holdings (**open-end funds**) or via the ability to trade shares in the funds on exchanges (**closed-end funds**). End investors in mutual funds are residual claimants and bear all the risk. Managers' remuneration is typically linked to the value of assets under management.

Asset allocation of an individual fund is generally fixed by the prospectus, especially in the case of specialized funds that invest in a given class of assets (domestic equities, foreign bonds, etc.[11]). The asset manager is thus responsible only for security selection. Accordingly, the size and asset allocation of the mutual fund sector largely reflect the asset preferences of households directly[12] as they choose between investing in different types of funds such as equity, bond, and money market funds. Note, however, that not all mutual funds are held by households; institutional holding of mutual funds is also sizable, especially as a means of accessing expert portfolio management in specialized fields (e.g., emerging market country funds). In the United States, 30% of mutual fund assets are held by other financial institutions, notably pension funds.

An important difference between open-end and closed-end funds is that open-end funds are obliged to sell and buy at current net asset value (i.e., the market value of the securities held less any debt, divided by the number of shares), while closed-end funds can and often do trade at a discount to net asset value. Ultimately, it is the threat of takeover that limits such discounts. Open-end funds have to sell securities to cope with redemptions and hence require much greater liquidity than closed-end funds. Money market mutual funds, by holding only liquid short-term money market assets, are able to offer redemption of holdings at par and hence provide payments facilities. They have been notably popular in the United States and France.[13]

---

11. There are also some balanced funds that hold a variety of assets at their discretion; these are notably popular in Continental European countries such as France (see table 3.13).

12. The existence of mutual funds may itself modify such preferences relative to a situation in which direct securities holdings are the only options, for example by reducing risk aversion.

13. As we discuss in chapter 5, fiscal incentives have been important underlying factors in France. In the United States, the initial growth of money market funds in the 1970s was linked to low regulated yields on bank deposits; improved technology allowing checking facilities has also been important.

Another special type of closed-end fund is a **hedge fund**, a private unadvertised mutual fund that is limited to wealthy investors[14] who are willing to incur high short-term risk in exchange for high return potential.[15] Managers often have capital themselves in the funds they manage. Hedge funds may engage in unlimited short-term trading, take short positions, and borrow to a greater extent than other institutions. They are usually in the legal form of either onshore investment partnerships or investment funds based in tax havens such as the Caribbean and are in each case unregulated and not subject to disclosure requirements.

Because of their ability to leverage and willingness to take risks, hedge funds may create sharp market movements and thereby provoke other institutions to similar action (e.g., in exerting pressure on currency pegs). They may also become highly vulnerable in bear markets owing to their leverage, as the experience of the Long Term Capital Management revealed (see Davis (1999d) and chapter 5). BIS (1998) reported assets of hedge funds at the end of 1997 to be $90 billion, with annual growth of 40% being witnessed since 1990. An extensive discussion of the hedge fund sectors' structure, investment strategies, and effects on market dynamics can be found in Eichengreen et al. (1998).

1.2.3 Risk Bearing and Regulation

A key distinction between types of institution, which warrants further comment, links to the **locus of risk bearing**. In a defined benefit pension fund and a life insurance contract having guaranteed returns, the risk of market volatility is taken by the sponsoring company and the life insurer, respectively. In contrast, in the case of a defined contribution pension fund, a mutual fund, and a variable-linked life insurance contract, the risk is borne wholly by the individual (except for a rather low guaranteed amount for the life contract).

There appears to a widespread tendency in recent years for institutional investors to switch from **bearing risks themselves to transferring them to the household sector**, whereby the institutional investor offers less or no insurance. Life insurance companies, as

---

14. In the United States, individuals must have $1 million in investable assets to be permitted to invest in onshore hedge funds.
15. See Basel Committee (1999).

discussed in section 2.2.2, are increasingly offering forms of policy in which the bulk of the return is not guaranteed but depends on investment returns (such as variable-life or unit-linked policies). In the United States, the volume of defined contribution assets for the corporate sector now exceeds defined benefit funds; defined contribution assets in 1998 were $2199 billion, while defined benefit plans had assets of $2132 billion. Similar trends are apparent for coverage.[16] Whereas in 1975, private sector membership of defined contribution funds in the United States was 11.2 million and defined benefit fund membership was 26.1 million, by 1995 the respective figures were 36.6 million and 27.2 million, and in 1997,[17] they were 40.2 million (40%) and 27 million (27%), respectively.[18] Note, however, that most public sector employees who are covered by pension plans have defined benefit coverage.

In the United States, much of the growth in pension assets in recent years has tended to come from 401(k)[19] plan assets, some of which result from terminations of defined benefit funds, although equally important have been extension of coverage in small firms and overall employment growth[20] (Berlinski and Western 1997). Nevertheless, the bulk of U.S. mutual fund assets are not retirement related. In a 1997 survey, around 50% of the United Kingdom's top 350 companies were considering switching to defined contribution (Investors Chronicle 1997). Twenty-five percent of U.K. employers used defined contribution in 1998, up from 11% in 1994, with the projection for 2003 being 35%. Meanwhile, over 20% of the workforce was covered by personal pensions.

Corporate sponsors favor defined contribution, as their risk stemming from pension obligations is sharply reduced, which may be beneficial to their cost of external funds. The household sector appears content to accept risk, given the recent good performance of

---

16. For details of the trends in pension provisions that this shift has entailed, see Mitchell (1999).

17. Source: Employment Benefit Research Institute Web site: www.ebri.org.

18. Note, however, that it is common for individuals to have both a defined contribution and a defined benefit plan.

19. 401(k) plans are a form of defined contribution plan offered to employees of a U.S. company, to which both employers and employees contribute and in which the individual determines the distribution of assets. The administrative costs of such funds are low, in part because of this delegation of asset allocation to the individual.

20. Note that the figures above show a constant level of defined benefit coverage rather than a decline over 1975–1997.

equity markets and also the advantages of defined contribution pension plans in terms of job mobility,[21] in a context in which jobs for life are much less prevalent than was hitherto the case. They may also prefer the ability, offered by some defined contribution arrangements, to control the disposition of their investment—an arrangement that also reduces asset management costs by eliminating the need for the fund to undertake asset allocation. The defined contribution fund has also been at the core of many recent pension reforms in developing countries such as Chile and Argentina (Davis 1998b, 1998e, 1998f) as well as OECD countries such as Australia and Italy. In the early 1990s, the shift to defined contribution in the United States was thought to have accompanied less aggressive portfolio distributions, which could threaten overall returns in the long term (Rappaport 1992). More recently, equity proportions have risen, but the reaction of the household sector to a prolonged bear market has yet to be seen. Certainly, it was the 1970s bear market that drove the earlier shift *away* from defined contribution arrangements in countries such as the United Kingdom and led to a collapse in holdings of equity mutual funds in the United States.

In combination with the growth of mutual fund investment per se, the rise of defined contribution plans means that **households are tending to have an increasing influence on asset allocation**. More generally, it can be argued that, as in the rest of the financial sector, there is a **blurring of distinctions** between types of institutional investor, as mutual funds in particular are being used as a vehicle for retirement saving and pension saving often has a life insurance aspect.[22] Insurance companies are tending to launch their own investment funds, either to run unit-linked policies or as separate profit centers. As we noted, they are also widely involved in pension provision, in provision of annuities and guaranteed insurance contracts for pension funds, and in segregated asset management for pension funds. Meanwhile, banks themselves are becoming active in this area, by purchasing or launching their own insurance companies

---

21. The U.S. General Accounting Office (GAO 1989) simulated equal-cost defined benefit and defined contribution plans with identical earnings and work histories and found pensions with five jobs with companies with identical defined benefits plans to be $9,800, those with jobs with identical defined contribution plans to be $12,100, and those with one job covered by the defined benefit plan to be $19,100. The last figure may reflect cross-subsidies from early leavers within the defined benefit plans.
22. Defined benefit funds often include survivors' benefits and life insurance.

(where regulations permit) to form financial conglomerates, selling their own mutual funds and personal pensions, and setting up or purchasing fund managers. Pension funds and, to a lesser extent, life insurers are linking more closely to the rest of the financial system via their choices of external fund managers.

There are considerable **differences in the regulation** of the behavior of the various types of institutional investors (see also section 6.3.2). The tightness of regulation in turn tends to reflect the differences in fiduciary obligations and in the above-mentioned contractual obligations and their implications for risk bearing. In particular, regulation reflects differences in the degree to which insurance features are bundled with asset management. Mutual funds are rather lightly regulated. The main regulations of mutual funds link to information disclosure to holders (as well as various other investor protection provisions). Reflecting the nature of obligations, life insurers and defined benefit pension funds are generally subject to forms of solvency or minimum funding regulations and may also have restrictions on the disposition of assets.[23] Defined contribution pension fund regulation is typically intermediate in terms of tightness.

1.3 Institutional Investors and the Functions of the Financial Sector

Section 1.1 showed that institutional investors play an increasing role in the financial sector. As will be detailed in the rest of the book, this entails collecting saving, investing in securities and other financial assets, cross-border investment and ownership of companies.

To facilitate understanding of the causes and implications of growth of institutional investors, we consider it is useful to adopt a **functional approach to the financial system**. Such an approach seeks to define functions that the financial system is always called upon to fulfill, regardless of its institutional form. It thus provides a set of constant features of long-term developments and of more recent trends; evolution of institutional forms and of financial structure such as the growth of institutional investors may be seen as a

---

23. Pension funds are subject to a variety of additional regulations with respect to liabilities, such as rules regarding portability, vesting, indexation, and benefit insurance. However, the main focus here is on assets. For a broad discussion of pension regulation, see Davis (1995a); for an assessment of the specific regulatory situation for pension funds in the United Kingdom, see Davis (2000b).

form of adaptation and improvement in the ways these functions are fulfilled, under pressure of competitive forces.

Various paradigms have been proposed;[24] here, we highlight and utilize the one proposed by Merton and Bodie (1995). They distinguish the following key functions:

• The provision of ways of clearing and settling payments to facilitate exchange of goods, services, and assets

• The provision of a mechanism for pooling of funds from individual households to facilitate large-scale indivisible undertakings and the subdivision of shares in enterprises to facilitate diversification

• The provision of ways to transfer economic resources over time, across geographic regions, or among industries;

• The provision of ways to manage uncertainty and control risk. Through securities and through financial intermediaries, risk pooling and risk sharing opportunities are made available to households and companies. There are three main ways to manage risk: hedging, diversifying, and insuring.

• The provision of price information, thus helping to coordinate decentralized decision making in various sectors of the economy

• The provision of ways to deal with incentive problems when one party to a financial transaction has information the other does not, or when one is agent of the other, and when control and enforcement of contracts is costly

In the context of this framework, growth of institutional investors is explicable in terms of either a changing comparative advantage in the functions they fulfill (related to the characteristics described above) or an increased demand for certain functions on behalf of end users. To illustrate this, we briefly consider the role of institutional investors under the heading of each individual function. A number of these points are addressed at greater length in succeeding chapters (see also Davis 1996a, Davis 2000a):

1. **Clearing and settling payments** to facilitate exchange of goods, services, and assets. Banks, for example, may offer checking accounts, cash cards, and wire transfers, while nonfinancial firms may offer credit cards. Systems for transferring payments and for

---

24. See Sanford (1993), Hubbard (1994), Kohn (1994), and Rose (1994), for example.

trading, clearing, and settling securities transactions may also fall under this heading. As regards institutional investors, owing to technological advances and the innovation of money markets themselves, money market mutual funds have been able to develop and to offer transactions accounts, based on units that are redeemable at par (see chapter 5). Note, however, that growth may have been facilitated by regulations and reserve requirements on banks or fiscal incentives. Furthermore, institutional investors have themselves influenced the structure of markets, for example by encouraging development of wholesale money markets, as well as influencing the form of trading and settlements systems more generally (see chapters 7 and 8). The resulting structure enables financial and nonfinancial institutions to hold, obtain, and transfer liquidity much more readily.

2. The provision of a mechanism for **pooling of funds** from individual households so as to facilitate large-scale indivisible undertakings and **the subdivision of shares** in enterprises to facilitate diversification. Financial intermediaries, including banks, provide means to pool funds, while securities markets and securitization of claims are examples of subdivision. As we noted, pooling is a fundamental characteristic of institutional investors, which, given their size and consequent economies of scale, they can perform much more readily than households can (see chapter 2). In this context, one may note the mutually reinforcing development of securitization of individual assets (such as loans), which has provided a ready supply of assets in which institutional investors may invest in competition with banks.

3. The provision of ways to **transfer economic resources** over time, across geographic regions, or among industries. By these means, households may optimize their allocation of funds over the life cycle, and funds may be optimally allocated to their most efficient use. A capital market facilitates the efficient separation of ownership and control of capital, thus aiding specialization in production. A range of financial intermediaries are active in these processes, thus facilitating saving for retirement and finance of corporate investment. The most crucial point is that aging of the population, combined with curtailment of, and/or growing lack of confidence in, the promises of social security pension systems, has led to increased demand for transfer of resources over time via growth of pension funds per se and also to retirement savings held in life insurance companies and

mutual funds (see section 1.5.3 and Huiser 1990). More generally, there is in OECD countries an increased demand for long-term saving, related to accumulation of wealth. This function does not typically entail maturity transformation; as we noted, institutional investors, unlike banks, typically have matched assets and liabilities. As regards transfer across space, one may highlight the increased amplitude of international portfolio investment by institutional investors, which has supplanted the bank-driven flows that were typical of the 1970s (see chapter 6).

4. The provision of ways to **manage uncertainty and control risk**. Through securities and through financial intermediaries, risk-pooling and risk-sharing opportunities are made available to households and companies. There are three main ways to manage risk: hedging, diversifying, and insuring. The role of derivatives in this process has come to the fore in recent years. More generally, separation of providers of working capital for real investment (personnel, plant, equipment) from providers of risk capital that bear financial risk facilitates specialization in production. Institutional investors are well placed to use derivatives and other means of risk control on their portfolios; many of the related innovations have been introduced or developed especially to cater for institutional demand (see chapters 2 and 5). On the liabilities side of their balance sheet, they may provide forms of insurance to clients (life insurance, defined benefit pension funds).

5. Provision of **price information**, thus helping to coordinate decentralized decision making in various sectors of the economy. Financial markets provide not only means to trade but also information useful for decision making; for households, yields and securities prices provide information in consumption-saving decisions and in allocating portfolios. Firms may equally make investment and financing decisions on the basis of market prices. Not only prices per se but also implied volatility (derived from options prices) may be relevant in this context. The ability of institutional investors to employ information has been highlighted above, and this is an important additional reason for their growth. Moreover, the existence of institutional investors has important implications for the financial system as a whole. On the one hand, they should facilitate the efficient allocation of resources. On the other, there has been some criticism that they may be responsible at times for disruption of

financial markets by heightening market volatility and leading to collapses of liquidity (see chapters 5 and 6).

6. Provision of ways to **deal with incentive problems** when one party to a financial transaction has information that the other does not or when one is agent of the other and when control and enforcement of contracts are costly. Moral hazard and adverse selection are inevitable in such cases, but features of the financial system, such as delegation of monitoring by households to specialized financial intermediaries, may reduce such problems. The issue remains, however, of how households may monitor the intermediaries themselves or whether the latter have the right incentives to act in line with the interests of investors. Institutional investors have a comparative advantage over individual investors in dealing with issues of corporate governance, given the size and voting weight that they can wield. More generally, institutions as a whole exert influence on governments not to adopt lax fiscal or monetary policies, for fear of the market consequences (see chapter 6). On the other hand, it should be stressed that there are limits to institutional involvement; banks' comparative advantages in overcoming asymmetric information in loans for small firms has ruled out securities market intermediation of their liabilities to date. And there are important incentive problems in the fund management relation itself.

1.4   Institutions and Financial Development

To further aid in understanding the role of institutional investors in the financial system, it is worthwhile also to sketch in a stylized manner how financial markets develop over time and the stage at which institutions become viable and important.

1.4.1   Development of Corporate Financing

The processes whereby an economy develops from an informal financial system through banking to securities markets can be analyzed by use of **theories of corporate finance**. Whereas an entrepreneur can begin a firm by relying on his or her own funds and retained earnings, rapid growth of the enterprise requires access to external finance. The simplest form of this is from the entrepreneur's family, who will be able to monitor the entrepreneur closely and hence protect their own interests. Beyond this, **banks** tend to be the first to offer funds, as they have a comparative advantage in monitoring and control of entrepreneurs who lack a track record, for example in terms of access to information, ability to take security, and ability to exert control via short maturities (see Diamond 1984, Hellwig 1991). They are also able to offer benefits to depositors in terms of pooling across investments and "liquidity insurance," that is, the ability to offer access to deposited funds at any time, at a positive interest rate (see Diamond and Dybvig 1983). This may then dominate the alternatives of extremely undiversified finance of enterprises or hoarding.

Share issuance becomes important when bank debt becomes sizable in relation to existing own-funds. This is because the high resultant level of gearing gives rise to conflicts of interest between debt holders and equity holders, as for example owner-managers have the incentive to carry out high-risk investments (see Myers and Majluf 1984). Banks may also protect themselves by means of covenants or even the acceptance of equity stakes, which internalizes the associated agency costs. Apart from banks, at the initial stages of development of share markets, securities are typically held by wealthy individuals as an alternative, diversifiable, liquid, higher-return albeit riskier alternative to bank deposits.

Corporate bond markets are viable only when firms have a very high reputation, as this then constitutes a capital asset, that would depreciate if the firm engaged in opportunistic behavior (Diamond 1991). High credit quality is needed because bond market investors are likely to have less influence and control over management than equity holders or banks, even if one allows for the existence of covenants. Rating agencies help to alleviate associated information problems and may thereby open the bond market for firms with poor reputations or volatile profitability ("junk bonds").

The pattern is completed by development of **institutional investors**, which by their nature have a comparative advantage over banks and individuals in equity and corporate bond financing. These advantages link in turn to aspects such as pooling, price sensitivity, and superior leverage in corporate governance. Note, however, that institutions do not typically develop before securities markets are present. (The relationship of institutional investors to capital markets is discussed in more detail in chapter 5.)

1.4.2   Three Phases of Financial Development and the Role of Banks

An alternative, complementary paradigm is provided by Rybczynski (1997), who divides the evolution of the financial system into three phases: bank-oriented, market-oriented, and securitized. With respect to the functions of the financial system outlined above, in all phases of evolution, banks are largely responsible for the functions of provision of payments services and liquidity. On the other hand, there is an adjustment in the locus of collection and allocation of saving; monitoring and disciplining users of external finance; and assumption, measurement, pricing, and management of risk. In all of these areas, institutional investors become of increasing importance as financial development proceeds.

In the **bank-oriented phase**, the external funding of nonfinancial firms is obtained from banks in the form of nontradable bank loans, with banks monitoring the performance of borrowers and disciplining them as necessary. Banks also collect the bulk of savings of the economy. Money markets are not very developed and are almost exclusively interbank. During this phase, the banks play a dominant role in the economy; most financial intermediation goes through banks and shows up in their balance sheets. They may even, if permitted, hold equity stakes in nonfinancial firms. This dominance of financial flows as well as of balance sheet components reinforces banks' position, as they are uniquely placed to access private information about borrowers, evaluate risk of prospective borrowers, and price and diversify risks. Most of banks' income is interest income, and there can be cross-subsidization between different bank products. Most emerging market economies remain in the bank-oriented phase.

During the **market-oriented phase**, banks face more competition from other providers of savings media and financing products (in particular reflecting the growth of institutional investors as well as direct holdings of securities by households). But banks remain the major source of external funding to the nonfinancial sectors. The size of money markets increases, although they are still dominated by interbank activities. Capital markets start to develop, but they mainly provide bond financing to government as well as a certain number of new issues of equity. Nevertheless, this phase is characterized by a relative decline in the traditional direct role of banks in terms of the importance of deposits as an asset for households, loans as a source of external finance to companies, and on-balance sheet versus market financing activities. Households build up securities holdings both directly and via institutional investors. Monitoring begins to be shared between banks and institutional investors (via the rise of the takeover mechanism).

With respect to financial innovations, other market participants than banks may take a leading role and new products may emerge that compete with traditional banking products. In the banks' balance sheets, this will lead to a decline in the share of traditional bank lending, an increase in the holding of tradable assets on the assets side, and a shift from retail to costlier wholesale liabilities. Consequently, the income structure shifts toward a larger share of trading and underwriting income, while the impact of competition from investment banks and institutional investors means that cross-subsidization has to diminish. Europe and Japan may be judged to have reached this phase, as have some of the advanced emerging markets such as Chile.

In the third, **securitized phase**, the market provides the bulk of financing to the nonfinancial and also the financial sector. Corporate bonds and commercial paper substitute for bank loans, while mortgages and consumer credit may be securitized. Collecting and allocating savings, monitoring, and disciplining are undertaken mainly by financial markets (in the form of rating agencies, investment banks, and institutional investors) rather than banks, with financial assets held increasingly on the balance sheet of institutional investors. In this context, new financial products develop, such as derivatives, that allow for segmentation, unbundling, and thus separate pricing and trading of various risks, and new expertise and institutional players emerge in the financial markets. From banks' point of view, this means that trading, underwriting, advisory, and asset management activities come to center stage while traditional banking loses importance. The United States, the United Kingdom, and Canada may be judged to have reached this stage of development, and European Monetary Union will accelerate its advent in Continental Europe (see chapters 4 and 6).

1.4.3 Preconditions for Financial Development

Evidence from history suggests that the progress of an economy through the stages described in the sections above depends on a number of **preconditions** (see Davis 1998e). Partly, these relate to

macroeconomic and structural factors. Without a satisfactory framework for enforcing property rights and financial contracts, as well as
for providing public information, securities markets will not tend to
develop. Rather, forms of relationship banking with equity stakes
held mainly by banks in borrowers are likely to be the limits of
financial development.[25]

Institution of limited liability for equity claims, a structure for col-
lateralizing debt, satisfactory accounting standards, and appropriate
protection against securities fraud (listing requirements and insider
trading rules, for example) are also important for public securities
markets (see Stiglitz 1993). Moreover, the development and satisfactory regulation of the banking system may be a precondition for
growth of securities markets and institutional investors, given the
role of banks in providing credit to underwriters and market makers,
even when they do not take on security positions themselves (Blommestein and Spencer 1996).

1.5   Supply and Demand Factors Underlying the Growth of Institutional Investors

In this section, we seek to elucidate further the reasons for the recent
rapid growth of institutional assets that were outlined in section 1.1,
viewed also in the context of the functions of the financial sector and
stylized patterns of financial development outlined in section 1.4. We
consider the extent to which institutional growth arises from:

• **supply-side factors** (institutions have offered their services relatively more efficiently, thus fulfilling the functions of the financial
system more effectively) or

• **demand-side factors** (households have enhanced requirements for
the types of financial functions that institutional investors are able to
fulfill).

1.5.1   Household and Institutional Balance Sheet Composition

Since the vast majority of institutional assets are held on behalf of the
household sector, such an investigation requires one to assess the

---

25. This point raises the issue of whether structural aspects of financial systems are
self-perpetuating or what shocks could lead to structural change. One current issue is
whether European monetary union will radically change E.U. financial sectors (Davis
1998d).

role that institutions have played in the context of household sector balance sheets.

Table 1.8 shows that **household assets and liabilities have increased** in all of the countries studied, with gross financial assets rising from around 130% of GDP in 1970 to over 230% in 1998 and liabilities from under 40% to around 60%. Net financial wealth has also risen strongly, from around 90% to 180% of GDP, reflecting the more rapid growth of gross assets than liabilities. Patterns are re-markably similar in the Anglo-Saxon countries and in Europe and Japan (although both assets and liabilities tend to be lower in the latter). As is shown in table 1.9, **within gross financial assets**, there has been a decline in the share of deposits and (in the Anglo-Saxon countries) direct holdings of bonds and equities, while there has been a universal sharp rise in the portfolio share of institutional assets. The relative decline in equity holdings is reflected in steady decu-mulation in flow terms, with outflows on a net basis occurring every year in the United States and the United Kingdom.

A **comparison of these patterns for households with the portfo-lios adopted by institutional investors** allows one to gain a view of the effects of institutionalization on households' portfolios in terms of the instruments that are ultimately held. Reflecting the character-istics outlined in section 1.2.2, notably the long-term nature of liabil-ities, institutions such as pension funds hold far more equities and foreign assets as a proportion of the portfolio than households do and fewer liquid assets (table 1.10). This is true to a lesser extent for life insurers (table 1.11) but even more so for mutual funds, with the exception of money market funds (table 1.12). Mutual funds tend to hold more equities and foreign assets than pension funds do, while life insurers hold more nominal assets such as loans and bonds. Whereas mutual funds concentrate largely on securities, life insurers and pension funds in many countries hold considerable shares of property and loans.

We now go on to **assess the supply and demand factors** underly-ing growth of institutional investors in more detail. Applied specifi-cally to households, the supply-side factors are those that encourage households to hold their saving in the form of institutional liabilities rather than other types, namely, bank deposits and direct holdings of securities. The demand factors outline why households' own char-acteristics or other background features are changing so that they may increase their demands for institutional saving. In effect, these

Table 1.8
Household Assets and Liabilities/GDP

		1970	1980	1990	1995	1997	1998	Change 1970–1998
United	Assets	1.82	1.16	2.07	2.75	3.11	3.22	1.41
Kingdom	Liabilities	0.39	0.35	0.80	0.75	0.74	0.75	0.36
	Net financial wealth	1.43	0.82	1.27	2.00	2.38	2.47	1.04
United States	Assets	1.90	1.66	2.20	2.57	2.84	3.10	1.20
	Liabilities	0.48	0.55	0.68	0.72	0.71	0.73	0.24
	Net financial wealth	1.42	1.11	1.52	1.85	2.13	2.37	0.95
Germany	Assets	0.78	1.01	1.26	1.35	1.47	1.50	0.72
	Liabilities	0.38	0.50	0.54	0.56	0.61	0.62	0.24
	Net financial wealth	0.41	0.51	0.72	0.80	0.86	0.88	0.47
Japan	Assets	0.98	1.44	2.20	2.42	2.42	2.52	1.54
	Liabilities	0.38	0.54	0.77	0.77	0.75	0.77	0.38
	Net financial wealth	0.60	0.91	1.43	1.66	1.68	1.76	1.15
Canada	Assets	1.48	1.54	1.74	1.97	2.05	2.08	0.60
	Liabilities	0.51	0.56	0.63	0.66	0.68	0.70	0.20
	Net financial wealth	0.97	0.98	1.11	1.31	1.37	1.37	0.40
France	Assets	1.14	1.05	1.42	1.59	1.87	1.99	0.88
	Liabilities	0.42	0.44	0.57	0.42	0.42	0.43	0.01
	Net financial wealth	0.72	0.61	0.85	1.17	1.45	1.56	0.87
Italy	Assets	0.92	0.87	1.68	1.91	2.08	2.23	1.30
	Liabilities	0.07	0.06	0.19	0.24	0.25	0.20	0.12
	Net financial wealth	0.85	0.80	1.49	1.67	1.83	2.03	1.18
G-7	**Assets**	**1.29**	**1.25**	**1.80**	**2.08**	**2.26**	**2.38**	**1.09**
	Liabilities	**0.38**	**0.43**	**0.60**	**0.59**	**0.59**	**0.60**	**0.22**
	Net financial wealth	**0.91**	**0.82**	**1.20**	**1.49**	**1.67**	**1.78**	**0.87**
Anglo-Saxon	**Assets**	**1.73**	**1.46**	**2.00**	**2.43**	**2.67**	**2.80**	**1.07**
	Liabilities	**0.46**	**0.49**	**0.70**	**0.71**	**0.71**	**0.73**	**0.27**
	Net financial wealth	**1.27**	**0.97**	**1.30**	**1.72**	**1.96**	**2.07**	**0.80**
Europe and	**Assets**	**0.96**	**1.09**	**1.64**	**1.82**	**1.88**	**2.07**	**1.11**
Japan	**Liabilities**	**0.31**	**0.39**	**0.52**	**0.49**	**0.50**	**0.50**	**0.19**
	Net financial wealth	**0.64**	**0.71**	**1.12**	**1.32**	**1.38**	**1.57**	**0.93**

Source: National flow-of-funds balance sheet data; for detailed sources, see table 1.1.

Table 1.9
Household Sector Balance Sheets (Proportions of Gross Financial Assets)

		1970	1980	1990	1995	1997	1998	Change 1970–1998
United	Deposits	0.34	0.43	0.31	0.22	0.22	0.21	−0.13
Kingdom	Bonds	0.07	0.07	0.01	0.02	0.01	0.01	−0.06
	Equities	0.24	0.12	0.12	0.15	0.17	0.15	−0.09
	Institutions	0.23	0.30	0.48	0.51	0.53	0.55	0.31
United States	Deposits	0.28	0.33	0.23	0.16	0.14	0.13	−0.15
	Bonds	0.13	0.10	0.11	0.10	0.07	0.06	−0.07
	Equities	0.36	0.21	0.14	0.22	0.24	0.23	−0.12
	Institutions	0.22	0.28	0.39	0.42	0.47	0.50	0.28
Germany	Deposits	0.59	0.59	0.48	0.43	0.40	0.40	−0.19
	Bonds	0.08	0.12	0.16	0.16	0.14	0.13	0.06
	Equities	0.10	0.04	0.07	0.05	0.08	0.09	−0.01
	Institutions	0.15	0.17	0.21	0.29	0.30	0.32	0.17
Japan	Deposits	0.55	0.69	0.60	0.60	0.62	0.60	0.04
	Bonds	0.06	0.09	0.09	0.05	0.03	0.02	−0.03
	Equities	0.12	0.07	0.09	0.06	0.05	0.04	−0.07
	Institutions	0.14	0.13	0.21	0.29	0.31	0.28	0.14
Canada	Deposits	0.31	0.38	0.36	0.32	0.30	0.30	−0.01
	Bonds	0.14	0.08	0.05	0.06	0.05	0.04	−0.09
	Equities	0.27	0.24	0.21	0.25	0.28	0.30	0.03
	Institutions	0.22	0.21	0.28	0.30	0.32	0.34	0.13
France	Deposits	0.49	0.59	0.38	0.35	0.32	0.29	−0.20
	Bonds	0.06	0.09	0.04	0.05	0.03	0.02	−0.03
	Equities	0.26	0.12	0.26	0.23	0.29	0.32	0.07
	Institutions	0.06	0.09	0.26	0.33	0.32	0.31	0.26
Italy	Deposits	0.45	0.58	0.35	0.28	0.23	0.23	−0.22
	Bonds	0.19	0.08	0.19	0.21	0.22	0.18	−0.02
	Equities	0.11	0.10	0.21	0.21	0.25	0.30	0.19
	Institutions	0.08	0.06	0.08	0.10	0.10	0.10	0.02
G-7	**Deposits**	**0.43**	**0.52**	**0.39**	**0.34**	**0.32**	**0.31**	**− 0.12**
	Bonds	**0.10**	**0.09**	**0.09**	**0.09**	**0.08**	**0.07**	**− 0.04**
	Equities	**0.21**	**0.13**	**0.16**	**0.17**	**0.20**	**0.21**	**0.00**
	Institutions	**0.16**	**0.18**	**0.27**	**0.32**	**0.34**	**0.34**	**0.19**
Anglo-Saxon	**Deposits**	**0.31**	**0.38**	**0.30**	**0.23**	**0.22**	**0.21**	**− 0.10**
	Bonds	**0.11**	**0.08**	**0.06**	**0.06**	**0.05**	**0.04**	**− 0.07**
	Equities	**0.29**	**0.19**	**0.16**	**0.21**	**0.23**	**0.23**	**− 0.06**
	Institutions	**0.22**	**0.26**	**0.38**	**0.41**	**0.44**	**0.46**	**0.24**
Europe and	**Deposits**	**0.52**	**0.62**	**0.45**	**0.42**	**0.39**	**0.38**	**− 0.14**
Japan	**Bonds**	**0.09**	**0.10**	**0.12**	**0.12**	**0.10**	**0.09**	**− 0.01**
	Equities	**0.15**	**0.08**	**0.15**	**0.14**	**0.17**	**0.19**	**0.04**
	Institutions	**0.11**	**0.11**	**0.19**	**0.25**	**0.26**	**0.25**	**0.15**

Source: National flow-of-funds balance sheet data; for detailed sources, see table 1.1.

Table 1.10
Pension Funds' Portfolio Composition, 1998 (Percent)

	Liquidity	Loans	Domestic Bonds	Domestic Equities	Property	Foreign Assets
United Kingdom	4	0	14	52	3	18
United States	4	1	21	53E	0	11E
Germany	0	33	43	10	7	7
Japan	5	14	34	23	0	18
Canada	5	3	38	27	3	15
France	0	18	65	10	2	5
Italy	0	1	35	16	48	0

E = Estimated.
Sources: National flow-of-funds balance sheets, Mercer (1999).
Numbers do not always add to 100 owing to "miscellaneous assets."

Table 1.11
Life Insurers' Portfolio Composition, 1998 (Percent)

	Liquidity	Loans	Domestic Bonds	Domestic Equities	Property	Foreign Assets
United Kingdom	5	1	25	48	6	13
United States	6	8	52	26	0	1
Germany	1	57	14	17	4	0
Japan	5	30	36	10	0	9
Canada	7	28	55	26	7	3
France	1	2	74	15	7	0
Italy	0	1	75	12	1	0

Source: National flow-of-funds balance sheets, OECD.
Numbers do not always add to 100 owing to "miscellaneous assets."

Table 1.12
Open-End Mutual Funds' Portfolio Composition, 1998 (Percent)

	Liquidity	Loans	Domestic Bonds	Domestic Equities	Property	Foreign Assets
United Kingdom	4	0	8	56	2	33
United States	17	0	30	51	0	N.A.
Germany	10	0	22	18	0	29
Japan	23	18	27	9	0	22
Canada	20	3	18	31	0	23
France	29	0	37	20	0	14
Italy	19	0	54	22	0	0

N.A. = not available.
Source: FEFSI, National flow-of-funds balance sheets.

sections draw out the economic implications of the features and functions of institutions that were set out in sections 1.2 and 1.3.

1.5.2   Supply-Side Factors Favoring Growth of Institutional Investors

The link between the "supply side" and the functions of the financial system is clear; institutional investors prove, in a competitive financial system and with current technology, to **fulfill financial functions** (section 1.3) **better than other arrangements**. We begin by outlining some longer-term structural advantages of institutional investors that have come to the fore as the sector develops before going on to assess some recent developments that compound such advantages.

As a baseline for considering the supply-side effects, it is worth noting **patterns of asset holdings that held before institutional investors developed**. Wealthy individuals were able to hold diversified securities portfolios at high cost, while shareholding tended to be uneconomic for those with lower wealth. Traditionally, and still to some extent in Europe and Japan, this led middle- and low-income individuals to hold bank deposits as a preferred means of saving, despite lower rates of return. The pattern as institutional sectors develop has been for the household sector to reduce holdings of deposits, bonds, and equities while increasing holdings of mutual funds, pension funds, and life insurance. Middle- and low-income individuals shifted out of deposits, and high-income individuals moved out of bonds and equities held directly (see table 1.9). Note that mutual funds in particular are attractive to the household sector because they typically offer a rather low level of minimum holding, for which the reduction in transactions costs would be particularly marked. With mutual funds, unlike life insurance or pension funds, there is also no need for a long-term savings contract.

1.5.2.1   Structural Aspects
Institutions can offer the possibility of **investing in large-denomination and indivisible assets** such as property that are unavailable to small investors. **Professional asset management costs** are shared among many households and are markedly reduced as a consequence. Institutions may as a consequence of professional management offer a superior risk-return profile. Hence, the direct

costs to households of acquiring the information and knowledge needed to invest in a range of assets is eliminated (although costs of monitoring the asset manager remain). **Customer services**, including record keeping and the ability to move money around among funds, is an attraction notably for mutual funds.

Individual investors find it difficult to **control the companies** in which they hold shares. As is discussed in greater detail in chapter 6, institutional investors are much more readily able to exert leverage on firms than individuals are, be it via "exit" (seeking out and selling to takeover raiders) or "voice" (exerting direct influence on corporate management). Indeed, lack of legal protection for shareholders in many countries tends to discourage direct equity investment by households altogether (see La Porta et al. 1999). In both contexts, institutions can make a major contribution to provision of equity finance to the corporate sector, thus allowing companies to benefit from a lower cost of equity capital.

Institutional investors, by specializing in certain types of asset, can offer a **wider range of options** to their holders on a cost-effective basis. The development of country funds, for example, has proved attractive not only to households but also to other institutional investors.

A particular feature of open-end mutual funds is that, like banks, they offer **liquidity insurance** to customers by allowing redemption of funds pro rata to the net assets of the fund without notice. Such liquidity is absent for most other types of institutional investors (although policy loans offered by life insurers are akin). They impose a cost on the fund—and on long-term holders—by forcing it to hold more cash and liquid assets than would otherwise be the case. Fee structures are often designed to reduce the incidence of withdrawals (Chordia 1996). Improvements in liquidity to customers may go beyond those linked solely to transactions costs. In the United States, checks can be written on long-term assets of mutual funds such as equities and bonds. Also, transactions or sales may be made by phone or by the Internet at the end-of-day net asset value; and the investor can costlessly exchange shares of one mutual fund for those of another within the same fund-family, thus changing the entire balance of the portfolio.

Institutions can also offer other forms of **insurance** that are not available to individual investors, as a consequence of the pooling of risks (as in the case of an insurance company), with a backup in terms of capital (for an insurance company or pension fund) or by investing in very liquid and high-quality instruments (for money market funds).

Fiscal advantages have often been accorded to institutional investors, thus increasing their attraction to investors.[26] The tax advantage of exemption of contributions and asset returns is common for pension funds where provision of such funds is voluntary for companies or individuals. But life insurance contributions also benefit from tax exemption in a number of Continental European countries, and mutual funds do in some countries also.[27] Money market funds' growth in France in the 1980s links to fiscal benefits.

Historically, the **transactions costs** that would need to be incurred for a household of average means to diversify via direct securities holdings[28] on an individual basis have been extremely high. Excess risk incurred if diversification is insufficient would not be compensated by higher return (as such risk is diversifiable to the market as a whole). Despite the relatively low levels of commission costs in the United States, estimates based on data for the early 1990s suggest that costs amounted to 1.2–9.8 percentage points per year on a seven-year holding period, depending on the size of the holding. Even for an investor with $100,000 to invest, 150–200 basis points (bp)[29] of commission would be incurred per year (Sirri and Tufano 1995). Such figures were typically much higher elsewhere in the G-7 and beyond. Even deregulation at times led costs of individual investment to increase: The deregulation of fixed stock market commissions typically favored large investors and eliminated cross-subsidies to small investors. This was the case both for the New York Stock Exchange (NYSE) deregulation of commission rates in 1975 and the U.K. "Big Bang" of 1986. Jarrell (1984), for example, points out that whereas institutional commissions on the NYSE fell by 50% in the five years after deregulation, the charge for transacting under 1000 shares by members of the public rose by 17% (see table 1.13).

---

26. The power of tax privileges is also illustrated by the decline in institutional assets that may follow radical tax reform, such as removal of pension funds' tax benefits in New Zealand.

27. In some countries, such as Germany, money market funds (in Luxembourg) have been an instrument of tax evasion.

28. Typically, around forty shares are needed to offer the same volatility as the market as a whole; in the United States, the "round-trip" commissions needed would in the early 1990s have amounted to 12% of value, even for a person of median wealth (Sirri and Tufano 1995).

29. A basis point is 1/100 of 1%.

Table 1.13
Effective Commission Rates on the NYSE for Public and Institutional Orders

Order Size (Number of Shares)	0–199		200–999		1000–9999		10000+	
Trade	Public	Instit	Public	Instit	Public	Instit	Public	Instit
1975	50.1	59.6	32.6	45.7	19.5	27.6	8.8	15.0
1980	59.3	47.3	38	30.9	17.3	14.8	4.3	7.5
% change	+18.4	−20.6	+16.6	−32.4	−11.3	−46.4	−51.1	−50

Public = public trades; Instit = institutional trades.
Source: Jarrell (1984).

In this context, institutional investors such as mutual funds and pension funds tended to offer much **lower costs of diversification by proportional ownership**. This has historically been of particular importance given minimum size investment barriers. Fees for managing such investments, as is discussed further in chapter 3, can be as low as 25 bp for (company) pension funds, 15 bp for index mutual funds, and 100 bp for actively managed mutual funds. One reason for this is that there are lower proportionate commissions[30] for large transactions, although this may be offset by other costs such as a wider bid-offer spread (chapter 8). Institutional investors can compound this advantage by negotiating lower commission costs and custodial fees.

More recently, the development of online brokerage in the United States and online trading elsewhere has tended to reduce costs of direct investment in securities on the part of households, making the transactions cost benefit of institutional investment less decisive.[31]

The **regulatory structure** that is applied to certain institutions such as mutual funds and wholesale investment managers has not typically sought to limit entry and competition but has sought rather to ensure sufficient disclosure, encourage prudent asset structures, and prevent fraud. This has ensured keen competition, as is discussed in chapter 3. In addition, regulation has focused on protection of investors against fraud and conflicts of interest and thus has helped to maintain consumer confidence.

---

30. Note, however, that institutional commissions are often distorted by so-called soft commissions, which pay for unrelated services such as research (see chapter 8).

31. Earlier, in the 1970s and 1980s, there was the growth of discount brokerage in the United States and the United Kingdom following deregulation of stock market fees and commissions, and benefits accrued of computerization in back-office processing.

It is in the context of these favorable structural factors that the declining share of households' portfolios held in the form of securities and the rising proportion of equities and bonds held via institutions can be explained. Institutional investors offer superior forms of pooling and liquidity and more generally have broadened the availability of investment options to the household sector. Institutionalization has in particular enabled households that were previously confined to deposits and life insurance to participate in the securities markets.

These **benefits have needed to be sufficient to offset some of the costs** that institutional investment imposes vis-à-vis direct securities holdings. For example, there are direct sales and marketing costs of mutual funds, charges for investment management and other ongoing services (which have been rising recently), and tax options forgone (e.g., in terms of timing of capital gains for tax efficiency). In some countries, these costs may be artificially high owing to entry barriers (such as control of distribution networks) that block competing firms from the market. More generally, households face a variety of principal-agent problems in monitoring and controlling asset managers that, if not resolved, may result in poor investment performance as managers act in their own interests rather than those of investors (chapter 2). As we have noted, direct securities' holdings relative costs have diminished recently, even for small transactions, owing to the growth of online brokerage and trading.

The net structural attractions have been enhanced by a number of more recent changes, which have enabled institutions to perform their investment role with even greater efficiency relative to the alternatives.

1.5.2.2   Recent Developments

Deregulation of the activities of institutions in the past two decades has added a dynamic aspect to the overall regulatory approach noted in section 1.2.3. In the 1970s and 1980s, institutions gained from deregulation of securities market commissions, since they have been able, first, to press for deregulation of fixed commissions by disintermediating the regulated market and, second, following deregulation, to exert bargaining power to reduce the commissions they pay. (See Jarrell (1984) for an account of this process in the context of the NYSE in the 1970s.)

More recently, deregulation of some restrictions on the portfolios of institutions, in particular in terms of international investment, has offered wider possibilities of diversification, as has deregulation in terms of production and distribution of their respective products. By removing remaining barriers to competition in asset management, deregulation has ensured that market forces have been able to fully operate, which has ensured low costs to the end user. (See the discussion of U.S. and U.K. asset management fees in chapters 3 and 4.) Another factor underlying heightened competition has been deregulation of the activities of banks and securities firms and banks' interest after the Basle capital adequacy accord in fee income generating that economize on the use of capital. As detailed in chapter 3, costs are higher in Continental Europe, where deregulation has been slower or aspects of market structure, such as domination of distribution by banks, have inhibited competition.

Institutions have benefited from recent **technological advances** in communications technology and information technology (IT), including efficient trading, clearing, and settlement systems, which enabled funds to be managed at lower cost. It would clearly be uneconomic for individual households to make the investment in IT that would be typical of an institution and can hence be shared (although development of Internet-based services is now narrowing the gap). Equally, technological advance has facilitated the development of checkable money market funds.

New financial instruments such as mortgage-backed securities and collateralized mortgage obligations, which require immense data-processing capabilities to make them viable, have been heavily utilized by institutions; in this context, one may note also enhanced possibilities of risk management via use of derivatives (see section 2.3.3).

Products offered by competing suppliers of savings products have proven increasingly unattractive. This is notably the case for bank deposits vis-à-vis money market funds. Historically, banks offered low or administered rates that failed to protect against inflation, while more recently, banks offered lower interest rates than were obtainable in the market owing to the banks' higher fixed costs (such as branch networks), capital requirements, reserve requirements, and repeated loan losses. In this context, institutional investors are not typically subject to minimum reserve requirements, an

Table 1.14
Social Security Benefits and Institutional Investment

	Social Security Replacement Ratios	Institutional Investment/ GDP (%), 1998
United Kingdom	60–33	197
United States	71–45	176
Germany	45–43	35
Japan	N.A.	63
Canada	57–26	105
France	67–51	90
Italy	78–75	54

N.A. = not available.
Note: Replacement ratios—pensions as a percentage of final salary—are for final salaries of $20,000 and $50,000. The data are for 1997.
Source: Watson Wyatt (1997), table 1.6.

implicit tax on banks, although portfolio regulations on institutions may at times act in a similar way.[32]

Among institutional investor sectors themselves, life insurance sectors have often faced difficulties in competing with pension funds and mutual funds. This is because life insurance sectors are often heavily regulated, have traditionally nominal fixed returns and high commission charges for remunerating salesmen, and in some countries face tight asset regulations that limit returns.

Social security benefits are also an alternative product to institutional investors for retirement income provision. As Davis (1997a) argues, generous social security is likely to constrain institutional growth, especially in the form of pension funds. This is especially the case, as in Continental Europe, where social security provides generous benefit promises to higher-income individuals (see table 1.14). On the other hand, growth in institutional investment is particularly marked where social security provides only a basic pension to alleviate poverty but does not have an important income insurance element, as in the Netherlands[33] and the United Kingdom.

Increasingly, however, it is the generous social security pensions that are seen as unsustainable in the light of demographic developments. (See the demand-side factors discussed below.) On balance, the governments that introduced such systems did not sufficiently

---

32. In the Euro area, ECB regulations permit the imposition of reserve requirements on money market mutual funds.
33. For a discussion of the Dutch pension system, see Davis (1996c) and Clark (2000b).

consider risks in terms of birth rates, sustainable economic growth rates, and death rates. Growing public concern about sustainability, as for example in Japan, encourages institutional saving as a precaution, notably via life insurance and mutual funds. Elsewhere, as in Australia and Chile, the growth of private pensions following a reform of social security has ensured high coverage and large, steady inflows to institutional investors. This has fed back strongly on the costs of asset management, leading to economies of scale and a wider range of services being offered also to nonpension clients.

Finally, an important environmental factor has been the **bull market** in both equities and bonds for much of the 1980s and 1990s. This has made investment in securities via institutional investors seem yet more attractive than the above supply-side factors might suggest. There has been a two-way process; in effect, the growth of institutions and, notably, mutual funds has helped to create a widespread equity culture. How such a culture will survive a bear market remains to be seen. Certainly, as Jorion and Goetzmann (1999) show, the real rates of return on equity in the 1990s are well above historical averages in the United States and the United Kingdom, and these themselves have been atypically well-performing equity markets over the longer term.

1.5.3 Demand Factors

The key demand-side factors underlying the growth of institutions are **demographic developments and their link to saving patterns**. The basic argument is simply stated: The population is aging, owing to a decline in birth rate and rise in life expectancy; saving for retirement is increasingly taking place via institutional investors (owing to various supply factors summarized below); such saving naturally tends to follow a life cycle pattern; and hence both aggregate saving and institutional saving are currently being boosted because the "baby boom" generation is at the time of maximum saving. We address these arguments one by one, with a particular focus on demographics. These patterns may drive institutional growth for many years to come as the entire population ages in the light of falling birth rates and existing social security systems become unsustainable. Benefits from this effect are not confined to pension funds. Nonpension saving via life insurance and mutual funds is strongly boosted where pension funds are less well established.

Table 1.15
Life Expectancy at Birth

Years	1970–1975	1980–1985	1990–1995	2000
United Kingdom	72	74	76	78
United States	73	75	77	77
Germany	71	73	76	77
Japan	74	77	79	81
Canada	73	76	78	79
France	72	75	78	79
Italy	72	75	78	79

Source: World Bank (1996), U.S. Department of the Census.

1.5.3.1 Past Demographic Factors and Institutional Saving

As regards **demographics**, OECD countries have all witnessed an increase in life expectancy and a decline in the birth rate in recent decades. These have already given rise to an aging population, with a high proportion of the population in the high saving age groups and also an increasing burden of dependents relative to the population of working age.

The higher **life expectancy** is, the longer individuals expect to live after retirement and the greater the need for long-term saving. As table 1.15 shows, the life expectancy at birth in the G-7 countries has risen from around 72 to 78 between 1970 and 2000. Life expectancy in Japan is now 81. Underlying these patterns are better health care, medical advances, and improved overall living standards.[34]

Except in the United States, there has also been a decline in **birth rates** since 1970, which has reduced the size of the younger generations who would otherwise borrow and offset the saving of their older counterparts (see table 1.16). In 2000, there were exceptionally low fertility rates[35] (of below 1.5) in Germany, Italy, and Japan, while the rate in France, Canada, and the United Kingdom was around 1.7 and that in the United States was 2.1. Only in the United States is the fertility rate sufficient alone (i.e., without immigration) to generate a stable population. Underlying the decline in fertility is the emerging pattern of later marriage and greater activity of women in the labor market, which has increased the opportunity cost of having children,

---

34. Accompanying these is a pattern of early retirement, thereby also lengthening the potential retirement period (Davis 1997c).
35. Fertility rates indicate the number of children born to an average woman over her lifetime.

Table 1.16
Fertility Rates (Number of Children per Female)

	1970–1975	1980–1985	1990–1995	2000
United Kingdom	1.8	1.8	1.8	1.7
United States	1.8	1.8	2.0	2.1
Germany	1.5	1.4	1.2	1.4
Japan	1.9	1.8	1.5	1.4
Canada	1.8	1.7	1.9	1.6
France	1.9	1.8	1.7	1.7
Italy	2.2	1.4	1.3	1.2

Source: World Bank (1996), U.S. Department of the Census.

as well as more general social and attitudinal changes.[36] Reflecting the decline in fertility, the generation born in the European Union in the 1970s is 17% smaller than that of the 1960s, and the 1980s generation is 25% smaller. In all of the G-7, as well as the European Union, the retirement of this baby boom generation offers a particular challenge to systems of retirement income provision.

Broadly speaking, these patterns have already influenced institutional saving by **increasing the proportion of the population in the high saving age groups** (roughly 30- to 60-year-olds). A strong effect of demographics on saving to date is found by many studies, most of which in turn attribute this to a life cycle pattern of saving.[37] For example, Masson et al. (1995), in econometric work on savings patterns across countries, find that consistent with the life cycle view, the total dependency ratio is negatively associated with total private saving, in both OECD countries and developing countries. The other main determinant of saving in their econometric estimates is income growth. Interest rates and terms of trade have positive but often statistically insignificant effects on saving in the econometric estimates; income per head raises saving at low income levels but reduces it at higher levels.

36. Davis (1997c) notes that the highest fertility rates among E.U. countries today are in Scandinavian countries, which provide comprehensive and subsidized child care facilities, thus spreading the burden of child care from the family to the economy as a whole.

37. The life cycle hypothesis assumes that consumers derive utility from a smooth pattern of consumption over both their working and nonworking life. As regards the implications of retirement, this entails the accumulation of assets during the working life, which will be decumulated after retirement.

Table 1.17
Projections of Elderly Dependency Ratio to 2030

Population 65 and Over as a Percentage of Population Aged 15–65	1960	1990	2010	2030
United Kingdom	17.9	24.0	25.8	38.7
United States	15.4	19.1	20.4	36.8
Germany	16.0	21.7	30.3	49.2
Japan	9.5	17.1	33.0	44.5
Canada	13.0	16.7	20.4	39.1
France	18.8	20.8	24.6	39.1
Italy	13.3	21.6	31.2	48.3
Memo:				
E.U. average	16.5E	21.4	25.9	40.3

E = estimated.
Source: Bos et al. (1994).

1.5.3.2 Future Demographic Changes

All demographic projections for OECD countries show a **continuation and intensification of the ongoing process of aging** in the future. These patterns provide a stimulus to institutionalization from a number of angles. First, existing funded systems will face higher demands for retirement saving. Second, governments with generous pay-as-you-go social security realize that they are no longer viable and seek to encourage private funding instead. Third, even absent government action, individuals lose confidence in social security promises and begin to save for retirement autonomously, be it via pension funds, life insurance, or mutual funds.

Highlights of a **recent demographic projection** for the G-7 by the World Bank are provided in table 1.17.[38] The table assumes that fertility rates converge gradually from current levels to replacement in 2030; that life expectancy tends gradually toward peaks of 83.3 and 90 for men and women, respectively; and that migration remains around current levels—generally zero. Clearly, the fertility assumption could be too high. Nevertheless, at least for the next fifty years, such projections can be made with reasonable precision, given the fact that many of the individuals concerned are already born, while birth rates and life expectancy change rather slowly. The dominance of the first of these factors is shown by the fact that projections are similar for some time with fertility rates of 2.5 or 1.7 and abstracting from migration.

38. Source: Bos (1994).

Table 1.17 shows that the demographic shift will be **particularly marked in the years from 2010 onward**. Whereas in 1990, the average G-7 dependency ratio was around 21%, it is expected to rise to over 25% in 2010 and 40% in 2030. In Germany and Italy, the elderly dependency ratio will be over 45% in 2030. The aging of the population is also anticipated in the United States, but the level expected in 2030 remains somewhat lower than that in the rest of the G-7 and the European Union. There is also expected to be an increasing proportion of very old individuals, who may need additional, and costly, health care as well as pensions. The share of young dependents is expected to be flat, but they tend to be less costly than the old.[39] The total dependency ratio (including those under age 15 and over age 65 in the numerator) will be over 70% in 2030 in Germany and Italy, according to these projections. Note that the burden of dependency ratios is also affected by shifts in the start and finish of working life and of unemployment. There have been tendencies, notably in Europe, for the average retirement ages to fall and for education to increase in length, while unemployment has also tended to increase (Davis 1997c).

1.5.3.3 Pressures on Pension Systems in the Wake of Population Aging

Roseveare et al. (1996) of the OECD have estimated **future pension expenditures** for G-7 countries on a comparable basis. They constructed detailed simulation models for each country based on known features of the pension schemes (retirement age, indexation provisions, etc.) as well as utilizing demographic projections (which were those from the World Bank illustrated above). Estimates cover a broad range of welfare benefits and complementary pension plans as well as basic social security pensions. The projection horizon is 2070. The calculations assume a discount rate of 5%, and productivity growth is assumed to be 1.5%. Naturally, such estimates omit some of the more detailed aspects of national economies and institutional features of social security schemes, but they do have the advantage of a uniform methodology and assumptions. As table 1.18 shows, the estimates suggest that pension expenditure will rise by 7% or more of GDP over 1990–2040 in Italy, Japan, and Germany and will more

---

39. Heller et al. (1986) accordingly estimate that social expenditures will rise in the major industrial countries even if savings in education and family benefits are taken into account.

Table 1.18
Projections of Pension Costs (OECD Estimates)

Pension Expenditure/GDP	1995	2000	2010	2020	2030	2040
United Kingdom	4.5	4.5	5.2	5.1	5.5	5.0
United States	4.1	4.2	4.5	5.2	6.6	7.1
Germany	11.1	11.5	11.8	12.3	16.5	18.4
Japan	6.6	7.5	9.6	12.4	13.4	14.9
Canada	5.2	5.0	5.3	6.9	9.0	9.1
France	10.6	9.8	9.7	11.6	13.5	14.3
Italy	13.3	12.6	13.2	15.3	20.3	21.4

Source: Roseveare et al. (1996).

than double in Japan relative to GDP. Peak ratios of old-age pension payments to GDP in 2040, with unchanged policies, would be over 15% of GDP in Italy and Germany. At the same point, they would be 5% or less in the United Kingdom[40] and below 10% also in the United States and Canada. Assuming unchanged policies on benefits and maintenance of pay-as-you-go financing, contributions would have to increase sharply. With unchanged contribution rates,[41] social security pension contributions would fall far short in most E.U. countries and in Japan, implying sizable public sector deficits.

Using the same methods, Roseveare et al. (1996) have also estimated the current and future **discounted liabilities of social security** pension systems for the G-7 countries. These indicate the capitalized value of identified flows over the period up to 2070. The results are shown in table 1.19. Estimates of gross liabilities range from 142% to 401% of 1994 GDP, equivalent to at least three times conventional government debt as a percentage of GDP. Note that in the gross calculation the OECD, no offset is allowed for future contributions in calculating net liabilities. An attempt is also made to assess projected contributions and hence net liabilities, assuming that current contribution rates are maintained. In general, future contributions were found to be well below present and future obligations, to an extent varying from 18% to 153% of 1994 GDP, even allowing for social security assets. There are net liabilities of over 100% of GDP in France and Canada. But as the net liabilities are the

---

40. Details of the U.K. reforms that have led to this situation are provided in Davis (1997b).
41. This would, of course, be contrary to the principle of pay-as-you-go, according to which contribution rates should be amended regularly so as to equalize expenditure and revenues.

Table 1.19
Present Value of Public Pension Liabilities as a Percentage of 1994 GDP
(OECD Estimates)

	Pension Payments	Contributions	Balance
United Kingdom	142	118	−24
Germany	348	286	−62
Japan	299	192	−70
Canada	204	97	−101
France	318	216	−102
Italy	401	341	−60
United States	163	134	−23

Source: Roseveare et al. (1996). French estimates exclude "fictive contributions"; German estimates exclude statutory transfers from the federal government.

Table 1.20
Present Value of Net Pension Liability, 1995–2050 (IMF Estimates)

As % of 1994 GDP	Net Pension Liability	Memo: Contribution Gap
United Kingdom	5	0.1
Germany	111	3.4
France	114	3.3
Italy	76	2.5
United States	26	0.8

Source: IMF (1996). The contribution gap is the difference between the contribution rate that is needed to reduce the net asset position to zero and the current contribution rate.

difference between two large and offsetting numbers, the calculations *are* sensitive to the choice of discount rate.

A further set of calculations has been prepared by the IMF, as presented in their World Economic Outlook for May 1996. These are presented in table 1.20. The real interest rate is assumed to be 3.5% and productivity growth 1.5%; the projection horizon is 2050, and the demographic projections are those of Bos (1994). Results are broadly equivalent to those of the OECD. The United Kingdom is always in the best position. The IMF also calculates the contribution gap, that is, the difference between the sustainable and actual rate of contributions, as a proportion of GDP. In each case, the difficulties of the systems in Germany, France, and Italy are highlighted.

We noted above that besides simple cuts in social security benefits, increased funding of pensions will be an important aspect of the policy response (see Davis 1997c). This in turn will increase the scope of institutional investment via pension funds. Even in advance of reforms, individuals in countries with generous pay-as-you-go systems are increasing their long-term saving via mutual funds and life insurers, owing to expectations of future difficulties and consequent reform, and are thereby already boosting the institutionalization of capital markets. Cross-country comparison using the data in table 1.6 indicate the enormous scope of pension fund asset accumulation that would be involved if Europe and Japan were to converge on U.S. levels of funded pension provision; mutual fund and life insurance growth would likely boost these figures further.

1.5.3.4 Saving Projections in the Light of Demographic Shifts

As regards **projections of saving** in the light of such patterns, focusing on Europe, Miles and Patel (1996) suggest that as long as the baby boom generation remains in the labor force, an increase in private saving should be expected in the European Union, building to a maximum of 2.5% in 2020, after which saving declines as individuals retire. This implies a continued high rate of institutional saving. The rise in private saving would, in the view of Miles and Patel, be more than enough to offset changes in government saving. This projection is based on a life cycle view of saving, whereby assets are accumulated over the working life and run down during retirement.[42] Börsch-Supan (1996) comes to a conclusion similar to that of Miles and Patel for major OECD countries regarding the profile of private saving, taking into account different saving propensities of cohorts and population growth. However, he concludes that increases in governments' demand for funds arising from population aging will outstrip the rise in private saving after 2005.

Not all studies suggest that private saving will rise. Roseveare et al. (1996) assess two scenarios that differ in the size of the assumed negative effect of the dependency ratio on saving and in the question as to whether there is Ricardian equivalence (private sector saving to offset public sector dissaving). They see private saving as a proportion of GDP across all industrial countries falling 3–6 percentage points between 2000 and 2030, depending on the scenario, and national saving declining by 8–16 percentage points, given unchanged

---

42. In a separate paper, Miles (1996) notes that cross-sectional evidence of individual households appears to be inconsistent with the life cycle, as saving is rarely negative after retirement. But he considers that this is largely a measurement error problem, as the decline in value of pension assets is rarely allowed for in cross-sectional data. Hence the predictions based on the life cycle—of falls in aggregate saving as the population ages—remain robust.

pension policies and assuming a partial response of private saving to government dissaving. In France, net national saving is forecast to be negative in 2030 in both scenarios. Cutler et al. (1990a) and Heller and Sidgwick (1987) reach similar conclusions.

Masson and Tryon (1990) use the IMF's global econometric model MULTIMOD to assess the combined effect of future aging on private saving, public deficits, and overall production (where production is assumed to link to the labor supply, i.e., the size of population of working age times the participation ratio). Their model generates large decreases in national saving in Germany and Japan from 2000 onward, as both private and public sectors reduce their saving, while in France, Italy, and the United Kingdom, the net effect is positive, with increased private saving more than compensating for a rise in the fiscal deficit. The difference in private saving links to the differences in demographic profiles. (Note that the model includes endogenous tax increases rather than assuming fixed contribution rates.)

These various simulations suggest that there is a need for caution in assuming that demographic trends will always drive increased private saving. On the other hand, given the need for retirement income and the likelihood of pension reform in some countries, it is quite likely that the composition of saving will continue to shift in favor of institutional investors, even if the overall level were to decline. (This subject is discussed further in chapter 6.)

1.5.3.5 Nondemographic Aspects
A separate factor from demographics is **wealth accumulation**. As table 1.8 shows, household sector balance sheets have seen an increase in both assets and liabilities relative to GDP, while in all cases, net financial wealth has also increased relative to GDP. Within gross holdings, there has been a universal increase in asset holding via institutional investors (table 1.9). As wealth increases, households want an increasing share of their assets to be held in the form of long-term and higher-return and higher-risk instruments, as their liquidity needs can be catered for by a relatively small proportion of the portfolio. Even the latter may be in money market mutual funds if they are available and suitably competitive vis-à-vis bank deposits.

Owing to this change in wealth, the political climate has arguably become more investor-friendly. The increased number of wealthy individuals has changed the demand for financial services. Traditional banking services or products, while maintaining a strong position in liquidity provision, are not adequate for people who are interested in diversification and maximization of return subject to risk in the context of long-term investments. The associated rise in demand for securities has entailed an increased importance of brokerage, fund management, and consultancy activities.

Conclusions

Institutional investors have grown strongly in the past few decades, as a consequence not only of the overall expansion of financial claims relative to GDP, but also of a boost in their share of total claims. This phenomenon can be traced to various supply and demand factors that have made institutions attractive to households. On the demand side, we have highlighted demographics and growing wealth. On the supply side, there is, inter alia, the ease of diversification, liquidity, improved corporate control, deregulation, ability to take advantage of technological developments, and enhanced competition, as well as fiscal inducements and the difficulties of social security pensions. It is argued that such underlying factors are best understood in light of the features of institutions and their expanding scope for fulfilling various functions of the financial sector. It is only at a certain stage in financial development that an institutional sector becomes feasible and these advantages come to the fore.

Whereas it is difficult to find the precise balance between the supply and demand factors in explaining growth of institutions to date, it is clearer that in the future, the key factor will be demographic change linked to difficulties of social security, which will likely lead to a vast further expansion of institutional investing. In this context, in many countries (notably in Continental Europe), future demographic pressures on pay-as-you-go social security are likely to lead governments to seek to stimulate further growth of private pensions as a substitute for social security. This could have a major effect on financial systems. For example, if France and Italy were to develop funded pension assets of the same value relative to GDP as in the United Kingdom, the sums involved would be over a trillion dollars. And following the example of countries such as Chile, Singapore, and Malaysia, developing countries also have considerable scope for development of pension funds. A preexisting level of development of capital markets and of administrative skills is needed.[43]

---

43. See Davis (1998f).

2   Investment Behavior and Performance of Institutional Investors

Introduction

The crucial test of the economic efficiency of a system of financing based on institutional investors lies in the rate of return and risk offered to investors relative to those that could be obtained by households directly in the capital markets or via the banking system. The issue for asset managers is not a simple one of maximizing return, since institutional investors and their underlying beneficiaries have different needs for income streams or certainty of repayment value. Hence the appropriate trade-off of risk and return will vary. Rates of return and risk depend crucially on asset allocation and security selection, which in turn have a major influence on the behavior of capital markets more generally.[1] At a most basic level, such an influence on capital markets arises because institutional investors may be more diversified and have a lower risk aversion in their investment than households would. This is due to features such as insurance, diversification, longer maturity of liabilities, and risk sharing. Correspondingly, as is shown in chapter 1, in most cases

---

1. Other influences on returns are fees and administrative costs, reviewed in the following chapter, and costs of trading, reviewed in chapter 8.

mutual funds, life insurers, and pension funds hold a greater proportion of capital uncertain and long-term assets, and fewer short-term liquid assets than households.

In this context, this chapter first reviews fund management objectives and constraints, that is, economic influences on portfolio behavior, both in general terms and for the main types of institutional investor. We do not seek to present an authoritative and comprehensive text on this matter (see Bodie et al. 1999), but rather to present some key aspects that are relevant to an understanding of the role of institutional investors and their impact on the capital market. In the second section, the chapter goes on to consider the main results in the literature regarding the performance of fund managers at a micro level (in terms of performance of individual asset managers relative to the market and to their peers). In the final section, we provide an illustration of institutional investors' performance at a macro level (in terms of average asset allocation), in the form of a case study focused on the performance of pension funds in different national markets.

2.1 Asset Management Objectives and Constraints

In this introductory section, we begin by spelling out some basic considerations that apply to any asset manager, and we outline the main techniques of investment. We then note the special considerations that apply to asset management of each type of institutional investor: mutual fund, life company, defined contribution pension fund, and defined benefit pension fund. The final subsections cover the considerations that apply to the asset classes of equity, foreign assets, and derivatives by institutional investors.

2.1.1 The Risk-Return Trade-Off

The most basic aim of investment is to achieve an **optimal trade-off of risk and return** by allocation of the portfolio to appropriately diversified combinations of assets (and in some cases liabilities, i.e., leveraging the portfolio by borrowing). The precondition for such an optimal trade-off is the ability to attain the frontier of efficient portfolios, in which there is no possibility of increasing return without increasing risk or of reducing risk without reducing return. Any portfolio in which it is possible to increase return without raising risk is inefficient and is dominated by a portfolio with more return for the same risk. The exact trade-off that is chosen will depend on objectives, preferences, and constraints on investors.

In this basic sense, asset managers acting for institutional investors face the same problem in investment as other agents in the economy do, be they households, companies, banks, or the government. The main distinction is that whereas the other types of investor invest largely on their own behalf, institutional asset management is a service involving management (by a securities firm, insurance company, or mutual fund) of an investment portfolio (bonds, equities, property) on behalf of a client (individual investor, company, bank, or pension fund). This disjunction requires communication and appropriate incentives or control mechanisms between the parties to ensure an optimal outcome.

2.1.2 Steps in Institutional Investment

There are common features of all types of institutional investment (Trzcinka 1997, 1998; Bodie et al. 1999) that form a useful introduction to an assessment of performance. First there is identification of the investors' objectives or preferences and constraints.

In terms of **objectives**, there is a need to assess where on the above-mentioned optimal risk-return trade-off the investor wishes to be—in other words, the investor's risk tolerance in pursuit of return. These issues are discussed for individual types of institutional investor in the sections below.

As regards **constraints**, these may include liquidity, investment horizon, inflation sensitivity, regulations, tax and accounting considerations, and unique needs. All of these may link to the nature of the liabilities; for example:

• liquidity-based constraints link to the need for investors to withdraw funds as a lump sum or the current needs for regular disbursement;

• the investment horizon relates to the planned liquidation date of the investment (e.g., retirement) and is often measured by the concept of effective maturity or duration;

• inflation sensitivity relates to the need to hold assets as inflation hedges, such as index-linked bonds (or, in their absence, equities or real estate);

Table 2.1
Asset Restrictions on Pension Funds and Life Insurers (Percentage)

	Pension Funds			Life Insurers		
	Equities	Bonds and Loans	Foreign Assets	Equities	Bonds and Loans	Foreign Assets
United Kingdom	P	P	P	—	—	Max. 20%
United States	P	P	P	Max. 15%	—	Max. 10%
Germany	Max. 30%	—	Max. 20%	Max. 30%	—	Max. 20%
Japan	Max. 30%	Min. 50%	Max. 30%	Max. 30%	—	Max. 30%
Canada	—	—	Max. 20%	Max. 25%	—	Max. 20%
France	—	Min. 50%	—	Max. 65%	—	Max. 20%
Italy	P	P	P	Max. 20%	—	Max. 20%

Note: P indicates that the prudent man rule applies.
Source: Davis (1998a), Dickinson (1998), European Commission (2000).

• institutional investors are often constrained by portfolio regulations. These may link to asset allocation such as a prudent man rule
(the rule that assets should be invested in a manner that would be
approved by a prudent investor). In other cases, there may be quantitative restrictions on portfolios that may in effect prevent asset
managers from achieving the efficient frontier. These often limit
equity and foreign investment of life insurers and pension funds
(see table 2.1 for regulations in the late 1990s). Regulations may
also affect liabilities, for example, by enforcing indexation of repayments or minimum solvency levels, and thereby affect desired asset
allocations;

• tax considerations may change the nature of the trade-off; and

• accounting rules can generate different "optimal" portfolios, although market value accounting is needed to produce an appropriate portfolio in an economic sense. Finding a market value may itself
be problematic for illiquid assets such as loans, artworks, and even
real estate.

After these considerations are taken into account, **investment
strategies** are developed and implemented. A primary decision is to
choose the asset categories to be included in the portfolio—usually
money market instruments, shares, bonds, real estate, loans, and
foreign assets. Market conditions are monitored, using historic data
on macroeconomic and financial variables as well as economic fore-

casts, to determine expectations of rates of return over the holding period. The efficient frontier can be derived between risk and return, depending on the probability distribution of holding period returns. An optimal asset mix may then be derived by selecting the portfolio that is efficient, meets the required trade-off of risk and return, and satisfies the constraints. Portfolio adjustments are made as appropriate when relevant variables change (such as market conditions, relative asset values and forecasts thereof, and the evolving nature of investor circumstances). Institutions vary in the weight that is put on different aspects of the process; for example, an index fund takes much less note of market conditions than a hedge fund. Such differences may also link to the nature of the client. But the process is common to all institutional investors.

The investment process is often divided into several components, with **asset allocation** (or strategic[2] asset allocation) referring to the long-term decision on the disposition of the overall portfolio, while **tactical asset allocation** relates to short-term adjustments to this basic choice between asset categories in light of short-term profit opportunities, so-called market timing.[3] Meanwhile, **security selection** relates to the choice of individual assets to be held within each asset class, which may be both strategic and tactical.

2.1.3 The Role of Liabilities

The **nature of the liabilities is the key** to understanding how institutions differ in their operations. A liability is a cash outlay made at a specific time to meet the contractual terms of an obligation issued by an institutional investor. Such liabilities differ in certainty and timing, from known outlay and timing (bank deposit) through known outlay but uncertain timing (traditional life insurance), uncertain outlay and known timing (floating rate debt), and—the main focus in this book —uncertain outlay and uncertain timing (pension funds, mutual funds, endowment/unit-linked life insurance, property and casualty insurance). Certainty needs will vary within groups; for example, a pension fund may require greater certainty than a mutual fund holder does. In this context, an institutional investor will seek to earn

---

2. Note that strategic choices include not only the disposition of the portfolio, but also the choice of active versus passive management (section 2.1.6) and domestic versus international (section 2.3.2).

3. As is shown in section 2.4, institutional investors tend not to time markets correctly.

a satisfactory return on invested funds and to keep a reasonable surplus of assets over liabilities. Risk must be sufficient to ensure adequate returns but not so great as to threaten solvency. The nature of liabilities also determines the institutions' liquidity needs.

2.1.4 Alternative Approaches to Asset Allocation

The above considerations are based broadly on the **mean-variance model**, which assumes that the investor chooses an asset allocation based solely on average return and its volatility. Certain considerations with respect to liabilities allow us to derive a number of further alternative paradigms of asset allocation (Borio et al. 1997):

1. **Immunization** is a special case of the mean-variance approach that implies that the investor tries to stabilize the value of the investment at the end of the holding period, that is, to hold an entirely riskless position; this is done typically with respect to interest rate risk by appropriately adjusting the duration of the assets held. **Matching** is a particular case of immunization in which the assets precisely replicate the cash flows of the liabilities, including any related option characteristics.

2. **Shortfall risk**[4] and **portfolio insurance** approaches put a particular stress on avoiding downward moves, for example, in the context of minimum solvency levels for pension funds or insurance companies. Hence, unlike mean variance and immunization, they are not symmetric with respect to the weight put on upward and downward asset price moves. Shortfall risk sees the investor as maximizing the return on the portfolio subject to a ceiling on the probability of incurring a loss (e.g., by shifting from equities to bonds as the minimum desired value is approached). In portfolio insurance, the investor is considered to want to avoid any loss but to retain upside profit potential. This may be achieved by replicating on a continuous basis the payoff of a call option on the portfolio by trading between the assets and cash (dynamic hedging) or by use of futures and options per se. By these means, the value of a portfolio may be prevented from falling below a given value (such as that defined by the value of liabilities of an insurance company or the minimum funding level of a pension fund).

---

4. See Leibowitz and Kogelman (1991).

3. A further issue is whether the benchmark for investment is seen in nominal terms, as we implicitly assumed above, or real terms. The benchmark may also be defined relative to the liabilities of the institution such as defined benefit pension or insurance claims. Asset management techniques that take into account the nature of liabilities are known as **asset liability management techniques** and are discussed further in section 2.2.3.2 (see also Blake 1999). They may be defined as investment techniques wherein the long-term balance between assets and liabilities is maintained by choice of assets with return, risk, and duration characteristics similar to those of liabilities. Equities are a matching asset when liabilities grow at the same pace as real wages, as is typical in an ongoing pension fund aiming for a certain replacement ratio at retirement, because the labor and capital shares of GDP are roughly constant and equities constitute capital income. Bonds are not a good match for real-wage-based liabilities, although they do match annuities for pensions. This approach may affect, among other things, the appropriate degree of diversification of the portfolio.

2.1.5   The Role of Conventions

Besides risks and returns and the nature of liabilities, actual investment may be strongly **influenced by conventions and peer group pressure** among asset managers (see also chapters 3 and 5). In highly competitive markets such as the United States and the United Kingdom, this reflects a desire to gain or maintain a place in the top two quartiles of performance, implying a need to stick close to the average portfolio but seek to improve on its performance slightly, possibly by increasing risk. On the other hand, in less competitive markets, as in Continental Europe and Japan, the issue tends to be more one of ensuring that performance is not far out of line with others lest the asset manager be criticized for excessive risk. Resulting consensuses of asset allocation are slow to change. Often, they evolve as markets perform differently, with higher capital gains in one market leading to a sustained shift in portfolio allocation. The advent of European Monetary Union is a interesting shock that is affecting such established patterns in the European Union (see section 4.3).

2.1.6 Investment Techniques: Active and Passive Management

Active management entails an attempt to seek out and purchase misvalued securities, with the implicit assumption that the market is inefficient and that not all relevant information is present in securities prices. **Passive management** assumes that the market is efficient and hence that returns are maximized by "holding the market."[5] Reflecting transactions and management costs, active management invariably entails higher fees than passive management does.

In discussing these approaches to investment, we return to the distinction between asset allocation and security selection, which we introduced in section 2.1.2. The former choice applies only when the institutional investor is free to diversify across asset classes, which would not be the case for a mutual fund investing in specific assets.

We have already dealt with considerations relating to **strategic asset allocation**. Such asset allocations may be set passively, for example, by the pension fund sponsor or mutual fund deed, or also employed as part of active management via so-called tactical asset allocation. It will be recalled that **tactical asset allocation** involves deviations from a benchmark asset allocation (e.g., the bond/equity choice) to take advantage of undervalued markets. A key question is whether managers have any ability at timing the market, for example, in switching from cash to risky assets[6] or from equities to bonds. Switching may often be undertaken by overlay[7] strategies using the futures market so as not to interfere with the underlying asset portfolio. Models of appropriate asset valuation supplemented by judgment are key ingredients. An intermediate type of investment choice involves switching between undervalued and overvalued national markets in a given instrument. This may employ a set benchmark and tactical allocation, in this case between national markets within

---

5. As Grossman and Stiglitz (1980) and Cornell and Roll (1981) noted, the efficient markets hypothesis does not rule out small abnormal returns as an incentive to acquire information, but those acquiring costly information should have only average net returns after the costs of acquiring information are taken into account.

6. To illustrate this, Bodie et al. (1999) show that whereas $1000 invested in commercial paper in 1927 would have cumulated to $3600 by the end of 1978 and the same amount in the New York stock market would have raised $67,500, appropriate switches at thirty-day intervals would have realized $5.36 billion.

7. Overlay strategies adjust exposure via purchase and sale of index futures without any transaction in the underlying. As we note in section 2.3.3, they facilitate an unbundling of the components of the investment process (such as currency versus stock selection).

equities and bonds. Currency selection is commonly split from market selection, a procedure that is facilitated by use of overlays.

Forms of matching of assets and liabilities, including immunization, are forms of **passive asset allocation strategy**. Passivity with respect to asset allocation may extend to the holding of international assets within each instrument in the form of a global portfolio, weighted by GDP or market capitalization. But the results of such exercises have not been promising, as for example capitalization weights recommended a 40% holding of Japanese equities before the crisis of the 1980s. More generally, market capitalization may be distorted by the varying proportions of the corporate sector that is publicly traded and because corporate cross-holdings overstate the amount of equity outstanding.

Security selection may also be either passive or active.[8] **Active security selection** assumes that there are mispriced securities in the market and that they can be systematically detected. One can distinguish a number of types of active security selection (see Blake 1997). Traditional active asset management is discretionary and based on the views of the asset manager regarding the types of securities to buy or sell. There are two types of traditional asset management: **continuation (or momentum) strategies and contrarian strategies**. The former seeks to exploit a presumed positive serial correlation in securities prices. Hence a continuation strategy would seek to purchase securities that have done well in the recent past and are expected to do so in the future and would sell securities with recent poor performance, assuming positive correlation of asset prices.

Contrarian strategies assume that the market overreacts initially to news, so price rises are followed by price falls. There is considered to be a negative serial correlation or mean reversion in asset price movements.[9] The contrarian investor buys securities when prices are falling in the expectation of later rises, and vice versa for sales when prices are rising. It is considered that naive investors extrapolate good or bad news too far into the future, giving arbitrage opportunities as resulting mispricing is corrected. In this context, **value strategies** involve the purchase of securities that have low market prices relative to fundamental measures of value such as dividend

---

8. They are not necessarily alternatives and indeed can be optimally combined as set out in the Treynor and Black (1973) model outlined in Bodie et al. (1999).

9. Tactical asset allocation is also often a form of contrarian approach, as it typically assumes a form of mean reversion in market prices and yield relations.

yields or involve switches from shares to bonds when the yield ratio reaches a certain level.

These active strategies are grounded in some well-known observations of financial economists. First, the **market may overreact to past performance** (over three to five years) of a firm and ignore the fact that performance in fact tends to revert to a mean level (De Bondt and Thaler 1985). This has led on the one hand to so-called **growth investing**, in which investors seek to take advantage of a period of overreaction, and on the other to the focus of so-called value investing on stock with bad past records, on the theory that the market is surprised when their performance reverts to the mean (Lakonishok et al. 1993a). It may be added that the value phenomenon is often blamed on inefficiencies in the asset management process, whereby fund managers are unwilling to hold unattractive securities of firms that have done poorly for presentational reasons. On the other hand, Fama and French (1996) suggest that higher returns to value investment arise because value stocks are more risky.

On the other hand, there may be **short-term underreaction**, with winners and losers over short periods of up to six months tending to persist for the next period (Jagadeesh and Titman 1993). It takes investors some time to react to news, in other words. Other evidence of underreaction is that stock prices respond to earnings announcement for up to a year (Bernard and Thomas 1990). Portfolios with stocks that have good positive earnings announcements earn positive returns for up to a year. Indeed, Davidson and Dutia (1989) found that there was marked positive serial correlation of the shares in the New York Stock Exchange, supporting the idea that investors underreact to new information. This last observation has led to a heightened focus on so-called **earnings momentum** (see Chan et al. (1996)).

As regards **passive strategies for security selection**, portfolio indexation involves holding securities in an index that reproduce the characteristics of the index. One may distinguish **replication**, which matches the index precisely by holding all its constituents; **stratification**, which seeks to economize on holdings by holding smaller number of stocks of various subtypes (such as by industrial sector); and **optimization**, which seeks to replicate the index by selecting a smaller number of stocks with certain risk and return characteristics. Costs are minimized by keeping portfolio switches to a minimum. Such portfolios should behave identically to the index concerned.

Whereas much of quantitative asset allocation is passive (e.g., indexing or immunization), there remain hybrids such as "rocket science" (which attempts to predict asset price movements over a short time horizon) and value-based quantitative analysis (which carries out value investment on a rule-based rather than discretionary framework, using models of asset pricing).

The growing importance of passive investment may actually increase the scope for profitable active management by making markets less efficient. An obvious example is to buy ahead a stock that is likely to be incorporated in an index, which will then be mechanically purchased by index funds.

2.1.7   Style Analysis

A recent phenomenon in the United States is so-called style analysis, whereby money managers identify precisely the type of security to be focused on and/or approach to active management and adhere to it (see Trzcinka 1998). Pension fund sponsors or mutual fund investors then allocate their funds to managers on the basis of such styles. Style management may be of particular importance in view of the increasing role of individuals in asset management. This is because such styles may be helpful to the household itself in constructing an appropriate portfolio of mutual funds. A style may also be chosen because of constraints on portfolio selection, for example requiring a certain proportion of assets to be in smaller companies. Authors such as Sharpe (1995) and Brown and Goetzmann (1997) have sought to systematize in financial terms how styles may be controlled for.[10]

One use of style analysis is in **communication and evaluation**. The investment style makes the sponsor or individual investor better informed about the type of stocks the manager considers and is able to evaluate whether the organization of the money manager is effective for the investment style (i.e., contacts, administration). It provides a basis for ongoing discussion. Clearly, for this to be effective, the style must put the manager in an identifiable subset of investors such as "value" or "growth," these must be related to useful charac-

---

10. Sharpe (1995) uses a set of passively managed funds as regressors in a constrained regression on fund returns with the coefficients limited to sum to 1 and the weights to be nonnegative. Brown and Goetzmann (1995), use a generalized stylistic classification algorithm, a class of clustering algorithm that sorts multivariate observations into discrete classes, conditional on a given number of classes.

teristics such as types of securities purchased, and the manager must not deviate from the style.

A second use is to **measure managers' performance** precisely by the use of style benchmarks. Using such benchmarks, investors can assess, for example, whether poor absolute performance relates to poor management or a style that is performing poorly. For this purpose, it is essential that a benchmark such as a market index or passive management style should be readily identifiable against which the manager's performance may be evaluated. In addition, the performance of the style must be observable independently of the behavior of the manager; and again the manager must have a stable style.

Style management may also **assist diversification** if the correlation between styles is more stable over time than that between individual securities. Choosing managers with different styles may be a better way of diversifying than simply choosing different stocks; and it may be defensible in court where the institutional investor has to adhere to a prudent man rule. If risk is also more stable for groups of stocks than for individual ones, then style management may increase **accuracy of risk control**, relative to having a number of managers in the entire universe of stocks. Risk control is aided if the style is related to systematic risks of securities. Sponsors may believe that they have useful information about markets and hence use style management as a **means of control** over the total portfolio. They do this by allocating more money to styles that are expected to do well. This is another form of second-guessing market timing, albeit with switches occurring between styles rather than between cash and securities. Obviously, choosing a manager who performs well within a style will add extra value—if the attempts at timing are accurate.

A difficulty with style management is that it is **not easy to classify managers**. Portfolio-based approaches, which focus on the stocks a manager holds, may ignore some information. An alternative is a returns-based approach, which measures a style by returns over a benchmark. Choice of benchmark as well as the time period and model may strongly affect the results; but once these are agreed, the results are objective in the sense of being replicable. A weakness of this means of classification is that statistical models used are unstable, and managers may change styles without this being detected. Arguably both tools should be used.

The efficient markets hypothesis suggests that **style management should not add value**; any evidence that style management adds value requires market inefficiency (Fama 1991).[11] Even if a style does well, not all money managers who adopt a style will achieve its excess returns, suggesting a need for intensified monitoring of managers. Note that as it entails less-than-complete diversification, adoption of an individual style has **costs** in terms of higher risk than would otherwise be feasible. That said, even in an efficient market it may be useful as noted above as a communication tool and for facilitating diversification across styles.

A cynical view applying to defined benefit pension funds (Lakonishok et al. 1992a) is that corporate treasurers like to allocate such funds across style-based asset managers because it gives them **scope for empire building** in terms of staff resources needed for monitoring while also protecting them from criticism for missing out on any type of investment that may do well. The fact that most corporate treasurers are following this approach offers double protection. In the view of the authors, style-based investment covering all possible styles is a poor and costly substitute for indexation per se. Meanwhile, money managers find styles a useful means to help them differentiate their products from others and seek to attract mandates. They may use styles as a means to convince sponsors that poor absolute performance relative to the overall market index is actually a good performance relative to a special or unique style-based index. The corollary for the individual investor is that styles may be used in a similar way in advertising.

2.2   Investment Considerations for the Main Types of Institutional Investor

We now trace the economic influences on portfolio distributions of different types of institutional investors that would operate freely in the absence of portfolio and funding regulations and if there were appropriate accounting methods. A general point is that the objectives of the different types of institutional investors are quite different in terms of motives and attitudes to risk. In principle, a market that is

---

11. On the other hand, Roll (1997) suggests that there is an extra return per unit of risk as a reward for paying attention to style if risk measures meet certain technical requirements.

characterized by such institutions should be sufficiently diverse[12] to ensure effective market functioning and liquidity. In chapter 5, we explore why there may instead be destabilizing herding, in which institutions all behave similarly despite their distinctions.

2.2.1 Mutual Funds

Both the **risk tolerance and the return requirement of mutual funds are predefined** for each fund and **can vary sharply** between funds. Hence investment objectives for mutual funds are straightforward in that they design investment strategies to allow their shareholders control over overall allocations by instrument or asset class. They are more specialized than pension funds or insurance companies. They have to maintain their declared profile of investments, designing the portfolio process directly for the asset class. Changes in the composition of the mutual fund sectors' assets will then reflect changes in the portfolio preferences of the household sector, which the household sector chooses in light of the remaining assets and liabilities. For example, U.S. households have increased their share of equity mutual funds in recent years from 23% of the total in 1990 to 54% in 1998, possibly reflecting a decline in risk aversion or merely a belief that equities will continue to do as well as they did in the 1990s.

There are major differences between mutual funds in their **portfolio strategies**. Following the discussion in section 2.1.6, a key distinction is between actively managed and passive or index funds. Within actively managed funds, there are a large number of subcategories dividing strategies, notably value versus growth strategies. And there are, of course, subdivisions with respect to the type of assets funds may invest in—and the strictness with which such subdivisions are to be maintained.

A special kind of mutual fund is the **hedge fund**,[13] as introduced in chapter 1.[14] Hedge funds may take short positions and borrow to

---

12. Besides such attitudinal differences, there may also be differences in information itself. In the survey that was undertaken to accompany this volume (see chapters 4 and 8), the asset managers were asked how often markets were liquid because buyers and sellers receive different information about stocks. The mean answer suggested investors felt this was "sometimes" the case.

13. It is estimated that in mid-1998, there were between 1000 and 4000 such funds, with total assets of as much as $400 billion.

14. See Basel Committee (1999).

a greater extent than other institutions.[15] There are several types of hedge fund, which differ in their modus operandi in markets. Macro funds seek to profit either from changes in economic developments at a national or global level. Relative value funds adopt arbitrage strategies aiming to profit from anomalies in market pricing.

2.2.2   Life Insurers

For life insurance, it is fundamentally a matter of actuarial calculation (notably using mortality tables as well as assumptions on asset returns) to assess and project how much a policyholder may be paid in the case of a claim. Life insurance company **liabilities tended historically to be defined in nominal terms** and hence could be matched or immunized in the sense described in section 2.1.4, usually by using long-term bonds. These nominal liabilities would include those arising from term policies (purchased to provide a certain sum in the event of death), whole-life policies (term policies with a saving element), and annuities (to give a fixed income for the remainder of the insured person's life). Guaranteed investment contracts (GICs), a form of zero coupon bond typically sold to pension funds, are a modern variant. Insurers may also offer insured defined benefit pension plans. These nominal policies remain an important component of life companies' business; the main risks are that interest rate assumptions or mortality assumptions will be incorrect.

However, life companies are **increasingly also offering variable policies** such as variable-life policies, variable annuities, endowment, and unit (mutual fund) linked policies. These typically combine a term policy with a saving element aimed at capital appreciation, where for the latter there is no explicit guarantee as to the size of the bonus to be disbursed. Such policies may offer higher returns—and also risks—to policyholders, while posing less shortfall risk to the surplus of the life insurer (see below). In many countries, including the United States, there is a deferred-taxation benefit to such investment. Targets for the size of bonuses are typically determined by the need to attract new business in light of competition in the market. (In contrast to the case for pension funds, discussed in the section below, there is no specific objective for capital appreciation defined in terms

---

15. In the United Kingdom, closed-end funds are able to leverage, but open-end funds are not.

of inflation or average earnings.) Unlike traditional policies, these variable policies are increasingly giving rise to active investment in equities.

Besides the popularity of variable policies, another factor increasing equity investment is that insurance companies are heavily involved in investing pension monies. This may occur directly on a defined contribution basis or externally as asset managers invest in so-called "segregated accounts" on behalf of defined contribution or defined benefit funds. An additional feature affecting life companies' portfolios is that they need some short-term liquidity to cover early surrender of policies and policy loans.

Overlaying the distinct effects identified above, which arise from the different types of product offered by the firm, the investments of life insurance companies are heavily influenced by the volume of **surplus assets**, where the surplus measures the extent to which assets exceed the value of liabilities that are contractually guaranteed. To protect firms from insolvency, supervisory rules[16] typically impose stricter regulations on assets backing technical reserves (i.e., guaranteed liabilities) than for the surplus (Dickinson 1998). Hence the assets backing technical reserves are more likely to be invested in bonds, with only the surplus including a share of equities.[17] A similar issue arises for defined benefit pension funds, which are discussed in section 2.2.3.2. Assets corresponding to nonguaranteed liabilities (such as the bulk of variable-life or unit-linked policies) may be relatively freely invested.

2.2.3 Pension Funds

Unlike the situation for mutual funds, asset allocation considerations, linked notably to the bond/equity choice, arise strongly for pension funds.[18]

---

16. Surplus calculations are affected by valuation methods (e.g., whether assets are valued at market value or book value) and discount rates used to calculate the present value of future liabilities. Life company sectors having low discount rates and book value accounting for the assets tend to have smaller surpluses and correspondingly lower allocations to equities than those with high discount rates and market value accounting.

17. Shortfall risk considerations are likely to entail cautious investment or hedging for these assets also.

18. For an extensive set of readings on the topic of pension finance see Bodie and Davis (2000).

The crucial point is that for pension funds, the portfolio distribution and the corresponding return and risk on the assets held, in relation to the growth of average labor earnings, determine the replacement ratio (pension as a proportion of final earnings) obtainable by purchase of an annuity at retirement financed via an occupational or personal defined contribution fund[19] as well as the cost to a company of providing a pension in a defined benefit plan.[20] This **link of liabilities to labor earnings** points to a crucial difference with insurance companies as well as households, in that pension funds face the risk of increasing nominal liabilities (for example, due to wage increases), as well as the risk of holding assets, and hence need to trade volatility with return. In effect, their liabilities are typically denominated in real terms and are not fixed in nominal terms. Hence they must also focus on real assets that offer some form of inflation protection. This implies a particular focus on equities and property.

An additional factor that will influence the portfolio distributions of an individual pension fund is **maturity**—the ratio of active to retired members. The duration of liabilities (that is, the average time to discounted pension payment requirements) is much longer for an immature fund having few pensions in payment than for a mature fund for which sizable repayments are required. A fund that is closing down (or "winding up") will have even shorter-duration liabilities. Blake (1999, 2000b) suggests that, given the varying duration of liabilities, it is rational for immature funds having "real" liabilities as defined above to invest mainly in equities (whose cash flows have a long duration), for mature funds to invest in a mix of equities and bonds, and for funds that are winding up to invest mainly in bonds (whose cash flows have a short duration).

Pension funds are more subject to pressures to invest according to nonfinancial objectives than are life insurers and mutual funds. Notably, there is often pressure to invest in "socially responsible"

---

19. The growth of receipts under funding with defined contributions depends on the rate of return on the assets accumulated during the working life. The actual pension received per annum varies with the number of years of retirement relative to working age (the passivity ratio).

20. Under full funding, the contribution rate to obtain a given defined benefit replacement rate depends on the difference between the growth rate of wages (which determines the pension needed for a given replacement rate) and the return on assets, as well as the passivity ratio (the proportion of life spent after retirement).

ways[21] (although there is also a growing mutual fund sector specializing in socially responsible investment). Funds may also be directed to invest in local infrastructure projects (see Clark 2000a). There is a potential conflict between such restricted or directed investment and risk-return optimization from the beneficiary or sponsors' point of view. For example, Mitchell and Hsin (1994) noted that public pension plans at a state and local level in the United States were often obliged to devote a proportion of assets to state-specific projects to "build a stronger job and tax base." These funds tended to earn lower overall returns than others, suggesting inefficient investment.

Further key distinctions arise in the investment approach of defined contribution and defined benefit funds, as we discuss below.

2.2.3.1 Defined Contribution Pension Funds

As we noted in section 1.2.2, in a defined contribution pension fund, the sponsors are responsible only for making contributions to the plan. There is no guarantee regarding assets at retirement, which depend on growth in the assets of the plan. In some cases, the portfolio distribution is chosen solely by the sponsor and the investment managers it employs. But increasingly (e.g., 401(k) plans in the United States), employees are left also to decide the asset allocation (see also section 2.2.4).

As regards **portfolio objectives**, a defined contribution pension plan should in principle seek to **maximize return for a given risk** so as to attain as high as possible a replacement ratio at retirement. This implies following closely the standard mean-variance portfolio optimization schema outlined in section 2.1.1. As Blake (1997) noted, to choose the appropriate point on the frontier of efficient portfolios, it is necessary to determine the degree of risk tolerance of the scheme member; the higher the acceptable risk, the higher the expected value at retirement.[22] The fund will also need to **shift to lower-risk assets for older workers** as they approach retirement,[23] thus reducing

---

21. In the United Kingdom in 1999, 19% of private sector funds and 31% of public sector funds said that they took ethical considerations into account in investing (Targett 2000).

22. Blake (1997) conceptualizes this as maximizing risk-adjusted expected value: the expected value of pension assets less a risk penalty, defined as the ratio of the variance of the funds assets to the degree of risk tolerance.

23. Booth and Yakoubov (2000) cast doubt on the need for such "lifestyle investment."

duration as outlined above and reducing exposure to market volatility shortly before retirement, which might otherwise risk to
sharply reduce pensions.

Until the approach of retirement necessitates a shift to bonds, the
superior returns on equity will likely ensure that a significant share of
the portfolio is accounted for by equities, depending on the **degree
of risk aversion**. Where employers choose the asset mix, the degree
of risk aversion is likely to be related to the fear of litigation when
the market value of a more aggressive asset mix declines;[24] as we
discuss below, where employees choose the asset allocation, the risk
aversion is more direct.[25] A more detailed assessment of these issues
and their effects on returns is provided in section 2.3.

2.2.3.2   Defined Benefit Pension Funds

Defined benefit fund liabilities are, owing to the sponsor's guarantee,
basically a form of corporate debt (Bodie 1990b). Appropriate
investment strategies will depend on the nature of the obligation
incurred, whether pensions in payment are indexed, and the demographic structure of the workforce. Real earnings will affect the
replacement ratio that can be financed by the pension fund in the
same way as for defined contribution funds. Liabilities will also be
influenced by interest rates. Investment strategies will also be influenced by the minimum-funding rules imposed by the authorities,
which determine the size of surplus assets. These, as for life insurers,
imply a focus on shortfall risk as defined in section 2.1.4.

To further elucidate the nature of the defined benefit pension
obligation, a number of definitions are needed. The wind-up definition of liabilities, the level at which the fund could meet all its current obligations if it were to be closed down completely, is known as
the **accumulated benefit obligation**. The **projected benefit obligation** implies that the obligations to be funded include a forward-

---

24. Meanwhile, the constraint for defined benefit funds in the United States is the fear
of litigation under the prudent man rule if bond shares fall below a market norm, such
as 40%.

25. In the United States, there is some evidence for "excessive" risk aversion, which
could seriously damage the value of pensions, but it may be declining. Traditionally,
defined contribution funds had much lower equity shares (Rappaport 1992). But now
defined contribution plans and defined benefit plans both hold around 60–70% in
equities (table 2.8). Within this total, beneficiaries of defined contribution plans are
often forced to invest a high proportion in their own companies' stock, implying a high
exposure to diversifiable risk.

looking element. It is assumed that rights will continue to accrue and will be labor earnings-indexed up to retirement, as is normal in a final salary plan. The **indexed benefit obligation** also assumes price indexation of pensions in payment after retirement.

If the sponsor seeks to fund the accumulated benefit obligation and the **obligation is purely nominal**, with a minimum-funding requirement in place, it will be appropriate, as for life insurers, to **immunize the liabilities** with bonds of the same duration to hedge the interest rate risk of these liabilities. Unhedged equities will merely imply that such funds incur unnecessary risk (Bodie 1995), although as for insurance companies, they may be useful to provide extra return on the surplus over and above the minimum funding level.

With a **projected benefit obligation target**, an investment **policy based on diversification** may be most appropriate, in the belief that risk reduction depends on a maximum diversification of the pension fund relative to the firm's operating investments (Ambachtsheer 1988). Moreover, it is normal for defined benefit schemes that offer a certain link to salary at retirement for the liability to include an element of indexation. Then fund managers and actuaries typically assume that it may be appropriate to include a significant proportion of real assets such as equities and property in the portfolio as well as bonds.[26] By doing this, they implicitly diversify between investment risk and liability risk, which are largely risks of inflation (see also Daykin 1995). To protect the sponsor from financial difficulties when volatile markets in these instruments generate temporary shortfalls of assets relative to liabilities, it is common for regulators to allow gradual amortization of shortfalls[27] or even focus in solvency calculations on income from assets rather than market values.[28] Allowing inflation indexation of pension to be discretionary is another way to reduce the risk of shortfall; implicitly, it is a form of risk sharing between firm and workers.

There are also **tax considerations**. As Black (1980) showed, for both defined benefit and defined contribution funds, there is a fiscal

---

26. See the discussion of equities and inflation below.
27. This is the case for U.K. pension funds since the Pensions Act of 1995, which introduced a minimum funding requirement for the first time (see Davis (2000b) and Blake (2000a)).
28. In the United Kingdom, the Pensions Act of 1995 retained elements of this traditional approach to asset valuation, which contrasts strongly with the market-value-based approaches that are common in other countries.

incentive to maximize the tax advantage of pension funds by investing in assets with the highest possible spread between pretax and posttax returns. In many countries, this tax effect gives an incentive to hold bonds. There is also an incentive to overfund with defined benefit to maximize the tax benefits, as well as to provide a larger contingency fund, which is usually counteracted by government-imposed limits on funding.

As Blake (1997) notes, minimum funding levels and limits on overfunding provide tolerance limits to the variation of assets around the value of liabilities. If the assets are selected in such a way that their risk, return, and duration characteristics match those of liabilities, there is a **liability immunizing portfolio**. This protects the portfolio against risks of variation in interest rates, real earnings growth, and inflation in the pension liabilities.[29]

Such a strategy, which determines the overall asset allocation between broad classes of instrument, may be assisted by an **asset-liability modeling exercise**. This is a quantitative technique that is used to structure an asset allocation in relation to the maturity structure of liabilities. It forecasts liabilities over a particular time horizon (such as ten years), combining the size of currently accrued liabilities with projections based on assumptions about salary growth, staff turnover, and the age and sex composition of the workforce. These forecasts can then be compared with projected contributions and asset returns to assess potential changes in funding status. Usually, several scenarios are generated to show the extent of risks. The asset-liability modeling exercise can be used both to show the various consequences of a given investment strategy and to discover alternative strategies that would help to achieve fund objectives, such as to minimize the present value of future contributions and risk of fluctuations therein (see Peskin 1997, Blake 2000b).[30]

The importance of **pension liabilities as a cost to firms**, and hence the benefit from higher asset returns, is underlined by estimates by the European Federation for Retirement Provision that a 1% improvement in asset returns may reduce companies' labor costs by 2–3%, where there is a fully funded, mature, defined benefit pension plan.

---

29. Note that this is distinct from classic immunization, which relates to interest rate risk only.

30. Note that as described, the asset-liability modeling exercise does not integrate the pension fund with the company balance sheet, as may be warranted by its status as a collateral for the firm's guarantee, but treats it as an entirely separate financing vehicle.

2.2.4   The Role of Individual Investors in Determining Institutional Behavior

The growth of defined contribution pension funds, particularly those investing via mutual funds, entails a **growing influence of individuals** on the asset allocation of institutional investors (see also section 1.2.3). More generally, this links to the fact that the lower the insurance component of the product the institution provides, the greater the degree of discretion the individual typically demands, as he or she also takes the risk. Influence on asset allocation is increased to the extent that individuals have moved discretionary funds out of deposits and into mutual funds. Note, however, that individuals have control over asset allocation only for some defined contribution pension funds, such as U.S. 401(k)s, that are structured to provide the employee with options. In many defined contribution funds around the world, the asset allocation is wholly in the hands of life insurance companies or corporate sponsors.

Bajtelsmit and VanDerhei (1997) and Goodfellow and Schieber (1997) investigated the issue of whether investments that are controlled directly by individuals tend to be **excessively risk averse**, threatening retirement income security.[31] Greater conservatism by individuals could result from a number of factors, such as:

• sheer ignorance of risk and return characteristics of different investments,

• balancing out risky assets elsewhere in the household's portfolio, and

• risk aversion per se, which is partly rational owing to the concentration of investment risk on the individual.[32]

In fact, the authors found that wealthier and higher-income people hold a greater proportion of equity in their pension plans. There is a nonlinear relation of age to risk, with risk increasing up to a certain age, after which individuals switch back to less risky assets as retirement approaches. Similar results were seen for job tenure, controlling

---

31. Such concerns may be aggravated by the tendency of individuals to dissipate their pension assets when they are distributed to them on changing jobs.

32. All of these features would tend to be absent for a manager of a defined benefit plan, concerned to meet the employer's benefit obligation in a low-cost manner. Such managers are likely to be risk neutral and can pool risk among an age-diversified set of employees.

for age.[33] Initially, asset allocation is cautious, after which it becomes more aggressive. Women tend to invest more cautiously than men, perhaps reflecting a less continuous career structure. For the most part, these are consistent with rational portfolio choice.

As regards outturns, in the late 1980s and early 1990s, the raw data supported the conclusion of risk aversion, with defined benefit funds in the United States holding an average of 42.9% in equities as opposed to 26.6% in defined contribution plans (although another 38.5% of the latter is held in employer securities). Trzcinka (1998) noted that "when employees select the assets [in defined contribution funds] they choose a much higher percentage of fixed income than when employers select assets."

More recently, the evidence has been less clear, with the latest data[34] showing 401(k)s holding 50% of their assets in equities and another 18% in employees' own-company stock. This equity exposure is similar to the national average for defined contribution funds and ahead of defined benefit funds (see table 2.8 in section 2.5.1). This could be a cyclical phenomenon and may be reversed if markets enter a bear phase. It could also link to demographic changes within the groups holding shares, for example, as more reach the peak age for holding shares.

Bodie and Crane (1997) looked at the total asset holdings of individuals both inside and outside retirement accounts and found that behavior was in line with economic theory and the "best advice" of investment professionals. They hold a proportion of cash that declines with wealth and a proportion of equities that declines with age and rises with wealth.

Finally, a number of papers by the Investment Company Institute (1995, 1996, 1998) have examined **mutual fund investor behavior during periods of severe financial turbulence**. They tended to find that investors did not panic and seek to liquidate their portfolios suddenly. On the other hand, their analyses do not cover the severe bear market of the 1970s, when holdings of equity mutual funds contracted sharply (see section 5.3.6).

---

33. As Bodie et al. (1992) noted, as human capital is a large proportion of wealth in the early years and the ratio declines with age, it may be optimal to hold a large proportion of stocks early on in the life cycle, but only if human capital risk is low early in the career.
34. These data, for 1998, are the most recent available (see Investment Company Institute 2000).

2.3 Topics in Investment

2.3.1 *Issues in Equity Investment*

Important issues arise from the underlying **justification for a strategy of equity investment** for institutional investors.[35] Is equity a hedge against inflation, or does it merely raise expected returns and offer benefits of diversification? Bodie (1995) shows that stocks are not a good hedge against inflation; rather, index-linked bonds and, to a lesser extent, floating-rate bonds could fulfill that objective as their returns are positively correlated with inflation. In contrast, the real rate of return on equity is unaffected by the rate of inflation, since real profits are unaffected by inflation.

Another common idea is that stocks are a good **inflation hedge** over the long term, since their expected real returns are high and hence the probability of a shortfall relative to the cumulated risk-free rate declines over time. But Bodie also challenges this, on the grounds that risks (in terms of the size of the potential shortfall) also increase over such a long period. If the measure of riskiness of an investment is taken to be the cost of insuring it against earning less than the risk-free rate over the investors' time horizon, such risks increase over a longer time horizon, even if returns follow a mean reverting[36] as opposed to a random walk process.

Ely and Robinson (1997) present some counterevidence over a long period, using a cointegration approach to the relationship between share prices and goods prices. They find that there is a tendency for stocks to retain their value relative to movements in the overall price index and that this is the case regardless of the source of shocks. The main exception is that there is a loss of real value of stocks following real output shocks in the United States. In addition, there is evidence that purchasing shares at regular intervals, as is typical of a pension plan, may significantly reduce risk by evening out rises and falls in valuation.

Also of interest is the suggestion that the **premium in returns** of equities over bonds has historically been more than can be explained by relative risk (Mehra and Prescott 1985), which, if correct, implies

---

35. Note that in some countries, institutional investors such as life insurers and pension funds face regulatory constraints on their equity investments (see table 2.1).

36. Malkiel (1990) is one of those who argues that mean reversion is a reason for stocks being less risky over a long time horizon.

that risk-neutral investors such as pension funds can gain from holding equities. Blanchard (1993) noted that the risk premium was tending to decline—a phenomenon that he ascribed to the growth of risk-neutral institutional investors—but remained positive. More recent evidence (Bank of England 1999) shows that the risk premium was close to zero in late 1999. But this may link to the existence of a "bubble."

Generally, it is important to note that finance theory shows that equities should not be assimilated with long-term indexed bonds; there is no guarantee of value, whether real or nominal, at any time in the future. At most, the value of equities is uncorrelated with inflation, rather than providing a hedge.

Jorion and Goetzmann (1999) strike a **cautionary note regarding assumptions that are commonly made about the long-term returns to equity**. They show that the historical average results for the United States are atypically high, with a real return of 4.3% (excluding dividends[37]) since 1921 compared with only 3.4% in other world markets (table 2.2). This takes into account, for example, that German stocks fell by 72% and Japanese stocks by 95% in 1944–1949. Accordingly, it is suggested that the high risk premiums that Mehra and Prescott estimated for the United States are subject to distortion due to survival bias.[38] The actual outturns for the United States ex post are consistent with a low or zero risk premium ex ante, with a positive expectation of a disastrous outcome, as has indeed befallen many stock markets in this century.

2.3.2   International Investment

2.3.2.1   Arguments Favoring International Investment
Modern portfolio theory (Solnik 1988, 1998) suggests that holding a diversified portfolio of assets in a domestic market can eliminate **unsystematic risk** resulting from the different performance of individual firms and industries but not the **systematic risk** resulting from the performance of the economy as a whole.[39] In an efficient

---

37. With dividends, real returns were 8.22%, 8.16% in the United Kingdom, 7.13% in Sweden, 5.57% in Switzerland, 4.88% in Denmark, and 4.83% in Germany.

38. Survival bias entails inaccurate estimation of a financial return owing to the exclusive focus on those markets, institutions, or instruments that survived throughout the evaluation period, ignoring those that failed or closed down.

39. See, for example, Frost and Henderson (1983).

Table 2.2
Performance of Global Stock Indices, 1921–1996 (Percent)

Index	Real Return (Arithmetic)	Standard Deviation	Real Return (Geometric)
United States	5.5	15.8	4.3
Non-U.S.	3.8	10.0	3.4
Global	4.6	11.1	4.0

Source: Jorion and Goetzmann (1999).

and integrated world capital market, systematic risk would be minimized by holding the global portfolio, wherein assets are held in proportion to their distribution by current value between the national markets. In effect, the improvement in the risk-return position from diversification more than compensates for the additional element of volatility arising from currency movements.

Several ways may be envisaged whereby a strategy of **international diversification** should reduce risk. Crucially, to the extent that national trade cycles are not correlated and shocks to equity markets tend to be country specific, the investment of part of the portfolio in other markets can reduce systematic risk for the same return.[40] In the medium term, the profit share in national economies may move differentially, which implies that international investment hedges the risk of a decline in domestic profit share and hence in equity values.[41] And in the very long term, imperfect correlation of demographic shifts should offer protection against the effects on the domestic economy of aging of the population.[42]

Jorion and Goetzmann (1999) provide evidence for the returns and risks to international equity investment over the period 1921–1996, using GDP to weight portfolio holdings. The results, shown in table 2.2, show that there is a major reduction in risk; even the inclusion of markets that failed (i.e., ceased to function entirely) does not greatly reduce the global total return.

---

40. Consistent with this, Harvey (1991), shows that markets tend to have correlations of 0.16–0.86, with a majority in the range 0.4–0.7.

41. This will be of particular importance to defined benefit pension funds in which liabilities are tied to wages and hence rise as the profit share falls. Similarly, at an individual firm level, investment in competitors' shares hedges against a loss of profits due to partial loss of the domestic market.

42. Erb et al. (1997) show how asset returns vary systematically with a country's demographic characteristics, with an older population being more risk averse and demanding a higher premium on equity investment.

2.3.2.2   Reasons for Home Asset Preference

Given the force of these arguments, the puzzle for finance theorists is that global diversification is not pursued to its logical extreme; instead, institutions tend to invest at least 60% of their assets in the home market, and in most, the figure is over 90%.[43] Enormous differences is expected yields would be needed to account for such portfolios in the context of the theory of efficient markets.[44] Reasons for this **home asset preference** include the following:

• **Liabilities** may play a role. The arguments above apply best to a portfolio that is following a mean-variance approach. The simple nature of mutual fund liabilities gives the most scope for international investment. For pension funds, inflation-linked liabilities may make international investment attractive, as they act as a hedge if the currency depreciates. As we noted above, life insurers and pension funds with money fixed liabilities may optimally seek an immunized portfolio, which would tend to be in domestic assets, given their higher correlation with a benchmark akin to domestic long-term bonds. Shortfall risk may also be best minimized by holding domestic assets. There are also some fiscal and regulatory barriers (see table 2.1).

• The arguments about global diversification may be considered to apply to different degrees in the cases of **equities, property, and bonds**. They apply most precisely to equities, although one counterargument is that diversification may be obtained by investment in the domestic market if domestic companies carry out foreign direct investment. Bond markets are more globally integrated, and hence there is less benefit from diversification out of domestic markets. Property is a real asset similar to equity but is less liquid and more reliant on imperfect local information. This makes international diversification more difficult, although as Eichholz (1996) argued, returns are for that reason less internationally correlated, and hence property company shares offers considerable diversification benefits.

---

43. In the United States, international assets for pension funds account for 11% of their total assets and 16% of equities.

44. For example, French and Poterba (1990) suggest that the low level of Japanese investment in the U.S. stock exchange could be rationalized only by a five percentage points higher than expected annual yield in Japan compared with the United States.

• Foreign investment will not overcome **systemic risks** to world capital markets. Solnik et al. (1996) showed that downside market movements, notably in equity markets, occur much more in parallel than do upside ones. Institutions that are adverse to downside risk (e.g., owing to minimum funding or solvency requirements) will therefore be cautious in assuming diversification benefits. Again, the argument for the global portfolio assumes efficiency of markets. If markets are inefficient, for example showing bubbles, then global indexation by market capitalization will not be an efficient strategy, as those who built up holdings of Japanese stocks in the late 1980s and early 1990s discovered.

• There are the issues of **information and other costs**. Better information on home markets may be a reason why investors choose to concentrate their investments there.[45] Consistent with this, Kang and Stulz (1995) show that foreign investors in Japan concentrate on larger stocks, which are better known. Frankel and Schmukler (1995) showed that prices of Mexican stocks declined more than closed-end funds traded in the United States, suggesting that investors in Mexico were better informed about fundamentals than are those in the United States. There will be sunk costs of setting up access the information that institutions may choose not to incur, as they cannot be recovered when emerging from the market. Equally, higher transactions costs, linked also to clearance, settlement, and custody, may limit investment in foreign markets.

• International investment poses **additional risk** compared with domestic investment—settlement, liquidity, transfer, and exchange rate risk. But settlement, liquidity, and transfer risks may be avoided by appropriate choice of markets. Exchange rate risk can be hedged,[46] and, viewed in the context of modern portfolio theory rather than in isolation, contributes to, rather than offsetting, the benefits of offshore investment in terms of returns and diversification of risk, notably for equities.

Section 2.5 shows estimates of the benefits of diversifying between equities and bonds and into international securities. Actual strategies and techniques of international investment used by U.K. pension funds are described in Davis (1995a).

---

45. See Gehrig (1993).
46. On the analytics of hedging, see Solnik (1998).

2.3.3 Derivatives

The demand for derivatives by institutional investors **links partly to the portfolio objectives** set out above. For example, immunization strategies of defined benefit pension funds—themselves largely a consequence of the nature of (minimum-funding) regulation—entail a demand for fixed duration securities as well as for index options and futures.[47] Pension funds writing call options on equities can be seen as converting them into short-term fixed-income securities for matching purposes. Portfolio insurance or contingent immunization —holding assets in excess of the legal minimum in equities, as long as their proportion is reduced when the market value of pension assets falls—has entailed the use of index options and futures markets and of program trading more generally. Also in defined contribution funds, a mixture of cash and equity options can offer downside protection as retirement approaches instead of switching to bonds, which would reduce returns.

In **domestic markets**, derivatives may also be used for controlling risk by increasing or reducing exposure to an asset class and for cutting costs, especially in index funds, in which a large change of asset allocation is anticipated. There are uses in cash flow management, whereby positions may be adopted before assets are purchased (by buying futures and selling put and buying call options). They also have a function in tactical asset allocation; use of derivatives allows asset managers to change asset allocations more cheaply and rapidly than by selling or buying a large volume of assets. When managers are changed, options can be used to replicate the original position when assets are shuffled to reflect the new manager's preferences. Finally, holding stock while selling a call option allows income enhancement.

In **international markets**, a general observation for all institutional sectors is that, whereas equity holdings are often left unhedged, bond investments are routinely hedged against currency risk. As Borio et al. (1997) noted, this could be justified by the fact that foreign exchange gains and losses are closely correlated with those

---

47. The recent introduction of a minimum funding rule for U.K. pension funds may increase the use of derivatives for hedging against shortfall risk, such as the use of cap and collar instruments that have a minimum return set in advance as well as a maximum.

on bonds but much less so with those on equities.[48] On the other hand, hedging of this type is more prevalent in the United States, the Netherlands, and Australia than in the United Kingdom and elsewhere in Continental Europe. In international investment, derivatives might also be used for long-term strategic movements into markets or stocks if they enable such shifts to occur without moving the market against the fund. This will be the case if the derivatives markets are more liquid than the underlying markets. At a tactical level, temporary adjustments in international exposure could be obtained by purchase and sale of index futures without any transaction in the underlying (overlay strategies), thus avoiding disturbance of long-term portfolios (see Cheetham 1990). Such overlay strategies facilitate unbundling of fund management into currency, market, and industry exposure and allow the institution to control risk precisely (Beschloss and Muralidhar 1998). Institutions might invest cash flow awaiting long-term investment in derivatives, as it ensures that the manager is always invested and will not miss an upturn.

2.3.4   Performance Measurement

The development of performance measurement is a prerequisite for effective investment. It is essential for all institutions, but in different ways. The asset manager will wish to evaluate its own performance, and so will the ultimate risk holders. In mutual funds and defined contribution funds, performance measurement is essential to enable individuals to assess whether their funds are being well managed. When they conclude that this is not the case, their option to shift to another manager ensures that a form of competitive pressure is enforced on managers to perform well, lest they lose their customers. Concerning insurance companies and defined benefit funds, when the company or sponsors bear the risk of shortfall, there is a clear interest in assessing the quality of asset management to ensure that costs and risks are minimized. As we discussed in chapter 3, performance measurement is widespread in the Anglo-Saxon countries but less so in Europe and Japan.

Performance measurement in practice entails a precise calculation of the returns on a portfolio over a given period, followed by further

---

48. Froot (1993) shows that the benefits of hedging are exhausted at horizons of five years for equities and eight years for bonds for investors that are concerned with real returns.

assessments, which may include calculations of risk, of performance relative to other comparable portfolios, of performance relative to the market, and of performance relative to an absolute benchmark. Performance measurement has major conceptual and practical problems, as discussed in Bodie et al. (1999), such as dollar-weighted versus time-weighted rates of return, dealing with inflows, use of arithmetic versus geometric averages, risk-adjusted performance measures (simple alpha, comparison with similar portfolios, Sharpe's measure, Treynor's measure, Jensen's measure, and the appraisal ratio), and the problems of shifting portfolios that change the portfolio mean and risk.

There is scope for various forms of **window dressing and selective quotation** of performance figures in advertising. The U.S. Association of Investment Management and Research (AIMR) has devised guidelines to ensure that performance measures are comparable across managers.[49] Derived from it is the worldwide standard known as the global investment performance standards (GIPS). Among the stipulations are that returns should be total returns (income and capital appreciation); annual returns should be provided for all individual years; returns should be on a composite of similar portfolios or, ideally, a companywide basis, not for individual managers or portfolios; and once selected, a composite should not change, for example by reclassifying or excluding underperforming or closed portfolios from the past data. Moreover, performance should be before fees, composite returns should be provided over at least a ten-year period, and results for accounts using leverage should be restated in a no-leverage manner. A control method is that the results need to be independently verified—and verification is essential to consultants' recommendation in the United States. At the time of writing, the GIPS standard appears to be being adopted widely. Difficulties (Financial Times 2000) are that there are national differences in the details of the guidelines and the "company" is harder to define for European-style financial conglomerates than for the U.S. boutiques for which the original AIMR guidelines were designed.

2.4   Asset Manager Performance at a Micro Level

In light of the section above, we now go on to discuss the results in the literature on the efficacy of **asset management in pension funds**

---

49. See www.aimr.com for the latest version.

and mutual funds. We do not attempt to provide an exhaustive overview of all the results in the literature, but rather we offer a broad view encompassing the main results for the United States and the United Kingdom. This reflects the fact that these are the most developed markets, where correspondingly most of the extant research has been undertaken. The results should generalize to other markets in which asset management is competitive and portfolio regulations do not unduly limit freedom to vary asset holdings.

Following the argument presented in section 2.1.6, the key issue addressed in the literature is simple: Given that higher fees are paid for active management, does it offer a superior return in terms of either asset allocation or security selection? The efficient markets hypothesis suggests that, given that prices already incorporate all available information, there is no net benefit from spending extra cash to try to beat the index rather than "holding the market." If markets are less than perfectly efficient, active management can earn more than passive, even after allowing for fees. It may be noted that the efficacy of active asset allocation depends on inefficiency *between* markets, while active security selection assumes inefficiency *within* markets, in each case inclusive of fees and transactions costs.

It may be noted at the outset that Fama (1991), reviewing all the evidence on the efficient markets hypothesis for the United States, found that the securities market is extremely efficient and there is no evidence that any strategy or money manager can earn more than a normal return. Reflecting this, as we show below, **active managers tend on average to underperform**, especially when one allows for fees.

2.4.1   Asset Manager Performance: Mutual Funds

Active management of mutual funds, given the circumscribed nature of the assets in which they invest, is mainly in terms of security selection rather than asset allocation.

For actively managed mutual funds in the United States, the evidence since Jensen (1968) is that, on average, their **activities do not earn a risk-adjusted return superior to that of the market**. Even a simple assessment of the proportion of equity funds beaten by unadjusted returns on the S&P 500 shows an average of 57.3% over 1971–1995. Adjusted for risk and for fees, the figure would be much higher, although it may be acknowledged that a few years of bad performance can be made up in one good year.

In this context, a recent article by Gruber (1996) shows that average funds over 1985–1994 underperformed by between 65 and 194 bp, depending on the index that is used for comparison.[50] As expense ratios averaged 113 bp, active mutual funds appear to be a poor investment. In comparison, index funds would exactly match the index and charge 22 bp. A structural reason for underperformance is that open-end mutual funds must hold a proportion of cash to cover early withdrawals. But many studies find underperformance even allowing for this (see, for example, Malkiel (1995)).

Daniel et al. (1997) sought to assess performance of equities held by mutual funds by comparison with returns on portfolios of stocks with equivalent characteristics, that is, similar to style analysis. They found that any excess returns that were earned over and above the passive strategy were not greater than the average fee. There was no evidence that managers were able to switch styles appropriately to maximize returns. Bogle (1998) also extended the analysis to cover different styles of investment. He examined fund performance over 1992–1996 in each of nine styles distinguished by the fund rating service Morningstar (value, blend/mixed, and growth-based for large, medium, and small caps). He found a strong negative relationship between investment performance and expense ratios. Most crucially, he showed that index funds would in all cases except for small cap growth investment provide risk-adjusted returns that were superior to actual actively managed funds over 1992–1996. The **high level of risk taken by active funds** compared to passive strategies was particularly noteworthy, implying that the shortfall of risk-adjusted performance of active management is even more sizable than in terms of the return alone.

Mutual funds also **fail to time the market accurately**. Neither mutual fund managers nor investors show any ability to sell at peaks and buy at troughs. Rather, they appear to have negative timing ability and tend to invest when the asset or market is at a peak (see Trzcinka and Shukla 1992, Carhart 1997). On the other hand, Ferson and Schadt (1996) caution that most results for market timing are based on misspecified models in that relevant expectations are not conditioned on publicly available information variables.

---

50. Underperformance was 194 bp relative to the market index, 156 bp for risk-adjusted returns relative to a risk-adjusted model, and 65 bp for risk-adjusted returns relative to a four-index model.

Despite these results, on the basis of the average performance across funds, there has been some work suggesting that there is **persistence in performance of individual mutual funds** (funds with high or low returns continue to do so). Over short (1- to 3-year) time horizons, this is found, inter alia, in Brown and Goetzmann (1995), while in Elton et al. (1996), it is also seen over periods as long as five to ten years. The results tend to be stronger for persistence in performance of the lowest-performing funds (Hendricks et al. 1993) and is more equivocal for the high performers. Malkiel (1995) suggests that there was persistence in the 1970s but it broke down in the 1980s.

Gruber (1996) found persistence of performance for individual mutual funds to be strong, with alpha[51] from the four-index model giving the best predictors of future performance. On the other hand, Carhart (1997) suggests that the adjustment of the data for funds that go out of business (so-called survivorship bias) tends to eliminate much of the apparent persistence in performance. Common factors in stock returns, mutual fund expenses, and transactions costs tend to explain predictability in mutual fund returns. More generally, **expenses have a particular impact** on fund performance in general, with higher-fee funds performing less well than lower-fee ones. Carhart's evidence was not supportive of the existence of skilled or informed mutual fund managers with superior stock-picking skills, but rather indicated that short-term persistence is due to the one-year momentum effect in stock prices detected by Jagadeesh and Titman (1993), with much of the remaining persistence linked to the worst-performing funds.

Investors may be able to select "winners." Gruber (1996) shows that investors seem to be able to detect funds with superior performance, since variables that predict performance also link econometrically to subsequent cash flows to such funds. Because of persistence, investors gain from focusing on past performance. He hypothesizes that there are two classes of investors: those who actively pursue performance and those who are disadvantaged in switching, for example by lack of information, institutional barriers (as when pension monies can only be invested in a given set of funds), or tax factors (when capital gains tax makes it inefficient to

---

51. Alpha measures the systematic element of return on an asset or portfolio that is not related to the moves in the overall market.

move between funds). The existence of disadvantaged investors helps to explain why underperforming funds do not quickly go out of business. Zheng (1999) finds evidence that funds that receive more inflows subsequently perform significantly better than those that suffer outflows, an effect that is short-lived and is attributed to a strategy of betting on winners.

However, Sirri and Tufano (1998) cast doubt on whether investors act as rationally in selecting funds as Gruber (1996) and Zheng (1999) suggest. They note that funds that receive greater media attention and that belong to larger complexes grow more rapidly than other funds and the performance-flow relationship is most marked among firms with the highest marketing effort as reflected in higher fees, which lower consumers' search costs.

Given that clients tend to favor the best-performing funds with new inflows, as we discussed in chapter 3, while asset manager fees are proportional to the size of the fund plus a flat amount,[52] there are **incentives for mutual fund managers to increase the risk** on their portfolios when investment performance is poor. This may help to explain the high risks seen by Bogle (1998). Tendencies to incur risk may be increased if, as per Sirri and Tufano (1992), there are also asymmetries in outcomes such that outflows are less in the case of underperformance than are gains from outperformance. This hypothesis was verified by Brown et al. (1996), who noted that such active changes in strategy in response to poor performance may run contrary to clients' long-term interests, as a fund may take on higher risk than the client expected, as well as adopting a shorter-term perspective than is appropriate. This pattern may link to the level of competition; such "strategic increases in risk" were not detectable for 1980–1995, when the industry was less competitive, but did hold for 1986–1991, as the industry became more competitive and when performance data were more readily available. Meanwhile, Chevalier and Ellison (1995) found that such heightened risk taking was partly seasonal, being most apparent over the September to December period as mutual funds sought to ensure adequate year-end performance.

One consequence of desire for performance at any cost, including biases to increase risk, is that mutual funds may **deviate strongly from their professed objectives** in terms of style, risk, and return

---

52. The flat amount gives a floor to remuneration, protecting managers against downside risk.

and may thus hinder investors' abilities to build diversified portfolios of mutual funds. Indeed, diBartolomeo and Witkowski (1997) show that 9% of all equity mutual funds are seriously misclassified and 31% are somewhat misclassified.

Finally, there is the question of whether individual mutual fund **managers' characteristics** may have an impact on their performance. Chevalier and Ellison (1999a) found that differences in performance across managers link to behavioral differences across managers and selection biases (e.g., higher systematic risk, expenses, and survivorship biases) and not to observable differences such as differences in age, SAT scores, and MBA degrees. On the other hand, some systemically higher risk-adjusted excess returns are found for managers who attended higher-SAT undergraduate institutions. In another paper, the same authors (Chevalier and Ellison 1999b) note that managerial turnover is performance sensitive for younger fund managers, consistent with the idea that management companies learn gradually about managers' abilities. This induces younger fund managers to take on lower unsystematic risk and deviate less from typical behavior than older counterparts.

All of the above results come from data for the United States. Evidence shows that there is also considerable variance in performance between mutual fund asset managers in the United Kingdom, even within the same risk class. This is, as Blake (1997) noted, of particular relevance to defined contribution pension fund members who invest in mutual funds, particularly if there are high costs of transfer to alternative funds, as is the case in the United Kingdom. Table 2.3 shows that there is, for example, a 4.1 percentage point difference in the U.K. equity growth sector between the top and bottom quartiles

Table 2.3
Distribution of Returns by U.K. Mutual Funds (Unit Trusts), 1972–1995 (Percent)

Sector	Top Quartile	Median	Bottom Quartile	Ratio of Fund Sizes
U.K. Equity Growth	16.0	13.6	11.9	3.2
U.K. Equity General	14.3	13.4	13.1	1.4
U.K. Equity Income	15.4	14.0	12.4	2.3
U.K. Smaller Companies	18.7	15.5	12.8	5.3

The ratio of fund sizes is that based on forty years of investment at the returns of the top and bottom quartiles.
Source: Blake and Timmermans (1999).

and a 5.9 percentage point difference for smaller companies. If sustained for forty years, such performance could lead to accumulated funds 3.2 and 5.3 times larger for choosing the top rather than the bottom quartile. Moreover, research on the **closure or takeover of underperforming mutual funds** shows that the elimination of such funds is a long and uncertain process (Blake and Timmermann 1999). Of the 973 trusts that were closed or merged between 1972 and 1995, the average duration was sixteen years, over which period these funds underperformed the industry average by 2.4 percentage points per annum.

The **performance of hedge funds** has been less well studied than that of public mutual funds, but the increased focus on hedge fund investment in recent years has also increased interest in their investment performance. For example, Brown et al. (1997) looked at the performance of offshore hedge funds, including those that did not survive, over 1989–1995. Over this period, the value of funds in their sample grew from $4.7 billion to $40.3 billion and from 78 to 399 funds. On average, funds earned 13.3% compared with the 16.5% that could be earned on the U.S. equity market (S&P 500 index), while risks were also lower, at 9.1% compared with 16.3%. They found that there was a high attrition rate of funds (few lasting more than three years) and little evidence of differentiated manager skills (despite highly performance-related reward systems).

Ackermann et al. (1999) examined data on a wider range of hedge funds over 1988–1995. They found that hedge funds consistently beat U.S. mutual funds in terms of risk-adjusted returns but could not beat the equity market (i.e., index funds) adjusted for fees. They nevertheless show very low betas (i.e., low correlation with the U.S. stock market), suggesting that hedge funds could play a useful role in terms of risk diversification. Incentive fees (which are paid only if a certain return level is reached) were found to be strongly related to improvements in risk-adjusted performance. The authors concluded by noting that the 1998 crisis revealed risks in hedge funds beyond those observed in the sample, implying in turn that the apparent superiority of hedge funds over mutual funds may reflect an underestimate of true hedge fund risk (see also section 5.3.)

2.4.2   Asset Manager Performance: Pension Funds

As we outlined in section 2.3, pension funds differ from mutual funds in that they invest in a range of assets rather than a defined

Table 2.4
U.K. Pension Funds: Long-Term Returns on Equity Relative to Benchmark Indices

Percentage Points	1981–1998		1981–1989		1990–1998	
	Average	Standard Deviation	Average	Standard Deviation	Average	Standard Deviation
United States	−2.3	2.1	−3.7	2.0	−0.9	1.0
Japan	0.3	7.5	−2.0	9.9	2.5	3.2
Continental Europe	−1.0	3.1	−1.8	4.0	−0.2	1.6
World	−1.6	6.0	−3.1	5.1	−0.2	6.7
United Kingdom	−0.4	0.7	−0.4	0.9	−0.3	0.6

Note: Before 1987, local indices for the United States and Japan, MSCI for Europe. After 1987, FT-A indices.
Source: WM (1999a).

type of assets. This means that asset allocation as well as security selection are relevant to investment performance. In some cases, such as U.K. "balanced management," asset allocation has typically been delegated to external asset managers. In the United States, the sponsors usually retain control of asset allocation and delegate only security selection.

Commencing with the **United Kingdom**, the picture is broadly similar to that of mutual funds in terms of **underperformance in terms of security selection**. Underperformance is illustrated by data from the performance measurers WM for the investment performance in individual markets by U.K. pension funds, shown in table 2.4. These show that even in the home market, funds tend to underperform the index, but underperformance is particularly severe in foreign markets.[53]

Similarly, Blake et al. (1997) show that over 1986–1994, the average U.K. pension fund underperformed the market for all its component assets by 0.45% per annum before management fees are taken into account, and this is also true for 57.2% of individual funds. This underperformance was largely a consequence of underperformance in equities, as highlighted in table 2.4.

Meanwhile, WM (1999a) show that there is a consistent underperformance by external managers relative to internal managers

---

53. This may be due to poor information on trading practices and company research compared to local managers, as well as high turnover and transactions costs.

Table 2.5
U.K. Pension Funds: Performance by Management Method, 1989–1998 (Percent)

	1998	3 Years	5 Years	10 Years	Memo: Average Management Cost (bp)
Internal management	14.8	14.4	11.5	13.3	6
(excluding property)	(14.9)	(14.4)	(11.6)	(14.2)	
External management	13.7	13.6	10.8	13.4	17
(excluding property)	(13.7)	(13.6)	(10.8)	(13.7)	

Source: WM (1999b).

(table 2.5). The advantage is compounded by much higher fees for external managers. Davis (1995a) shows, using data for the late 1980s and early 1990s, that average returns are again lowest for external managers, which is in turn inversely correlated with turnover. These results are consistent with principal-agent problems; managers that are under the most tenuous control of the trustees have higher turnover and lower returns.

In the context of the U.K. tradition of balanced management, whereby the fund manager carries out both asset allocation and security selection across international markets (chapter 3), underperformance in security selection may justify an indexed approach to national stocks, in which the fund manager's skill is employed in tactical asset allocation, picking undervalued markets rather than stocks and employing stock index futures to gain rapid exposure to such markets (Howell and Cozzini 1991).

Indeed, Blake (1997) shows that for U.K. pension funds, over **99% of total returns link to asset allocation**, 2.7% was linked to security selection, and market timing was value deducting by around 1.6%. It was noted that the active component of asset management contributed just over 1% to total return, less than the fee that active managers charge. A typical illustration of the importance of asset allocation is the suggestion in Financial Times (1998) that "underweighting of the U.S. cost U.K. funds £20 bn in 1994–7." Blake et al. (1999) come to a similar conclusion regarding the importance of asset allocation, while noting that the low relative contribution of security selection compared to asset allocation reflects managerial behavior. In effect, they suggest that it reflects the lack of extensive attempts at active management by U.K. pension fund managers, rather than the relative economic importance of security selection.

The importance of asset allocation is one reason why U.K. funds are typically compared with the average of all funds rather than with the market.[54] But even in such a **peer group comparison**, outperformance is rarely sustained. Investors Chronicle (1997) shows that of over 50% of U.K. managed funds that outperformed the average in 1990–1991, only half continued to do so in 1991–1992, a third in 1992–1993, and well below 10% in subsequent years. As regards the three-year periods over which pension fund managers are often evaluated, 40% outperformed the average over 1986–1989, 20% over 1988–1991, and below 10% from 1991–1994 onward. According to Blake et al. (1997), some persistence in performance was present for U.K. funds in equities over their 1986–1994 sample; those in the top quartile had a 37% chance of being there next year, while those in the bottom quartile had a 32% chance of remaining there. Some similar results were found for cash holdings but not for other asset classes or the portfolio as a whole, nor over longer time horizons than a year. The justification for choosing asset managers on the basis of their past performance is still shown to be a tenuous one.

Whereas the above comments link mainly to average or median funds, there is also a **significant degree of variation about the mean**. Blake et al. (1997, 1998) show, for example, that on the one hand, the interquartile range for U.K. pension fund portfolios[55] is quite small, being around 2% for most asset classes and just over 1% for the whole portfolio (table 2.6). On the other hand, the extremes of the distribution are extremely wide apart. Blake (1997) attributed the quite narrow interquartile range to herding among funds, following the suggestion that they do not wish their relative performance to get too far out of line. This phenomenon, which links to the industrial

---

54. A broader form of indexation, which also covers asset allocation, is so-called consensus management, whereby a pension fund manager is obliged to hold the average portfolio of instruments that is held by all other funds in the same national market. Such an approach seems designed to generate herding. An emerging trend that avoids such a consensus-chasing approach is the use of strict benchmarks for proportions to be invested in each asset class, tailored to the liabilities of the fund. In the United Kingdom, use of individual benchmarks for pension funds has increased from 5% in 1990 to 40–45% in 1999.

55. Blake et al. note that the bulk of the portfolios during the sample period were invested by the largest U.K. asset managers: Mercury, Phillips and Drew, Schroders and Gartmore (see chapter 3). In other words, the table does not show the variation in performance across a large number of independent asset managers, as would be the case in the United States.

Table 2.6
U.K. Pension Funds: Fractiles of Total Return by Asset Class, 1986–1994 (Percent)

	U.K. Equities	International Equities	U.K. Bonds	International Bonds	U.K. Index Bonds	Cash	U.K. Property	Total
Minimum	8.6	4.4	6.6	−0.6	5.6	2.7	3.1	7.2
25%	12.4	9.6	10.4	8.3	7.9	9.0	8.0	11.5
50%	13.1	10.7	10.8	11.4	8.2	10.3	8.8	12.1
75%	13.9	11.8	11.2	13.4	8.5	11.7	10.0	12.6
Maximum	17.4	14.7	17.2	26.3	10.1	19.7	13.5	15.0
Difference 25%–75%	1.5	2.2	0.8	5.1	0.6	2.7	2.0	1.1
Difference maximum − minimum	8.8	10.3	10.6	27.0	4.5	17.1	10.5	7.8

Note: The rows do not represent individual funds, so the total does not link to the individual asset returns.
Source: Blake et al (1997).

structure and dynamics of the market as discussed in chapter 3, may lead to herding and consequent volatility of equity markets as assessed in chapter 5. Consistent with this, Blake also showed that the return on the median fund is extremely close to the average market return on assets and that 80% of funds were within 1 percentage point of the median fund. It is suggested that this shows that U.K. funds not only are herding, but also are matching the index closely, despite claiming to (and charging of fees for) active management.

Meanwhile, large funds are represented disproportionately among the poor performers, with 32% of the size quartile of the largest funds being in the lowest performance quartile (a random distribution would give 25%), while only 15% of the quartile containing the smallest funds is also in the lowest performing quartile. This may link to the difficulties of large funds in outperforming the market, given the limitations of liquidity (although it may also be related to the poor performance of property over the 1986–1994 period).

For the **United States**, where delegation of asset allocation to managers as opposed to security selection is much less common than in the United Kingdom, there are **similar results of underperformance** on the part of pension fund managers. Studies include that of Beebower and Bergstrom (1977), who found underperformance of 150 bp on equity holdings over 1966–1975. In 1981, Pensions and Investments reported that 74% of U.S. pension funds underperformed the S&P over 1971–1980. Brinson et al. (1986) found 110 bp underperformance relative to the S&P over 1974–1983. McCarthy and Turner (1989) found that inactive funds (with a rate of turnover of under 15%) obtained a 30 bp premium in returns over funds with a turnover of over 70%. Ippolito and Turner (1987) came to similar conclusions.

Lakonishok et al. (1992a) show that the equity proportion of U.S. funds (excluding the management fee) underperforms the S&P 500 index by an average of 1.3% per annum over 1983–1989, or 2.6% if returns are value weighted, that is, putting a greater weight on large funds. If managers overperform in some periods, this is virtually never sustained. Such underperformance excludes management fees, which would worsen performance by a further 50 bp. Underperformance was common across virtually all styles except yield-based, which was adopted by only 11% of managers. It is also shown that, measured on a value-weighted basis, money managers would have performed much better had they frozen their portfolios and not traded[56] (the loss is 42 bp on a portfolio frozen for six months and 78 bp on one frozen for twelve months).[57]

However, Bodie (1991) suggests that such findings may still be consistent with profit maximization by the sponsor if he or she is seeking forms of immunization and portfolio insurance, requiring higher turnover, whose cost is the reduction in returns. In particular, U.S. defined benefit funds are obliged to **hedge to a greater extent** than would a risk-neutral investor, **owing to the shortfall risk** created by strict minimum funding requirements. This would tend to lead to some underperformance owing to the "insurance" costs that need to be paid against a sharp fall in the stock market. Moreover, evidence is not unequivocal. Coggin et al. (1993) find some evidence of outperformance on a risk-adjusted basis.

Meanwhile, as in the United Kingdom, a survey of over 1000 U.S. pension fund sponsors showed that internally managed defined benefit funds tend to outperform those managed by external managers (Institutional Investor 1996) and may also outperform the market index. Yet at the time of the survey, only 25% of U.S. funds had internal management.

As in the United Kingdom, the lesson drawn from these analyses—and the many thousands of others showing that securities markets are efficient—is that indexation will be optimal for most pension fund assets, with the caveat that the benefits arising from active management are likely to increase with the number of funds adopting such predictable passive strategies and with the inefficiency of the market more generally. According to Riley (2000), 35% of U.S. pension fund equity assets are indexed, accounting for 22% of

---

56. On the other hand, Lakonishok et al. (1992a) found that turnover was correlated positively with return in their sample.

57. Analyzing the factors underlying such patterns, Lakonishok et al. suggest that the persistent use of active management despite such evidence is related to agency problems. In particular, they suggest that these may arise within the management structure of the sponsor; corporate treasurers seek to bolster their own positions vis-à-vis their managers and hence seek fund managers that can offer good excuses for poor performance, clear stories about portfolio strategies, and other services unrelated to performance. They avoid indexation, as this would reduce their own day-to-day responsibilities, as well as internal asset management, as this would give them too great a responsibility for errors. Lakonishok et al. suggest that these agency costs are additional to the difficulties (as noted above) that arise between a (rational profit-maximizing) sponsor and the fund manager and that a shift to defined contribution plans would help to overcome the difficulties.

Table 2.7
Pension Fund Sector Asset Allocation (Percentage of Total Assets)

	Year	Bonds	Equities	Liquidity	Property	Foreign	Loans
Australia	1970	58	15	25	2	0	0
	1995	15	41	20	9	14	0
Canada	1970	53	22	5	1	0	8
	1995	40	29	6	4	14	5
Denmark	1970	72	0	3	0	0	6
	1995	63	27	1	6	0	1
Germany	1970	19	0	3	12	0	31
	1995	51	0	2	7	0	40
Japan	1972	11	6	3	22	0	58
	1993	53E	20E	2	2	10E	13
Netherlands	1970	13	6	1	16	7	48
	1994	24	13	2	10	24	25
Sweden	1970	76	0	0	0	0	22
	1995	83	1	6	3	0	7
Switzerland	1970	25	3	7	16	0	48
	1994	28	14	7	16	0	34
United Kingdom	1970	31	49	4	10	2	3
	1995	12	53	4	4	19	0
United States	1970	45	45	1	0	0	6
	1995	27	45E	6	0	8E	1

Source: National flow of funds balance sheet data. Totals do not add to 100 owing to "miscellaneous assets."

assets (the total indexed share is somewhat higher—around 28%—reflecting indexation of bond holdings); 62% of the largest 200 have indexed equity funds; and 34% have indexed bond funds.

2.5   Asset Manager Returns at a Macro Level: A Case Study of Pension Fund Sectors

In this section, we provide a case study of the asset allocation of institutional investors at a macro level, based on data for pension fund sectors in OECD countries from 1967 to 1995. Patterns of portfolio distributions over time for pension funds and their determinants are discussed extensively in Davis (1995e). Table 2.7 shows actual portfolios in 1970 and 1995.

Pension funds have differing appropriate portfolio distributions, reflecting differences in liabilities, accounting, and so forth, as is discussed in section 2.5.1. Hence it is not surprising that the returns also differ somewhat, as is discussed in section 2.5.2. As Borio et al. (1997)

stressed, given the importance of liabilities, it is hard to make a judgment of optimality based solely on relative returns and risks. Nevertheless, some useful comments and comparisons can be made.

2.5.1 Influences on the Portfolio

In line with the discussion in section 2.1.3, **liabilities** have a major influence, for example on the share of bonds, in that:

• the **duration**[58] of liabilities in combination with the strictness of minimum funding rules will set a benchmark for the duration of assets—or, if they are not matched, for the scope of interest rate risk;

• the **inflation sensitivity** of liabilities will determine the demand for assets acting as inflation hedges such as index-linked bonds, as well as assets whose return is unaffected by inflation, such as real estate and equities (see also section 2.3.1);

• the need for **cash flow** will play an important role by determining the need for liquidity to meet (known or uncertain) cash flows, for example in the context of growing maturity.

As regards duration, the U.K. experience is instructive, as funds have tended to shift toward bonds, owing to growing maturity. Whereas in 1995 the equity share was 76% and bonds 14%, by the end of 1998 the figures were 72% and 19%, respectively (WM 2000). However, since 1995, an increased focus on duration matching has also been mandated by the introduction of a minimum funding rule (Davis 2000b). (Minimum funding rules are discussed further below.) Meanwhile, U.S. funds, which have always been subject to such rules, have generally held more bonds than their U.K. counterparts (see table 2.7). Danish and Australian funds tend to be defined contribution, which may imply tighter constraints on duration.

Turning to inflation sensitivity, in countries such as Canada, with a high share of bonds, pension payments are generally fixed in nominal terms, while in the United Kingdom, where bond holding is lower, a degree of inflation protection both before and after retirement is expected. On the other hand, similar indexation promises are made by the Swedish, German, and Swiss pension funds, despite which the share of inflation hedge assets is extremely low, suggesting that influences other than liabilities are operating.

---

58. Duration is the average time to an asset's discounted cash flows.

Moreover, the general rise in the share of equities that is apparent in table 2.7 is not consistent with the growing maturity of pension funds and hence the need for cash flow. On balance, therefore, liabilities alone are insufficient to account for cross-country differences in portfolios, leading us to seek further underlying factors.

Historically, the higher **taxation** on bonds than equities made the former an attractive investment to tax-exempt investors such as pension funds, but the high shares of equity actually held suggest that this is not a strong explanation. In the United States, cross-fund comparisons (as in Gallo and Lockwood 1995) show that there is little relationship between the scope for a pension fund to exploit tax benefits and a larger proportion of tax-disadvantaged assets, that is, bonds.[59] Elsewhere, portfolio regulations often force funds to hold tax-disadvantaged assets, as in Denmark, where pension funds must effectively hold 60% fixed-interest assets (European Commission 2000), despite the real interest tax on such assets.

Ownership and control of pension funds may influence portfolios, via the degree of risk aversion of those controlling the fund and the degree to which those holding residual risks (i.e., benefiting from a surplus or funding a deficit) can control asset distributions.

For private funds in the United States and the United Kingdom, the surplus of a pension fund is more clearly at the disposal of the sponsor than elsewhere (Davis 1995a). This may explain the more aggressive and less risk-averse portfolios with a large share of equities. In contrast, in corporate pension funds in the Netherlands, equity holding has historically been low (20%) despite the absence of portfolio restrictions. Van Loo (1988) suggests that this may relate to risk aversion of pension fund trustees[60] but may also link to the fact that sponsors benefit less from surpluses than in the United States and the United Kingdom. Employee trustees may also move the balance toward risk aversion,[61] and the small size of the Dutch equity market may be another factor discouraging equity investment. This is now changing, not least with the advent of the Euro-

---

59. Note, however, that recent analyses suggest that equities are now less advantaged in the United States and hence should be more attractive; indeed, bond shares in the United States have declined somewhat.
60. Also according to Wyatt (1993), there are unofficial tolerance limits for equity exposure of 30%, imposed by the supervisors.
61. Research on U.S. funds by Mitchell and Hsin (1994) suggests that employee representation reduces returns even for defined benefit funds, although in principle the employer is bearing the risk.

pean Economic and Monetary Union (EMU). Defined benefit pension funds sponsored by public agencies (local government and public corporations) seem historically to have held more bonds than private funds in the United States and the United Kingdom (Davis 1995a); although this may be related to risk aversion and an inability to utilize surpluses, it could also reflect self-interest by favoring public sector assets.[62]

Similar considerations of control and risk aversion may arise for defined contribution funds. Lower proportions of equities in defined contribution funds are partly rational, given the lack of risk sharing between member and sponsor, and workers nearing retirement will be anxious for low-risk assets to be held.[63] For example, the equity share in Denmark, where funds are largely defined contribution, is exceptionally low. This pattern holds despite the Danish tax on real returns to debt instruments, which encourages substitution of equities for bonds. Whereas the low share of equity may partly reflect portfolio regulations, it is probably also due to the funds' defined contribution basis and conservatism of managers (since the regulatory limits do not currently bind). U.S. defined benefit plans tended historically to hold more equities than defined contribution funds do, reflecting the greater risk tolerance of sponsors, but this pattern has been reversed since 1990 (table 2.8). For personal pensions in the United Kingdom, there is anecdotal evidence that people who are free to choose their asset backing often select highly cautious combinations of assets.

Funding rules and their interaction with associated accounting arrangements may play a crucial role in influencing portfolios. This is because they determine the size and volatility of the surplus, as well as defining the rules for dealing with a corresponding deficit (section 2.2.3.2). They influence the likelihood and cost of any deficiency and hence the importance for pension funds of maintaining a stable valuation of assets relative to liabilities.

In the United States, minimum funding regulations make it optimal to hold a large proportion of bonds to protect against shortfall

---

62. This is also true of the Dutch ABP pension fund for civil servants, which historically was obliged to hold almost all of its assets in the form of bonds and loans, as well as for the Swedish fund.

63. This point indicates the inflexibility of company-based defined contribution plans that seek to cater to both risk-seeking young workers and risk-averse older ones. Some funds, such as BT in Australia, overcome this by offering four separate funds at different levels of risk.

Table 2.8
U.S. Private Pension Funds' Assets

	1988	1990	1992	1994	1996	1998
Defined Benefit ($ billion)	810	879	1038	1159	1523	2132
Percent of total assets:						
Equities	41.2	37.0	44.1	45.3	53.5	60.4
Bonds	34.2	40.3	37.3	36.6	31.0	27.0
Liquidity	8.0	6.7	4.8	4.7	3.7	3.1
Defined Contribution ($ billion)	595	730	972	1193	1629	2199
Percent of total assets:						
Equities	38.8	41.2	48.6	52.0	61.1	68.6
Bonds	16.5	18.7	18.3	19.9	18.3	17.2
Liquidity	10.4	11.8	8.5	6.7	4.7	3.5

Source: U.S. Flow of Funds data.

risk; despite their weakness in the past as an inflation hedge, bonds form around 40% of pension funds' portfolios.[64] Traditionally, in the United Kingdom, there was no strict minimum funding rule, and therefore equities could be held without risk. The new U.K. minimum funding regulation (Davis 1997b, 2000b) has obliged funds to hold much larger proportions of bonds to minimize shortfall risk, although elements of the actuarial income based approach are retained. In Switzerland and Japan, a requirement to post minimum returns leads to conservative investment, not least since in Switzerland, the requirement explicitly excludes capital gains. Swiss bonds offer low returns, but given the low target yield of 4% nominal, fund managers there historically saw little need to diversify into equities. Desire for a stable return is reinforced in Japan by a desire for an income flow from pension funds to finance recreation and leisure facilities. On the other hand, recent experience has seen huge deficits in Japanese pension funds, requiring large top-up payments by companies (section 5.3.7).

As regards **accounting standards**, in Japan, assets have to date been held at book value,[65] and a fixed return on the fund (based on

---

64. Bodie (1991) suggests that given such funding rules, it is a paradox that U.S. defined benefit funds invest in equities, since a drop in market values can cause underfunding that has to be reflected in the employer's profit and loss account. He suggests that it occurs because management sees a plan as a trust for employees and manages assets as if it were a defined contribution plan (i.e., for employee welfare), with a guaranteed floor given by the benefit formula.
65. Book value accounting was abolished in Japan in April 2000 in favor of market value.

interest and capital gains) is targeted for every year. This gives perverse incentives to sell well-performing equities as general share prices fall and retain those showing price declines, as well as to hold more bonds that portfolio optimization would imply (Tamura 1992). In Germany and Switzerland, Hepp (1990, 1992) suggests that application of strict accounting principles, which are more appropriate to banks than pension funds, restrains equity holdings by funded plans independently of the portfolio regulations (evidenced, in Switzerland, by the fact that funds' equity holdings were historically far below the ceilings permitted). These conventions, for example, insist on positive net worth of the fund at all times, carry equities on the balance sheet at the lower of book value and market value, and calculate returns net of unrealized capital gains. In the Netherlands, equities are accounted for at market value and bonds at book value, leading to a potential bias against the former.

In contrast, the United Kingdom accounting standard permits long-run actuarial smoothing of equity returns and focuses on dividends rather than market values and hence enables funds to accept the volatility of equity returns. Until recently, when the above-mentioned minimum funding rule began to play a decisive role, the concern of some commentators in the United Kingdom was rather whether equity holdings were too high given the risks. Paradoxically, an additional factor that has been operative in reducing adequacy of funding since 1997 has been the reduction in the actuarial returns on pension funds in the United Kingdom due to the abolition of the credit on advanced corporation tax, despite the fact that market values were unaffected.

Portfolio regulations as set out in table 2.1 give a ceiling to holdings of a given asset class, although the degree to which such limits bind appears to vary (see Davis 1998a), suggesting that other influences, as mentioned above, based on minimum funding and accounting may be more important (see Borio et al. 1997). Whereas portfolio restrictions are aimed to prevent overconcentration of risk in individual assets, portfolio regulations may operate contrary to this; Swedish and Danish funds have considerable exposure to housing markets via mortgage-related bonds and loans to housing credit institutions. Together with mortgages, these amounted to no less than 35% of Swedish funds' assets in 1998, while Danish funds had 60% of assets in mortgages or mortgage association bonds in 1996.

These imply an enormous exposure to potential effects of recession and falling house prices.

There are many other examples of the effects of portfolio restrictions. The decline in bond holding in Australia in the 1980s parallels the removal of portfolio requirements that formerly required the majority of assets to be held in government securities. As regards equities, a rise in equity holdings of the Dutch ABP fund for civil servants has been permitted by the abolition of previously binding asset restrictions. In 1996, the strong Danish equity market forced pension funds to disinvest to comply with regulations (Financial Times 1998). German funds are currently limited to a maximum of 30%[66] equities by regulation, and Japanese funds were until very recently limited to 30%; hence at 7% and 18%, respectively, in 1998, the ceilings were not binding. Canadian funds are close to their ceilings for international assets. Unlike other sectors, which have decreased holdings of property in recent years, Swiss funds retain around a fifth of their assets in property; one of the few assets that were relatively free under their pre-1993 portfolio restrictions. This focus may drive up the price of land, it does not contribute to capital formation, and funds may face decreasing returns on (domestic) property in the future, as the population declines.

Even countries with prudent man rules may not leave equity investment entirely unrestricted. Trzcinka (1998) maintains that U.S. defined benefit fund managers target a fixed income ratio of around 40%, owing to the prudent man rule (although the minimum funding regulation may be more influential). Davis (1995a) reports that Dutch funds were, at least until the early 1990s, subject to unofficial tolerance limits for equity exposure of 30%, imposed by the supervisors.

As we noted in section 2.3.2, **international diversification** can offer a better risk-return trade-off to fund managers, by reducing the systematic risk of investing in domestic markets arising from the cycle or medium-term shifts in the profit share. In a longer-term context, international investment in countries with a relatively young population may be essential to prevent battles over resources between workers and retirees in countries with an aging population (Blake 1997). In small countries such as the Netherlands and Ireland, the assets of pension funds may exceed the entire domestic equity market,

---

66. Note that historically the ceiling was much lower.

and hence simple liquidity considerations necessitate international investment.

Foreign asset holdings have grown sharply over the 1980s and 1990s in the United Kingdom, Australia, and Japan. In all three countries, this pattern followed abolition of **exchange controls**, also in the United Kingdom and Japan when the economies were generating current account surpluses and overseas investment returns looked attractive. In Japan, portfolio restrictions on overseas investment were also progressively eased over the 1980s. Meanwhile, Dutch funds have long held a significant proportion of assets abroad, partly owing to the large volume of pension fund assets compared with domestic security and real estate markets. Growth in international investment has been much less marked in the other countries; in Germany, Switzerland, Denmark, Sweden, and Canada, this is partly due to portfolio restrictions.

The structure of **asset management** and related levels of competition is likely to affect the efficiency of investment. In particular, protection of fund managers from external competition, as was the case in Japan until recently (see section 3.7) may lead to a suboptimal investment strategy from the point of view of plan beneficiaries and most recently have led to huge topping-up requirements for sponsors (see section 5.3.7). Equally, suboptimal returns may result from sectors that, owing to oligopoly, are dominated by a small number of firms, while there are barriers to entry, as has historically been the case in Continental Europe (see section 3.6). This point links to the more general issue of lack of an equity culture, which characterizes the bank-dominated as opposed to market-based financial systems (see chapter 5). Certainly, the preexisting financial structure may be seen to have an influence on the relatively low equity investment of the pension funds in bank-dominated systems. But conversely, by investing in equities, the pension funds may also play an active role in a financial system's transition to a more capital markets-based one, as was the case in Chile (see Holzmann (1997a) and section 5.1.1).

Whereas in principle, capital market activity should ensure that asset returns are equalized across countries, owing to international investment restrictions, exchange controls, and so forth, this has not always been the case in the past, resulting in markedly **different real returns on assets**. In this context, intercountry differences in strategic bond holding may also relate to asset returns. As shown in table 2.9,

Table 2.9
Real Asset Returns and Risks over 1967–1995

Average Real Return (and Standard Deviation)	Loans	Corporate Bonds	Shares	Government Bonds	Mortgages	Short-Term Assets	Property	Foreign Equities	Foreign Bonds
Australia	4.8 (5.2)	1.9 (22.4)	8.3 (19.9)	−0.1 (18.5)	3.4 (4.2)	1.8 (4.3)	4.4 (18.7)	7.5 (20.7)	4.4 (17.8)
Canada	4.2 (3.1)	3.3 (12.9)	5.0 (15.8)	2.0 (13.3)	5.5 (2.9)	2.7 (3.3)	9.4 (8.3)	8.2 (17.8)	5.1 (15.0)
Denmark	6.6 (3.5)	5.3 (12.2)	5.9 (25.6)	4.4 (19.1)	6.2 (3.5)	2.3 (2.8)		5.2 (21.4)	2.1 (17.7)
France	3.3 (3.3)	3.2 (16.2)	7.7 (18.4)	2.5 (15.8)	4.0 (2.5)	2.9 (3.4)	4.3 (14.5)	6.9 (17.2)	3.8 (14.5)
Germany	6.8 (2.0)	4.4 (15.4)	10.8 (23.8)	3.9 (15.7)	4.7 (1.4)	3.1 (2.1)	10.9 (11.5)	5.5 (21.4)	2.4 (17.4)
Italy	4.3 (3.7)		4.1 (32.5)	−2.0 (20.8)		−0.3 (4.4)		7.9 (16.3)	4.9 (14.5)
Japan	1.4 (4.7)	3.4 (16.3)	8.5 (20.9)	3.1 (19.5)	2.7 (4.7)	−0.2 (4.5)	11.5 (19.4)	7.8 (20.4)	4.4 (12.8)
Netherlands	4.0 (3.4)	2.8 (16.1)	8.8 (26.6)	2.6 (14.1)	4.4 (2.4)	2.1 (3.8)	5.9 (8.3)	6.2 (18.7)	3.1 (13.9)
Sweden	4.4 (3.8)	1.7 (15.3)	14.1 (31.4)	1.4 (16.3)	4.3 (3.3)	2.1 (3.9)	10.3 (27.1)	7.7 (17.6)	4.6 (15.4)
Switzerland	2.8 (2.0)	0.4 (20.3)	7.8 (22.8)	0.0 (18.7)	1.6 (2.2)	1.3 (2.0)	1.7 (9.1)	5.3 (19.9)	2.2 (15.9)
United Kingdom	1.7 (6.1)	2.1 (14.7)	8.3 (17.8)	1.0 (14.9)	2.7 (5.1)	2.1 (4.6)	1.5 (15.3)	8.0 (17.7)	4.1 (15.7)
United States	3.8 (2.3)	1.7 (13.0)	6.2 (14.8)	1.2 (15.2)	4.7 (2.9)	2.0 (2.3)	5.6 (22.1)	8.5 (18.7)	5.5 (14.9)

Source: OECD, BIS.

partly owing to low and stable inflation, real returns on bonds and other fixed-interest assets have historically been relatively high in Germany, Denmark, and the Netherlands, thus motivating a high portfolio share. But in Sweden and Switzerland, bonds have a high portfolio share owing to portfolio regulations, despite poor returns.

The above comments apply to long-term strategic asset allocations. Davis (1988) made estimates of the determinants of the scope of **tactical asset allocation** for pension funds in the United States, the United Kingdom, Germany, Japan, and Canada. These estimates showed that changing portfolios are strongly influenced by relative asset returns (implying tactical asset allocation) where there are few regulations governing portfolio distributions and low transactions costs, as in the United States and the United Kingdom. Adjustment to a change in such returns in these countries is generally rapid. Assuming adequate information and appropriate incentives to fund managers, this should imply an efficient allocation of funds and correct valuation of securities. In Davis's research, these results did not all hold where transactions costs are high and regulations are strict— for example, in Germany, Japan, and Canada. In these countries, adjustment to a change in returns is somewhat slower, implying that portfolios are relatively invariant to changes in asset market conditions. The results also contrast with corresponding estimates for households and companies, where adjustment to changes in returns tends to be slow, owing to higher transactions costs and poorer information. Examples of responses to relative returns include the high levels of liquidity held temporarily after stock market collapses, as in the United Kingdom in the mid-1970s, and in the longer term owing to structural changes in yields arising from deregulation and expansion of short-term markets, as in the United States and Canada. One caution should be noted in interpreting such results: that pension funds acting together may be sufficient to move the market in their direction.

2.5.2   Returns and Risks on the Portfolio

Data for risks and returns on assets can be used in combination with those on portfolio distributions to derive **estimates of the returns and risks on portfolios**. The results illustrate the ex post cost to the sponsor of providing a given level of pension benefits (for a defined benefit fund) or the return to the member (for a defined contribution fund). Using annual data for 1970–1995, we weighted for each year the annual real rate of return on each asset by the relevant portfolio share, thus giving on aggregation a series of annual portfolio rates of return. Transactions and management costs were ignored; actual returns would be lower if these were included. (See the discussion of fees in chapter 3 and the discussion of trading costs in chapter 8.) Annual holding-period returns on marketable fixed-rate instruments were used instead of redemption yields. In our view, the holding-period returns are the more relevant measure for an ongoing portfolio, since they take full account of losses or gains due to interest rate changes (although other assumptions regarding holding periods could also be made).

Although such calculations of risk and return are of some interest, their meaning is **subject to some caveats**. It is not straightforward to use them to reach conclusions on the optimality of the portfolio distribution of a pension fund sector, given the myriad influences on portfolios that were set out in the section above. Simple comparisons of returns without consideration of risk are relevant only if risk is wholly diversifiable, which is not the case for individual pension funds. Even calculation of a risk-adjusted rate of return assumes that a simple mean-variance approach is relevant, with no consideration of the influence of liabilities on the strategic asset allocation (in an asset-liability management context) or desire of managers to invest on the basis of shortfall risk, portfolio insurance, or matching techniques (as described in section 2.1.4). Nevertheless, we do derive a simple common measure of risk-adjusted return, namely the Sharpe ratio (real return/standard deviation of real return).

As regards the appropriate asset returns to use in such calculations, one should in principle judge optimality by the best informed guess that the asset manager might make under uncertainty about expected returns, risks, and covariances over the investment time horizon. Even a 30-year period (as illustrated in table 2.9) may not be sufficient to accurately judge whether realized returns are best informed guesses or not. Also, the returns that are available differ sharply for funds that remain largely confined to domestic markets—and even international returns in domestic currency are influenced by currency depreciation. Hence it is best merely to note the differences ex post rather than seeking to form an explicit evaluation.

As regards **returns** (table 2.10), the estimates suggest that pension funds in the United Kingdom and Germany obtained real returns

Table 2.10
Returns and Risks on Pension Fund Sector Portfolios: Average Real Return (and Standard Deviation)

	1970–1995				1980–1995			
	Pension Funds	50–50 Bond Equity	Global Portfolio	Real Average Earnings	Pension Funds	50–50 Bond Equity	Global Portfolio	Real Average Earnings
Australia	1.8 (11.4)	3.5 (17.5)	6.1 (18.2)	1.0 (3.4)	6.1 (8.6)	8.8 (15.8)	10.2 (17.8)	−0.1 (2.2)
Canada	4.8 (10.0)	4.0 (12.1)	7.1 (14.7)	1.3 (2.4)	7.5 (10.6)	6.6 (13.1)	10.6 (14.1)	0.3 (1.2)
Denmark	5.0 (11.1)	6.1 (19.0)	3.7 (18.5)	2.4 (3.5)	9.2 (10.6)	8.8 (17.9)	9.1 (18.8)	0.7 (1.9)
Germany	6.0 (5.9)	6.4 (17.7)	3.9 (18.4)	2.7 (2.7)	6.7 (6.9)	10.4 (18.4)	9.3 (18.4)	1.4 (1.4)
Japan	4.4 (10.2)	6.1 (16.9)	6.9 (16.0)	2.4 (3.0)	6.9 (9.4)	9.6 (14.5)	8.9 (9.8)	1.4 (1.3)
Netherlands	4.6 (6.0)	5.5 (18.3)	4.8 (14.7)	1.4 (2.6)	6.3 (6.7)	11.4 (19.5)	9.9 (13.7)	0.1 (1.7)
Sweden	2.0 (13.1)	8.0 (20.1)	6.3 (14.8)	1.4 (3.5)	4.9 (15.9)	10.3 (21.7)	10.4 (15.3)	0.3 (2.4)
Switzerland	1.7 (7.5)	2.4 (18.1)	3.7 (17.0)	1.5 (2.1)	1.8 (7.7)	3.4 (18.6)	9.2 (15.8)	0.8 (1.3)
United Kingdom	5.9 (12.8)	4.7 (15.4)	5.9 (15.0)	2.8 (2.3)	9.8 (9.7)	9.2 (11.9)	10.2 (15.2)	3.0 (1.2)
United States	4.5 (11.8)	4.4 (13.3)	7.5 (15.2)	−0.2 (1.9)	8.4 (10.9)	8.7 (12.6)	10.0 (15.5)	−0.8 (1.4)

Source: Authors' calculations.

Table 2.11
Sharpe Ratios (Real Return/Standard Deviation)

	1970–1995	1980–1995
Australia	0.2	0.7
Canada	0.5	0.7
Denmark	0.5	0.9
Germany	1.0	1.0
Japan	0.4	0.7
Netherlands	0.8	1.0
Sweden	0.2	0.3
Switzerland	0.2	0.2
United Kingdom	0.5	1.0
United States	0.4	0.8

Source: Authors' calculations.

of 6% or more per annum over 1970–1995 and those in Canada, Denmark, Japan, the Netherlands, and the United States earned 4–5%, while those in Australia, Sweden, and Switzerland earned 2% or less. We also show for comparison the shorter period 1980–1995, when markets and regulations were more liberalized. Then, returns of over 8% were gained in Denmark, the United Kingdom, and United States, with over 6% being achieved in Australia, Canada, Germany, Japan, and the Netherlands. Swedish funds managed nearly 5%, but Swiss funds were still below 2%.

As regards **risk**, standard deviations of real returns were below 10% over 1970–1995 only in Germany, Japan, and the Netherlands. Elsewhere, standard deviations tend to be 10–12%. Sharpe ratios, shown in table 2.11, give a better summary of the risk-return trade-off. German and Dutch funds had the best Sharpe ratios, consistently, while the performance of the other sectors improved in the later period.

Finally, we calculated the **differentials between real returns obtained and various benchmarks**. The most crucial is the growth rate of average earnings, which determines the replacement ratio. If a pension fund is unable to exceed this benchmark, it is in a sense value deducting, and the pension system would be better off as a pay-as-you-go system. (This follows from the so-called Aaron (1966) condition, which shows that funding is superior to pay-as-you-go as long as asset returns exceed the growth rate of average earnings.) Two other benchmarks of potential interest are the 50–50 equity-bond split in the domestic market and an estimate of the global

Table 2.12
Real Returns Relative to Benchmarks (Percentage Points)

	1970–1995			1980–1995		
	50–50	Global	Real Average Earnings	50–50	Global	Real Average Earnings
Australia	−1.7	−4.3	0.8	−2.7	−4.1	6.1
Canada	0.8	−2.3	3.5	0.9	−3.2	7.2
Denmark	−1.0	1.4	2.6	0.5	0.1	8.5
Germany	−0.4	2.1	3.3	−3.7	−2.6	5.3
Japan	−1.6	−2.5	2.1	−2.7	−2.0	5.5
Netherlands	−0.9	−0.2	3.2	−5.0	−3.5	6.2
Sweden	−6.0	−4.3	0.6	−5.4	−5.6	4.6
Switzerland	−0.6	−1.9	0.2	−1.6	−7.4	1.0
United Kingdom	1.2	0.0	3.0	0.6	−0.4	6.9
United States	0.1	−3.0	4.8	−0.3	−1.6	9.2

Source: Authors' calculations.

portfolio return[67] comprising again 50% bonds and 50% equities in international markets. The former gives an idea of the costs of any portfolio restrictions which may limit funds to a lower share of equities than 50%, while the latter gives a comparison with a fully diversified portfolio.

Funds from Canada, Germany, the Netherlands, the United States, and the United Kingdom obtain considerable headroom above **real average earnings** growth (over 3%) over 1970–1995 (see table 2.12). This was also true to a lesser extent in Denmark and Japan (2–3%). But in Australia, Sweden, and Switzerland, the excess was less than 1%, which may be insufficient to offset transactions costs. Following the arithmetic of funding, these results must be reflected in either funding costs for sponsoring firms or the level of benefits offered. It is notable that in the 1980–1995 period, the Australian funds gave a much better performance, which may correspond to a switch to a prudent man rule for asset allocation in the early 1980s.

Concerning the **benchmark of 50–50 domestic equities and bonds**, only Canadian and U.K. funds exceeded this by any considerable amount. U.S. and Danish funds were broadly in line, while the others could have achieved higher returns from such a passive port-

---

67. Global portfolios were estimated from capitalization-weighted returns on the foreign countries' equities or bonds, adjusted for inflation and the annual change in the effective exchange rate of the country concerned.

folio. In the Swedish case, the shortfall is as much as 6 percentage points. However, as table 2.10 shows, in most cases such a switch would be at a considerable cost in terms of risk relative to that which was actually incurred. Similar comments can be made about the benchmark of a **global portfolio**. In most cases, both returns and risks on an estimated "global portfolio" are higher than they would be in the case of actual outturns.

Several further observations can be made regarding the results. The publicly sponsored Swedish fund does poorly, despite the structure of independent fund boards. The Swedish and Swiss systems—and latterly the Australian system—are also compulsory, thus in principle reducing competitive pressures. In the case of Australian and Danish funds, occupational defined contribution funds imply that those who select the managers—companies themselves—do not bear the risk. The Japanese, Swiss, and Germans have generally had little competition in fund management (as we discussed in chapters 3 and 4). But as the results for Germany show, good economic performance—or international diversification—can overcome such handicaps.

Comparison of the risks and returns on pension fund portfolios with table 2.9 shows the benefits of diversification in terms of lower standard deviations on the portfolio than individual assets. Comparison of the results and risks with risk-free yields suggests that the funds generally outperformed government bonds in terms of return and in many cases also for risk.

Conclusions

Asset management has been shown to involve a number of discrete tasks, the most crucial of which are asset allocation and security selection. Whereas all types of asset management have a large number of elements in common, certain specialized considerations apply in the case of mutual funds, life insurance, defined contribution pension funds, and defined benefit pension funds. These in turn give rise to differing requirements in terms of portfolio strategy. Equity investment and investment in foreign assets also raise some important issues for all asset managers. In a number of countries, the degree to which the benefits of these instruments in terms of returns and diversification may be utilized for portfolio objectives is limited by regulation, to the detriment of performance of institutional investors.

Analyses of performance at a micro level show that security selection may actually be value-deducting in efficient capital markets. The implication is that the use of index funds would seem to be recommended in most cases, given that active investors are unable to beat the index net of transactions costs in any consistent manner. On the other hand, active asset allocation across the portfolio seems to be profitable. For pension funds, internal management is also seen to be superior to external management, a finding that in turn supports the argument that principal-agent problems are important in fund management (since internal managers are subject to closer monitoring). As regards the macro analysis, a myriad of influences can be identified that affect pension funds' portfolios. The outcomes differ markedly across countries in terms of rates of return and risk, in a way that is dependent both on these factors affecting asset allocation and on the returns on assets themselves. Conclusions concerning optimality of strategies cannot, however, be simply derived from data on returns and risks given the additional constraints (such as the need to hedge against shortfall risk) affecting some sectors. Nevertheless, the exceptionally poor results for countries such as Switzerland and Sweden suggest a need for further investigation, notably of the influence of the interaction of asset manager competition, accounting rules, portfolio regulations, and minimum-funding or minimum-return rules. The fact that the systems in question are mandatory may also be relevant (see Davis 1998f).

II

The Industry of Asset
Management:
Present and Future

3

The Industrial Structure and Dynamics of Asset Management

Introduction

This chapter focuses on the nature of competition in the asset management industry, viewed in light of the main structural features of the sector. It employs the concepts of industrial organization theory as applied to financial markets and institutions. The first section develops an analytical framework; the second looks at wholesale and retail fund management in general terms in light of the framework. In the following sections, we undertake case studies of fund management in the United States, the United Kingdom, and other E.U. markets.[1] Finally, we consider as a case study of transition the Japanese wholesale asset management sector. This has historically been dominated by a virtual cartel, but this pattern may now be breaking down owing to deregulation and poor performance of incumbent managers. In the following chapter, the overall prospects for asset

---

1. As background to our choice of focus in this section of the book, note that the pattern of institutional equity investment by the ten largest financial centers shows that London was the largest center in 1998, with $2.2 trillion, followed by New York with $2.0 trillion, Boston with $1.5 trillion, Tokyo with $1.1 trillion, San Francisco with $0.6 trillion, Zürich with $0.5 trillion, Los Angeles and Paris with $0.4 trillion, Philadelphia and Chicago with $0.3 trillion (British Invisibles Web site: www.bi.org.uk).

management in the United States, the United Kingdom, and Continental Europe, including the effects of Monetary Union in Europe are considered. These assessments of prospects are illuminated by the responses to a questionnaire that was sent to asset managers.

3.1 What Is Asset Management?

Asset management (also referred to as fund management, investment management, money management and portfolio management) defines the **process whereby assets collected by institutional investors are actually invested in the capital markets**. The fund management sector is an integral part of institutional investment process, although the asset manager may or may not be a part of the institutional investor in a legal sense. In effect, asset management may be either internal or external[2] to the institution itself; fund managers may be in the trust department of banks or securities houses, in separately capitalized fund management firms owned by banks or insurance companies, in independent fund management firms, or internal to large pension funds or life insurers themselves. There is increasingly fierce competition among asset managers.

Two observations may be added: first, that the number of asset managers is smaller than the number of institutional investors, given that many small funds may be managed, often on a pooled basis, by a single external manager. Second, the total amount of managed funds exceeds that of institutional investors, owing to the importance of assets of high-net-worth individuals, banks' and securities firms' proprietary trading, nonfinancial companies' treasury operations, charities, and other endowments.

As is detailed in British Invisibles (1997), the **function of fund managers** may be divided into **front office functions and back office functions**. Front office functions include the following:

• Marketing new products and developing products

• Fund management, the main focus of this section, including strategic fund management (long-term asset allocation and risk management), operational fund management (security selection, tactical asset allocation, decision making, and implementation), research

---

2. The tendency in recent years has been for outsourcing, especially for pension funds. This also applies to ancillary functions in the fund management process. For example, custody is increasingly being outsourced.

(fundamental and technical economic and company analysis), trading (buying and selling investments, pretrade broker liaison), and cash management (placing deposits and foreign exchange)

Back office functions include the following:

• Transaction processing and settlement (deal administration and control, post-trade liaison with brokers and custodians), safe custody (security safekeeping and control), and stock lending (arranging and processing loans)

• Systems support: systems maintenance (operational and technical maintenance of existing IT) and systems development (planning and implementation of new IT and major enhancements to existing systems)

• Accounting and administration: investment accounting (provisions of valuations and client reports, tax reclaims, management information), performance measurement (provision of investment performance reports, attribution analysis of returns), and mutual fund administration (client dealing and associated administration, including contract notes, distribution and trustee-director liaison)

• General administration: compliance (regulatory reporting and in-house monitoring activity), financial accounting (corporate accounting and reporting), and corporate management (training, personnel, and staff and premises management)

The degree to which these functions are bundled together differs across regions. They are more bundled in Continental Europe, where fund management often includes execution of trades, investment advice, custody, and marketing, all typically provided by a universal bank. In contrast, these services tend to be provided separately in the United States and the United Kingdom. The degree of bundling also varies between sectors, with life insurers typically providing more bundling than pension funds and mutual funds.

Finally, note that there is an important chain element to much asset management, with delegation of asset management to a core manager entailing further delegation to country specialists.

3.2   Aspects of the Industrial Economics of Financial Institutions

This section sets out **aspects of the theory of industrial organization** that are considered relevant to an assessment of the behavior of financial sectors such as the asset management sector. For a more detailed overview of industrial organization theory, see Tirole (1989). For earlier applications of a similar approach to the primary eurobond market, see Davis (1988), and for an industrial analysis of financial instability, see Davis (1995b). For an approach to competition in asset management based on spatial concepts in economic geography, focusing also on the process of decision making in pension fund management, see Clark (2000a).

3.2.1   The Structure-Conduct-Performance Model

The traditional approach to competition and pricing in industrial economics may be characterized as the structure-conduct-performance (SCP) paradigm. The **key to understanding and predicting the performance of an industry** in terms of profits, growth, technical progress, and so forth is **found in the industrial structure.** Structure is defined to include product market concentration, (influenced by the relative and absolute size of firms), product differentiation, ease of entry, and elasticity of demand for the output of the industry. Conduct, which covers aspects of firm behavior and objectives, in turn generates the performance of the industry in terms of profitability. In practice, in SCP studies, examination of conduct is often minimal, and direct links are assumed between structure and performance. Short-term profit maximization is assumed to be the objective of performance, and firms are seen both as passive agents and as homogeneous (i.e., there is no distinction in the mind of the customer between similar goods or services offered by different firms). Dynamic aspects (growth of the firm, penetration of new markets) are largely ignored.

At the simplest level, through the analysis of **concentration and other structural factors**, it is possible to categorize industries as being in a state of **perfect competition, monopoly, or some gradation** between. The most commonly identified intermediate state is monopolistic competition, in which atomistic firms sell somewhat differentiated products but are unable to make monopoly profits. The point on the spectrum can be used to make predictions about performance, in particular relating to profitability. The basis of this is that in atomistic competition when there are many firms, individual firms are unable by their own actions to influence the price of the product significantly. As a consequence, they earn only the "normal profits," which are just sufficient to keep them in the industry. Power over pricing is assumed to increase inversely with the number of firms, as well as being linked to the degree of homogeneity of the product.

Industrial concentration is typically taken to be exogenous and beyond individual firms' control. An important determining factor is the ease of entry, notably the capital required by a potential competitor to set up in business to challenge existing firms. An increasing minimum efficient scale is seen as raising the level of monopoly, ceteris paribus. Other entry barriers that are of relevance in many financial markets include legal restrictions or regulations, often imposed or approved by governments. The growth rate of the market and the size of the market have also been found in various studies to influence concentration (a small or slow-growing market is more likely to be concentrated), while there is usually a positive relationship between expenditure on advertising and concentration. The homogeneity of the product will also influence industrial structure.

The SCP approach is basically a **short-run static approach that takes firms to be passive agents**. With a given structure of single-product firms, firms are taken to be maximizing short-term profits. Structure is assumed to determine performance, not vice versa. This approach ignores both the effects of potential competition and the possible endogeneity of industrial structure to firms' activities. Many industrial economists would suggest that the traditional approach remains relevant to some extent for stagnant or heavily regulated markets, which were characteristic, at least until recently, of domestic banking in some countries.[3] Meanwhile, dynamic theories relating to growth of the firm are particularly applicable in growing and liberalized markets. Arguably, globalization of financial markets and measures of liberalization such as domestic financial deregulation, the General Agreement on Tariffs and Trade, and the European Single Market are making dynamic concepts of increasingly general relevance to financial markets, including fund management.

Such dynamic aspects are addressed by recent theoretical developments, notably those regarding contestable markets and strategic competition. Implicitly, these revive the importance of conduct, often

---

3. Such markets may be most vulnerable to excess capacity when competitive conditions change (see Davis and Salo 1998).

ignored in the traditional approach, and the heterogeneity of individual firms. The theories can apply only where there is no restrictive regulation on entry.

3.2.2   Contestable Markets

According to the theory of contestable markets, many **seeming oligopoly situations may be characterized by competitive behavior** on the part of existing firms because of the potential for new firms to **enter in a hit-and-run manner** in response to excess profits. Contestable markets may thus benefit from both efficient industrial structures and competitive behavior. Strictly speaking, to induce competitive behavior, there has to be an absence of significant lags between a decision to enter and entry occurring, an instant response of demand to changing prices, and an absence of losses on exit due to sunk costs (e.g., capital specific to the industry that cannot be used if the firm decides to withdraw). The entrant knows that if the incumbent has sunk costs, it will always be worth the incumbent's while to deter entry.

According to this theory, **economies of scale need not be a barrier** to entry; firms can produce at minimum efficient scale for a short period and sell (storable) output over a long period.[4] It is clear that in practice, entry into oligopolistic industries is often easier for established firms in related industries than for startups, given the frequent importance of economies of scope (joint costs). Such cross-entry is typically ignored in the more traditional approach but is obviously important in financial markets. The degree of contestability will, of course, change over time with shifts in parameters such as demand, technology, and regulation.

It seems unlikely that all financial markets in the real world fit the assumptions, notably that there are no sunk costs (or that they are equal between entrants and incumbents) and that an entrant can come into a market and set up at full scale before existing firms respond to changing prices. Obviously, unlike goods, services such as asset management are not storable. **Sunk costs** such as expertise, relationships, and reputations (including brand names, which may

---

4. If there are neither economies of scale nor sunk costs, the paradigm collapses to that of competitive equilibrium.

constitute the principal asset of a financial intermediary itself) are often important in financial markets. This implies that demand will not respond instantaneously to prices. Nor are firms identical, as the theory implicitly assumes.

3.2.3 Discretion and Managerial Approaches

A key element in a dynamic approach to industrial analysis is recognition of the **discretion of firms to deviate from short-run profit maximization**, particularly in the case of multiproduct firms in situations of oligopoly (such as banking and finance in many countries). This may be particularly common when there is no close oversight of managers by shareholders. Discretion arises from the divorce of ownership from control in public limited companies, which enables managers to change the objectives of firm behavior. It also links to sunk costs themselves, which offer excess profitability, enabling currently unprofitable activities to be cross-subsidized. Managerial behavior is limited by the possibility that the share price of a firm that is not maximizing profit will decline, the firm will be taken over, and the managers will be fired or at least that corporate governance pressures will more generally increase (see chapter 6). In the financial sector, deregulation has permitted more discretion to firms to merge and to enter new markets (although some intermediaries—notably public and mutual ones—remain protected from takeover). On the other hand, to the extent that deregulation reduces entry barriers, it has also tended to reduce excess profitability from oligopoly.

Managerial theories have typically assumed that, given discretion, managers will aim to **maximize an objective such as sales revenue growth**, which enters the managerial utility function, rather than maximizing profit in either the short or long run. Indeed, the behavior of financial institutions (seeking growth in balance sheet size, assets under management, or market share) suggests that this may be a common objective. Nevertheless, the substitutability of profit and growth should not be exaggerated. Profits may in any case be essential for growth, given the use of retained earnings to invest in extra capacity and—in some financial markets such as banking—the need for reserves and capital adequacy. And an increasing focus on profitability by shareholders has been witnessed in recent years (see section 6.2).

3.2.4 Strategic Competition

The focus in the "new industrial economics" (Tirole 1989) is rather different from that in the managerial theory of the firm literature. **Discretion is used for strategic purposes**, where a strategic move is one designed to induce another player to make a choice that is more favorable to the strategic mover than would otherwise occur. The principal **goal of managers is again assumed to be (long-run) profit maximization**.

The principles of strategic competition can be illustrated by reference to entry deterrence. The traditional theory of industrial structure (limit pricing) suggested that price or output levels of the incumbent could be set to discourage entry, whereby existing firms sell as a price level just below that at which an entrant can obtain adequate profits. This may be unrealistic, as the incumbent firm may reduce its output in the event of entry. Instead, to deter entry, the incumbent(s) typically vary instruments that have a lasting and irreversible effect on cost or demand conditions—that create sunk costs. The incumbent **commits itself to a course of conduct that would be detrimental to an entrant**. Short-run profit maximization is traded for the long-run benefits of avoiding entry. On the cost side, there could be overcapitalization, such that the output produced by the incumbent could have been produced more effectively with a low level of capital or more variable factors of production. The same may hold for research expenditure; high levels may offer a credible threat to entry. By a further strategic move, a firm may be able to raise a rival's costs, for example by setting high wage rates in the industry. Preemptive patenting is a fourth approach on the cost side that could be used in strategic entry deterrence.[5] Finally, if there are **intertemporal dependencies** of cost—the so-called "experience curve" whereby a firm's cost level is a declining function of its cumulative output (experience itself being a sunk cost)—then even price or output choice can deter entry.

On the demand side, firms may act strategically by advertising expenditures, product differentiation or brand proliferation to deter entry. Again, there may be intertemporal dependencies on the

---

5. In fact, patents tend to lack force in finance, as products are easily copied in such a way as to avoid patent infringement.

demand side arising from sunk costs such as relationships and a reputation built up by being first or by being trustworthy. It should be emphasized that entry barriers built up over time in this way need not be due to active planning on the part of the firm but may result from historical accident due to short-run profit-maximizing behavior.

The analysis, which applies to cases of perfect information on existing firms' behavior, can be extended to imperfect information, that is, informational asymmetries such that the entrant is unable to predict the incumbent's responses. In such cases, limit pricing may be used to deter entry, since the potential entrant is, according to the hypothesis, uncertain about the incumbent's cost level. An incumbent may signal with a low price to indicate efficiency, whether the firm is actually efficient or not. Predatory pricing in cases of imperfect information, that is, selling at a price below marginal cost, may be a worthwhile way of building up a reputation as a committed fighter for markets, thus deterring competition, especially if the incumbent is active in a series of markets.

3.2.5 Summary

Summarizing the analysis above, the static approach applies mainly to markets that are stagnant and/or subject to structural regulation limiting cross-sectoral competition. In this SCP view of market behavior, barriers to entry and hence reasons for excess profitability (besides the existence of regulatory barriers) could include insufficient capital (as a result of economies of scale that necessitate entry at a large scale of production), advertising and product differentiation more generally, and limit pricing (i.e., pricing by incumbents below the level at which new entrants make profits).

For **liberalized financial markets that are subject to economies of scale, dynamic theory will provide a more appropriate framework** than SCP. In such liberalized financial markets, the key determinant of intermediaries' profitability is the level of sunk costs (i.e., costs that cannot be recovered in exiting the market). In the presence of such costs, firms may exert market power; in its absence, they will make normal profits even if there are economies of scale. A crucial distinction may be made by employing the concept of sunk costs. Markets may be classified as contestable or noncontestable, depending on whether significant sunk costs, that is, irrecoverable expenditures, are needed to enter the market. If sunk costs are not important, hit-and-run entry is possible, and potential competition is a discipline on incumbent firms. As long as there are supernormal profits, penetration of contestable markets is always possible even if there are economies of scale; the number of firms in equilibrium will depend on technology and demand.

Are liberalized financial markets always contestable? Following the discussion in section 3.2.4, there are clearly potential sunk costs in financial markets, which may in principle deter entry. Intertemporal dependencies such as reputation, relationships, and expertise are likely to be of particular importance. Advertising, product differentiation, brand proliferation, and excessive research may buttress such advantages. Arguably, information itself may be a form of sunk cost generating competitive advantages in financial markets. On the other hand, financial services tend to be "commoditized" homogeneous products, with any innovations easily copied; technical advances are easing penetration, and firms tend to be multiproduct, which facilitates cross-entry. On balance, these latter factors tend to favor contestability.

3.3   Generic Aspects of the Asset Management Industry

We now go on to outline some **broad structural features of asset management sector** and the **nature of competition** in the industry in the light of the discussion above. We deal successively with wholesale management (management of assets on behalf of an institutional investor such as a pension fund) and retail management (management of assets, by mutual funds or for personal pensions, directly on behalf of the household sector). It will be seen that in each case, the nature of competition in the market is related to that market's technology, regulation, and demand.

An important structural feature of all asset management that influences the nature of the industry is the **division of principal** (the owner or sponsor of the funds) **and agent** (the asset manager). This gives rise to a need for monitoring of the manager's performance. In the absence of monitoring, the managers might churn the portfolio, "front run" by buying a line of stock ahead of a privileged order, give preferential treatment to one fund over another, or simply not

strive to optimize performance[6] in light of the principal's requirements. Monitoring costs will tend to be higher, the weaker the reputation of the manager or the relationship with the client. This is
largely because reputation and relationships are implicitly capital
assets that would depreciate if established fund managers did not
align their interests with those of the client, although in addition a
new firm may lack expertise.

3.3.1   Wholesale Asset Management

Following the description of approaches to asset management presented in chapter 2, three types of wholesale fund management may
be distinguished. **Generic asset management** refers to strictly quantitative and nondiscretionary operations in asset management such
as indexation, immunization of portfolios, provision of annuities,
and guaranteed insurance contracts (GICs). **Specialized management** involves the manager carrying out only discretionary security
selection (choice of individual securities within given asset categories), with asset allocation (choice of markets and instruments to
invest in) being carried out by the sponsor, advised by consultants.
Balanced management entails the asset manager carrying out, on a
discretionary basis, both asset allocation and security selection. Note
that these may be either complements or substitutes from the point
of view of a sponsor, which also may have the option of internal[7]
management of funds.

    We now go on to characterize "industrial" features of these types
of asset management in a competitive market (i.e., without entry
barriers created by monopolistic aspects or by regulation).

3.3.1.1   Generic Asset Management

Since generic asset management is by nature **nondiscretionary and
quantitative**, monitoring the quality and performance of the manager is not a major problem. It can **readily be verified** whether

---

6. Conflicts of interest may be rife in multiproduct financial firms, such as conflicts
between the institutional and broker-dealer operations (sometimes called the buy and
sell side of the firm), the use of discretionary funds to influence corporate outcomes,
the use of privileged information, conflicts between management of private funds and
collective funds, conflicts between research departments and interested parties in
stocks, and when one side of the firm is buying and the other side is selling.

7. In practice the trend has been away from internal management, partly owing to
difficulties in integrating "City" or "Wall Street" remuneration into salary structures.

indexation has been carried out in an accurate manner for example, and as long as a firm has a reputation to maintain, there can be reasonable confidence that such performance will also be maintained. Hence there are no significant asymmetries of information and little need for monitoring. Generic asset management firms tend to be subsidiaries or branches of large, established financial institutions. Given that little discretion is involved in investment, there is little need for special investment skills; rather, there is a need for a reputation for stability and quality built up over many years in the market. Given that the product is rather homogeneous, turnover of firms by sponsors may correspondingly be rather low.

The cost structure of this sector tends to be typified by **rapidly declining average costs** (Lakonishok et al. 1992a), owing inter alia to economies in management, custody and trading costs relative to active management.[8] This leads to a potential for high concentration and stability of market shares, a form of oligopoly underpinned by benefits of reputation and economies of scale. Nonetheless, given that generic services are easily copied and portfolios are easily taken over, there is little opportunity for raising prices to gain supernormal profitability; hit-and-run entry by diversified financial institutions is an ever-present threat. Hence such "commodity" markets are also likely to be broadly contestable.

3.3.1.2   Specialized Asset Management

Specialized asset management, entailing discretionary security selection within a given asset category, is at the opposite extreme of generic products. Here the discretionary business of selecting and managing portfolios of specific types of assets gives rise to a major **difficulty of observing quality of fund management**. The past performance of firms must be both observed and interpreted for its implications for future performance, thus putting an important emphasis on standardized and comparable means for assessing performance (see section 2.3.4). Beyond the inherent differentiation between firms based on quality of management, a form of deliberate product differentiation by managers is also typically employed as a marketing tool. Firms that are already operating in distinct sectors (e.g., offering

---

8. They may also save costs by internal cross-trades and by replicating an index's characteristics with a subset of stocks.

expertise in management of small firm equity portfolios) will seek to distinguish themselves further by an appeal to past performance and other types of product differentiation at least in terms of presentations. The results of the questionnaire reported in section 4.5 cast further light on this.

The sponsor is thus often faced with a large number of specialized managers. Ongoing monitoring employs, among other things, short mandates as a **control mechanism** (thus offering incentives to perform well[9]). Fees related to the stock of funds can also be seen as an incentive to good growth performance without undue risk; as we noted, these may sometimes be supplemented by performance-related fees. These aspects of fee structure tie fund managers' profits to the level and change in the market, respectively. Turnover of managers can potentially be rather high, given that consistent over-performance is inherently difficult to maintain (see section 2.4) and sponsors are likely to focus sharply on such performance. As for generic products, it is technically simple for another firm to take over investment of publicly quoted securities.

There are rather **few economies of scale in this sector**; indeed, the need for intensive interaction between key employees and sponsors of funds tends to limit the number of mandates that can be managed. Equally, there are some potential diseconomies of scale such as loss of staff motivation in large organizations, remoteness from decision makers, preference of sponsors for independent firms that may be less vulnerable to conflicts of interest,[10] and difficulties for market liquidity with large trades (Chan and Lakonishok 1995). Also the growing importance of consultants in the manager selection process puts an emphasis on performance and quality of service in the wholesale field more than advertising and branding (where the latter could otherwise lead to growth of firms).

As a consequence of these features, **free entry may lead to a very unconcentrated industry** with—given the instability of

---

9. Arguably, it may also increase the incidence of herding, with managers all adopting similar investment strategies, and the possibility that managers who underperform may take high risks to recover a good position.

10. If the fund manager is linked directly to a corporate finance provider, for example in a large, integrated investment bank, there is a danger of conflict of interest, which may be another form of diseconomy of scale. Broby (1997) notes that of all the many participants in the 1997 Deutsche Telekom issue, only one, BZW, wrote an adverse report on prospects for the issue.

performance[11]—perceptions of the qualities of firms varying over time and between customers. As a consequence of uneven performance, reputations may be hard to maintain. These structural elements imply that the sector may be typified by monopolistic competition, with product differentiation but inability of firms to make supernormal profits by pricing above a standard rate for their services. In the words of Lakonishok et al. (1992a), it is likely to be "a highly specialized service business which does not have a well-defined quality aspect and hence lacks a stable configuration of market shares for its differentiated products."

3.3.1.3 Balanced Management

The third type of sector that one may distinguish is the balanced manager; in this sector, the **asset manager carries out both asset allocation and security selection**. Characteristics of such a sector are intermediate between those of generic and specialized management. Monitoring is clearly more important than that for generic products, given the discretionary nature of the asset management product. On the other hand, to the extent that balanced managers follow a consensus approach in terms of asset allocation, performance will be rather predictable. Given that balanced managers seek to maintain a large number of mandates, they will focus sharply on reputation, thus providing additional protection to the client. Typically, a sponsor will deal with only one balanced manager for all needs. Included in balanced management may be some formal or informal portfolio indexation; that is, there may be elements of generic management.

Compared to the specialized manager, the balanced manager may **benefit from economies of scale**, owing to sharing of research staff between types of asset or national economy and spreading of IT outlays, the ability of large firms (with large average fund sizes or standard types of fund) to pool risk and reduce transactions costs, and the fact a large manager who is highly active in the market will tend to benefit from better information than will a smaller player (there may be a size-information trade-off) (Feldman and Stephenson 1988). Large managers are also most likely to be included in distribution of initial public offerings on favorable terms, which may give

---

11. This may be a key reason for herding within the sector (i.e., firms all adopting similar investment strategies), as management firms seek to avoid the risk of deviating from "average behavior."

a fillip to performance. There may, however, be diseconomies of scale at some point, given the difficulties of staff management within large firms and inability to trade in large quantities without moving the market.

Given economies of scale, a competitive balanced management sector may well have a rather **concentrated market structure**. Moreover, the market structure may also tend to be rather stable. This links to the fact that it can be costly to switch between balanced managers, given the scope and bundled nature of services offered. Also, there may be slow decumulation of relationships and reputation. Poor performance may thus have a less rapid effect on market share than for specialized managers. Nonetheless, opportunities for supernormal profits may be rather limited, as the options of switching to internal management to specialized or generic management still remain. Firms would also risk spoiling their reputations and relationships by raising prices. As is the case for generic products, a contestable market paradigm would seem appropriate.

3.3.1.4   General Features of Wholesale Management
Some general comments may be added in respect to competitive fund management markets. For all three types of sector, it is clear that the most common objective of investment managers' conduct is to **increase the volume of funds under management**; since fees are usually proportional to assets, this is seen as the way to sustain profitability. Growth may be sought either internally (by attracting funds or growing existing funds) or externally (by buying other managers).

Internal growth is dependent on the performance of the asset manager (notably for specialized managers and to a lesser extent for balanced managers), development of reputation, and the marketing strategy. Notably for specialized and balanced managers, internal growth generated by price competition is typically of second-order importance. This is partly because, given the primacy of performance, new mandates cannot be obtained by cutting fees. Also, following the logic of competition, to the extent that supernormal profits are absent, there should be no scope for firms to lower prices in the long term (although cross-subsidization within conglomerates cannot be ruled out).

External growth faces obvious legal and organizational risks. In particular, the industry is highly personality based, and a poorly handled takeover can lead to loss of staff, with mandates following them to other firms. Even if staff does not leave, mandates may be reviewed owing to fears of unannounced changes in investment approach. U.S. evidence suggests that relative performance deteriorates by around a decile for some time after a takeover, and managers who sell out their equity stakes to large conglomerates may also become demotivated. Such problems are particularly acute for equity managers, whereas for bond managers, mergers may improve performance.[12]

Not all wholesale fund management sectors are competitive. Barriers to competition may be internal to the industry, linking to the scope of relationships between sponsors and asset managers, which may limit the possibility of new entry (e.g., in the context of relationship banking links between corporations and universal banks). Equally, there may be a lack of performance measurement, which may again limit firms' ability to monitor asset managers in an informed manner. A stagnant market may be less competitive than one that is growing. There may be barriers to entry arising from regulatory features such as controls on entry of foreign managers.

3.3.2   Retail Asset Management

The structure of a retail asset manager, for example, of an individual mutual fund, is **best seen as a set of contracts** between the trustees and various organizers selling specific services (Fortune 1997). These include a sponsor, which organizes the launch of the fund; a distributor, which acts as investment banker and issues new shares; an advisor, which carries out portfolio decisions and borrowing/lending; an administrator, which keeps accounts and monitors cash flow and transactions; a custodian, which keeps records of securities held and traded, establishes their prices, and keeps general accounts; and a transfer agent, which keeps records of individual ownership, receives and pays cash from purchases and sales, and distributes dividends. Sales of mutual funds are typically by a sales force (i.e., on the recommendation of third parties such as banks or financial advisors) or by direct marketing (sales direct to customers on their

---

12. Phillips (1997) suggests that inefficiencies in the fixed income market and its tilt toward macroeconomic trends may make large bond portfolios easier to manage.

initiative). Sales forces may be compensated by front load changes on purchase and/or ongoing annual charges.

Retail funds differ from wholesale funds in that retail funds must have a **prospectus**, which outlines fundamental policies relating, inter alia, to portfolio management and hence sets limits to freedom to vary the portfolio's composition. Whether the asset manager carries out asset allocation or only security selection depends on the narrowness of the definition of eligible assets and the overall objective of the fund. Typically, employees of the fund itself may not transact in securities with it, lend to it, or borrow from it. Open-end funds generally have regulatory limits to leverage. Standards of diversification and liquidity are generally also set by regulators. In most countries, mutual funds are subject to corporation tax on their profits, but capital gains, dividends, and interest income are "passed through" and taxed at the level of the fund holder.

A number of key structural differences obtain between retail management of mutual funds (United States), SICAVs (France), or unit trusts (the United Kingdom) and external management of wholesale funds. In some markets, information asymmetries between investors and managers are great; relative performance evaluation after purchase is less common (although performance figures are often used to attract new investors), and investors are often guided by financial advisers whose interest lies in earning commission. On the other hand, where there are informed investors and established and objective measures of performance, benefits of branding can be unstable and vulnerable to poor performance (Phillips 1997). But in all cases, bargaining power of investors over managers is virtually nonexistent.

Faced with a mixture of informed and uninformed investors, **inflows to a fund** in the retail sector tend to **reflect not only performance but also marketing and product-packaging skills**, access to distribution networks, and the culture of the firm. Clearly, of these, access to distribution networks may be a barrier to entry, although new technology (e.g., fund supermarkets and the Internet) are offsetting this and making entry easier. Marketing, branding, and expertise developed over time are forms of sunk cost barrier. However, as we have noted, the level of information and knowledge available to the client base is likely to influence how important brand names will be in attracting customers.

As retail mutual funds are often **organized in families of funds** (bond fund, equity fund, money market fund, global fund, etc.), they may **benefit from economies of scale** and scope, in terms of shared research staff, spreading of IT outlays, shared advertising and branding costs, and offering an attractive service to fund holders in switching between types of fund within the family, saving on commissions. For retirement funds, this is of particular importance, given that they may thereby avoid taxation. Further economies of scale may arise if investment management firms can cross-subsidize wholesale business from the retail side. In particular, if bad performance causes a loss of wholesale mandates, it may be optimal for firms to have retail arms to smooth profitability. In the absence of segregated funds and/or appropriate regulation, it is also possible for firms to take advantage of inertia on the retail side to shift high-performing assets into wholesale funds.

The industrial behavior of competitive retail asset management sectors typically reflects a balance between these forces. Generally, a **large number of asset managers** tend to be present, suggesting that the economies of scale and barriers to entry should not be exaggerated. Large and small firms typically coexist, and the large firms may account for a significant proportion of the market. It is relatively inexpensive to set up a new mutual fund, and distribution channels are increasingly available. On the other hand, price competition, although present, does not seem to be sufficient to drive firms from the market; informed investors focus more on expected performance than on fees; uninformed investors may not be aware of differentiation of fees within the sector.

An increasing trend is for **mutual funds to be held as part of employer-sponsored defined contribution pension funds** (such as 401(k)s in the United States). These may have different requirements from those of regular mutual funds. There is a need for the management firm to be selected by the employer and then for the funds to be selected by the employee. To be selected by the corporate sponsor requires the technological ability to cope with the needs of a potentially very large base of employees at low unit cost. It must offer the potential to invest monies not only in its own funds, but also in funds from other competing asset managers. To win over the employees requires good funds and brand recognition. As Moon et al (1998) of Goldman Sachs argue, such requirements favor larger firms and put an emphasis on economies of scale. Their growing importance may foreshadow greater concentration (see section 4.4).

3.4   The U.S. Asset Management Sector

Having set out the industrial organization framework for analyzing asset management sectors in sections 3.2 and 3.3 above, we now go on to highlight developments in the United States, the United Kingdom, and Continental Europe. The differing patterns of structure and behavior **as they stand at present** give evidence on the overall nature of the industry. Note, however, that in **looking forward**, it is widely suggested that sectors will in the future become more homogeneous and a handful of giant firms will dominate the world financial system. Size is often considered essential on the grounds that only companies with a great deal of capital will be able to afford the product and distribution capacity necessary to expand globally, while only firms with brand names will be able to attract the attention of clients at a global level. We address these issues in chapter 4.

It is appropriate to begin with the United States, which is both the **largest asset management market** in the world and the one that has been **most closely studied**. With regard to value of assets, institutional assets were estimated in 1998 to be around $15.7 trillion (Conference Board 1999). Institutional assets account for 20.3% of outstanding U.S. financial assets. Institutional investor growth in the United States is a long-standing development but one that has accelerated since 1980. From 1980 to 1998, total U.S. financial assets grew sixfold, while institutional assets grew eightfold. Institutional assets tripled in the 1980s, then grew 140% over 1990–1998, an annual growth rate in the 1990s of 11.8%.

Since 1990, the U.S. sectors that have seen the **strongest growth are mutual funds and state and local pension funds**, which grew at annual rates of 17% and 14%, respectively (see table 3.1). Annual revenue of the institutional fund management sector is around $43 billion. Equity holdings of the institutional sector are high, albeit not as high as those in the United Kingdom; around 50% of pension and mutual fund monies are held in this form.[13] U.S. institutions in 1998 owned more than 47% of U.S. equities outstanding, up from 6% in 1950.

---

13. Up to the early 1970s, equities were even more popular than they are now (Sellon 1992), but there was a shift away from them in the wake of the bear market of the early 1970s, which is only just swinging back.

Table 3.1
Growth of U.S. Institutional Assets Held

	1990 ($ billion)	1998 ($ billion)	Compound Annual Growth Rate (%)
Pension funds:	3124	7409	11.4
Private	1668	4060	11.8
Insured	636	1005	5.9
State and local	820	2344	14.0
Mutual fund	967	3396	17.0
Insurance companies	1328	2537	8.4
All institutions	6322	15432	11.8

Source: Conference Board (1999). Assets held differ from assets under management owing to delegation of management between sectors (see table 3.2).

The 401(k) and mutual fund sectors, technically retail sectors, are the only areas of institutional investment to witness positive cash flows over the past five years (of around 3% and 5%, respectively). These are discussed in section 3.4.2. First, we assess the wholesale sector.

3.4.1 Wholesale Asset Management in the United States

3.4.1.1 Overview

In the United States, wholesale fund management includes management of the assets of **company and public (state and local) pension funds**. Assets of these sectors amounted to $7.4 trillion in 1998. Company pension funds at that time were $4 trillion, while public pension funds were $2.3 trillion. Private insured funds placed with insurance companies accounted for a further $1 billion. The public sector funds have grown more rapidly in recent years, with average growth over 1990–1998 being 14% in contrast to 11.8% for company funds. Corporate downsizing and restructuring help to account for slower growth of company defined benefit funds (new firms that have absorbed the unemployed have tended to set up defined contribution plans). Another factor underlying slower growth is the negative cash flow of the defined benefit sector. Although it is partly a reflection of flat or falling coverage, it also reflects the performance of asset markets, which led to pension plans becoming overfunded. More generally, the wholesale sector has grown less strongly than the retail sector in recent years. Nevertheless, at $7.4 trillion, the wholesale fund management sector is vast; it remains the primary market for most U.S. money managers.

Table 3.2
U.S. Institutional Investor Holdings Versus Management, 1998 (1993)

Institution	Percent of Assets Held	Percent of Assets Managed	Percent Internally Managed
Pension funds:	48.0 (49.2)	22.3 (21.9)	46.4 (44.5)
Private trusteed	26.3 (28.0)	14.8 (16.6)	
Private insured	6.5 (9.1)	0.0 (0.0)	
State and local	15.2 (12.2)	7.4 (5.3)	
External investment advisers	0.0 (0.0)	5.5 (8.5)	
Investment companies	22.0 (18.1)	33.1 (23.8)	
Insurance companies	16.4 (18.2)	20.6 (26.4)	
Banks	11.7 (12.3)	17.6 (19.0)	
Foundations	1.9 (2.1)	1.0 (0.4)	
Total	100 (100)	100 (100)	

Source: Conference Board (1999).

Regarding **composition**, although the share of defined contribution funds is growing rapidly, more than half of U.S. pension assets (including state and local government) remain defined benefit.[14] A part of defined contribution assets are managed by retail asset managers in mutual funds; the rest is managed at a company level and hence may be categorized as wholesale.

The Employee Retirement Income Security Act (ERISA)[15] **of 1974** had an important influence on the structure of wholesale management by prompting defined benefit pension plans to diversify their assets and to appoint independent master trustees. By increasing reporting requirements, it raised the cost of administration for internally managed funds. All of these provisions encouraged increased employment of external managers; less than 25% of U.S. funds manage assets in-house.[16] Remaining internally managed funds are nevertheless relatively large. They account for 46.4% of pension assets,[17] according to data from the Conference Board (1999) (see table 3.2).

The asset management firms that have come to dominate the industry are **specialist managers**, offering special expertise in secu-

---

14. The share of private pension assets is about 50-50 (see table 2.8).
15. ERISA was a key U.S. pension law that defined fiduciary responsibilities, set minimum funding standards and vesting rules, and set up a benefit insurance scheme.
16. One reported reason is inability to afford the salaries needed for in-house management (Institutional Investor 1996).
17. The calculation assumes that insured funds are internally managed.

rity selection within narrowly defined asset classes. Twenty-five percent of the 200 largest defined benefit funds use ten or more managers
for domestic equity alone, and 65% use between four and nine. The
mean number of managers in 1999 was thirteen (Targett and Wine
2000), compared with seventeen in 1995. Balanced management is
not common, accounting for only 4% of mandates (although it was
predominant up to the 1970s), with delegation of security selection,
or specialized management, being the most common type of arrangement for asset management. Consultants are employed by sponsors
to advise on asset allocation across the portfolio as a whole.

One reason for this multimanager pattern is that ERISA might see
the use of a single manager as a lack of diversification. Corporate
treasurers may also favor large numbers of external managers, as
this justifies a large staff for them. This may help to account for the
popularity of so-called diversifying across styles (see section 2.1.7),
which implies as a corollary that both value and growth management remain in demand even when the performance of one of these
styles relative to the market is quite poor. Note that these comments
apply mainly to large funds; small funds are often managed on an
insured basis by insurance companies.

Indexation and the use of other generic products is important,
with 35% of equity assets being indexed, accounting for 22% of total
portfolios[18] (see Riley 2000).[19] Sixty-two percent of the 200 largest
defined benefit funds use indexation. It is more prevalent for public
than private funds, with indexation accounting for 54% of public
funds' domestic equity and 24% of that of corporate funds.[20] Immunization strategies are common in defined benefit funds, given the
minimum funding requirement (see chapter 2). Defined contribution
funds are heavy users of GICs. **Equity** investment has risen with the

---

18. Note that since bond holdings are also indexed, the total share of the portfolio
covered by indexation may be higher—around 28%.

19. Note, however, that Lakonishok et al. (1992a) argue that indexation is used less
than is optimal, owing to principal-agent problems affecting the sponsor. In a nutshell,
the corporate treasurer's office that is responsible for investment of defined benefit
monies may be more interested in bolstering its own position than in maximizing
return. Passive management is hence avoided, as it reduces the demand for services
from the office concerned, while internal management would give too much responsibility. Active, external management is hence preferred, even though the performance
of active managers is on average inferior to indexing—as one would expect in an efficient market (see also chapter 2).

20. A corollary of greater indexation by public funds may be greater interest in
corporate governance, as discussed in section 6.2.

bull market to around 64% of the portfolio but is below the level in the United Kingdom. **International** investment of U.S. funds is growing, but levels are again lower than those in the United Kingdom. The average is around 11% of the portfolio, but this is skewed; the twenty-five largest funds have 18% international. The latter account for 66% of the total foreign equity of U.S. pension funds.

3.4.1.2   Structural Aspects

Perhaps reflecting the preference for specialized management, the market structure of the industry is of **low concentration**, with a large number of small and medium-size firms representing a considerable proportion of assets under management. Excluding mutual fund managers (who totaled 533), there were no fewer than 2840 money managers as of March 31, 1997, of whom 1256 managed $500 million or more in discretionary pension and endowment assets. Ennis (1997) reports that there is also product proliferation, with 9000 products on offer in 1997 to tax-exempt investors, up from 6000 in 1993. By simple arithmetic, each firm offers around three products to the market.

Table 3.3 shows the **largest managers** to be mostly insurance companies and banks that focus partly or largely on **generic products**. The top ten firms accounted for 30% of the total in 1998, but if generic products other than annuities are excluded, the concentration

Table 3.3
Top Ten U.S. Wholesale (Tax-Exempt) Money Managers, 1998

Name	Tax-Exempt Assets ($ billion)	Internally Managed Tax-Exempt Assets	Percent of Tax-Exempt Market	Percent of Assets in Generic Products
State Street Global	334.4	332.5	5.1	57
Barclays Global	329.7	329.7	5.0	93
Fidelity Investments	250	242.3	3.8	N.A.
Bankers Trust	217.9	217.9	3.3	67
TIAA-CREF	213.4	213.4	3.2	37
Northern Trust	153.6	153.6	2.3	27
Prudential Insurance	139.5	139.5	2.1	19
J. P. Morgan Investment	120.7	120.7	1.8	4
Vanguard Group	116.1	73.0	1.8	53
Morgan Stanley/Miller	112.2	98.2	1.7	3

N.A. = not available.
Source: Pensions and Investments (1998b).

Table 3.4
Concentration in Tax-Exempt U.S. Asset Management Sectors, 1998

Sector	Total Assets ($ billion)	Percent Managed by Five Largest Firms
All sectors	6604	20.4
Defined contribution plans	1388	43.4
U.S. equity passive	625.9	80.2
U.S. bond passive	99.9	68.3
U.S. equity enhanced indexation	184.4	73.8
U.S. bond enhanced indexation	77.6	61.5
Dedicated and immunized portfolios	53.1	67.6
Active international	452	28.2
Passive international	122	87.6

Source: Pensions and Investments (1998b).

would be much lower. Indeed, as table 3.4 shows, the concentration in generic products such as indexation is very high; for example, the top five firms in equity indexation account for 80% of the total in 1998, compared with 28% for active international investment and 20% for the market as a whole.

There has tended to be a **slight increase in concentration** in recent years, with the top ten firms' share rising from 22% in 1990 to 30% in 1998, as we noted above. Large pension funds are reportedly reducing the number of managers that they deal with (perhaps reflecting agency problems where there are many managers). Indexation reduces the number of specialized managers needed, replacing them with a small number of generic managers. Moreover, advances in information technology, the scale of investments required for up-to-date information systems, and fiercer competition are increasing pressures on the profitability of medium-size firms. Nevertheless, the overall picture remains one of proliferation.

With regard to other structural features, there is frequent **performance evaluation**, in the context of mandates typically lasting three years (thus offering incentives to perform well). Performance measurement services are almost universally used to evaluate the performance of asset managers, and managers are chosen almost exclusively on the basis of past performance relative to market- or style-based benchmarks. Lakonishok et al. (1992a) suggest that this may be reasonable, as there would appear to be some persistence in performance if it is measured over a three-year horizon[21] (see also section 2.4.2). On the other hand, studies have also shown that such performance data are not immune to manipulation by asset managers, with, for example, window dressing of portfolios before evaluation (Lakonishok et al. 1991b), that is, getting rid of poorly performing stocks. Alternatively, asset managers may seek to lock in performance once they are ahead of the index by shifting the portfolio to resemble it and raise risk when they are below it.

As we noted in section 2.3.4, the Association of Investment Management and Research (AIMR) has established **standard evaluation methods** that should help to overcome some of these problems, defining the calculation basis and the pool of funds, to generate numbers that are comparable among fund managers over time. Managers will no longer be able to drop poorly performing portfolios from calculations. Verification services will be provided by performance measurers and accountancy firms. Without verification, U.S. asset management firms find it difficult to be selected for consultants' shortlists. Unfortunately, as the Financial Times (1999) noted, many asset managers choose only to be assessed on the basis of subgroups of funds rather than for firmwide verification, which may bias the results. The AIMR has a new international counterpart, the global investment performance standards (GIPS), which is effective from 2000. It may be added that performance mandates are often specified in terms of performance relative to a market index.

Turnover of managers is high and increasing. In a survey noted in Phillips (1997), only 50% of U.S. sponsors had not terminated any mandates in the last twelve months. Twenty-five percent had terminated one mandate, and 25% had terminated two or more, generally because of dissatisfaction with current performance. Obviously, there are a variety of competitors always seeking the mandate. Choices of new managers are usually made from a pool of those who have outperformed the median manager over the last five years (Lakonishok et al. 1992a).[22] Since maintenance of strong performance

---

21. Over this periodicity, the gain from hiring a manager in the top quartile was 2.1 percentage points per annum more than hiring one in the bottom quartile and 1 percentage point more than the average, using data over 1983–1989. But the best-performing manager may still not beat the index over time, net of transactions costs.
22. Lakonishok et al. (1992a) calculate that for every 100 bp of superior performance over the average of managers over a three-year period, a firm would gain 2.6% more accounts. As the difference between the ninetieth percentile and the average in their sample was 450 bp, 11.7% more accounts could be gained over the next three years.

Table 3.5
Evolution of Leading Wholesale Asset Management Firms by Type of Firm

	1	2	3	4	5
Insurance Companies					
1980	Prudential	Equitable	Aetna	Metropolitan	CIGNA
1984	Equitable	Metropolitan	Prudential	Aetna	Travelers
1987	Prudential	Equitable	Metropolitan	Aetna	New England
1990	Prudential	Metropolitan	Aetna	Equitable	New England
1998	Prudential	Metropolitan	Aetna	Nationwide	New York Life
Banks/Trust Companies					
1980	J. P. Morgan	Bankers Trust	Harris Trust	Citicorp	Mellon
1984	Bankers Trust	J. P. Morgan	Citicorp	Man Han	Wells Fargo
1987	Bankers Trust	J. P. Morgan	Wells Fargo	Mellon	State Street
1990	Bankers Trust	Wells Fargo	Mellon	State Street	J. P. Morgan
1998	State Street	Barclays	Bankers Trust	Northern Trust	J. P. Morgan
Independent Investment Counselors					
1980	Alliance	Scudder Stevens	Fayez Sarofim	Lionel Edie	T. Rowe Price
1984	Batterymarch	Jennison	Criterion	Fayez Sarofim	Fischer Francis
1987	GE Investments	Mitchell Hutchins	Boston Co.	Miller Anderson	Lehman
1990	Fidelity	GE Investments	Miller Anderson	Boston Co.	Lincoln Capital
1998	Fidelity	Vanguard	Pacific	Alliance	Merrill Lynch

Source: Lakonishok et al. (1992a), Pensions and Investments (1998b).

is extremely rare,[23] the market structure of the specialized managers is not only unconcentrated, but also unstable, with the top firms rarely retaining their positions. The situation in the generic sector is, by contrast, extremely stable. These results are confirmed for the more recent period by Ennis (1997) and by the data in table 3.5.

As we have noted, less than 25% of defined benefit pension fund sponsors do **in-house management**, despite evidence of better performance (see chapter 2). Even the U.S. life insurance companies are beginning to outsource their investment management and in 1997 had done so for $300 billion of assets (Broby 1997). It is often claimed that few sponsors can afford the salaries of high-caliber in-house

---

23. See Kahn and Rudd (1995).

managers. But there may be deeper forces at work, linking to agency problems within the sponsor (see the discussion of Lakonishok et al. (1992a) in chapter 2).

With regard to **economies of scale**, there is evidently room for large numbers of specialized niche players (which may be facilitated by the large size of the market relative to other countries), suggesting that economies of scale are rather minor in the specialist sector. Indeed, as transactions costs may, even in the United States, beyond a rather low level vary inversely with trade size (Perold and Salomon 1991), there is a diseconomy of scale for large, active managers. Mobility of key staff resources is another difficulty for large and successful firms.

In contrast, there are clearly benefits for large firms in the generic sector and rather few diseconomies of scale for giant firms, given large and liquid markets. The product is consistently deliverable and undifferentiated. Large indexers develop broad and integrated products, which make it easy, cost-effective, and defensible under ERISA for a single indexer to be used by clients for all their passive investment needs. Such firms can also offer ancillary services such as portfolio rebalancing without transactions costs, given the opportunity of "crossing" trades between the firm's clients. In contrast, small firms would suffer from higher average costs, a limited product line with fewer ancillary services, and difficulty of differentiating the product.

3.4.1.3   Conduct and Performance
Specialized managers advertise on their **past performance**, although **league tables of assets** are also frequently used to indicate the firm's popularity. Firms seek to distinguish their products as much as possible, mainly by their performance but also by a focus on a style, narrow type of security, investment philosophy, and the like. As sponsors prefer small and specialized firms, it is rather easy for a new firm to gain a track record, implying, together with lack of economies of scale, that barriers to entry are not insuperable. In general, because the market is still growing, there is apparently scope for an increasing number of firms. This increases the opportunity of new entrants to develop a reputation by gaining mandates with new funds (which in turn are more likely than existing funds to accept new managers given their own lack of established relation-

ships). The scope for large firms to lose assets owing to poor performance is greater.

Meanwhile, **price competition** in the specialized asset management sector in the United States is of **second-order importance**. New active management mandates typically cannot be obtained by low fees.[24] This is partly because of the primacy of performance and also clients' belief that superior performance is available. Indeed, Halpern and Fowler (1991) report no correlation between fees and performance, although in line with product differentiation, different fees were charged for similar services. Competition from index funds has not (yet) changed this situation. Fees in the United States are around 45 basis points (bp) for separate account or segregated equity management and 30 bp for bonds, diminishing for larger accounts. Halpern and Fowler report median fees for active equity management of 50 bp for a $10 million portfolio, falling to 30 bp for $250 million, and Trzcinka (1998) reports 40–60 bp for active management for pension funds. These levels have remained broadly stable over the 1990s. As we note below, this is higher than the level for defined benefit funds in the United Kingdom, despite the appearance of intense competition in the U.S. market.[25] For comparison, actively managed mutual fund-based pension fund investments charge around 100 bp or more on average (see Investment Company Institute 2000).[26]

The situation in **generic products**, such as indexation services, again differs. With a homogeneous product, buyers are **price sensitive**, and so price competition is intense. As Ennis (1997) argues, price is likely to follow average cost, which, with economies of scale as outlined above, is declining. The going rate can be as low as 2 bp (Ennis 1997), although Trzcinka (1998) suggests that 5–10 bp is typical. Dominance by large firms is a corollary.

The **profit performance** of firms in the U.S. fund management sector is difficult to assess, given that many are part of multiproduct firms, but in general, the recent picture has been one of rather high

---

24. In the words of Ennis (1997), "rational if optimistic buyers realize they cannot expect something for nothing."
25. Explanations for this differential could include the ability to cross-subsidize from retail business in the United Kingdom and not in the United States and/or a higher risk of loss of mandate in the United States, which means that fund managers require higher fees to break even. Another possible explanation is the prevalence of "soft commissions" in the United Kingdom, although they are also common in the United States (chapter 8).
26. Trzcinka (1998) quotes a higher figure of 140 bp.

profitability, despite intense competition. Indeed, it is widely suggested that investment management is currently the most profitable industry in the United States. Moon et al. (1998) quote a figure of 30% for pretax margins of publicly quoted firms, with small private firms posting margins as high as 70%. On the other hand, index funds are not highly profitable, reflecting contestability. Profits fell from 1.8 bp per dollar of assets in 1996 to 1.4 bp in 1998.

Share prices of fund management firms have often been bid up by other financial institutions' desire to buy into fund management. A number of European banks have bought into U.S. fund management in recent years. In line with the last point, specialist fund managers have rather high price/earnings ratios (albeit average dividend yields).

3.4.1.4 Summary
The market for specialized wholesale management in the United States is characterized by large numbers of buyers and sellers, ease of entry and exit, and slightly differentiated products. It is not highly concentrated, and there is little evidence of oligopoly or excess profitability, although equally, there is neither competition to lower prices nor scope to raise them to exploit good performance. **Competitive features** of the fund management sector include:

• the willingness of trustees to switch between managers on the basis of performance evaluation;

• the increasing role of consultants, who may even attract foreign clients to small domestic managers;

• the lack of bargaining power of fund managers in their relationships with trustees;

• the availability of other external managers to take over mandates and the relatively low costs of such switches;[27]

• the available alternatives of passive indexation as opposed to active management, as well as internal management; and

• the rather low sunk costs that are incurred in entering the sector.

Firms **seek to differentiate their products** from those of competitors by reference to performance records, the markets focused on, the

---

27. It is cheaper to take over a pool of funds in a given instrument (such as Japanese equities) than to have to reorganize the disposition of an entire portfolio across a number of instruments (domestic bonds, international equities, etc.).

philosophy of investment, and the like. Product differentiation is facilitated by pension funds' demand for a variety of investment styles and willingness to measure performance against specialized benchmarks. As we have noted, firms are also becoming multiproduct, which, according to Ennis (1997), links to the fact that in an efficient market, a firm is unlikely to be able to excel in one area all the time. If a firm has only one product, periods of underperformance would threaten its survival, whereas having several products gives it a chance to continue by focusing on the currently successful product at any one time.

There is room for some limited sunk cost factors, such as an influence of expertise and reputation (in terms of asset size and performance) as well as relationships with clients, which may enable firms to retain mandates despite occasional lapses in performance.

On balance, competition in U.S. wholesale asset management is best seen as **monopolistic**, akin to restaurants or hotels all with some unique features that distinguish them from each other. Nevertheless, in line with the paradigm of monopolistic competition, the features of the market offer little scope for established fund managers to exploit existing clients.

In contrast, the market for **generic**, nondiscretionary asset management services is dominated by few firms, with economies of scale and intense price competition, thus giving evidence of **contestability**. New entry by large, established firms is feasible, thus limiting the scope for supernormal profits. There is steady growth in this sector, but the majority of wholesale asset management remains active. This may imply either a belief in inefficient markets on the part of sponsors or an objective other than simple maximization of return relative to risk, as we suggested in section 2.1.7.

3.4.2   Retail Asset Management in the United States

3.4.2.1   Overview
The U.S. retail sector has seen the **most dynamic growth** in recent years owing to the expansion of mutual fund investment (see, for example, Pozen 1998). Assets under management have increased at an annual rate of 26% over the past eighteen years. In 1998, the total value of mutual funds was $5.5 trillion (Investment Company Institute 1999b), of which money market funds accounted for $1.4 trillion, bond funds $0.8 trillion, equity funds $3 trillion, and mixed bond/

equity funds $0.4 trillion. Mutual funds own around 20% of U.S. equities and 10% of corporate bonds. The United States accounts for over 50% of global mutual fund assets (see table 1.7). It should be noted at the outset that the U.S. asset management sector should not be seen as entirely divided into watertight retail and wholesale sectors. One hundred thirty-two of the top 200 asset managers sell at least some mutual funds (Moon et al. 1998), owing to growth opportunities of the retail sector. Moreover, besides households, mutual funds are commonly held by other institutional investors. The proportion held by sectors other than households was over 30% at the end of 1998.

As we discussed in chapter 1, **factors underlying the growth** of the retail sector in the United States include the aging of the baby-boomers, concern about the sustainability of social security, decline in the attractiveness of traditional savings products, and growing realization of the benefits of diversification offered by institutional investors. Accordingly, the proportion of households having at least one mutual fund rose from 6% in 1980 to 47% in 1998. One distinctive feature of the United States is a sizable money market fund sector, accounting for 25% of mutual fund assets. This grew up when bank interest rates were regulated in the 1970s (see chapter 5). It incidentally allowed the retail asset management industry to survive the period of the 1970s when equity markets suffered sharp declines. Bond funds too grew strongly after the bear market in equities of the 1970s.

Equity funds have grown much more rapidly than other funds in recent years; they were only a quarter of mutual fund assets in 1985[28] but are over 50% now. This pattern partly reflects the good performance of stock markets, boosting the value of existing holdings as well as new investments. Expansion of equity funds has important implications for industry structure because it benefits firms that specialize in equities and because fees on equity funds tend to be higher. Index funds are still relatively small, but cash flow is strong, rising from 2% of net cash flow to mutual funds in 1994 to 31% in 1999. Besides the focus on equities, a growing share of mutual fund assets are invested internationally (12% in 1998, with 17% for equities).

---

28. Following a similar pattern to pension funds, mutual funds were 87% equity-based over 1952–1970 but switched sharply into bonds and money market instruments thereafter.

At the end of 1998, 34% of U.S. mutual fund assets were held in forms of **retirement funds (401(k) funds and IRAs)**, up from 19% in 1990 (Investment Company Institute 1999a). In 401(k)s, firms make an agreement with asset managers to provide a selection of funds to workers, with firms merely providing oversight and making contributions. IRAs are tax-free assets that may be held in a variety of instruments, including mutual funds, and that are ring-fenced up to retirement. In 1998, 35% of non-money-market inflows were for retirement purposes. The mutual fund sector itself accounted for 17% of total pension assets in 1998, compared with 5% in 1990.

The total assets held in 401(k) plans has risen from $385 billion in 1990 to $1407 billion in 1998, while the value of mutual funds held in 401(k)s has grown from $35 billion to $593 billion. Of 401(k) funds, on average at the end of 1998, 49.8% of total plan balances were invested in equity funds, 17.7% in company stock, 11.4% in guaranteed insurance contracts (GICs), 8.4% in balanced funds, 6.1% in bond funds, 4.7% in money funds, and 0.3% in other stable value funds (Investment Company Institute 2000). The growth of 401(k)s is part of the overall growth of defined contribution pension funds relative to defined benefit in the United States; defined contribution funds accounted for 9% of all private pension assets in 1984 and over 50% in 1998, of which 401(k)s were 27% in 1984 and 64% in 1998. The 401(k) market is dominated by firms such as Fidelity and Merrill Lynch, which also dominate the wider defined contribution market, while small companies are often served by life insurers, such as Principal Mutual, which services 32,000 company accounts. The 401(k) sector is in a sense a convergence of retail and wholesale. It has benefited the industry by smoothing fund flows, because, unlike normal discretionary contributions to mutual funds, 401(k) inflows arrive regularly on a contractual basis.[29]

3.4.2.2 Structural Aspects

There has been a **rapid expansion in the number of funds**, with long-term (bond and equity) funds totaling 6288 in 1998 and money market funds totaling 1026.[30] The corresponding figures for 1990, 1980, and 1970 were 2362 and 743, 458 and 106, and 361 and 0,

---

29. According to Moon et al. (1998), the mean monthly flow to equity funds as a proportion of the standard deviation was 1 in 1984–1990 and 1.95 in 1990–1997.
30. There are also 4700 hedge funds, available only to high-net-worth individuals and not to the general public (Ennis 1997).

respectively. Historically, as Wohlever (1993) noted, the number of funds tended to outpace the number of shareholders, so the average fund has a declining average number of shareholder accounts. But since 1995, this tendency has been reversed.[31] The average size of a mutual fund is currently $755 million (long-term funds average $664 million and money market funds $1318 million). There were 533 management firms in 1997 compared with 252 in 1985. Since there were only 1528 funds in 1985, firms have become much more multi-product, with a rise in the average number of funds per company from six to twelve. Six thousand funds have assets in excess of $25 million.

Despite these patterns, there is quite **high, albeit declining, concentration** in retail fund management; the five largest mutual fund companies accounted for 38% of the market in 1986 and 34% in 1999. The twenty-five largest accounted for 80% of the market in 1986 and 65% in 1999.[32] Factors accounting for this pattern of relatively high concentration are the frequency of mergers, the growth of large firms offering large numbers of funds, and the resultant skewed size distribution of funds, with a few giants such as the Fidelity Magellan fund and a very long "tail" of small funds.

There are nevertheless some factors that **keep small funds and fund groups viable** and that indeed lower barriers to entry. These include the growth of supermarkets (which avoid the need for a sales force) as well as the growing sophistication of investors who seek a high degree of choice. No-load funds in particular are finding supermarkets crucial to their success. Setting up a new fund per se is not costly and is not restricted for U.S. firms by regulation, which focuses on disclosure and "fit and proper" criteria.[33] Rather, as Wohlever (1993) noted, the difficulty may be to distinguish a new product from the large number of existing ones.

Despite the attractive size and growth of the U.S. market, it can, according to Broby (1997), be **difficult for foreign firms to penetrate**

---

31. Whereas in 1995, the average number of shareholders was 22,900, it was 26,500 in 1998.
32. Broby (1997).
33. In the United States, since 1996, fund companies valued over $25 million are regulated by the Securities and Exchange Commission and those valued under $25 million by the states. The former account for 95% of assets, but according to Walter (1999), the latter account for most of the abuses. Investors also have scope for class action suits against managers and directors in case of dereliction of duties to investors.

the U.S. market, given the complexity and cost involved in the need to register under the 1940 Investment Company Act and the 1933 Securities Act. This leads most foreign funds to aim for the so-called private offering exemption, which means that they cannot advertise in the United States, and most comply with restrictions on size of client and income requirements. Alternatively, they may simply take over U.S. groups. But, as we discuss below, this restriction on foreign entry does not blunt competition in the sector.

The bulk of U.S. mutual funds are run by **specialist mutual fund companies**, such as Fidelity and Vanguard, or subsidiaries of investment banks, such as Merrill Lynch and Salomon Smith Barney. New entrants in the 1990s have been insurance companies and commercial banks. There have been important mergers in the sector in recent years, such as Zurich Kemper-Scudder, Steven and Clark, and J. P. Morgan-American Century.

A small but growing proportion of mutual funds are **held in insurance products called variable annuities**, variable life insurance, and variable universal life insurance. Such products are held in separate accounts to avoid portfolio restrictions on life insurance companies. They comprise mutual fund and mutual-fund type assets, in which the client bears the risk and has none of the guarantees associated with normal life insurance. A significant proportion of such variable annuity accounts are actually institutional fund managers that subadvise a mutual fund for a share of the fund's advisory fee.

Commercial banks are in a relatively weak position with respect to mutual funds. Historically, this reflected not only the Glass-Steagall Act restrictions on banks' securities activities, dating from the 1930s, but also an unwillingness to cannibalize the deposit base. Because of these factors, the independent asset managers gained a reputation and market share that was difficult to counter. Since the early 1980s, banks have sought to circumvent the Glass-Steagall restrictions by entering into agreements with separately controlled mutual fund distributors. This arrangement offered a legal means for the distribution of proprietary mutual funds offered by banks, which also acted as investment advisers. Banks may also act as brokers for nonproprietary mutual funds. Mellon Bank has the most important mutual fund business relative to its size, accounting for 14% of earnings.

In the United States, the **investor base** for mutual funds is more informed than in the United Kingdom or Continental Europe and hence is not as susceptible to brand name manipulation. This focus is aided by well-developed analytical services that rate funds and track their performance, such as Morningstar and Fortune. In the context of these patterns, the influence of analytical services can be judged by the fact, as noted by Walter (1999), that in 1993–1996, 85% of mutual fund inflows went to funds that were rated four- or five-star by Morningstar Inc., and the same funds had 75% of mutual fund assets in 1996.

Goetzmann et al. (1992) show from household surveys that investment performance was the crucial input into the choice of funds in which to invest. Sirri and Tufano (1992) show that it is mutual funds earning the highest return within the latest annual assessment period that get the largest rewards in terms of new inflows. On the other hand, clients may not be willing to disinvest in a fund that performs poorly to the same extent.[34] As is the case for wholesale management, clients nonetheless appear to believe that there is some market inefficiency, that they can select managers with superior performance, and that transactions and management costs are not large enough to absorb all the potential gains. Otherwise, they would choose index funds. (Note that there was a notable shift to index funds as active managers underperformed the S&P in 1996 and again in 1998.) More generally, as funds become more and more spread across the less financially sophisticated parts of the population, name recognition and branding may become more important again. Walter (1999) reports that in a recent U.S. survey, only 20% of potential investors could pass a test of basic investment skills.

There has been some research into **economies of scale in the sector**. Ferris and Chance (1987) and Trzcinka and Zweig (1990) found a negative and significant relationship between a fund's asset size and its expense ratio. Consistent with this, Wohlever (1993) found that a doubling of the size of a fund would reduce the expense ratio by 8 bp. Collins and Mack (1997) found economies of scale up to $4–6 billion for bond funds, $0.6–0.8 billion for equity funds, and $10–12 billion for money funds.

---

34. This may link on the one hand to the structure of mutual fund charges, in particular front-end and exit fees, and on the other to cognitive dissonance, whereby investors are unwilling to acknowledge that they have made a poor investment. Nevertheless, losses of clients may occur in the case of prolonged poor performance; a recent example is Fidelity's major loss of clients when performance deteriorated in the mid-1990s.

Using data for 1998, Investment Company Institute (1999e) found that the operating expense ratio for funds with over $5 billion in assets was 70 bp, compared with 139 bp for funds with $250 million or less. This is suggestive of economies of scale. This relationship also held when fund objectives were controlled for (i.e., it does not link to the large size of low-expense index funds). A similar decline in average costs was apparent in examining funds that grow over time. Investment Company Institute (1999d) also finds that costs in the industry as a whole tended to decline over the 1980–1998 period. For equity funds, the decline was 91 bp, or 40%. Corresponding declines for bond and money funds are respectively 45 bp, or 29%, and 13 bp, or 24%. Finally, Moon et al. (1998) find that there may also be scale benefits on the demand side operating via reputation, in that fund size is an important independent determinant of fund inflows.

Besides individual funds, families of funds may offer economies of scale and scope, in terms of shared fund managers, research staff, stockholder and custodial services, spreading of IT outlays (e.g., in providing daily information to clients on the value of assets), shared advertising and branding costs, legal costs, directorships, and offering an attractive service to fund holders in switching between types of fund within the family. They may also offer savings in costs of maintaining tax records,[35] notably for retirement funds. Wohlever (1993) found that a $10 billion increase in assets for a family of funds would raise profit margins by 1.5 percentage points. A doubling of group assets reduces the management fee by 2 bp. Analysis by Collins and Mack (1997), studying mutual fund complexes using a translog cost function, suggests that the optimal size for a multi-product fund complex is around $20–40 billion (although the largest benefits would arise from expansion of fund families with assets of under $1 billion).

On balance, it appears that there are indeed some economies of scale, but firms of uneconomic scale manage to survive, given the growth of the industry, implying in turn a potential for hidden excess capacity. Cessation of such growth could bring problems of excess capacity more into the open, leading to pressure for merger or closure of smaller firms.

The economics of 401(k) accounts differs from that of the rest of the industry. There may be somewhat greater economies of scale when

---

35. Note that in the United States, unlike in Europe, mutual funds are obliged to report all income and capital gains to the Internal Revenue Service.

one takes into account the need for sophisticated record keeping, education of the workforce, telephone help lines, and the need for brand recognition, as well as the intense competition and the countervailing power of the sponsoring company in getting the best deal for its workforce.

3.4.2.3 Conduct and Performance

One of the salient aspects of industry conduct, similar to that for the wholesale sector noted above, is the **proliferation of products**. Firms' growing multiproduct orientation may be justified by the focus of a large part of the investor base on performance, in the context of efficient securities markets. Consistently beating the market is hard to do and risky for the survival of a single-product firm. The probability of having at least one product with a successful ten-year experience rises sharply when many products are offered (Ennis 1997). If the probability of outperforming a benchmark is 0.45 in any one year, the probability that a single-product firm will have a successful ten-year experience is 38%. With five products, the potential for at least one successful product is 90%. Multiproduct approaches may also be helpful in simply providing enough baskets for gathering assets in the environment of rapid growth that has been seen in the United States in recent decades. This is in addition to the economies of scale and scope offered by families of funds outlined in section 3.3.2 and discussed further below.

Distribution channels for mutual funds are traditionally via captive channels and direct sales. Banks accounted for 8% of mutual fund sales in 1996 compared with 31% for full service brokers, 32% for direct sales forces, and 20% insurance agents and advisors (Walter 1999). Whereas these methods may benefit existing firms, an innovation that is improving market access for small firms is so-called supermarkets such as Charles Schwab's OneSource and Fidelity's Funds Network, also available on the Internet, which offer a wider choice than the commission-based agents involved in direct sales.[36] Accordingly, in the mid-1990s, 9% of sales were from such discount brokers. As we have noted, banks have been restricted from activity

---

36. Whether they also lower costs is open to dispute. Tam (1998) notes that supermarket fees rose in 1998 to stand at 0.35% of invested assets, up from 0.25–0.3% in 1997. Such fees are effectively distributed across all investors. There are also concerns that supermarkets make it difficult for funds to contact, or even identify, their investors. Supermarkets may also increase volatility of cash flow.

in this area by regulatory constraints, but the 1999 Financial Modernization Act has liberalized them for some institutions.

Pricing of products shows some variation even in a given instrument or sector owing to varying front-end fees, regular management fees, and exit fees. Front-end[37] and exit fees may be justified by the costs that early redemptions impose on other investors by forcing the fund to hold more cash (Chordia 1996). Actively managed equity products command the highest fees, while fees on money funds, bond funds, and generic products such as index funds are low. Around 150 bp of assets per annum is typical of active equity funds, and 110 bp for bond funds, while index funds charge 20 bp. There is some downward pressure. Moon et al. (1998) show that retail advisory fees are 72 bp for domestic equity, 88 bp for international equity, 52 bp for taxable bond funds, and 30 bp for money funds.

The fact that funds with higher than average fees may still enjoy inflows suggests that consumers feel that they are being compensated by superior performance. Alternatively, the consumer base is segmented with the informed consumers going for the low-priced funds and the uninformed accepting the commission-based salesman's advice and also paying higher annual fees (such as so-called 12b-1 fees, which are explicitly earmarked for marketing).

Consistent with the suggestion that less informed consumers are willing to pay for services that are unrelated to risk and return, Kihn (1996) showed that the level of fund marketing fees is determined econometrically not just by financial variables such as past return, future return, and past risk but also by service variables such as availability of transactions by phone and a low minimum purchase level. He took this as implying that, given uninformed consumers, firms would be justified in focusing on marketing and low-cost service-related expenditures as well as financial performance. Marketing charges, conversely, were found not to add any value to the financial performance of mutual funds;[38] nevertheless, funds with high expense ratios continue to sell.

The **profitability performance** of firms in the U.S. mutual fund sector is difficult to assess, given that many are part of multiproduct firms, but in general, the recent picture has been one of rather high

---

37. As was mentioned, no-load fees are also common.
38. Indeed, as Smyth (1994) showed, no-load funds outperform load funds.

profitability.[39] (Bear in mind that revenue is linked to new inflows—for load funds—and assets under management, and hence firms do well when they attract new funds and/or markets are strong.)

3.4.2.4 Summary

On balance, the U.S. retail asset management sector would appear to be in a **state of monopolistic competition**, as with the specialized wholesale sector. There are large numbers of buyers and sellers, ease of entry and exit, and slightly differentiated products. The sector is not highly concentrated, albeit more so than in wholesale management, and there is little evidence of oligopoly or excess profitability, although equally there is neither competition to lower prices nor scope to raise them to exploit good performance. There are some economies of scale, notably in the field of 401(k)s, but the growth of the industry makes it feasible for small firms of inefficient scale to survive. A cessation of growth in inflows could bring such economies of scale more to the fore and lead the industry toward a situation of contestability comparable to that of the generic sector.

3.5 The U.K. Asset Management Sector

The value of **assets under management** in the United Kingdom in 1998 was estimated at $4.1 trillion (Institutional Investor 1999). Around 25% is managed on behalf of foreigners, 65% for U.K. institutional clients, and 10% for private client funds (see table 3.6). The City of London is widely used as a base for pan-European or global investment, a position that it enjoys owing to advantages such as critical mass, reputation, a pool of skilled staff, innovativeness, and a light regulatory touch (see Davis and Latter 1990).[40] The fund management sector is thought to account for 0.4% of U.K. GDP and 35,000–45,000 jobs. Forty-one of the 250 largest asset managers outside the United States are U.K.-based (British Invisibles 2000). The

---

39. Focusing on an earlier period, Wohlever (1993) noted that returns on equity in the late 1980s were, for example, generally in excess of 20% for publicly quoted mutual fund firms. Whereas a slight decline in returns on equity was detectable in the early 1990s, this was seen as being due to a buildup of equity capital to finance new acquisitions. Profit margins were high and stable.
40. The corollary is that a sharp tightening of regulation could unravel London's advantages.

Table 3.6
Assets under Management in the United Kingdom, End of 1998

Institutional Funds	U.K. Clients (£ Billion)	Overseas Clients (£ Billion)	Total (£ Billion)
Pension funds	699	208	907
Insurance	875	60	935
Unit trusts	272	49	221
Investment trusts	51	11	62
Money market funds	7	21	28
Other	0	193	193
Less double counting	−132	0	−132
Institutional total	1672	542	2214
Private clients	291	50	341
All clients	1963	592	2555

Source: British Invisibles (2000).

wholesale sector is much larger than the retail sector,[41] with pension fund assets amounting to $1165 billion in 1998, compared with $363 billion for open-end and closed-end mutual funds (known in the United Kingdom and unit trusts and investment trusts, respectively).

An outstanding feature of the U.K. industry is its strong **bias toward equity and international investment**, with 60% of assets under management being in equities and 20% in overseas assets. Another is the tendency of foreign firms to purchase U.K. asset managers in recent years, which means that most major European banks are represented. Recent takeovers included ING/Barings, Deutsche Bank/Morgan Grenfell, UBS/PDFM, SBC/Warburg, Dresdner Bank/Kleinwort Benson, Merrill Lynch/Mercury, and Nationwide Mutual/Gartmore. The 1999 UBS/SBC merger and that in 2000 between Schroders and Salomon Brothers/Citibank made for further change. U.S. firms also play a sizable direct role in the United Kingdom, with, for example, Citibank and J. P. Morgan managing their international assets from London. There is marked concentration, with ten asset management firms controlling half of the domestic wholesale business and 25% of the capitalization of the equity market.

41. Pension funds' share of institutional assets rose from 29% in 1965 to 42% in 1998, and unit trusts (open-end mutual funds) rose from 3% to 10% over the same period. The share of pension funds in institutional assets peaked at 48% in 1990. The life insurance sector is also extremely large in the United Kingdom (see table 1.6).

3.5.1 Wholesale Asset Management in the United Kingdom

3.5.1.1 Overview

U.K. pension funds employ far **fewer managers** than their U.S. counterparts, the average in 1999 being three compared to thirteen in the United States (Targett and Wine 2000). **Balanced management**, in which the asset manager takes decisions on both asset allocation and security selection, has historically been the key structural feature of pension fund management in the United Kingdom. Delegation of security selection alone (for a given market or asset), comparable to specialized management in the United States, is also common, however. According to Financial Times (1999), in 1998, 80% of funds had a balanced structure, either employing wholly balanced management or in conjunction with specialist and internal management. WM (1999a) record that in 1998, balanced management accounted for 71%[42] of mandates from U.K. segregated pension funds, and specialist management accounted for 29%. As we discuss in section 4.2, balanced management seems at the time of writing to be under pressure from other paradigms, but the process of loss of mandates is a gradual one.

Balanced investment management may be top-down (i.e., looking at macroeconomic data and selecting markets to invest in, often at a global level) and/or bottom-up (selecting individual stocks that are expected to perform well). Balanced management is typically seen as simple, cost-efficient, and facilitating a coherent approach to investment, at a possible risk of overdiversification. It seems that most pension fund sponsors believe that investment performance tends to be determined by asset allocation rather than security selection, suggesting that they believe that individual markets are efficient but there are inefficiencies between markets.

Specialist management is quite prevalent for large funds (British Invisibles 1997); 35% of those with assets of over £1 billion use exclusively specialist management, while only 26% use exclusively balanced management. Of funds with assets of under £100 million, 70% use balanced management only and 13% use specialized man-

---

42. Of the balanced funds, 38% were on a fully discretionary basis, while 33% were internally managed on a balanced basis, used consensus or index tracking in line with a peer group asset allocation.

agement. British Invisibles (2000) reports a sharp increase of around 20 percentage points in the number of funds using specialist management between 1997 and 1999. An estimated 20% of pension funds by value are thought to be internally managed, and 80% externally. **Indexed funds** accounted for around 25% of pension assets in early 2000 (Financial Times 2000), sharply up from the 16% seen in 1998. In 1998, index funds accounted for 49% of pension fund inflows, with 39% of private pension funds and 49% of public pension funds using index tracking for some of the portfolio. Index funds often focus on corporate governance issues.[43] Whereas annuities are common, and indeed are compulsory for the bulk of pensions accumulated in defined contribution plans, other forms of generic management that are common in the United States, such as GICs and portfolio immunization, are not.

There is frequent **performance evaluation**, in the context of mandates typically lasting three years (thus, as in the United States, offering incentives to perform well). Performance measurement services are almost universally used by investment managers, trustees, and consultants to verify the standard of performance that is attained in terms of absolute return, return relative to the industry mean, and against a benchmark that reflects liabilities of the fund. Measurement also informs the sponsor of the extent to which superior performance is due to asset allocation or security selection. Use of performance measurement is underpinned by the statutory requirement to trustees to disclose information about performance annually to members; independent performance measurement is recommended by the industry body the National Association of Pension Funds (NAPF) as best practice; and there is a general realization of the importance of performance for the cost of providing pension benefits. As the Financial Times (1999) noted, the GIPS will bring the types of standards and verification typical of the U.S. AIMR rules (see section 2.3.4) to the United Kingdom.

Mandates may often be specified in terms of a certain position in the ranking[44] or in terms of a certain excess return above the indus-

---

43. For example, a successful firm in recent years has been Legal and General, which has focused on indexation of funds and therein on corporate governance issues similar to CALPERS (see section 6.2).
44. Such benchmarks may of course be highly inappropriate for a fund whose liabilities differ from the industry average.

Table 3.7
Concentration in U.K. Wholesale Asset Management

	Five-Firm Concentration Ratio	Number with over 5% of the Market	Herfindahl Index*	Numbers Equivalent $(1/H)^{\dagger}$
1985	47%	8	0.07	14
1990	55%	7	0.08	12
1997	67%	7	0.11	9
1998	65%	6	0.10	10

*The Herfindahl Index is the sum of the squares of the market shares of the firms in an industry and thus measures the inequality in the size of firms. The data are evaluated for the top twenty firms in U.K. pension fund management.
†The numbers equivalent shows the number of equal-size firms that would give the same concentration.
Source: *Financial Times* (various issues).

try mean.[45] (According to Broby (1997), the latter was the case for 15% of U.K. mandates.) Note the contrast with the United States, where the more objective benchmark of beating the overall market index or an appropriate style-based benchmark is preferred. This is, of course, a feasible method for specialized managers but not so straightforward for balanced managers that are active in many markets, for which the performance of competitors is considered a more convenient benchmark.

3.5.1.2 Structural Aspects

The **range of competitors** for investing pension fund monies in the United Kingdom includes not only specialized asset managers, but also commercial banks, investment banks, and life insurance companies. The last also benefit from considerable "captive" retail business from the management of personal pensions—possibly enabling cross-subsidization to occur.

The market structure of the industry features quite **high and (until recently) increasing concentration**, especially if funds originating from foreign clients are included (table 3.7). The top five firms accounted for 47% of assets in 1985, peaking at 67% in 1997 before falling to 65% in 1998. The numbers equivalent, that is, the number

---

45. Such benchmarks risk being totally unrealistic; Harrison (1997) quotes CAPS as saying that trustees ask managers to beat the average by 1% on a three- or five-year rolling period, whereas in practice, such consistent outperformance is virtually impossible; no manager in their sample of ten years ever beat the average for more than seven of those years.

Table 3.8
The Five Largest U.K. Pension Fund Managers

	1	2	3	4	5
1985	Mercury	Schroders	Fleming	P & D	County
1990	Mercury	P & D	Barclays	Schroders	Prudential
1997	Mercury	Schroders	P & D	Barclays	Gartmore
1998	Mercury	Schroders	P & D	Barclays	Morgan Grenfell

Source: *Financial Times.*

of equal-size firms that would give the same concentration (a measure of skewness in relative size of firms) declined to nine in 1997 before rising to ten in 1998. The top quarter of fund managers accounted for 59% of institutional assets in 1992, 66% in 1996 and around 70% in 1999[46] (IFMA 1996, FMA 1999).

Another feature—at least until recently[47]—has been that **dominant firms have tended to stay dominant**. There has tended to be little fluidity, implying a degree of stickiness in mandates that is absent from the U.S. specialized sector and more typical of the generic sector in that country.[48] Even the rankings have changed little (table 3.8). Of course, although the names of firms have stayed the same, there have been changes of ownership following takeovers. This pattern of stability is apparent from the rather long periods between changes in mandates. (Blake et al. (1999) report an average length of mandate of 7.25 years.) Stability has tended to prevail despite the willingness of a variety of firms, including foreigners,[49] to enter the industry, the fact that many players and potential entrants are part of multiproduct firms (able to cross-subsidize entry), and the large number of niche players that are constantly entering and leaving the sector.

Concerning **economies of scale**, whereas it would seem that there is room for niche players, there appear to be benefits for large firms and some diseconomies of scale for giant firms. According to British Invisibles (1997), firms that grow to £7.5 billion reap particular economies of scale. Balanced management is likely to favor large

---

46. The corresponding figure for domestic clients in 1999 was 62%.
47. For an account of the recent difficulties of the dominant balanced managers, see section 4.2.
48. Over 1984–1990, the top twenty asset managers included only twenty-nine firms; fourteen firms remained in the top twenty throughout, and only two of the nine new entrants were able to establish themselves in a durable manner.
49. Foreigners tend to enter mainly via takeovers.

firms that have the analytical capacity to monitor a number of markets simultaneously and can share some costs, such as those of macroeconomic research and analysis. The growth of regulation and the rising costs of information technology may have helped to increase minimum efficient scale. On the other hand, giant firms in the United Kingdom's narrower markets would be more likely to face difficulties of moving the market during large trades.

3.5.1.3 Conduct and Performance

In general, U.K. wholesale asset management firms **advertise** to pension funds on the basis of their past performance, although league tables of assets are also frequently used to indicate the firm's popularity. Both of these features can **act as barriers to new entry**, because new entrants have no performance record and no existing stock of assets. It is hence difficult to obtain mandates for the first time. The scope for large firms to lose assets owing to poor performance was historically rather limited. U.S. firms such as Fidelity and J. P. Morgan have been in the United Kingdom for twenty years but have only slowly managed to gain significant market share among U.K. institutions. On the other hand, as we discuss in section 4.2, the Financial Times (1999) reports something of a breakthrough in 1998.

Fees for wholesale management in the United Kingdom are rather low (despite being partly composed of hidden charges). Without charges, historically a £100 million pension fund typically paid an annual fee equal to 12 bp, with charges of 22 bp (Davis 1993c). The range is reportedly narrow: around 10–35 bp. (Smaller funds may pay more, for example 50 bp for funds up to £10 million and 25 bp from £10 million to £25 million.) Booth and Wrighton (1999) suggest that the level for fees on active management remains around 30 bp (and 1–10 bp for index funds). As we have noted, a U.S. fund pays 40 bp, despite the appearance of intense competition in the U.S. market. Moreover, according to Graham (1997), investment management fees for large U.K. pension funds roughly halved over the 1990s.

Such estimates need to be treated with caution, given the **prevalence of so-called soft commissions**, the situation in which an investment manager may strike a deal with a brokerage house to provide an amount of business and provides a certain kind of service such as research or computer software. This practice makes the amount of an investment manager's remuneration opaque. It may give a reason to deal with a broker even when it is not the cheapest means. Other distortions may arise via use of in-house unit trusts and higher charges for international investment, in particular for transactions. Such practices could help to explain the difference between U.S. and U.K. fees (although "soft dollars" are also important in the United States; see Greenwich Associates (1998)[50] and chapter 8). Other explanations for this differential could include greater ability to cross-subsidize from retail business in the United Kingdom and/or a higher risk of loss of mandate in the United States, which means that fund managers require higher fees to break even.

Performance measurement is used as a marketing tool, both directly and via newspaper reports. The NAPF have highlighted problem areas in this regard: omission of relevant information that would enable comparisons to be evaluated correctly (omission of returns on property for example) and provision of figures that are not capable of independent verification (particularly information that is released too early to be authenticated). But the role of performance alone should not be exaggerated. According to Investors Chronicle (1997), it comes fifth in terms of ability to get on consultants' shortlists, after the actual investment process, quality of personnel, security selection philosophy, and corporate strength of a fund manager. (Note that charges are not mentioned in this list.)

An increasing trend is for there to be **individual benchmarks** tailored to the specific nature of funds' liabilities. This practice accounted for 40–45% of U.K. pension fund assets in 1999, up from 4% in 1990 (Financial Times 2000). The benchmarks are usually set in terms of guidelines for asset allocation, implying that balanced fund managers are not free to choose asset allocations at will. This implies that direct comparisons with the consensus or average return will become less meaningful. Besides the fact that pension funds are becoming increasingly divergent in their liabilities per se, an important spur for specialized benchmarks is the U.K. Minimum Funding Requirement (see Davis 2000b), which requires closer asset-liability matching than was hitherto the case. It is stimulating use of asset-liability management, as described in chapter 2.

Meanwhile, **price competition** in the United Kingdom is reportedly of **second-order importance**. This is partly because, given the

---

50. In 1997, they accounted for 24% of listed commissions.

primacy of performance, new mandates cannot be obtained by low fees. And such price competition is, in any case, limited by the low prevailing level of fees. Innovation and product differentiation (quantitative techniques) are often deployed as means of competing, though success in creating barriers to entry by such strategic investments is limited by ability of other firms to copy them and drive down profitability.

As in the United States, the performance of firms in the U.K. fund management sector is difficult to assess, given that many are part of multiproduct firms, but in general, the recent picture has been one of rather **high profitability**, reflecting the strength of stock markets. However, competition and increasing costs of labor, premises, and regulation have acted as restraints on profitability. Costs have reportedly risen sharply in recent years, from 0.18% of assets in 1992 to 0.23% in 1995, despite the rise in asset values over this period.

Share prices of fund management firms have often been bid up by the desire of other financial institutions to buy into fund management. In line with the last point, table 3.9 shows that specialist fund

Table 3.9
Market Data for U.K. Asset Managers, Third Quarter 1999

	Beta	Market Cap	Yield	P/E Ratio
Asset Managers				
Aberdeen	0.88	190	4.1	29.9
Amvescap	1.62	3792	1.5	35.9
Edinburgh	0.97	116	6.6	14.7
Ivory and Sime	1.05	268	3.9	21.3
M and G	1.24	1870	2.1	35.1
Paragon	1.18	297	1.4	11.2
Perpetual	1.3	987	2.4	19.7
Rathbone	1.23	268	2.7	19.6
Investment Banks				
Schroder	1.39	2929	1.4	22.6
Singer and Friedlander	1.26	284	4.4	9.5
Sectors				
Life assurance	0.86	11223	2.9	22.1
Banks	1.36	28575	2.8	19.7
Investment banks	1.33	1928	2	18.8
Asset managers	1.4	2415	2	27.5
FT-All share	1	1965	2.3	27
FTSE-100	1.02	12780	2.2	28.8

Source: LBS risk measurement service.

managers have rather high price/earnings ratios and low dividend yields. The relative instability of earnings and the close correlation of earnings with the stock market is reflected in betas of well over 1. Investment banks have similar features.

3.5.1.4 Summary

Wholesale fund management in the United Kingdom appears to have many of the **features of a contestable market**. Owing to threat of entry, firms behave as if they were in a competitive situation, in terms of pricing and hence profitability, despite the high concentration of the sector. The concentration may be explained partly in terms of economies of scale, but also in terms of certain noncontestable features that are sufficient to limit new entry to the upper echelons of the sector without being enough to enable them to act as an oligopoly.

Contestable features of the U.K. wholesale fund management sector include:

• the variety of managers available to take on mandates;

• the willingness of trustees to switch between managers on the basis of performance evaluation;

• the increasing role of consultants;

• the lack of bargaining power of fund managers in their relationships with trustees;

• the willingness of other managers to take over mandates and the relatively low costs of such switches; and

• the available alternatives of internal management and of passive indexation as opposed to active management.

These offer little scope even for large, established fund managers to exploit existing clients.

An explanation is still required for the structure of the industry, with rather few dominant firms and little new entry to the upper echelons. (Recent changes to this overall pattern are discussed in section 4.2.) In our view, the evidence on costs noted above makes it difficult to regard economies of scale as the sole explanation. Our preferred approach is to **relate concentration to the importance of reputation** (in terms of asset size and performance); **relationships** with clients, which may enable firms to retain mandates despite occasional lapses in performance; and **expertise**. To some extent, it may be easier to differentiate the product for balanced management than for specialized management—and more belief that markets are inefficient at the level of asset allocation than security selection. Moreover, herd instinct among trustees is clearly strong—a variant on "no one was ever fired for buying IBM." The increasing role of consultants, which ensure that performance is brought to the fore in new mandates,[51] has till recently tended to favor existing fund managers that already have a track record and established relationships elsewhere.

Another factor is expertise with derivatives. Already, 70% of U.K. pension funds permit the use of derivatives directly or by their external managers.[52] Skills with derivatives may become more important in the context of the introduction of a minimum funding rule for U.K. pension funds. Such skills are concentrated in large firms.

The prevalence of **balanced management may limit switching** in that it means that changing the manager puts the performance of the whole portfolio into play. U.K. performance measurement service CAPS suggests that a change of fund manager can cost as much as 2% of assets, including fees, taxes, and dealing costs. For some types of mandate, for example management of a large volume of funds in a specialist market, only a few firms may have the necessary capability. Finally, although funds under management have grown, the number of mandates have not. This reduces the opportunity of new entrants to develop a reputation by gaining mandates with new funds (which in turn are more likely than existing funds to accept new managers, given their own lack of established relationships).

It is suggested that these features may help to **explain the maintenance of rankings**, although they are not strong enough to support excess profitability. In this context, takeovers of fund management groups can be seen as means of buying positions in the ranking that are otherwise unobtainable. The lack of excess profits may be compensated by synergies such as ability to use the expertise, relationships, and reputation in other markets. Such synergies could also

---

51. Consultants tend to be active in asset liability modeling, regular monitoring of the manager, and strategic investment advice, as well as manager selection.

52. In fact, the proportion actually using derivatives in 1998 was only 26% of private funds and 44% of public ones. Forty-one percent of private funds and 26% of public funds did not use derivatives despite being allowed to at their discretion, while 33% of private funds and 30% of public funds are forbidden to use derivatives (Investment and Pensions Europe 1999b).

help to explain the paradox of lack of exit from the sector by firms that are making losses, although fear of loss of reputation may also be important.

3.5.2 Retail Asset Management in the United Kingdom

3.5.2.1 Overview

Compared with its wholesale counterpart, the U.S. wholesale and retail sectors, the assets of the U.K. retail sector are **relatively small**, with assets under management in unit trusts[53] (open-end mutual funds) of around $285 billion in 1998 and net inflows of $23 billion.[54] The sector nonetheless warrants consideration for offering a further illustration of the nature of competition in asset management. Active firms include specialist unit trust managers, banks, and insurance companies. The average group managed around $1.9 billion in eleven trusts with an average fund value of $170 million. The distribution of funds is mainly to equities (which account for $238 billion, or 84% of the total). Of the remainder, $22 billion each are in bond and mixed funds, and only $1.5 billion are in money market funds. Only about 50% of the units outstanding are actually held by retail clients, the rest being held by other institutional investors. Insurers will often invest personal pensions in their own unit trusts.

So-called Personal Equity Plans (PEPs)—a form of limited tax free saving—increased the popularity of unit trust saving in the 1990s, although there was also a degree of substitution from taxed unit trusts. In 1998, nearly 100% of unit trusts sales were via PEPs, PEP funds under management were £43 billion, and unit trusts had the majority of the PEP market. PEP money is rather immobile, owing to its tax privileges, which are lost if they are sold. The replacement of PEPs by Individual Savings Accounts[55] (ISAs) in 1999 forced firms to adapt and regain public interest.

3.5.2.2 Structural Aspects

The industry is quite **fragmented**, with 1689 unit trusts alone provided by 153 groups and no one group controlling more than 9% of the industry (see HSBC Securities 1998). One reason for this structure

---

53. There are also investment trusts (closed-end mutual funds) valued at $78 billion.
54. Source: FEFSI.
55. ISAs are a similar type of tax-free saving account offering scope for investment in a wider range of assets.

is that costs of an individual manager and overheads are apportioned at the level of the asset management group. Hence there is a form of cost sharing in which the size of small funds is absorbed into the overall operational structure of the parent group. Equally, setting up a trust per se is quite inexpensive, and the independent broker network is available to distribute new trusts. Hence, as in the United States, there are rather low barriers to entry for new unit trusts.

Also, the **distribution channels** in the United Kingdom, as in the United States, are diverse and are not all tied to defined families of funds. Indeed, independent advisors, who are charged under the Financial Services Act to offer best advice to clients and are not tied to companies, account for over 40% of sales. Bank branches are relatively unimportant, as in the United States, while direct and dedicated sales forces account for 50%.

Two **barriers to mergers** of unit trusts are, first, the possible liability to stamp duty (a stock exchange transactions tax of 0.5%) in the case of a unit trust merger. Second, there is the fee structure, whereby no fund management group wishes to subcontract the management and the fee involved to another group (Broby 1997). In the case of investment trusts, takeovers are more straightforward. Vulture funds buy stakes in underperforming funds and seek to initiate shareholder action to fire the managers and replace them with themselves (this happened in the mid-1990s to Kleinwort Benson European Privatization Trust).

According to the broker James Capel (1995), the retail market **suffers from overcapacity**, with too many firms chasing the same customers and homogeneity and too little to distinguish between firms and products. It was considered that transparency of fees would require firms to compete in investment performance, advertising and costs, and charges. A further process of rationalization was hence envisaged. Consistent with this, there is a growing concentration at a firm level, with the share of the top five firms being 29% in 1997 compared with 19% in 1990. Sales fall off rapidly outside the top five firms. Foreign firms account for 21% of the market (Moon et al. 1998).[56]

---

56. A structural change to the U.K. industry, albeit one that was slow to have a major effect, is the advent of open-end investment companies (OEICs), which have a corporate form rather than being based on trust law. They have the advantage over unit trusts of lower switching fees between funds and could hence increase barriers to entry. They are also familiar in structure to Continental European and hence may facilitate cross-border selling. Many U.K. unit trusts are expected to convert to OEICs.

3.5.2.3   Conduct and Performance

The **investor base** for mutual funds in the United Kingdom is **typically rather uninformed** and hence is susceptible to brand name manipulation and advertising. These are indeed heavily employed by the larger groups, as well as the blandishments of commission-based salespeople. Fees for unit trusts were traditionally a 5% front-end fee and up to a 1% annual fee. Investment trust fees are much lower; no front-end charge and a 0.5% annual charge are typical. Unit trust and personal pension fees are now coming under pressure, owing to new entry, but remain considerably higher than those in the United States. Investors often seem to lack awareness of the high costs involved in unit trust saving, focusing only on past performance. A survey by the unit trust association AUTIF (1998) showed that only 14% of retail investors cite reasonable charges as a justification for choosing a given fund. This is irrational, given that high explicit charges have a strong and predictable negative effect on performance (see Carhart (1997), cited in chapter 2). A penetrating analysis by James (2000) on behalf of the Financial Services Authority has shown that one needs to invest £1.50 in an actively managed unit trust or life fund to obtain a market rate of return of £1 as compared to £1.10 to £1.25 in an index tracker fund.[57]

On the other hand, the market has proved very **sensitive to the "pricing" issue** of even higher commission on endowment life insurance and personal pension funds. For these sectors, front-loaded commissions (to compensate salespeople) are so high as to use up contributions for some time after the start of the contract and hence mean that there are particularly low returns for those who cease contributions at an early stage. Even on average over a full contract period, personal pensions charge around 2.5% of contributions in administrative charges and up to 1.5% of assets in fund management charges. As Blake (2000b) notes, the average personal pension over a twenty-five-year period takes 19% of contributions in charges, and the worst schemes take 28%. Some of the charges may be hidden, also raising issues of information. (Occupational pension charges are much lower, by a factor of 3 or 4.) Disclosure, enforced at the begin-

---

57. James (2000) suggests that the dominant strategy for a new active fund appears to be to seek to beat the market for the first few years by increasing portfolio risk, thus gaining strong inflows, then taking advantage of investor inertia to profit from high charges. This strategy dominates the alternative of offering low charges.

ning of 1995, along with the pensions misselling scandal[58] led to a collapse of life and pension sales. This was considered to have triggered major structural change in the retail sector, as it challenged the existing means of selling via sales force.

One response was to shift to bancassurance, with sales occurring through bank branches. Second, U.S. discount brokers and fund supermarkets such as Schwab Corporation, entered the market, as did the conglomerate Virgin and the store group Marks and Spencer. Third, some groups entered other area of financial services to seek to give customers a better service and to prevent them from taking funds out of the organization (e.g., life insurers buying banks). A further development is a focus on greater transparency of products, with a classification into high, medium, and low risk, led by the U.S. consultant Micropal (Broby 1997). Performance figures for U.K. mutual fund managers are shown in table 3.9. (Asset management firms are typically active in both retail and wholesale management.)

3.5.2.4 Summary

The U.K. mutual fund sector shows features similar to those of its much larger cousin in the United States: a large number of firms, low to medium concentration, and pressure on profit margins, although price competition is still marginal. The U.K. retail sector seems, as in the United States, to be characterized by forms of **monopolistic competition**.

3.6 The Continental European Asset Management Sectors

The total value of funds under management in Europe—including the United Kingdom—is over $10 trillion, of which the United Kingdom accounts for 40% (see Institutional Investor (1999) and table 3.10). This implies an annual revenue of around $55 billion. In Continental Europe, life funds are estimated to be valued at around $2.2 trillion and pension assets at $2 trillion, with mutual funds being $2.5 trillion (about a third of global mutual funds). Of the total assets, around 4% is private client business. (This is much more im-

---

58. In the 1980s, salespeople for life insurance companies persuaded large numbers of individuals to leave their company pensions for personal defined contribution schemes, which had much larger commissions and did not benefit from employer contributions. They are now ordered to pay compensation, which may run to $18 billion (see Davis 2000b).

Table 3.10
European Money Management Centers

	$ billion	Percent of Total
United Kingdom	4132	40
Switzerland	1997	19
Germany	1456	14
France	938	9
Netherlands	936	9
Italy	306	3
Sweden	257	2
Spain	154	1
Belgium	82	1
Ireland	38	0.4

Source: Institutional Investor (1999).

portant in countries such as Switzerland.) Many markets are **dominated by a small number of banks**, with the banks controlling 94% of German domestic assets and 73% each in France and Italy. Insurers manage 11% of assets in France and 16% in Italy.

Walter (1999) suggests that the main **drivers of institutional asset management** in Continental Europe include the trend toward professional management of household assets, the recognition that pay-as-you-go pension systems are unsustainable as they stand, the move from defined benefit to defined contribution pensions in the private sector, and the shift of portfolios into equities and foreign assets. Although these factors are also present elsewhere, European countries are among those that have the greatest scope for growth in this respect, having less well developed mutual fund sectors, ongoing pay-as-you-go pension systems, and little funding except in the United Kingdom, Ireland, Denmark, the Netherlands, Sweden and Switzerland. There is also a predominance of defined benefit occupational pensions and generally highly restrictive regulations in respect of portfolio choice for pension funds (and life insurers), see Davis (2000c). Europe has also featured growth in overall personal financial assets of 11% per annum over the period 1987–1996, compared with 8% in the United States and Japan. More generally, owing to the dominance of pay-as-you-go pensions (Davis 1997a), scope for expansion is arguably even greater than in the relatively mature markets of the United States and the United Kingdom, where pension systems already have major funded elements. Institutional saving is likely to increase sharply over the next twenty years as individuals seek to provide for their retirements.[59] These elements help to explain the considerable attention being paid to European markets by the industry in general. The scope for change is enhanced by the process of Economic and Monetary Union in Europe (generally referred to more briefly as European Monetary Union or EMU), as outlined in chapter 4.

3.6.1   Wholesale Asset Management in Continental Europe

3.6.1.1   Overview

Pension assets in Europe are only around half of those in the United States, despite a much larger population. Within the total, and consistent with the relative size of pension fund sectors, the bulk of pension assets (around 40%) are in the United Kingdom,[60] while there are 17% in the Netherlands, 9% in Switzerland and Germany, 7% in Sweden, and the others account for 20% (Mercer 1999). As we showed in chapter 1, there are also extremely large life insurance sectors, not least in the countries where pensions are provided mainly by social security. Indeed, half of pension funds in Europe are insured—typically offering a guaranteed return of around 4% (Financial Times 1999).

European fund management has traditionally been strongly based on domestic bond investment (table 3.11), linking, inter alia, to:

• the relative risk of taxation being imposed on equities, which is less feasible for anonymous bearer bonds;

• historic-cost-based accounting systems;

• portfolio regulations;[61] and

• investor caution resulting from past experiences of equity risk (e.g., after World War II when equities became worthless in many countries; see Jorion and Goetzmann (1999)).

Notably in Spain, Germany, and France, there has been suspicion of international investment, for example, owing to concern about currency risk, liquidity risk, and lack of information. But there are

---

59. Indeed, Intersec predict annual growth in pension assets in the European Union of around 14% in coming years.
60. Figures are based on 1998 outturns from the William Mercer pension fund managers' survey.
61. See Davis (1998a) and section 2.5.

Table 3.11
European Pension Fund Managers' Asset Allocation, 1998 (Percent)

	Domestic Equity	Domestic Bonds	Foreign Equity	Foreign Bonds	Property	Cash
Austria	4	54	19	14	1	8
Belgium	20	29	28	12	5	6
Denmark	23	59	9	2	6	1
Finland	11	69	2	3	7	8
France	10	65	2	3	2	18
Germany	10	43	5	2	7	33
Ireland	34	13	37	7	6	4
Italy	16	35	0	0	48	1
Netherlands	20	43	17	12	6	2
Norway	11	47	10	19	7	6
Portugal	18	61	6	5	2	8
Spain	16	56	5	1	1	23
Sweden	21	60	10	3	6	0
Switzerland	17	29	8	9	26	11
United Kingdom	55	9	17	6	3	10

Note: Data differ from those in Table 1.10 owing to different definitions, sources, and methods.
Source: Mercer (1999).

signs that this is changing to a more equity-based and internationally based approach, as the appreciation of the benefits of diversification and the yield pickup available from equities becomes more widely appreciated, and EMU has eliminated currency risk for the participating countries (see section 4.3). Portfolio indexation is growing rapidly, albeit accounting for only around 4% of assets in 1999 (although indexation is more prevalent in the Netherlands, Ireland, and Switzerland).

3.6.1.2 Structural Aspects

E.U. **capital markets and institutional sectors remain fragmented**. In most countries, it is still **domestic managers** who are dominant, while they in turn are little represented abroad. They tend to be balanced managers, offering investment management services for whole portfolios, as in the United Kingdom, rather than specialists as in the United States.

However, generalization is risky, as the **sectors are by no means homogeneous**. In the Netherlands, Sweden, and Switzerland, the size of capital markets—and institutional sectors—is comparable with that in the Anglo-Saxon countries. But structurally and behaviorally, the wholesale asset management sectors are rather different. In several countries, it is the bank of the pension fund sponsor that would be the investment manager, for relationship reasons, almost regardless of performance.

The **manager selection process** differs sharply from that in the United Kingdom, where it is dominated by consultants. In the Netherlands, the selection process may be managed by members of the board itself who are investment professionals and have a background in academia or finance. There, there is intense competition among asset managers. In Switzerland, there may be a senior bank representative on the board who selects and recommends managers. Perhaps reflecting this, 80% of pension assets are in pooled vehicles managed by Swiss banks, and about 20% are in segregated funds. Equally, performance measurement is not particularly prevalent.

Size of asset managers differs widely, largely reflecting the size of the domestic markets; hence in countries such as Ireland and in Scandinavia, firms are generally quite small. In Southern European countries, including Spain, Italy, and Portugal, there are only six companies that feature in the largest 150 in Europe.

One reason consolidation is slow is the **difficulty of takeovers**; rather few independent fund managers are available, most being linked to or part of banks or insurance companies. As we noted in section 3.3, takeovers of asset managers in any country may face problems such as loss of valuable staff. But cross-border takeovers of fund managers in Continental Europe have particular difficulties. These include different accounting traditions, which hinder assessment of the worth of a fund, management business, and integration of business. Taxation, use of market data, and advertising rules on presentation of performance also vary widely.

Following the argument made for the United Kingdom, there would tend to be economies of scale for balanced management. Broby (1997) argues that the minimum efficient scale for fund managers is around $5 billion.

3.6.1.3   Conduct and Performance

According to Harrison (1997), **fees** for wholesale business such as pension fund asset management are 100–200 bp per annum in Belgium, 25–75 bp per annum in Denmark, and 30–75 bp below IEP 1 million and 10–20 bp above IEP 30 million in Ireland; in the Netherlands, equity managers may charge 25 bp and bond managers

12.5 bp or less. In Switzerland, fees may be 50 bp, but overall costs may also include income on turnover charges, and turnover may be 50–75% per annum.

There is a major **problem of hidden fees**, as noted by John (1999) summarizing a Towers Perrin survey. In the survey, there is particular criticism of German asset managers for hiding management, transactions, and safekeeping costs. Universal banks that dominate investment management in that country do not separate out the cost of services; they have cut visible asset management fees to ward off competition while keeping hidden charges high. Clients may "think they are paying less than 20 bp for management services but end up paying 160 bp, mainly due to high commission charges." Only large international investors have been able to negotiate lower fees. Belgium is also singled out for criticism, and only the Netherlands approaches Anglo-Saxon levels of transparency of charges.

Clearly, there are considerable variations, but also in most cases, fees are above those in the United States and the United Kingdom. There is also more scope for conflict of interest when, for example, the asset manager is a subsidiary of the bank providing the transactions services. Growth of global custodians, as well as more competition in asset management after EMU, may help to remedy the situation.

As we have noted, use of **performance measurement** is much less common in Continental Europe than in the United States and the United Kingdom, although there are also sharp differences between countries. Broadly speaking, most funds use a measurement service in Ireland, and this is also becoming the rule in Belgium and the Netherlands. In Switzerland, it is beginning to catch on, although the bulk of performance measurement is undertaken by the banks on their own behalf. In Germany, performance measurement is rare for pension funds (Pensionskassen) but more common for wholesale corporate investment funds (Spezialfonds). To a considerable extent in Switzerland and Germany, it is the investment management firm that measures its own performance, with scope for falsification (although reportedly practices have improved since the 1980s). Finally, in Scandinavia, Austria, Italy, Luxembourg, Spain, and France, performance measurement is virtually unknown. Even in such an important and mature market as Denmark, banks use their own past performance claims for competitive purposes, rather than independent performance measurement services (Harrison 1997). One reason for the absence of performance measurement may be relatively undiversified asset composition in bonds, which requires less performance measurement than more sophisticated portfolios. Prescribed asset returns, such as 4% for Swiss pension funds, make performance less important than risk control. In addition, the fund is not always independent of the sponsor; or, as we noted above, there may be representatives of the investment manager on the fund board; hence their performance is less often questioned.

The **profit performance** of Continental asset managers is not possible to judge separately, as they are parts of financial conglomerates. But high prices paid for U.K. asset managers by Continental universal banks suggest that returns are attractive.

3.6.1.4   Summary

In most Continental European countries, the key contestable or competitive features that are present in the United States and the United Kingdom are weak or absent. This has ensured not only that rankings are maintained, but also that there is excess profitability. For example:

• there is much less new entry, even at the niche level;

• relationships are much more important, particularly where an industrial firm has relationships with a financial conglomerate or "relationship bank" in all areas of business (there often being no independent trustees);

• there is less performance evaluation and/or it is less sophisticated;

• prescribed asset returns make performance of even less importance, while bringing risk control, the province of insurance companies, to the fore;

• the bargaining power of fund managers is greater, given the lack of local alternatives,[62] as well as their absolute size (e.g., universal banks and life insurers); and

• regulatory barriers may prevent new entry either directly or by preventing pension fund investment in the securities markets, where potential entrants have a comparative advantage.

Moreover, expertise in the typical investments of European funds—domestic bonds—is less widespread than equity/international invest-

---

62. This of course begs the question of why foreign managers are not seen as alternatives.

ment where a variety of international houses are ready to enter. In this sense, it is portfolio restrictions, not just restrictions on foreign entry, that are barriers to competition. EMU is removing this historic advantage, as we discuss in section 4.3.

With regard to paradigms of industrial organization, it is suggested that the Continental asset management sectors are **oligopolies**, partly as a consequence of regulatory factors as noted above, but also owing to structural entry barriers entailing significant sunk costs (e.g., owing to strong relationships). Market power means that the firms concerned obtain higher profits than in a competitive market. It will be interesting to see how long pension fund sponsors on the one hand and consumers on the other will be content with such structures, given the shortfall in performance. Some movements are underway already that have begun to change the market situation in Continental wholesale asset management, and EMU is further altering the situation (see chapter 4).

3.6.2   Retail Asset Management in Continental Europe

3.6.2.1   Overview
Mutual funds' assets in Europe stand at around $2.7 trillion, around 30% of the global total (table 3.12). France accounts for 23% of the total, Luxembourg for 19%, and Italy for 16% (see table 3.13). It is owing to its status as a tax haven that Luxembourg has developed as the major center for E.U. mutual fund companies, with most of the inflows to its mutual funds coming from elsewhere (especially

Table 3.12
Mutual Funds' Net Assets, 1998 ($ Billion)

	Equities	Balanced/ Hybrid	Bonds and Loans	Money Market	Total
European Union	854	353	942	476	2659
United States	2978	365	831	1351	5525
Japan	146	—	147	123	417
Number of funds					
European Union	6916	3892	6110	1635	18898
United States	3513	525	2250	1026	7314
Japan	N.A.	N.A.	N.A.	N.A.	4584

N.A. = not available.
Source: Investment Company Institute, FEFSI.

Germany and Belgium). As table 3.13 shows,[63] the distribution between different types of funds differs sharply between E.U. countries, with equity funds dominating in the United Kingdom but being less important elsewhere, although the weight of equities is growing. The French market features a sizable money market fund sector (historically for tax reasons), while in Italy, there is a preponderance of bond funds, reflecting investor preferences and the less developed state of equity markets than elsewhere.

3.6.2.2 Structural Aspects

On the retail side in Continental Europe, the **absence of an independent broker network**[64] provides a **barrier to entry**; financial institutions typically offer only their own products, and their customers are rather unadventurous. In Germany and France, the five biggest banks have market shares of 60% or more, and banks as a whole have shares of 70–80%, the rest is largely accounted for by domestic life insurance companies. Around 80–90% of all mutual fund sales in France and Germany take place via banks and insurers. Entry to domestic retail markets is hindered by the density of the bank branch network, combined with a lack in most countries of other sales channels such as the U.K. financial advisers (see table 3.14). Only in Italy, apart from the United Kingdom, do independent advisors play an important role (accounting for around 50% of sales, with the other 50% via bank branches).

Large banks and insurance companies, while they may be willing to sell products of smaller overseas fund managers, may for defensive reasons refuse to sell the products of large or global firms. On the other hand, smaller banks, which do not have their own asset management subsidiaries, are proving increasingly willing to sell foreign products. It is notable that Fidelity and other U.S. firms entered the German market partly by direct selling but also by selling through the small local savings banks (Sparkassen); Schroders are selling products in Italy via regional banks. Fidelity has begun direct sales in Germany, using German nationals based in the United Kingdom as telephone salespeople.

---

63. In Spain—not shown in the table—the distribution is 50% money market funds, 46% bonds, and 2% each equities and balanced.
64. Independent distributors account for 5% of sales in France and 15% in Germany.

Table 3.13
Distribution of European Mutual Fund Assets, 1998 ($ Billion)

	Total Net Assets	Percent of Total Net Assets	Equity Funds	Bond Funds	Balanced Funds	Money Market Funds	Funds of Funds	Other
Austria	64	2.3	7	37	17	3	1	0
Belgium	57	2.1	31	9	15	2	4	0.02
Czech Republic	1	0.02	0.007	0.1	0.2	0.2	0	0
Denmark	19	0.7	9	11	0.2	0	0	0
Finland	6	0.2	2	1	1	1	N/A	0
France	626	22.8	107	191	143	184	0	0
Germany	196	7.1	84	78	7	27	0	0
Greece	32	1.2	2	6	3	21	0	0.1
Hungary	1	0.1	0.01	1	0.3	0.2	0	0
Ireland	24	0.9	7	7	8	2	0	0
Italy	436	15.9	79	220	34	82	0	21
Luxembourg	510	18.6	145	236	40	81	0	8
Netherlands	88	3.2	51	20	8	7	0	2
Norway	11	0.4	6	2	0.4	3	0	0
Poland	1	0.02	0.1	0.1	0.3	0.002	0	0
Portugal	23	0.8	3	9	2	7	5	2
Spain	239	8.7	48	88	44	59	0	0.5
Sweden	55	2.0	41	6	8	incl.	0	0
Switzerland	72	2.6	50	22	0	0	0	0
United Kingdom	286	10.4	238	22	23	1	8	0.4
Total	2745	100	911	966	354	479	18	34

N/A = data not available.
Source: FEFSI. Note that the total exceeds that in Table 3.12 owing to the inclusion of non-E.U. countries.

Table 3.14
Percent Distribution Channels for European Mutual Funds

Country	Bank	Broker	Insur-ance	Direct	IFA	Tied Sales Force	Other	Mixed
France	74	0	10	0	5	0	11	0
Italy	53	0	0	1	4	10	0	32
Germany	74	0	7	2	17	0	0	0
United Kingdom	0	6	0	7	41	46	0	0
Spain	92	4	2	0	0	2	0	0
Netherlands	31	0	0	34	1	1	47	0
Switzerland	90	0	0	0	10	0	0	0
Austria	90	0	5	0	5	0	0	0
Belgium	75	0	0	0	0	0	25	0
Sweden	86	0	7	1	6	0	0	0
Greece	86	0	9	1	4	0	0	0
Portugal	0	95	0	0	0	5	0	0
Denmark	96	0	0	3	1	0	0	0
Norway	86	0	7	7	0	0	0	0
Finland	43	0	0	55	2	0	0	0

Source: Cerrulli; Lipper; Bernstein; FEFSI; Goldman Sachs.

Product regulations in Continental Europe often have a protectionist effect. For example the new German pension product known as the Altersvorsorge Sondervermögen,[65] introduced in 1998, is restricted to investing in mutual funds whose managers are based in Germany. France applies a similar restriction to its Plan d'Épargne Action (Eaglesham 1998).

As the Economist (1997) noted, a more significant barrier may be, on the one hand, **caution regarding the risks of equities**, as outlined in the section above, and, on the other, at least historically, a **lack of interest in relative performance**. The Economist (1997) reports that whereas an institutional fund manager in Europe can expect 3% more assets if performance is improved by 10 bp, for retail clients the return is only 1% more clients (see also Moon et al. (1998)) Reflecting these features, foreign managers have a rather small share of European markets, illustrating lack of integration. According to Moon et al. (1998), they account for 4% in Germany and 1% in France, although they have captured 19% of the market in Italy.

---

65. This is basically a balanced fund with equity proportions to be between 21% and 75%, limits of 30% on foreign assets, and no use of derivatives permitted. There are no tax advantages.

On the other hand, the overall **economics and costs of the sectors** are not different from those of the United States and the United Kingdom. Notably, Dermine and Röller (1992) found results for economies of scale and scope for French mutual funds similar to those quoted above for the United States, with economies of scale present for small and medium fund complexes but not for large fund complexes.

3.6.2.3 Conduct and Performance

As we have noted, sale of mutual funds **tends to be through bank branches** that have, at least until recently, offered only their own funds. In general, fees for mutual funds in Continental Europe are higher than those in the United States and the United Kingdom, and they remain even more subject to the hidden charges noted above than wholesale funds. There are **local idiosyncrasies** in product preferences. Broby (1997) notes an equity index product in the Netherlands with downside protection afforded by purchase of put options. Another example is an Italian fund focusing on property developers' shares and real estate investment trusts. Walter (1999) notes that in the European Union, the fiscal environment of high tax rates and lax enforcement relative to the United States has encouraged **tax avoidance**. The use of mutual funds for this objective has been rife, prompting interest in tax harmonization and an E.U.-wide withholding tax.[66] Walter notes that elimination of fiscal differences could be helpful for the growth of pan-European mutual funds also, along the lines of those in the United States.

Cross-border competition is only just developing, hindered by distribution problems. Broby (1997) sets out some criteria for successful penetration of Continental retail markets. These include the quality of the parent's name and its prominence in the country concerned (which can obviously be enhanced by advertising); past performance of funds, risk adjusted, in terms of the local currency (which U.S. and U.K. funds often find a major advantage); risk and volatility being tailored to local preferences; investment selection being carefully explained (e.g., benefits of international diversification); financial backing and safety of assets in the case of cross-border sales of funds; a competitive pricing structure for the country concerned; an efficient and consumer-friendly dealing system; and

---

66. Note that an earlier initiative in this area collapsed in 1989.

comprehensive service more generally. Clearly, local knowledge is essential for many of these. Product literature in the local language offers considerable benefits, which, surprisingly, are not always taken advantage of. Walter (1999) sees targeting of specific client segments and superior products to traditional vendors as essential by for effective cross-border competition.

3.6.2.4 Summary

As for wholesale management, retail management in most of Continental Europe is an **oligopoly**, partly as a consequence of protectionist legislation, but also owing to structural entry barriers entailing significant sunk costs, notably via control of channels of distribution. Market power means that the firms concerned obtain higher profits than they would in a free market. EMU may undermine these oligopolies, as we discuss in section 4.3, but the process is likely to be gradual.

3.7   The Evolution of Wholesale Asset Management in Japan

3.7.1   The Historical Situation

Assets of Japanese pension funds amounted to 85 trillion yen at the end of 1998, equivalent to $650 billion. The Japanese wholesale asset management sector, despite its large size and rapid growth, has historically been dominated by a mere twenty-nine institutions: eight trust banks and twenty-one life insurers (see Clark 1994, Lee 1994). Until the mid-1990s, the top fifteen pension fund managers controlled 94% of the pension monies, compared with 22% in the United States. Fees were high. Trust banks were able to charge as much as 60–180 bp, while life insurers charged 2–5% of the inflow.

Three main features explain this **pattern of oligopoly**: regulation, accounting, and traditional relationships. Regulations have permitted foreign fund managers to enter the market only relatively recently. Only since 1990 have they been able to act on restrictive terms[67] for Employee Pension Funds (EPFs). Even then, regulations limited foreign ("discretionary") managers to 20% or less of EPF money. And

---

67. There was a limit of one third of an EPFs assets to be managed by a foreign discretionary manager; limits of 50% in equities and 70% in foreign assets; only new money could be invested by discretionary advisers; and only EPFs that had been in existence for eight years could use such discretionary investment advisors.

until the late 1990s, foreigners were not permitted to act on behalf of Tax Qualified Pension Funds (TQPPs)[68] or public pension assets. Asset restrictions on pension funds meant that funds had to invest half of their assets in bonds, and equity and international investment was limited to 30%, and property to 20%.[69] This obviously also reduced the scope for international managers to undertake asset allocation. Meanwhile, defined contribution plans are only just being permitted at the time of writing in 2000.

A number of **accounting features** made it difficult for asset managers to compete for business on the basis of superior investment performance. Notably, accounting regulations valued assets at book value rather than market value, but when a pension fund changed managers, capital gains and losses were realized. Moreover, lack of disclosure provisions meant that poor performance was often obscured.

As in much of Continental Europe, **relationships historically tended to dominate choice** of asset managers rather than performance. The small number of life insurers and trust banks that dominated investment of pension assets are often part of the industrial group (Keiretsu) that includes the pension fund sponsor. To manage pension assets, Japanese companies usually chose fund managers that were large and faithful shareholders of firms or good customers (Clark 1994). Such shareholders would, for example, be firm holders of the shares, would be content with low dividends, and would not interfere with the running of the firm in question. The companies often dealt with large numbers of managers for relationship reasons (as many as fifty), but the service was not provided on a competitive basis.

Competition among asset managers was also rendered more difficult because there tended to be a **lack of available performance records** of money managers. Performance measurement was little used, partly owing to resistance by existing managers (Lee 1994). "New" foreign competitors lacked a track record. Meanwhile, the existing managers tended not to compete on performance, rather offering the same service of a guaranteed annual return (5.5% until 1994, 4.5% until 1996, and 2.5% since then), window dressing their portfolios at the times of measurement to ensure this.

---

68. TQPPs are available to firms with fifteen or more employees; EPFs are available only to larger firms with 500 or more employees. Only the latter can contract out of the earnings-related social security for an equivalent pension benefit.
69. These rules were known as the 5-3-3-2 rule (50%, 30%, 30%, 20%).

Until 1998, their portfolios were constrained by the 5-3-3-2 **investment restrictions** noted above, and their actual performance was obscured by the above-mentioned book value accounting practices. They tended to sell assets showing book value gains to ensure that the rate of return targets were met, acting entirely contrary to what would be needed for a long-term sustainable return. The regulations on discretionary managers meant that these did not historically pose a significant competitive threat. And given that mandates were usually awarded for relationship reasons as noted above, incumbents did not need to compete actively with each other in any case.

There was some evolution even before the mid-1990s. Whereas in 1982, 76% of EPF assets were managed by trust banks and 24% by life insurers, in 1993 trust banks managed 59% of EPF assets, insurance companies 37%, and discretionary advisors 4%. The change was not due to competition in the normal sense of the word. Rather, life insurers gained market share because they pool pension and non-pension reserves. Following the logic outlined above, they were able to take profits on shares bought long ago to back individual life policies to boost their pension fund returns.

As Clark (1994) noted, the net effect of this oligopoly situation and associated lack of competition, as well as distortions caused by book value accounting and portfolio regulations, was to **sharply reduce potential rates of return** to Japanese pension funds (see section 2.5). As long as the boom of the 1980s continued, this was not viewed with much concern, as even poor performance on the part of an asset manager would obtain a reasonable absolute return. But since 1990, the bear market in shares and property has led to concerns about underfunding and sharpened the focus on asset manager performance. Indeed, pension funds were vastly underfunded at the time of writing, with a 40% shortfall of assets to liabilities, according to the accounts of Japanese firms that are listed in the United States (see section 5.3.7). Japanese pension funds cover the same proportion of the workforce as in the United States and the United Kingdom, but they have only a seventh of the assets.

3.7.2   Recent Changes

Change is underway; the trigger appears to have been the **reduction in returns which are guaranteed** by life insurers to pension funds to 2.5% in April 1996, in contrast to 5.5% required by pension funds to avoid underfunding (Economist 1997). In addition, there are concerns about the solvency of life insurers themselves after the failure of Nissan Mutual in April 1997.[70] The public fund Nenpuku took the lead by withdrawing 5 trillion yen from life companies at the beginning of 1996. The restrictions on EPFs' use of investment advisory firms were eased so that half of their money could be managed by them. And the 5-3-3-2 portfolio regulations were relaxed for the largest EPFs.

The consequence of these developments was, on the one hand, a major **swing back to trust banks**, which, unlike life insurers, were able to show returns of 5% in 1996. On the other hand, there was a major shift to **investment advisory companies**. Whereas in March 1996, investment advisors managed 4.9 trillion yen in pension money, the figure was 11.6 trillion yen by March 1997 and 17.5 trillion yen by December 1997. Of the total run by advisors, the proportion handled by foreign firms rose from 16% to 26%, and the number of EPFs using foreign managers rose from 120 to 261. The independent managers accounted for 7.6% of the market. On the other hand, the foreigners experienced something of a setback when the yen started to strengthen in 1998, as this reduced the attractiveness of foreign assets. Their share fell back somewhat during that year.

Some **further deregulatory acts** are increasing competition. In particular, the portfolio regulations were abolished altogether effective from April 1998; TQPPs are now allowed to use investment advisory companies, and book value accounting was abolished in April 2000 in favor of market value. The shift from book value accounting will make switches of asset manager much more feasible. A Japanese version of the U.S. 401(k) personal pension was introduced in 2000. Finally, as we discuss further in chapters 5 and 6, Japanese firms are unwinding their cross-shareholdings (Tett 1999), and there are signs that the so-called Keiretsu groups are also beginning to break down. These will further weaken the traditional links of asset managers to pension fund sponsors.

3.7.3 The Mutual Fund Sector

Japan accounts for 9% of global mutual fund assets, in the form of so-called **securities investment trusts**. Their distribution was, until

---

70. See section 5.3.7. The companies had promised high returns in the 1980s, which could be financed only by new money inflows, given the fall in yields. Once new money dried up, failure loomed.

the end of 1998, still largely in the hands of local investment banks, although a few foreign asset managers and insurance companies were allowed to offer funds. Mutual funds in Japan suffer from a bad performance reputation. This is partly linked to historical restrictions on international investment. But it also reflects the tendency of salespeople to induce customers to shift between funds to increase competition and the tendencies of investment banks both to churn portfolios to generate commission and to "stuff" investment trusts with unsold inventories of securities (Smith 1998).

Deregulation incorporated in the Foreign Exchange and Foreign Trade Control Act of 1998 is facilitating mutual fund development. Banks and insurance companies are now allowed to sell mutual funds, opening new distribution channels also for foreign funds.[71] Indeed, sales of investment trusts by banks and insurance companies was nearly 3 trillion yen in November 1999, having been below 0.5 trillion yen before February 1999. The traditional providers of such funds, such as Nomura, are launching so-called monster trusts aimed at value investment in sunset industries, which are gaining large inflows. Meanwhile, foreigners are developing direct sales; for example, Merrill Lynch took over thirty branches of the bankrupt securities house Yamaichi and hired 2000 staff members with the intention of selling mutual funds. Fidelity and Mercury are also marketing directly. The introduction of a law permitting 401(k)-style defined contribution pensions is a further step forward. But low tax benefits, red tape, a 2% commission charge, and lack of consumer information may make progress slow.

Conclusions

Asset management sectors differ sharply in terms of structure and behavior among the major OECD countries. There is a divide between the Anglo-Saxon countries on the one hand and Continental Europe and Japan on the other, in terms of the scope of competition. These are reflected in turn by differences in fees and performance generally. Both regulatory and structural reasons may be responsible for weaker competition in Europe and Japan, the role of relationships, distribution channels, and investor attitudes to equity being among the factors highlighted in Continental Europe and also regulation in

---

71. In late 1998, Fidelity announced an agreement with twenty-three Japanese banks to sell its funds through 1000 branches. Putnam has linked to Nippon Life, and Franklin/Templeton has linked to Sumitomo Life.

Japan. There are in addition marked contrasts between the United States and the United Kingdom in terms of active wholesale asset management. In the former, specialist managers are dominant, whereas in the latter, it is the balanced managers that predominate. Meanwhile, the retail sectors in the United States and the United Kingdom are much more comparable, as are the sizable generic sectors that focus particularly on indexation.

With regard to paradigms of industrial organization, Continental and Japanese sectors to date are oligopolies. Generic (nondiscretionary) management in the United States and the United Kingdom, as well as balanced wholesale management in the United Kingdom, are contestable markets, with large firms predominating owing to economies of scale but potential competition and low sunk costs limiting fees to a competitive level. Specialized wholesale management in the United States and retail asset management in the United States and the United Kingdom are better characterized as monopolistic competition, with rather few economies of scale or entry barriers and a proliferation of firms with differentiated products.

4   Influences on the Future of the Asset Management Industry

Introduction

Chapter 3 focused largely on the current situation in the various asset management markets and their analysis in an industrial organization context. This chapter focuses on future prospects in the light of current trends. We look successively at pressures on existing patterns of asset management in the three main sectors examined in chapter 3: those of the United States, the United Kingdom, and Continental Europe. In the case of Europe, we focus on the impact of the recent introduction of the Euro. We then go on to examine the hypothesis of globalization of asset management that is favored by a number of investment bankers and industry experts. Finally, we look at the responses to a questionnaire that was specially undertaken for this book, which casts light on asset managers' own views with respect to the analyses presented in chapters 3 and 4.

4.1   Challenges in the U.S. Market

4.1.1   Wholesale Asset Management

The **pattern of demographic change** has to date fueled the growth of the wholesale asset management industry via the saving of baby boomers. But the situation will soon change. Those in the prime saving age group of 40–60 will peak as a proportion of the adult population in 2006, at around 36% of the total population. Flows to institutional saving will moderate.[1] In the case of occupational pension funds, these trends mean that there will be negative cash flow as the population ages and begins to draw on its pension funds. Asset managers will have to compete intensively for existing assets rather than taking a share of rising assets.

In this context, commentators suggest that plan sponsors will want to deal with fewer managers (and hence carry out less monitoring) than has been the case hitherto. Ellis (1992) suggested that this will entail a switch to **management by large investment management firms**, the so-called **new paradigm**. He suggests that they could do this, without changing their objectives in terms of diversification, by moving relatively toward balanced or "core" management (see the discussion of the United Kingdom in chapter 3). Firms wishing to be chosen as core managers would have to develop their sales forces and investment products. And at the same time as these tendencies would raise the cost of competing, average fees for products would fall as sponsors demanded volume discounts from managers. Following this, Hurley et al. (1995) and Berlinski and Western (1997) have argued that there will be increasing merger activity and consequent rising concentration. They forecast that there will be twenty to twenty-five active managers with over $150 billion under management and many firms with under $5 billion—a contrast to the structure in the late 1990s of over 200 firms with over $5 billion and only three with active assets of over $150 billion.

The **counterthesis** (Phillips 1997) points out that the number of mergers among money managers has remained fairly steady at around forty per year since 1988, while the number of U.S. institutions using balanced managers is rather small (around 4% in 1999, down from 7% in 1997). There is concern that employing a single asset management firm could lead to concentration of risk (for example, if it takes a certain view on inflation that influences all its decisions). Such a concentration could be seen as contrary to the prudent man principle under ERISA. If fees are linked to asset allocation, it may give rise to risks and conflicts of interest. And sponsors are

---

1. This was also the case in the 1970s, when the ratio of prime savers to the population fell from 30% in 1970 to 25% in 1986.

conscious that large, active firms may face higher costs of transactions for their large trades in efficient markets, given liquidity
problems (Ennis 1997).

In a recent Pension Forum survey of 1050 U.S. pension plan sponsors, more than 25% of sponsors expected to increase the number
of managers they employed. Moreover, 76% of sponsors preferred to
use employee-owned (and hence small) money management firms
rather than subsidiaries of larger financial services organizations. A
focus on the U.K. experience may be relevant to the resolution of this
debate. Indeed, Moon et al. (1998) suggest that there will be a bifur-
cation in the U.S. asset management industry between large, retail-
oriented asset managers seeking growth (see below) and smaller
firms managing institutional assets, which will trade growth for
stable profits.

The **future of active management** is a key issue with regard to the
U.S. wholesale markets. Lakonishok et al. (1992a) commented that
the specialized sector appears to be "value subtracting" given poor
average performance (1.3–2.6% below the S&P 500 was achieved
over the 1980s) and considered that the industry could not survive in
its current form. After adjusting for risks and active management
costs, Ambachtsheer and Ezra (1998) found a "risk adjusted net value
added" of −0.5% for forty-eight U.S. pension funds in 1992–1995. We
noted in chapter 3 that there has been considerable growth in indexation. The issue is how far the current trend toward indexation can
proceed. A natural limit may be reached at which indexation is so
prevalent that the predictability of the behavior of indexed strategies
facilitates superior performance by active managers. The alternative
is for active managers to increase their efficiency and effectiveness
(Ambachtsheer and Ezra 1998).

4.1.2   Retail Asset Management

On the retail side in the United States, we noted in chapter 3 that
defined contribution pension funds are growing strongly relative to
defined benefit, and this may be expected to increase. This implies a
growing retail focus of the industry and so-called **instividualization**.
Berlinski and Western (1997) give a prognosis for retail asset management that suggests that despite the growth of assets, competition
will also increase, in line with costs of gathering and retaining assets.

Notably, there is the need, as we pointed out in chapter 3, to satisfy both a corporate sponsor and the employees to gain 401(k) mandates.

Following the logic of the paragraphs above, a **slowdown in growth** as baby-boomers start to retire would **accelerate such trends**. Customer expectations in regard to service as well as quality of asset management have increased. These imply a need for considerable expenditures on technology to generate performance reports, voice recognition systems, Web sites, and so forth. Costs of selling via sales forces are rising, given the costs of experienced professionals, while advertising costs in the direct channel are also increasing. Banks and insurance companies are now permitted to enter the sector and are boosting competition. Supermarkets have offered opportunities, as noted, to small, independent asset managers and have lowered entry barriers. But given the increasing number of mutual funds, so-called shelf space in mutual fund supermarkets is getting crowded, implying that the supermarkets have increasing pricing power.[2] The Internet could account for an increasing proportion of sales and thus offer both an opportunity and a threat to the status quo. The opportunity is for established firms to reach an increasing number of consumers by this route. The threat is that it lowers the entry barriers to new asset managers.

Exchange traded funds are baskets of stocks that are traded continuously on an exchange. Introduced by such firms as State Street, they are widely seen as a threat to traditional mutual funds. The funds are much cheaper than index funds, with fees of 12 bp, in contrast to 18 bp for index funds. Being tradable, they can be cashed at any time during the day; the investor need not wait until the end of the day. And they can be for specific sectors, such as the German equity market or U.S. health care stocks. Introduced in 1993, this sector accounted for $40 billion in assets at the time of writing.

Even more radically, some observers have noted that the low stock transaction fees charged by Internet discount brokers facilitate the creation of **personal mutual funds** with assets of as low as $100,000 and with much lower fees than the average mutual fund. This could be a distant threat to the whole industry.

---

2. Charles Schwab charges managers 35 bp, up from 25 bp originally. Load fees have also fallen from around 8% to 4.5%. On the other hand, without the supermarkets, small funds could not afford the sales forces, customer service centers, and so forth needed to reach such a large and diverse customer base.

As in the wholesale sector, individuals are becoming increasingly **aware of the benefits of indexation**, with index funds accounting for 5% of assets of U.S. mutual funds and 13% of inflows in 1997; by 1999, the share of inflows had risen to 31%. Retail investors are also becoming interested in alternative investments such as real estate, commodities, insurance-based products, and various hedging strategies, whose returns are orthogonal to the market (see for example Goldman Sachs (1998)). There is also likely to be an increasing focus on income rather than growth, given the desire of the elderly for a stable source of income and a lesser willingness to take risks. These trends put pressure on active managers of traditional equity and bond funds to deliver both performance and service (Moon et al. 1998). Middle-tier firms may be notably at risk given the continuing scope for new entry by small firms with lower overheads.

These factors imply that retail fund managers will **seek higher scale to spread costs**. In 401(k) pension management, it is firms that bundle record keeping with investment management that have grown most successfully in recent years (Phillips 1997), thus reaping economies of scale, although the advantage that this gives may now be fading as investors focus more on performance. Meanwhile, only the less economical small firms do not yet have 401(k)s. Elsewhere (Moon et al. 1998), asset managers will compete for existing assets, which in the context of retail markets puts emphasis on branding, product differentiation, and distribution. Overall, consolidation is expected in the U.S. retail market as well as the wholesale market.

Walter (1999) argues that there are forces arguing both **for and against industry concentration** in the future in the retail sector. He agrees that concentration might be aided by economies of scale and brand name concentration among increasingly unsophisticated investors, notably in the context of retirement saving and given the large number of extant funds. On the other hand, shifts in performance track records, the link of size to performance problems, and the role of mutual fund supermarkets will militate against excessive concentration. Star managers may prefer not to work for large conglomerates.

Walter (1999) sees **competition as likely to increase** considerably, with mutual fund companies and broker dealers adding banking-type services to mutual funds and securities firms seeking a more stable source of income than in the competitive and volatile wholesale investment banking activities. Insurance companies and banks, too, see the mutual fund sector as offering profitable opportunities in the face of strong competition in their traditional areas of business. The recent abolition of the Glass-Steagall separation of commercial and investment banking could herald further structural changes, with further scope for consolidation in asset management, as banks and insurers seek to recapture business from independent asset management companies, via acquisitions[3] or development of their own asset management companies. According to Moon et al. (1998), there is particular scope for insurance companies to profit from mutual fund development, as they have sales forces and offer annuities that are complementary to mutual funds as the population ages.

4.1.3   Social Security Privatization

The **U.S. social security** pension system has **built up reserves** that were valued at around $625 billion in mid-1997. A buffer fund, the reserves aim to protect against large increases in contributions or falls in benefits during the future aging of the population. These assets are currently held in the form of nonmarketable government bonds. The volume of assets is scheduled to peak at around $2.9 trillion in 2018 and then to decline rapidly, to be depleted in 2029. Economists have extensively analyzed privatization of social security; they argue that it would improve long-term productive capacity at the cost of a higher fiscal burden for generations that will be alive during the transition (Kotlikoff 1996, Feldstein and Samwick 1998). It could also have marked effects on intragenerational income distribution (Kotlikoff et al. 1998).

As Merrill Lynch (1997) reported, the U.S. President's Advisory Council came up with a number of **options for reform** in January 1997. All of the three plans suggested that part of the social security asset should be invested in instruments other than Treasury bonds. One suggestion was for a centralized system whereby 40% of the assets would be invested in equities by 2014, supervised by an investment policy board nominated by the President and confirmed by the Senate. A second proposal would create individual accounts with a 1.6% supplement to social security contributions. These could be invested in index funds or other types of mutual fund. Whereas

---

3. Examples in the 1990s included Mellon Bank's acquisitions of Dreyfus, Boston and Founder's and Fleet's acquisition of Columbia.

these proposals would retain the current earnings-related social security pension, a third proposal would reduce this to a flat rate system and hypothecate 5% of earnings to mandatory personal savings accounts, which would be privately managed.

It is clear that the second and third of these proposals would **add extra business to the retail asset management sector**, developing from its existing 401(k) plans, although the amounts involved would be sizable only for the third proposal. The first proposal would seem to be more likely to benefit wholesale asset managers, depending on whether the funds were internally or externally managed.

4.2   The Future of U.K. Asset Management

With regard to prospects for U.K. wholesale asset management, the Financial Times (1999) notes that the **balanced manager paradigm is under some pressure** from specialists; 34% of funds had at least one specialist in 1997 and 42% in 1998, and those having three or more specialists accounted for 46% of the total.[4] According to Greenwich Associates (1999a), the proportion of pensions assets managed on a balanced basis fell from 78% in 1997 to 70% in 1999; 18% of funds anticipated hiring new specialist managers and only 1% a balanced manager. Targett and Wine (1999) report a survey by the National Association of Pension Funds according to which, the number of balanced managers hired by the top 430 U.K. pension funds fell 6% to 579 in 1999, and the number of specialist managers rose by 31% to 595.

Indexation has proven to be a popular alternative to balanced management. Its market share has risen to 25% of equities under management and 7% of the market as a whole. Indexation is used by 39% of private funds and 49% of public funds, with a total value of $270 billion. Barclays index fund managers alone gained £11 billion in indexed money in 1998; Legal and General has $85 billion in indexed assets. There were further losses of business by the balanced managers in 1999 (Financial Times 2000), while specialist firms such as those from the United States saw dramatic increases in business.

---

4. Growth of specialist multimanager strategies would further strengthen consultants, which already control 95% of manager appointments, and also provide asset liability modeling and set performance benchmarks. They could come to play a greater role in asset allocation also.

The trend toward specialized and passive management partly **links to the bad performance** of the leading balanced funds in 1997–1998, when they tracked one another and collectively missed out on rises in the United States, which they considered overvalued. Their skills in midrange stocks were not useful. Philips and Drew were particularly adrift, as its value-based approach underperformed. Unilever Pension Fund has threatened Mercury with legal action for underperformance, relative to contract, seeking damages of £100 million (Targett 1999); such disputes link partly to the flawed concept of "tracking errors" of asset managers on the basis of past levels of volatility, that was often built into contracts. But as we noted in chapter 3, the inherent strengths of the leaders means that attrition is slow and could be reversed.

Besides competing with active managers, specialized and passive managers are also competing with each other. For example, in 1998 the specialized managers themselves did badly, with only 26% beating the FTSE index (Booth and Wrighton 1999), and lost some of their business to indexers. On the other hand, specialized and passive managers may also act as complements rather than substitutes in the increasingly popular **core-satellite approach**, in which a passively managed core is complemented by specialist "satellite" portfolios. The former controls overall risk, while the latter target outperformance. Asset allocation is undertaken largely by using index funds. Balanced managers are seeking to compete by offering both core and satellite without the cost of a multimanager approach (Investors Chronicle 1998) while advising on asset allocation and improving their specialist skills. Meanwhile, passive managers are themselves facing challenges such as the need to cope with "mega-shares" such as Vodafone, which at the time of writing accounts for over 10% of the U.K. domestic (FTSE) share index.

U.K. balanced managers are also seeking to regain business from indexers using performance-related fees, bonuses based on beating the index and not a peer group average, focusing on the sectors such as Internet and telecommunications firms that at the time of writing were driving the index, limiting managers' freedom to deviate from index components, and, as we noted, offering index funds themselves. A possible difficulty is that they could find the potential for outperformance sharply reduced. Passive performance for active fees is unlikely to be attractive to sponsors.

The **shift to defined contribution** is expected to gather pace in the United Kingdom, with growth from $45 billion in 1998 to $105 billion in 2003 being anticipated. U.K. companies appear to be attracted to the U.S. 401(k) bundled approach to asset management and record keeping. Nevertheless, brand names will be important, as in the United States. Financial Times (1998) reports a study by Watson Wyatt, which suggests, 68% of asset managers are focused on defined contribution in their new business strategies. The Financial Times (1998) also notes that the balanced, defined benefit managers have a comparative advantage in capturing defined contribution mandates, as the trustees and consultants are used to dealing with them.

A reform in April 2001 will introduce stakeholder pensions: personal pensions that have charges capped at 1% per annum[5] and that all companies with over five employees and no alternative occupational pension fund must offer (see Davis 2000b). This is a major challenge but also an opportunity for efficient providers. Some, however, will face difficulties in adjusting to this low level, as witness the fact that at the time of writing, the annual charge equivalent for personal pensions was as high as 5% (Timmins 1999). Providers are pointing out that advice to pension holders may not be financeable at only 1% per annum, which may lead to inappropriate investment decisions.

Finally, Rajan (2000) conducted a survey of seventy-seven U.K. investment managers and thirty-five follow-up interviews to assess the **coming challenges to asset managers** in the United Kingdom. Interpreting the answers, he suggests that the various forces identified above will drive asset managers in the United Kingdom to one of four types of specialization:[6]

---

5. Stakeholder pensions must also be readily transferable between providers without the charges of as much as 25–33% of assets that are often imposed for current personal pensions (Blake 2000a).

6. From his survey, Rajan found that top executives and senior business managers in asset management firms were considered by their colleagues to be most lacking in strategic thinking, ability to inspire trust, and motivation and awareness of information technology as a business development tool. In contrast, investment managers were most lacking in teamwork, broader business awareness, and personal skills. Following these observations, Rajan suggests also that to be successful in the twenty-first century, U.K. asset managers would need to develop a leadership group that can understand the new market dynamics, "demystify the craft of investment management" without constraining creativity, make it multiskilled, and temper individualism with team discipline.

- the brand management model, focusing on consistent investment performance and convenience for retail clients;
- the business excellence model, providing high investment performance to institutional and high-net-worth clients;
- the global hybrid model, seeking to use a domestic retail brand name to sell multiple products in foreign institutional markets; or
- the virtual fund management model, establishing a low-cost service in direct competition with established institutional asset managers.

These trends, less sharply distinguished, can also be discerned in the predictions of globalization of the industry set out in section 4.4.

4.3   Europe: European Monetary Union and Institutional Investors

The fundamental pressures for growth of Continental European asset management were discussed in chapters 1 and 3, that is, the aging of the population in the context of generous pay-as-you-go pension schemes (see also Davis 1999a, 1999b). Changes are already taking place in the structure of asset management owing to deregulation and autonomous developments. There are also a number of ways in which European Monetary Union (EMU) will tend to accelerate the growth of institutional investors.

4.3.1   Ongoing Forces for Change

Many administrative and regulatory barriers have been removed by the **Investment Services Directive (ISD)**, which since the beginning of 1996 has, inter alia, offered a European "passport" for the first time to fund managers, thus permitting a level playing field in cross-border marketing of investment management (excluding mutual funds; see below). It also imposed capital requirements on investment firms that are intended to allow firms in difficulty an orderly run-down period of three months[7]. The basic requirements for approval under the ISD are that directors must be of good reputation

---

7. Franks and Mayer (1989) question the need for capital requirements for asset managers, suggesting they are an inappropriate barrier to entry and that consumer protection would better be served by conduct-of-business rules (some of which are also mandated under the ISD).

and have adequate experience, the firm must be a legal entity, at least two people must take part in the decision-making process, and the head office must be in the same member state as the registered office. On the other hand, there has been much delay in the ISD's implementation, which has hindered cross-border competition. In addition, loopholes in the Directive have been widely used for protectionist purposes (see Steil 1996).

Another important force for liberalization is the **UCITS Directive**, which opened the way for cross-border marketing of mutual funds authorized in a member states. Under UCITS, which came into operation in 1989, general rules are specified for mutual funds' investments and sales. The home country is responsible for regulatory requirements for fund management and certification, while rules regarding disclosure and selling practices are a host country matter. Permitted funds include synthetic funds based on derivatives, which were previously forbidden in some centers. Under UCITS, 90% of mutual fund assets must be invested in publicly traded companies, the fund may not own more than 5% of a single company's stock, and there are limits on borrowing. Real estate, commodity, and money market funds are excluded from the Directive. There remain problems with UCITS, notably the requirement to publish prospectuses and the like in local languages, protectionism against foreign managers as a consequence of the host country basis of the Directive, and exclusion of funds of funds (i.e., mutual funds that invest solely in other funds) and some cash and venture capital funds. These are being addressed in a new Directive.

Insurance companies also benefit from Single Market Directives, which allow services and products to be offered across the European Union. Single banking licenses under the **Banking Directives** are valid also for institutional investment, for the case of banks including asset management and advice and trading in securities.

The European Commission drafted a **Pension Fund Directive** to complement these acts, but it was ultimately abandoned in the face of irreconcilable differences over the appropriate liberalization of international investment (see Davis 1996b). The European Commission is currently planning a new attempt at a Directive on prudential rules for occupational pension funds, with a bias toward a prudent man principle and mutual recognition of supervisory systems, thus allowing cross-border provision of services and cross-border membership. Progress will also be sought on removal of obstacles to labor mobility (seeking to facilitate pan-European schemes) and appropriate coordination of tax systems with regard to pensions (abolishing tax discrimination on pension and life insurance products offered cross-border). See the Commission Communication of 11 May 1999 for details (European Commission 1999).

European countries are **developing professional bodies** of asset managers and analysts that, by contributing to the understanding of financial markets, risk, and return, are tending to enhance competition. The European Federation of Financial Analysts' Societies is in the process of developing a single European examination of fund manager competence. Further development of performance measurement, shifts toward equities/international investment, and use of derivatives are aiding competition. And the tendency toward cross-border acquisitions of fund managers (notably of U.K. managers by German and Swiss banks) is already facilitating consolidation at a European level, although the motivation of such mergers may be partly a desire to consolidate entrenched positions at home.

Some autonomous developments are also relevant. One point is that Continental European pension funds are often willing to **invest in mutual fund shares** (using bargaining power to reduce fees), hence reducing the sharpness of the distinction of the retail and wholesale sectors. Moreover, there is considerable **interest in passive or indexed funds** for cost reasons, in which foreign managers typically have a comparative advantage. According to Broby (1997) indexation is used by 15% of E.U. pension funds. Wells Fargo Nikko has attracted $6 billion in funds in the Netherlands despite strong local competition. Use of derivatives, mainly for risk control, is increasing; in 1995, the WM company reported that a third of 1455 European pension funds that it monitored made use of derivative markets (although most were in the United Kingdom). Related to this, there is an increasing focus on the so-called middle office, which seeks to monitor investment risk.

Another trend that may start to break traditional patterns is **the growth of international investment**, which is also promoting foreign managers. According to Intersec (1995), 40% of specialist international mandates in E.U. countries and two thirds of cross-border mandates (valued at $30 billion) went to foreigners based in the United Kingdom. Deregulation of portfolio restrictions will accelerate this process, as will EMU (see below). Moreover, there is a **shift to independent managers**, accounting for 22% of external manager appointments by E.U. pension funds and life insurers, implying a decline in the strength of banking relationships. Mercer (1996) noted that specialist mandates at E.U. pension funds had doubled in the four preceding years. Nondomestic firms accounted for 13% of mandates in Belgium and 7.5% in the Netherlands.

4.3.2 EMU and Pension Provision

The EMU context enhances **pressure for reform of public pension systems**. This links to fiscal integration in EMU, notably because in the context of an effective Stability and Growth Pact, there would be much less scope than would otherwise be the case for governments to run large deficits to cushion rises in taxes when aging becomes an acute burden on social security. This would be the case even if such deficits are desired as part of a strategy of reform that aims to distribute the burden of transition to funding between generations.[8] To avoid sharp rises in taxation, governments will seek to deal with their social security obligations and switch to funding of pensions at an earlier stage.

Furthermore, owing to the so-called "no-bailout clause" in the Maastricht Treaty,[9] financial markets in general and rating agencies in particular are putting an increasing focus on general government obligations, of which pension liabilities are the largest part (De Ryck 1997). Furthermore, transparency in terms of differences in prices and costs, for example owing to social security contributions, together with enhanced capital mobility is tending to put countries imposing high taxes on employers for social security purposes under greater pressure to adapt their systems. The risk is that companies will shift operations elsewhere, where such taxes are less onerous. Meanwhile, pay-as-you-go hinders international labor mobility, which will be of crucial importance in EMU.

Finally, firms in Germany with **book-reserve pension liabilities** are keen to shift to a fully funded basis, given the ongoing shift to market value accounting, which will make such liabilities apparent, as well as the impact of such liabilities on their credit ratings, where

8. Note that reforms that seek to distribute the costs of transition from pay-as-you-go to funding between generations may in principle involve heavy government borrowing and deficits. Pure tax financing leaves all the burden on the current generation of workers. See Holzmann (1997).
9. Both the monetary authorities and other fiscal authorities are debarred under the Treaty from rescuing a country in fiscal crisis.

ratings are increasingly crucial to the cost of capital in the securitizing EMU capital market. The proposed tax reform of 2000 should
make it easier for pension assets and liabilities to go into separately
capitalized pension funds.

4.3.3 Improved Conditions for Institutional Investment under EMU

Macroeconomic and financial conditions in EMU also favor growth
of institutions. Since monetary integration seems likely to give rise to
sustained lower inflation, at least in some countries, it will make it
easier for defined benefit pension funds to finance inflation indexation, while pension benefits from defined contribution funds will
also more readily retain their purchasing power (Dickinson 1992).

Financial integration is also making institutional investment more
attractive by leading to a **better risk-return trade-off** being attain-
able. One aspect is increases in the range of instruments available,
owing, for example, to broader availability of corporate bonds and
securitized loans, especially as the supply of government bonds
diminishes. Increased liquidity and lower transactions costs resulting
from market integration in EMU are increasing institutions' comparative advantage over bank intermediation. If, as some analysts
argue, EMU is accompanied by a reduction in the risk and return on
"domestic" bonds and an increase in the risk and return on equity,[10]
there would be a beneficial widening out of the frontier of efficient
portfolios in the euro area[11], increasing the potential combinations of
risk and returns that may be sought.

---

10. Return and risk on long bonds could well be lower in the longer term than in the
absence of EMU, owing to elimination of exchange rate risk, correction of budgetary
difficulties, a reduction in perceptions of inflation risk, in some countries a decline in
expected inflation, and lower short-term rates. Corporate restructuring, by increasing
efficiency, may raise the return on equities. Companies desiring to issue in the integrated euro area equity markets may face greater pressure to act in the interests of
investors, again tending to boost returns. However, heightened vulnerability of local
economies in EMU to asymmetric shocks could increase risks on equity for companies
that are dependent on the domestic economy. And integration reduces the diversification benefit of different national markets (Beckers 1999).

11. The euro area or euro zone comprises the 11 countries which adopted the Single
Currency, the euro, on January 1st 1999. These are Austria, Belgium, Finland, France,
Germany, Ireland, Italy, Luxembourg, the Netherlands, Portugal, and Spain. The
European Union countries not adopting the euro at that time were Denmark, Greece,
Sweden, and the United Kingdom.

Regulations limiting international investment have ceased to be effective in the context of the euro zone, with accompanying increased correlation of national markets leading to sectoral investment across the whole of the euro zone.[12] Besides eliminating the effects of home bias and diversifying portfolios across the euro area, a sectoral approach necessitates a major restructuring of portfolios as for example industrial stocks are 45% of the German market and 11% of the Spanish market.

EMU is leading to **increased competition among asset managers** that previously monopolized national markets, with those having pan-euro-zone expertise having a decisive advantage. Since asset managers are increasingly competing in euro-area-wide investment, the scope to compare their performance also increases, thus strengthening forces of competition. An aspect of this is cross-border activity. Mercer (2000), for example, notes that in 1999–2000, forty-one of the top European money managers operate in five or more countries, whereas in 1996, the corresponding number was only seventeen. Besides benefiting returns, competition should mean that the high fees and hidden charges noted in section 3.6.1.3 should diminish. One factor putting pressure on costs is the popularity of indexation, with European indexed pension funds growing by 28% in 1998 and further following EMU. Passive managers apparently benefit from the lack of an entrenched equity culture. In EMU, active managers are finding it hard to compete with indexers, since the main focus of cross-border investment is on the top 200 shares in EMU, and it is harder to find undervalued stocks among such giants than among smaller firms. Also the scope for active management diminishes, owing to the loss of currency risk in EMU (Beckers 1999).

Overall, EMU should also increase demand for the product of asset management as well as provoking an immense merger wave in E.U. asset management (Wrighton 1998).

Investors and corporate sponsors are perceiving that freedom for institutional investors to invest across the euro area offers beneficial results for risks and returns. This may encourage them **to exert pressure on governments for broader deregulation**, especially of international investment outside the European Union and investment in equities. (See Pragma Consulting (1999) for a survey of cur-

---

12. Beckers (1999) showed increased correlation to be an established trend even before EMU.

rent opinion in the industry.) Sponsoring firms in particular may press for this to reduce costs of their own pension provision in the context of heightened product market competition following EMU. Further weight may hence be put behind the European Commission's plans to liberalize pension fund investment and institute a full prudent man approach. Note, however, that for multinationals, a key issue is tax divergences that prevent a pan-European pension fund. At the time of writing, a group of companies (the Pan European Pensions Group) are challenging tax inequalities regarding funded pensions in the European Court of Justice.

In due course, in a deeper securities market, there may arise **financial innovations** that are tailored to institutions' needs. These could include currently unavailable instruments such as bonds with returns linked to average earnings, which could be useful for life insurers and pension funds in matching assets to liabilities.

4.3.4 Pressures on Banks' Traditional Business

Banks in Europe are facing **challenges to their traditional business** under EMU that will lead them to seek to expand their asset management activities to maintain profitability. An immediate aspect is the elimination of commissions for foreign exchange transactions within the euro area. Lower inflation in some countries due to monetary integration has reduced interest rate margins,[13] owing to the elimination of the so-called endowment effect profit from zero-interest sight deposits in a context of positive rates of inflation. Moreover, as financial integration increases, competition between banks for wholesale deposits and loans is also tending to intensify. For example, EMU gives multinationals the opportunity to consolidate treasury operations that were formerly spread across different currency zones (McCauley and White (1997), White (1998)). In addition, the transparency generated by the single currency is also allowing bank customers generally to compare rates and fees more readily across borders, thus threatening traditional relationship banking links. In the longer term, formerly insulated national retail banking markets in which domestic competition is already intensifying may also become subject to intensified cross-border competition in a single-currency environment.

---

13. The margin is the difference between the average rate on loans and the average rate on deposits.

The scope for **disintermediation of traditional banking activities is increasing**, as witness the rapid growth of corporate bond issuance by E.U. firms in 1999. By issuing bonds, firms are avoiding the "cost and relative inflexibility of the covenant burden of bank loans" (Bishop 1998). Disintermediation could be of considerable importance, since banks' current share of lending to companies is 73% in France, 77% in Germany, and only 22% in the United States. Lower-quality firms may also be able to obtain bond market financing if the higher-yield bond market develops further[14] as predicted by Cooper (1998), among others. The integrated money markets generated by EMU are facilitating the use of commercial paper for short-term borrowing by companies and security repurchase agreements (repos) and commercial paper as alternative repositories for liquidity to bank deposits.

For all of these reasons, Continental universal banks are increasing their **focus on asset management and other investment banking services** as a result of EMU, as the means to ensure continuing profitability and taking advantage of their distributional advantages. This is particularly marked in countries such as Germany, where the major commercial banks are seeking to redefine their business focus toward investment banking and aim to downplay or even eliminate their traditional—and relatively unprofitable—domestic retail and corporate banking.

4.3.5 The Scope of Potential Change in Financing

The thrust of the points made above is that the euro zone will increasingly feature much less banking activity and more securities market financing and institutional investment. In this context, the massive growth in bond issuance in 1999 (see Bank of England 1999) shows that the new securitized system is developing much more rapidly than had previously been predicted. Pragma Consulting (1999) have predicted that pension assets in Europe will rise $2–5 billion per annum over the next ten years.

---

14. A helpful contribution to this development is that EMU may lower public information costs, owing to the integration of markets for goods and services across the European Union (IMF 1997). This is because in such a situation, there will be less need for detailed knowledge of local market conditions; sectoral specialization by equity or credit analysts across the union would be sufficient for pricing of equity and debt claims.

Table 4.1 gives an idea of the **scale of the likely shift in financing** that would be entailed should the euro area resemble the United States in terms of the value of instruments relative to GDP. Institutional investment would rise markedly except in Luxembourg, the United Kingdom, and the Netherlands. There would also be enormous growth of equity market capitalization and bonds outstanding, offset by a major contraction of the banking sector. The overall change in total assets is very small, because financial assets outstanding are equivalent to just over 300% of GDP in both the United States and the euro area (see table 5.3). Of course, the absolute adjustment in terms of money values (in particular the contraction of the banking sector) shown in the table is most unlikely to occur. Rather, it would take place over time in terms of differential growth rates. Moreover, the U.S. banking system was historically more strictly regulated in terms of products and geographical location than the European one. Equally, there are various structural factors that would limit balance sheet convergence with the United States and within Europe, such as the absence of a government-backed mortgage-backed securities market in Europe (Bishop 1998), differing liquidity preferences of the household sector, fiscal differences, and residual regulatory differences.

4.4   Globalization of the Industry?

The asset management industry is one of the world's key growth industries and has reached an impressive size. As we showed in chapter 1, current estimates suggest that assets under management are approaching $30 trillion. Already, the assets of the top five global asset managers are equivalent to the combined GDP of the United Kingdom and France, while the top thirty-five have assets equivalent to U.S. GDP.

Although portfolios tend to be invested mainly in domestic markets, **cross-border investment is growing more strongly than average**, with portfolio flows into the United States of $200 billion per annum in recent years and outflows of around $100 billion. In parallel, financial markets are themselves becoming more global and integrated, while domestic markets are becoming more open to foreign competition. Global agreements are also helpful, such as the GATT, which declares that "no party may adopt any measure

Table 4.1
Adjustment to Financial Structure in E.U. Countries if There Were Convergence on the U.S. Pattern ($ billion/% of GDP)

	Equities (Market Cap)	Percent of GDP	Government Bonds	Percent of GDP	Private Bonds	Percent of GDP	Bank Assets	Percent of GDP	Total	Percent of GDP	Institutional Investors	Percent of GDP
E.U. −15	5093	62	3298	40	1963	24	−11695	−134	−1223	−14	5962	71
E.U. −11	5733	82	2846	41	1828	26	−9246	−133	0	0	5890	86
Belgium	173	69	−42	−17	15	6	−657	−253	−522	−201	234	87
Denmark	127	75	46	27	−73	−43	−65	−36	32	18	135	78
Germany	2024	88	1253	57	315	14	−2893	−127	433	19	2395	99
Greece	104	95	7	6	59	60	−15	−12	173	143	N.A.	N.A.
Spain	528	80	353	53	341	53	−554	−99	320	57	605	107
France	1278	80	802	51	382	24	−2235	−132	271	16	1082	70
Ireland	41	63	35	53	19	57	−113	−156	9	13	N.A.	N.A.
Italy	1004	93	−247	−23	249	23	−1173	−96	49	4	1394	125
Luxembourg	−12	−64	15	90	0	−1	−590	−3552	−592	−3566	−341	−1797
Netherlands	51	14	146	40	154	42	−498	−131	−171	−45	−52	−13
Austria	224	102	131	61	58	27	−354	−160	38	17	258	110
Portugal	79	89	40	45	36	40	−149	−139	41	38	114	111
Finland	74	64	59	50	33	28	−45	−37	121	98	120	95
Sweden	50	20	90	36	−13	−5	−79	−32	−2	−1	67	29
United Kingdom	−344	−29	723	60	504	42	−2267	−180	−1399	−111	−188	−17

N.A. = not available.
Source: Davis (1999b) based on 1996 data; see table 5.3 for levels.
Note: the E.U. −11 refers to the eleven European countries which have adopted the Single Currency, the euro, while the E.U. −15 refers to the whole of the European Union. See footnote 11 of this chapter.

restricting any type of cross-border trade in financial services by financial service providers that is permitted to another party."

In chapter 3, we showed that each national market has a distinctive profile shaped by factors such as local regulations, taxation, and legal provisions as well as demand and distribution. For this reason, we treated the United Kingdom, the United States, and Continental Europe as separate entities. But S.I. Davis (1997) foresees **growing globalization of asset management**. He argues that this will be driven largely by performance, with a product that can outperform the market being attractive across borders, depending of course on how penetrable markets prove to be. Other developments that would prove attractive in less developed markets include fund supermarkets, benchmarking of performance, superior product and performance information for small investors, and segregation of fund management if it takes place within a financial conglomerate. Global or regional marketing organizations such as those created by Fidelity and Merrill Lynch will create a growing consciousness of the global nature of the market. Furthermore, there is the growing liberalization of investment for pension funds (such as that which will be triggered by EMU), which will increase the scope for global institutions to offer a full range of products.

Berlinski and Western (1997) of Goldman Sachs also argue strongly that globalization of the industry is on the cards. The reasons are:

• the progressive aging of the population, necessitating increased funding;

• the increased focus on equity investment, expertise in which is rather concentrated in the United States (and the United Kingdom); and

• the expertise in defined contribution pensions, which is concentrated in the United States.

This has led global financial service companies wishing to expand asset management to acquire U.S. asset managers. For example, the French AXA Group now owns the Equitable company of the United States, which has around $200 billion under management. More generally, over 20% of the assets under management globally have seen their managers change ownership since 1989, which suggests that a degree of consolidation within the industry is underway. It may be added that mergers have also taken place from outside the industry, with investment banks and commercial banks being keen to increase the share of their profits earned from relatively stable asset management fees, given declining and volatile profits in sectors such as trading and underwriting.

According to the view of Berlinski and Western (1997), globalization of investing—including growing international investment—is seen as creating in due course a **single global market for asset management**. Those that succeed will need access to capital resources to finance such strategies (fund management personnel, distribution, systems, technology, and new product research and development). They will also need a trustworthy brand name and long track records of successful international experience. A broad-based franchise is needed to weather the volatility that is a feature of international business. For asset management firms, the only alternative to tailoring products for the global market will be establishment as niche competitors in domestic markets.

As we outlined in chapter 1, **aging of the population** is clearly an important driving force for increased demand for asset management and may be increasingly so in the future, even more so in Europe and Japan than in the United States. Berlinski and Western (1997) estimate that the demographic effect may raise assets of pension funds at a global level from $7.3 trillion in the mid-1990s to $12 trillion in the early twenty-first century. There will be a need for $2 trillion of new investments (the rest being organic growth), of which Goldman Sachs estimates that half will be cross-border equity investment and a third will be domestic equity investment. The pressures on pension systems will stimulate both growth of funded provision and deregulation of investment markets. It will also help to generate further globalization of capital markets, further fueling consolidation of the industry on a global scale. Goldman Sachs estimates that the outcome could be six to ten major global players.

Another argument for globalization is the **difficulty for medium-sized firms** of controlling costs. As Graham (1997) noted, marketing costs in both wholesale and retail sectors have risen strongly, while salaries for star analysts and fund managers have soared. Price pressures are arising from dissatisfaction with performance, particularly by pension funds, and the competition from passive management.

Certainly, there have been a number of **international takeovers**, such as Zurich Insurance for Kemper Securities, and Barclays of

Wells Fargo Nikko.[15] More recently, there has been the $5 billion takeover of Mercury Asset Management by Merrill Lynch, aimed at exploiting opportunities in the European markets; the SBC-UBS merger, which created the world's largest investment management firm; and Schroders-Salomon Brothers/Citibank. Only the largest of global firms have been able to afford the prices involved in such deals. Experience of past merger waves in other industries suggests that such a trend may well continue, regardless of the underlying economic justifications, as firms seek not to be left out for strategic reasons—not least to avoid being taken over themselves.

A recent recapitulation of the case for globalization is in Moon et al. (1998), again of Goldman Sachs. Besides the points made above, they note that U.S. firms' competitiveness has been sharpened by intense competition and the shift to retail management, and they also benefit from economies of scale gained at home. Consequently, they will seek opportunities abroad where there are similar fundamentals but less developed markets for asset management. But they acknowledge that these opportunities may not be available at present. There is believed to be an even higher minimum efficient scale for global companies than for U.S. domestic ones, meaning that very few will be able to adopt a global strategy. The most attractive route to a global strategy may be in partnership with local universal banks in Continental Europe.

There are also **counterarguments to the globalization hypothesis**. **Diseconomies of scale** may arise for giant firms. In the short term, there may be costs of mergers in terms of performance and staff defections. In the long term, the risk of moving markets against a firm, given that liquidity may be insufficient to cope with the largest deals, may tell against size. The advantages to specialized niche players[16] may continue to constitute important barriers to the domination of markets such as that in the United States by giant firms. Financial Times (1998) notes that whereas 43% of managers claim that their firms wish to be global, only 34% of managers would like to be in such companies. Regulatory provisions such as ERISA will continue to favor wide diversification of external managers by pension funds.

---

15. This coincided with Goldman's acquisition of Van Kampen American Capital for $21.5 billion in 1995.
16. These include the importance of personal contact, suspicion of conflicts of interest, and difficulty of retaining star managers within large firms.

Agency costs could be severe in giant asset management organizations. When the predator is an investment bank, there is particular concern that it might use its fund management arm to dispose of poorly performing securities issues (in the traditional manner of Continental universal banks). Taxation and regulation constitute barriers to progress in cross-border sales, requiring dedicated systems and products in each country and little opportunity to exploit economies of scale. Indeed, seemingly global firms such as AXA may be characterized as collections of ring-fenced national asset pools. It is also notable that UBS-SBC left the Philips and Drew firm as a separate entity at the time of the merger, given its strong position in the United Kingdom. Even switches to defined contribution, as in the "stakeholder pension" in the United Kingdom, may not require U.S.-style integrated asset management and administration.

Moreover, **changes in investor preferences will also be needed** to make an evolution toward global standard products viable;[17] no firm has yet managed to create a global brand and strength in all global markets. Also the limitations of available distribution channels will form a barrier to expansion in the retail sector, notably in Continental Europe, where local oligopolists—usually big banks—control distribution (see table 3.11). Indeed, Moon et al. (1998) conclude that the retail distribution issue is "so vexing" that the best opportunities for entry there are in institutional wholesale management and in 401(k)-type plans, in which the integrated product of U.S. houses should offer an advantage. In other words, there may exist a demand for global investor skills but not necessarily for global asset management companies in the sense of firms with asset management and distribution operations in many countries.

4.5   Questionnaire Answers Relating to the Structure and Dynamics of Asset Management Sectors

A questionnaire was circulated to a large number of institutional investors' chief investment officers in early 1998, posing questions relating to market structure, conduct, and performance as well as future prospects. Part of the questionnaire was designed to illustrate some of the issues raised in chapters 3 and 4 from the investors' own

---

17. The severity of the pensions crisis could lead to such a shift, that is, toward equities.

points of view. Further aspects of the questionnaire, relating to the demands of institutions with respect to securities market performance, are outlined in Schwartz and Steil (2000) and chapter 8.

4.5.1 Sample Characteristics

Completed responses were obtained from seventy-two institutions of 850 contacted; that is, the response rate was 8.5%. This is comparable with other such samples, and the funds under management of the firms in the sample are substantial. A total of $2066 billion was declared by the respondents, a figure that, if accurate, accounts for around 15% of world mutual and pension funds and around 10% of the total institutional assets as identified in section 1.1.2.

The **features of the sample** are set out in table 4.2. With regard to the geographical coverage of the sample in terms of number of responses, there is a majority of U.S. asset managers (54%), with a further 19% and 11% coming from Canada and Australia, respectively. U.K. coverage is 8%, and Continental Europe 7%. Accordingly, the sample is almost wholly composed of Anglo-Saxon-based managers, whose approach may differ from that of managers in Continental Europe and Japan. Furthermore, of these Anglo-Saxon managers, the vast majority are based in North America (73%). These may share specific views and preconceptions that are not present elsewhere.

The pattern may be compared with the assets under management figures provided in chapter 1 to illustrate that the structure of the sample is to some extent unrepresentative of global patterns of asset management. There we showed that the North American share of all institutional investors is around 60%, with Japan accounting for 15% and Europe 25%. On the other hand, the sample is more accurate for mutual funds and pension funds alone (i.e., disregarding life and non–life insurance companies). The share of North America in these sectors is indeed 70%, with Japan accounting for only 8%. Europe is then 20%, which is again not far from our sample's coverage. Australia and Canada are clearly overrepresented, however. With regard to the sample characteristics by region, U.S. firms had on average $18 billion in assets under management (median: $6.5 billion), Canadian and European investors are larger (around $60 billion average), and Australians are smaller at around $5 billion on average.

Table 4.2
Questionnaire Sample Characteristics (Total Number of Respondents: 72)

Region	Percent
United States	54
Canada	19
Australia	11
Non-Europe	85
Europe	15
United Kingdom	8
Primary Investment Approach	
Value/growth	68
Quant-driven active	11
Indexation/passive	7
Asset allocation (e.g., country funds)	3
Other	6
Asset Allocation	
Equities	63
Bonds	29
Cash/property	7
Foreign assets	13
Percentage of Funds Invested in Equities	
Under 50%	21
50% or more	64
Percentage of Funds Invested Abroad	
Under 20%	58
20% or more	29
Value of Assets under Management	
Under $1 billion	14
$1–10 billion	42
Over $10 billion	33
Type of Organization	
Independent investment management firm or mutual fund operation	38
Subsidiary of bank insurance company or brokerage firm	29
Department of a bank insurance company or brokerage firm	12
Corporate pension fund	6
Public pension fund	7
Responsibility for Share Trading in the Organization	
Centralized dealing desk	81
Portfolio manager	16
Trader/trading desk	3
Other	3
Percentage of Funds Deriving Directly from Individual Investors	
Under 50%	53
50% or more	19
Percentage of Funds Subject Wholly to Company's Discretion	
Under 50%	26
50% and over	58

Note: numbers may not add to 100 owing to duplicated or omitted responses.

Turning to the primary investment approach of the asset managers in the sample, as shown in table 4.2, this is overwhelmingly traditional value- or growth-based active management (68%). The shares of quant-driven active management (11%) and asset allocation/indexation/passive (10%) are much less. This is broadly in line with the shares of the different approaches in terms of numbers of managers, as set out in chapter 3, but may somewhat underweight passive management in terms of the proportion of assets that are invested by this means. Indeed, the detailed results of the survey show that the active asset managers have an average of $21 billion in assets under management, while the quant-driven managers have $31 billion, and the passive/indexers have $135 billion. This is in line with the greater economies of scale for indexers as hypothesized in chapter 3.

The share of assets under management in the sample accounted for by firms with assets under management of less than $1 billion is 14%, with 42% being by firms with $1–10 billion and 33% managed by firms with over $10 billion. This result tends to underpin the results of the survey in terms of the share of the market accounted for, albeit not in terms of the numbers of managers. For, as we note in chapter 3, the size distribution of managers is actually much more skewed toward the smaller end. In effect, we received a preponderance of responses from the larger managers, which account for a greater proportion of assets under management.

The types of organization involved in the sample are mainly either independent investment managers/mutual fund operations (38%) or subsidiaries of banks, insurance companies, or brokerage firms (29%). The other categories were departments of banks, insurance companies, or brokerage firms (12%) and corporate or public pension funds (13%). Thirteen percent is somewhat smaller than the proportion of pension funds invested internally, but bearing in mind that mutual funds are all externally managed (in terms of this classification), the proportions are reasonable. Eighty percent of the sample have a centralized dealing desk that is responsible for equity trading.

Turning to the asset distributions of the firms in the sample, there is a preponderance of equity investment, in line with the market pattern for pension funds and mutual funds worldwide, weighted by assets (see tables 1.10 and 1.12). The equity share is 63% on average across the sample, while the bond share is 29%, the remainder being cash and property. The share of foreign assets is 13% on average, with the European share being much larger at 30–40% and the U.S. share lower at around 9%. This is as would be anticipated from the aggregate figures shown in chapter 1. In the sample as a whole, two thirds have less than 20% of assets invested abroad, and two thirds have 50% or more in equities.

The question of "instividualization" was addressed by asking the asset managers the proportion of assets derived from individual investors. Of those responding, around three fourths had under 50% so derived. In other words, we have a largely wholesale sample. Interinstitutional investments may, of course, be not only company pension funds, but also managers that operate on behalf of pension and mutual funds. Finally, the percentage of funds that are subject wholly to the asset management companies' discretion is typically 50% or more. This may, of course, entail only security selection and not asset allocation.

4.5.2 Elements of Competition in the Market

A first question related to the key elements of competition in the respective markets. For this and the following questions, the responses were classified by the strength of conviction, from 1 (unimportant) to 5 (very important) for each factor. The percentage of firms responding to each set of questions is variable (although for each question, a minimum of two thirds responded). The responses are summarized by the mean response, on which we mainly focus. In the text, we supplement the average results shown in the tables with insights derived from subsamples by region, size of firm, and type of activity.

As table 4.3 shows, the most **important elements in competition are seen to be performance relative to other institutions and relationships with consultants and advisors**, both of which have a mean score of 4 or more. These are the core of the manager selection process, or so-called beauty contest. This pattern is highly consistent with the view, on the one hand, that asset managers are competing with one another as much as or more than with the market (which, as shown in chapter 5, may give rise to herding behavior) and, on the other hand, that the reputation with the public is less important than the reputation with the facilitators who engage asset managers for other institutional investors (as discussed in chapter 3). There is

Table 4.3
What Are the Key Elements of Competition in Asset Management?

Answers Ranked from 1 (Unimportant) to 5 (Very Important)	5	4	3	2	1	Mean	Percent Response
Low fees and charges	12	26	45	14	3	3.31	90
Performance in terms of absolute return	39	36	14	3	8	3.97	92
Performance in terms of risk-adjusted return	17	38	29	15	2	3.53	92
Performance relative to other institutions	55	31	9	5	0	4.37	90
Specialization in terms of asset class or sector	14	25	49	9	3	3.37	90
Use of innovative portfolio management techniques (including index tracking)	8	11	34	39	8	2.72	89
Advertising/name recognition	12	35	25	20	8	3.25	90
Level of assets under management	6	31	34	25	5	3.09	90
Reputation with consultants and advisors	39	38	16	3	5	4.03	89
Other (please specify)							

no geographical pattern to the responses regarding relative performance, whereas the importance of consultants and advisors is shown to be somewhat greater in Europe and Australia than in North America. The passive/indexation managers give rather lower scores to performance and reputation, as might be expected, given the mechanical nature of their investment activities. Finally, the smaller managers (with funds of under $6.2 billion) have a greater need for reputation than their larger counterparts, but the relative performance scores are identical, showing that even the largest managers are not immune to losses of business from poor relative performance.

With regard to other factors that are seen as important, there is a high score for absolute performance and a somewhat lower one for the risk-adjusted return (consistent with the view that risk is not yet accorded as much importance as normal portfolio considerations set out in chapter 2 would suggest). Despite the expected high score for absolute return, the considerable shortfall compared to relative return is noteworthy. Absolute return scores highest in the United States and Australia, albeit in each case falling short of relative return. Scores in the United Kingdom, Canada, and Continental Europe are relatively low for absolute performance, suggesting strongly comparison-driven markets for asset management there. This may link to the predominance of balanced managers, whose performance, as argued in chapter 3, is relatively hard to assess in absolute terms. Meanwhile, Australia shows an unusually high ranking (4) for risk-adjusted returns, which may relate to the predominance of defined contribution plans in that country and consequent focus on risk as well as return, given that such risks are borne by individuals.

The lower ranking of absolute return compared to relative return also holds for all the types of primary investment approach, even the growth/value-based managers, although the absolute level of the score for absolute performance is higher for growth/value-based traditional managers than for the others. Reflecting the size pattern (in which traditional active managers tend to be small relative to others), the smaller managers also put a higher premium on absolute performance than the larger ones do.

Scores of slightly above moderately significant (i.e., an average mark of 3) are gained for low fees and charges, specialization in terms of asset class or sector, and advertising/name recognition. The result for fees is consistent with the view set out in chapter 3 that fees are not seen as decisive in terms of awarding of mandates for asset management (bearing in mind that the vast majority of managers in the sample are taking funds not directly from the public but from other institutions). As might be expected, the fees and charges are seen as a more important plus point for the passive and quant-driven managers, averaging a score of around 4 in each case compared to 3.33 for the sample as a whole. Scores for specialization and advertising are evenly distributed both geographically and by investment approach; advertising is thought to be more important for the smaller firms, showing a need to develop reputation by this means.

Factors that are thought to be of rather less significance are levels of assets under management and use of innovative portfolio management techniques. To some extent, such responses might be expected from a sample that is largely formed of traditional active asset managers. Accordingly, the importance of techniques is seen as high by the quant-driven and passive managers but not the others. Interestingly, there is no distinction between small and larger asset managers in terms of the importance accorded to size (bearing in mind that benefits of size may accrue indirectly via the other factors such as reputation and name recognition).

4.5.3 Barriers to Entry in Domestic Markets

Industrial economics, as set out in chapter 3, puts a great deal of emphasis on barriers to entry in markets that are based on sunk costs as a structural feature that may influence performance and profitability. If there are no entry barriers, markets will be competitive or contestable (depending on economies of scale), and hence profitability will be at a minimum needed to keep firms in the industry. Otherwise, some monopoly profits can be obtained. Evidence on entry barriers also casts further light on the nature of competition—by highlighting the factors that might prevent firms from competing in a given market in the first place.

We asked firms what factors might hinder them from entering markets in their home country where they are not currently active. As table 4.4 shows, the responses indicate a **decisive importance for incumbent firms' distribution channels/selling networks, relationships with clients, and their reputations more generally**. All of these have mean scores of over 3.5. These responses are consistent with the view that there are intertemporal dependencies in the sector that give rise to sunk costs: Existing firms can hold on to their clients unless their performance becomes exceptionally poor. The creation of

Table 4.4

What Are the Main Barriers for Your Firm in Entering Domestic Sectors Where It Is Not Currently Active?

Answers Ranked from 1 (Unimportant) to 5 (Very Important)	5	4	3	2	1	Mean	Percent Response
Reputation of existing firms	14	43	29	9	5	3.52	78
Existing firms' relationships with clients	20	38	32	5	5	3.61	78
Existing firms' distribution channels/ selling networks	29	36	27	5	4	3.8	78
Existing firms' expertise/technical capabilities	9	43	30	14	4	3.39	78
Existing firms' lower unit costs	2	24	40	24	11	2.82	76
Capital or marketing costs	4	18	53	20	6	2.95	76
Existing firms' local information	6	18	40	24	13	2.8	76
Established investor preferences	6	29	51	11	4	3.22	76
Regulatory barriers	0	9	36	38	16	2.38	76
Other (please specify)							

distribution channels and selling networks could act as a strategic investment discouraging entry (although realistically, they are more likely to be a by-product of regular business). These factors were thought to be of particular importance in Canada and Europe (including the United Kingdom). They were less crucial (albeit still scoring highest) in the United States and Australia. The index/ passive funds saw them as being of greater importance than did the others; also, the smaller firms saw such barriers as more important than did the larger ones, except for distribution networks and selling channels, in which the importance was considered equal.

The next most important barriers were the expertise and technical capability of the existing firms and established investor preferences. The latter may be seen as a product of the reputation and relationships of existing firms highlighted above; but it scored much lower in the United States than elsewhere, suggesting a degree of "footlooseness" for (institutional) investors vis-à-vis fund managers that was not present elsewhere. Meanwhile, expertise and technical capability cover the quality of the investment management process and its outcome in terms of returns. This element was highlighted notably in the United Kingdom and Europe. It is worthy of note that whereas we saw in section 4.5.2 that relative performance is given somewhat greater weight than reputation as a means of competing in existing markets (i.e., in gaining a larger share of the available assets under management), reputation is more important than relative performance for cross-market entry.

A number of factors are shown to be relatively unimportant as barriers to entry. These were the lower unit costs of existing firms, capital or marketing costs that might need to be incurred, existing firms' local information, and, particularly, regulatory barriers. The responses in terms of information and regulation are perhaps to be expected given that the question related to entry into different sectors in the domestic market (e.g., a pension fund asset manager entering the mutual fund sector). But the responses in terms of costs are more revealing. Lower unit costs were highlighted only by the passive/indexers, which, as we noted in chapter 3, is precisely the sector in which economies of scale are most marked. The implication is that in other sectors, economies of scale are not important barriers to entry.

Table 4.5
What Are the Main Barriers for Your Firm in Entering Foreign Markets?

Answers Ranked from 1 (Unimportant) to 5 (Very Important)	5	4	3	2	1	Mean	% Response
Reputation of existing firms	20	48	20	2	11	3.63	64
Existing firms' relationships with clients	29	38	18	4	11	3.69	64
Existing firms' distribution channels / selling networks	40	36	13	0	11	3.93	64
Existing firms' expertise / technical capabilities	7	33	35	13	13	3.07	64
Existing firms' lower unit costs	7	7	50	17	16	2.48	61
Capital or marketing costs	4	28	43	13	13	2.98	63
Existing firms' local information	15	38	28	6	13	3.36	65
Established investor preferences	11	38	34	9	9	3.34	65
Regulatory barriers	13	24	31	18	13	3.07	63
Other (please specify)							

4.5.4 Barriers to Entry in Foreign Markets

The same question concerning barriers to entry was also posed with respect to foreign markets (see table 4.5). Cross-border entry would, of course, need to be an important component of the globalization of the industry as forecast by some commentators (section 4.4). The response rate on this question was lower than that for domestic entry (around 65% as opposed to 75%), suggesting that a greater number of firms are considering expansion in their domestic market than in foreign markets.

The interest in this question lies largely in any contrasts with the domestic responses. In fact, the **most important factors are the same: existing firms' distribution channels or selling networks, relationships with clients, and reputation**. Scores in each case were somewhat higher than those for entry to domestic markets, suggesting that barriers to entry based on incumbents' infrastructure, reputation, and relationships are higher in cross-border entry. The barriers to globalization are underlined by these responses.

With regard to second-rank factors that are still considered to be of more than average importance (i.e., scoring well over 3), established investor preferences again come to the fore. But equally important is thought to be existing firms' local information, while existing firms'

Table 4.6
Will There Be More or Fewer Asset Managers in Your Principal Market Five Years from Now?

	Percent
Over 50% more	0
15–50% more	17
Roughly the same	36
15–50% less	45
Over 50% less	2

expertise and technical capabilities comes much lower in importance as a barrier to entry than for domestic firms. In other words, prospective entrants to foreign markets appear to consider themselves capable of competing with foreign firms in terms of their expertise but also perceive that there are important information asymmetries that would hinder them. Meanwhile, regulatory barriers are also seen as more important for foreign than domestic markets, albeit still scoring barely in excess of 3. Regulatory barriers are seen as particularly relevant in Europe (including the United Kingdom) and Canada, possibly implying regulatory problems for entrants in the European Union and United States, respectively. Costs are again seen as being of minor importance, with lower unit costs scoring particularly low as an entry barrier. Potential entrants appear not to perceive a major cost disadvantage relative to incumbents.

4.5.5   Expectations Regarding Industry Structure

Respondents were asked for a view on **how many firms there will be in the industry** in five years' time (table 4.6). Obviously, declines in the number of firms may occur via mergers and closures, while increases typically result from new entry from other sectors or de novo start-ups. As background, 18% of the respondents had been involved in a merger or acquisition in the year before the survey. Over a longer period, the number would obviously be higher. (For a discussion of consolidation in Europe, see Wrighton (1999).)

For the principal domestic market in which the managers are currently operating, the overall view was that there would be fewer firms in five years' time than today. Forty-seven percent took this view, 36% saw a similar number, and 17% saw more firms. Firms in the United States and the United Kingdom held most strongly to the

Table 4.7
Will There Be More or Fewer Asset Managers Servicing an Intercontinental Client Base
Five Years from Now?

	Percent
Over 50% more	3
15–50% more	51
Roughly the same	18
15–50% less	28
Over 50% less	0

Note: 18% of managers were in a merger last year.

view that numbers would contract; elsewhere, views were more evenly balanced. The implication is that the process of industry consolidation has farther to go in the main global markets.

The same question was posed with respect to an intercontinental client base (table 4.7). In this case, consistent with the views expressed in section 4.4, there was a major expectation that the industry would become more globalized. Fifty-four percent saw an increase in the number of managers acting transcontinentally, with 18% seeing the same number and 28% seeing fewer. Of course, it cannot be ruled out that the response implies intellectual assent with the arguments of Goldman Sachs outlined in section 4.4 rather than intentions on behalf of the firm in question. But the response remains a powerful indicator of sentiment in the industry at present.

4.5.6 Economies of Scale

Managers were questioned about the features that they thought tended to benefit large firms and also about costs. Note that the question was not posed directly in terms of whether large firms are thought to have an inherent competitive advantage; nonetheless, the responses give some important clues with respect to this issue.

With regard to the **benefits of size** in terms of assets under management (table 4.8), the most important is **name recognition**, with a score close to 4. **Costs come second**, the score for lower average operational costs (e.g., by duplicating portfolios) also scoring over 3.5. The cost factor is emphasized particularly by European managers and by quant-driven/passive managers, the latter of whom might already benefit from such an advantage. Ability to attract top portfolio managers also scores around 3.5, contrary to the view that

Table 4.8
What Are the Main Benefits of Large Size for Asset Managers in Terms of Assets under Management?

Answers Ranked from 1 (Unimportant) to 5 (Very Important)	5	4	3	2	1	Mean	Percent Response
Greater name recognition	27	42	26	5	0	3.92	92
Lower average operational costs (e.g., by duplicating portfolios for different clients)	12	41	36	11	0	3.55	92
Ability to negotiate price with broker-dealers	11	20	47	21	2	3.17	92
Overview of market prices, trading pattern, order flow, etc.	5	23	42	30	0	3.02	92
Ability to offer international coverage to clients	11	23	31	23	13	2.97	86
Ability to take on primary issues	5	25	34	28	8	2.91	89
Greater ability to attract top portfolio managers	17	30	35	14	4	3.41	92
Greater ability to communicate direct with clients	11	28	40	15	6	3.22	91

top managers are often alienated by large firms. The other factors that are of above-average importance are ability to communicate with clients and ability to negotiate price with broker dealers (the latter indicating a role for bargaining power). Superior information on market prices, international coverage to clients, and ability to take on primary issues are seen as relatively unimportant. The result for international coverage is an interesting counterpoint to the idea of globalization of the industry. It is seen as very important in Europe (including the United Kingdom), however.

The advantages of size seem in most cases to be more appreciated by the larger firms than by the small ones, with one interesting exception: The small ones emphasize the advantage to large firms of being able to attract top portfolio managers, perhaps as a result of bitter experience of loss of their own "stars."

Turning to the **costs of large size** (table 4.9), the most important factor is **the market impact of large transactions**. All the other factors that were mentioned—costs from the market impact in trading of the firm's name, higher regulatory costs, inability to retain portfolio managers, lack of personal contacts with clients, and client perceptions of conflicts of interest—are considered to be of relatively minor importance (scoring less than 3). Costs of moving the market

Table 4.9
What Are the Main Costs of Large Size for Asset Managers in Terms of Assets under Management?

Answers Ranked from 1 (Unimportant) to 5 (Very Important)	5	4	3	2	1	Mean	Percent Response
Costs from market impact of large transactions	26	42	29	3	0	3.91	91
Costs from market impact of the firms' name	6	19	42	31	3	2.94	91
Higher regulatory costs (external and internal)	5	8	40	42	5	2.63	91
Costs from inability to retain top portfolio managers	3	20	34	30	12	2.72	89
Costs from lack of personal contact with clients	6	20	33	28	12	2.8	89
Costs from client perceptions of possible conflicts of interest	5	19	31	32	13	2.71	86

score close to 4 in all the subcategories of the sample and on average. As might be expected, the U.S. managers see this as less important than the others, since they benefit from relatively liquid markets. One other result that is worthy of mention is that the impact of the firm's name is seen as quite important by the quant-driven active managers, suggesting that their activities play a signaling role to which market makers are sensitive.

Adding together and comparing the tables 4.8 and 4.9, one can infer that there are considered to be some advantages of scale in asset management but that reputation is more important than operating cost advantages (i.e., "economies" of scale), while market impact of large transactions is the key cost.

4.5.7 Influences on the Asset Management Sector over the Next Five Years

The final question (table 4.10) addresses the theme of chapter 4 directly, by seeking views on the main factors that are likely to affect asset management in the future. A large number of potential issues were suggested, including questions relating to regulatory barriers to entry, mergers, benefits of size, trading costs, supply of funds (globally and in specific markets), and miscellaneous factors (the Internet, bank activity, social security privatization, and EMU).

Table 4.10
Influences on the Asset Management Industry over the Next Five Years

Answers Ranked from 1 (Unimportant) to 5 (Very Important)	5	4	3	2	1	Mean	Percent Response
Reduced regulatory barriers to entry for domestic fund managers	0	25	33	35	7	2.77	84
Increased regulatory barriers to entry for domestic fund managers	0	24	36	27	14	2.69	82
Reduced regulatory barriers to entry for foreign fund managers	5	31	36	24	5	3.07	82
Increased regulatory barriers to entry for foreign fund managers	3	17	32	34	14	2.63	82
Domestic mergers of fund management firms	16	46	33	5	0	3.74	85
Cross-border mergers of fund management firms	15	43	32	10	0	3.63	83
Growing competitive benefits to large fund management firms	12	45	28	13	2	3.52	83
Growing competitive benefits to small fund management firms	2	15	37	42	3	2.69	82
Growing competitive benefits to "global" fund management firms	17	40	23	18	2	3.52	84
Declining security trading costs	3	25	38	33	2	2.95	85
Rising security trading costs	3	15	20	41	20	2.41	82
Growth in supply of investable funds	15	45	30	10	0	3.65	84
Decline in supply of investable funds	14	14	17	42	14	2.71	82
Growth in small cap stock markets	0	25	50	22	3	2.97	84
Growth in emerging market securities	5	25	45	25	2	3.05	84
Growth in Internet use (e.g., for selling mutual funds)	20	23	42	13	2	3.47	84
Greater participation of commercial/ investment banks in asset management	18	36	38	8	0	3.64	85
Social security privatization	22	28	24	17	9	3.38	81
European Monetary Union	9	29	34	25	3	3.14	82

Overall, the **key factors** that were seen as likely to influence the industry were **domestic and cross-border mergers, competitive benefits to large and global firms, growth in supply of funds, and the growing participation of commercial and investment banks in asset management**. All of these scored over 3.5. There was no distinctive pattern with respect to the subcategories of the sample, scores being similar across geographical regions, primary investment approaches, and values of assets under management. The Internet and social security privatization were the only others to receive marks significantly over 3; these elements were highlighted particularly by U.S. managers.

Of the other factors, E.U. managers anticipated a lowering of barriers to cross-border entry (consistent with the introduction of the Single Market), but U.K. firms also anticipate increased regulatory barriers to entry for domestic firms. The latter perhaps reflects pessimism about the impact of the changing U.K. regulatory structure. Australian managers anticipate greater competitive benefits to small firms, perhaps reflecting the growth of boutiques in that country. Continental European managers are notably optimistic about lowering of securities trading costs, as seems likely with EMU. U.S. managers seem to be relatively optimistic about prospects for small cap and emerging markets. And unsurprisingly, EMU is emphasized notably by European managers.

Note that one feature that was not included in the questions—nor proposed by the managers themselves—as a challenge to both domestic and global asset managers is the diminishing supply of government bonds. This may require considerable adaptation toward lower credit quality and less liquid debt instruments. It also distorts the benchmark against which such instruments are typically priced. The caveat is, of course, that structural effects will arise only if the decline is sustained. In the United Kingdom in the 1980s, there was a budget surplus and widespread predictions of "paying back the national debt." But the underlying pattern of sectoral financial balances—a public surplus and twin deficits for the external and private sectors —proved cyclical, linked to what proved to be overborrowing in the context of financial liberalization. Such a pattern could hold again in countries such as the United States (Bank of England 2000).

Overall, these answers are broadly compatible with the globalization hypothesis set out in section 4.4. Managers' responses imply that mergers will proliferate, as will entry by banks, in a context of growing competitive benefits to large and global firms, while the supply of funds is expected to go on increasing. The Internet is seen as another key factor.

Conclusions

Driven by the supply and demand factors outlined in chapter 1, prospects for institutional asset management are favorable, but considerable structural change in the industry is likely. Indeed, a global merger wave is already underway. There are harbingers of potentially major shifts in the organization and behavior of the industry in the United States and the United Kingdom. A marked impact of EMU on European sectors is already becoming apparent. Globalization of the industry is widely predicted, owing to factors such as the growing demand for equity investment, expertise in which is rather concentrated in the United States (and the United Kingdom), and the demand for expertise in defined contribution pensions, which is concentrated in the United States. Globalization is not inevitable; there are a number of arguments suggesting that it is less likely than consolidation of individual domestic sectors. Among these are diseconomies of scale for giant firms and barriers to entry, such as monopolization of distribution channels by local banks. Nevertheless, both globalization and domestic consolidation raise important issues. One is how large firms will cope with market liquidity problems. Furthermore, it is important that consolidation—be it at a national, regional, or global level—should occur in a situation in which potential competition has a strong influence on pricing, lest market power be exploited. This in turn implies a need to eliminate any regulatory or structural factors that constitute barriers to entry and that discourage competition. In this context, a challenge to both domestic and global asset managers is the diminishing supply of government bonds—if it is sustained.

Briefly, the responses to the questionnaire show that the key elements of competition in asset management are relative returns and relationships with customers and advisers. Entry barriers in both domestic and foreign markets include existing firms' distribution channels, relationships, and reputations, with foreign entry being seen as a tougher hurdle than domestic entry. Marked consolidation and globalization are foreseen. Benefits of size are mainly by way of reputation, with lower operating costs being offset by costs of the market impact of large trades. The future is seen as being strongly influenced by mergers, advantages of large firms, and participation of commercial and investment banks in asset management. Overall, these are consistent with a nuanced view of some of the prognoses shown in earlier sections of the chapter, in that whereas major structural change is seen as likely, the influence of some of the structural elements identified in chapter 3 (relative return, reputation, relationships, expertise, and distribution channels) will have rather durable effects in preserving existing patterns of asset management.

III

Institutional Investment, the Financial Sector, and the Economy

5   Implications of the Growth of Institutional Investors for the Financial Sectors

5.1   Implications for Capital Markets
5.2   Implications for Banks
5.3   Institutionalization and Financial Stability

Introduction

We now assess the broader economic and financial implications of the growth of institutional investors. These implications affect—positively or negatively—the ability of the financial system to fulfill its overall functions as set out in section 1.3. Given the massive growth of institutional investors and prospects for such expansion to continue, as highlighted in chapter 1, it is appropriate to probe these wider implications in some detail.

This chapter focuses on effects on the rest of the financial sector, subdivided into implications for capital markets, for banks, and for financial stability. Functions of the financial system that we highlight in this chapter include provision of payments services, pooling of funds, risk control, and price information. Chapter 6 looks at implications for the wider economy, dealing particularly with the financial functions of transfer of resources and overcoming incentive problems.

In each case, increased institutionalization will have novel implications only if asset allocation, security selection, and trading activity were to differ from the case in which individuals invested on their own behalf.[1] Such differences will in turn stem from contrasts in costs of financial activity, motivation, and perceptions of risk or reward

---

1. This argument abstracts from the implications for the relative size of financial institutions.

between individuals and asset managers. Chapters 7 and 8 focus more narrowly on the effects of institutional investor development on market structures and on trading.

5.1   Implications for Capital Markets

5.1.1   *Institutional Investors and the Growth of Capital Markets*

5.1.1.1   Patterns of Institutional and Capital Market Developments

In recent years, consistent with the stylized descriptions of **financial development** set out in section 1.4, securities markets have grown in terms of market capitalization quite significantly, entailing a rise in the ratio of securities to bank deposits and loans (see table 5.1). Capital markets have grown even more in terms of turnover. (Table 5.2 shows data up to the early 1990s.) But in addition, there has been a growing segmentation between retail and wholesale/institutional business, while in foreign exchange markets, the importance of institutional investors has increased. There has been a sharp increase in financial innovations in securities markets and technological advances in trading systems (for an overview of recent financial change, see Blommestein 1996).

These developments strongly **reflect the growing size and activity of institutional investors**. One indicator of their increasing role in securities markets is that the ownership of shares and bonds has changed sharply from being the province of individuals to holdings via institutions, with such holdings often concentrated in rather few hands.[2] Such changes may have broader implications—which are explored elsewhere in this volume—given the importance of capital markets for the real economy and corporate finance as well as indirect effects on banks.

It is relevant first to ask **how the growth of institutions relates to that of capital markets** in general terms. Following the discussion of the functions of the financial system in section 1.3, securities markets are, conceptually, means whereby claims may be subdivided to facilitate diversification and transfer between holders. The contrasts between countries in the size of both institutional sectors and securities markets raises the issue as to whether securities markets are a

---

2. However, the ongoing shift from defined benefit to defined contribution pension funds constitutes a partial return to control via individuals (see section 2.2.4).

Table 5.1
Volume of Financial Instruments Outstanding (Percent of GDP)

		1970	1980	1990	1995	1997	1998	Change, 1970–1998
United Kingdom	Deposits	0.87	0.64	1.50	1.44	1.58	1.58	0.71
	Equities	0.83	0.43	1.14	1.92	2.17	2.35	1.52
	Bonds	0.37	0.30	0.32	0.82	0.92	0.99	0.63
	Loans	0.66	0.44	1.16	1.63	1.73	1.75	1.10
United States	Deposits	0.65	0.67	0.64	0.55	0.55	0.56	−0.09
	Equities	0.85	0.58	0.63	1.15	1.60	1.81	0.96
	Bonds	0.68	0.69	1.19	1.39	1.41	1.48	0.80
	Loans	0.80	1.00	1.17	1.11	1.14	1.13	0.33
Germany	Deposits	0.89	1.08	1.21	1.25	1.40	1.47	0.59
	Equities	0.28	0.23	0.47	0.49	0.72	0.87	0.59
	Bonds	0.23	0.35	0.62	0.93	1.06	1.14	0.92
	Loans	0.97	1.27	1.44	1.54	1.71	1.78	0.81
Japan	Deposits	0.97	1.44	2.12	2.12	2.09	2.19	1.23
	Equities	0.27	0.40	0.75	0.71	0.59	0.59	0.31
	Bonds	0.26	0.64	0.77	1.05	1.04	1.19	0.93
	Loans	1.13	1.54	2.23	2.19	2.03	2.06	0.93
Canada	Deposits	0.74	0.99	0.92	0.92	0.96	0.97	0.23
	Equities	0.94	0.82	1.07	1.56	1.76	2.00	1.06
	Bonds	0.77	0.70	0.79	1.09	1.12	1.15	0.38
	Loans	0.79	1.04	1.04	1.07	1.09	1.12	0.34
France	Deposits	1.05	1.62	1.77	1.92	2.07	2.02	0.97
	Equities	0.92	0.69	1.77	1.46	2.26	2.75	1.83
	Bonds	0.15	0.23	0.51	0.74	0.82	0.85	0.70
	Loans	2.10	1.94	2.05	2.02	2.04	2.05	−0.05
Italy	Deposits	0.95	1.17	1.08	1.05	1.01	0.98	0.03
	Equities	0.37	0.61	0.81	0.85	1.09	1.37	0.99
	Bonds	0.45	0.41	0.71	1.06	1.24	1.30	0.86
	Loans	1.19	1.16	1.05	1.20	1.22	1.07	−0.12
G-7	Deposits	0.87	1.09	1.32	1.32	1.38	1.40	0.52
	Equities	0.64	0.54	0.95	1.16	1.46	1.68	1.04
	Bonds	0.41	0.47	0.70	1.01	1.09	1.16	0.74
	Loans	1.09	1.20	1.45	1.54	1.57	1.57	0.48
Anglo-Saxon	Deposits	0.75	0.77	1.02	0.97	1.03	1.03	0.28
	Equities	0.87	0.61	0.95	1.54	1.84	2.05	1.18
	Bonds	0.61	0.56	0.77	1.10	1.15	1.21	0.60
	Loans	0.75	0.83	1.12	1.27	1.32	1.33	0.59
CEJ	Deposits	0.97	1.33	1.54	1.58	1.64	1.67	0.70
	Equities	0.46	0.48	0.95	0.88	1.16	1.39	0.93
	Bonds	0.27	0.41	0.65	0.94	1.04	1.12	0.85
	Loans	1.35	1.48	1.69	1.74	1.75	1.74	0.39

Source: National balance sheet data; see table 1.1 for details.

Table 5.2
Capital Market Turnover (Percent of GDP)

	1977	1980	1985	1990	1993
United Kingdom	70	50	70	160	220
United States	110	130	420	430	620
Germany	10	10	30	70	110
Japan	20	50	320	320	220
France	10	10	20	60	120
Italy	10	10	20	50	290[†]
Euromarkets*	10	10	30	40	130

Estimates of the annual value of secondary market transactions in equities and bonds, including over-the-counter transactions. A purchase and corresponding sale count as a single transaction.
*Total transactions settled through Euroclear and Cedel as a percentage of total GNP of G-10 countries in U.S. dollars.
[†] 1992.
Source: BIS.

precondition for development of institutional investors or whether institutions may emerge first and then stimulate capital market development.[3]

In fact, there would appear to be a **two-way relationship**. Although institutions could develop on the basis of loans or property investment, their greatest comparative advantage is in the capital market. Loans require intense monitoring, so the customer relationship may give banks a comparative advantage there. Trading and risk pooling are more efficiently undertaken in the capital markets, in which transactions costs are lower. Hence, for example, capital markets facilitate the growth of mutual funds and may encourage development of funded pensions.

But institutional investor growth may also spur further growth of capital markets, as recent experience following pension reform in Chile has confirmed (Holzmann 1997a). Major changes ensued, affecting capital market structure, liquidity and volatility of markets, and demand for capital market instruments. There were also changes to financing patterns for nonfinancial companies.

Why do such effects arise? In pay-as-you-go social security schemes, there is no stimulus to the capital market, as such schemes are based solely on transfers. When institutional investors replace pay-as-you-

---

3. Note that these arguments are broadly "closed economy" based, a bias that may be justified given the tendency to date of institutions to invest domestically even in globalized financial markets.

go, assets are built up as the schemes mature, and this stimulates investment and the development of securities markets. Given their focus on real returns, institutions should be particularly beneficial to the development of equity markets. Certainly, there seems from table 5.3 to be a correlation in OECD countries between equity market capitalization and the size of institutions. Indeed, the correlation coefficient of institutional assets and equity market capitalization across all of the countries shown is no less than 0.97. Equally, institutions are ready customers for bonds and securitized debt instruments.

5.1.1.2   Experience in Chile

We dwell on the Chilean example in some detail because of the lessons it offers about the **benefits for capital markets of development of institutional investors** both to other emerging market economies and to OECD countries without funded pensions. The Chilean pension system, set up in 1981, is a decentralized mandatory retirement scheme that replaced an insolvent social security scheme. The system is defined contribution; it requires employees to contribute 10% of their salaries (an extra 3% covers fees and compulsory term life insurance). Assets are invested on an individual basis by private investment management companies on a basis of one account per worker. Workers are allowed to transfer if they are dissatisfied with the manager's performance. Fund management companies (known as AFPs) are allowed to offer only one type of pension account. On retirement, workers are obliged either to buy an indexed annuity with the bulk of their accumulated funds—a system facilitated by long-standing and credible use of indexed debt in Chile—or to carry out programmed withdrawals. There is a complex regulatory structure to protect workers—and the government, given its minimum pension guarantee (see Davis 1998f). Existing old age security obligations are being honored by a reduction in the budget surplus and by use of so-called recognition bonds that offer a real return of 4%.

Holzmann (1997a) points to the fact that Chilean pension funds grew from zero in 1980 to 39% of GDP in 1995 and 42% in 1998. They may have played a major role in stimulating the rise in private saving observed over this period (Morandé 1998).[4] This accompanied an

---

4. However, Holzmann (1997a) notes that the initial effect on private saving was low or even negative.

Table 5.3
European Union and G-7 Financial Structure Indicators, End of 1996 ($ billions/% of GDP)

	Equities	% GDP	Government Bonds	% GDP	Private Bonds	% GDP	Bank Assets	% GDP	Total	% GDP	Institutional Assets (1995)	% GDP	Listed Domestic Companies	Listed Foreign Companies
EU-15	4518	55	4617	56	2945	36	18,066	207	30,146	345	6214	74	3997	2972
EU-11	2447	35	3818	55	2391	34	14,321	206	22,976	331	4041	59	2769	2115
Belgium	120	48	282	113	133	54	846	326	1381	532	156	58	146	145
Denmark	71	42	118	69	175	103	196	109	560	313	116	67	237	12
Germany	667	29	857	39	1034	46	4556	200	7113	312	1113	46	681	1290
Greece	24	22	99	90	1	0	103	85	227	188	N.A.	N.A.	217	0
Spain	244	37	286	43	45	7	962	172	1537	274	215	38	357	4
France	591	37	708	45	573	36	3471	205	5343	315	1159	75	686	187
Ireland	35	54	28	43	1	3	166	229	230	318	N.A.	N.A.	61	10
Italy	259	24	1277	119	401	37	2065	169	4002	327	223	20	244	4
Luxembourg	33	181	1	6	11	61	602	3625	647	3897	369	194	54	224
Netherlands	378	103	205	56	66	18	775	204	1426	376	626	158	217	216
Austria	33	15	75	35	71	33	516	233	695	314	82	35	94	35
Portugal	25	28	45	51	18	20	227	212	315	293	35	34	158	0
Finland	61	53	54	46	38	32	135	110	288	233	63	50	71	0
Sweden	243	97	150	60	163	65	259	105	815	332	267	116	217	12
United Kingdom	1733	146	434	36	216	18	3187	253	5569	442	1790	162	557	833
Canada	366	65	581	103	93	16	516	91	1556	275	493	87	N.A.	N.A.
United States	8458	117	6965	96	4327	60	5580	73	25,330	331	10,501	145	7755	708
Japan	3003	71	3409	81	1453	34	160	62	8026	311	3035	59	1766	67

N.A. = not available.
Source: Dermine (1998), OECD (1998), BIS (1998).

expansion of overall financial assets from 28% of GDP in 1980 to 68% in 1993 (Fontaine 1997), with pension assets accounting for a third of this total. Initially, funds were invested mainly in debt securities, owing to regulatory prohibition of equity investment, but they did not invest solely in government paper; they also accumulated bank certificates of deposit (CDs) and mortgage bonds. As a consequence of the development of pension funds, debt maturities became unusually long for an emerging market economy: 12–20 years by 1990. Equity investment was permitted in 1985, and holdings have grown to over 30% of assets. This accompanied and encouraged a marked expansion of equity market capitalization from 32% of GDP in 1988 to 90% in 1993; in the early 1990s, private companies were encouraged by high price/earnings ratios to go public and accept standard record keeping and auditing practices, thanks to better access to pension fund financing. In 1991, the pension funds held one third of public bonds, two thirds of private bonds, and 10% of equities. Holzmann (1997a) shows econometrically that the development of financial markets in Chile correlates with strong development of the real side of the economy, via rising total factor productivity and capital accumulation. Holzmann also estimates that long-term growth in Chile is 1–3% higher, owing to the effects of the pension reform operating via financial markets, although he also points out that the structuring of the transition may have played an important role.[5]

As table 5.4 shows, pension fund growth was accompanied, inter alia, by rising stocks of corporate bonds, often placed directly by large companies into pension funds, the bond market having been improved by a new risk classification and credit-rating industry. The life insurance sector grew to provide annuities as well as survivorship and invalidity reinsurance as required by the new system. And other investor groups, such as mutual funds and foreign investor funds, have emerged, increasing the diversity of market participants.

Fontaine (1997) also notes that pension fund development **facilitated internal resource transfers**. It enabled the Chilean government to service its international debts without extreme fiscal adjustment (which was elsewhere damaging to the real economy), by providing a domestic source of borrowing without requiring excessively high

---

5. The tight fiscal stance may have contributed to economic performance by crowding in of private investment and offering a higher credibility to the reform program within and outside the country.

Table 5.4
Developments in the Chilean Financial Sector

Percent of GDP	1980	1986	1992
Fixed income instruments	0.2	26	60
Stock market capitalization	30	24	88
Corporate bonds	0.2	0.4	5
Mutual funds	3	1	2
Foreign capital country funds	0	0	3
Insurance company reserves	N.A.	3	7
Pension funds	0	13	32

N.A. = not available.
Source: EBRD (1996).

interest rates (in fact, the debt was generally CPI-indexed). Correspondingly, public sector debt rose from 5% of GDP in 1980 to 28% in 1990. Later, the demand of pension funds enabled debt conversion—by both private and public institutions—to occur smoothly. In addition, the fact that pension funds were not permitted to invest internationally until 1989, and then only in a limited way, explains why the capital markets in Chile grew in size and depth so rapidly. Again, given the existence of domestic long-term institutions and the high domestic saving that pension reform helped to stimulate, Chile is probably better insulated from the shifting behavior of international investors, as shown by the lower correction after the Mexican crisis, than are other Latin American markets.

Hansell (1992) suggests that development of pension funds has been a major factor behind Chile's bonds being rated investment-grade, the first Latin American country's bonds to be so rated since the debt crisis. Disclosure standards are higher than elsewhere in Latin America. Corporate governance has been improved by requirements that pension fund managers vote for independent directors. On the other hand, Chileans have been rather unsuccessful at ownership dispersion, one reason being unwillingness of closely held companies to accept dilution of control. Rating regulations have until recently prevented funds from investing in start-up companies and venture capital.

5.1.1.3 Estimates of the Relationship of Institutionalization to Capital Market Development

We now go on to use data on financial structure indicators for the G-7 countries shown in chapter 1 to investigate further the potential

effects of growth in institutional investors on capital markets. The simple estimates shown in tables 5.5 and 5.6 utilize the variables in tables 1.1, 1.2, 1.3, 1.9, 5.1, and 6.5 (five yearly over the period 1970–1995) as a panel (pooled cross section and time series) data set. The dependent variables that are included are the size indicator, equity as a proportion of financial assets, components of household assets, and components of corporate liabilities. An additional dependent variable was monthly equity market volatility averaged over five-year periods (table 5.9). The independent variables are household institutional assets as a proportion of total household financial assets and institutional assets as a proportion of total financial assets.

There are, in effect, forty-two observations for each series, with six observations each for seven countries. We then regressed the above-mentioned indicators of the size of the institutional sector on the indicators of financial structure. We used both of the standard panel data estimation techniques: testing for random and fixed[6] effects. The latter being considered more appropriate, we report only results of this (while noting that the random effects results are very similar). The work thus differs from otherwise comparable work such as that of Demirgüç-Kunt and Levine (1996), which estimated correlations on purely cross-sectional data. It should be emphasized that the results will not have any causality implication, but rather show what patterns or changes in financial market structure and behavior have accompanied institutionalization. It cannot be ruled out that other causes have affected both dependent and independent variables (such as liberalization generally and technological change). Finally, the data sets are small, so again conclusions must be drawn cautiously; outliers may have a disproportionate effect. Further and more systematic investigation is needed.

With these caveats in mind, the **results for the G-7** (table 5.5) tend to indicate the following: higher levels of institutionalization (measured by the share of total financial assets) accompany a larger size of the financial superstructure (total financial assets/GDP), even when national differences in levels of the latter are taken into account by the dummies. Second, higher institutionalization accompanies a higher share of equity in total financial assets. Third, there is no significant link of the level of institutionalization to volatility. Of course, a low level of average volatility may still be consistent with occasional disruptive peaks of volatility (see section 5.3).

---

6. That is, with country-dummy variables in each equation.

Table 5.5
Results of Correlation Analysis for the G-7 (Fixed Effects Regressions, Variables Significant at the 95% Level)

Dependent Variable	Independent Variable	Coefficient (*t* Value)
Size indicator	Institutional assets / total financial assets	47.9 (9.1)
Equity / total financial assets	Institutional assets / total financial assets	0.8 (2.8)
Volatility of share prices (monthly S.D.)	Institutional assets / total financial assets	
Household equity / household financial assets	Household institutional assets / household financial assets	
Household bonds / household financial assets	Household institutional assets / household financial assets	−0.13 (2.0)
Household deposits / household financial assets	Household institutional assets / household financial assets	−0.63 (4.4)
Corporate equity / corporate liabilities	Institutional assets / total financial assets	1.8 (3.4)
Corporate bonds and market paper / corporate liabilities	Institutional assets / total financial assets	
Corporate loans / corporate liabilities	Institutional assets / total financial assets	−1.4 (2.9)

Concerning household sector portfolios, the share of institutional investment in households' portfolios appears to be negatively related to the share of deposits and bonds, suggesting some substitution. In looking finally at company liabilities, the share of institutional investment in total financial assets tends to accompany higher levels of the share of equities in corporate liabilities and lower levels of loans. Concerning bonds, the coefficient is insignificant. It is notable that strong substitution for institutional assets is indicated for both key elements of banks' balance sheets: household deposits and company loans. Implications of growth of institutional investors for banks are probed further in section 5.2.

We **split the sample** between the Anglo-Saxon countries, that is, the United Kingdom, the United States, and Canada (with eighteen observations) and Europe and Japan, that is, Germany, France, Italy, and Japan (twenty-four observations), as shown in table 5.6. Splitting the sample in this way enables one to judge whether the overall results were driven by only one subgroup of countries, with results being inapplicable to the other subgroup. A priori considerations

Table 5.6
Results of Correlation Analysis for Subgroups (Fixed Effects Regressions, Variables Significant at the 95% Level)

Dependent Variable	Independent Variable	Anglo–Saxon	Europe and Japan
Size indicator	Institutional assets/total financial assets	42.5 (5.6)	54.3 (7.5)
Equity/total financial assets	Institutional assets/total financial assets		1.28 (3.2)
Volatility of share prices (monthly S.D.)	Institutional assets/total financial assets	−35.2 (3.7)	
Household equity/ household financial assets	Household institutional assets/ household financial assets	−0.4 (3.4)	
Household bonds/household financial assets	Household institutional assets/ household financial assets	−0.24 (3.8)	
Household deposits/ household financial assets	Household institutional assets/ household financial assets	−0.45 (4.0)	−0.9 (3.4)
Corporate equity/corporate liabilities	Institutional assets/total financial assets	1.1 (1.9)	2.6 (3.2)
Corporate bonds and market paper/corporate liabilities	Institutional assets/total financial assets		0.35 (1.8)
Corporate loans/corporate liabilities	Institutional assets/total financial assets	−0.56 (2.0)	−2.3 (2.8)

suggest that this is possible, bearing in mind that institutional investor growth has been much more marked in the Anglo-Saxon countries. In fact, there are a number of results that appear consistently for both groups when they are examined separately. In each case, a higher level of institutions in total financial assets has accompanied a larger overall financial superstructure as shown by total financial assets/GDP; the growth of institutions' share of household portfolios has accompanied a decline in deposits; and a higher level of institutional assets as a proportion of total assets has accompanied a higher level of corporate equity and a lower level of corporate loans.

Some differing econometric results across subsamples were nonetheless obtained. It was found that in the Anglo-Saxon countries, but not in Europe and Japan, a larger institutional sector is associated with a lower average level of capital market volatility (see section 5.3). Moreover, the results imply that there is consistently strong substitution from equities and bonds to institutional assets in households' portfolios in the Anglo-Saxon countries but not in Europe and Japan. There is also some evidence of higher bond shares in company liabilities in Europe and Japan as institutions increase in size and importance, which was not apparent in the Anglo-Saxon countries.

5.1.2   Institutional Investors and Securities Market Structure

5.1.2.1   General Considerations
The development of institutional investors has had a **pervasive effect on capital market microstructure**, increasing the efficiency with which the function of clearing and settling payments is fulfilled and aiding the accurate pricing of financial assets. Their key demand is **liquidity**, which may be defined in terms of four dimensions:

• width, which is the bid-offer spread between buying and selling prices for securities transactions;

• depth, the amount of securities that can be traded at given bid and offer prices;

• immediacy, the time needed to carry out a transaction; and

• resiliency, the time the market needs to return to previous prices after absorbing a large trade (see Kyle 1985[7]).

For a broader discussion of liquidity in the context of changing capital market structures, see chapter 7.

Note that besides market structure per se, liquidity may also be linked to the activities of institutions themselves, in that their own arbitrage, trading, and diversification helps to increase liquidity further. More generally, liquidity is a form of economy of scale (network externality), as larger markets in which institutional investors participate generate more trading, and hence such markets may have an advantage over small ones even with the same technology.

---

7. Kyle also cites Black (1971), who states that "the market for a stock is liquid if (1) there are always bid and asked prices for the investor who wants to buy or sell small amounts of the stock immediately; (2) the difference between the bid and asked prices (the spread) is always small; (3) an investor who is selling a large amount of stock, in the absence of special information, can expect to do so over a long period of time at a price not very different, on average, from the current market price; (4) an investor can buy or sell a large block of stock immediately, but at a premium or discount that depends on the size of the block." The larger the block, the larger the premium or discount. In other words, a liquid market is a continuous market, in the sense that almost any amount of stock can be bought or sold immediately, and an efficient market, in the sense that small amounts of stock can be bought or sold very near the current market price and in the sense that large amounts can be bought or sold over long periods of time at prices that are, on average, very near the current market price.

Liquidity of wholesale capital markets was aided by deregulation and elimination of fixed commissions, which institutions have proven to be well placed to press for (although they have often been willing to pay "soft commissions" to brokers; see chapter 8). Increases in liquidity should in turn be beneficial more generally to the efficiency of capital markets and should lead to a reduction in the cost of capital.

Essential **complements to liquid wholesale capital markets** are advanced communication and information systems, reliable clearing and settlements systems, and efficient trading systems, all of which help to ensure that there is efficient arbitrage between securities and scope for diversification. Given the role of banks in providing credit to market makers and to underwriters, they are also essential ingredients for sound capital markets (see Blommestein and Spencer 1996). Adequate public disclosure of information, a market-oriented accounting system, and a proper legal framework for the institutional and financial sectors are also important features of markets if they are to attract institutional trading.

Institutional investors are relatively unconcerned by the firmness of investor protection regulation, as they have sufficient countervailing power to protect their own interests against market makers and other financial institutions. But they are also extremely footloose and willing to transfer their trading to markets that offer improved conditions. In effect, this feature renders the market for institutional securities trading services contestable, regulation permitting (i.e., the threat posed by potential new entrants ensures that prices remain at a perfectly competitive level), as we discussed for some investment management sectors in section 3.2.2.

5.1.2.2 Institutional Investors and Equity Market Structure

In spite of the massive recent growth in online retail brokerage in the United States, institutional investors continue virtually year on year to account for an increasing proportion of U.S. equity holdings. A mere 12% in 1960, they reached 34% in 1980, 47% in 1998, and 48% in 1999.[8] Whereas **exchange trading rules and architectures are subject to more regulatory control in the United States** than in most European markets, institutions have nonetheless had a **significant effect on their development**. Over half of New York Stock Exchange

---

8. Source: U.S. Federal Reserve Flow of Funds Accounts (http://www.bog.frb.fed.us/releases/Z1) and Conference Board (1999).

trades are blocks (over 10,000 shares), generally arranged "upstairs" with exchange members, although subject to the exchange's interaction rules for floor participation.[9] In the NASDAQ (over-the-counter) market, over three quarters of institutional volume is executed via broker-dealers, on either an agency or a principal basis, but this is more a reflection of the fact that NASDAQ was established as a dealer market than the choice of institutions.[10] The remainder is executed via so-called electronic communications networks (ECNs), the largest of which is Instinet.[11] A discussion of the development of ECNs and their relation to institutions is given in chapters 7 and 8.

The **European markets have evolved in a very different manner**, owing largely to far less regulation of interexchange competition. Institutional trading was key in driving significant volumes of continental European share trading out of the local, mainly open-outcry floor-based, markets to London's SEAQ International dealer market in the mid to late 1980s. By 1990, London accounted for 10–65% of trading volume in major continental stocks. Reversal of trade flows in the early 1990s, particularly for smaller trades, back toward the home markets after the introduction of continuous electronic auction systems ultimately led to the demise of the London-based dealer market. After the introduction of the SETS system on the London Stock Exchange in 1997, the convergence toward electronic auction trading across Europe was complete. London in particular, however, still shows a higher percentage (over 50%) of volume executed away from the electronic order book than in other European markets. Pagano and Steil (1996) provide an analysis of the evolution of the European equity markets from the "Big Bang" deregulation of the London market in 1986 through to the launch of the European Union's Investment Services Directive in 1996. Steil (1996) offers an analysis of the Directive itself, and Schwartz and Steil (1996) evaluate the findings of a major empirical study of European institutional trading. We examine the interaction of institutional trading and market structure development in chapters 7 and 8.

---

9. Source: New York Stock Exchange (http://www.nyse.com/marketinfo/marketinfo.html).
10. Agency trades are those in which the broker-dealer intermediary crosses buy and sell trades among its customers. Principal trades are those for which the broker-dealer commits its own capital to buying shares from, or selling them to, the customer.
11. See Greenwich Associates (1999b) for data on institutional ECN use.

A further change to market structure induced by development of institutional investors is **cross-border listing of companies** (see table 5.3 for the scope of this in 1996). Whereas this was partly a quest for new sources of financing, notably by expanding the investor base in export markets and to enhance public image, it also linked strongly to the growing international diversification of institutional investors that were eager to minimize the cost of portfolio rebalancing by trading foreign stocks on their home exchanges.[12]

5.1.2.3 Institutional Investors and Debt Market Structure

As discussed in IMF (1994), governments have in recent years also sought to **modernize the infrastructure of their public bond markets**, driven by the desire to make their debt more attractive to international institutional investors (in effect, emulating U.S. market practices). Governments hoped thereby to reduce financing costs of their public deficits. The need for such measures became acute in the context of abolition of exchange controls, which meant that governments could no longer rely on captive domestic investors but had instead to attract foreign investors. But by modernizing bond market infrastructure, governments also facilitated private issuance in the form of corporate bonds and securitized loans. Measures taken by OECD governments included:

- the introduction of primary dealer systems;
- auctions;
- issue calendars;
- vehicles for financing positions (such as repos);
- the abolition of withholding taxes;[13]
- derivatives markets;
- the tailoring of issues to specific investor needs;
- benchmark issues;
- improvements in clearing and settlement systems; and
- "global bonds."

---

12. Hence, for example, thirty-one French companies are listed on seventeen foreign stock exchanges, and forty-six are regularly traded on SEAQ.

13. When New Zealand abolished withholding taxes, the immediate fall in the bond yield was reportedly more than sufficient to cover the loss of tax revenue.

For example, the modernization of the French government bond market, innovations such as OATs and the futures market MATIF, were motivated by the need to attract foreign institutional investors by offering them suitable, highly liquid instruments for hedging against interest rate risk and foreign exchange risk (Benos and Crouhy 1996).

The advent of EMU has stimulated development and integration of government bond markets across the Union, which also promotes private issuance by providing benchmarks against which private issues can be priced (Davis 1999a). It has also enhanced competition among EMU government bond markets, prompting further modernization and innovation (such as the French government's program of index-linked bonds similar to those in the United States and the United Kingdom). However, full integration of repo markets is hindered by fiscal and regulatory barriers as well as lack of full integration of securities settlement (see European Central Bank 2000b).

5.1.2.4 Derivatives and Other New Markets

The process of **financial innovation**—the invention and marketing of new financial instruments that repackage risk or return streams— has also been closely related to the development of institutional investors, with respect to both individual instruments and the effect of institutional demand on the dynamics of innovation generally. Financial innovation in capital markets was rapid in the 1980s and 1990s. Indeed, Merton and Bodie (1995) characterize the process that has been witnessed as an "innovation spiral," whereby innovations drive the financial system to greater efficiency, in turn spurring further innovations. Particularly noteworthy was the growth of derivatives markets (table 5.7) and the development of commercial paper (CP). But one could also highlight the recent expansion of securitized debt, when, for example, the stock of U.S. federal agency debt rose from $2199 billion in 1994 to $3320 billion in 1998 and private asset-backed securities outstanding rose from $570 billion to $1395 billion over the same period.

Before the mid-1980s, most innovations originated in the European markets; after the mid-1980s, they originated in the U.S. domestic market. In the **1980s, innovations tended to arise to serve international banks' needs** for improved risk management. BIS (1992), for example, showed how swaps, forward rate agreements (FRAs),

Table 5.7
Financial Derivative Instruments Traded on Organized Exchanges
(Trillions of U.S. Dollars)

	1992	1993	1994	1995	1996	1997	Notional Amounts Outstanding at the End of 1997
Interest rate futures	141.0	177.3	271.7	266.3	253.5	274.6	7.5
On short-term instruments	113.3	138.9	222.1	218.2	204.8	223.2	7.1
Of which:							
3-month eurodollar rates	66.9	70.2	113.6	104.1	97.1	107.2	2.6
3-month euroyen rates	14.0	24.6	44.2	46.8	34.7	29.9	1.6
3-month euro-DM rates	7.5	12.9	18.5	18.4	23.9	25.3	1.0
3-month PIBOR	5.8	10.4	12.0	15.9	13.7	12.3	0.2
On long-term instruments	27.7	38.5	49.6	48.2	48.7	51.4	0.4
Of which:							
U.S. Treasury bonds	7.1	8.0	10.1	8.7	8.5	10.1	0.1
Japanese government bonds	9.7	14.2	13.8	16.2	12.3	10.6	0.1
German government bonds	3.2	5.1	8.9	9.3	12.3	14.5	0.1
French government bonds	2.8	3.2	4.6	3.4	3.4	3.1	0.0
Interest rate options	25.5	32.8	46.7	43.3	41.0	48.6	3.6
Currency futures	2.3	2.8	3.3	3.3	3.0	3.5	0.1
Currency options	1.4	1.4	1.4	1.0	0.9	0.7	0.0
Stock market index futures	6.0	7.1	9.4	10.6	12.9	16.4	0.2
Stock market index options	5.7	6.3	8.0	9.2	10.1	13.0	0.8
Total	181.9	227.8	340.5	333.9	321.5	356.8	12.2
In North America	102.1	113.1	175.9	161.1	154.2	182.7	6.3
In Europe	42.8	61.4	83.9	87.5	100.1	114.9	3.6
In Asia	36.9	53.0	77.8	81.1	63.8	56.3	2.2
Other	0.1	0.4	2.9	4.2	3.4	2.9	0.1

Source: BIS.

interest rate options, and short-term interest rate futures have complemented and substituted for traditional international interbank deposits in the context of volatile interest rates and asset prices. But increasingly over time, innovations have also proved essential complements to asset management (see section 2.3.3). Innovations were increasingly tailored to institutions' needs. Institutional investors (notably from the Anglo-Saxon countries) have also tended to press foreign markets to adopt innovations that they use at home (equity and bond futures markets, etc.). Once in place, these innovations have themselves further encouraged international investment by facilitating hedging and position taking.

The uses of derivatives by institutions were highlighted in section 2.3.3. Concerning estimates of the spread of their use, according to a survey by Intersec, 61% of E.U. pension funds and insurance companies use derivatives directly or via their external fund manager, although there were sharp cross-country differences. Of those using derivatives, 75% use them for tactical asset allocation as noted above, 50% to hedge currency risk, and 33% to take positions on interest rates. U.S. institutions' use of derivatives is even more comprehensive. Institutions are also key investors in securitized debt instruments, which have in turn been an important aspect of disintermediation of the banking sector (see section 5.2.3). Institutional holdings of U.S. agency securities amounted to $1100 billion (a third of the total) in 1998.

Wholesale money markets have benefited from the development of money market funds. These markets have been a crucible for many of the financial innovations of recent years, notably CDs, CP, deposit notes, swaps, and repurchase agreements (Stigum 1990). In the U.S. money market, mutual funds held 35% of the CP outstanding at the end of 1998.

An emerging development of interest in the context not only of innovation but also of cross-border investment and corporate finance is the creation of **synthetic shares**, which replicate the dividend and price behavior of existing shares while circumventing foreign ownership restrictions. These can increase liquidity for issuers without changing control structures. Other types of synthetic share can enable investors to create and unwind controlling blocks of shares at low cost; this would facilitate changes to corporate governance and control structures (Berglöf 1996).

Credit derivatives, which enable credit risk to be transferred separately from the underlying bonds or loans,[14] are also arousing interest among institutional investors because they are well placed to absorb credit risk at an appropriate price. EMU in particular is putting an enhanced focus on credit risk management at a European level. This is partly because it eliminates other distinguishing aspects of government debt (notably exchange rate risk). Also, by limiting government bond issuance under the Stability and Growth Pact while broadening the pool of investors, EMU promotes the growth of corporate bond markets, again increasing the focus on credit risk.

---

14. Conceptually, securitization is another form of credit risk transfer akin to credit derivatives, but it also entails transfer of market risk.

Trading techniques such as portfolio insurance put heavy demands on liquidity in the securities and derivatives markets; such liquidity is at times vulnerable to collapse (see section 5.3). Access to cash through the banking system is a vital backup for such strategies.

5.2 Implications for Banks

Growth of institutions has led to **increased competition for household savings** and has affected the profitability of traditional financial instruments. These trends have had a **marked effect on banking sectors**, leading them to shift the focus of their activity away from traditional lending business and toward investment banking and other types of activity that generate noninterest income. (See also the paradigms of financial development outlined in section 1.4.) In some cases, especially where regulation constrained banks from such adaptation, as in the United States, institutional competition led to heightened risk taking on the part of banks as they sought to maintain the profitability of the traditional lending business. In this section, we deal successively with trends in banking and institution-bank competition on the liabilities and the assets side.

5.2.1 Trends in Banking

Table 5.8 shows trends in bank activity during the period of rapid growth of institutional investors from 1980 to the late 1990s. Banks' balance sheets tended to grow rapidly in the 1980s but leveled off in the 1990s. Interest margins narrowed; banks' income streams have tended to shift toward fee income, while major increases in bad debts have occurred. Relative stocks of financial instruments in the G-7 economies, as shown in table 5.1, indicate a relative decline in the importance of bank assets and liabilities. As a share of total financial claims, the volume of securities outstanding has risen, notably in terms of bonds and money market paper, while the share of deposits and loans has declined. On the other hand, reflecting the growth in the overall financial superstructure, all types of financial claim have risen relative to GDP.

Such patterns are **widely taken as indicative of a "decline of banking,"** under pressure from disintermediation by institutional investors, among other things. However, an objection to this view is that the size of **the balance sheet is a poor measure of the output of**

Table 5.8
Banking Sector Developments

(a) Change in Lending/GDP Ratio

	1970–1975	1975–1980	1980–1985	1985–1990	1990–1995	1995–1998
United Kingdom	−0.22	0.00	0.28	0.44	0.47	0.12
United States	0.06	0.15	0.08	0.09	−0.06	0.02
Germany	0.14	0.16	0.15	0.01	0.10	0.24
Japan	0.23	0.18	0.33	0.36	−0.04	−0.13
Canada	0.11	0.14	−0.09	0.10	0.03	0.05
France	−0.16	0.00	0.02	0.10	−0.03	0.03
Italy	0.17	−0.20	−0.06	−0.05	0.15	−0.13

(b) Noninterest Income/Total Income (Percent)

	1979–1984	1985–1989	1990–1992	1993–1996
United Kingdom	31	37	41	42
United States	24	30	34	36
Germany	19	21	25	21
Japan	18	32	20	−1
Canada	22	27	31	35
France	15	16	26	43
Italy	27	29	24	24

(c) Interest Margins/Assets (Percent)

	1979–1984	1985–1989	1990–1992	1993–1996
United Kingdom	3.2	3.0	2.8	2.3
United States	3.0	3.3	3.6	3.8
Germany	2.2	2.1	1.9	2.1
Japan	1.1	0.9	0.8	1.4
Canada	2.5	2.9	3.0	2.5
France	2.5	2.3	1.7	1.2
Italy	2.7	2.9	3.2	2.8

(d) Provisions/Assets (Percent)

	1979–1984	1985–1989	1990–1992	1993–1996
United Kingdom	0.41	0.86	1.2	0.43
United States	0.35	0.83	0.89	0.36
Germany	0.41	0.37	0.38	0.43
Japan	0.02	0.04	0.08	0.33
Canada	0.49	0.74	0.64	0.45
France	0.55	0.53	0.54	0.56
Italy	0.66	0.48	0.52	0.76

Source: OECD Bank Profitability.

banks as financial institutions, since it excludes off-balance-sheet items and fee-earning services, which also contribute to banks' functional importance to the economy. For example, Kaufman and Mote (1994) show that the simple addition of trust services, nonbank subsidiaries, and bank-operated mutual funds to balance sheets goes some way toward eliminating the statistical decline in banks' share of financial services in the United States. In addition, there are sources of bank income that are unrelated to owning or managing assets but are nonetheless often founded upon banks' traditional advantages in credit evaluation, such as lines of credit, letters of credit, futures, options, and swaps, as well as activities based on unbundling of financial assets, including origination of loans that are later securitized. The increasing importance of these is reflected in an increase in the share of bank income accounted for by noninterest income (for cross-country E.U. data, see European Central Bank (2000a)). On the basis of these measures, Kaufman and Mote conclude that there is little evidence of a decline in banking, though they acknowledge that the sector might have grown faster in the United States had it not been restricted from certain activities by regulation.

Boyd and Gertler (1994) sought to adjust U.S. bank assets systematically for off-balance-sheet activities. One method is to transform those services involving credit risk—loan commitments and letters of credit—into asset equivalents using their Basel risk weights,[15] thus giving a level of assets that would give the same risk exposure. An alternative is to assume that all sources of noninterest income offer the same rate of return as net interest income and calculate implicit non-interest-earning assets that may be added to the balance sheet. When these methods are used, virtually all the decline in bank "assets" share in the United States disappears.

So although it is clear that banks' share of traditional intermediation has declined relative to that of institutional investors, banking is shown to be in a state of evolution rather than outright decline. We now go on to probe the developments underlying these patterns and the role of institutional investors in more detail. Competitive pres-

---

15. The Basel risk weights are regulatory bank capital requirements that vary to crudely reflect the different credit risks from varying types of bank exposure. For example, the weight for a corporate loan is 100%, and for an interbank loan it is 20%. These weights, introduced in the mid-1980s, are at the time of writing being amended to reflect credit risk more sensitively (see www.bis.org for information on the progress of the reform).

sure is exerted by institutional investors on banks on both the liabilities and assets sides.

5.2.2   Competition on the Liabilities Side

On the liabilities side, banks have faced strong **competition in some countries from money market mutual funds**. The latter are diversified open-end investment companies that invest in short-maturity and highly rated debt securities. They seek to maintain a stable asset value per share of par, which is facilitated by the type of short-term, low-risk money-market securities in which they invest. Shareholders are often allowed to redeem funds by use of checks, thus giving transactions services identical to those of bank accounts. Besides being a major financial innovation per se, money market funds have two important effects on financial structure, namely, providing competition to bank deposits and spurring the growth of money markets. Their growth has been a particular feature of countries such as the United States and France (see table 1.12); their development has been much less marked elsewhere, to date. Competition on the liability side is an important aspect of the competition faced by banks' traditional business in these countries. It has led to a narrowing of profit margins, higher deposit rates, and greater risk taking (see section 5.2.3). Concerning risks, there is a debate about possible risks of runs from money market funds in the event of sharp price changes and a decline in market liquidity (see section 5.3.4).

Money market mutual funds developed rapidly in the United States in the 1970s, a period of high money market rates. They disintermediated bank deposits, whose interest rates were subject to government control, unlike the return on money funds. Disintermediation led to a crisis of profitability for banks, which was followed by the abolition of controls on interest rates for banks and thrifts in the early 1980s. But growth of money funds continued. This is because yields remained higher than banks would offer, owing to the effect of reserve and capital requirements on banks' spreads. Similarly, in France, there has been a major expansion of money funds, stimulated partly by tax incentives. Since money market funds in France are run largely by banks, the degree to which banks suffered loss of income due to disintermediation was diminished (although fees from money market funds fall short of the spread income from the equivalent value of traditional deposits).

Longer-term mutual funds may also compete with bank deposits. For the United States, Mack (1993) argues that even longer-term mutual funds may provide effective competition for banks, given their liquidity, despite capital uncertainty. Fortune (1997) notes that checks may be written even on equity or bond funds in the United States. In Japan, medium-term bond funds (Chikoku) have offered effective competition with bank deposits owing to their liquidity and higher yields than deposits.

5.2.3 Competition on the Asset Side

Disintermediation by institutional investors on the asset side of banks' balance sheets can be viewed in various ways. One point is that institutional investors broadened the scope of borrowing options for corporations beyond bank credits. A second is that institutional competition raised the efficiency of intermediation as loan and deposit rates became tied more closely to capital market rates. But equally, the story of securitization and of the banking difficulties of the 1980s—and the intense competition that still characterizes banking markets—are intimately linked. Institutional investors were crucial players in the overall developments that occurred: "competition-driven disintermediation into securitized money and capital markets" (IMF 1991).

The process of bank-institution competition on the asset side developed from the **long-term growth** of pension funds, insurance companies and mutual funds. The beginning of securitization took place in 1975, when the U.S. government sponsored the packaging of illiquid individual mortgage loans held by thrifts to sell to institutional investors and guaranteed investors against credit risk. This was intended to raise the flow of funds to the housing market and improve diversification for lenders that were obliged by interstate banking restrictions to focus on lending to local markets. But it also furthered the process of disintermediation.

Factors underlying balance sheet developments that led to major losses by banks in many OECD countries at the end of the 1980s and in the early 1990s cannot omit the **less developed country debt crisis**.[16] Losses incurred led to a reduction in banks' credit ratings and hence increased their cost of funds vis-à-vis their major corpo-

---

16. For a description of the crisis, see Davis (1995b).

rate customers, as well as leading to a need for wider spreads on loans to rebuild capital bases. Such pressure on spreads was aggravated by tightened regulation of capital bases. This itself promoted securitization by putting the heaviest risk weights on corporate loans and the lowest on government bonds, as well as requiring less capital for trading than banking activities.

Both loss of credit rating and wider spreads reduced banks' competitiveness as suppliers of funds to highly rated companies as compared with institutional investors operating via the securities markets. Companies accordingly switched part of their demand for debt finance to the money[17] and bond markets. In parallel, as we noted above, depositors often found that their needs could be served more cheaply by the use of money market instruments and money market mutual funds. Note that in the absence of alternative sources of funds such as institutional investors in securities markets, banks' customers would simply have had to pay higher spreads in the 1980s. This was indeed the case for small companies, which are confined to bank finance by information asymmetries.

The loss of rating by banks is only half the story, however. **Competitiveness of the securities markets was sharply improving**. This was partly due to the growth in institutional investors themselves, following a shift by the household sector asset demand away from deposits (which led to a boost for money market funds on the one hand and expanded the supply of long-term funds for insurance companies and pension funds on the other).[18] Supply-side factors also played a role in improving securities market competitiveness. These included large government deficits and privatization, improved distribution technology (e.g., for CP), and other developments partly related to institutionalization such as improved trading technology (see section 5.1.2 and chapter 8) and deregulation of domestic securities markets. A further supply-side element was the growth of information services and rating agencies (which supplanted banks' credit assessment for many borrowers, thus reducing the value of bank relationships).

17. Note that whereas initially, money market funds tended to invest heavily in bank CDs, by the 1980s and 1990s, they were mainly invested in commercial paper and other short-term credit instruments, disintermediating banks (see F. Edwards 1995, Wojnilower 1997).

18. Hargraves et al. (1993) trace this pattern in the United Kingdom, the United States, and Japan in the 1980s.

Financial innovations to service needs of institutions **played a key role** in this process. Financial products in effect migrated from banks to markets once they proved sufficiently standardized and high volume. (The higher funding costs of banks also proved to be an important incentive.) Because funds were thus increasingly supplied by institutional investors (who rely on public information) rather than banks (which rely on private information), such migration was accompanied by an enhanced focus on public information disclosure (Bisignano 1995). Examples of this pattern are low-grade bond and medium-term note markets, which have enabled a broader range of companies than before to benefit from securities market financing and have facilitated highly leveraged corporate restructurings. A further innovation was the expansion of packaging and securitization of a wide range of loans without government guarantees (including mortgages, student loans, commercial loans, and consumer debt). Besides involving institutions as investors, these innovations led to competition for commercial banks from investment banks for origination and servicing fees. The growth of money markets as highlighted above has in turn encouraged corporations to switch to money markets for their short-term financing needs, thus disintermediating banks also on the asset side and undermining the profitability of their short-term business lending. CP could be issued directly by large and creditworthy companies, while lower-quality credits could borrow from finance companies, which themselves would be financed by CP issue.

Besides the general demand of institutions for securitized assets, demand for some securitized instruments that disintermediated banks is closely linked to **specific regulations**. For example, as we noted in section 2.3.3, minimum funding requirements for U.S. and Canadian pension funds sharply increased the demand for hedging (Bodie 1990). This stimulated the development of immunization strategies (to match assets to liabilities) based on long-term bonds. The requirement of a fixed duration[19] for investment instruments in the context of such strategies in turn stimulated innovations in the

---

19. Bodie (1990) suggests that fixed-duration securities (and associated strategies) have little role in terms of household utility maximization, as they are unable to hedge against the inflation risk to future consumption. U.S. (and Canadian) defined contribution funds nonetheless tend to hold significant quantities of fixed duration instruments, partly owing to the risk aversion of the members.

United States and Canada tailored to pension funds' needs, such as zero-coupon bonds, collateralized mortgage obligations, and guaranteed investment contracts (GICs) offered by life insurers. This in turn spurred the overall process of securitization involving mortgages in the case of collateralized mortgage obligations and loans and private placements in the case of GICs.

The patterns of disintermediation by institutional investors, putting pressure on banks' profits, **coincided with deregulation, liberalization, globalization, and technological advance**. These entailed increased competition even in areas of traditional banking business in which securities issuance was less viable (such as for small to medium-size business loans). Competition increased between banks themselves both in domestic markets and across borders, as well as between banks and nonbanks such as finance companies. The factors are very much interrelated, and authors differ in the emphases they put on what are often interlocking or mutually reinforcing causal relations (see Revell (1997) for some recent in-depth studies). These developments have entailed changes in the structure of the financial system. Following the classification in section 1.4, financial systems are departing from the bank-oriented phase and becoming more market-oriented or even securitized.

5.2.4 Banks' Responses to Disintermediation

In sum, the challenges on the liabilities and assets side of the banks' balance sheets involved increasing competition for deposits and diminishing returns on traditional loans. They took place while the banks were also facing deregulation of their own activities and difficulty of restructuring to remove excess capacity that emerged as competition increased (Davis and Salo 1998). Their responses were threefold.

First, there was a much greater focus on **off-balance-sheet and fee-earning activity** (see table 5.8) to economize on capital and share in the increase in securities market activity, taking advantage of their distribution networks and customer relationships. The activities in question included underwriting, brokering, market making, and insurance business, as well as services related to institutional investment and fund management itself. As we noted in chapter 1, banks themselves are becoming active in purchasing or launching their own insurance companies (where regulations permit[20]) and selling their own mutual funds and setting up or purchasing fund managers. Index fund management operations of banks in the United States have been particularly successful. They also benefit from the growth of fund management in terms of custody,[21] payment, and foreign exchange services. In effect, institutionalization gave a spur to the universalization of banking even in countries such as Japan and the United States (and, to a lesser extent, the United Kingdom) where activity of banks has been traditionally restricted (Rybczinski 1995). There was also increased penetration of previously segmented lending markets, particularly where their branch networks could be used (e.g., for mortgage lending).

Second, there was **intensified cost cutting** to eliminate the excess capacity that emerged as disintermediation and increased competition affected banking markets. This has entailed branch closures and reductions in staff, often following mergers.

Third, there was **increased balance sheet growth**, focusing particularly on higher-risk borrowers, to maintain profitability. Higher-risk lending included loans to real estate development companies, loans to finance leveraged takeovers, and cross-border lending. Often, these patterns accompanied a shift from relationship to transactions banking (in parallel to the trend toward transactions-driven securities finance). In principle, shifts to higher-risk and unfamiliar markets should have been possible without major increases in solvency risk to the banks if the associated credit risk had been priced accurately and reserves had been built up accordingly.

The fact that **major losses** were incurred in the 1980s and early 1990s by banks in many OECD countries suggests that risk pricing—or quantity rationing—was not accurate. Competition from institutional investors may have aggravated this tendency, since the latter can lend at much lower spreads. Three main cases can be outlined as to how this could come about: accurate risk pricing ex ante but unexpected developments generating losses ex-post, deliberately inaccurate risk pricing to generate competitive advantages and thus profits in the future, and inaccurate risk pricing due to errors in

---

20. It should be emphasized that regulations have until recently limited the scope for such diversification by banks in countries such as the United States.

21. In the United States, pension funds are obliged to subcontract custody, and in the United Kingdom, the proportion rose from 28% in 1992 to 38% in 1996 (British Invisibles 1997).

credit assessment. Experience suggests that the second and third played important roles (Davis 1995b); mispriced government safety net protection may have encouraged such errors, as they meant that the cost of funds did not rise with risk (Kane 1986).

The **response by banks** to the above-mentioned difficulties in the 1990s included a further wave of mergers, as excess capacity was removed (Berger et al. 1995). Given the coincident recession of 1990–1991 and existing asset quality problems, U.S. banks in particular found it hard to raise additional capital either from the public or from increased earnings. The response was to reduce on-balance-sheet risk assets, notably loans. Accordingly, the introduction of the Basle capital ratios gave a strong additional impetus to the process of securitization of loans. In the words of Wojnilower (1997), "the sale of securitized packages of consumer and other loans, which improved capital ratios by removing these assets from balance sheet totals, accelerated greatly. Since they were trying to reduce rather than expand assets, banks also bid much less aggressively for deposits and other funds, opening wider the door for mutual funds." A further effect was to encourage the expansion of securities activity by banks such as market making and proprietary trading to increase profitability.

Further such waves of securitization and institutionalization can be envisaged, following further the lines set out above. Market making has already become less profitable. Hence proprietary trading is becoming more important to both commercial and investment banks, which, as was observed in the Russia/LTCM crisis of autumn 1998, could increase risks (see section 5.3.4.5).

5.2.5 The Future of Banking

The assumption of most financial market analysts has been that although there may be excess capacity in the banking sector, there will remain a role for depository institutions making nonmarketable loans at fixed terms. Some economists would, by contrast, suggest that **all of banks' functions could be taken over by institutions** such as pension funds, life insurers, and mutual funds operating via securities markets (together with rating agencies and other specialized monitors). They would point to the successful securitization of personal loans, the ability of bond and commercial paper markets to serve an expanding range of companies, the development of corporate banking and treasury operations, and the success of money market mutual funds in countries such as the United States in providing market-based means of transactions as well as saving.

One **counterargument** would point to the shift of banks into fee-earning business as noted above. This includes not only their traditional role in the payments system, but also provision of backup lines of credit, brokering and market-making fees and commissions, credit assessment, underwriting, foreign exchange, advice on mergers, proprietary trading in capital markets, custody, income from origination and servicing of securitized loans, and institutional fund management itself. Securities and derivatives markets require access to liquidity through the banking system to ensure timely delivery of cash. Indeed, as we noted above, analysts such as Boyd and Gertler (1994) show that if balance sheets are adjusted to allow for some of these services, much of the "decline of banks" in the United States disappears.

Banks' advantages in overcoming asymmetric information may also form a basis for a continuing role for banks in an institutionalized financial system. Recent studies of banks' uniqueness would seem to underpin this suggestion. Direct evidence of comparative advantages of bank loans over other forms of finance include the following:[22]

• Bank lending relationships are important to small firms, and such firms rely on banks that are geographically close (see Elliehausen and Wolken 1990, Hannan 1991).

• Borrowers and not depositors tend to bear the tax of reserve requirements (Fama 1985, James 1987). This suggests that borrowers obtain services from banks that are not obtainable elsewhere; otherwise, they would shift to avoid the burden of the tax.

• There is evidence of a positive market value of banking relationships; Slovin et al. (1993) found that borrowers from Continental Illinois had negative excess stock returns during its crisis and positive returns during the bank's rehabilitation. The size of the excess returns varied with the importance of the relationship between the

---

22. For a broader discussion of the links between banking, corporate finance, and monetary policy, see Davis (1994b).

bank and the borrower. Petersen and Rajan (1994) found positive effects of close and committed banking relationships on firms' value.

• There are signaling effects of bank lending relationships on the cost of other forms of finance, as other providers of external finance appear to take existing lending relationships and the associated agreement on the part of the firm to be monitored as a positive signal about firm quality (James 1987, James and Wier 1990).[23]

• Securitization has not reduced the importance of banks as monitors of debt claims, since loans that are securitized are often held by other banks rather than direct investors (Berger and Udell 1992).

These studies suggest that banks do have a clear comparative advantage over other financial institutions for certain types of transaction, implying that they will retain a role in the financial system despite the growth of institutional investors.[24] There may still be a reduction in the scope of bank lending, however, in that the above evidence suggests that their comparative advantage is most marked for small, highly idiosyncratic, and information-intensive borrowers and transactions. Other financings will increasingly take place via capital markets and will be held as assets on the balance sheets of institutional investors.

In this context, one may add that institutions, having matched assets and liabilities that are usually marked-to-market and being generally well diversified, should help to improve financial stability relative to a system dominated by banks. Runs and insolvencies are less likely to occur for institutional investors than for banks. But as we discuss in the next section, there are counterarguments relating to securities market instability that could be generated by institutional investors.

---

23. Note, however, that banks may not be able to capture the profits from such monitoring as markets free ride on information about lending relationships.

24. Our main focus in this section is on effects of institutionalization on commercial banks. Investment banks also had to adapt their business to cope with the fact that retail investors that wished to invest directly in stocks and bonds began increasingly to switch to institutional investing. This reduced the profitability of specialized intermediaries in retail brokerage with large research departments, particularly once securities commissions were abolished owing to pressure from institutions (in New York in 1975 and in London in 1986). Consolidation and diversification were the consequence. The winners were the discount brokers and those seeking to specialize in wholesale business serving pension funds and mutual funds. This included trading expertise, risk management, product advice, and development of financial innovations and strategies to control risk for pension and mutual funds.

5.3   Institutionalization and Financial Stability

5.3.1   Institutions and Securities Market Turbulence: General Considerations

The tendencies for important changes to occur in the structure of capital markets as a consequence of the development of institutional investors have **implications equally for the accuracy of asset pricing**. It is often popularly suggested that the growing dominance of financial markets by institutional investors has led to heightened volatility, thus weakening the performance of this key function of financial systems.

Such hypotheses must, however, be formulated with care. In normal times, institutional investors, having good information and low transactions costs, are likely to **speed the adjustment of asset prices to fundamentals**; this should entail price volatility only to the extent that fundamentals are themselves volatile. Moreover, the growing diversity in types and sizes of institutions—in their liabilities, incentives, and consequent attitudes to risk—should be **stabilizing to financial markets** (see chapter 2). In the words of BIS (1998), a financial system's stability depends on "the coexistence of participants with divergent objectives and mutually complementary behavior." Diversity should be increased by the growth of diverse types of institutional investors and increased further as ultimate responsibility for asset allocation is handed back to individual investors in the context of defined contribution pension funds and mutual funds.

Certainly, the concept of **superior information** of institutions is underpinned by studies showing that initial public offerings that are largely subscribed by institutions tend to do well, while those that are largely purchased by the general public tend to do badly (Trzcinka 1998). This suggestion is also supported by econometric analysis (Davis 1988) of the portfolio distributions of life insurers and pension funds, which shows that asset holdings relate strongly to relative asset returns, as we noted in section 2.5.1. Such market sensitivity generates an efficient allocation of funds and also acts as a useful discipline on lax macroeconomic policies. Institutions are also to some extent attracted to more volatile securities, as they are likely to offer higher returns to accompany higher risk, while idiosyncratic risk is eliminated in a diversified portfolio.

Table 5.9
Market Price Volatility (Standard Deviation of Monthly Percentage Changes)

		1965–1970	1970–1975	1975–1980	1980–1985	1985–1990	1990–1995	1996–1999
United Kingdom	Bond total returns	1.2	3.4	3.5	2.6	2.4	1.9	2.8
	Share prices	4.0	8.7	5.1	3.3	5.2	3.3	3.4
	Exchange rates	1.2	1.3	1.9	2.0	1.8	1.7	1.7
	Industrial production	1.0	2.4	2.1	1.3	1.3	1.0	0.7
United States	Bond total returns	2.0	1.7	2.5	3.0	2.3	1.8	3.8
	Share prices	3.4	4.3	3.2	3.5	3.9	2.2	3.6
	Exchange rates	0.2	1.3	1.2	1.8	1.6	1.6	1.6
	Industrial production	0.8	1.2	0.8	0.9	0.6	0.5	0.5
Germany	Bond total returns	1.1	1.4	1.7	1.6	1.5	1.4	3.3
	Share prices	4.3	4.3	2.5	3.2	6.0	3.6	5.1
	Exchange rates	0.9	1.6	1.1	1.1	0.8	1.0	0.6
	Industrial production	2.0	1.7	1.7	2.5	1.6	1.4	1.4
Japan	Bond total returns	0.1	0.6	2.1	2.1	3.5	1.9	14.6
	Share prices	3.3	4.7	1.9	2.8	5.2	5.0	4.9
	Exchange rates	0.2	1.6	2.6	2.1	2.5	2.5	2.9
	Industrial production	1.1	1.5	1.3	1.2	1.4	1.6	2.2
Canada	Bond total returns	1.2	1.5	1.9	3.4	2.1	2.0	4.0
	Share prices	4.0	5.1	5.1	5.2	4.7	3.0	4.6
	Exchange rates	0.5	0.7	1.3	0.9	1.1	1.1	0.6
	Industrial production	0.9	1.4	1.2	1.5	0.9	0.7	1.0
France	Bond total returns	0.7	1.0	1.6	1.9	2.2	1.7	2.8
	Share prices	3.9	4.0	4.2	4.8	6.2	4.0	4.7
	Exchange rates	1.1	1.3	1.1	1.2	0.7	0.9	0.5
	Industrial production	6.1	2.0	1.7	1.3	1.5	1.2	1.1
Italy	Bond total returns	0.9	1.8	1.9	2.0	1.9	2.6	3.3
	Share prices	3.8	7.3	6.2	7.0	7.0	5.7	6.3
	Exchange rates	0.3	1.3	1.7	0.7	0.6	2.2	0.8
	Industrial production	2.3	3.9	3.0	2.5	3.2	3.5	1.4

Source: BIS.

The **liquidity** that institutional activity generates may dampen volatility, as is suggested by lower share price volatility in countries with large institutional sectors (see table 5.9 and the results in section 5.1). It can be argued that securitized financial systems have important stabilizing features (notably ease of marking to market, distance from the safety net, and wider opportunities to diversify and spread risk).

In a global context, enhanced **cross-border portfolio investment** undertaken by institutional investors as discussed in chapter 6 should enhance the efficiency of global capital markets by equalizing total real returns (and hence the cost of capital) between markets. Such a process occurs as investment managers shift between overvalued and undervalued markets via tactical asset allocation. Increased efficiency enables capital to flow to its most productive use and savers to maximize their returns.[25] It is aided by the increase in speed of information flows and the ability of institutions to conduct cross-border arbitrage using derivatives markets (stock index futures for equities, FRAs for money markets, and swaps for bond markets).

We now go on to assess how the picture above, of increased financial stability as a consequence of institutional investor development, could prove incorrect. This could occur in particular if the risk and reward structures in a delegated portfolio management relationship impair managers' ability or willingness to adopt contrarian positions and institutions instead adopt mimetic portfolio positions, herding into and out of markets in a disruptive manner.

5.3.2   Asset Price Volatility

As table 5.9 shows, overall price volatility has not shown a marked increase on average over five-year periods in bond, equity, and forex markets, despite growth in institutional investors. There is rather a correlation with volatility of fundamentals such as industrial production. Some results of financial economics analysis nonetheless suggest that securities markets—dominated by institutional investors —show **"excess" volatility on average** over long periods:

• Stock prices are too volatile to be justified by the volatility of cash flows[26] (Shiller 1990, Leroy and Porter 1981).[27]

• The rate of return in any market is negatively related to the unexpected change in market volatility (French et al. 1987, Haugen 1997). When volatility increases, the price falls, thus increasing future

---

25. There is some evidence (Howell and Cozzini 1990) that international investment has tended to reduce the dispersion of real returns, although a longer run of data and more disparate economic performance between countries would be needed to prove it. It is clearer that nominal covered returns have tended to equalize, notably as capital controls are abolished (Frankel 1992). Indeed, Bisignano (1993) argues that gross flows alone will tend to equalize only nominal returns; net flows of saving and investment are needed to equalize real returns. But net flows have also been sizable for some time, such as the flows between Japan and the United States.

26. Roll (1984a) finds that futures prices for orange juice are too volatile to be justified by the volatility of temperature—the main determinant of price—although they do predict temperature better than the U.S. Weather Service.

27. Ackert and Smith (1993) counter that if merger premiums are included in cash flows, then the excessive volatility result disappears.

returns and vice versa. Price changes thus appear to not anticipate future returns but rather react to changes in volatility.

• Unexpected changes in economic and financial variables explain only 18% of differences in monthly market returns, while the other 82% do not react to measurable factors[28] (Cutler et al. 1990a).

• The activity of noise traders may undermine market efficiency and generate volatility. An efficient market relies on arbitrage by informed investors to return the price of securities to equilibrium levels. Transactions costs and risk aversion may limit this activity if prices may be driven far from equilibrium values by traders who are irrational and think prices should differ from equilibrium levels.[29]

The analyses above link to considerable work on **foreign exchange markets**. As became apparent in the ERM crisis (IMF 1993, Davis 1995a), these are increasingly influenced, if not dominated, by institutional investors, notably hedge funds. For example, Evans and Lewis (1993) show that there are persistent excess returns in spot and forward currency markets and in bond markets. They suggest that "informed traders" are more risk averse than "trend chasers" or "noise traders" and hence are unwilling to take large positions even when currencies are far from their equilibrium values. Alternatively, there may be a range of values of the exchange rate within which a precise equilibrium rate is not defined and within which sharp movements can occur in response to herding, as the influence of noise traders predominates, but also margins beyond which the rate is definitely considered contrary to the fundamentals, and the judgments of informed traders prevail (De Grauwe 1989). Clearly, the width of the range may itself change as uncertainty increases. In a fixed rate system, such heightened uncertainty may ultimately shift the range of plausible values beyond the bands that the authorities seek to defend.[30]

---

28. But this may neglect the possibility that risk compensation varies over time in a predictable manner. Ferson and Harvey (1992, 1993) argue that when this is allowed for, stock returns do become predictable relative to economic variables.

29. In support of this hypothesis, it can be argued that the discount in closed-end funds links to the demand by the market for compensation from risk generated by noise traders. Other interpretations are possible, however.

30. See also Cartapanis (1993), who favors an explanation of heightened volatility based on an initial situation of dispersed expectations and heightened uncertainty, which increases the weight of noise traders relative to informed traders, as informed traders, lacking confidence in their own judgment, find it rational in such circumstances to follow the rest of the market. In such a situation, a loss of credibility by the authorities—for whatever reason—may lead to a crisis, with all market opinion moving in the same direction, and a rapid shift in the rate, overcoming any resistance by authorities.

Lakonishok et al. (1991a, 1992b) examined the investment behavior of U.S. **pension funds** and its potential effects on market price volatility. They found only weak evidence of herding but stronger evidence of positive feedback trading in smaller stocks. There was little evidence of positive correlation between changes in institutional holdings and excess returns; therefore no support is lent to the idea that institutions destabilize markets in individual stocks on average. But they could not rule out marketwide herding, which is of most relevance to this section[31].

Sias (1996) examined directly the relationship between the **volatility of securities returns and the level of institutional ownership** generally. He found a positive contemporaneous relation between institutional ownership and securities market volatility after accounting for capitalization.[32] This is surprising, given that institutions are subject to prudent man rules and seem to avoid the more volatile smaller stocks (see section 6.2.5). The relationship could be consistent either with institutions seeking high volatility stocks, owing to the high return they offer (and because informed trading is easier to conceal for large stocks), or because higher volatility results directly from institutional ownership. Sias suggests that the latter is the case. This is contrary to the view that institutions play a stabilizing role owing to their superior information[33] and rationality compared to individual investors. Possible reasons for a linkage of higher volatility to institutional ownership may include larger average trade size of institutions, which may induce volatility by overwhelming market liquidity and the greater use of program trading by institutional investors. It may also reflect a greater tendency for institutions to engage in noise trading or herding, as we discuss in the next section.

5.3.3 Herding by Institutional Investors

A considerable volume of theoretical research focuses on the implications of principal-agent problems to which institutions are prone

---

31. See also Chan and Lakonishok (1993, 1995) and Lakonishok et al. (1993b) on short-term market responses to institutional trades.

32. The adjustment is needed, since institutions focus on larger stocks; the result is that within each decile of size, the stocks most held by institutions are also the most volatile.

33. Also because higher institutional involvement may generate more interest among analysts.

for financial structure and behavior outlined above. It examines in particular potential effects on price volatility. As outlined in the surveys by Devenow and Welch (1998) and Bikhchandani and Sharma (2000), this literature suggests that institutional investors may be subject to **rational herding**, all seeking to buy or sell assets at the same time. In effect, although institutions are usually best seen as merely a conduit through which investors' changing moods are transmitted to financial markets, in exceptional circumstances herding behavior may induce capital market volatility beyond what would be generated by similar reactions in a more traditional investor base composed of individuals.[34]

In other words, the hypothesis is that institutionalization, in the context of modern capital markets, may **amplify market dynamics** by virtue of institutions' size and common behavior. Such herding may be a **periodic rather than continuous** phenomenon, being much more marked in periods of market stress than in the case of normal market conditions, which in turn makes it more difficult to detect by using standard statistical techniques[35] such as are used by the studies cited in the section above.

As detailed in chapter 2, fund management is a service involving management of an investment portfolio on behalf of a client. Unless the manager is perfectly monitored and/or a foolproof contract is drawn up, the manager may act in his or her own interests (e.g., in generating excessive commission income) and contrary to those of the fund. Various features of fund management can be seen as ways to reduce **principal-agent problems**. For example, pension fund managers in countries such as the United States and the United Kingdom are offered short (three-year) mandates, with frequent performance evaluation;[36] fees related to the value of funds at year-end and/or performance-related fees. At least in countries where performance figures are widely used, open-end mutual fund and life insurance managers will suffer loss of new business if they underperform, while closed-end mutual funds may be taken over.

Principal-agent problems and the means that are used to resolve them could give rise to institutional behavior that induces capital

---

34. See also Haugen (1995, 1997), and on the principal-agent issue see Golec (1992).
35. Nevertheless, Blake et al. (1997) found evidence from a study of individual pension portfolios in the United Kingdom that is consistent with forms of herding.
36. Note that performance evaluation over a short period contrasts sharply with the nature of liabilities, whose maturity may extend to twenty-five years or more for life insurers and pension funds.

market volatility.[37] One underlying mechanism is **reputation**—the desire of managers to show they are of good quality, for example in the context of short mandates. In the model of Scharfstein and Stein (1990), herding, whereby all managers move in the same direction to buy or sell assets, occurs because the market for fund management skills takes into account both the success of investment strategies (based on skills and information) and the similarity to others' choices. The first is not used exclusively, since there are systematically unpredictable components of investment, while good managers are expected to receive correlated signals (they all observe the same relevant pieces of information); hence all good managers may be equally unlucky. On the other hand, a manager who alone makes a good investment may be a lucky but poor-quality manager. So mimicking others is the best way to show quality.

A related factor that could induce volatility is **regular performance checks** against the market benchmark. This may induce similar behavior and hence herding to avoid performing significantly worse than the median fund, not least because fund managers' bonuses, like performance checks, are typically provided annually.[38] For mutual funds, the incentive arises from the desire of managers to be the best performer and hence attract high volumes of inflows (Brown et al. 1996); conversely, net cash outflows may lead to dismissal of managers.

Overall, the result of monitoring may be a preference to follow the leadership of the successful managers, with the danger of a contrarian bet going wrong being much more severe than that of performing badly along with the rest of the market. In each case, such monitoring may, as a corollary, lead to short time horizons (Benartzi and Thaler 1995). As a consequence, institutions may, for example, adopt similar portfolio shifts even if their own information suggests that a different pattern could yield better returns. This may in turn amplify shocks to prices. A corollary is that if managers avoid posi-

---

37. These effects may also apply to equity market researchers on whose earnings forecasts institutional investors rely. If they also herd, as the research of Olsen (1996) suggests, then mimetic institutional behavior will be reinforced.

38. See Davis (1995a), who, after interviewing twelve fund managers on international investment strategies in London in 1991–1993, found that "Most of the managers, but particularly those who are external managers, felt some pressure not to under perform relative to their peers, for fear of losing the management contract. Managers who could afford to act more freely, perhaps because of their firm's reputation, still felt a need to know the consensus in order to act in a contrarian manner."

tions that could result in a large deviation from the benchmark because of the risk-reward structure of incentives, they will not seek contrarian positions that might otherwise help to stabilize markets.

It is notable in this context that according to the Financial Times (1999), 75% of U.K. pension funds still use a peer group benchmark. We also saw in the results of the questionnaire for institutions outlined in section 4.5 that relative rather than absolute return was one of the crucial aspects of asset manager competition.

Short time horizons may affect **information acquisition** and hence market dynamics (Froot et al. 1992). If assets were to be held forever, it would be rational to seek to gain information not held by others, but with a short time horizon—for reasons as described above—it may be rational to concentrate on the same information as others, even if it is extraneous to fundamentals. This is because the larger the number of investors who study the information, the more quickly it enters the market and the greater the benefit from early learning. Use of chartism is an illustration of this point.

Mutual fund managers may **transact repeatedly** to generate commission income in uncompetitive markets such as Switzerland, thus generating market volatility.[39] Other reasons for herding by institutions could include institutions' **inferring information from each others' trades**, about which they are relatively well informed compared to individuals, and herding as a result as information cascades (Shiller and Pound 1989, Bikhchandani et al. 1992). This may be a marked feature if some managers have a reputation for being well informed. Moreover, they may be **reacting to news**, which they all receive simultaneously, in a similar manner.[40]

The **risk management framework** may also play a role. If defined benefit pension funds have minimum funding limits, as have now been introduced in the United Kingdom, they are subject to heightened shortfall risk if asset values decline. This may encourage herding either via direct sales of equities for bonds or by the effects of hedging in so-called dynamic hedging, contingent immunization, or portfolio insurance strategies on market prices. It also severely limits funds' stabilization role, that is, the degree to which they are free to act in a contrarian manner. As Borio et al. (1997) noted, dynamic

---

39. Certainly, De Bondt and Thaler (1994) observe that the turnover rate for institutional investors exceeds that of individual investors.
40. News may cause sizable portfolio shifts in a world characterized by uncertainty if it causes funds to change their views about the future.

hedging can be disruptive for at least two reasons: the mechanical impact of large volumes of sales and because other market participants may infer changes in sentiment from what are actually mechanical, value-insensitive strategies and revise their own expectations accordingly (see Genotte and Leland 1990).

More generally, as Frijns et al. (1995) show, tighter solvency requirements will shorten time horizons, with possible consequences as noted in this section. Credit quality standards, which may be imposed by regulators or by the institution itself, may limit the scope for taking contrarian positions. Hence a downgrading of a certain borrower may lead to a liquidation of positions even if the risk of default is considered remote, and such a withdrawal may itself worsen credit quality.[41] There may also be multiplier effects from contribution holidays for defined benefit pension funds, which are taken when investment performance is sufficiently good to avoid the necessity of further contributions. This would be the case if they lead to higher corporate earnings and thereby boost share prices.

Further elements of the overall framework of asset allocation dominated by institutional investors as outlined in chapter 2 may, while not strictly involving herding, still give rise to positive feedback mechanisms that increase market price momentum. The increasingly **narrow style distinctions** being employed by mutual fund managers as a means of communicating with investors may imply that swings in investor sentiment lead to more leverage on market prices as they switch between such narrowly defined asset classes. The increasing focus on the "best-performing fund" over a recent period, combined with managers' desire to stick to a narrowly defined style, can lead to disproportionate rewards for good performance of a style, which lead on to sharp price rises in the asset class concerned. The popularity of momentum trading, which was seen as highly profitable in the bull market of the late 1990s, illustrates this point.

A simpler mechanism may underlie sharp movements by open-end mutual funds: simple **purchases and sales by households**, which oblige the manager to liquidate assets immediately to redeem the units or in an upturn to purchase stocks. This may be a powerful mechanism if households are risk adverse and subject to major shifts in sentiment. It may be increased by the shift to defined contribution pension funds; the assets are typically held in mutual funds and

---

41. See also Schleifer and Vishny (1990).

their disposition is often at the discretion of the individual investor (assets are "instividualized"). Risk-averse investors may sell funds in response to short-run moves, contrary to appropriate long-run time horizons of their (retirement) assets. However, evidence from the Investment Company Institute (1995, 1996, 1998) tends to suggest that U.S. mutual fund shareholders have at least in the last two decades not sought to liquidate en masse when markets fall.

The **use that is made of benchmarks** may also have destabilizing consequences. If asset managers are seeking to replicate the benchmark and benchmarks are based on capitalization weights, then there may again be self-reinforcing tendencies. For example, the IFC index weights for Latin America and emerging Asia were 34% and 45%, respectively, in January 1997, whereas in the wake of the Asian crisis they changed to 41% and 24%, respectively, following sharp falls in Asian share prices and exchange rates. To the extent that managers were following such benchmarks by selling Asian stocks, this may explain why there were no rapid reflows back to Asian markets after prices fell.

Herding is more likely to have a market impact when no investors take offsetting contrarian positions. But not all institutions are at liberty to **act in a contrarian manner**. Mutual funds must adhere to the asset allocation strategy set out in their prospectus. Moreover, whereas the overall strategy of leveraged institutional investors, such as hedge funds, is precisely to adopt contrarian positions, they may at times of market stress have limited scope for maneuver. They may, in effect, be forced to herd, owing to the way in which credit that is freely available in the upturn in asset prices may be sharply withdrawn in the downturn. This was apparent in the bond market crisis of 1994 as well as after Russia/LTCM in 1998 (Davis 1995c, 1999d). Pension funds and life insurers have the greatest freedom to act as contrarians.

Herding by institutions need not always be destabilizing; it may **speed the market to a new equilibrium** price. Indeed, Wermers (1999) suggests that U.S. mutual funds on average tend to speed the price adjustment process for individual stocks to which they herd (although overshooting of equilibrium levels could not be ruled out). This is so-called rational positive feedback trading. What is needed for herding to be of concern is for institutions also to follow strategies that may be **contrary to fundamentals** and profit maximizing

—buying high and selling low—which is "irrational" positive feed-back trading.[42]

Cutler et al. (1990a) suggest that institutions may themselves act in this manner. This may be a consequence of biases in judgment under uncertainty by fund managers, which leads to extrapolative expectations or trend chasing rather than focus on fundamentals. Such approaches may help the money manager by "adding winners" to the portfolio and removing embarrassments for the sponsor, that is, window dressing (Lakonishok et al. 1991b). Certain investment strategies may also induce such behavior, such as stop-loss orders, purchases on margin, and dynamic hedging strategies. These may be common when there are minimum funding limits. Institutions may also seek indirectly to provoke positive feedback trading (DeLong et al. 1990), since in the presence of less-informed investors such as households, it is rational for institutions (such as hedge funds) to buy in the knowledge that their own trades will trigger further feedback trading by less-informed investors, thus amplifying the effect.

The potential **effects of herding** are discussed below, namely, heightened volatility of market prices and quantities and/or liquidity failures in debt markets at specific times. But one might add that herding may also entail a loss of diversification benefits (as markets move together) and expose institutions themselves to major losses as prices deviate from fundamentals. Market liquidity failures also pose major problems to monetary policy makers, in that loss of liquidity in debt securities markets caused by herding may engender systemic risks for leveraged institutions such as commercial and investment banks as well as hedge funds. In effect, central banks have to consider whether large shifts in securities prices are the consequence of a well-functioning market responding to a change in fundamentals or whether they arise from liquidity problems that could, in extreme circumstances, be a matter of serious policy concern.

5.3.4   Capital Market Instability

5.3.4.1   Overview

There have been periods of securities market instability whereby relatively thin securities markets have tended to undergo crises of

---

42. Evidence for destabilizing herding would be a later correction of market prices, with no change to the "fundamentals."

illiquidity, while liquid markets have undergone large perceived deviations of prices from fundamentals. These patterns appear to be **linked to episodes of one-way selling** by institutions, which may generate securities market instability; in the context of increasingly integrated markets in which institutions are active, they may readily spread between markets and internationally. Recent episodes of instability are listed in table 5.10.[43] The table shows that although there have also been major banking crises, the types of crisis that are linked at least in part to the activity of institutions have become more common in recent years.

BIS (1986) suggested a number of reasons for one-way selling to occur more frequently in a financial system dominated by institutional investors, including the following:

• Portfolios are increasing concentrated in the hands of few institutional investors, which may react similarly and simultaneously to news, transmitted increasingly rapidly by global telecommunication links.

• Such investors have a fiduciary role.

• They see their holdings of money market and debt instruments as short-run, low-risk, high-liquidity assets.

• They may have less detailed information than would a bank on which to base a credit decision.

• They have less of a relationship reason (than banks) to support a particular borrower or keep a particular market functioning.[44]

In section 5.3.3, we also noted various incentive-based reasons why institutions may herd. A complementary explanation—which may amplify the effect of such herding—is that buying or selling pressure may **overwhelm the available liquidity** in the market (Genotte and Leland 1990). Also sophisticated trading and investment strategies using derivatives and leverage—which often program in identical responses to a given price change (Wojnilower 1997)—may lead small changes in expectations to generate large price shifts. Certainly, Borio et al. (1997) noted, a fragile anchor for expectations, increasingly weak liquidity constraints (notably in an upturn) due to availability of credit for leveraged trading, and strong pressure to

---

43. For descriptions and analyses, see Davis (1994a, 1995b, 1995c, 1999d).
44. Because of the loss of positive externalities from liquid markets, they may be induced to display clublike supportive behavior.

Table 5.10
Selected Episodes of Financial Instability, 1970–1998

Date	Event	Main Feature
1970	U.S. Penn Central Bankruptcy	Collapse of market liquidity and issuance
1973	U.K. secondary banking	Bank failures following loan losses
1974	Herstatt (Germany)	Bank failure following trading losses
1982	LDC debt crisis	Bank failures following loan losses
1984	Continental Illinois (U.S.)	Bank failure following loan losses
1985	Canadian Regional Banks	Bank failures following loan losses
1986	FRN market	Collapse of market liquidity and issuance
1986	U.S. thrifts	Bank failures following loan losses
1987	Stock market crash	Price volatility after shift in expectations
1989	Collapse of U.S. junk bonds	Collapse of market liquidity and issuance
1989	Australian banking problems	Bank failures following loan losses
1990	Swedish commercial paper	Collapse of market liquidity and issuance
1990–1991	Norwegian banking crisis	Bank failures following loan losses
1991–1992	Finnish banking crisis	Bank failures following loan losses
1991–1992	Swedish banking crisis	Bank failures following loan losses
1992–1996	Japanese banking crisis	Bank failures following loan losses
1992	ECU bond market collapse	Collapse of market liquidity and issuance
1992–1993	ERM crisis	Price volatility after shift in expectations
1994	Bond market reversal	Price volatility after shift in expectations
1995	Mexican crisis	Price volatility after shift in expectations
1997	Asian crisis	Price volatility following shift in expectations and bank failures following loan losses
1998	Russian default and LTCM	Collapse of market liquidity and issuance

For detailed accounts, see Davis (1994a, 1995b, 1995c, 1999d).

conform due to high competitive pressures on asset managers help to explain incentives to herd and why there may be strong externalities between individual portfolio choices. The fact that liquidity constraints typically harden abruptly when conditions become adverse helps to explain why market adjustments can be extremely sharp. Borio et al. argue that the new financial environment, with greater market integration, may make a common shock across markets more likely by increasing access to similar sources of information and homogeneity of views and approaches. In finance theory terms, it increases the common factor in asset returns.

5.3.4.2 Herding and Price Volatility
One consequence of herding behavior seems to be the observation of occasional **sharp price shifts following medium-term deviations of asset prices from levels consistent with fundamentals**, generally in

highly liquid financial markets, which raise concerns for monetary and financial stability (Davis 1995c). Examples are the stock market crash of 1987, the ERM crises of 1992–1993, the global bond markets in 1993–1994,[45] the Mexican crisis of 1994–1995, and to some extent the East Asian crises of 1997. Common features of these events included heavy involvement of institutional investors in both buying and selling waves,[46] bank lending being rather subordinate, cross-border investment flows, signs of overreaction to the fundamentals and excessive optimism before the crisis (i.e., herding), at times inappropriate monetary policies, a shock to confidence that precipitated the crisis, albeit not necessarily sufficient in itself to explain the scale of the reaction, and rapid and wholesale shifts between markets, often facilitated by derivatives in the wake of the shock. Such volatility may have important macroeconomic consequences of concern to monetary policy makers (see section 6.3.3), raise borrowing costs for companies and the government, increase uncertainty and thus reduce investment,[47] generate inefficient resource allocations, and lead to systemic risk via losses incurred by leveraged investors.

As an example of systemic risk, one may cite the 1987 stock market crash (F. Edwards (1995), Fortune (1993)), when on October 20, 1987, in the wake of sharp institution-driven declines in share prices, traders of equity futures and options contracts had to meet massive margin calls. Largely because of timing problems associated with these margin flows, some large brokers experienced a liquidity squeeze, which threatened to send the clearing and settlement system into gridlock. Because it was unclear whether firms were illiquid or insolvent, banks were unwilling to extend credit. So to avoid a systemic collapse, the Fed announced its readiness to "serve as a source of liquidity to support the economic and financial system."

5.3.4.3 Market Liquidity Risk

A second consequence of herding behavior on the part of institutions is the tendency of **debt securities markets that are rather thin and illiquid to face complete liquidity failure** when institutions begin to sell heavily (Davis 1994a). Examples are the ECU bond market crisis

---

45. On the role of dynamic hedging during the bond market crash, see Fernald et al. (1994).
46. For example, Wojnilower (1997) notes that the key propellant for the stock market crash was selling by fifteen portfolio insurers, institutional investors that were following a program of selling futures automatically in response to falls in market prices.
47. See Hu (1995).

of 1992, the FRN market in 1987, junk bonds in 1987, Swedish commercial paper in 1990, and the Penn Central crisis in the U.S. commercial paper market in 1970, as well as Russia/LTCM in 1998. Financial crises typically feature changes in both prices and liquidity, so there is a continuum between such episodes and those noted above. For example, the ERM crisis entailed sharp falls in liquidity in certain derivatives markets, and in the 1994 bond market break, there were a number of financial failures owing to a panic and liquidity failure in the market for mortgage-backed securities (Wojnilower 1997). Equity markets may also suffer from illiquidity in crises, as for example the stock market crash of 1987 led to sharp changes in market liquidity.[48] But the main focus here is on markets in short- and long-term debt and derivatives.

In general, market liquidity depends on all other asset holders not seeking to realize their assets at the same time; in other words, there are externalities to individual behavior. If doubt arises over the future liquidity of the securities market for whatever reason (it could be heightened credit risk or market risk), it is rational to sell first before the disequilibrium between buyers and sellers becomes too great and market failure occurs (i.e., yields are driven up sharply, and selling in quantity becomes extremely difficult). The associated decline in liquidity of claims is likely to sharply increase the cost of raising primary debt in such a market (i.e. there will effectively be heightened price rationing of credit), or it may even be impossible to gain investor interest at any price (quantity rationing).

The nature of such liquidity failure may be further clarified by analysis of the **role of market makers**, which buy and sell on their own account, increasing or reducing their inventories in the process,[49] at announced bid (buy) or ask/offer (sell) prices. A market maker provides (to buyers and sellers) the services of immediacy and a degree of insurance against price fluctuations. To be able to satisfy buyers of the asset, the market maker must have an inventory of the asset in question (although the securities may be borrowed rather than purchased), together with access to finance for such inventories; the spread must obviously cover the cost of finance. There is a risk of a capital loss on the inventory through unforeseen changes in prices. Accordingly, the response of market makers to one-way selling when

---

48. Indeed, Amihud et al. (1990) show that the price decline itself reflected in part the revision of investors' expectations regarding equity market liquidity.
49. Unless they are able to "cross" individual buy and sell orders.

the new equilibrium price is uncertain is often simply to refuse to quote firm prices, for fear of accumulating stocks of depreciating securities, which itself generates a collapse of liquidity. Uncertainty is crucial; if there is a new market-clearing price at which buyers reemerge, the market makers will adjust their prices accordingly without generating liquidity collapse.

Market collapse in dealer markets, even in the absence of generalized uncertainty, may also result from perceptions of asymmetric information (Glosten and Milgrom 1985). Market makers face a mix of investors who are more or less informed than they are. Those who are more informed are "insiders," and those who are less informed are "liquidity traders." A relative increase in insiders leads market makers to widen spreads to avoid losses. This discourages liquidity traders, who withdraw, increasing adverse selection. Some dealers may cease to operate. Once the insiders are too numerous and if their information is too good, bid and ask prices may be too far apart to allow any trade. Since a wide spread in turn prevents the insider from revealing his or her information by trading, shutting down the market will worsen subsequent adverse selection (i.e., the proportion of insiders relative to liquidity traders) and widen the spread further.

Bingham (1992) argues that such liquidity collapses in debt securities markets and derivatives markets are particularly likely when returns to market making are low and hence investment banks are unwilling to devote large amounts of capital to it. In such cases, the secondary market, in effect, ceases to function (see also section 6.3.2). These patterns pose major risks to securitized financial systems, given the central importance of liquidity to financial institutions (such as banks' funding via CDs, companies via CP, dealers/brokers via repos, money market funds on the asset side, etc.).

5.3.4.4 Why Are Market Liquidity Crises of Concern?

One reason why market liquidity in debt and derivatives securities markets is of greater concern than it was in the past is that **banks are more actively engaged** in securities business, including not only issuance but also trading, underwriting, and providing backup facilities. Hence a securities market collapse could lead to a liquidity crisis for a bank.[50]

Equally, **failure of a major securities house** could occur during a market liquidity crisis. There could be withdrawal of bank credit

---

50. For a more detailed discussion, see Davis (1994a).

lines as a consequence of perceptions of exposure to the market concerned, loss of confidence in the wholesale money markets where such firms obtain much of their funding, collapse of liquidity in those markets, or demands by banks for greater collateral at a time when its asset value is falling sharply (OECD 1991). Failure could in turn lead to further defaults, given the varied and sizable exposures of firms to each other in several markets.

Furthermore, securities markets are increasingly relied on as repositories for liquidity. Money market mutual funds, for example, find liquidity of money markets essential to maintain the ability to maintain par (section 5.3.6). Sharp declines in liquidity may lead to cash flow difficulties due to inability to sell or increased difficulties obtaining credit due to the lower value of collateral. Bankruptcies and defaults may ensue.

The process of securitization has entailed a much greater reliance on securities markets by a range of institutions. Banks, for example, may rely on the ability to securitize loans to realize liquidity. They are also tending to hold portfolios of securitized assets themselves. There is a wide range of nonbank financial institutions such as finance companies, whose funding (as in Sweden) relies mainly on securities markets and whose default following securities market collapse may lead to wider difficulties in the financial sector. Nonfinancial companies are also increasingly reliant on securities markets to raise short-term working capital (via CP) and long-term finance (via bond issuance).

Liquidity difficulties may arise just as readily in derivatives markets as in underlying securities markets. As the IMF (1993) noted, of credit, market, and liquidity risk in derivatives markets, "the most difficult to counter is liquidity risk." Banks are tending to use markets in derivative products, notably forward rate agreements and swaps, instead of the traditional interbank markets to manage their own interest rate risk. Besides exposing banks to interest rate risk, the collapse of liquidity in derivatives markets may entail heightened uncertainty over banks' exposures (given that derivative exposures are in any case off balance sheet) and thus heighten the potential for runs.

5.3.4.5   Institutional Investors and Liquidity in the Russia/LTCM Episode

The financial market turnaround seen in 1998 in OECD countries, which led to both sharp asset price falls and declines in liquidity, was heavily influenced by institutional investor behavior (see IMF (1998) and Davis (1999d) for detailed accounts). Over the period of upturn in the bull market, there appeared to have been an increase in risk tolerance, manifested in a willingness by institutional investors (and households) to hold equities on much lower required returns than had hitherto been the case, as well as a narrowing of credit-quality spreads on bonds.

This pattern may have been influenced by overoptimism and an **increase in risk tolerance** on the part of asset managers (belief in a new era of growth), albeit equally influenced by overoptimism on the part of retail investors in mutual funds[51] (implying that the bull market was partly "instividual"). The latter's confidence in the sustainability of historically extreme market valuations was shown by their willingness to avoid selling equities via their mutual funds, notably in the United States, during the market break recorded in October 1997 and in the succeeding years up to the time of writing in spring 2000 (see Bank of England 2000). Their willingness to underpin the market led to liquidity and confidence being maintained (in contrast to episodes in 1987 and 1989), paving the way for a further rise in prices until the year's peak in July 1998, which was itself underpinned by massive further inflows to mutual funds, while wholesale asset managers were more restrained.

Other factors may have been important besides an increase in risk tolerance. As noted by BIS (1998), declining yields on substitute assets may also have played a major role, whereby the decline in inflation-adjusted bond yields tended to outpace required returns. Also lower inflation rates could help to justify lower required returns, via a lower volatility of short-term interest rates and a less distortionary effect of tax systems. Meanwhile, the bull market in bonds was also influenced by the expectation of higher growth at low interest rates, as well as in 1997–1998 by a flight to quality from Southeast Asian and other emerging markets.

More generally, the **decline in supply of both bonds and equities** in the mid-1990s owing to fiscal retrenchment and share buybacks, at the same time as institutional portfolios were growing rapidly, may also have played a role in boosting prices. These may have led to an

---

51. It is not clear whether behavior would have been identical in the case of direct holdings of shares by households or whether the portfolio diversification and expert management of mutual funds helped in itself to underpin investor confidence.

increase in demand for riskier and less liquid assets independently of risk tolerance per se. Surveys show that leveraged buyout funds, international private equity, and venture capital rose considerably in importance in pension funds portfolios, with holdings of these types of instrument by U.S. and Canadian pension funds amounting to over $70 billion in 1998. Hedge funds, often speculating in a leveraged manner on "renormalization" of spreads, were very active market participants. Corporate bonds and emerging market instruments also increased in attraction (see below). Not that all such assets need to be high risk. Synthetic securities that reproduce the risk and return characteristics of government bonds and securitized debt are examples of relatively low-risk substitutes for government debt, albeit with some liquidity risk attached.

The severe financial market turbulence that shook the OECD financial markets in late 1998 was widely linked to a **reversal from risk tolerance to extreme risk aversion**, with severe falls in share prices and corporate bond prices, further turbulence in emerging markets, and a contraction of liquidity. One trigger was the Russian default in August, but the crisis was aggravated by the insolvency and rescue of the hedge fund LTCM in September. The IMF (1998) highlighted the fact that it was simultaneous sales by leveraged players such as hedge funds and investment banks that helped to precipitate such large and wide-ranging price and liquidity collapses in the wake of these shocks.[52] Institutional investors, which could have cushioned market price falls and enhanced liquidity by taking contrarian positions, failed to do so as a consequence of risk aversion following earlier losses.

Whereas longer-term institutional investors (other than hedge funds) were thus rather inactive in the crisis, their **role as stock lenders** was important. They created a pool of lendable securities, which through custodian banks usually provide liquidity to leveraged players such as hedge funds. Hedge funds in turn take short positions using this liquidity. These positions may be outright bear strategies or relative value/arbitrage strategies. So institutions may facilitate such leveraged position taking by providing liquidity to securities markets in this manner. Markets as a consequence become more efficient and perhaps more volatile.

---

52. See also BIS (1998), chapter 7.

5.3.5   Institutional Behavior and Emerging Markets

As we detail in section 6.1.3, there was a large **increase in capital flows to emerging markets** in the 1990s[53], driven by mutual funds and other institutional investors. Such investment was expected to bring increased liquidity and reduce price volatility, but instead the result appears to have been heightened volatility. This was particularly apparent in the wake of the Mexican crisis, when a number of other emerging markets whose fundamentals had not apparently changed also experienced sharp price falls. Similar patterns were observable in the Asian crisis of 1997, although in this case, the role of institutional investors appeared to have been less central.

In this context, there is an **important asymmetry** between the **location and size** of institutional investors—very large in cash terms and mainly in OECD countries—and the emerging markets and their relatively small size (BIS 1998). In the context of the cyclical nature of investment in emerging markets, a marginal portfolio adjustment in the context of global investment by institutions can thus be a first-order event for the emerging market. According to 1995 data, 1% of domestic equity holdings by institutional investors in the G-7 countries is equivalent to slightly over 1% of global stock market capitalization but would be equivalent to 27% of market capitalization of the emerging Asian economies and 66% of Latin American ones. Hence if portfolio shifts on the scale of only 1% of domestic equities were to be focused solely on the emerging markets, the effects could be very disruptive.

Aitken (1996) found that the degree of autocorrelation of total returns in the overall emerging market index,[54] as indicated by the variance ratio,[55] increased sharply in the period of increased capital inflows (1992–1995) compared with the previous period (1989–1991).

---

53. See also Gooptu (1993).

54. The IFC index for all emerging markets, for Latin America, and for Asia.

55. In an efficient market in which asset prices reflect all available information about fundamentals, prices will tend to follow a random walk, the current price being the best forecast of the future price. A random walk generates actual future prices that are within a range that widens linearly over time. The variance of the rate of return increases proportionally with the time assets are held. The variance ratio tests whether this is the case. A positive variance ratio shows positive autocorrelation, and a negative variance ratio shows negative autocorrelation. Positive autocorrelation indicates that conditions for bubblelike behavior are present; that is, whether price increases or declines would signal further increases or declines in the future.

This is contrary to the movement that would be expected if inflows had led to greater liquidity, longer investment horizons and market efficiency. Moreover, the composite indices showed larger increases in variance ratios than the individual national markets, suggesting that such indices have a separate importance from that of their components. The estimate of the variance ratio of the composite index was 3.7 over 1992–1995, where any ratio above 2 shows that excess rates of return increase or decrease in an accelerating manner.

Froot et al. (1999) sought to assess the potential **role of institutional investors in destabilizing emerging markets** over a more recent period, using a data set of custodial holdings over the 1994–1999 period to assess flows into and out of forty-six countries. The authors found that there was a statistical effect of (foreign) inflows on prices in the emerging market. Following the logic of the efficient markets hypothesis, that prices encapsulate all relevant information, this suggests that foreign investors are better informed than domestic ones. They found that flows into and out of countries are highly correlated across international investors and seem to occur in response to global trends such as inflation and exchange rate expectations rather than changes in local conditions in the country concerned. Also, although investors' withdrawal did not strongly correlate with falls in prices (i.e., it was not direct pullouts that caused price collapses), a marked deceleration in inflows did tend to depress prices, consistent with the idea that they are often marked up in the expectation that recent trends in inflows will continue. We consider that the results are not entirely conclusive in suggesting that foreign institutions destabilize emerging markets but offer strong circumstantial evidence.

It would appear from this evidence (as well as from independent interview surveys (Davis 1995a)) that institutional investors often **treat emerging markets as a separate asset class**. This is also shown by research by Buckberg (1996), who, assessing emerging markets' stock returns data over 1989–1995, showed that a standard one-factor model of asset returns (in which returns on the asset relative to the global portfolio is the only relevant factor) is dominated by a two-factor model including also the return on emerging market stocks. The implication is that investors indeed follow a two-step portfolio allocation process; they first determine the share to allocate to emerging markets as a whole, then allocate it to individual markets within that group. Underlying this pattern, institutional investors or their portfolio managers who are uninformed about individual countries, or who do not seek to differentiate, may allocate funds evenly across emerging markets to ensure diversification. Inflows thus tend to lead to increases in stock prices across all emerging markets, regardless of the variation in underlying structural and macroeconomic performance.

The use of managers with general expertise in emerging markets rather than specialists in individual countries is reportedly partly[56] driven by the difficulty of comparing the performance of such narrowly defined specialists. In contrast, general or "balanced" expertise in emerging markets may be readily compared. But the latter may generate herd behavior, as managers seek not to diverge from mainstream asset allocation for fear of performing below the median. The behavior thus stems directly from the fundamental need for monitoring in the portfolio management process. It may be added that such bloc behavior is not limited to emerging markets; interviews that the author conducted with portfolio managers in 1991–1995 (Davis 1995a) showed that even before EMU made it appropriate, Continental Europe was commonly treated as a bloc. Equally, as Wojnilower (1997) noted, selling of government bonds in the 1994 market break led to distress selling worldwide, with little respect for the fundamentals underlying each government bond market.

Judgments on emerging market investments are often not only undertaken in a manner that is correlated across markets but are also made on the **basis of historical evidence of correlations and returns**, without reference to the effects of recent inflows on such patterns. As inflows themselves generate price rises, the process may **become self-generating**, destabilizing the market. The corollary is that when there is a crisis in one emerging market, such as **Mexico** in 1994, a reassessment occurs, and the allocation across the asset class as a whole is reduced. Given the size of institutional investors relative to the emerging markets, this generates volatility across the sector as a whole. Such behavior is contrary to the efficient markets hypothesis, with allocation not following fundamentals of an individual asset but rather investor sentiment about the class of assets as a whole, whose fundamentals may be unrelated. Indeed, such behavior is likely to drive prices away from fundamentals in many markets.[57]

---

56. Other reasons may include restrictions on asset allocations to emerging markets and strong risk aversion, which leads investors to avoid high-risk assets.
57. See Beckaert and Harvey (1995).

At least in the early stages, correlated behavior was less apparent in the 1997 crisis in **East Asia**, suggesting that a degree of learning had taken place. Institutional investors appear to have read the signs correctly well ahead of the banking sector and had already reduced their exposure when the crisis began in Thailand in July 1997. As BIS (1998) noted, portfolio allocation data for pension funds from the Netherlands, the United States, and the United Kingdom showed that pension fund managers from these countries had embarked on a reduction of their Asian exposures as early as the last quarter of 1996. Meanwhile, banks continued to invest heavily in the sector until the second quarter of 1997. Some commentators have pointed to the fact that institutional investors are typically not covered by any form of safety net[58] and hence were not subject to moral hazard in the way that banks were, although desire on the part of banks not to disrupt customer relations may also have played a role. There was also little evidence that hedge funds as a group were heavily involved in triggering or intensifying the series of Asian currency depreciations. According to BIS (1998), although there was considerable exposure in early 1997, long positions were substantially reduced in the months preceding the crisis, while exposures to Latin America were built up.

Nevertheless, regardless of possible turning points, there is certainly evidence that Southeast Asia underwent a generalized withdrawal of funds by both banks and nonbanks in the second half of 1997. The severe consequences for financial stability in the region showed again how, given the size of institutional portfolios, combined one-way shifts of this nature could lead to sharp adjustments or even dysfunction of the market price mechanism. Moreover, it was seen that in late 1997, mutual fund investors also began to sell Latin American funds, thus generating contagion across emerging markets in a way that was less present in 1994. Finally, in the autumn of 1998, there was a generalized withdrawal from emerging markets by institutional investors in the wake of Russia/LTCM, driven on the one hand by the generalized increase in risk aversion and on the other by a key component of this increase: the financing difficulties of leveraged investors.

---

58. Besides considering themselves protected from failure by their own authorities, banks from OECD countries may have anticipated safety net assistance by local governments on behalf of the banks in the Far East to which they lent or the willingness of the international community to bail out the countries concerned.

5.3.6   U.S. Mutual Funds and Financial Stability

So far, this section has focused mainly on fund managers' behavior and its potential for triggering asset price volatility. But **households**, the ultimate owners of institutional assets, may also by their behavior **induce financial instability**. On the one hand, they are more likely to have diverse views than is a select group of large institutional investors. But on the other, they are vulnerable to fads and fashions in investing that may oblige managers to focus on a single approach or philosophy of asset management. The popularity of growth and momentum investing at the time of writing is one example. In the context of mutual fund investment, households can often shift from one fund to another in a fund family at low or zero cost. Withdrawal of households by this means from a style of investing (as discussed in section 2.1.7) could generate instability.

At the time of writing, a concern in the United States is **whether the boom in mutual fund ownership is leading to overshooting of equilibrium levels of share prices** (see, for example, Shiller 2000). Such a situation could, it is argued, culminate in a market collapse that could be damaging to the real economy, raising unduly the cost of capital. In this context, although asset manager behavior may have an impact, the mutual funds have to be viewed as largely a transmission mechanism for the increased enthusiasm among the public for the seeming high returns and low risk that equities have offered in recent years. In particular, Fortune (1997) shows that the rise in equity holdings by mutual funds results from a portfolio shift by investors into mutual funds rather than increased saving or a shift into equities by mutual funds independently.

The gap between the redemption of units and receipts from sales of securities, noted in chapter 1, could pose stability problems for mutual funds. Default of a large number of mutual funds on their implicit obligation to repay in cash could clearly lead to a financial panic. To cover redemption needs, funds hold a certain amount of cash-equivalent assets, such as short-term bonds, for sale or repurchase.

The size of such **on-balance-sheet liquidity** is a matter of portfolio choice. In a highly competitive environment, there is an incentive to reduce liquid asset holdings to a minimum, lest performance decline (although there is a limit on explicitly illiquid assets, which cannot be sold at net asset value in seven days, to 15% of the portfolio). Indeed,

Fortune (1997) shows that whereas U.S. equity mutual funds held 10% of their portfolios in liquid form in the early 1990s, this fell sharply to 5.5% at the end of 1996 (although this was partly linked to a reduction of settlement periods from five days to three days) and to just over 4% in 2000. Another factor may be the greater size of mutual funds, which offers economies of scale in cash balances (a tendency that may be partly justified given the law of large numbers).

Fortune (1997) points out that there are three further ways of providing liquidity to cover redemptions:

• credit lines with banks (either committed, when the bank is obliged to make a loan in certain circumstances, or standby lines, when there is a willingness but not an obligation to lend);

• credit from within a family of funds (when, for example, if individuals are switching from the equity to the money market fund, some temporary recycling may be appropriate to cover the payments gap); and

• the fact that funds have the possibility to redeem in shares rather than cash.

For each of these sources of liquidity, there are limits to the availability of the facility. Bank credit lines will depend on the health of the lending institution and, as we have noted, are wholly reliable only in the case of committed lines. Inter-fund-family lending is severely restricted by regulation in the United States, owing to the risk of inappropriate loans with insufficient collateral and return. The option of in-kind redemption is thought to be dangerous for a firm's future reputation and future business; many funds have committed themselves, under a 1971 rule of the Securities and Exchange Commission (SEC), to redeem in cash[59] and hence do not have this route available.

One can envisage a **scenario in which heavy redemptions may exhaust liquidity**, leading to securities sales, even ahead of redemptions to rebuild liquidity. By drawing on credit lines, mutual funds could become highly leveraged, and hence net asset values could become more sensitive to securities market fluctuations. In a sharp decline in securities prices with heavy redemptions, there may be a

---

59. Redemption in kind remains possible for individuals wishing to redeem over 1% of net assets or whose redemptions over ninety days exceed $250,000.

higher proportion of failed or misrecorded trades, for which mutual funds themselves might ultimately have to accept responsibility.

One protection against such massive redemptions that could threaten financial stability is that assets in mutual funds are transparent, unlike those of banks, which reduces the overall risk of runs. Investors also are subject to inertia and seek to avoid selling units until prices have recovered. Moreover, the increased use of mutual funds for retirement saving (34% of the U.S. total in 1998) makes a large proportion of mutual fund assets unlikely to move out of the sector as a whole in response to short-term market movements. The ease of switching within families of funds, for example from the equity to the money market fund, may attenuate this stabilizing factor, however.

Experience of the 1987 crash (Fortune 1997) was favorable, in that there were no major problems of financial difficulty among funds, although some did adopt delays in repayment. Sales of equity mutual funds accounted for only 3.2% of equity transactions on October 19, 1987, and only 2% of equity mutual funds were redeemed (most of which were exchanges into other funds).[60] More generally, the Investment Company Institute (1995, 1996, 1998) notes that U.S. mutual fund shareholders have, at least in the last two decades, not sought to liquidate en masse when markets fall. On the other hand, Fortune (1997) detected an apparent tendency for U.S. mutual fund investors to invest in a positive feedback manner (a correlation of new money flows to capital value as high as 0.5 for equity funds), which, if amplified in a crash, could be highly destabilizing. Moreover, as Wojnilower (1997) notes, Japanese mutual funds were decimated in the 1990s bear market in that country, and a similar pattern occurred for U.S. and U.K. equity funds in the 1970s.

A second risk arising from mutual funds could be a form of **"snowball" decline in market prices**, whereby an initial shock leads to accelerating redemptions by mutual fund holders, which feeds back in turn to generate an accelerating fall in prices and further redemptions. Fortune (1998) found at least some evidence supportive of this hypothesis. He found that changes in U.S. bond and equity prices are predictors of flows of net new money to corresponding mutual funds. The evidence of reverse causality was weaker.

---

60. F. Edwards (1995) notes similar patterns of low redemptions for the 1994 bond price collapse and the Mexican crisis of 1994.

Although flows into bond funds help to predict equity and bond prices and flows into "equity and bond funds" predict equity prices, there was no evidence that flows into equity funds shape current returns on stocks or bonds. Using a similar methodology, Edwards and Zhang (1998) found that inflows to mutual funds did not explain the rise in U.S. stock prices in the 1990s. However, they did find that net redemptions of mutual funds over 1971–1981 caused a fall in stock market prices. It could not be ruled out that this pattern would be repeated in a future bear market (see also Warther 1995).

A third possible reason for concern is that **losses on money market mutual funds could lead to a run by money fund shareholders** (F. Edwards 1995, 1996). Money funds in the United States are highly exposed to the CP market, which accounted for 42% of their assets in 1998. Defaults in CP, particularly if they lead some funds to break par and redeem shares for less than a dollar, could lead to investors redeeming their shares. This would force money funds to liquidate their assets, including CP, entailing a drying up of liquidity in the CP market, more breaking of par, and further redemptions. Commercial paper issuers would find it hard to roll over their paper, leading potentially to more defaults. The cycle would also lead to price falls in CP, leading to more losses for money fund shareholders.

F. Edwards (1995) points to the fact that whereas there were rather few CP defaults from the time of the Penn Central crisis of 1970 (see Davis 1994a) to 1989, since then there have been a significant number. In 1989–1992, twenty-six issuers defaulted on $2.4 billion in CP in the United States and Europe, nine in the United States alone, accounting for $1.0 billion. Following CP defaults, losses were recorded by two money funds in 1990 (Value Line Cash and Liquid Green Trust), but neither broke par, as the advisors injected funds by buying the defaulted paper at par value rather than market value. Similar bailouts occurred for derivative-based losses by other funds. In 1997, Strong Capital Management repurchased CP from three of its money funds after a default by used car lender Mercury Finance. There has been some discussion in the United States of privately insuring money funds, although the effects on performance would be significant.

Gorton and Pennacchi (1992), however, found no evidence that money fund shareholders responded to defaults in CP by selling their money fund shares. The U.S. regulator, the SEC, responded to defaults in the early 1990s by tightening portfolio regulation of money funds so that a single issuer may not account for more than 5% of assets, nor may paper of below the highest rating be over 5% or a single issuer of this type over 1%. The weighted average maturity of fund assets may not exceed ninety days. The CP market is characterized by backup lines of credit, meaning that rollover difficulties are unlikely to entail failure.

F. Edwards (1995) contends that despite these changes, the stability of money funds "remains an issue." On the other hand, he concludes that proposals to extend banklike regulation to money funds (D'Arista and Schlesinger 1993) are misconceived. The history of money funds suggests a marked degree of stability. Also the transparency of money funds makes bank runs based on uncertainty about solvency unlikely. Furthermore, money funds are not vulnerable to the moral hazard that the so-called safety net has created for banks.

5.3.7   The Threatened Insolvency of Japanese Institutional Investors

At the time of writing, a key ongoing policy issue in Japan was the **negative net worth of life insurance companies and a number of pension funds**. The pattern shows the downside of institutional investment when there are guarantees on returns to beneficiaries (i.e., in defined benefit pension funds and traditional life insurance) in combination with restricted investment of assets, low levels of competition in asset management, and poor returns on the assets available. The problem has been overshadowed by the difficulties of the Japanese banks and the economy but is now coming increasingly to the fore as the authorities come to grips with the banks.

Traditionally in Japan (Clark 1994), **book value accounting**[61] **has obscured poor performance** of pension funds and life insurers and has prevented a clear assessment of solvency[62] (see section 3.7). It has also prevented funds from selling poorly performing shares and has prevented switching of asset managers (as both would entail realization of losses). Pension funds used to use a wholly unrealistic

---

61. A reform is currently shifting funds to market value accounting (Pensions and Investments 1997).
62. Book value accounting has also been at the root of various scandals in Japan, such as those related to so-called tobashi-deals, CSFB derivatives operations, and Princeton Economics.

discount rate of 5.5%, imposed by the government, which led to further underfunding. Accounting reform that involves a move of pensions onto the balance sheet, a realistic discount rate, and a switch to market values (in April 2000) has brought solvency to the fore (see Nakamae and Harney 1999).

Concerning **pension funds**, market estimates of the shortfall on pension assets in 1998 were $663 billion[63] (implying that around 50% of liabilities are uncovered). Sumitomo Chemicals announced that it would use half its free cash flow for a year to halve its pension liability, but most Japanese firms did not have such resources. Hitachi reduced employee benefits. Sony created a separate pension trust into which it moved cross-holdings while retaining voting rights; it hired foreign asset managers (see section 3.7) to help manage the fund. Toyota reported in November 1999 a $5.7 billion shortfall in its pension fund as of March 1999 under new Japanese accounting rules, using a so-called conservative 3% interest rate, a figure that was double the one previously announced. Nissan had announced a comparable figure earlier. Toyota announced, in common with other Japanese companies, that it would be selling cross-shareholdings or using cash reserves to replenish the deficit. In April 2000, the merging Sakura and Sanwa banks announced that they would use unrealized gains on their share portfolios to tackle underfunding.

Sales of cross-holdings seem likely to be a significant contributor to the shift of Japanese corporate finance toward a more Anglo-Saxon basis—under pressure from without by funds such as CALPERS (see section 6.2.3) and from within from the failings of Japanese institutional investors. The pattern of difficulties for defined benefit funds is likely to encourage the growth of defined contribution funds, now that these are permitted.

Pension liabilities have not led to corporate bankruptcies, since underfunding can be recouped gradually (although they could be restraining business fixed investment). The solvency situation for **life insurers** is in some ways more threatening (see Bank of England 1999). At the time of writing, one firm, Toho Mutual, had gone bankrupt, with negative equity of 200 billion yen, and in doing so had used up half of the investor protection fund. In June 1999, the major life funds acknowledged a shortfall of 1320 billion yen on their core business (Nakamae 1999). As Japanese long-term interest rates

---

63. An estimate for early 2000 is 70 trillion yen.

remained at around 1–2%, the firms were unable to make returns sufficient to meet guarantees to policyholders, which had been set at a time when long rates were three times higher than at the time of writing but that regulations prevented the firms from reducing. (Guaranteed policy dividends were on average around 3.8–4.1% at the time of writing.) Personal and corporate new business was, in the meantime, falling sharply, and policy cancellations were rising owing to both poor economic conditions and a lack of confidence in the industry's ability to honor policies in the long run. The life insurers also faced huge bad debts on loans, amounting to 1110 billion yen. On the other hand, some perspective is provided by the fact that the bad debt figure was only 0.6% of assets. The assets of the eight major companies remained sizable, and their solvency margins were above the 200% minimum. Demutualization may be encouraged for companies to enable them to recapitalize.

These difficulties **may not be unique to Japan**. There has been comment on possible difficulties of life insurers in southern European countries such as Italy, Spain, and Portugal that may have guaranteed returns based on formerly high nominal interest rates. According to Bishop (1998), the problem even extends to Belgium, where life insurers guarantee a 4.75% return, which for some time in 1999 was above the government bond yield. France is also thought to be affected; the difficulties of the U.K. life insurer Equitable Life have a similar basis.

Conclusions

In this chapter, we have showed that institutional investor development has a major impact on capital market size, microstructure, and innovation. Institutionalization may by this route make a contribution to the broader efficiency of the economy, by ensuring that the functions of the financial system are carried out in an effective manner. However, there may be an effect not just on capital market structure per se, but also on the banking sector and on the dynamics of capital markets. We have examined the hypothesis that the banking sector may been weakened by the development of institutional investors and found that competition on both the asset and liability sides has intensified. We note, however, that heightened risk taking is not the only feasible response, and many banks have taken the route of offering noninterest fee-based services to institutions themselves.

An increase in average asset price volatility is not detectable with institutionalization; indeed, there is evidence of increased market efficiency. On the other hand, institutionalization does seem to be linked to a rise in volatility for stocks held by institutions. Moreover, one-way selling of assets by institutions occurs sporadically, usually following a longer wave of buying and price increases. In liquid markets, this may lead to sharp price fluctuations, while in less liquid markets, illiquidity may be the consequence. Such patterns may be linked in turn to herding behavior by institutions, induced by the types of incentives that portfolio managers face. Further issues for financial stability are raised by the development of mutual funds in the United States, by the effects of institutional investment on the emerging markets, and by the ongoing problems of life insurers and pension funds in Japan. All of these indicate that regulators and monetary policy makers need to focus closely on institutional investor behavior. (We return to this issue in section 6.3.)

6

Implications of the Growth of Institutional Investors for the Nonfinancial Sectors

6.1   Macroeconomic Implications of Institutionalization
6.2   Corporate Finance Issues
6.3   The Public Sector and Policy Iissues

Introduction

This chapter assesses the broader implications of the growth of institutional investors for the economy as a whole as they fulfill functions such as transfer of economic resources across time and across national borders, as well as overcoming adverse incentive problems. These effects are deep and wide-ranging, reflecting the importance of institutions as a repository of household saving and holders of financial instruments such as government debt and corporate equity and their preeminent position as cross-border portfolio investors.[1]

The chapter is subdivided into implications for the macroeconomy, for the corporate sector, and for regulatory and monetary authorities. Among the topics addressed in the first two sections are the effect on saving, the composition of the demand for financial assets, international capital flows, corporate finance and corporate governance, short-termism, and small firm finance. Policy issues are considered briefly in the third section. Those that are raised include the effect on public financing and privatization (for the fiscal authorities), the appropriate regulation of institutional investors (for regulatory authorities), and the appropriate adaptation of policy in relation to monetary and financial stability (for monetary authorities). Note that issues relating institutional investors to market microstructure and

---

1. See tables 1.9, 6.2, 6.3, and 6.4 for an indication of the importance of institutions with respect to these types of financial claim for the G-7 countries.

development of securities trading systems are considered in chapters 7 and 8.

6.1 Macroeconomic Implications of Institutionalization

6.1.1 Institutions and Saving

In the context of saving, we are discussing how institutions facilitate performance of the financial function of **transfer of economic resources over time**. Development of institutional investors—notably those such as pension funds and life insurance in which savers enter into long-term savings contracts—has often been linked to changing patterns of long-term saving. It is commonly suggested that the development of institutional investors could in principle have caused both a switch of asset holdings toward longer maturities and also an increase in saving per se. This section deals with effects on total saving, and the next deals with its composition.

It may be noted at the outset that a strong effect of institutionalization on saving appears **a priori unlikely** to hold. Empirically, the countries where institutions are most important—the United States and the United Kingdom—are also known for low personal saving. There are also theoretical objections. The basic argument against any effect of institutionalization on saving is that individuals choose a lifetime savings pattern separately from its distribution, so a rise in one component of wealth (such as pension funds, mutual funds, or life insurance claims) will be fully offset by falls elsewhere, either by reducing forms of discretionary saving or by borrowing. This offset will be particularly likely to occur when pension wealth and discretionary savings are close substitutes.

In principle, growth of long-term institutional investors could generate increased saving via the following channels (for an overview, see Kohl and O'Brien 1998):

• Illiquidity of long-term institutional (life insurance and pension) assets may mean that other household wealth is not reduced one-to-one for an increase in wealth held in the form of claims on such long-term institutional investors, because households do not see such claims as a perfect substitute for liquid saving such as deposits (Pesando 1992).

• Liquidity constraints whereby some households are not free to borrow may imply that any forced saving (such as life insurance or pension contributions) cannot be offset either by borrowing or by reducing discretionary saving (Hubbard 1986).

• The interaction between the need for retirement income and retirement behavior may increase saving in a growing economy, as workers increase saving to provide for an earlier planned retirement (Feldstein 1974).

• As unfunded social security is typically seen to reduce saving,[2] because it implies an accumulation of implicit claims on future income, a switch toward funding of pensions should increase it (World Bank 1994, Feldstein 1977, 1995).

• Tax incentives that raise the rate of return on saving via life insurance or pension funds may encourage higher aggregate saving. (Smith (1996) discusses issues relating tax provisions to saving.)

On the other hand, one should note that taxation provisions boosting rates of return will influence saving at the margin only for those whose desired saving is below that provided by social security and tax-favored institutional saving. For those whose desired saving exceeds this level, the increased returns on saving[3] will have an income effect but no offsetting substitution effect. Hence their saving will tend to decline. Moreover, even if tax provisions and the other mechanisms outlined above increase private sector saving, this could be more than offset at a macroeconomic level by the government's revenue loss due to tax concessions.

Most of the research on institutions and saving links to the **introduction of pension funding** (although the results could also apply to life-insurance-based saving). On balance, research suggests that growth in funded pension schemes does appear to boost personal saving, but not one-to-one. A significant offset arises via declines in discretionary saving.

• Much of the literature[4], such as Pesando (1992), which is focused on U.S. defined benefit funds, suggest an increase in personal saving

2. However, analysts in countries such as Germany dispute this effect (Pfaff et al. 1979) and suggest that social security had no effect on saving.
3. Note that increased returns may link not only to the tax concession but also to increased underlying returns on saving via institutions relative to the alternative.
4. For important earlier studies, see Feldstein (1978) and Munnell (1986).

of around 0.35–0.5 results from every unit increase in pension fund assets, though the cost to the public sector of the tax incentives to pension funds reduces the overall benefit to national savings to around 0.2. Hubbard (1986) suggests a larger effect on personal saving of 0.84, Gale (1997) around 0.5.

• Effects would plausibly be less marked for defined contribution funds, in which the worker is more likely to be able to borrow against pension wealth and participation is generally optional. On the other hand, Poterba, Venti, and Wise (1993, 1996) suggest that 401(k) accounts in the United States have added to aggregate saving. Tax incentives are one important reason, but employer matching of contributions, payroll deduction schemes, and information seminars may also be relevant factors in encouraging net saving by this route.

• Similarly, Joines and Manegold (1995) find that IRAs have also raised saving in the United States (by around 0.2), while Attanasio and De Liere (1994) found that 40% of contributions to IRAs by new contributors were new saving and IRAs raise saving by 0.2. Venti and Wise (1994) found that RRSPs (a kind of personal defined contribution pension) raises saving in Canada.

• These results do not extend to shorter-maturity nonpension saving instruments, even if they are tax privileged. Banks et al. (1994) found that tax privileged equity accounts (PEPs) (see section 3.5) as well as tax free deposits (TESSAs) had no effect on personal saving in the United Kingdom but only generated portfolio substitution.

• In developing countries, Corsetti and Schmidt-Hebbel (1997) and Morandé (1998) find that the pension reform replacing pay-as-you-go with funding boosted saving in Chile; World Bank (1994) finds similar effects in Singapore. These effects may link to the prevalence of credit constraints for low-income households that would not otherwise have saved.

• Unfunded social security appears to lower private saving in developing countries (S. Edwards 1995); Feldstein (1995) suggests that personal saving rises 0.5 for every unit decrease in U.S. social security wealth (and vice versa). Neumann (1986) gives similar estimates for Germany, and Rossi and Visco (1995) find a figure of 0.66 for Italy. Lower figures than Feldstein's, of 0.1–0.3, are found by other studies of the United States, such as Gale (1997), who found 0.11, and Hubbard (1986), who found 0.33; King and Dicks-Mireaux

(1988) found 0.17 for Canada. Kohl and O'Brien (1998) argue that the displacement of private saving by pay-as-you-go is more likely, the more imperfect capital markets are.

All these estimates abstract from effects on public saving in the transition to a privately funded system (e.g., in deficit financing of existing social security obligations) that may be fully offsetting at a national level (see Holzmann 1997b). Even tax-financed transitions may, according to some authors, have at most a small positive effect on saving in the long term (Cifuentes and Valdes Prieto 1997).

Institutional investment may have side effects on saving in the **case of financial liberalization**. It is plausible that there would be an institutional effect on saving before such liberalization owing to liquidity constraints as outlined above. This might disappear after liberalization. Indeed, it is notable that the household sectors in countries with large pension fund sectors, such as the United States and the United Kingdom, have also been at the forefront of the rise in private sector debt in the 1980s, as shown in tables 1.8 and 1.9 (see also Davis 1995b, 1995d). The familiar story underlying this is that rationing of household debt diminished following financial liberalization, which allowed households to adjust to their desired level of debt. But in the context of preexisting accumulation of wealth via institutions and high returns to institutional assets, this adjustment could be partly seen to rebalance portfolios, thus entailing borrowing by households to offset earlier forced saving through institutional investors.

On the other hand, even in a liberalized financial system, credit constraints will affect lower-income individuals particularly severely, as they have no assets to pledge and less secure employment. Therefore forced institutional saving will tend to boost their overall saving particularly markedly (for evidence, see Bernheim and Scholz (1992)). This point is of particular relevance in countries that have or are currently introducing compulsory private pensions, such as Australia (Bateman and Piggott 1993), which could thus anticipate a rise in personal saving ceteris paribus (Edey and Simon 1996, Morley and Subbaraman 1995). There may also be a link to education; Gale (1995) indicates that the displacement of private saving by social security is twice as large for the educated as for the uneducated.

One other important empirical result in this area should be noted. Bernheim and Shoven (1988) show that the development of defined benefit pension funds may change the volatility and relationship between saving and real interest rates. Data from the United States show that a rise in real interest rates may reduce saving if it makes more defined benefit schemes fully funded (where institutions are target savers) and hence reduces the need for contributions. There is also evidence for this in the United Kingdom in the 1980s. This pattern may itself give a further boost to market valuations, since it raises profits. Other sectors, of course, need to take up the shares for this boost in valuations to be realized.

The effect of institutional investor growth on personal saving may be offset at the level of national saving by the impact on public finances of tax subsidies to personal saving. However, a switch away from social security to pension funding would probably have a major effect on overall saving, given that the former has been shown significantly to depress saving in a number of countries, notably for the first generation that has not contributed to pay-as-you-go.

It may be added that population ageing will of itself, as noted in chapter 1, generate changes in saving which may have a major macroeconomic impact (see for example Cutler et al (1990b), Makin (1993), Roseveare et al (1996) and references in Davis (1997c)). These changes will undoubtedly be channeled via institutional investors, but institutions may not always be themselves a causal factor in such shifts.

6.1.2 Institutions and Financing Patterns

Abstracting from the likely increase in saving and wealth, the implications of growth in institutions, notably life insurers and pension funds, for **financing patterns** arise from differences in behavior from the personal sector, which would otherwise hold assets directly. As we showed in tables 1.10–1.12, portfolios of long-term institutions vary widely, but in most cases, they hold a greater proportion of capital-uncertain and long-term assets than households. For example, equity holdings of pension funds in 1998 were 68% of the portfolio in the United Kingdom (including foreign equities) and 64% in the United States. But in each case, they compared favorably with personal sector equity holdings, which were 15% and 23%, respectively, in 1998 (table 1.9). On the other hand, the personal sector tends to hold a much larger proportion of liquid assets than institutions do. These differences can be explained partly by time horizons, but institutions also have a comparative advantage in compensating for the increased risk of long-maturity assets by pooling.

The implication is that institutionalization could increase the supply of long-term funds to capital markets and reduce bank deposits, even if saving and wealth do not increase, as long as households do not **increase the liquidity of the remainder of their portfolios fully to offset growth of institutional assets**. As we showed in table 1.9, total deposit shares have indeed tended to decline in most countries over the last thirty years. Some offsetting shifts were apparent in the econometric results of Davis (1988), which suggested that over 1967–1985, the growth of institutions was accompanied by a greater holding of deposits than would otherwise have been the case, albeit insufficient to prevent an overall shift toward long maturity assets.

On the other hand, King and Dicks-Mireaux (1988) found little such offsetting effect in Canada. Moreover, radical changes in financial structure—inconsistent with full offsetting—have been widely observed to accompany growth of funding, not least in Chile (Holzmann 1997a). On balance, results are consistent with an increased demand for long-term saving as institutional investors grow, implying that institutionalization has indeed accompanied a shift in the composition of households' overall portfolios. As we discussed in chapter 1, besides demographics, this may be related to rising overall income and wealth (where only a certain volume of saving is needed to cover contingencies). Interestingly, a shift to defined contribution plans in which individuals determine their own asset allocations may reduce or eliminate these shifts to longer-term assets (Friedman 1996).

Blanchard (1993) suggests that the increased supply of long-term capital market instruments, which he attributes to the development of institutional investors, may be leading to a **compression of the yield differential** between equities and bonds, which may have significant implications for corporate capital structures by making issuance of equities cheaper relative to bonds than was the case in the past. Recent trends and market comment suggest that there has been considerable further compression of the equity risk premium since 1993 (Bank of England 1999), although this may partly be a cyclical rather than a structural phenomenon.

As regards the **broader economic effects** of overall shifts to long-term assets, they should tend to reduce the cost and increase the availability of equity and long-term debt financing to companies, while the accompanying growth of capital markets should also increase allocative efficiency. There may hence be an increase in productive capital formation.[5] Economically efficient capital formation could in turn raise output and, endogenously, growth itself (Holzmann 1997a), thus potentially contributing to resolving the problem of financing retirement as the population ages by increasing the volume of future resources available. Higher growth will feed back onto saving. Endogenous growth effects of an increase in capital investment on labor productivity may be particularly powerful in developing countries if a switch from pay-as-you-go to funding induces a shift from the labor-intensive and low-productivity "informal" sector to the capital-intensive and high-productivity "formal" sector (Corsetti and Schmidt-Hebbel 1997).

Equity market development per se has also been shown to enhance overall economic development (Demirgüç-Kunt and Levine 1996). Levine and Zervos (1996) show how stock market development may aid growth potential, for example, by increasing liquidity and thus facilitating the financing of long-term, high-return projects; enabling international diversification of portfolios to take place and thus encouraging investment in riskier long-term projects; increasing incentives to acquire information about firms; facilitating the tying of management compensation to share prices via stock options; and facilitating takeovers to resolve corporate governance difficulties. But they point out that there are often counterarguments to these. Meanwhile, Demirgüç-Kunt and Maksimovic (1996) show that access to an active stock market also increases firms' ability to borrow at long maturities, especially in developing financial markets (see also Caprio and Demirgüs-Kunt 1998). Finally, access to a range of securities in domestic currency should limit the incentive for companies to borrow in foreign currency, which was a feature of the recent Asian crisis (Davis 1999c).

One note of caution is that if governments force pension funds to absorb the significant issues of government bonds that may be needed in a debt-financed transition strategy, or if government debt issuance crowds out corporate issues, many of the benefits of long-term financing from funding may not be realized.

---

5. This result also requires allocation of funds to their most profitable uses and adequate shareholder monitoring of the investment projects; as detailed in section 6.2, this should also tend to occur in capital markets that are dominated by institutional investors.

Table 6.1
International Investment Flows

	1975–1979		1995	
Share (%)	Outflows from OECD Countries	Inflows to OECD Countries	Outflows from OECD Countries	Inflows to OECD Countries
Banking	49.5	72.0	9.2	5.4
Equities	5.1	3.2	35.0	35.7
Bonds	9.8	13.3	41.7	48.2
Direct investment	35.6	11.5	14.2	10.7

Source: Howell and Cozzini (1995).

6.1.3   International Capital Flows

6.1.3.1   Trends in Portfolio Investment

Recent trends in **international portfolio investment**—the financial function of transfer of resources in the form of securities across national borders—are intimately linked to growth of institutional investors. As table 6.1 shows, cross-border flows have been transformed since the late 1970s, from dominance by banks to a situation in which securities represent over 75% of both inflows and outflows from OECD countries.

This pattern links partly to **adverse developments in international banking**, namely, that before the less developed country (LDC) debt crisis in the 1970s, banks were active lenders, intermediating the funds deposited by Organization of Petroleum Exporting Countries (OPEC) countries to LDCs. After the crisis, banks' willingness to lend to LDCs collapsed, banks' capital bases were weakened owing to the need to provision against losses, and the fall in oil prices reduced inflows from OPEC. But saving/investment imbalances between countries persisted, notably between the United States and Japan. The resulting net capital flows, the size of which was determined by macroeconomic developments, tended to be less than gross institutional flows, so portfolio flows dominated the financing of saving/investment imbalances. As a by-product, portfolio flows also strongly influenced exchange rates, helping, for example, to drive the dollar to a peak in 1985. These gross institutional flows reflect a sharp expansion of international investment by pension funds in recent years, as well as for life insurers in some countries. The expansion of

Table 6.2
International Diversification of Institutional Investors, 1996

Percent of Asset Class	Pension Funds		Insurance Companies		Mutual Funds		Market Cap. as a Percent of Global
	Securities	Equities	Securities	Equities	Securities	Equities	
United States	11	16	7	4	7	10	45
Japan	23	35	13	10			16
Germany	4	21					4
France			1	1			3
Italy			15	40	16	34	1
United Kingdom	28	28	18	19	15	16	9
Canada	17	37	26	30	37	40	3
Australia	20	27	22	29			2
Netherlands	30	58	18	21	7		2
Sweden	6	27	16	36	20	23	1
Switzerland	16	33			49	51	2

Source: BIS (1998).

mutual funds and hedge funds has entailed a sizable proportion of specialized funds investing only in foreign markets.

There are marked **differences in international investment between types of institutional investor** (table 6.2; see also tables 1.10–1.12[6]). Pension funds have a higher level of diversification than life insurers do; also, the trend for pension funds is for diversification to increase, while life insurers appear to be at an equilibrium level of diversification. Life insurers are often focused on fixed income securities, for which benefits of international diversification are less than for equities; both types of institution are often restricted by regulation from international investment. These patterns are also explicable in terms of liabilities; life insurance claims tend in most countries to have fixed income characteristics, which limit the potential benefits of international investment. Mutual funds are focused largely on equity investment, reflecting directly the portfolio choices of the household sector. In most countries, they are more internationally diversified than life companies or pension funds are. Overall, the level of diversification is higher in Canada, Japan, and the United Kingdom (as well as smaller OECD countries) than in

6. The differences in levels of international investment between these two sets of tables are explicable by different sources, sectoral definitions, and years of observation.

Table 6.3
Holders of Government Bonds by Sector (Percentage), 1998

	Households	Companies	Public Sector	Foreign	Financial Institutions of Which:	Banks	Life Insurance and Pension Funds	Mutual Funds
United Kingdom	6.8	1.1	0.0	20.0	72.1	8.5	61.1	2.2
United States	11.0	1.6	7.2	35.3	44.8	5.7	15.5	8.9
Germany	17.6	2.2	0.6	26.4	53.2	35.9	4.7	12.6
Japan	2.3	6.0	45.6	8.3	29.1	16.3	10.8	2.1
Canada	6.4	0.5	22.3	33.9	44.6	11.9	27.9	4.8
France	4.9	4.6	1.9	18.3	70.3	19.6	36.1	14.6
Italy	30.9	1.7	0.9	24.2	41.9	35.2	6.8	N.A.

N.A. = not available.
Source: National flow of funds data; see table 1.1 for details.

Table 6.4
Holders of Corporate Equities by Sector (Percentage), 1998

	Households	Companies	Public Sector	Foreign	Financial Institutions of Which:	Banks	Life Insurance and Pension Funds	Mutual Funds
United Kingdom	21.7	3.6	0.1	29.9	44.7	2.1	33.4	N.A.
United States	39.8	0.0	0.7	7.2	52.3	3.6	31.8	16.3
Germany	15.0	30.5	1.9	15.6	37.0	10.3	13.8	12.9
Japan	19.2	24.4	0.7	13.1	42.6	25.8	15.1	1.4
Canada	30.9	15.2	2.8	20.3	31.1	5.6	9.5	5.1
France	13.3	19.2	7.4	27.3	32.8	15.6	7.8	9.4
Italy	49.6	16.6	5.7	11.9	16.2	12.8	3.5	N.A.

N.A. = not available.
Source: National flow of funds data; see table 1.1 for details.

Germany and the United States. But there is a clear upward trend in the United States.

International investment has also been apparent in terms of the scope of foreign holding of securities. The current picture is shown in tables 6.3 and 6.4 for government bonds and equities. Table 6.3 shows that foreigners hold over 20% of government bonds in all of the G-7 countries except Japan and France. Table 6.4 shows that for-eign holdings of domestic equity fall short of 10% only in the United States, while in the United Kingdom, Canada, and France, foreigners hold more than 20% of equities. These figures have increased signi-ficantly in recent decades. As recently as 1979, foreign holdings of French and German bonds were zero and 5%, respectively.

Data in table 6.2 show that equity holdings of institutional inves-tors tend to be more diversified internationally than do bond hold-ings, because after adjustment for currency risk, bonds do not offer the same long-run diversification benefits as equities do. Bonds are also more likely to be required for matching of domestic currency liabilities, for example, for annuities and life policies. Meanwhile, aggregate data suggest that international investment tends to be focused in OECD countries, despite growth in holdings in emerging markets.

6.1.3.2 International Investment and Portfolio Strategies

Internationalization has been accompanied by an increasingly **active approach to international portfolio investment** on behalf of institu-tions. Whereas in 1982 U.K. pension funds held foreign equities for two years on average, in 1998 the average holding period was just over one year (WM 1999), while the stock of foreign equities held by U.K. pension funds had risen from around $20 billion to over $175 billion. The turnover rate for foreign shares has always exceeded that for U.K. shares, which in 1998 had an average holding period of 2.5 years.

In addition to securities markets, international activity of institu-tions has also **affected the foreign exchange market**. Whereas it has traditionally been the preserve of the banks,[7] participants in foreign exchange markets have become more diverse, with the entry of insti-

---

7. In foreign exchange markets, banks are increasingly limited in position taking by prudential requirements as well as internal risk management rules; they are tending to focus on their role as intermediaries in the foreign exchange markets, providing liquidity, innovative portfolio strategies, and advice to customers.

tutional investors as direct players. They have also been involved in periods of financial turbulence. In assessing the 1992–1993 crisis in the European Exchange Rate Mechanism (ERM), the IMF (1993) suggested that the involvement of mutual funds, pension funds, and life insurers was the most novel feature. The IMF estimated that before the crisis, institutional investors and banks held around $300 billion in convergence trades, which entailed the purchase of higher-yielding bonds of ERM countries, speculating on the convergence of bond yields when EMU began. The rapid unwinding of these trades explained why speculative pressures grew so quickly during the crisis. The crisis underlined the fact that the resources available to institutional investors far exceed national foreign exchange reserves and that relatively small percentage shifts in the disposition of their portfolios could lead to major pressures on exchange rates.[8]

6.1.3.3 Causes of Increased International Investment

As we noted in chapter 2, the benefits of international investment for institutions, particularly in terms of risk diversification, have always been present. Why did diversification of institutions' portfolios increase so significantly in the 1980s and early 1990s? Dailey and Motala (1992) show that factors underlying growth in foreign asset holdings of institutions include those underlying retirement saving itself and growth of the relative size of institutions in domestic markets. But these do not explain growth in portfolio shares. Key autonomous factors include improved global communications; liberalization and increased competition in financial markets, which have reduced transactions costs; improvement of hedging possibilities via use of derivative instruments; and marketing of global investment management services by asset managers.

Abolition of exchange controls was an important factor underlying growth of international investment in countries such as Japan, the United Kingdom, and Australia (see also section 2.5). But equally, it cannot be a complete explanation, as Germany, where life

8. Long-term institutions' involvement was not the only novel feature. Also active were hedge funds, which seek to profit from movements in exchange rates and interest rates by leveraged investments, either by selling vulnerable currencies forward, using their capital to finance margin requirements, or by establishing interest rate positions via futures to profit from an interest rate decline after a crisis. Corporate treasury operations have also expanded, meaning that their funding, positioning, and hedging operations can also lead to exchange rate pressures.

insurers and pension funds tend to hold few foreign assets, abolished exchange controls in the 1959. It is **portfolio regulations** that are the key remaining factor that limit international investment by life insurers and pension funds (see table 2.1). Such regulations do not apply to mutual funds, thus helping to explain the relatively high levels of international investment shown in table 6.2. Taking the example of pension funds (see chapter 2; see also Davis (1995a, 1998a)), U.S., U.K., Dutch, and Australian pension funds are unrestricted or subject to a prudent man rule that requires the managers to carry out sensible portfolio diversification and that is taken to include international investment. German, Swiss, Japanese, and Canadian pension funds have been subject to quantitative restrictions. Taxation of international investment (especially withholding taxes) may limit its attractiveness even where there are no formal restrictions. This is reportedly a disincentive to international diversification by Australian pension funds.

6.1.3.4 Macroeconomic Implications

In a macroeconomic context, international portfolio investment by institutions may be an important **conduit for saving** to flow to countries with demand for capital in excess of domestic saving and thus high returns to capital (as well as balance of payments deficits). For example, institutional investors in Japan, once exchange controls were abolished, played a key part in financing trade imbalances between the G-3 countries over the 1980s and 1990s, by investing heavily in U.S. bonds. This may be seen conceptually as facilitating a form of consumption smoothing[9] that would not be possible in closed economies, whereby Japanese savers were able to postpone consumption via international investment while allowing U.S. consumers to advance it via international borrowing (Bisignano 1993). This in turn helped to equalize covered returns on financial assets, making the world market portfolio more efficient. However, such inflows may allow countries to pursue ultimately unsustainable policies for longer than is desirable. An example is expansionary fiscal policy in the United States in the early 1980s. Another is the growth in U.S. private sector debt accompanying a fiscal surplus and

---

9. Such consumption smoothing as is highlighted here for the G-3 is a general feature of capital flows among advanced countries, according to research by Brennan and Solnik (1989); they suggest that in recent decades, it has yielded benefits in eight advanced countries equivalent to 4–8% of total annual consumption in the early 1970s.

balance of payments deficit in the late 1990s. This pattern has been seen as contributing to a virtuous circle of U.S. growth and buoyant asset prices. But a break in confidence by foreign investors could lead to a collapse of asset prices and the dollar, necessitating a rapid cut in net borrowing by both the household and corporate sectors and possibly inducing a major recession (Bank of England 1999). Certainly, the United Kingdom found in the late 1980s that a private sector deficit combined with a balance of payments deficit and a public sector surplus could not be viewed merely with benign neglect, as the pattern unwound in the early 1990s, provoking a major recession.

International investment may also act as a safety valve to relieve excessive pressure on asset prices. For example, in the United Kingdom, the 1981 appreciation of sterling, which damaged the domestic economy, might have gone much further in the absence of capital outflows from U.K. institutions after exchange controls were abolished.

In the 1990s, around 50% of **flows to emerging markets** were portfolio flows by institutional investors (the rest being largely direct investment or official flows). Reasons for institutional interest in emerging markets included:

• an improvement in macroeconomic conditions as economies recovered from the LDC debt crisis,

• cyclical value-driven flows, and

• the structural shift by institutions in the direction of global diversification.

Empirical research on the determinants and dynamics of portfolio flows to emerging markets is surveyed in section 5.3.5.

There remains a great deal of **scope for expanding international investment** of institutions. Current portfolio shares of international assets are well below those that would minimize risk for a given return and even below those that would appear optimal, taking into account the share of imports in the consumption basket.[10] Home bias and regulation, as discussed in chapter 2, are partly at the root of this, although liabilities of institutions may also justify a domestic bias. Whereas the impact of liabilities will tend to be durable, home

---

10. Such a limitation of international investment might be justified if purchasing power parity were not considered to hold in the long run.

bias and the effects of regulation seem to be diminishing. The uneven pace of demographic changes, as well as differences in saving and investment between countries (Grundfest 1990), suggest that net cross-border flows are likely to accompany, and accentuate, further shifts by institutions. Such an expansion would magnify the effects of existing cross-border investment as outlined above.

6.2   Corporate Finance Issues

The role of institutional investors in corporate finance is not only related to provision of finance per se—the financial function of transfer of resources—but also linked to their role in overcoming principal-agent problems that plague both the creditor-borrower relationship and the shareholder-manager relationship. This links to the financial function of overcoming adverse incentive problems. This section on corporate finance is structured as follows: First, we assess corporate financing in general terms with a reference to institutions' role in debt finance before passing to our main topic of equity finance. In this context, we first consider the issue of agency costs in equity and the way in which they are overcome in a number of paradigms of corporate governance. Then we consider successively the U.S. corporate governance movement by institutional investors and issues raised by the evolution of corporate governance in Europe and Japan, with particular reference to the role of institutional investors. Finally, we examine two special topics: the short-termist hypothesis and small firm financing.

6.2.1   Corporate Financing Patterns and Debt Finance

Corporate financing patterns for the G-7 are shown in table 6.5. There has been an overall increase in financial liabilities relative to GDP, and this has entailed a rise in both debt and equities (valued at market prices). In countries other than the United Kingdom and Italy, there has been an increase in money market and bond financing, while the loan ratio has declined except in Germany and Canada (and for Germany, this appears to be linked to reunification). The equity ratio has risen except in those two countries, implying a fall in the debt-equity ratio. In this context, one indication of the importance of institutional investors is that equity holding is heavily weighted toward institutional investors, either domestic or foreign

Table 6.5
Corporate Sector Balance Sheets (Proportions of Gross Liabilities)

		1970	1980	1990	1995	1997	1998	Change, 1970–1998
United Kingdom	Bond	0.07	0.02	0.00	0.06	0.07	0.07	0.00
	Equity	0.49	0.37	0.53	0.67	0.69	0.72	0.23
	Loan	0.15	0.22	0.21	0.22	0.22	0.21	0.06
United States	Bond	0.14	0.17	0.18	0.14	0.11	0.12	−0.02
	Equity	0.55	0.49	0.39	0.59	0.61	0.64	0.10
	Loan	0.15	0.13	0.18	0.11	0.10	0.09	−0.05
Germany	Bond	0.03	0.02	0.02	0.03	0.02	0.02	−0.02
	Equity	0.27	0.20	0.31	0.27	0.32	0.36	0.09
	Loan	0.47	0.52	0.42	0.49	0.46	0.44	−0.03
Japan	Bond	0.02	0.03	0.06	0.07	0.07	0.07	0.04
	Equity	0.16	0.22	0.29	0.24	0.20	0.21	0.04
	Loan	0.48	0.45	0.45	0.46	0.45	0.45	−0.03
Canada	Bond	0.12	0.08	0.13	0.17	0.17	0.17	0.05
	Equity	0.46	0.41	0.41	0.49	0.50	0.51	0.05
	Loan	0.15	0.22	0.22	0.18	0.17	0.17	0.01
France	Bond	0.03	0.04	0.04	0.06	0.05	0.05	0.02
	Equity	0.41	0.34	0.56	0.47	0.58	0.63	0.22
	Loan	0.54	0.60	0.38	0.28	0.22	0.19	−0.35
Italy	Bond	0.08	0.04	0.03	0.02	0.01	0.01	−0.07
	Equity	0.32	0.52	0.48	0.48	0.53	0.54	0.22
	Loan	0.60	0.43	0.41	0.43	0.38	0.37	−0.22
G-7	Bond	0.07	0.05	0.07	0.08	0.07	0.07	0.00
	Equity	0.38	0.36	0.43	0.46	0.49	0.52	0.13
	Loan	0.36	0.37	0.32	0.31	0.29	0.28	−0.09
Anglo-Saxon	Bond	0.11	0.09	0.10	0.12	0.12	0.12	0.01
	Equity	0.50	0.42	0.44	0.58	0.60	0.62	0.12
	Loan	0.15	0.19	0.20	0.17	0.16	0.16	0.01
Europe and Japan	Bond	0.04	0.03	0.04	0.04	0.04	0.04	−0.01
	Equity	0.29	0.32	0.41	0.37	0.41	0.43	0.14
	Loan	0.52	0.50	0.41	0.41	0.38	0.36	−0.16

Bonds include short-term paper.
Source: National flow of funds data; see table 1.1 for details.

(table 6.4). If one assumes that foreign holders of shares are largely institutional investors, their overall holdings range from 15% in Italy to 60% in the United Kingdom. A similar pattern holds for corporate bonds.

The bulk of this section focuses on institutional investors' holdings of equity and its implications for corporate governance. But first we consider **institutional provision of debt finance**, which has traditionally been the preserve of banks. To address this issue, we introduce aspects of theory of intermediation, which analyzes why some financings take place via capital markets while others are intermediated by banks (see Davis 2000a).

There are four main factors that divide borrowers from banks and markets (Davis and Mayer (1991)):

• Economies of scale: Owing to transactions costs, small investors and borrowers use banks, while wholesale users can access bond markets.

• Information: Banks have a comparative advantage in screening and monitoring borrowers to avoid problems of adverse selection and moral hazard that arise in debt contracts—market finance is available only to borrowers that have a reputation.

• Control: Banks are better able to influence the behavior of borrowers while a loan is outstanding and seize assets or restructure in the case of default.

• Commitment: Banks can form long-term relationships with borrowers, a situation that reduces information asymmetry and hence moral hazard.

Analysis of debt financing by institutions and banks suggests that these **differences continue to hold, but boundaries are shifting** between financings undertaken by banks and by markets. The development of rating agencies, junk bonds, and securitized debt are indicators of increased availability of market debt financing. Institutional investors in the United Kingdom and Australia tend not to invest significant amounts in corporate debt. In contrast, in the United States and Canada, institutions invest in instruments such as corporate bonds and securitized debt, employing the services of rating agencies to assess credit quality (screening and monitoring). As recorded in Carey et al. (1993), U.S. life insurers have been significant investors in private placements[11] in recent years, employing their own credit-screening and monitoring facilities. In the Netherlands, as for U.S. life insurers, institutions are active as both lenders and monitors.

In Germany, where debt constitutes the major part of institutional portfolios, most of the loans by institutional investors are made to banks and public authorities and only indirectly to firms. Thus banks retain the role that theory of intermediation outlined above highlights. Similarly, in Japan, many loans are arranged and guaranteed by the trust bank that manages the funds or the commercial bank in the life insurer's industrial group, thus again leaving banks in the controlling position.

As we discussed in section 4.3, the introduction of EMU has induced a marked shift in corporate financing in Europe toward bond issuance and away from bank lending, which will be reflected in institutional investors' portfolios. Further pressure in the same direction may be induced by the falling supply of government bonds (which reduces crowding out of corporate bonds and makes institutions interested in alternative forms of debt instruments). Besides holding corporate bonds, institutional investors may be expected to develop their own credit assessment capabilities in light of these stimuli.

6.2.2 Corporate Governance and Institutional Investors in the United States

6.2.2.1 Agency Costs and Equity Finance
Turning to our main theme, equity finance, we note that the development of institutional investors and their growing dominance as owners of corporations have had a pervasive influence on corporate governance. In this context, they help the financial system to fulfill its function of providing ways to deal with incentive problems when one party to a financial transaction has information that the other does not or when one is an agent of the other and when control and enforcement of contracts are costly.

---

11. In effect, a hybrid between bank loan and public bond financing, requiring extensive screening and monitoring and negotiation of covenants (although since 1990, under SEC rule 144a, institutions have been able to transact freely in such bonds, thus aiding liquidity).

Given the divorce of ownership and control in the modern corporation, shareholders cannot perfectly control managers acting on their behalf. Hence **principal-agent problems arise**. Managers have superior information about the firm and its prospects and at best a partial link of their compensation to the firms' profitability.[12] As a consequence, they may divert funds in their own interests and to the disadvantage of shareholders. Forms of diversion of funds may include expropriation[13] or diversion of cash flow to unprofitable projects.

Evidence for such agency costs includes the frequent observation that share prices of bidder firms fall when acquisitions are announced (Roll 1986), resistance of managers to takeovers that threaten their positions (Walkling and Long 1984), and the premium offered to shares with voting rights (Zingales 1995). As Schleifer and Vishny (1997) noted, shareholders are much more vulnerable than other stakeholders in the firm, such as workers and creditors. Workers can withdraw labor, and creditors can refuse debt finance and apply pressure on the managers by those means. Whereas it may be argued that managers' desire to maintain reputation in the market will help to protect shareholders (Kreps 1990), it may not be sufficient.

Principal-agent problems in equity finance imply a **need for shareholders to exert control over management** while also remaining sufficiently distinct from managers to let equity holders buy and sell shares freely without breaking insider trading rules. If difficulties of corporate governance are not resolved, equity finance will tend to be unduly costly and often subject to quantitative restrictions.[14]

A key to all successful forms of corporate governance is mechanisms for **legal protection of shareholders**. (These include the right

---

12. Performance-related pay, the use of share options, and similar devices may help to align managers' and shareholders' interests. But such contracts may themselves worsen the governance problem by leading to heightened incentives for self-dealing, with managers negotiating such contracts when they know that performance may improve.

13. Beyond theft, transfer pricing, and asset sales, expropriation may take forms such as perquisites, high salaries, diversion of funds to pet projects, and general entrenchment even in cases in which managers are no longer competent or qualified to run the firm.

14. Investor overoptimism may play a periodic role in the provision of external finance. See, for example, evidence on the overvaluation of junk bonds used to finance U.S. takeovers in the 1980s in Kaplan and Stein (1993) and of new equity issues by Ritter (1991). But this sentiment tends to be highly cyclical.

to vote on important corporate matters, notably mergers, as well as elections of boards of directors.) There may also be a legally enforceable duty of loyalty by managers to shareholders (see Schleifer and Vishny 1997). Boards of directors, in particular nonexecutive directors, act as shareholders' representatives in monitoring management and ensuring that the firm is run in their interests. Shareholder influence is ensured by their right to vote on choice of directors (as well as other elements of policy proposed by management). On the other hand, if boards are weakly supervised by shareholders, they may act in managers' interests rather than those of shareholders (Jensen 1993), or they will be passive in all but extreme circumstances (Kaplan 1994).

Hence effectiveness of corporate governance typically also requires the **presence of large investors**, be they banks, other companies, or institutional investors. They will have the leverage to oblige managers to distribute profits to providers of external finance. They are needed because individual investors may find it difficult to enforce their rights, even if these are legally enshrined. Underlying these difficulties are information asymmetries vis-à-vis managers, the difficulty of forming coalitions to act in a concerted manner against management, and free rider problems. Large investors may find it easier than small investors to enforce their rights in court.[15]

There is also a downside to large investors, as they may override the interests of minority shareholders (La Porta et al. 1999). Consistent with this downside, Morck et al. (1988) found that profitability is higher for firms with shareholders that have up to 5% stakes. Beyond that, profitability falls. This pattern may indicate that larger, blockholding investors seek to generate private benefits of control that are not shared by minority shareholders. Institutional shareholders are often limited, either by regulation or by a desire to maintain liquidity, to holding a maximum 5% of a firm's equity.

In most of the world outside the Anglo-Saxon countries, Germany, and Japan, absence of minority shareholder protection means that external equity finance is relatively uncommon and most firms are family owned and financed (La Porta et al. 1999).

---

15. Note that this argument suggests that households will be justified in being more willing to provide equity finance via institutions than they would directly.

6.2.2.2 Four Paradigms of Corporate Governance

There are well-known contrasts in the behavior of financial institutions and markets in the major OECD countries, notably as they relate to the financing and governance of companies. The general division is between the Anglo-Saxon systems of the United Kingdom, United States, Canada, and Australia on the one hand and the systems that have prevailed historically in Continental Europe and Japan on the other. We would characterize the traditional distinction between the two systems in terms of the finance and control of corporations, distinguishing between direct control via debt and market control via equity (see Davis 1993b, 1995a).

Direct control via debt implies relationship banking along the lines of the German or Japanese model. This typically involves companies having exclusive financing relationships with a small number of creditors and equity holders. There is widespread cross-shareholding among companies.[16] Banks are significant shareholders in their own right and in Germany are represented on supervisory boards both as equity holders and as creditors.

In these countries, banks exert corporate governance most decisively via their control rights as creditors. They may influence the firm by varying the maturity of debt as well as taking control when firms default or violate debt contracts.[17] They may also provide rescue finance to firms in financial difficulty, recouping the expense by charging higher spreads when the firm recovers. Nonetheless, banks in these countries have also been able to exert control through the voting rights conferred on them by custody of bearer shares of individual investors who have surrendered their proxies. The influence of other (institutional) shareholders is often limited by voting restrictions, countervailing influence of corporate shareholders, and lack of detailed financial information, as well as the right of other stakeholders (such as employees, suppliers, and creditors) to representation on boards. Implicitly, monitoring of managers is delegated to a trusted intermediary: the bank. In practice, equity holders are often discriminated against in such systems, to the advantage of the creditors, for example in terms of dividends. Such discrimination

---

16. However, bi-directional cross-holdings are typically means of cementing alliances or collusion rather than exerting control.
17. Hoshi et al. (1993) show how profitable Japanese firms sought to avoid the costs of bank links when access to public debt issuance was liberalized.

may make minority investors unwilling to invest, leaving equity markets themselves underdeveloped.[18] However, as we noted in section 6.2.4, this pattern is changing, partly owing to pressure by institutions from the Anglo-Saxon countries.

As regards **market control via equity**, the principal advantage of hostile takeover activity, which is a distinguishing mark of Anglo-Saxon systems, is that it can partly resolve the conflict of interest between management and shareholders: The firms that deviate most extensively from shareholders' objectives—and that consequently tend to have lower market values as shareholders dispose of their holdings—have a greater likelihood of being acquired. Indeed, there is evidence that takeovers act to address governance problems (Jensen 1993). The threat of takeover, as much as its manifestation, acts as a constraint on managerial behavior. Institutional shareholders, both directly and via nonexecutive directors, can have an important role to play in this context, both in complementing takeover pressure as a monitoring constraint on management behavior and in evaluating takeover proposals when they arise. Focusing on the period 1986–1990, Clyde (1997) found that institutional concentration among shareholders was positively correlated with the frequency of takeovers.

The willingness of banks—and institutional investors, via junk bonds—to finance highly leveraged buyouts (LBOs) and takeovers in the 1980s in the United States and the United Kingdom brought to the fore **market control via debt** (Jensen 1986). A key source of conflict between managers and shareholders stems from firms' policies in dividing profits between dividends and retained earnings. The suspicion is that managers may waste retained earnings or "free cash flow" on unprofitable projects. Debt issue can ease tensions, since by increasing interest payments, the free cash flow at managers' disposal is reduced. If free cash flow is preempted by interest payments, managers must seek external financing via either debt issue or equity issue for each new project undertaken. This forces them to obtain an adequate rate of return on such projects. Besides this benefit, the equity stakes that managers usually take on in LBOs align their incentives with those of other equity holders.

---

18. Note that there is also evidence that banks may be inadequate as monitors, not seeking to discipline managers as long as the firm is far from default (Harris and Raviv 1990).

A disadvantage of increased gearing is that potential conflicts between shareholders and debt holders become more intense.[19] Jensen and Meckling (1976) show that shareholders in highly leveraged firms have an incentive to engage in projects that are too risky and so increase the possibility of bankruptcy. Given this risk, monitoring of managers by creditors may become so intense as to preclude investment altogether. Indeed, it is commonly argued that LBOs are a transient form of corporate organization that may be helpful in unwinding earlier excesses in terms of diversification.

The question arises as to **whether institutions have actively encouraged increased leverage**. Research on the influence of institutional investors on debt levels is inconclusive. Firth (1995) shows that the presence of institutional shareholders tends to have a positive influence on the debt/assets ratio. But Grier and Zychowicz (1994) find a negative effect. They suggest that direct discipline by institutional investors (see the discussion below of direct control via equity) acts as a substitute for debt. One possible reason for the difference is that Firth's data are from the peak of the popularity of leverage (1987–1989), while Grier and Zychowicz cover a longer period (1984–1988) including years when pressure for leverage was less intense.

Research on the best form of corporate governance is inconclusive (Mayer 1996). The insider model of direct control via debt, with its emphasis on private information and on stakeholder relationships rather than public disclosure and liquidity, may be superior at implementing policies that need consensus among stakeholders. Such consensus policies may in turn encourage high levels of fixed investment by the firm and of the employees in firm-specific skills, in the context of long-lived corporations. On the other hand, the outsider models in which institutions play a greater role may be better at responding to change and building up new firms. As Allen and Gale (1995) argued, capital market financing could well be economically beneficial in emerging industries with high financial and economic risks and in which knowledge about industry is uncertain

---

19. Perhaps more important, high leverage is likely to have various deleterious consequences. By raising the bankruptcy rate, it increases the incidence of deadweight bankruptcy costs arising from legal costs, diversion of managerial energies, and breakup of unique bundles of assets, for example. And at a macro level, increased corporate fragility is likely to magnify the multiplier in the case of recession (Davis 1995b).

(e.g., IT, biotechnology). In contrast, banking may have a comparative advantage in industries in which markets are mature and innovation and uncertainty are low, as banks can then accurately monitor and diversify risk among companies.

Taking a broader view, Allen and Gale (1997) show that Anglo-American capital markets dominated by institutional investors may have a disadvantage in terms of risk sharing, whereby competition and opportunities for arbitrage constrain intermediaries to carry out only cross-sectional risk sharing—exchanges of risk among individuals at a given point in time. This leaves individuals vulnerable to undiversifiable risks arising over time, for example, owing to macroeconomic shocks. In contrast, financial systems in which banks have some monopoly power over savers facilitate the elimination of such intertemporal risks by accumulation of reserves and smoothing of returns over time. These benefits may be lost as openness to global markets increases via pension fund growth. (There is an obvious application to the current situation in Germany.) In Anglo-American countries, the focus on cross-sectional risk sharing may help to explain the intense focus on risk management via derivatives (Allen and Santomero 1999).

6.2.2.3   The Corporate Governance Movement in the United States

There are a number of **shortcomings to market control via equity** as practiced in the Anglo-Saxon countries. As Schleifer and Vishny (1997) noted:

• takeovers are so costly that only major performance failures are likely to be addressed;

• they may increase agency costs when bidding managers overpay for acquisitions that bring them private benefits of control;

• and they require a liquid capital market (e.g., for junk bond issuance) to provide finance.

These problems came increasingly to the fore in the United States as the boom of the late 1980s turned to recession, leveraged firms started to default, and the junk bond market collapsed in 1989.[20] Dissatisfaction with the takeover mechanism was increased by abuse

---

20. The junk bond market has proven highly cyclical, with a collapse of issuance occurring in 1989–1991 and again in 1998 (see Davis 1994a, 1999d).

of takeover defenses by managers of weak companies and/or pay-offs of raiders, regardless of shareholders' interests. Managerial compensation and performance under the protection of such devices was acknowledged to be unrelated to profitability.

As a consequence of these concerns, institutions in the United States began to seek new means to exert corporate control. This discontent brought to the fore a corporate governance movement based on **direct control via equity**.[21] The dominance of institutions as shareholders gives ample scope for leverage: They own 50% of the top fifty U.S. companies, and the top twenty U.S. pension funds own 8% of the stock of the ten largest companies. Such influence may be exerted via the right of shareholders to select boards of directors, as we noted above. But this right may be supplemented by direct links from institutional investors to management[22] either formally at annual meetings or informally at other times. This is precisely what has been observed in recent years. As is discussed below, the movement was facilitated by new Securities and Exchange Commission[23] (SEC) regulations allowing institutions to collaborate more readily to form coalitions to exert pressure on management. It can be argued that the development of stock options has facilitated this trend by increasing the incentives of mergers to perform in line with institutions' expectations, even in the absence of takeovers and leveraged buyouts.

A further important motivation for direct control via equity has been the development of **indexing strategies** (chapter 2). Indexation by its nature obliges institutional investors to hold shares in large companies that form the index. It thus encourages them, following their fiduciary duty as well as in the interests of returns, to improve management of underperforming firms, (see Monks 1997).[24] Even

---

21. Note that the argument presented here from an institutional investor's point of view generalizes to the extent to which any large shareholder, be it an individual, bank, or company, may exert direct influence on a firm and thereby overcome corporate governance problems. Schleifer and Vishny (1997) note a number of studies showing effective exercise of governance in Germany, Japan, and the United States.

22. Note that in countries such as Italy, direct control via equity is exerted in pyramidal groups of companies, in which those (larger firms) higher up hold shares in those (smaller) lower down (OECD 1995).

23. The SEC is the regulatory body for U.S. securities markets.

24. This is an important observation, since it is often suggested in countries such as the United Kingdom that the longer-term relationships, close monitoring of company performance, and large shareholdings needed for alternatives to takeover to operate will not be present in the case of indexation.

active investors that hold large stakes in a company must bear in mind the potentially sizable cost of disposing of their shareholdings, thus again encouraging activism. In effect, they are driven to seek direct control owing to illiquidity (see Coffee 1991).

Coalition building is essential for effective institutional control to be exerted; institutions typically do not seek to hold large stakes in firms, while influence is obtained only when a significant proportion of shareholders act together.[25] With growing institutionalization, it becomes much easier and cheaper to reach a small number of well-informed key investors who will command a majority of votes. But SEC regulations had historically limited the ability of institutions to build coalitions. The U.S. shareholder activist movement was hence encouraged in the early 1990s by a new rule from the SEC that liberalized the coalition-building restrictions. It enabled investors to collude more readily; now any number of shareholders could communicate orally without restriction, as long as they were not seeking to cast votes for others.

A further SEC rule aided the movement by improving information available to shareholders. It enforced comprehensive disclosure of executive pay practices (salary, bonuses, and other perks for the top five officers over a three-year period) and policy regarding the relationship of executive pay to performance of the company as a whole.

A number of other changes help to explain the increased focus on corporate governance in the United States. A 1988 ruling by the U.S. Department of Labor (the "Avon letter") stated that decisions on voting by pension funds were fiduciary acts of plan asset management under ERISA, which must be either made directly by trustees or delegated wholly to external managers. Note, however, that despite mutual funds' growing importance, there is no equivalent to this fiduciary obligation for them. Second, there were shareholder initiatives on social issues (South Africa, the environment) in the late 1980s, which stimulated increased interest by public pension funds in the importance of proxy issues generally. The collapse[26] of the

---

25. If collaboration is ruled out, institutions are likely to be in a prisoners' dilemma situation with respect to corporate governance, with each finding that acting in their own interests (e.g., selling the shares in an underperforming company) leads to a worse outcome than could be realized by acting collectively (e.g., by requiring improvements to management structure and performance).

26. This was attributable to such factors as recession, which made target companies less attractive to bidders, and the retrenchment of banks from takeover finance following their losses on property, as well as the antitakeover strategies noted above.

takeover wave itself at the turn of the decade helped to boost activism by removing an alternative means of corporate control. Under the lead plaintiff provision of the U.S. Private Securities Litigation Act of 1995, large shareholders can seek to be named controlling parties on class-action shareholder lawsuits against company management.

Since these developments, U.S. pension funds have **consistently voted** on resolutions that they might previously have ignored. Public pension funds such as the California Public Employees Retirement Scheme (CALPERS) and the New York Employees Pension Fund (NYEPF) have been particularly active. They have sought, for example:

- to challenge excessive executive compensation and takeover protections,
- to seek to split the roles of chairman and chief executive,
- to remove underperforming chief executives,[27]
- to ensure independent directors are elected to boards,[28] and
- to ensure that new directors be appointed by nonexecutives.

These ends are reached by filing proxy resolutions and directing comments and demands to managers, either privately or via the press. CALPERS in 1997 also drew up corporate governance standards relating in particular to the role of the independent directors and graded the 300 largest holdings on this basis.

Private pension fund trustees and mutual fund managers have been more restrained. In the case of mutual funds, Roe (1992) suggests that restraint in corporate governance activities may reflect regulations that limit activism by restricting large holdings of firms' equity and regulating or prohibiting activities with affiliates.

Broadly similar tendencies toward shareholder activism by pension funds is also apparent in the United Kingdom and Canada, often aided by U.S. involvement (Davis (1995a), Simon (1993)). Besides pension funds, value-based asset managers such as Phillips and Drew have become active on their own behalf in the United

---

27. Examples in the early 1990s include those of IBM, Westinghouse, Kodak, Amex, and General Motors.

28. Celebrated cases include the CALPERS agreement to back Texaco management in a takeover bid if the management agreed to support independent directors and pressure by CALPERS and the NYEPF on General Motors to accept a resolution for more than half the directors to be independent.

Kingdom, taking large stakes in underperforming firms with a view to improving management or provoking takeovers (Martinson 1998).

6.2.2.4 Effectiveness of Shareholder Activism

The **effectiveness of such shareholder activism** remains a question of lively debate in the United States; the bulk of empirical work seems to justify a degree of skepticism. **On the positive side**, Wahal (1996), in a sample of forty-three cases, found that efforts by institutions to promote organizational change via negotiation with management (as opposed to proxy proposals) are associated with gains in share prices. Strickland et al. (1996) report that firms that were targeted for pressure by the United Shareholders Association[29] experienced positive abnormal stock returns, although corporate governance proposals per se had no effect.

Del Guercio and Hawkins (1999) analyzed shareholder proposals of large and active funds over 1987–1993. They sought to take into account the fact that the tactics adopted by different institutional investors may vary as a consequence of the constraints on their investment strategies. For example, an index fund might seek via shareholder proposals to boost the overall performance of the whole market (for example, by improving overall governance standards) rather than solely seeking to improve performance of those firms in which they invest. Externally managed funds are more likely to seek publicity for their governance aims than those that are internally managed, for which activism and trading can be profitably coordinated. Del Guercio and Hawkins (1999) found that companies receiving shareholder proposals experienced a higher frequency of governance events such as turnover of top managers, shareholder lawsuits, asset sales, and restructuring. CALPERS initiatives had much more leverage than those for other funds. Contrary to popular belief, the results suggested that funds are value maximizing in their corporate governance activities and are not politically motivated.

On the negative side, Del Guercio and Hawkins found no evidence that activism had a significant effect on stock returns over the three years following the proposals. Wahal (1994) surveyed activism by nine public pension funds over the 1987–1993 period and also concluded that there was no evidence of improvement in the long-

---

29. Note that this is actually a coalition of small investors rather than an institutional investor per se.

term stock price performance of targeted firms, which rather continued to decline for three years after targeting. Gillan and Starks (1995) found some positive returns in the short term but no statistically significant positive returns over the long term, leading them to question the overall effectiveness of shareholder activism. M. P. Smith (1996), looking at the firms that had been targeted by CALPERS, found that activism again led to no statistically significant improvement in performance of the companies concerned. On the other hand, activism had led to changes in that 72% of targets had adopted proposed governance structure resolutions or made changes sufficient to warrant a settlement. Moreover, there was a statistically significant increase in shareholder wealth; CALPERS gained an estimated $19 million over 1989–1993 at a cost to itself of $3.5 million. Karpoff et al. (1996) found that shareholder initiatives were well targeted on firms with atypically poor prior performance but had little effect on operating returns, company share, values, and top management turnover; the only exception was a significant improvement in returns on assets for the targets relative to a control group.

Monks (1997) explains the ineffectiveness of corporate governance activity in raising returns by reference to the political nature of public pension funds. While they are well placed to raise fairness issues such as excessive managerial remuneration, the incentive structure of trustees is not such as to encourage the long-term pressure on management that is needed to obtain positive excess returns in the long term. More effective institutional pressure may be exerted by so-called relationship investors such as Warren Buffett and the LENS fund. The effectiveness of such funds is underpinned by the background of their managers in business, commitment, and unwillingness to be distracted. But as Monks (1997) noted, partnerships between relationship investors and public funds have at times been profitable.

Evidence from outside the United States on the effectiveness of corporate governance initiatives is sparse, but Faccio and Lasfer (2000) show that the monitoring role of U.K. pension funds is concentrated among mature and low-performing firms and that in the long run, the firms in which pension funds have large stakes markedly improve their stock returns.

An additional factor of major interest, which has been little researched, is the **role of governance of the institutional investor itself** in the context of the activism it carries out. It is well known in the United States that public funds are the most active. O'Barr and

Conley (1992) suggest that such activism relates partly to the size of the funds, which makes selling shares in poor performers potentially expensive, and indexation (which is more common in public funds than in private funds). But also by being active on shareholder rights, public pension fund managers can preempt the pressure from politicians to use funds for social ends; and as public figures themselves, managers of public funds reap benefits from activism in terms of publicity. Managers of private pension funds have been much less active in corporate governance and generally support incumbent management of firms in which they hold shares. O'Barr and Conley (1992) concluded that there was an underlying desire not to trouble other firms lest their pension fund retaliate and thus cause difficulties for the fund managers vis-à-vis the sponsor's management. They would also see dangers of conflicts of interest if they become too heavily involved in running businesses. Mutual funds are again "reluctant activists" (Pozen 1998).

6.2.3   Corporate Governance in Europe and Japan: A Revolution in Corporate Financing?

6.2.3.1   Institutional Investors and Bank-Based Systems of Corporate Finance

Even in bank-dominated countries such as Germany and Japan, **U.S. pension funds have introduced shareholder activism.**[30] U.S. funds' leverage is apparent from the size of their international holdings ($410 billion in 1999) and concentration ($265.5 billion in the twenty-five largest funds). CALPERS, which in 1998 had $2 billion in Japanese stocks and $4 billion in French stocks, has issued guidelines for corporate governance. As noted in Financial Times (1998), CALPERS stated that "the Japanese market will only become attractive to investors if it adopts corporate governance standards that are more representative of shareholders' interests," while France "needs to begin meeting market expectations and requirements" and must develop "a greater focus on the role of shareholders when defining the corporations interests."

Other factors are facilitating institutional activism. Many firms in Continental Europe and, to a lesser extent, Japan are already seeking

---

30. Monks (1997) comments that greater activism of even private U.S. funds abroad may show a lower fear of commercial reprisal.

access to relatively low-cost international equity finance. They are accordingly being obliged to meet the needs of Anglo-Saxon pension funds for market-value-based accounting,[31] information disclosure and higher dividend payments (see Schulz 1993).

Important **fiscal and regulatory changes** are taking place in Europe and Japan that are improving the scope for corporate governance activity by international institutional investors. The German government announced in December 1999 that companies would be able to decumulate shareholdings without incurring capital gains tax. This promises to reduce cross-shareholdings,[32] thus reducing the influence of block shareholders, which has tended historically to favor incumbent management. French law has been amended to protect minority shareholders in takeovers, owing largely to pressure from institutional investors. Reform has taken place of insider information restrictions (in countries such as Germany), limits on dual classes of share (an important issue in countries such as Switzerland), and equal treatment of creditors in bankruptcy (to protect corporate bond holdings).

German firms over 1985–1995 raised DM 200 billion in equity, more than double the amount of equity raised in 1950–1985, adjusted for inflation; and since 1995, equity issuance has accelerated further, especially for start-up firms. A larger volume of equity issuance increases the potential leverage of institutional investors. Germany saw its first hostile takeover, of Mannesmann by Vodafone, in 2000. New flotations in Germany are at a record level, reflecting the growth of the Neue Markt (new market) for start-ups. In Japan, firms and banks are decumulating their cross-shareholdings, partly under pressure from their own pension liabilities (see chapter 5), thus, as in Germany, weakening the influence of block shareholders. In Japan, there has also been a successful takeover of the domestic telecommunications firm ICD by Cable and Wireless of the United Kingdom, despite a competing offer by Japanese telecommunications company NTT. Decisive sales to Cable and Wireless were made by the corporate cross-holder Toyota and the trading house Itochu, contrary to Japanese tradition favoring domestic firms. The latter may have been

31. Based on the U.S. Generally Accepted Accounting Principles.
32. Cross-shareholdings are mutual holdings of each other's shares by two usually nonfinancial firms to cement corporate relationships. They have not usually been a channel for corporate governance activity.

under pressure from foreign shareholders to take the more attractive bid.

Structural change to the entire system of corporate financing appear to be underway in both **Germany and Japan**. Particularly in Germany, universal banks are switching away from the traditional lending that underpinned direct control via debt to investment banking activities and decumulation of shareholdings. These shifts partly link to pressures for better performance from banks' own shareholders. They also reflect increased competition for lending; as Petersen and Rajan (1994) argued, exclusive credit relationships, which are a feature of traditional corporate financing in Germany and Japan, may be vulnerable to increased banking competition. This is because competition gives rise to a risk of poaching of borrowers by other lenders and reduces spreads. Then it is no longer profitable for banks to rescue firms that are in financial distress, since they cannot charge higher spreads in good times to pay for this insurance. A special feature in Japan was the weakening of banks owing to the real estate crisis of the 1990s, which reduced their ability to rescue firms in difficulty.

Nonfinancial companies in Germany and Japan are also seeking to reduce dependence on relationship banks, to avoid the risk of exploitation[33] (see Edwards and Fischer 1991, 1994, Hoshi et al. 1993). The growth of securities markets enables them to substitute bond for bank finance, at a cost in terms of greater vulnerability to financial distress (Hoshi et al. 1990, 1991, Elston 1993).

As regards empirical evidence of a decline in direct control via debt, Gorton and Schmid (1996), attribute a disappearance of the favorable effects of German bank equity holding on firm performance between 1974 and 1985 to disintermediation, reductions in equity holdings by banks, and greater interbank competition. All of these were thought to weaken banks' oversight over management.[34]

6.2.3.2 Barriers to Change

The potential for convergence of German and Japanese corporate governance with systems in Anglo-Saxon countries should not be exaggerated (Berglöf 1996), not least because of the **large proportion**

---

33. See also Hellwig (1991) for a discussion of risks of exploitation in the context of an exclusive financing relationship.
34. Block holding was still found to have a favorable influence on companies' performance.

of corporate firms that are private in Continental Europe and Japan (although flotations of such firms are accelerating as heirs of the founders seek to realize their wealth). Even for listed firms, there can be strong **worker resistance** to corporate governance and "shareholder value," for example, from workers having book reserve pension funds, who may perceive a conflict between their own interests and those of shareholders. The representation of workers on boards gives scope to express such opposition.

Certainly, radical change will take time. For example, company statutes in some countries would need to be reformed if stakeholders were no longer to have a say in management. And company secrecy is to some degree protected by law, thus maintaining banks' comparative advantage over markets as a source of finance. Large blocks of shareholdings by banks, families, or other firms will disperse at most only gradually. The example of the Netherlands, where pension funds do not have a strong voice in corporate governance, shows that pension fund growth alone is not sufficient to ensure radical change in this area (Bolt and Peeters 1998, Hoogduin and Huisman 1998).[35]

6.2.3.3 EMU and Corporate Governance

EMU is compounding pressures for change to corporate governance in Europe in a number of ways. Owing to EMU, institutional investors, which are no longer confined by portfolio regulations to national markets, are seeking to diversify much more widely across the Union. As highlighted in chapter 4, asset managers are under increased competitive pressure to offer high returns. In this context, investors and asset managers wish to ensure that corporate management performs in line with shareholder value, be it via development of hostile takeovers or direct shareholder pressure.[36]

Meanwhile, companies are seeking to issue more equity, both to finance restructuring and to increase the robustness of their balance sheets in a context of weaker bank relationships. Desire to issue equity implies a need to satisfy the expectations of institutional investors

---

35. Dutch pension funds do apparently monitor their own debt exposures rather than delegating the task to banks.

36. Among the most interesting outworkings of a shift in corporate governance will be in the governance of banks per se, which Dermine (1996) sees shifting from market-share-based to value-based strategies in the EMU context under pressure to maintain returns to shareholders.

regarding dividends, information disclosure, minority protection, and profitability.

In the wake of EMU, hostile takeovers have been undertaken in Germany, France, and Italy. Development of a euro corporate bond market (Bishop 1999) has helped to underpin a shift in modes of corporate governance by facilitating leveraged buyouts and takeovers as a means to discipline management. For example, Olivetti was able to issue 9.4 billion euros in bonds to finance its majority control of Telecom Italia.

As we have noted, companies, under pressure to maximize profits, are divesting their cross-holdings, thus eliminating a proportion of currently passive shareholders. Banks equally are seeking to further reduce equity holdings, partly owing to capital adequacy considerations. Book-reserve-based pensions are giving way to Anglo-Saxon-style externally funded pensions. Daimler-Benz has shifted $4 billion of pension liabilities from balance sheet book reserves to an external equity-based trust, partly because of the adverse effects of book reserves on credit ratings (Burt 1999).

The reduced willingness of banks to undertake rescues, which we discussed above in a German context, has intensified following EMU. This reflects both increased interbank competition and the enhanced ability of firms to avoid the costs of banking relationships by issuing bonds[37] in the rapidly growing euro corporate bond markets.

Foreign shareholders continue to play a major role in transforming corporate governance in Europe. For example, the dependence of companies on foreign equity holders in the absence of well-developed domestic institutional sectors (see table 6.4) is making takeover bids easier to undertake.[38] Pressure for change may be sustained in the longer term as domestic institutions develop more strongly, when governments reform social security pension systems (Davis 1993a). The discussion of section 4.3.2 suggests that EMU will provide a considerable stimulus for such reform. Introduction of pension funds in Italy in the wake of social security reform (OECD 1995)—a country that Schleifer and Vishny (1997) highlight as having particularly

---

37. Firms are proving willing to use euro-denominated bonds for the main source of their regular debt financing and not only to finance takeovers.
38. In France, the three-cornered merger battle between Société Generale, Paribas, and BNP showed the growing influence of foreign institutional holders relative to the government.

poor legal protection for shareholders—may hence be a forerunner of changes elsewhere.

6.2.3.4   Risks in the Transition

If one accepts the above arguments, then during a transition to a more Anglo-Saxon financial system, there is the issue of whether **alternative means of corporate control** (hostile takeovers and direct influence by institutional investors) as well as means of reducing asymmetric information and aiding control by debt holders (rating agencies, changes in credit structure and possibly a lower debt/equity ratio) can rapidly develop. Otherwise, a vacuum could arise in corporate governance and corporate finance, with possible misallocation of investment, heightened agency costs, and increased credit rationing. There will also be a need for adequate adaptation of information to creditors and investors. Whereas banks rely on private information derived from ongoing credit relations, knowledge of the borrowers' deposit history,[39] and use of transactions services, securities markets must rely on public information.[40]

Theoretical and empirical work in financial economics underline the potential importance of this issue. The risk that a fragmented group of shareholders will all free ride, and corporate governance will therefore be inadequate, is a standard critique of capital-market-based financial systems (Grossman and Hart 1980). There may be similar free riding in bond markets, which would discourage monitoring, owing to the public good features of information about the borrower (Diamond 1984). Equally, initial lenders may be less careful regarding monitoring and credit risk in the case of loan packaging, while investors in asset-backed securities may be less able than banks to deal with rescheduling problems (Hellwig 1991). Syndicated loans may suffer from the interest of lead managers in their fees and their low exposure to credit risk (thus indicating difficulties for corporate finance). Again, U.S. experience shows that bond markets generally find rescheduling after financial distress difficult, and banks generally play a major role in restructuring, acting in many

---

39. Note that disintermediation may disturb these information sources.
40. In IMF (1997), it is argued that EMU will lower public information costs, owing to the integration of markets for goods and services across the Union. This is because in such a situation, there will be less need for detailed knowledge of local market conditions; sectoral specialization by equity or credit analysts across the Union would be sufficient for pricing of equity and debt claims.

ways like German or Japanese relationship banks (Gilson et al. 1990). Policy action could be considered in this respect, notably in terms of appropriate regulations to buttress shareholders' rights, although market forces (notably pressures of institutions on issuers for information disclosure) should also be an effective catalyst for change.

6.2.3.5 Summary

The growing **dominance of equity holdings by institutional investors**, both domestic and international, is casting a **sharp focus on their activities as owners and monitors of firms**. It was useful to separate discussion of the developments in the Anglo-Saxon countries and in Continental Europe and Japan. Anglo-Saxon countries are witnessing an increase in direct influence of institutions to complement reliance on the takeover mechanism to discipline managers. This has arguably led to improved corporate performance. Europe and Japan remain more firmly in the bank-relationship-based governance paradigm. On the other hand, such differences should not be exaggerated, and some convergence is discernible to a modified form of the Anglo-Saxon paradigm in which institutions are the primary actors in corporate governance generally. In Europe, EMU will provide a major spur to such convergence.

It may be added that in emerging markets, protection of shareholders is typically more primitive than that in Continental Europe and Japan, with minimal legal protection of investors (La Porta et al. 1999). Here again, institutions are active investors (Singh 1995), albeit with small proportions of their portfolios and at considerable risk of incurring the types of agency costs mentioned at the start of this section in extreme form. Schleifer and Vishny (1997) suggest that they have to rely on desire for reputation on the part of firms and prospects of soon returning to the market for finance until the institutions and legal protections are put in place.

6.2.4 Short-Termism

The **short-termist hypothesis** maintains that equity markets dominated by institutional investors tend to undervalue firms with good earnings prospects in the long term but low current profitability. This in turn is held to discourage long-term investment or research and development (R&D) as opposed to distribution of dividends, because firms that undertake long-term strategies may be undervalued and/or taken over. Underlying the hypothesis is the willing-ness of institutional investors to sell shares in takeover battles, in combination with regular performance evaluation of asset managers by trustees, which is said to make managers impatient for returns.

Whereas such a phenomenon could reflect irrational undervalua-tion of long-term investment projects, this is not necessarily the case. Schleifer and Vishny (1990) show that given information asymme-tries, risk-averse managers could prefer short-term investment proj-ects in a situation in which arbitrageurs have limited funds and hence mispricing of long-term projects by the market is only gradu-ally removed.

In support of the short-termist hypothesis is research by Miles (1993), who undertakes tests of whether discount rates implicit in market valuations applied to cash flows that accrue in the long term are too high both in absolute terms and relative to the rates applied to cash flows in the near term. The result seems to confirm the exis-tence of such effects in the United Kingdom, with long-term discount rates being too high. An earlier study by Nickell and Wadhwani (1987) came to similar conclusions. Evidence of mean reversion in stock prices in the United States is seen in the same light by Poterba and Summers (1992).[41]

Against the short-termist hypothesis, Marsh (1990) notes that in the absence of information relevant to valuations, excessive turnover will hurt performance of asset managers, and reaction to relevant information on firms' long-term prospects, which itself generates turnover, is a key function of markets. High stock market ratings of drug companies, with large R&D expenditures and long product lead times, would seem to tell against the hypothesis. More recently, the willingness of institutional investors to hold shares in Internet companies, despite their being expected to make losses for some years, is further contrary evidence. Indeed, markets seem to favor capital gains over dividends (Levis 1989), and some research sug-gests that announcement of capital expenditure or R&D boosts share prices (McConnell and Muscarella 1985).

The corporate governance movement of recent years, as discussed in section 6.2.2.3, reflects dissatisfaction among institutional inves-tors with the costs of the takeover mechanism and preference for

41. See also Schleifer and Vishny (1990).

direct influence as equity holders on incumbent management (see Davis 1995a). The link of the movement to the growing use of portfolio indexation, itself a form of long-term holding, was highlighted above. Even when there is not indexation, the costs of trading for large investors mean that they are effectively locked into a firm for the long haul, absent a bid, in any case.

Moreover, the data for holding periods of equity by institutional investors do not indicate excessively short holding periods. U.K. pension funds, for example, had a turnover rate for domestic equities of around 40% in 1998, implying an average holding period of around 2.5 years. But these numbers may not be an accurate indication for the overall portfolio; trading of the core portfolio may be low, or it may even be indexed, while those securities that are actively traded may turn over more rapidly than these estimates would suggest.

On balance, **current evidence does not appear to favor the short-termism hypothesis**, but two caveats should be mentioned: First, it may be that the recent enthusiasm for Internet and IT firms that were expected to make profits only in the long term was a bull market phenomenon. Second, even if the short-termist phenomenon does not exist, effects may ensue if managers behave as if it does, which Marsh (1990) admits may be the case in countries such as the United Kingdom.

6.2.5 Small Firm Finance

A further issue arising from the corporate financing behavior of institutional investors is their **attitude toward investment in small firms**, which are important for economic growth and employment. Institutional investors are in principle well placed to accept the risk and illiquidity of small company shares in the context of a diversified portfolio. But arguments are often put forward, particularly in the United Kingdom and Continental Europe, that institutions are reticent in undertaking such investment, with deleterious economic consequences.[42] On the evidence presented below, there is a **ranking of countries** in terms of the issue. It applies least to the United States, to

---

42. Besides affecting growth and employment, neglect of small firms could bias the economy toward sectors with larger firms, such as financial services, which may be contrary to the comparative advantage of the economy as a whole.

a greater extent in Continental Europe, and most strongly[43] in the United Kingdom.[44]

What **economic factors** could underlie the avoidance of small cap stocks? For all institutions, such a tendency could link to illiquidity or lack of marketability of shares, levels of risk that may be difficult to diversify away, difficulty and costs of researching firms that lack track records, and limits on the proportion of a firm's equity that may be held. For pension funds and life insurance companies—but not mutual funds—low levels of small firm investment may also link to investment restrictions on higher-risk assets. Prudent man rules on pension funds could discourage investment in small firms if prudence is interpreted not only to link to a need for diversification, but also to favor "seasoned" issues that are also acceptable to other funds. In other words, trustees could protect themselves from liability by tilting their portfolios toward high-quality assets that are easy to defend in court. Del Guercio (1996) finds some evidence of this in the United States for banks running personal trusts and pension funds but not for mutual funds.[45] Of course, avoidance of individually high-risk assets that could improve the overall risk and return profile of the portfolio may actually be contrary to beneficiary protection, which was the intention of prudent man rules. Such interpretations may also encourage a focus on portfolio indexation. Indexing to narrow core market indices (such as the FTSE-100 and the S&P 500) artificially drives up the value of the firms that are included. Consistent with this, inclusion of a stock in the index tends to drive up its value sharply, owing to the activity of index funds (Harris and Gurel 1986). Even indexation of the wider market, except

---

43. Indeed, the U.K. government has at the time of writing launched an enquiry into institutional investor behavior, with a particular focus on small firm and venture capital financing, see Myners (2000).

44. A possible reason for the relative neglect of small firms in the United Kingdom is the concentrated structure of asset management and focus on balanced management (section 3.5). Large asset managers who are focused on asset allocation both domestically and internationally and seek not to deviate too much from the consensus portfolio may be more likely to neglect small firms than specialist operations involved solely in stock selection, which are relatively more important in the United States. In addition, regulation of pension funds hinders them from investing in limited partnerships—the main form of venture capital fund—unless they are registered as investment managers with the Financial Services Authority.

45. She found that bank managers hold 31% of their equities in stocks of companies rated A+ by Standard & Poor's, while the corresponding figure for mutual funds is 15%. Alternative explanations to prudent man rules for this behavior—namely passive indexing and limits in allowed portfolio positions—were rejected.

for indexing of small cap indices themselves, can be undertaken with a sole focus on the large core stocks in the market, as small stocks are not needed to replicate the overall index with reasonable accuracy.

Clark (2000a) offers a detailed analysis of **pension fund trustee decision making** that offers background to this issue. He argues that the situation of trustees is best seen in the context of three frames of reference in decision making, based on habits, rules, and norms, respectively. These help the trustees—who are typically neither trained investment professionals nor among the key decision makers in the sponsor—cope with the risk and uncertainty related to investment in financial markets, delegation of responsibilities, and related principal-agent problems.

Habits of prudence are the immediate response to risk and uncertainty. They may lead trustees to adopt many of the "irrational" biases that are predicted in the behavioral finance literature, such as loss aversion (displeasure at losing money exceeding pleasure of winning the same amount), preference for certainty and preference for similarity (to other trustees), and regret for lost opportunities. Second, there are rules of proprietary conduct that regulate the process of collective decision making by trustees. These involve fiduciary duties, regard for beneficiary interests, impartiality, and, increasingly, the requirement for diversification set out by modern portfolio theory. Rule-based decision making is seen as a means of justifying past investment decisions, but the rules are themselves often vague and inconclusive. Finally, there are norms of relationships that govern trustees' interactions with others outside the fund, such as consultants and investment managers. A key norm is that of reliance, whereby trustees must rely on others to actually discharge their responsibilities and use appropriate tests of commitment and sincerity. Then there is reciprocity, including an element of loyalty to the service provider. Underpinning these is mutual respect, that trustees have a major burden of responsibility and rely on expert advisers to discharge it. These norms underpin longer-term relationships, overlapping the rules of proprietary conduct and prudential habits. The point arrived at is that all of these habits, rules, and norms in the context of risk and uncertainty can help to sustain **conventional decision making**—and thus decisions against holding alternative investments such as small firms, private equity, and equity in urban infrastructure.[46]

---

46. Another difficulty of such investments is that all too easily, those undertaking them can be accused of corruption.

Table 6.6
Institutional Ownership and Market Price Volatility in the United States (New York
Stock Exchange Firms, 1977–1991)

Capitalization Decile	Institutional Holding (%)	Standard Deviation of Weekly Returns
1 (smallest)	7.6	0.0646
2	12.7	0.0512
3	17.2	0.0488
4	23.9	0.047
5	26.8	0.0452
6	31.2	0.0426
7	35.6	0.0417
8	40.9	0.0397
9	45.6	0.0378
10 (largest)	47.5	0.0353

Source: Sias (1996).

The data are indeed suggestive of a bias of institutional investors against **small listed firms**, albeit to an extent that differs between countries. Table 6.6, from Sias (1996), shows that for the United States, institutional holding of the largest firms on average over 1977–1991 was over 47%, and for the smallest it was under 8%.[47] In the United Kingdom, Revell (1994) shows that U.K. pension funds in 1989 held 32% of large firms and only 26% of smaller ones. (The smaller difference in the United Kingdom is partly linked to greater institutional ownership overall in the United Kingdom than in the United States as well as the lesser importance of smaller listed firms in the United Kingdom.)

Of course, a relative lack of interest on the part of institutional investors would not be a problem if the household sector were willing holders of small firm stocks. Here the United States, with much higher equity ownership by households (table 6.4) and willingness to invest in IPOs, is at an advantage.[48] In contrast, and reflecting lack of demand by household investors, U.K. small firms are becoming concentrated in specialist hands, with the proportion of the FTSE

47. There are also sharp differences within the deciles, with, for example, the highest institutional holding of a firm in the largest decile being 64% and the lowest being 30%. For decile 5, the highest institutional holding was 53% and the lowest was 8%; for the smallest decile, the highest was 23% and the lowest was 1%.

48. On the other hand, empirical work by Falkenstein (1996) shows that in the United States, mutual funds are commonly adverse to certain kinds of stock such as those with lower liquidity or higher risk. This aversion can lead to institutional herding (see also section 5.3.3).

Small Cap index held by the thirty-five largest specialist fund managers rising from 43% in 1997 to 54% in 1998. Small firms are relatively unimportant in the U.K. equity market, as witness the fact that the largest companies account for 96% of the U.K. equity market and 63% of the U.S. one; the top twenty-five corporations account for 17% of the U.S. stock market and 38% of the U.K. The market capitalization of small stocks in the United Kingdom outside the FTSE-100 index amount to half of the value of a single stock, BP-Amoco. These data, as well as the choice of a number of U.K. entrepreneurs to launch IPOs in the United States, suggest that some small firms that are quoted on Nasdaq would not be able to float in the United Kingdom for lack of demand.

The returns on small and large companies in the United Kingdom have mirrored relative demand in recent years, with U.K. small firms returning 2% per annum in 1997 and 1998, for example, while the top thirty stocks returned 31% each year. This is a reversal of the traditional pattern, whereby the small firm effect up to the mid-1990s gave rise to a higher return on small firms than on large firms. A similar pattern is apparent in the United States. Liquidity is low and falling for small firm stocks, with the proportion of U.K. equity market turnover accounted for by small firms falling from 12% in 1997 to 8% in 1998. Time is needed to assess whether these patterns reflect structural or cyclical influences.[49] Meanwhile, the U.K. minimum funding requirement, by discouraging holdings of volatile assets, is widely seen as a further disincentive to holdings of small firm stocks.

Institutional interest in private equity, LBO funds, and venture capital also differs across countries. In the United States, the average allocation to such **alternative investments** having high returns and uncorrelated with markets by private and public pension funds and endowments is 7.3% of the portfolio, accounting for $152 billion. Of this total, 46% are LBO funds and 19% are venture capital funds (Goldman Sachs and Frank Russell 1999). The largest U.S. funds are seeking allocations to investments that are uncorrelated with stock markets of around 10%, with CALPERS allocation $11.25 billion to hedge funds in 1999.

---

49. Note also that in the United Kingdom, the small firm sector is widely seen as having been hit by low inflation and relatively slow growth, while large firms are protected by their brand name or ability to cut costs. Over 1989–1997, small firm dividend growth in the United Kingdom was 3.4 percentage points a year lower than that of large firms.

In Europe, allocations are much lower; the corresponding portfolio share is 2.5%, accounting for $13.8 billion. The distribution of alternative investments in Europe is 44% venture capital and 40% LBO funds. The U.K. portfolio share is lower than that in Continental Europe, at 2.2% compared with 2.8%.

The **integration of EU equity markets** following EMU may paradoxically increase the cost of equity for some types of small to medium-size firms and make flotation more difficult, even though it will increase the scope of equity finance generally (see Peel 1999, Davis 1999b). This is because large institutional investors are tending to treat the market as a bloc, and indexers then tend to buy only the large firms that comprise the index. Small stocks are consequently underperforming. There may also be fundamental reasons for underperformance of small caps in EMU, as they will not benefit as much as large firms from mergers and acquisitions and from the benefits of transparency; in addition, larger firms will have more scope to gear up in the context of the growing pan-EMU debt markets.

Note that these arguments apply most strongly to existing firms in older, established industrial sectors in the euro area. At the time of writing, they did not appear to hold for high-tech start-ups, for which IPOs are booming in specialist markets such as those recently established in Germany and France. Indeed, the development and improvement of such specialist stock markets for small company shares represent one initiative that may make such holdings more attractive to institutional investors. Close attention is also needed to the regulations imposed on institutional investors, to assess whether they discourage small firm financing.

6.3   The Public Sector and Policy Issues

6.3.1   Government Finance

At a **macro level**, international institutional investors seeking portfolio diversification provide a wider pool of saving for governments seeking to finance budget deficits. As table 6.3 shows, G-7 countries other than France and Japan all have at least 20% of government bonds held by foreigners. Institutional demand for government bonds will itself tend to increase in future as baby-boomers begin to retire and need annuities and lower-risk assets (Bishop 1998).

Whether access to a global pool of saving reduces the **cost of financing** budget deficits depends on the balance of two effects.[50] On the one hand, there is the portfolio effect, whereby investors demand higher returns to compensate for holding a larger proportion of their portfolios in a given asset. This should be lower for issuers in global markets than for those confined to a smaller domestic pool of saving. On the other hand, international investors will be more vigilant in requiring compensation for default risk and may also require compensation for currency risk (although the latter should be diversifiable).

Overall, fiscal authorities that are perceived as prudent by international institutional investors may indeed benefit from global issuance. But once market discipline begins to take hold, the process may be brusque; in effect, perceptions by international creditors of serious disequilibria in an economy can lead to major shifts of funds, and governments may face a situation akin to a bank run when the yield on government debt rises sharply and the exchange rate collapses. This pattern was witnessed in Mexico in 1994 and, on a lesser scale, in many OECD countries in the 1980s and 1990s. A point of controversy is whether correction of fiscal positions is delayed for longer than is desirable (see section 6.1.3). A possible reason for this is moral hazard following rescues by the International Monetary Fund of countries facing fiscal crises.

Institutional investors' relative preference for long-term instruments (section 6.1.2) may in itself benefit fiscal policy. Bond finance helps to ensure nonmonetary financing and thus aids counter-inflation policies. As table 6.7 indicates, there is considerable further scope for securitization of government debt in the sense of increasing the proportion that is tradable. In this context, the presence of institutional investors, both domestic and international, has also helped to ensure the success of privatization financings, which have become an important substitute for debt issuance, as well contributing to overall economic efficiency.

At a **micro level**, institutional investors' behavior may put government revenues under pressure via their desire to avoid stock exchange transactions taxes. Such taxes are increasingly found merely to trans-

---

50. The argument presented assumes that there are no exchange controls, which may otherwise force down the cost of financing budget deficits domestically.

Table 6.7
Potential Securitization of Government Debt

	Bonds as Percent of Maastricht Debt	Current Market Value of Bonds (ECU Billion)	75% of "Maastricht" (ECU Billion)
Germany	35	415	864
France	57	422	545
Italy	31	390	943
United Kingdom	58	376	503
Netherlands	62	146	171
Belgium	50	130	195
Spain	50	169	249
Denmark	97	92	67
Sweden	52	81	121
Austria	27	34	98
Finland	66	40	46
Ireland	41	17	31
Portugal	36	20	43
Total	44	2334	3876
United States	40	1822	
Japan	28	1007	

Source: Bishop (1998).

fer institutional business offshore, the outcome being widespread abolition of the tax as it applies to securities.[51]

The main issue at a micro level, however, is whether to exempt or subsidize institutional saving from taxation (see Dilnot and Johnson 1993). The basic choice in taxation of savings is between a regime in which asset returns are tax free (expenditure tax treatment) and one in which they are taxed (comprehensive income tax treatment). All taxes distort incentives in some way—one can only choose a "second best." The choice between income and expenditure taxes rests on contrasting views of the appropriate form of neutrality to aim for. Is it neutrality between consumption and saving (implying that returns are taxed) or between consumption at different points in time (in which case returns are tax free)?

For pension fund and life insurance saving, most governments appear to find neutrality between consumption at different points in time more appropriate. Most countries follow the logic of the expenditure tax for pension saving, exempting it from taxes on con-

---

51. However, it has been increased sharply with respect to transfers of immobile assets such as residential property transfers.

tributions and asset returns while taxing retirement income and lump sums drawn from such tax favored assets (see Davis 1995a). Life insurance has also tended to benefit from expenditure tax privileges in many countries, although these are being withdrawn in some cases (for example, the United Kingdom abolished tax relief on life insurance premiums in 1984). Some mutual fund saving that is not destined for life or pension use has been tax privileged in small amounts, as for PEPs and latterly ISAs in the United Kingdom.

Governments are typically **not consistent in their treatment** of different forms of saving. Forms of saving such as bank deposits, mutual funds, and direct equity holdings usually face an income tax treatment.[52] Reasons for taxing pensions and life insurance relatively leniently include:

• the need to assist people to save enough to maintain postretirement living standards,

• a desire to encourage people to save and thus cut the cost to the state of means-tested social security benefits,

• to raise the general level of saving, and

• the idea that long-term institutional investors are in some way superior to other types of financial institutions.

An element of skepticism seems warranted in regard to these arguments. We showed in section 6.1.1 that institutional saving and related tax privileges do not strongly boost aggregate saving. The alternative to encouraging saving for old age is to make it compulsory, in which case tax privileges may be reduced, as is the case for Australia and Denmark. And it is difficult to argue that the overall effects of institutionalization, as outlined in chapters 5 and 6 of this book, are so favorable as to warrant a tax subsidy. Rather, if the expenditure tax argument is found persuasive, the treatment is best extended to all forms of saving.

6.3.2 Financial Regulation

In assessing the relationship between institutional investors and financial regulation, one may distinguish aspects of the regulation of

---

52. The distortion to consumption and saving decisions is aggravated by the fact that tax is usually imposed on nominal returns, including the element that compensates for inflation.

institutions themselves from the broader forms of financial liberalization that their growth and behavior has helped to trigger. Note that we do not aim to provide detailed coverage of extant regulations for institutions, or indeed of financial deregulation generally. Useful references are as follows:

• on the overall regulation of nonbank financial intermediaries, see Kumar (1997) of the World Bank and Steil (1994);

• on pension fund regulation, see Davis (1995a, 1998a) and Wyatt (1997);

• on life insurance regulation, see OECD (1993, 1996) and Dickinson (1998);

• on mutual fund regulation, see Investment Company Institute (2000);

• on regulation of asset managers, see Franks and Mayer (1989);

• on securities market regulation, see Steil (1994, 1996, 1998);

• and on financial deregulation generally, see Reserve Bank of Australia (1991)[53], World Bank (1992), and Edey and Hviding (1995).

As regards **regulation of institutions**, there are important contrasts with banking regulation. For example, institutions lack capital and reserve requirements and hence may be able to offer finance to borrowers at a lower cost. Underlying this is the fact that institutions tend to have matched assets and liabilities that are marked to market frequently and hence do not need the safeguards that banks require against runs by depositors. Mutual fund regulation, in particular, is focused on information disclosure and self-regulation. Defined contribution pension funds are also largely regulated to ensure consumer protection. On the other hand, more or less strict minimum funding and portfolio restrictions apply in addition to life insurers and defined benefit pension funds, which means that their portfolio allocation is not entirely free. This is because these institutional investors offer guarantee or insurance features that imply a risk of insolvency. Asset managers, which should in principle be regulated from a purely conduct-of-business point of view since they do not take positions (Franks and Mayer 1989), are in some countries subject to unnecessary and distortionary capital requirements.

---

53. In this volume, see Bisignano (1991) on issues in European deregulation.

Table 6.8
Selected Patterns of Deregulation

	1960	1980	1987	1990	1995
United Kingdom	IEC	IC			
United States	I	I	I		
Germany	I				
Japan	IEC	IC	IC	IC	
Canada	I				
France	IEC	IEC	IE		
Italy	IEC	EC	EC	E	

I = interest rate controls, E = exchange controls, C = direct controls on credit expansion.

Some changes in regulation of institutions have induced shifts in behavior: The ERISA for U.S. pension funds led to a focus on long-term bonds and derivatives for immunization purposes, for example, as well as justifying international diversification. We noted above that new U.S. Department of Labor regulations helped to promote the corporate governance movement among U.S. institutions. Easing of restrictions on international investment by funds in Japan has had a major impact on their cross-border activity, independent of easing of exchange controls.

The way in which the asset management sector is consolidating, which was outlined in chapters 3 and 4, raises important regulatory issues. In particular, current regulatory structures remain fragmented along industry and national lines, whereas these boundaries are becoming increasingly blurred in the world today. Besides a need for consumer protection, important competition issues could arise if, for example, large asset managers were able to exert market dominance via control of distribution channels.

Institutions have also had an **impact on financial liberalization more generally**. Several major types of deregulation can be discerned (see Edey and Hviding (1995) and table 6.8):

• the abolition of interest-rate controls or cartels that fixed rates;

• the abolition of direct controls on credit expansion;

• the removal of exchange controls;

• the removal of regulations restricting establishment of foreign institutions;

- the development and improvement of money, bond, and equity markets;
- the removal of regulations segmenting financial markets; and
- the deregulation of fees and commissions in financial services.

Partly to offset these, there has been a tightening of prudential supervision, particularly in relation to capital adequacy and often harmonized internationally. This last point shows that liberalization is not a removal of all regulation but a shift in its locus from structural to prudential regulation.

The main motivations of the authorities have been:

- to increase competition (and hence to reduce costs of financial services),
- to improve access to credit for the private sector,
- to improve efficiency in determining financial prices and allocating funds,
- pressures from competition authorities to remove cartels,
- a desire to maintain competitiveness of domestic markets and institutions,
- increased flexibility and responsiveness to customers,
- facilitating financial innovations,
- securing a ready market for increasing sales of government bonds, and
- desire to secure stability of such a system against excessive risk-taking.

Note that these are broadly in line with the desire for an improvement in the way the various functions of the financial system set out in section 1.3 are fulfilled.

However, it would be wrong to see deregulation purely as a proactive shift by the authorities. In many cases, it was **necessitated by structural and technological shifts** that had already made existing regulations redundant. In this context, the role of institutional investors may be highlighted, whether indirectly or directly. Notably, it was the willingness of institutions to bypass domestic securities markets that led to deregulation of fee and commission structures that were contrary to their interests (as in the case of Big

Bang in the United Kingdom). As we noted, governments more generally have sought to improve the functioning of their domestic bond markets so as to satisfy the liquidity needs of institutional investors in the hope of thereby reducing their own funding costs. Abolition of exchange controls in countries such as the United Kingdom and Japan can be seen in the light of a desire to ease upward pressure on the exchange rate via capital outflows, in the context of growing pressure by institutions to invest offshore. The U.S. deregulation of secondary trading of private placements (Article 144a) showed a recognition that institutions do not require elaborate investor protection—and was a response to fear of competition for domestic securities issuance generated by offshore issues of bonds to institutional investors.

Some of the banking deregulation that occurred in the 1980s was seen as necessary owing to the intense competition that banks faced from institutions. The abolition of the U.S. interest rate regulations (Regulation Q) owing to competition from money market funds is a good example; easing of reserve requirements is another (although clearly, wholesale delocalization of banking was also an implicit threat). The fact that institutional competition left banks with lower quality credits made the removal of controls on credit expansion, on the one hand, and capital adequacy regulation, on the other, all the more urgent. Moreover, once the process of liberalization began, one measure quickly led to others, owing to the desire to maintain a level playing field (within countries) and competitive equality (between countries).

6.3.3 Monetary Stability

Following on from the previous section, the vigilance of international institutional investors against fiscal excesses is likely to benefit monetary policy, as it helps to ensure that a noninflationary policy mix is maintained (Browne and Fell 1994). Nevertheless, in some other respects, monetary policy making in an institutionalized and globalized environment is a **more difficult and uncertain process** than in a purely domestic and bank-based setting (see, for example, Deutsche Bundesbank 1996). In particular, to the extent that equity, foreign exchange, and bond market adjustments become recurrent features of international capital markets, monetary policy makers generally will need to be aware of the views and expectations of the global financial markets and their implications for the domestic economy.

Monetary policy makers typically wish to assess asset price developments for their overall **impact on monetary conditions and as an indicator**, among other indicators, of potential inflationary pressures. They do not in general use domestic asset prices as a target for monetary policy, as this could risk destabilizing the economy. For example, resisting a fall in equity prices by cutting interest rates beyond the level that is judged necessary to stabilize inflation may be a good recipe for boosting inflation as well as generating moral hazard among investors. Even pegging the exchange rate may be successful only in certain specific circumstances, as experience during the Asian crisis showed. Experience from European countries such as Denmark suggests that pegging tends to be effective only where inflation is low and fiscal performance is identical between currencies, cyclical trends are similar, and monetary policy in the satellite is wholly devoted to maintaining the parity.

In **assessing asset price developments**, policy makers have become aware that, whereas markets for the most part work on the basis of fundamentals and hence impose useful discipline on policy makers "undermining policies which are not credible or sustainable" (Bisignano 1995), at times they may be subject to bubbles or trend chasing, "amplifying the disruptive implications of collective misjudgments" in the words of BIS (1995). Massive and undetected overhangs of open positions may develop in markets, to be sharply unwound when the underlying market assumptions are proved incorrect. One example is the bond market bubble and reversal of 1993–1994. In using asset prices as monetary indicators, monetary authorities wish to distinguish between price changes that reflect fundamentals and those due to institutional herding. They are also aware that the incidence of such herding is not independent of economic performance. Experience suggests that countries that adopt fiscal consolidation, low inflation, and a nominal anchor are less likely to face asset price volatility than those that do not.

When there is **exchange rate pegging**, asset price volatility may present major dilemmas to the authorities as it may give rise to conflict between growth and counterinflation objectives, or indeed between monetary and financial stability more generally. During the 1992 ERM crisis, countries defending exchange rate pegs found that the rapidity with which markets are able to react to news shortens the reaction times required of central banks and necessitates action on the basis of less complete information. Reserves are likely to be wholly inadequate against the scale of transactions that institutions can undertake, particularly given the ability of hedge funds to borrow to gain leverage, and hence greater stress is placed on the interest rate.

Bond market globalization and the consequent tendency for foreign yields to have a greater influence on domestic bond markets may **diminish the leverage of domestic monetary policy** over the economy. Monetary conditions may be dictated more by globally pivotal short- and long-term rates[54] than by domestic short-term rates (see Fell 1996). More generally, market movements occurring for nonfundamental reasons reduce the clarity of the signals from bond yields. Conventionally, bond yields are seen as being composed of three components: real yields, inflation expectations, and a risk premium, where the use of index-linked bond yields enables the size and movement of the inflation component to be estimated and volatility of options prices facilitates estimation of the risk premium. But the possibility of overshooting of fundamental levels makes this potentially highly inaccurate. As an example of the effects of institutions on bond yields, it may be noted that in the United Kingdom at the time of writing, institutional behavior had driven bond yields below what are historically considered normal levels. This pattern reflects the influence of regulations; there is artificially high demand for long-dated bonds by pension funds, driven by the minimum funding provisions of the 1995 Pensions Act.

Despite such difficulties, as argued by Wojnilower (1997), the **yield curve or term spread** between short- and long-term rates remains one of the more robust indicators in an institutionalized financial system. As a number of authors have shown, this spread tends to be an accurate indicator of the real economy (Davis and Fagan 1997, Estrella and Mishkin 1995). The transmission mechanism between the term spread, inflation, and growth is conventionally explained in terms of investors' inflation expectations and the level of real short-

---

54. For example, until 1998, the configuration of world interest rates with low Japanese rates led hedge funds and other institutions to borrow heavily in yen and invest globally, unleashing funds that helped to boost asset prices worldwide (see IMF 1998). The unwinding of such yen carry trades in September 1998 was at root of an unprecedented 15% shift in the yen-dollar rate in one day.

term rates. But the transmission mechanism can be extended to take into account the activity of institutional investors. The argument is that a wider yield spread induces borrowing by hedge funds and other institutional investors to purchase bonds and equities, inducing rises in bond and equity prices and favorable conditions for economic growth. Conversely, a fall in the spread discourages lengthening of asset maturities and raises long-term rates.

6.3.4 Financial Stability

Unlike banks, institutional investors are not in general subject to panic runs, because they have assets and liabilities of similar maturity. Nevertheless, an institutionalized financial system may still raise concerns for financial stability. In this section, we note some of the issues raised and mention, without necessarily endorsing, some of the policy responses that have been suggested.

A **wider range of institutions may need to be covered by lender of last resort** assistance in the context of an institutionalized financial system. Federal Reserve policy during the 1987 stock market crash aimed to avoid systemic risk arising from failure of investment banks, which was ensured by a general easing of liquidity and moral suasion on commercial banks to lend. The private sector rescue of the hedge fund LTCM was undertaken with the good offices of the Federal Reserve Bank of New York because of fears of both the authorities and major financial institutions that serious disruption could follow an unwinding of LTCM's portfolios. It cannot be ruled out that nonbanks may need direct public sector rescues in the future.

As discussed in section 5.3.6 and F. Edwards (1995), the stability of money market mutual funds could be threatened in some circumstances. A fund that breaks par value could plausibly lead to a run on such funds, which could lead to a more general liquidity crisis in the money markets. There is an issue whether individuals realize that such funds are not subject to deposit insurance and whether demands for policy assistance could become loud if a crisis supervened.

A point of major debate in the wake of the Mexican crisis was whether an **international lender of last resort for countries** is also needed in a globalized and institutionalized financial system. The IMF rescues of Thailand, Indonesia, and South Korea have renewed discussion of this issue. As is the case for the domestic lender of last resort, the issue is linked to a trade-off between moral hazard created by such rescues and the damage that an ongoing financial crisis could cause. In this context, some have revived the well-known issue of a tax on gross foreign exchange transactions to slow the response of financial markets (Eichengreen et al. 1995); others point out the well-known shortcomings of this suggestion (Garber and Taylor 1995).[55]

Liquidity failure of securities markets (money, bond, and derivatives markets), which may be generated by institutional behavior, may raise prudential concerns. Notably, as we discussed in section 5.3.4, funding difficulties of banks and other intermediaries are a potential source of instability. Also markets are seen as a repository for liquidity. Derivatives markets are often vital for the smooth functioning of asset and liability management strategies, so failure of such markets may threaten wider defaults on the part of intermediaries.

If they consider that systemic risks are likely to arise from market liquidity failure in debt securities markets, **central banks may intervene**, either by offering liquidity assistance to market participants or even by maintaining market liquidity using their own assets. Clearly, moral hazard may arise for securities markets in the same way as for banks, with imprudent underwriting and market-making practices being followed on the assumption that liquidity will be maintained; nonfinancial companies would also be more willing to increase leverage via securities markets. Moreover, maintaining an incorrect level of market prices is a recipe for market distortion and, ultimately, inflation. Hence central banks have generally avoided such responses, using market liquidity failures as salutary lessons in prudence for the market. Such an approach was underpinned by that fact that, until 1998, liquidity crises were for the most part confined to peripheral markets such as the junk bond market (Davis 1994a). But experience after the Russia/LTCM crisis showed that traditionally highly liquid debt security markets, such as the U.S. bond and money markets, could also be vulnerable to liquidity difficulties.

---

55. Notably, that a country imposing such taxes unilaterally would face disintermediation, while a global tax could still be avoided by undertaking separate positions and transactions, particularly via use of derivatives, to mimic a foreign exchange deal, necessitating application to an ever wider range of instruments. And since success of such a tax would likely entail a decline in liquidity and liquidity tends to be stabilizing, it might have directly counterproductive effects on volatility.

Besides brokering a rescue of LTCM, the authorities acted to reduce interest rates (Davis 1999d).

The incidence of debt market liquidity crises may be reduced by **policy action that increases the robustness of markets**. For example, issuance of standardized benchmark securities by governments and avoidance of interest rate instability as a by-product of monetary policy[56] are strategies that can be helpful to ensuring market liquidity. Robustness of intermediaries requires adequate capital, encouraging clearing and settlement, adequate management and control procedures, and inducing firms to monitor each other. An obvious additional point is that both intermediaries and end-users of securities markets must diversify their sources of funds and of liquidity to protect themselves against problems in individual markets. Crisis scenarios could play an important role in such calculations.

As cited by Bingham (1992), a traditional view is that robustness of debt securities markets may also require some limits to competition between market makers, possibly via designation, recognition, and licensing rules. In this view, economic rents associated with market maker status may be needed to ensure that they devote sufficient capital to prevent frequent liquidity collapses. An alternative to limits on entry in this context is low levels of disclosure of trades and the ability to post indicative prices.

One reason why this approach has not typically been adopted (and indeed remaining cartels have been liberalized) is that such markets might be subject in the short term to oligopolistic abuses, with high fees, wide bid-offer spreads, and risks of price manipulation. In the longer term, trading in such markets would be disintermediated. More generally, the number of market maker markets, in the sense of there being an obligation to make markets, is declining. The more common type of market nowadays is the "dealer market" with no obligation to make markets (examples are the foreign exchange, bond, and OTC derivatives markets, as well as many equity markets). In such markets, high levels of capitalization might protect the dealer from bankruptcy but could not guarantee that market liquidity would always be maintained, since the dealer has no obligation to do so.

---

56. Volatile and unpredictable interest rate movements may undermine the profitability of market making, by increasing position risk as well as driving away liquidity traders.

Conclusions

It has been shown that institutional investors exert a major influence on the nonfinancial sectors as well as the financial sector. This chapter has identified effects on the portfolio behavior of the household sector, notably increasing holdings of longer-term instruments, a sea change in patterns of international investment, various effects on corporate finance and corporate governance, and an impact on government fiscal, regulatory, and monetary policies. On balance, the effects are favorable, as they tend in the direction of greater economic efficiency at a national and—for international investment—a global level. Some question marks arise in relation to the lack of investment in small firms in some countries and, more tentatively, the short time horizons of institutions.

With regard to public policy, institutionalization may make fiscal deficits easier to finance, but institutions are also vigilant against "excesses" of fiscal expansionism that generate default risk. Monetary policy makers benefit from this vigilance of institutions regarding countries' macroeconomic policies but also need to revise their own views, among other things, of how markets work and about indicator properties of yields. Regulatory policy must learn to cope with the potential for instability generated by an institutionalized financial system while also ensuring that the benefits of institutions for financial stability—in particular that, having balanced assets and liabilities, they are not subject to runs in the manner of banks—are safeguarded. All of these issues are of importance to the future performance of the economy as institutional investors grow and, as such, are important areas of further research.

IV

Institutional Trading

7

Automation, Trading Costs, and the Structure of the Securities Trading Industry
Ian Domowitz and Benn Steil

Introduction

This chapter examines the impact of advances in automated trade execution on the cost of institutional trading and the structure of the securities trading industry. The effects have been fundamental: The cost of providing exchange trading services has declined significantly, the means by which services can be delivered to investors have changed radically, and the natural industrial structure of the trading services industry has been transformed in consequence. These developments are affecting all classes of market participants: exchanges, broker-dealers, investors, and regulators.

This chapter is an updated version of a paper of the same name published in *The Brookings-Wharton Papers on Financial Services* (Domowitz and Steil 1999). It provides important background on the development of exchanges and trading systems that will be useful in understanding the changing market environment in which institutional investors buy and sell shares. It will therefore set the context for our discussion of institutional trading in chapter 8. However, the presentation will be somewhat more technical than that in chapter 8, and the reader may wish to revisit some of this material in more depth when references to it appear in chapter 8.

The chapter is organized as follows: At the outset, we provide an analytical description of recent industry developments in the context of the spread of technologies enabling automated trade execution. We then suggest theoretical paradigms to explain observed changes and to assist in anticipating future changes in trading market structure. Specific implications for the competitive behavior of industry incumbents and entrants are drawn out and compared to current and planned developments in exchange and industry structure. We then isolate those inputs into the theories that govern their predictions in order to guide empirical investigations of their significance in the development of the trading industry. Finally, we examine trading data corresponding to such inputs in order to evaluate the trajectory of market structure development.

Existing analyses of automated trading operations focus on the explicit trading rules of systems, the mechanics of trading under those rules, and the effects of the trading mechanism on the formation of prices. This description of the work corresponds precisely with the objectives of the various paradigms in classical financial market microstructure (O'Hara 1995, p. 1). Aside from clear statements of the mechanics of trading, it concentrates on the characteristics of traders. This emphasis persists even in work purporting to describe competition between exchanges.[1]

In contrast, our objective is to explain changes in the structure of the trading services industry. Our maintained hypothesis is that industrial structure cannot be explained by focusing on the demand side alone—that is, on traders—and that insufficient attention has been paid to the supply side. We shall not ignore trader behavior in the analysis, but the emphasis is decidedly on the provision of alternative technologies for trading services.

Exchanges operating in a competitive environment can be analyzed as firms.[2] Firms offer different technologies for trading, including traditional floors and computerized auctions embodying automated trade execution.[3] Through these alternative technologies, transaction services are produced. Traders are consumers of trading services. They choose technologies and associated bundles of trans-

---

1. See, for example, Ramanlal, Hargis, and McDonald (1997), in which competition depends only on the ratio of informed to uninformed traders and the degree of information revelation by market makers. Information asymmetries, for example, are not linked to trading mechanisms.
2. See also Arnold et al. (1999) for a similar perspective.
3. There may, of course, be product differentiation within a given technological class (such as automated continuous auctions and periodic call auctions).

action services, taking explicit costs, implicit trading costs, and liquidity effects into account. Through the interaction of technology choice and trader behavior, prices are produced.

We use a combination of network economics and contestability theory to unify developments. In section 7.1, we analyze the rapid entry of computerized exchanges into the world market for exchange services within a network theory paradigm. We focus in particular on the interaction of development costs, operating costs, and the direct costs of delivering trading services to customers. We examine liquidity effects, which are commonly held to account for the durability of the dominant national exchanges, as a form of network externality. The rise of automated exchange systems, in the face of such externalities enjoyed by incumbent floor exchanges, is examined in terms of significant shifts in relative costs, strategic penetration pricing, and competitive efforts to achieve compatibility among electronic systems and thus to expand new networks.

The impact of trading automation on the pricing behavior of exchanges is addressed through the framework of contestability theory in section 7.2. We argue that automation has significantly increased market contestability, in particular via its role in reducing sunk cost barriers to entry and exit. The effect is to reduce dramatically the ability of exchanges to cross-subsidize different types of trading activity, as such behavior is incompatible with the sustainability of prices in a contestable market. We illustrate this effect by reference to the competitive erosion of long-standing exchange cross-subsidization regimes—in particular, large trades by small trades, "on-exchange" by "off-exchange" trades, and retail trades by institutional trades.

The incentive structure under which an exchange operates is heavily influenced by its governance structure, which is itself a logical product of the trading technology employed. In section 7.3, we discuss the role of automation in determining the governance structure of exchanges, focusing on the motivations for and effects of exchange demutualization and the emergence of nonmember-based proprietary trading systems.

In the context of trading technology adoption, the determination of market structure depends on the relative quality of the technologies and cost. Debates over the viability and future of computerized auctions relative to the floor trading alternative traditionally focus on the issue of "market quality" (e.g., liquidity proxies, informational efficiency, and volatility). In contrast, we suggest that consideration of trading technology adoption and subsequent market structure development needs to move from issues of market quality to issues of cost. This conclusion stems from an examination of extant empirical evidence, which we carry out in section 7.4, comparing traditional trading venues to automated price-discovery systems. Overall, the evidence suggests that automated markets and traditional trading floors may differ in subtle and complex ways but that market quality is equalized across market structures.

Assessment of relative costs is a complex undertaking. Beyond the problems of valuing fixed-cost components and calculating marginal cost, trading entails a variety of implicit costs faced by the investor. In section 7.5, we evaluate explicit and implicit (execution) costs using a unique sample of five-year trading data from a large institutional user of proprietary electronic trading systems. Electronic markets dominate traditional brokers across the board for trading in over-the-counter (OTC) stocks. An analysis of total cost, including commissions, suggests that commissions are high enough to outweigh any possible gains in execution cost achieved by trading listed issues through a traditional broker. These conclusions are reinforced by an examination of costs sorted by a variety of trade characteristics.

7.1   Automation and Network Effects

Securities exchanges operating in a competitive environment can be analyzed, regardless of their actual governance structure, as firms offering trading products that embody particular technologies. The way in which the structure of the trading industry develops might then profitably be studied within the framework of industrial economics. Given the nature of the trading products offered in the marketplace, we argue that issues of technology adoption must be approached by using industry models in which network externalities feature prominently.

An exchange or trading system is analogous to a communications network, with sets of rules defining what messages can be sent over the network, who can send them, and how they translate into trades. This is more readily apparent for an automated system than for a floor-based one, but the principle applies equally for both models.

In the securities-trading industry, two important effects relate specifically to the network nature of the product. First, the benefit to an individual market participant of a specific trading system increases with the number of locations from which the system may be accessed. As in the operation of telephone and retail distribution systems, consumer benefit increases with the number of outlets at which a good or service is available.[4] Second, the benefit to an individual market participant increases with the number of other participants on the system. As the value to one trader of transacting on a given trading system increases when another trader chooses to transact there as well, such a system is said to exhibit network effects or network externalities. We believe that such network externalities are the source of the liquidity effect to which is commonly ascribed the durability of the dominant national trading markets.

The salient presence of network effects in the securities trading industry makes the adoption of technology a complex process. The cost of trading over a given system is a function of the timing of the operator's market entry compared with that of incumbents and not merely the marginal production costs of the system operator. Users derive significant positive external consumption benefits from the presence of other users and from the complementarity of the trading network with other systems designed to generate and process trades. Each of these factors has a major influence on the adoption of technology.

Network models yield important implications for the development of market structure. Clearly, traders have enormous incentives to coalesce around the system that minimizes trading costs. Yet the standardization of trading on a given system is far from straightforward. First, standardization may not occur even where it is optimal (Katz and Shapiro 1986).[5] Individual traders may disagree with respect to which trading technology is the more desirable, and traders take no account of negative liquidity effects on other traders when choosing a given trading platform in preference to standardization on another. Second, when standardization does occur, the optimal technology may not be selected. The existence of a network externality can confer a significant first-mover advantage on the technology that is available earlier or that is cheaper at the outset, and this advantage may not be overcome even when it is socially optimal to standardize on a newer alternative technology.

---

4. In the case of trading systems, this benefit can assume an additional dimension: As the number of locations increases, the variety of instruments available for trading may rise as well.

5. Optimality is social optimality or efficiency here, defined in terms of maximization of total economic surplus.

Given such a first-mover advantage, a potential entrant utilizing a technology of quality equal to that of the incumbent would have, at the least, to face a lower marginal cost of production. However, when the incumbent enjoys a significant network externality, this may not be sufficient. The entrant may have to engage in penetration pricing to establish its own viable network. Submarginal cost pricing to first-period traders can be optimal when their participation raises the value of the system to second-period traders.

For such strategic pricing to be a viable competitive option, the entrant must control property rights to some significant component of the underlying technology, or other entry barriers into the supply of that technology must exist. Otherwise, pricing above marginal cost in future periods, which is necessary to recoup initial losses, will not be possible. Katz and Shapiro (1986) refer to such firms as "sponsors" of a given technology. By engaging in below-cost pricing early in the technology's life, the sponsor can internalize the external benefits that are generated when first-period traders adopt its technology.

Models of sponsorship are complex and yield markedly different welfare outcomes depending on the cost structures, entry timing, and sponsorship powers of the competitors. In the context of trading system competition, strategic pricing capability in network markets can yield results that are important not only for understanding and predicting market structure developments, but also for guiding public policy toward the industry. In particular, trading system operators often face strong incentives to construct cartels among themselves to facilitate strategic pricing, and such cartels may actually be socially desirable. To the extent that cartels enable future period pricing above marginal cost, they generate incentives to invest in new trading technology in the presence of liquidity effects. This line of reasoning is pursued by Domowitz (1995), who notes that implicit mergers between providers are enabled in large part by the advent of automated trading system technology. Trading service providers may actually move to automated systems specifically to facilitate such cartel activity.

7.1.1 Networks in the Context of Automated Trading and Market Structure Development

7.1.1.1 Entry and Cost

In the early days of automated systems development, a quarter of a century ago, hardware and software development costs were much higher than they are today; developments costing $100 million were the norm at a time when listings were much fewer and turnover was much lower. Given that traditional trading floors already possessed functioning liquidity pools, or networks, the cost of trading automation had to fall considerably before it would be widely adopted. This was so even if automated trading would have been superior at existing levels of floor turnover, owing to the network externalities enjoyed by the established floor-based markets.

Development costs for computerized auction markets have declined dramatically over the past decade. Against a backdrop of static or rising costs for floor-based systems, we witness automated systems emerging as the model of choice in almost all new market development efforts. Across Western and Eastern Europe, virtually every stock exchange has now implemented an electronic auction system. It is only where the network power of floor-based and dealership markets was substantial in the 1980s that resistance to full automation has been significant. The world's five largest stock exchanges—New York, Nasdaq, London, Tokyo, and Frankfurt —have been the slowest to dismantle obligatory human trade intermediation.

It is exceptionally difficult to compare the costs involved in operating automated versus floor-based trading structures on the basis of cross-market expenditure comparisons. Trading volumes, ancillary services, and regulatory obligations vary markedly across exchanges. In terms of up-front construction costs, recent European automated and floor system development plans indicate that the latter are at least three to four times more costly.[6] The best we may be able to do in estimating the annual operating cost savings in switching from floor to automated trading is to rely on the proprietary estimates of exchanges that have undergone, or are undergoing, the transition. The most recent such published estimate comes from the Sydney

---

6. The London Stock Exchange and Deutsche Börse each spent more than $100 million implementing their new automated auction systems, SETS and Xetra, yet Tradepoint's system was developed for less than $10 million. Relative volumes cannot account for the difference, as Tradepoint could match the capacity of either with a further technology investment of around $5 million. Yet the cost of building and technologically equipping a floor is clearly much higher. LIFFE's floor development plan, abandoned in the spring of 1998, was priced at more than $400 million. A smaller bond futures trading floor at the Chicago Board of Trade was completed in 1997 at a cost of approximately $200 million. The New York Stock Exchange spent over $2 billion on trading technology between 1995 and 1999, much of it devoted to its SuperDOT order delivery system.

Futures Exchange, which expected to realize savings in human resources and ancillary services of at least 40% (Robinson 1998a).

Cost is undoubtedly the most significant factor driving the rapid expansion of automated trading in the past several years. Expansion often proceeds in the face of direct competition from well-established floor-based exchanges. It is not merely the decline in development and operating costs that has driven this process, however, but also a steep decline in the direct cost of delivering automated services to customers.

Distance costs in the provision of automated trading services are small or nonexistent, whereas the cost of access to floor systems generally increases with distance from the customer.[7] This derives from the requirement for the customer either to be physically present on the floor itself or to employ an agent to intermediate transactions on the floor. The removal of important legal barriers to direct cross-border electronic trading since 1996, both within the European Union and between the European Union and the United States, has allowed automated markets to expand their networks dramatically, attracting foreign traders whose cost of access to local floor markets was much higher.

Article 15.4 of the European Union Investment Services Directive gives "regulated markets" within the European Union the right to solicit "remote members" in other member states without having to secure any authorization from the foreign market regulator. Most E.U. screen-based equity and derivatives exchanges have now implemented remote membership. In 1997, the U.S. Commodity Futures Trading Commission granted the Frankfurt-based Deutsche Terminbörse (DTB, predecessor to Eurex) derivatives exchange the right to solicit remote members in the United States for trading in ten-year Bund futures contracts, making it the first non-U.S. exchange to be granted direct access authorization by a U.S. authority. DTB rapidly attracted two dozen new members based in Chicago and New York. Before the launch of U.S. trading, DTB's market share was about 35–40% for many years. The speed with which DTB moved to a 70% share by the spring of 1998 and a near 100% share by the summer is testimony to the power of "tipping" effects in network

---

7. The shift from open-outcry to electronic trading at the Sydney Futures Exchange was specifically motivated, according to the chief executive, by the competitive need to overcome the "tyranny of distance" (Robinson, 1998b), representing the cost of providing trading services to traders based at great distance from the exchange.

markets. Strong positive feedback elements in network markets generate a tendency for one system to achieve complete dominance rapidly once it has achieved an initial advantage. In dynamic network models, tipping is reflected in equilibria in which new placements of the losing system dry up once a rival system becomes accepted in the marketplace (Farrell and Saloner 1986, Katz and Shapiro 1992). This was clearly the case for the London International Financial Futures and Options Exchange (LIFFE) once DTB had surpassed the 50% market share barrier.

Furthermore, locally established E.U. automated exchange members have increasingly been transferring or expanding their screen access across national borders, even where explicit legal authorization has been lacking.[8] This has allowed them to reduce trading and support costs in automated markets by creating access points where they can be most efficiently exploited.

Table 7.1 lists transformations from existing floor-based or dealership trading systems to automated auction systems that were either implemented or initiated in 1997 and 1998. (Floor and dealership trading remains for some products on some of these exchanges.) Rapidly falling seat prices on floor-based exchanges—particularly derivatives exchanges, which have been most directly affected by cross-border automated competition—have accelerated the process.[9] The most dramatic cases of transformation involved LIFFE and MATIF (*Marché à Terme International de France*) in the spring of 1998. LIFFE abruptly abandoned a $400 million floor development plan in favor of accelerated development of an electronic system in the wake of the loss of the ten-year Bund futures market to DTB. MATIF had long resisted moving to screen-based trading as a precondition for a

---

8. Instinet and Lattice Trading direct electronic access from the United States into European automated exchange systems has never been formally authorized by the U.S. Securities and Exchange Commission (SEC). The SEC has decided not to challenge it, however, despite the fact that the European exchanges of which they are members are explicitly forbidden from placing their own screens in the United States. The disparity of treatment between exchange screens and exchange member screens would appear logically indefensible, since orders entered through either screen go directly to the exchange's electronic order book. Nonetheless, there is a legal logic of sorts, in that companies listed on non-U.S. exchanges do not necessarily meet U.S. Generally Accepted Accounting Principles (GAAP) reporting requirements. Non-U.S. exchanges offering to exclude non-GAAP-compliant stocks from direct access authorization have nonetheless been rebuffed by the SEC.

9. Seat prices on the Sydney Futures Exchange halved in the two years to April 1998. Seat prices on the Chicago Board of Trade halved in the first half of 1998 alone.

Table 7.1
Exchanges Moving to Automated Auction Trading, 1997–1998

Exchange
Athens Stock Exchange
Chicago Board of Trade
Chicago Mercantile Exchange
International Securities Market Association
LIFFE
London Stock Exchange
MATIF
Monep
Osaka Securities Exchange
SIMEX
Sydney Futures Exchange
Tokyo Stock Exchange
Toronto Futures Exchange
Toronto Stock Exchange

Note: Floor or dealership trading remains for some products or trading periods on some of these exchanges.

strategic alliance with DTB yet moved quickly to adopt it after DTB merged with the Zurich-based Swiss Options and Financial Futures Exchange (SOFFEX) to create a new electronic exchange, Eurex. MATIF's move created a fascinating case study of hybrid trading, as the floor was initially maintained in parallel with the new electronic system. The plan was formally abandoned within thirty trading days, after the electronic system rapidly achieved a 99% market share.[10]

7.1.1.2   Entry and Strategic Pricing

Automated exchanges have also applied strategic penetration pricing to undercut incumbents with established networks. DTB offered cut-rate memberships and fee holidays on the ten-year Bund futures contracts in 1997, when then-floor-based LIFFE still controlled about two-thirds of the market. After abandoning the floor for screen trading in 1998, MATIF began offering five- and ten-year U.K. gov-

---

10. Automated auction trading is also rapidly expanding in U.S. derivatives exchanges. For example, the Chicago Board of Trade canceled evening floor trading in bond contracts in favor of trading on its electronic Project A system. More recently, the exchange petitioned the Commodity Futures Trading Commission to allow Project A trading in bond contracts during the daytime floor trading hours.

ernment bond contracts at £0.17 per trade, 40% less than LIFFE was charging.[11] The start-up Cantor Financial Futures Exchange, a joint venture for electronic trading of U.S. Treasury futures launched by brokerage firm Cantor Fitzgerald and the New York Board of Trade, went live in September 1998, charging 50% less than the incumbent floor-based Chicago Board of Trade. Tradepoint undercut the London Stock Exchange (LSE) by 75% in the processing of pre-matched interdealer broker trades in the period preceding the LSE's launch of automated auction trading in 1997.

7.1.1.3 Adapters and Incompatible Networks

The proliferation of incompatible automated auction systems has encouraged the growth of enterprises that aim to reduce the costs of investor access by providing a standardized interface across different networks. These electronic brokerage firms correspond to the role of "adapters" in the network economics literature (see Katz and Shapiro 1994). They become members of different automated exchanges, constructing electronic interfaces into each from their own proprietary order entry systems. These systems are marketed to institutional investors, who use them to access multiple exchange order books directly via a single electronic entry point. Instinet, owned by Reuters, operates the largest such system, providing direct cross-border institutional access into U.S., European, and Asian stock exchange order books. Other cross-border adapters include Lattice Trading, owned by State Street Brokerage, and Credit Suisse First Boston's PrimeTrade system for listed derivatives.

7.1.1.4 Remote Cross-Border Trading

Examples of automated exchange systems offering remote cross-border access from the United States include the Chicago Mercantile Exchange's Globex (access in the United Kingdom, Hong Kong, Japan, France, and Bermuda), the New York Mercantile Exchange's ACCESS (United Kingdom, Australia, and Hong Kong), and the Chicago Board of Trade's Project A (United Kingdom, France, and Japan). Most European exchanges now accommodate remote cross-border access, but some, such as the Madrid Stock Exchange, still do not allow *remote membership*. The latter does not require members to

---

11. LIFFE's fee of £0.28 per trade was already a 33% reduction from its £0.42 charge earlier in the year (Calian 1998).

maintain an office in the exchange's home country and is frequently resisted by local members concerned with losing cross-border brokerage business to foreign intermediaries. As the example of DTB's U.S. expansion illustrated, remote membership can be a powerful tool for expanding networks and hence liquidity that is traceable to network effects. The fact that local members controlling an exchange often resist remote membership to protect their existing brokerage franchise raises important questions about exchange governance, which we discuss in section 7.3.

7.1.1.5 Mergers and Alliances

Exchanges have begun to cooperate in the construction of their own adapters in order to enable compatibility between their networks or in some cases to merge their networks outright. As investors expand their holdings of foreign securities and intermediaries expand the geographic scope of their activities in consequence, the externalities resulting from cross-border networking increase. The cost advantage in operating a cross-border system over multiple incompatible national systems thereby increases.

Concern has recently been spreading rapidly among exchanges in Europe and the United States that failure to participate in a major cross-border trading network will lead traders to abandon domestic systems in favor of single-entry-point access to a much wider international grouping of traders and products. This was particularly true in the wake of the July 1998 agreement between the London Stock Exchange and Deutsche Börse to develop a common trading system for blue-chip European shares (subsequently abandoned). The perception of first-mover advantages in network markets lends a sense of urgency to exchanges that are considering a competitive response to such initiatives.

Table 7.2 documents U.S. and European automated exchange linkage strategies implemented or launched between January 1997 and December 2000.[12] These are classified into four broad categories: strategic alliances and joint ventures, common access systems, common trading systems, and mergers. Given the size of this list, it is

---

12. We do not believe this list to be fully comprehensive, as new alliances are now almost a weekly development. More important, we recognize that this list will have evolved considerably by 2001. It is therefore provided primarily for illustrative purposes.

Table 7.2
Automated Exchange Mergers and Alliances, 1997–2000

Merger or Alliance	Status
Exchange Mergers	
AEX: Amsterdam Stock Exchange and European Options Exchange	I
HEX: Helsinki Stock Exchange and SOM	I
BEX: Brussels Stock Exchange and BELFOX	I
OM Stockholm Exchange: Stockholm Stock Exchange and OM	I
Wiener Börse and ÖTOB	I
Paris Bourse and Monep	I
Paris Bourse and MATIF	I
Borsa Italiana and MIF	I
Eurex: DTB and SOFFEX	I
NYBOT: Coffee, Sugar & Cocoa Exchange and NY Cotton Exchange	I
Singapore Exchange: Stock Exchange of Singapore and SIMEX	I
Euronext: Paris, Amsterdam, and Brussels exchanges	I
Hong Kong Stock Exchange and Hong Kong Futures Exchange	A
Bovespa (Brazil) and BVRJ	A
Archipelago ECN and Pacific Exchange (equities)	A
virt-x: Tradepoint and Swiss Exchange (blue chip equities)	A
Chicago Board of Trade and Chicago Board Options Exchange	N
MATIF and MEFF	N
Alberta Stock Exchange and Vancouver Stock Exchange	N
BVLP (Lisbon) and Oporto Derivatives Exchange	N
Euronext and BVLP (Lisbon)	N
Eurex Bonds and EuroMTS	N
Australian Stock Exchange and New Zealand Stock Exchange	N
Common Trading System	
Oslo Stock Exchange and OM (derivatives)	I
FUTOP (Denmark) and OM (derivatives)	I
Norex: OM Stockholm Exchange and Copenhagen Stock Exchange	I
Deutsche Börse, Wiener Börse, and The Irish Exchange	I
Eurex and HEX	I
Chicago Board of Trade and Eurex	I
NEWEX: Deutsche Börse and Wiener Börse	I
Norex and Oslo, Reykjavik, Tallinn, Riga, and Vilnius exchanges	A
International Petroleum Exchange and Nord Pool	A
Paris Bourse and Australian Derivatives Exchanges	A
Euronext and Bourse de Luxembourg	A
Globex Alliance: Chicago Mercantile Exchange, MATIF, MEFF RV, Singapore, Montreal, and BM&F (Brazil)	A
Common Access System	
MATIF and MEFF RV	I
Chicago Mercantile Exchange and LIFFE	I
Euro-Globex Alliance: MATIF, MEFF RV, and MIF	A
SWIFT-FIX access protocol: Amsterdam, Brussels, Frankfurt, London, Madrid, Milan, Paris, and Zurich	A

Table 7.2 (continued)

Merger or Alliance	Status
Strategic Alliance/Joint Venture	
Benelux Exchanges	I
Globex: Chicago Mercantile Exchange and MATIF	I
Cantor Financial Futures Exchange: Cantor Fitzgerald and N.Y. Board of Trade	I
MITS: London Metal Exchange and MG	I
OM Gruppen and NGX	I
Nasdaq Japan: Nasdaq and Osaka Securities Exchange	I
Nasdaq and Hong Kong Stock Exchange	I
Chicago Board Brokerage: Chicago Board of Trade and Prebon Yamane	I
Nasdaq and Australian Stock Exchange	A
NYMEX-SIMEX	A
ParisBourse, Swiss Exchange, Borsa Italiana, and Lisbon Stock Exchange	A
London Stock Exchange and Buenos Aires Stock Exchange	A
Nord Pool and Leipzig Power Exchange	A
Australian Stock Exchange and Singapore Exchange	A
Chicago Mercantile Exchange and Cantor Fitzgerald	N
International Petroleum Exchange and NYMEX	N
Eurex and NYMEX	N
GEM: Amsterdam, Australia, Bovespa (Brazil), Brussels, Hong Kong, Mexico, New York, Paris, Tokyo, and Toronto exchanges	N
Chicago Board Options Exchange and Osaka Securities Exchange	N
London Stock Exchange and Johannesburg Stock Exchange	N

I, implemented; A, agreed; N, being negotiated.

particularly notable that these types of consolidation initiatives were relatively few and far between before 1997.

An example of the strategic alliance strategy is that implemented by the Chicago Mercantile Exchange (CME) and MATIF. The CME has adopted the MATIF NSC-VF trading technology as the basis for its own electronic trading system, and MATIF has adopted the CME's clearing system. A deeper form of alliance is exemplified by the creation of a common electronic system to access multiple exchange systems, a strategy that was agreed to by eight European stock exchanges[13] but subsequently abandoned. The evidence to date suggests that common access systems are generally more complex and costly than was anticipated when they were first widely proposed in the late 1990s. The Norex alliance between OM Stockholm Exchange and the Copenhagen Stock Exchange goes a step further, producing a single trading system based on the Stockholm SAXESS

---

13. London, Frankfurt, Paris, Amsterdam, Zurich, Milan, Madrid, and Brussels.

technology to trade both Swedish and Danish stocks. Although the exchanges remain separate legal entities, members of one are offered free membership in the other. The Oslo, Reykjavik, Tallinn, Riga, and Vilnius exchanges are expected to join the common trading system beginning in 2001. The CBOT and Eurex agreed to a similar strategy, deepening an earlier one based on the model of a common access system. The most notable example of an actual exchange merger during this period is Eurex, which combined Deutsche Börse's DTB derivatives arm with the Swiss Exchange's SOFFEX derivatives arm into a single corporate entity, utilizing a common trading system.

7.2 Automation and Cross-Subsidization of Trading

State-owned or protected public utilities frequently engage in cross-subsidization of products and services, pricing above marginal cost in one area to keep prices below it in others. Among the more conspicuous examples is uniform national postal service pricing, which represents a subsidy from urban to rural users. Such cross-subsidization is usually defended on the grounds of distributive concerns, although it clearly distorts market incentives and generates deadweight efficiency losses. We suggest that increased automation is now leading to the disappearance of cross-subsidization in the trading services industry. Our argument is based on a link between automation of trading and market contestability.

In markets that are contestable, cross-subsidization is inconsistent with sustainability of prices; it always invites profitable entry into the subsidizing portion of the business, thus ensuring that the cross-subsidies cannot persist (Baumol et al. 1988). The trading services industry is showing clear signs of increasing contestability. Sunk cost barriers to entry have declined rapidly over the past decade, owing in particular to the following factors:

• System development costs have plummeted as basic auction market technology has become commoditized and computer processing power has expanded dramatically.

• The significance of geographic location has declined tremendously in tandem with the steep decline in the cost of constructing wide-area cross-border computer networks.

• Automated systems can now be tailored quickly and inexpensively to accommodate trading in a growing number of securitized products, such as equities, bonds, currencies, financial derivatives, pooled mortgages, agricultural commodities, electricity, pollution emission permits, and hospital bed allocations. This facilitates rapid and low-cost entry into different sectors of an expanding market for securitized products.

Perfect contestability requires not only the absence of sunk cost barriers to entry and exit, but also that entrants face no disadvantage vis-à-vis incumbents and that they be capable of undercutting incumbents before the latter can react. The proliferation of open architecture trading services systems has greatly facilitated the integration of new trading systems with existing information and support systems, thus reducing entrant disadvantage, and there is considerable evidence of price undercutting by entrants (see section 7.1.1.2). If the trading services market does now sufficiently approximate a contestable one, then we would expect to see evidence of the erosion of cross-subsidies employed by incumbent national exchanges.

In fact, the expansion of automated trading structures does appear to be imposing increasing external discipline on the way in which exchanges can price different types of trading. The cross-subsidy regimes that have traditionally been imposed by exchanges fall into three general categories: cross-subsidization of large trades by small trades, "on-exchange" by "off-exchange" trades, and retail by institutional trades. As automation significantly reduces the cost to system operators of focusing their competitive strategies on well-defined types of trading and traders and of extending their competitive reach across wide geographic areas, it enables automated competitors to avoid an incumbent's subsidized market segment and to focus instead on the profitable subsidizing segment. We discuss examples of this effect below.

7.2.1   Cross-Subsidization of Large Trades by Small Trades

Dealer markets rely on cross-subsidy by design. One class of market participant—market makers—is assigned specific obligations that are not borne by the wider market. Such obligations include the requirement to post firm two-way quotes for a minimum number of shares for the stocks they are assigned. In some markets (for example, London's SEAQ-I), maximum posted spread limits are assigned. No trader would be willing to take on such obligations without compensatory privileges. The most significant of these privileges is restrictions on public limit-order display, which allows dealers to maintain exclusive access to order flow information and prevents disintermediation. Some markets further mandate delayed trade publication when the market maker is dealing as principal in large size, a large minimum tick size (which generates profits deriving directly from the spread), and fixed minimum commissions.

In the case of the LSE's dealer market, disintermediation was forestalled by an exchange rule barring market makers from posting better prices publicly than they were posting on SEAQ screens. This significantly hampered Instinet, a member firm operating an electronic order-matching system, in its efforts to disintermediate SEAQ by matching natural buyers and sellers within the posted market maker spreads. It was only after Tradepoint, regulated as an independent exchange, began automated auction market trading in 1995 that the LSE began seriously reconsidering the sustainability of the dealer market structure. The U.K. regulatory authorities held that LSE market makers trading on Tradepoint could not be bound by LSE rules restricting public limit-order displays, thereby subjecting SEAQ to the same competitive forces that had already undermined SEAQ-I.

Data from the LSE in the early 1990s document high market maker profits on small transactions, in which dealer intermediation was rarely necessary. These profits subsidized losses on midsize blocks,[14] for which institutional clients appeared to have strong knowledge of market order flow. The continental European automated auction systems, many of which were implemented in the period 1989–1991, had the effect of undermining this structure. Small transactions in continental shares rapidly migrated from SEAQ-I back to the home markets, wiping out a major source of market maker subsidy and exposing many of them to large losses at the hands of well-informed institutional clients. SEAQ-I's quoted spreads more than doubled between 1991 and 1994 as dealers abandoned formal market making in continental stocks (Pagano and Steil 1996).

Given the experience of SEAQ-I, we would suggest that Nasdaq's experience in the face of Instinet's rapid rise to a 20% market share is also explicable in the context of conventional industrial economics. In particular, the "excessively wide" quoted spreads identified by

---

14. Six to ten times Normal Market Size (NMS), NMS being equivalent to approximately 2.5% of average daily trading volume.

Christie and Schultz (1994) do not necessarily require an explanation based on widespread collusion, and frequent reports of Nasdaq market makers dropping stocks in the midst of a bull market are not puzzling, as is sometimes claimed.[15] Both effects represent logical responses to the erosion of cross-subsidies in the dealer market.

7.2.2   Cross-Subsidization of On-Exchange by Off-Exchange Trades

Many auction market operators impose "interaction" rules on members, obliging block traders transacting away from the central limit-order book to satisfy all orders on the book at equivalent or better prices. This is commonly presented as an issue of fairness regarding order book users; whatever the merits of this position, interaction rules represent a clear subsidy by off-exchange traders of on-exchange traders.[16]

Paris Bourse interaction rules, created in 1989 after members were permitted to trade for their own account, were significantly relaxed in 1994 owing to the effect of regulatory arbitrage in favor of London. Block traders in Paris routinely executed their block trades in London to avoid having to expend capital or leak information by obeying the Bourse's interaction rules. Even under the current Paris regime, which requires only that block trading take place within a weighted-average measure of the order book inside spread, block trades are still often executed in London via screens in Paris to avoid the market impact risk that a dealer might take on in trading within the Paris spread limits.[17]

7.2.3   Cross-Subsidization of Retail Trades by Institutional Trades

NYSE and Nasdaq rules intended to accommodate small retail-size trades on uneconomical terms are being exploited by proprietary

---

15. The *Wall Street Journal* ran a story focused on this phenomenon in 1996 (Lohse, 1996). One observer's reaction was quoted as follows: "What you are seeing is [that] even in a huge bull market, you still have market makers cutting back on stocks when logic tells you they should be increasing" (Robert Flaherty, editor of *Equities* magazine).
16. A counterargument that traders must price their off-exchange deals based on order book prices, and are therefore free riding on price discovery, is valid only when the price and quotation data provided by the exchange to data dissemination systems (such as Reuters and Bloomberg) are not themselves priced at competitively determined rates. Given that data dissemination represents approximately 17% of European exchange revenues (Baggiolini 1996), this argument would not appear to us to have merit.
17. See Pagano and Steil (1996) for details.

trading systems focusing entirely on executing institutional orders. For example, Nasdaq market makers are subject to the requirements of the Small Order Execution System (SOES), which allows small orders (up to 1000 shares) to be executed electronically against market maker quotes. Although the system was set up to ensure that retail investors could achieve timely executions, SOES is exploited by firms known widely as "SOES bandits," which fire rapid streams of 1000-share orders at market makers before they are able to adjust their quotes to news or trading activity. Nonexchange systems such as Instinet can focus their business on profitable institutional order flow, leaving unprofitable executions to the traditional exchange systems.

7.3 Automation and Exchange Governance

Exchanges have traditionally been organized as mutual associations, operated by member-firm brokers and dealers, under varying degrees of state control. The member firms often are the legal owners of the exchange and, in some cases, actually own shares in the exchange as a corporate entity.[18] In other cases, the exchange is legally a government entity.[19]

This mutual structure is a remnant of the era before automation, when exchanges were of necessity floor-based. The inherent limitations of floor space required access limitations. Access was rationed through the sale of a fixed number of memberships (or "seats"). Since a nonautomated trading floor itself has little more than commercial real estate value, it is logical that the members themselves should operate the floor as a cooperative. These members necessarily become intermediaries for all others wishing to trade the exchange's contracts, and a portion of their profits derives from barriers to entry.

In an automated auction market, there is no inherent technological barrier to providing unlimited direct access. There is therefore no longer an economic logic to exchanges being organized as intermediary cooperatives. An automated system operator can sell access direct to all who wish to trade and can charge for this service on a transaction basis. The marginal cost of adding an additional user

---

18. Transference of such shares is generally strictly limited. In the case of Deutsche Börse AG, for example, the sale of shares must be approved by the supervisory board.
19. This was the case with the Italian Consiglio Di Borsa, the predecessor of the privatized Borsa Italiana.

to a network is virtually zero, thus negating any economic value to membership as such. Therefore we would expect the operator to select its governance structure on the same basis as a normal commercial enterprise.

Whereas an automated exchange *can* be organized along traditional mutual lines, it is questionable whether such a structure is optimal in the type of competitive environment that we have heretofore described. The optimality issue is beyond the scope of this chapter, however. We offer a set of more limited observations here. First, as we have already described, trading market automation permits demutualization, defined as separating ownership of the exchange from membership. Second, the incentive problems inhibiting demutualization are similar to some of those inhibiting the adoption of technology, namely, vested financial interests. Third, demutualization is now rapidly being adopted in practice, and all such examples begin with a conversion from traditional floor trading technology to automated trade execution. Finally, for trading service enterprises with no prior history of mutual governance structure, the mutual structure is routinely avoided in favor of a for-profit joint-stock corporation structure. As automation initiatives continue to proliferate, a revealed preference argument may indeed suggest the optimality of a demutualized exchange structure relative to its mutual counterpart.

It is clear that the incentive structure under which a mutualized exchange operates is different from that under which a demutualized one does. As exchange members are the conduit to the trading system, they derive profits from intermediating nonmember transactions. This, in turn, means that members may resist innovations that reduce demand for their intermediation services, even if such innovations would increase the value of the exchange. If the members are actually owners of the exchange, they will logically exercise their powers to block disintermediation when the resulting decline in brokerage profits would not at least be offset by their share in the increase in exchange value.

A number of exchanges, particularly in Europe, have in the past several years chosen to demutualize, detaching ownership from membership. This transformation of governance structure has had the effect of diluting the influence of member firms over the commercial activities of the exchange. To the extent that the financial interests of nonmember owners differ materially from those of members, such a transformation could have a significant impact on the exchange's behavior.

Stockholm was the first exchange in the world to demutualize, doing so in 1993. The initiative came on the back of major competitive inroads into Swedish equity trading made by London's SEAQ-I between 1987 and 1990, a period in which Stockholm's turnover declined by a third and its market share of global reported Swedish equity turnover dropped as low as 40%.

Half of the shares in the new Stockholm corporate structure were retained by the members, and half were allocated to listed companies. The shares became freely tradable in 1994, and in 1998 they were listed on the exchange itself. Following the demutualization, the exchange became the first in Europe to offer remote cross-border membership (1995) and direct electronic access for institutional investors (1996), although trades must still be notionally executed via a sponsoring member. Local Swedish members resisted both of these initiatives but could not block them, given their minority interest.[20] Nonmember owners, in contrast, had an unambiguous incentive to support these measures. The exchange as a commercial enterprise appeared to have performed well following the demutualization. Turnover quadrupled in the first two years of demutualized operation, and the exchange's share price rose nearly sevenfold.[21]

The Stockholm model has since been widely emulated by other automated exchanges. Table 7.3 documents demutualizations. The biggest difference among them has been in the initial allocation of shares. Helsinki and Copenhagen, for example, applied a 60–40 share split between members and listed companies. Amsterdam allocated 50% to members and auctioned off 50% to both listed companies and institutional investors. Australia allocated all shares to the members but listed them on the exchange itself the day after the demutualization.

Member-based exchanges are demutualizing to approximate better the incentive structure of a public company with a diversified shareholder base. In contrast, trading system operators in the United States and United Kingdom, which have entered the market with

20. Anecdotal evidence from exchange officials suggests that smaller local members did, in fact, suffer financially from a diversion of foreign order flow to the new, larger remote intermediaries.

21. The exchange itself credits part of the increase in turnover to the removal of a 1% transaction tax at the end of 1991, according to Rydén (1995).

Table 7.3
Exchange Demutualizations

Exchange	Year
Completed Demutualizations	
Stockholm Stock Exchange	1993
Helsinki Stock Exchange	1995
Copenhagen Stock Exchange	1996
Amsterdam Exchanges	1997
Borsa Italiana	1997
Australian Stock Exchange	1998
Iceland Stock Exchange	1999
Athens Stock Exchange	1999
Stock Exchange of Singapore	1999
SIMEX	1999
Toronto Stock Exchange	2000
Chicago Mercantile Exchange	2000
New York Mercantile Exchange	2000
London Stock Exchange	2000
Agreements on, or Board Proposals for, Demutualizations and Public Offerings in 2001	
Chicago Board of Trade	
Chicago Board Options Exchange	
Deutsche Börse	
Hong Kong Stock Exchange	
International Petroleum Exchange	
London Metal Exchange	
Nasdaq	
New York Stock Exchange	
Oslo Stock Exchange	
Euronext	
PCX Equities	
Sydney Futures Exchange	

automated auction products, have avoided the mutual structure entirely. Such companies are widely referred to as proprietary trading system operators (or, more recently, electronic communications networks). Instinet (owned by Reuters), POSIT (owned by ITG), and Lattice Trading (owned by State Street) are formally regulated as brokers but sell order-matching services on a transaction fee basis direct to institutional investor-clients.

The Arizona Stock Exchange (AZX) and London-based Tradepoint are classified by their respective national regulatory authorities as exchanges but operate in an identical manner. OptiMark and Bond-Connect (owned by State Street) have chosen a third route: Legally, they are neither brokers nor exchanges. The companies license their trading products to existing bodies that are classified by their regulators as exchanges.

We argued in section 7.1 that exchanges operating in a competitive environment can usefully be analyzed as firms offering trading products in a market defined by the salience of network externalities. The degree to which this formulation approximates reality depends on the level of contestability in the market for trading services and the incentive structure under which exchanges operate. As we have argued in section 7.2 and here in section 7.3, trading automation has, in fact, significantly increased both market contestability and the incentives of exchanges to exploit network externalities. These incentives are manifested, inter alia, in the transformation of exchange governance structures toward conventional corporate models.

7.4 Market Quality Comparisons

Network models rely largely on two factors for their explanatory power: the quality or efficiency of the alternative trading technologies and relative cost. Early conceptual arguments over the introduction of computerized markets focus exclusively on the issue of "market quality" relative to the floor trading alternative.[22] We argue that debates over the adoption of trading technology and the consequent development of market structure need to move from considerations of market quality to issues of cost. We offer evidence supporting this position in this section.

In the absence of a precise definition of market quality, we focus on liquidity, informational efficiency, and volatility. Liquidity is a multidimensional factor, which we address through consideration of the size of the bid-offer spread and measures of market depth. We would concede that all aspects of what we call "market quality" can ultimately be characterized by the term "cost," which is borne by some party in the trading process. This is most clear in the case of bid-offer spreads. In other cases, the link is not so easy to quantify. Consider informational efficiency, for example. Greater speed of value revelation through the trading mechanism should lower the cost of trading in terms of the formulation and implementation of order submission strategies, but the linkage is complex and indirect.

---

22. The earliest mention seems to be in SEC (1963), in H.R. Doc. 95, 88 Cong., 1 sess., pt. 2, pp. 358, 678. The Commodity Futures Trading Commission organized a conference around the topic in 1977, summarized in CFTC (1977) and Melamed (1977).

Table 7.4
Implicit Trading Cost Studies for Automated Markets

Study	Automated Market	Traditional Market	Instrument
Coppejans and Domowitz (1997)	Globex	CME floor	Futures
Franke and Hess (1995)	DTB	LIFFE	Bund futures
Grunbichler et al. (1994)	DTB	FSE	DAX futures
Kofman and Moser (1997)	DTB	LIFFE	Bund futures
Pagano and Röell (1990)	Paris Bourse	SEAQ-I	Stocks
Pirrong (1996)	DTB	LIFFE	Bund futures
Sandmann and Vila (1996)	OSE	SIMEX	Nikkei futures
Schmidt and Iversen (1993)	IBIS II	SEAQ-I	Stocks
Shah and Thomas (1996)	BOLT/NSE	Bombay	Stocks
Vila and Sandmann (1996)	OSE	SIMEX	Nikkei futures

Our cost measures applied in section 7.5, however, are much more direct and disaggregated than are those encompassed in market quality measures.

General conclusions, to the extent that they may be obtained, require intraday data and multiple market comparisons. The data requirements are too large for any single research project. We therefore rely on a variety of existing studies for our information. The relevant literature is not extensive, and we cover most of it in this section. Because our treatment proceeds by topic, not by individual study, table 7.4 summarizes the contributions for reference.

Some of these papers provide more direct evidence than others, and the emphasis in individual studies differs. Studies of the Bund futures contract benefit from the overlap of trading times on the automated DTB market and the LIFFE floor, as well as the close similarity of contracts traded in the two venues.[23] Comparisons of the automated Osaka Securities Exchange and floor trading on the Singapore International Monetary Exchange (SIMEX) share these advantages, but there are differences across markets that are not related to automation. Interpretation of a study of Globex and the CME floor is complicated by natural deficiencies in liquidity that are endemic to an overnight market. Work on India is in the form of a time-series study of the introduction of automation, as opposed to a comparison of automated and floor auctions operating over the same

---

23. Shyy and Lee (1995) also consider the Bund market, but the overlap of emphasis between their work and that of others considered here is large enough not to merit separate consideration.

time period. Analysis of computerized DAX futures trading relies on a comparison of the futures contract with aggregate trading in the underlying index, reflecting different forms of trading activity as well as variations in market structure.[24] Finally, comparisons of automated auctions with dealer markets have contrasted the Paris CAC and German IBIS auction systems with the London SEAQ-I dealer market. The findings of these studies are favorable to computerized markets but rife with ambiguities. Beyond problems of data interpretation, dealer markets are quite different from auction markets generally, whether the latter be automated or floor-based. Although we include these studies for completeness, we do not discuss details of the comparisons.[25]

7.4.1   Bid-Offer Spreads

The size of the bid-offer spread is the most commonly quantified measure of liquidity across markets. All studies, with the exception of those comparing auction and dealer markets, rely on the computation of realized, as opposed to quoted, spreads. The realized spread is an imputed measure of the difference between the best buy and sell prices in the market, inferred directly from the transaction prices themselves.

Studies of trading on DTB and LIFFE agree that spreads are smaller, or at least no larger, in the automated market than in the floor market. Pirrong (1996), for example, reports that spreads are 5% lower on DTB than on LIFFE. Results in Kofman and Moser (1997) vary, depending on the method of calculation, but they cannot reject the statistical equality of the spread across trading venues. Coppejans and Domowitz (1997) present similar findings for stock index futures trading.

Vila and Sandmann (1996) report substantially larger spreads in the Osaka market relative to floor trading on SIMEX.[26] The tick size in Osaka is twice that on SIMEX, however, biasing the comparisons. Orders also tend to be much larger in this automated market, naturally raising spreads in Osaka relative to SIMEX.

---

24. A similar contribution is made by Kempf and Korn (1996).
25. See Pagano and Steil (1996) for an overview of results and a detailed critique.
26. Coppejans and Domowitz (1997) also find larger spreads on Globex for currency futures, but this is explained by higher adverse selection costs due to operation of the overnight interbank currency market.

7.4.2 Depth of Market

Assessment of relative market depth is plagued by measurement problems. Depth cannot be measured solely by trading volume. Changes in volume can occur independently of market structure considerations.[27] Some studies simply use a measure of volatility, which conflates the information effects, depth, volume, and spread size. However, a variety of different market microstructure models relate the variance of price changes to a function of traded volume.[28] The coefficient quantifying the impact of volume on the variance of returns is an inverse measure of liquidity or market depth. As this parameter decreases, the sensitivity of price changes to volume falls, and the market is seen to be deeper or more liquid.

Some variant of this model is represented by regression formulations in studies of Bund and Nikkei 225 futures trading. The implied volume coefficient in the comparison of Osaka and SIMEX is lower in the automated market, based on Vila and Sandmann (1996), implying greater depth in Osaka. Pirrong (1996) splits volume into expected and unexpected components. He finds that the coefficient on unexpected volume is approximately zero for DTB while significantly positive for LIFFE. Similar results are obtained for expected volume. This implies a deeper market in the automated venue.[29]

7.4.3 Informational Efficiency

Relative informational efficiency across computerized and traditional trading venues has been a topic of debate since the work of Melamed (1977). It represents a facet of market quality in at least two ways. The first dimension pertains to asymmetric information considerations, captured in the adverse selection component of the bid-offer spread. The second pertains to the transmission of information into prices: Slower value revelation raises the cost of trading in terms of ex ante order submission strategies.

---

27. For example, Shah and Thomas (1996) report large increases in volume following automation of the Bombay market, but this effect can be ascribed to large numbers of new listings that had little, if anything, to do with the switchover.

28. See, for example, the trading models in Kyle (1985), Blume et al. (1994), Coppejans and Domowitz (1996), and Domowitz et al. (1997).

29. Only Franke and Hess (1995) suggest greater depth in the floor market. Their result is questionable, however. They use the volatility of prices, as opposed to the volatility of price changes, in their regressions, biasing statistical inference for technical reasons.

7.4.3.1 Adverse Selection

Asymmetric information effects may be exacerbated in automated markets relative to their floor counterparts. The perceived problems are the openness of automated limit-order books and the time required to cancel orders. One possibility is reluctance to submit limit orders in the face of potential adverse selection, inhibiting liquidity provision. For uninformed traders, the problem is one of the free option that a firm quote presents to the market, permitting trades that disadvantage the liquidity provider. For informed traders, the issue is information that might be revealed by submitting large orders to the book.

Indirect evidence contrary to this view is provided by Vila and Sandmann (1996), who show that the Osaka computerized system handles larger orders than are processed on SIMEX. The average number of contracts per trade is about fifty-two on the automated market, compared to fourteen on the floor. The comparison is even stronger in monetary terms, because SIMEX contracts are valued at 500 times the futures price, while the Osaka contract is worth 1000 times the price. Adverse selection problems that may be due to automated system design do not necessarily inhibit large orders and trades, as compared with a floor auction market.

Direct evidence on adverse selection as a cost of trading is given by Coppejans and Domowitz (1997). The adverse selection component of the bid-offer spread is estimated to be 17% higher on the CME floor than in the Globex trading system for stock index futures contracts. Since the index spreads are approximately equal across the two trading venues, adverse selection effects in absolute, as well as proportional, terms also are lower on the automated system.

Comparisons across markets are narrow and few in this regard. The free option problem is undoubtedly an issue in automated settings and deserves further examination.[30] For example, in reference to the study on the CME and Globex, the possibilities for adverse selection may be lower in the overnight market for the stock index than in day trading on the floor. In contrast, the Globex market for foreign currency futures operates in the shadow of the overnight interbank currency market. Trading in the latter exacerbates the

---

30. In fact, new technological developments in automated market design are oriented largely toward large-order processing and increased possibilities for liquidity provision.

potential for adverse selection on Globex. Indeed, in the case of currency futures, Globex adverse selection components exceed their floor counterparts by an average of 26% across currencies.[31]

7.4.3.2 Transmission of Information to Prices

The speed at which information is transmitted to prices is generally analyzed by calculating correlations between current and past returns. Shah and Thomas (1996), for example, compute such correlations over various time spans before and after the introduction of automated execution in Bombay.[32] The correlation between current and lagged returns drops sharply following automation, suggesting greater informational efficiency in an automated environment.

Vector autoregressive (VAR) models are used for much the same purpose by Kofman and Moser (1997) and by Sandmann and Vila (1996). The VARs allow an assessment of information transmission within a single market and between markets. In both studies, price adjustment within a single market and adjustment to shocks in the alternative market are found to be faster in the traditional trading venue, but differences are small. The flow of information through pricing is bidirectional. Both papers conclude that there is no obvious price leadership differentiated by market structure.

In contrast, Grunbichler et al. (1994) find that the automated market absorbs information much more quickly than the floor does. Coppejans and Domowitz (1997) attempt to control for the effects of asymmetric information, inventory control, and speculative demands based on order flow. They find no substantive difference in informational efficiency between automated and traditional market structures.

7.4.4 *Volatility*

Price volatility has conceptual links to information flow and liquidity. However, there is no theoretical reason to expect higher or

---

31. Kofman and Moser (1997) also find adverse selection effects to be stronger on DTB than on LIFFE. Their evidence is indirect, however. They find that serial correlation in expected returns is higher in the automated system and infer that informational asymmetry is greater in the automated market. Coppejans and Domowitz (1997) find no such correlation on either Globex or the Chicago Mercantile Exchange and therefore cannot support such inference.

32. This includes the introduction of the BOLT system on the Bombay Stock Exchange itself and the introduction of the fully automated National Stock Exchange.

lower volatility in automated markets, relative to their traditional counterparts.[33]

The available evidence suggests that volatility in an automated market is generally equal to, and sometimes less than, volatility in the traditional market (Shah and Thomas 1996).[34] Shah and Thomas present such results, based on daily returns. Kofman and Moser (1997) find that return volatility on a minute-by-minute basis is higher on LIFFE than on DTB. Corresponding calculations for those markets on a daily basis show no difference across venues; Vila and Sandmann (1996) obtain the same result. Only Coppejans and Domowitz (1997) contradict such findings, but their results are attributable to sharply lower liquidity in the overnight market in dimensions other than price variability.

Volatility comparisons with respect to dynamics involve severe interpretation problems in assessing cross-market characteristics.[35] We mention only two results, relating to cross-market information linkages and market share considerations.

First, Kofman and Moser (1997) model cross-market transmission of volatility. Volatility is transmitted bidirectionally across market structures. In two of five weeks, it appears that LIFFE responded much more sluggishly to volatility shocks originating from DTB. The evidence is too weak to suggest more efficient information handling in the automated market, but equality across markets may be a reasonable conclusion.

Second, several authors model the choice between automated and floor markets as a function of volatility. Given the theoretical correlation of information arrival and volatility, most possible explanations suggest the choice of floor venue. For example, higher volatility increases the value of the free option stemming from the provision of liquidity to the limit-order book. This might encourage traders to

---

33. The only work on this point seems to be the simulation study of Bollerslev and Domowitz (1991). They predict lower volatility in an automated market, compared to the floor, based on the smoothing of transaction flow through the electronic book.

34. Unconditional volatility dropped 2.2 percentage points after the introduction of automated trading in Bombay. Spread-corrected volatility measures showed no difference following automation. See also Kofman and Moser (1997), Franke and Hess (1995), Vila and Sandmann (1996), Coppejans and Domowitz (1997).

35. For example, it is tempting to ascribe high serial correlation in volatility to poor information transmission. However, a larger serial correlation coefficient in an automated market relative to its floor counterpart may simply be an artifact of the mechanics of limit-order books, having nothing to do with information effects (see Bollerslev and Domowitz 1991).

shift to the floor. Similarly, higher information intensity reduces the relative importance of order book information, given higher intensity of floor trading. Periods of higher information intensity and concomitant volatility also increase the likelihood of adverse selection, and adverse selection effects may be higher on automated systems.

Despite the logic of such arguments, the evidence is mixed. Studies by Franke and Hess (1995) and by Vila and Sandmann (1996) estimate identical models relating automated market share to lagged share and current and lagged values of price volatility. Higher volatility is found to decrease DTB market share. In the comparison of Osaka and SIMEX, higher volatility generates a move to the automated market (Franke and Hess 1995).[36]

7.4.5   What Have We Learned about Relative Market Quality?

Distinctions between various dimensions of market quality are not as sharp as our taxonomy might suggest. Whereas trade-offs may exist between some markets, our reading of the evidence is that market quality is roughly equal across automated and floor technologies.

Bid-offer spreads are approximately the same across automated and traditional trading venues. Considerations of market design tell us little about the anticipated size of relative spreads. The openness of automated limit-order books does, however, suggest higher costs in terms of the adverse selection component of the spread. Available evidence supports such intuition in environments characterized by a high probability of adverse selection effects. Theoretically, the spread is composed of the sum of adverse selection costs, inventory costs, and order-processing costs. Given that the inventory component is found to be very small in all studies that attempt to break it out separately, the results suggest that order-processing costs are generally lower in automated markets. These conclusions must be tempered by considerations of the relative size of processed orders and explicit costs that may or may not enter the spread calculations. It is

---

36. Vila and Sandmann (1996) offer the following resolution: In a larger market, uninformed traders may be less concerned with adverse selection risk and therefore do not reduce trading activity in periods of high volatility. They simply shift to the larger market. LIFFE and Osaka had market shares of approximately 65% and 60%, respectively, relative to the floor at the time of the studies. There is an obvious endogeneity problem with such reasoning, however, because the market's average size may be related to its structure.

not generally true that automated systems handle only small orders, however, as exemplified by the comparison of Osaka and SIMEX. Larger spreads are a feature of markets, automated or not, that process larger orders on average.

It is often argued that automated markets do not foster good market depth, owing to the high visibility of order book information and order cancellation delays. Neither average trading volume nor average volatility in isolation provides a good measure of depth, obviating some evidence on this point. On the basis of parametric estimates, using data on volatility and volume combined, market depth is generally found to be greater in the automated market.

Average volatility is at least as low in computerized markets as in floor-based markets. It is not clear exactly what dimension of market quality is being measured, however. This confusion may explain the mixed results on volatility dynamics and the effect of volatility on market share. There are also conflicting interpretations of volatility persistence, in terms of information and market design.

Mild differences in informational efficiency across trading technologies are observed, but these differences disappear once such models are augmented by additional trading information. There is no evidence supporting price information leadership across market structures with regard to either prices or volatility characteristics. Traders do not necessarily migrate to floors in the presence of high volatility, despite anecdotal arguments to the contrary.

One explanation of the equality of market quality across trading structures lies in a peculiar form of what statisticians call selection bias. The term is commonly reserved for situations in which the sampling information is not random in some dimension. This lack of randomness is exemplified here, since all cross-market comparisons depend on the survival and stability of two markets trading the same securities, usually with heavy overlap in terms of time zone. One might therefore reasonably conclude that both floor and automated auctions serve traders well, even if they do so along different dimensions. The quality of market may differ between competing structures in some aspect, which is offset in another.

This rough equality across auction mechanisms does not, however, imply that dual market structures will continue to exist over the long run. The consumers of trading system services also face a combination of implicit and explicit costs, and we now turn to some new evidence on this point.

7.5   Transaction Costs, Intermediation, and Market Structure

An important implication of automation is the potential for institutional investors to obtain direct market access.[37] Access to traditional trading floors requires the use of brokers with exchange membership. Intermediation in dealership markets is built into trading protocols by design. In contrast, an institutional trader can place orders directly in automated venues such as Instinet, POSIT, and the Arizona Stock Exchange.[38]

Why might this distinction matter in practice? The first answer concerns the choice of trading venue. In an intermediated setting, the broker determines where execution will take place. If the broker is representing the best interests of the trader, choice of trading location would be rationally based on price and quality of execution. This hypothesis appears to be refuted in practice. For example, most trades in NYSE issues that are executed off the NYSE floor happen when the execution venue is posting inferior quotes. This indicates that location is often determined for reasons other than best pricing (Blume and Goldstein 1997).[39]

Discussions with institutional investors suggest a second response, pertaining to information. Once an order is placed with a broker, information about the trade is no longer private, and information leakage can occur. If so, some information is reflected in quotes before trade execution, adversely influencing execution costs on the part of the original investor. Keim and Madhavan (1996) argue that such leakage is greater for trades in small capitalization stocks, large block transactions, and high-volatility environments.

A simple alternative explanation is that human intermediation services are often unnecessary. The investor is nevertheless obliged

37. Although this may eventually also be true for retail customers, capital requirements typically exclude direct access for noninstitutional traders.
38. Technically, an institutional trader cannot place an order directly on the Arizona Stock Exchange. Because the company is legally regulated as an exchange, the SEC requires intermediation by a registered broker. However, the broker merely places the order and receives only a small payment for the service.
39. U.S. law mandates that brokers provide "best execution," described by the SEC (1996) as to "seek the most favorable terms reasonably available under the circumstances for a customer's transaction." Macey and O'Hara (1996), however, note the absence of specific definitions of best execution or of an explicit best execution rule. A variety of studies also show that trades are often executed at prices superior to the posted quotes, suggesting the possibility that trades executed at the inside quote might have received better execution at an alternative venue (see Petersen and Fialkowski 1994, Bessembinder and Kaufman 1996, Blume and Goldstein 1997).

to pay for such services when trading through a traditional broker. Automated trading enables institutions to avoid paying for intermediation services they do not require. On simpler trades, the trading expertise of the broker may not be sufficient to compensate for the lower commissions that automated services invariably levy.

Common to each explanation is the importance of transaction cost, whether explicit or implicit. We have already stressed the contribution of cost considerations to theoretical predictions concerning market structure. We now examine explicit and implicit costs, concentrating on commissions and fees, realized bid-offer spreads, and price impact.

Except for the spread analyses in the previous section, work on transaction costs across trading venues has concentrated on comparisons among the NYSE, Nasdaq, and the regional exchanges in the United States.[40] Such studies do not compare costs across intermediated versus nonintermediated venues or traditional versus electronic trading arenas.[41]

We compare transaction costs for trades executed through traditional brokers with those incurred through nonintermediated trading in automated markets. Explicit costs in terms of commissions, as well as implicit costs embodied in the prices at which trades are completed, are considered.

There are two possible levels of interpretation for the results that follow. Cost comparisons are most directly interpretable in terms of intermediated versus nonintermediated trading. No ambiguity is associated with this particular exercise. The vast majority of trades handled through brokers are executed through the Nasdaq market and on the NYSE or regional floors. To the extent that broker order flow, representing institutional orders in particular, is not directed to automated venues, the comparisons may be interpreted as being between automated and traditional trading markets.

7.5.1   The Data

The data consist of information reflecting the trading activity of a U.S. mutual fund managing, at the time of this study, approximately

---

40. Keim and Madhavan (1998) provide a survey of the literature on transaction costs, with a brief review of individual contributions.
41. Bessembinder and Kaufman (1997) discuss the Cincinnati Stock Exchange, however.

$44 billion in equity assets. We refer to this institution hereafter simply as "the fund." The data are averages of cost components and related variables for trades over six-month periods between 1992 and 1996, as reported by their trading cost consultant, SEI. The data are available for thirty-five traditional brokers and four electronic brokers. The latter include Instinet's continuous order-matching system, the Instinet Crossing Network, POSIT, and the Arizona Stock Exchange call auction. Thus we have one continuous auction system, two periodic crossing systems, and one call auction in our sample of electronic brokers.[42]

We have identified as electronic brokers only those that specialize in electronic order execution. Those that use electronic systems exclusively to route orders to exchanges are classified as traditional brokers. The distinction is somewhat arbitrary for listed stocks. For example, Instinet is often used for order-routing on NYSE issues (through the DOT system), making it similar in function to some other brokers, which we have classified as traditional. Our categories distinguish, as accurately as the data allow, between brokers that intermediate trades and those that allow buyers and sellers to inter-act directly, without human intermediation.

For each broker and time period, trades are broken down into those in OTC issues (i.e., Nasdaq) and those in exchange-listed issues. Trade direction is identified. When we refer to buy trades, for example, we mean that the fund initiated the trade as a buyer. The number of trades of each type that enters the six-month averages is known. Information is available on shares per trade, market capital-ization of the stock traded, market beta of the stock, daily volatility of stock returns, and average stock price. Data on transaction costs are included in the form of explicit costs (fees) and implicit costs for each broker and time period. We return to the construction of implicit costs below.

Like some other proprietary databases, the data come from only a single trading entity. There is potential selection bias in the choice of brokers by time period or market conditions, which cannot be effec-tively corrected with the limited number of observations and vari-

---

42. It has been suggested, especially for the early period of our sample, that the Arizona Stock Exchange is effectively a crossing network, as orders entered into the system are almost invariably priced passively; that is, orders are typically placed at the NYSE closing price for the stock.

ables available. Similarly, variation in investment style cannot be used as an input to transaction cost benchmarks.[43] The analysis also is conditional on trade execution; that is, we exploit no information regarding delays in execution or whether an order was executed in the particular venue to which it was originally sent.

There are characteristics of these single-institution data that make them very appropriate for our analysis, however. First, the fund has no "soft commission" arrangements with brokers, as a matter of company policy. In effect, funds that pay soft commissions are paying for services that are not related to execution via trade execution fees, complicating the task of measuring the true costs of trade execution. The fund data are relatively immune to this distortion.[44] Second, the fund is an exceptionally large-scale user of nonintermediated electronic trading services. The fund accounts for approximately half the total trading volume going through such systems on the full SEI database, which comprises data from thirty-three institutional clients. It is one of the few funds in the world for which there are sufficient data to allow valid comparisons of trading cost between traditional and electronic trading mechanisms.

Finally, most cross-exchange comparisons are made using trade-by-trade data, while our information is restricted to activities across days. The conceptual cost experiment in the former case is one of immediate turnaround on the next trade.[45] In contrast, the data here compare costs embodied in prices against what would happen if turnaround occurred in one or two days, depending on the measure. Regardless of the reader's preferences with regard to this trade-off, our approach is the only one feasible. Available trade-by-trade information does not allow discrimination between automated and

---

43. As in Keim and Madhavan (1997), for example.

44. Soft commissions represent payments made directly from client funds to brokers for research and other services, which are effectively embedded in the fees that the fund pays for each trade. Generally, funds that pay soft commissions commit in advance to paying a minimum annual level of commissions to the broker in return for services. The fund does not commit to minimum volume levels with any broker to obtain research, information, or trading system services. This does not eliminate the possibility that the company is implicitly securing such services by de facto maintaining large volumes with a given broker, but it does mitigate the distortionary effects of explicit soft commissions.

45. More formally, the cost might include the difference between the actual posttrade value and the value if the investor had been instantaneously able to transact the desired quantity at a net price equal to the fair value of the asset.

traditional trading venues or between intermediated and noninter-mediated trades.[46]

7.5.2 The Definition of Transaction Costs

The appropriate construction of implicit cost measures is often debated. However, we have access only to the information provided to the fund by SEI and not to the underlying database. We must use the implicit cost measures provided by the consultant rather than developing our own. Nevertheless, the available measures corre-spond to commonly used definitions.

Let V_{it} denote the true economic value of security i at time t, for which some observable proxy must be used in applications. We define

effective half-spread $= 100D_{it}(P_{it} - V_{it})/V_{it}$

and

realized half-spread $= 100D_{it}(P_{it} - V_{it+n})/V_{it}$

where P is the transaction price of the security, n is a time increment, and D is a binary variable taking on the value of 1 for buy orders and -1 for sell orders.[47] The effective half-spread is a measure of the proximity of the trade price to the underlying value. This provides an estimate of the percentage execution cost paid by the trader. It has the advantage of reflecting savings due to trading inside the quoted spread. The realized half-spread is the difference between the effec-tive spread and decreases in asset value following sells and increases in asset value following buys. The latter measure, sometimes called price impact, reflects the market's assessment of private information conveyed by the trade (Bessember and Kaufman 1997). The realized spread may also be interpreted as a measure of the reversal from the trade price to posttrade economic value.

The cost measure supplied by the fund represents an interpretable combination of these concepts as well as proxies for the underlying

---

46. For example, in the TAQ database available from the NYSE, trades executed on Instinet are reported as NASD trades and cannot be identified separately. Trade-by-trade data also force the researcher to infer trade direction, introducing estimation error, while trade direction is unambiguously identified here.

47. Following Huang and Stoll (1996b), Bessembinder and Kaufman (1997).

true value of the security. Specifically, setting $n = 1$ day in the definitions above, we define

$$\text{execution cost} = D^*[(\text{effective half-spread}) (\text{realized half-spread}) - \text{index return}]$$

where the index return is calculated for the day after the trade, based on a specific industry index appropriate for the particular security under consideration. Effective and realized half-spreads typically are analyzed separately. This permits, for example, the price impact effects to be isolated directly through the difference between the two measures. In our case, for small movements in index returns within days, the cost measure is approximately the square of the geometric average of effective and realized spreads.

SEI uses the trading day closing price as a proxy for V_{it} and the next day closing price as a proxy for V_{it+n}. The product of the two half-spreads is then modified by a measure of the index performance of the relevant industry group with which the stock is associated from trade day until close of the next day. On the buy side, a positive value of the term within the brackets represents favorable execution cost, while the opposite is true on the sell side. For example, suppose this cost is computed for a buy trade as ninety-nine basis points. The impact is favorable: It may be a result of the stock price moving up on trade day and down by more the next, yet not by as much as the composite of stocks in the same industry group. In other words, the stock price performed well after the trade relative to the industry group performance, even though the investor actually lost money on the transaction. Thus D^* now takes on the value of -1 for buy orders and 1 for sell orders. The example above represents a savings of ninety-nine basis points. Finally, we define *total trading cost* to be the sum of execution cost and fees for the trade.

7.5.3   Average Trading Costs

Table 7.5 reports cost as a percentage of value traded. Data means are disaggregated into trading categories, differentiating between OTC and exchange-listed shares and between buy and sell activity. The percentage of dollar volume for all market categories and for individual electronic markets is also provided.

On the basis of unconditional average total trading costs, the automated systems outperform the traditional brokers across the board.

Table 7.5
Average Total Trading Costs

	Total Trading Cost	Fees	Percentage of Dollar Volume
OTC Buy Trades			
All brokers	0.22	0.04	100.00
Traditional	0.38	0.00	38.50
All electronic	0.12	0.06	61.50
Crossing/call	0.15	0.05	6.08
Instinet	−0.23	0.03	1.98
POSIT	0.25	0.06	3.52
AZX	0.83	0.04	0.58
Instinet continuous	0.11	0.07	55.40
OTC Sell Trades			
All brokers	1.37	0.05	100.00
Traditional	1.60	0.00	30.90
All electronic	1.27	0.07	69.10
Crossing/call	0.73	0.06	7.68
Instinet	0.61	0.04	2.47
POSIT	0.83	0.07	4.45
AZX	0.52	0.04	0.76
Instinet continuous	1.33	0.08	61.50
Listed Buy Trades			
All brokers	0.33	0.12	100.00
Traditional	0.37	0.13	88.60
All electronic	0.07	0.05	11.40
Crossing/call	0.09	0.04	7.38
Instinet	0.21	0.03	2.55
POSIT	−0.04	0.05	3.93
AZX	0.25	0.03	0.90
Instinet continuous	0.05	0.07	3.99
Listed Sell Trades			
All brokers	0.47	0.16	100.00
Traditional	0.48	0.17	88.30
All electronic	0.45	0.06	11.70
Crossing/call	0.33	0.04	6.63
Instinet	0.20	0.04	2.50
POSIT	0.42	0.05	2.86
AZX	0.39	0.03	1.27
Instinet continuous	0.61	0.08	5.10

For listed buys, traditional brokers generate costs 429% higher than electronic venues, while for OTC buys, the gap is 217%. For listed sells, traditional broker costs are only 6.7% higher than costs in the electronic markets, while for OTC sells the difference is 26%.

One might reasonably expect cost savings to be larger when disintermediation potential is larger, as it is in the OTC market. The evidence is consistent on the sell side but not for buy trades here. This intuition is better supported once trading characteristics are taken into account below. The volume data also reflect differences in potential cost savings. Dollar volume directed to electronic markets for OTC trades is about five times that of electronic brokerage in listed issues. Most of this variation is for trades using Instinet's continuous market. Relative dollar volumes on the periodic markets differ little and unsystematically between listed and OTC stocks.

Keim and Madhavan (1998) suggest that crossing systems offer substantially lower fees than commissions charged by traditional brokers; they mention a figure of $0.01 to $0.02 a share. We also observe large differences between traditional brokers and periodic automated systems in terms of fees calculated in percentage terms. Fees for Instinet continuous trading, even in OTC issues, are also substantially lower than those charged by traditional brokers for listed trades. Traditional brokers charge about twice as much as the continuous automated auction.

These preliminary results could be due to the special nature of our single-institution data. The range of the results is generally in accordance with that of other studies, however. Keim and Madhavan (1998) report average commissions of approximately 0.20% over the 1991–1993 period, which is close to that calculated by Stoll (1995) for 1992. Our data represent trading over more recent periods, and commissions have been falling. For listed stocks traded through traditional brokers, commissions are in the range of 0.13–0.17%.

The ratio of traditional broker commissions to crossing fees should be on the order of 3.73 based on other studies.[48] For listed stocks, we find the ratio to be 3.75 on average. It is more difficult to compare our numbers for execution cost to the half-spreads in the literature, given the different methods of computation. However, our geometric average of half-spreads for traditional broker trading activity is very

---

48. This rough calculation is based on Edwards and Wagner (1993), who find average commissions in dollar terms to be about $0.056. Compare this number with $0.015 per trade on a crossing network, as Keim and Madhavan (1998) suggest.

close to the effective spreads reported by Bessembinder and Kaufman (1997), for example.

The data also exhibit striking absolute and relative variation in performance across buys and sells. On average, trading cost is much higher for sells than for buys, and the difference is particularly marked for OTC stocks. Similar results are noted in other studies (Keim and Madhavan 1998). The finding is apparently unrelated to automation effects, and we simply continue to condition our subsequent analysis on buy and sell initiations separately.

7.5.4 A Benchmark Correction for Trade Difficulty

Execution costs differ with respect to the relative difficulty of making the trade. Trade characteristics matter in assessing costs, making unconditional comparisons less than fully informative. In this section, we construct a benchmark against which other costs may be measured. Although our variables and technique differ somewhat, the exercise follows the regression approach suggested by Keim and Madhavan (1997). The goal is to judge whether trading costs vary systematically between traditional brokers and electronic markets, controlling jointly for variation in a set of economic characteristics. The general approach is analogous to risk-adjusted return measures in the performance evaluation field. We estimate a panel data model of the form

$$C_{it} = \alpha_i + \beta' x_{it} + \varepsilon_{it}$$

in which the i's index variation over traditional brokers and electronic markets and t denotes time. We take C_{it} to be execution cost and use the full sample to estimate the slope coefficients.[49] The vector of trade characteristics, x_{it}, includes shares per trade (sh/tr), market capitalization of the stock ($mktcap$), the market beta of the stock, annualized daily standard deviation of returns for the traded issue (vol), and the inverse of the share price (p). This list is similar to that used by Bessembinder and Kaufman (1997) and others in the calculation of economic characteristics of trading costs. Execution

---

49. Qualitative results using total cost measures are very similar and are not reported. One could also use different regressions for different categories of trades, for example, for OTC versus exchange listed issues or for buys versus sells. Sample size and selection considerations make such estimates unstable, however.

costs may diminish with firm size, owing to relatively better liquidity and reduced informational asymmetries. Larger trades should be more difficult, and hence more costly, possibly owing to larger inventory costs in intermediated settings or because of information content. Costs rise with volatility, especially in intermediated venues, given some degree of risk aversion. Trading costs are related to price levels, and the use of the inverse follows Harris (1994).

There are some specific estimation issues to be addressed. The α_i represent individual broker effects. They are treated as fixed, as opposed to random, given potential correlation of the effects with other variables in the model. Our data are unbalanced; that is, we have different numbers of time-series observations for each broker and electronic market. The fixed-effects estimator for unbalanced panels discussed in Domowitz et al. (1997) is used, with one modification (Domowitz, Glen, and Madhavan 1998). The estimator is adapted to generalized least squares, given that all data are averages. The number of trades for each broker and for each time period is used in the weighting scheme, an otherwise standard correction for averaged data.

Estimation is based on a cross section of thirty-nine traditional brokers and electronic markets and an average of seventeen time periods per broker. The cost measure is calculated from the regression estimates as

$$\tilde{C}_{it} = 0.003(sh/tr)_{it} - 0.013(mktcap)_{it} + 0.001(beta)_{it} \\ + 0.009(vol)_{it} + 0.061(p)_{it}$$

We will refer to $\tilde{C}_{it}$ as benchmark cost.[50] Unlike Bessembinder and Kaufman (1997), we do not use estimated fixed effects as a measure of cost differences after adjusting for economic heterogeneity in trades.[51] Instead, we compare the benchmark to actual execution cost. Realized cost embodies any broker-specific attributes that may increase or decrease cost relative to the cost predicted by trade characteristics alone.

---

50. Since we are not interested in inference with respect to coefficient estimates, standard errors are omitted. They are generally small, with the exception of the coefficient on inverse price, and the regression R^2 is 0.09.

51. The conditioning set is incorrect for this interpretation, given our econometric method. Bessembinder and Kaufman (1997) transform their variables somewhat differently.

Table 7.6
Realized and Benchmark Median Execution Costs

	All Brokers	Traditional	Electronic
Overall Market Activity			
Execution cost	0.310	0.325	0.270
Benchmark cost	0.349	0.355	0.278
OTC versus Listed			
Execution cost			
OTC	0.520	0.660	0.350
Listed	0.220	0.220	0.195
Benchmark cost			
OTC	0.502	0.528	0.409
Listed	0.241	0.270	0.099
Buy versus Sell			
Execution cost			
Buy	0.175	0.220	0.105
Sell	0.520	0.480	0.555
Benchmark cost			
Buy	0.331	0.335	0.264
Sell	0.363	0.370	0.323

7.5.5   Execution Costs Relative to Benchmark Costs

Median execution costs (i.e., excluding commissions) and benchmark costs for overall market activity are reported at the top of table 7.6. The electronic systems are handling easier trades at lower cost. Execution cost is 20% higher for traditional brokers than for their electronic counterparts. On the other hand, benchmark costs in the electronic venue are about 22% less than those predicted for traditional brokers, indicating less difficult trades.

Next, we differentiate between OTC and listed trades. For OTC stocks, differences in trade difficulty, as measured by the benchmark, are small, but the transactions are done much more cheaply electronically. Execution cost for traditional brokers in OTC transactions is 89% higher than for electronic systems, while the benchmark cost difference is only 29%.

For listed stocks, the situation is reversed: Trades done electronically look extremely easy according to the benchmark, but trading costs are only slightly lower than those incurred by traditional brokers. Realized costs are only 13% higher for traditional brokers, while the benchmark is 173% higher relative to electronic venues.

Table 7.7
Median Ratio of Realized to Benchmark Execution Cost

	Traditional	Electronic
OTC	1.343	0.895
Listed	0.913	2.066
Buy	0.654	0.171
Sell	1.548	2.158
OTC buys	0.531	0.043
Listed buys	0.807	1.085
OTC sells	2.558	1.864
Listed sells	1.086	3.027

Benchmark costs are higher for sell trades than for buys. This observation provides one explanation for the cost asymmetry between buy and sell transactions. Sells appear to be done under more difficult conditions, on average.[52] On the other hand, percentage differences between the realized costs of buy and sell transactions, when type of broker is held constant, exceed those observed for the benchmark costs. Thus market conditions alone cannot explain the disparity between costs on the two sides of the market, regardless of the type of broker.

In table 7.7, we report the median ratio of execution costs to the benchmark by type of trade. We interpret this measure as cost relative to the difficulty of the trade. A ratio greater than 1 indicates costs in excess of those expected based on trade characteristics. Conversely, ratios less than 1 suggest that the trades are done more cheaply than would have been suggested by their relative difficulty.

For OTC stocks, the electronic systems are handling easier trades, but much more cheaply than traditional brokers, relative to trade difficulty. The traditional brokers' ratio is 50% higher than that observed for electronic systems. A breakdown of OTC trades into buy and sell transactions reveals superior performance of electronic systems in both cases, but much of the relative advantage is on the buy side.

For listed issues, however, it appears that traditional brokers outperform electronic systems. Traditional brokers exhibit a cost ratio close to 1, while the figure for electronic systems is just over 2. Rela-

---

52. This is consistent with Keim and Madhavan (1998), who attribute larger costs to larger sizes on the sell side.

tively lower cost compared to the benchmark characterizes traditional brokers' operations, regardless of whether the transaction is on
the buy or the sell side.

The contrast between the results for trades in OTC and listed
shares might not be surprising. The potential for cost savings
through disintermediation via the electronic systems is greater for
OTC trades than for trades in listed shares that already take place
in an auction environment. The complete reversal of results based on
the ratio of execution costs to the benchmark for listed trades is more
surprising, given the remainder of the evidence. We investigate this
point further in the context of individual trade characteristics.

7.5.6   Trade Characteristics and Total Trading Costs

As we have discussed, trades executed through traditional brokers
appear in the aggregate to be more costly than trades done electronically. Transactions on electronic systems are easier trades with
lower expected cost. Differences in trade difficulty account for some,
but not all, of the electronic markets' cost advantage, however.

Excluding commission costs from our analysis, the superior performance of electronic markets is evident only for OTC stocks. For
OTC trades, traditional brokers incur costs that are 34% higher than
expected, given market conditions, while trade costs on electronic
systems are more than 10% lower than would be predicted. Benchmark costs for OTC trades are more than double those for listed
issues, suggesting that electronic markets do well for more difficult
trades. For listed trades, however, electronic markets appear to fare
much less well vis-à-vis traditional brokers. On the basis of the ratio
of execution cost to the benchmark, electronic markets do poorly
relative to expectations and relative to the performance of traditional
brokers. We now attempt to shed further light on these results by
extending our analysis to total trading costs (including commissions)
and more disaggregated comparison data.

In table 7.8, total costs are sorted by values of several trade characteristics, including benchmark execution cost. The figures are constructed in the following manner. For a trading category (listed or
OTC), the median value of a trade characteristic (shares per trade) is
calculated. Observations for a type of broker (traditional or electronic)
are classified as being above or below this median value. For obser-

Table 7.8
Trading Costs Sorted by Market Conditions

	Below Median		Above Median	
	Traditional	Electronic	Traditional	Electronic
OTC Shares				
Shares per trade	0.543	0.452	0.967	0.825
Market cap	0.919	0.150	0.558	0.546
Beta	0.381	0.459	1.292	0.598
Volatility	0.324	0.508	1.181	0.595
Inverse price	0.502	0.461	1.016	0.714
Benchmark cost	0.386	0.524	1.053	0.649
Listed Shares				
Shares per trade	0.475	0.255	0.307	0.815
Market cap	0.506	0.291	0.231	0.263
Beta	0.241	0.179	0.522	0.341
Volatility	0.232	0.286	0.529	0.262
Inverse price	0.364	0.210	0.391	0.312
Benchmark cost	0.239	0.271	0.478	0.295
OTC Buys				
Shares per trade	0.255	0.293	0.017	0.051
Market cap	0.285	0.005	−0.137	0.254
Beta	−0.264	0.511	0.587	0.041
Volatility	−0.102	0.351	0.330	0.082
Inverse price	0.193	0.268	0.059	0.176
Benchmark cost	0.060	0.253	0.165	0.158
OTC Sells				
Shares per trade	1.156	0.622	1.689	1.452
Market cap	1.399	—	1.558	0.823
Beta	1.104	0.700	1.984	0.893
Volatility	0.834	0.660	1.970	1.198
Inverse price	0.996	0.894	1.824	0.633
Benchmark cost	0.877	0.832	1.849	0.755
Listed Buys				
Shares per trade	0.401	0.125	0.260	—
Market cap	0.472	0.106	0.149	0.137
Beta	0.061	0.018	0.601	0.207
Volatility	0.235	0.202	0.400	0.031
Inverse price	0.431	0.141	0.203	0.109
Benchmark cost	0.267	0.163	0.357	−0.227
Listed Sells				
Shares per trade	0.494	0.396	0.391	—
Market cap	0.537	0.445	0.315	0.396
Beta	0.419	0.337	0.451	0.459
Volatility	0.235	0.375	0.649	0.435
Inverse price	0.336	0.530	0.531	0.285
Benchmark cost	0.184	0.392	0.614	0.715

—, No observations within cell.

vations on either side of the median, average total trading costs are calculated.[53]

Costs by trade characteristic for OTC trades are contained in table 7.8. Electronic OTC trading costs are lower than those for traditional brokers, regardless of the size of the trade, market capitalization, or average share price. Electronic trade execution is also less costly for trades with volatility and expected cost above median values. These results support findings based on execution cost; in the OTC market and for relatively more difficult trades, electronic markets outperform traditional brokers. Figures reported in table 7.8, disaggregating OTC trades into buy and sell activity, yield the same basic conclusion. Electronic brokers tend to dominate across all categories on the sell side, which we have documented as representing more difficult market conditions in this sample.

In the case of listed issues, our results suggest that large savings in explicit trading costs from electronic executions outweigh possible gains in implicit costs from trading via traditional brokers. We earlier reported a ratio of execution cost to benchmark for traditional brokers that is 55% below that for electronic markets. On the other hand, for benchmark execution costs above the median, total costs for traditional brokers are 62% above those for electronic markets. The difference in findings stems from commissions charged by traditional brokers, which are over 100% more than fees charged by electronic markets.

We also note that for listed stocks electronic brokers exhibit lower total costs for high-volatility trades, for small sizes, all price ranges, and low market capitalization. Given such results, the apparent superiority of traditional brokers based specifically on the ratio of execution cost to the benchmark stands out as an exception. We now suggest that some ambiguities in the data simply obscure the basic finding that electronic systems constitute the less costly trading technology.

We disaggregate listed activity into buys and sells in table 7.8, and several significant findings emerge. First, all electronic trading in this sample of listed stocks is done for trade sizes below the overall median (conditional on whether the trade is a buy or a sell). This

---

53. In table 7.8, for example, average total cost is 0.919 for traditional brokers doing OTC trades in stocks whose market capitalization is below the median for all OTC trades in the sample. The corresponding value for trades in stocks with above-median capitalization is 0.558 for traditional brokers and 0.546 for electronic venues.

implies that benchmark execution cost is lower relative to sample averages for electronic systems, raising the ratio of execution costs to the benchmark for electronic markets. This is another way of expressing a result of the potential sample selection bias noted earlier. Second, average costs for traditional brokers fall for large trades relative to small trades. The expected relation between price impact and order size may be reversed by upstairs-facilitated block trades in listed stocks.[54] Yet the benchmark cost regression indicates that for the full sample—including electronic markets, traditional brokers, and OTC as well as listed stocks—cost increases with size. Benchmark costs for traditional brokers in listed issues rise as size increases, actual execution costs fall owing to block facilitation, and the ratio of execution cost to the benchmark declines.

Thus the execution cost results for listed stocks, which are favorable to traditional brokers, are due to a combination of sample selection problems and a bias in the benchmark calculations due to unobserved upstairs activity. This conclusion is supported by other information in table 7.8. Consider buy transactions in particular. Total trading costs are lower for automated systems for small trade sizes and for all levels of market capitalization, volatility, price level, and benchmark cost.

Owing to the complications involved in handling the listed trade data, we state our conclusions as follows: In the U.S. OTC markets, trading via electronic systems would appear to offer significant cost savings over trading via traditional brokers, even after adjusting for trade difficulty. Whereas considerably more ambiguities are present in the data for listed stocks, extending our analysis to encompass total trading costs and using more informative disaggregated data justify a similar conclusion in that market.

Conclusions

The classical financial market microstructure literature models exchanges as hierarchies of trading rules that determine the parameters within which heterogeneously endowed traders strategically interact. The explicit transaction costs that traders bear are presumed to be unaffected by the technology, operating costs, or organizational

---

54. Leinweber (1995) and Keim and Madhavan (1996) document similar findings in this respect.

structure of the exchange. Even such issues as competition between exchanges are assumed to be governed by the behavior and composition of traders. As such, the literature has little to say about the most important developments in the trading services industry today: namely, the impact of advances in computer and telecommunications technology on the cost of trading and the development of market structure. In this chapter, we address these issues directly by focusing on the characteristics of exchange trading products rather than on the characteristics of traders.

We argue that exchanges operating in a competitive environment should be analyzed as firms offering trading products that embody particular technologies. The liquidity effect, to which the durability of the dominant national exchanges is commonly ascribed, derives from the salience of network externalities in the securities-trading industry. Issues of trading technology adoption require analysis in the framework of network models of industrial organization. Such models serve to illuminate increasingly prominent features of exchange competition and market structure development.

Assuming roughly equivalent product quality as between incumbent (floor auctions) and entrant (computerized auctions), an assumption whose applicability we document, new technology adoption in the face of network externalities requires clear cost advantages for the entrant. Cost therefore features as the centerpiece of our quantitative study of electronic versus intermediated trading. Yet the diffusion of new trading technology involves more complex processes. Our review of recent competitive developments in the trading industry appears to reinforce the fundamental role of the network effects postulated by this branch of industrial organization theory. First-mover advantages exist but are being eroded by relative cost movements and strategic pricing behavior. The role of technology sponsorship appears to be important in abetting successful entry. We observe sudden and rapid adoption of the entrant's trading technology once apparently small advantages have been achieved (tipping). The spread of external adapter systems, such as Instinet, that integrate incompatible networks is further predicted by the theory. Finally, we examine the emergence of mergers and "cartels" among automated system operators, a development that may be socially optimal given the underlying tenets of network economics.

We discuss the role of cost in the pricing of exchange trading services in the context of increasing market contestability. Several factors bring the market for trading services much more closely into line with the assumptions of perfect contestability. These include a massive decline in the costs of developing automated systems, the elimination of distance costs in the provision of cross-border electronic trading services, and the expansion of securitized products. As cross-subsidization of products is inconsistent with sustainability of prices in a contestable market, this has important implications for the way in which exchanges price different types of trading. Among U.S. and European exchanges, we document salient examples of such cross-subsidization, such as large trades by small trades, "on-exchange" trades by "off-exchange" trades, and retail trades by institutional trades. We demonstrate how trading automation greatly facilitates specialization of service provision and, as a consequence, serves to arbitrage away cross-subsidies. We expect this trend to intensify. For example, limit-order traders benefit from exchange interaction rules obliging block traders to execute their orders. As automation increasingly facilitates the incursion of competitor block trading services, and thereby eliminates this subsidy for limit-order traders, exchanges will be compelled not merely to eliminate fees for such traders (as Tradepoint has already done) but actually to *pay* them (as, more recently, the Island ECN has done).

The behavior of exchanges is conditioned not merely by the competitive environment, but also by the incentive structure deriving from their internal governance arrangements. The traditional mutual structure of an exchange is a remnant of the preautomation era, when the space limitations inherent to trading floors necessitated the rationing of direct access to members. As members then became intermediaries for all nonmember order flow, exchange behavior came to be partly directed by the interests of members in maintaining intermediation profits. As trading automation has facilitated unlimited direct access, it is logical that new automated entrants have chosen to be governed not as intermediary cooperatives, but rather as for-profit joint-stock companies selling execution services on a transaction basis. Member-based exchanges are increasingly trying to replicate the incentive structures of such companies by demutualizing, or divorcing ownership from membership. The historical record of such initiatives is short, but the Stockholm experience in particular would appear to indicate that innovations such as foreign remote membership and direct investor access are more easily implemented when intermediaries are minority owners and that demutualization may therefore serve to improve the performance of the exchange as a commercial enterprise.

As commercial enterprises, exchanges compete on the basis of the "market quality" that they offer as well as the cost of their trading services. In this regard, the focus of academic research has long been on measures of market quality, whereas it is our contention that a true understanding of trading technology adoption and market structure development can now be achieved only by moving the focus to cost. This conclusion stems from an examination of extant empirical evidence comparing traditional trading venues to automated price-discovery systems. Market quality is assessed using a combination of information relating to liquidity, informational efficiency, and volatility characteristics. Overall, the evidence suggests that automated markets and traditional trading floors may differ in subtle and complex ways, but that market quality is equalized across market structures.

If this is the case, measuring the actual cost of trading across traditional intermediated markets and automated nonintermediated markets becomes an important exercise. Despite the many recent transformations from floor and dealer markets to automated auction markets that we have documented, the structures still coexist in many parts of the world. Lower development and operational costs for automated structures will undoubtedly influence competitive developments, but it is the explicit and implicit (execution) costs borne by traders in each type of market that is ultimately likely to be determinant. We evaluate explicit and implicit costs, using a unique sample of five-year trading data from a large institutional user of proprietary electronic trading systems.

Both categories of cost are lower for electronic systems than for traditional brokers across OTC (Nasdaq) and U.S. exchange-listed stocks. To account for differences in trade difficulty across electronic markets and traditional brokers, we construct a benchmark measure of execution cost based on trade characteristics. Analysis of execution costs, net of commissions, suggests that trades on the electronic systems are easier trades with lower expected cost. However, we also find that electronic markets are generally less costly than traditional brokers for more difficult trades.

For OTC stocks, electronic markets dominate traditional brokers across the board. For listed stocks, our conclusions are similar but more nuanced. The ratio of execution cost to benchmark cost is generally superior for traditional brokerage, but this statistic is not informative for listed stocks, owing to a number of features of the data which we detail in the text. An examination of total trading costs, inclusive of commissions, reveals electronic trading to be superior to traditional brokerage by any measure of trade difficulty for buy trades and to be comparable for sells. We therefore conclude that electronic trading generally yields considerable cost savings over traditional trade intermediation.

We have tried to demonstrate in this chapter the enormous impact that advances in computer and telecommunications technology have had both on trading costs and on the natural industrial structure of the securities-trading industry. The implications are far-reaching for the development of market structure and the design of effective public policy. In particular, exchanges are now compelled to compete in an increasingly international market for trading services and can no longer be seen as static repositories for rules governing the transfer of ownership of securities. In our view, researchers, regulators, and traders would benefit from taking an industrial economics approach in trying to understand and react to this new market environment.

8

Institutional Trading Costs: The Impact of Market Structure and Trading Practices

Introduction

This chapter examines the trading behavior of institutional investors and their interaction with evolving market structures. The focus is heavily on U.S. institutions, as U.S. data are plentiful and the trading and regulatory environments are more complex and rapidly changing than elsewhere. Nonetheless, most of the analysis is directly relevant to the European institutional sector, and we make frequent reference to survey findings and market developments that are particular to Europe.

We begin with a discussion of trading costs and how they are measured and analyzed. We then examine how trading costs are affected by the investment style of a given fund and by the order management practices of their trading desks. Next, we investigate how trading behavior and trading costs are affected by the actual market and regulatory structures in which institutions operate. We conclude with a discussion of how institutional trading is likely to change in the coming years.

8.1   The Significance of Trading Costs:
The Implementation Shortfall

As outlined in chapter 2, portfolio management involves the selection of securities that the portfolio manager wishes the fund to hold,
given market prices at the time. Institutional trading desks are then
charged with implementing portfolio adjustment decisions through
the actual purchase and sale of securities in the marketplace.[1] Trading securities is a costly process, however, and therefore affects the
return on the securities and the desirability of actually acquiring or
disposing of them.

The function of implementing portfolio decisions, the trading
function, results in a considerable divergence between what the
desired portfolio is worth "on paper"—that is, according to market
midquote prices—and what it actually costs to acquire the securities
in the market. A frequently cited example is the ValueLine fund, the
portfolio of which had an annualized return of 26.2% from 1979 to
1991 on paper but that had only a 16.1% return as implemented.[2]
This striking differential, often referred to as "the implementation
shortfall," illustrates the significance of trading costs.[3] In an international setting, cross-country differences in trading costs are so substantial that they can be shown to have a significant impact on the
composition of global efficient portfolios (see Domowitz et al. 2000).

8.2   Measuring and Decomposing Trading Costs

In this section, we discuss the primary components of the cost of
trading, how they are quantified, and their relative significance.
Later, in section 8.4, we will examine how institutions actually manage trading costs.

8.2.1   Explicit Costs

The actual measurement of trading costs is not a straightforward
exercise. Some costs generated in the trading process, such as commissions and taxes, are easily quantified. These are the direct costs of

---

1. In small fund management firms, the portfolio manager may handle the trading
function as well (see section 8.3.1).
2. See, for example, Leinweber (1995).
3. See, for example, Treynor (1981), Loeb (1983), and Perold (1988).

trading, or the **explicit costs**, as they are commonly referred to by trading cost consultants and researchers.

The fact that explicit costs are measurable tells us little, however, about their relative significance in comparison with trading costs that are less readily identifiable and quantifiable, or even their relevance in determining what it actually costs traders to execute trades. As we explain in section 8.4.2, brokerage commissions frequently comprise charges levied on investors that are unrelated to the actual buying and selling of securities. They may therefore overstate the actual cost of trade intermediation and undermine their relevance as an indicator of the cost of trading. More important, studies show that explicit costs in the U.S. markets are frequently much less significant than less visible costs generated in the trading process.

8.2.2   Implicit Costs

These less visible costs represent the **implicit costs** of trading. Domowitz et al. (2000) found that whereas explicit trading costs in Europe were on average three to four times higher than those in the United States, implicit cost advantages more than offset this differential between 1996 and 1998. This marked discrepancy may reflect a more competitive and efficient brokerage industry in the United States but more competitive and efficient trading systems in Europe.

Logically, implicit costs have a number of identifiable components, but they are difficult to isolate in practice. This difficulty has facilitated the growth of a trading cost analysis and consultancy industry, particularly in the United States, where each of the major firms applies a somewhat different methodology.[4] Below, we examine the measurement and significance of three implicit cost measures: spreads, market impact, and opportunity cost.

8.2.2.1   Bid-Offer Spreads

In continuous trading environments, a buyer-initiated trade will generally be executed at a higher price than a seller-initiated trade, and vice versa, at any given point in time. This **bid-offer spread** represents a deviation between the trade price and the actual underlying value of the security, but one that is very difficult to measure

---

4. The primary U.S. trading cost consultants are the Plexus Group, SEI, Abel/Noser, and Elkins/McSherry.

accurately. Using actual **quoted spreads** to measure such costs is problematic for a number of reasons, in particular:

• Trades are frequently executed inside the **inside spread**, or the best quoted bid and offer.

• The size and relevance of quoted spreads will vary systematically across different market structures. Organized dealer markets, for example, typically require market makers to post continuous bid and ask prices for a minimum number of shares.[5] This minimum is frequently greater than the number that would be available at the best bid or offer in an auction market, in which buyer and seller orders interact directly.[6] An auction market trader would therefore frequently have to accept offers outside the inside spread in order to transact the same number of shares as he or she could at the inside spread in a dealer market.

These observations imply that the **effective spread**, a logically more accurate measure of the spread based on actual transaction prices, is likely to be more similar between market structures than quoted spreads. Effective spreads must be estimated—they cannot simply be observed, as with quoted spreads—and a variety of techniques exist for doing so.[7] Owing mainly to the phenomenon of bid-offer bounce in transaction prices, as trades alternate between bid and offer prices, a negative serial covariance of successive price changes yields effective spreads that are generally lower than quoted spreads.

Furthermore, common features of dealer market trading—such as investor **preferencing** of orders to preferred dealers, who then **quote match** the best posted bid or offer—will generally result in quoted

---

5. The terms "dealer" and "market maker" are frequently used interchangeably, but there is a significant difference. Market makers are always dealers, but dealers are not necessarily market makers. Dealers commit their own capital to buying securities from natural sellers and selling them on to natural buyers. They do so wholly at their own discretion unless they are also market makers. Market makers must commit in advance, through a price quote dissemination system, to buying and selling shares at the prices they set, in accordance with the rules of the specific market in which they operate. Thus "dealer markets," such as Nasdaq or SEAQ International, might be termed more accurately "market maker markets."

6. This is strictly true only in auction markets without any specialist function, such as the computerized systems operated by most European exchanges. The NYSE auction market is actually a hybrid, as the specialist plays a counterparty role, similar to that of a Nasdaq market maker, in approximately 25% of trades.

7. See, for example, Roll (1984b), George, et al. (1991), Madhavan, et al. (1997), and Lee (1993).

spreads that are supranormal vis-à-vis those that would be expected in an auction market context.[8] As orders submitted to a dealer market are not executed on the basis of time priority, dealers have little incentive to compete on the basis of quoted prices. The practices of preferencing and quote matching instead induce dealers to focus on nontrade aspects of investor service, such as company research, in order to attract order flow. This rule structure governing dealer market competition, and the resultant "bundling" of broker-dealer services, make measurement of trading costs on the basis of spreads problematic.

It also severely complicates detection of "collusive" behavior among dealers. Academic and regulator allegations of systematic collusive behavior in the Nasdaq market have been based on quoted spreads (see Christie and Schultz 1994, Christie et al. 1994), but the theoretical and empirical basis for inferring collusion from quoted spreads is tenuous. Christie and Schultz (1994, p. 1835) maintain that dealers should compete using quoted prices to attract automatic executions through Nasdaq's Small Order Execution System (SOES). But this claim is inconsistent with the widespread reports of market maker losses to "SOES bandit" traders going back to 1988, and repeated NASD rule changes to limit SOES trading as a result.[9] Unlike with most electronic auction systems, SOES quotes are not anonymous. Auction system operators have long recognized that traders quote less aggressively when their identity is broadcast. The Nasdaq market is no exception.

8.2.2.2 Market Impact

The act of trading affects market prices. A small trade in a highly liquid market will have a small impact on prices. A large trade in a highly illiquid market will have a large impact on prices. This effect is known as the **market impact**, or **price impact**, of trading.

Measuring market impact involves difficult counterfactual analysis. Basically, one is interested in the degree to which the transaction price deviates from the market price that would have been observed had the transaction never occurred—a hypothetical price that is some-

---

8. See in particular Dutta and Madhavan (1997).

9. See, for example, "Day Trading's Father," *New York Post*, August 15, 1999 (*http://www.nypostonline.com/081599/business/1440.htm*), and "SOES Bandits Rain on Nasdaq Parade," *TheStreet.com*, February 27, 1997 (*http://www.wsaccess.com/theStreet/comment/easymoney/2278.html*).

times referred to as the "unperturbed price" (Keim and Madhavan 1998). This price must be estimated, and logically it can be done by looking at a price, or prices, before the trade or after the trade. Studies of block trading typically compare trade prices with the prior transaction price or closing price.[10] The results of such studies are very sensitive to the pretrade benchmark that is chosen (Keim and Madhavan 1996). Other studies use a posttrade benchmark price instead.[11] These have the advantage of avoiding possible "gaming" effects, where traders believing that their performance will be evaluated against a specific pretrade price condition their trading accordingly.

Typically, liquidity demanders, or those trading via market order,[12] will generate positive market impact costs; that is, when they buy (sell), the market price is lower (higher) the following day. Sometimes called a **realized spread**, this measure of market impact can be interpreted as the reversal from the trade price to posttrade economic value. Liquidity suppliers, or limit-order[13] traders, will tend to generate negative market impact costs, meaning that limit-order trading can be profitable in itself (see Handa and Schwartz 1996). Yet another methodology applies a weighted average of both pretrade and posttrade transaction prices to measure market impact (see Berkowitz et al. 1988).

Taken as a whole, market impact studies indicate that this "invisible" implicit cost of trading tends to exceed explicit costs by a ratio of about 1.5–3 : 1.[14] In spite of this, *Institutional Investor's* Pensionforum survey (July 1999) found that only 35.9% of U.S. pension plan sponsors monitored market impact costs, compared with 95.3% that monitored commissions. Since explicit commissions are not even levied on Nasdaq dealer trades,[15] much if not all of the cost of such

10. See, for example, LaPlante and Muscarella (1997).
11. See, for example, Domowitz and Steil (1999 and chapter 7 of this book).
12. Market orders are orders to buy or sell at the best price prevailing in the market at that moment.
13. Limit orders are orders to buy (sell) at a specified maximum (minimum) price. Limit-order traders hope to buy (sell) at a lower (higher) price than the best offer (bid) prevailing in the market and are willing to bear the risk that the market moves away from them while they wait.
14. See, for example, Plexus Group (1998) and Domowitz and Steil (1999 and chapter 7 of this book).
15. The trade price agreed between investor and dealer implicitly comprises a commission charge.

trades is represented by market impact, and is therefore entirely unmonitored by nearly two-thirds of U.S. pension sponsors.

8.2.2.3 Opportunity Costs

Opportunity costs represent the costs associated with incompletely filled or delayed trading orders. Logically, they can exist only for trades that are information-motivated, as information leaking into the market is incorporated into prices over time.

Opportunity costs are notoriously difficult to measure. Trade and market price data are not enough; one needs reliable time-stamped data following the evolution of an entire *order* from the moment it is submitted to the trading desk through to the last component trade that was executed. Trading desks must obviously manage market impact and opportunity costs simultaneously, as they tend naturally to be negatively correlated. The measurement complications are therefore considerable.

Wagner and Edwards (1993) estimate trade delay costs at 0.20% of value for so-called "liquidity-neutral" markets, or those exhibiting no momentum. They also find that 24% of orders go uncompleted, and that the nonexecution costs on the unfilled component average 1.80%. Putting aside methodological questions, which are considerable in dealing with opportunity costs, their finding on the proportion of orders uncompleted substantially exceeds the 4–5% unearthed by Keim and Madhavan (1998) and Perold and Sirri (1993). These two studies would suggest that nonexecution costs as a percentage of total costs are actually quite low.

Results of an international survey of institutional chief investment officers (CIOs) and head equity traders by Schwartz and Steil (2000)[16] cast further doubt on the Wagner and Edwards estimates of opportunity costs. Schwartz and Steil find that the demand for immediacy in trading that can be ascribed specifically to information is considerably less than is commonly assumed:

• When asked to indicate, in deciding whether to buy a stock, the weight they generally gave to their estimate of a company's share price a day hence, 65% of CIOs said that they gave it "no weight" at

---

16. Survey respondents represented seventy-two firms: thirty-nine U.S., fourteen Canadian, eleven European, and eight Australian. The survey was carried out in 1998. Further details on the survey are discussed in section 4.5 as well as in Schwartz and Steil (2000).

all, and none said that they gave it "very great weight." In contrast, 70% said that they gave "very great weight" to their share price estimates *two years* hence.

• Similarly, only 9% said that their buy orders were "regularly" or "very frequently" generated from a decision process lasting under one hour, which must be the case for information-driven trades, whereas 77% said that this was "never" or "infrequently" the case. In contrast, 49% said that the decision process was "regularly" or "very frequently" between a week and a month in duration, and 38% said that it "regularly" or "very frequently" took over a month.

• When trading because they believe a stock is mispriced, only 3% said that they "regularly" or "very frequently" expected the price correction to take place within an hour, and 8% said that they expected it to occur within an hour and a day. In contrast, 86% said that they "never" or "infrequently" expected the correction within an hour, and 84% said the same for corrections within an hour and a day. Fifty-one percent "regularly" or "frequently" expected the correction to take over *one year*.

These and related findings indicate that institutions rarely trade because they believe that they have nonpublic information. When they do not, they cannot logically bear any opportunity costs.

Given the considerable evidence documenting the inability of fund managers to outperform indexes over extended periods of time, institutions need to be cautious in assuming that patient trading will necessarily yield opportunity costs. If institutions behave as if they have information when they do not, then they will merely reduce their investment performance via excessive market impact costs.

Given the structure of trading in most markets, institutions may rationally seek to trade quickly for reasons that are entirely unrelated to information. In particular, continuous trading markets produce an endogenous demand for immediacy that owes to the effect of order revelation on prices. An institution trading in a dealer market, for example, must give up its identity when trading, thereby offering signals to broker-dealers as to its future buying or selling intentions. Such information leakage naturally induces a tendency to trade quickly. New electronic call market systems (see section 8.4.1) are designed to eliminate information leakage and encourage patient trading.

8.3   Trading Costs and Investment Style

There are two primary internal determinants of an institution's cost of trading; that is, given the structure of the marketplace in which it operates. The first is the portfolio strategy, or investment style, of the fund in question; the second is the way in which the strategy is implemented in the market.

Differences in investment strategy imply differences in the demand for immediate order execution. Faster executions imply larger trade sizes and temporary order imbalances in the market, which in turn imply higher execution costs. "Technical investors," who attempt to capture gains from short-term expected price movements, generally require a much higher degree of immediacy than do "value investors," who seek undervalued stocks on the basis of long-term fundamental valuations. All else being equal, the former should therefore expect to incur higher trading costs than the latter.

Keim and Madhavan (1997) document and measure this effect using trading data for twenty-one institutions over the period 1991–1993. Demand for immediacy among technical investors is manifested in a very high usage of market orders (97%), rather than limit orders. Value investors used market orders much less frequently (77%). The impact on their relative trading costs, with and without commissions, was substantial. As table 8.1 shows, technical investors bear significantly higher trading costs whether buying or selling and whether trading U.S. exchange-listed or Nasdaq stocks. For example, technical traders paid on average almost 2.5 times more than value investors to buy listed stocks (0.71% of principal versus 0.30%), and over ten times as much to sell them (0.87% versus 0.08%).

Table 8.1
Trading Costs and Investment Style

	Market Order Usage	Cost of Trading U.S. Exchange-Listed Stocks		Cost of Trading Nasdaq Stocks	
		Buys	Sells	Buys	Sells
Technical Investors	97%	0.71%	0.87%	1.39%	1.68%
Value Investors	77%	0.30%	0.08%	0.37%	0.61%

Source: Keim and Madhavan (1997).

Chan and Lakonishok (1995) similarly document higher market impact costs for growth-oriented investors than for value-oriented investors, and higher costs for investors with high turnover rates.

8.4 Trading Costs and Order Handling

8.4.1 Managing Information Leakage

Implementation of a given investment strategy still leaves considerable scope for better or worse order handling. Trading costs can be significantly influenced by the trader or trading system. A key factor is the degree of information leakage. Other players in the market use information associated with the identity of the transacting fund, the securities involved, the direction of the trades and the size of the orders to gauge movements in demand for securities, and condition their own trading activities accordingly. The performance of the fund is therefore harmed to the degree that market prices are pushed up by wider market knowledge that the fund is buying, or pushed down by knowledge that the fund is selling. The consequence is that fund managers naturally seek mechanisms whereby portfolio adjustments can be made without communicating their identity or intent to the wider market.

There are a number of ways in which this may be done. Traditionally, it has involved subcontracting the order execution to an outside broker-dealer firm, which is then charged with filling the order as cost-effectively as possible, often within certain time limits, in return for a commission payment. The absence of unambiguous benchmarks to gauge trading performance on each order, however, provides the broker-dealer with considerable opportunity to profit from its knowledge of the order. Such knowledge may inform the broker-dealer's own proprietary trading activity, legal restrictions on front-running notwithstanding, or may be passed on privately to other clients that may reward the broker-dealer for such information.

To limit the scope for information leakage and strategic exploitation, larger fund management firms increasingly operate their own internal centralized trading desks, staffed with professional traders, which intermediate between the internal portfolio managers and the external broker-dealers. In the process, orders from portfolio managers are frequently broken up, repackaged, and strategically allocated among multiple broker-dealers to disguise to the greatest degree possible the buying and selling intentions of the firm in the securities being transacted.

This division of labor between portfolio manager and trader, widespread in the United States and to a lesser extent in the United Kingdom began expanding rapidly in continental Europe only in the late 1990s.

More recently, many institutions have undertaken to internalize more of the order execution process through the use of electronic order-routing and trade execution systems. These systems either automate the brokerage process or effectively eliminate it altogether by allowing institutions to transact directly with one another or with broker-dealers.[17] Most such systems provide full anonymity to the trader, thus reducing or eliminating information leakage in the trading process. In so doing, adverse price movements before or after the trade, deriving from inferences drawn in the market about the trader's positions or strategies, are mitigated or eliminated. This effect would appear to be a significant component of the trading cost savings that we ascribed to nonintermediated electronic trading in chapter 7.

Newer systems coming onto the market are now aiming to automate what are traditionally the most difficult and costly trades: large block trades in a given security or trades involving a portfolio of securities. Until recently, such trades required human broker intermediation.

Traditional trading structures, whether auction or dealer markets, can only process orders in two dimensions; that is, the trader may indicate only that he or she is willing to buy or sell so many shares of a given security at a specified price or better. This means that an institution wanting to trade a large block of shares, even anonymously, will move prices adversely merely in revealing its interest. Knowledge of this interest in the market leads participants to infer that the current market price does not accurately reflect demand. Bids and offers will thus adjust accordingly even without any transaction taking place, thereby precluding the trader from filling only

---

17. Systems such as Instinet allow institutional traders to transact either against other orders on the system itself or against orders posted on exchanges to which the system has electronic access. Interconnectivity among different broker and institutional trading and messaging systems has been greatly improved by widespread adoption of the FIX (Financial Information Exchange) messaging protocol across the industry.

part of the order at the price that prevailed before the block order was revealed.

However, new automated call market[18] systems with extremely high processing capacity are able to process complex contingent orders in three or more dimensions, facilitating "trial-and-error" approaches to order matching among large numbers of participants without disclosing any information to the market until a trade is actually executed.[19] For example, a trader with a downward-sloping demand curve for a stock could offer to buy a million shares for up to $50 a share, but otherwise accept 10,000 shares at a price of $49 a share. This ability enables both block and portfolio trading without generating adverse price movements from information leakage. If the block cannot be executed on the buyer's terms, the computer can attempt to find matches for less preferred price and size combinations without revealing the buyer's intentions. At the time of writing, these systems are in their early years and have not yet attracted the volumes of orders necessary to make them a dependable block-trading facility for institutional investors.

8.4.2 Managing Commissions

Domowitz and Steil (1999 and chapter 7 of this book) found institutional trading commissions to be, on average, three times higher with traditional telephonic brokers than with electronic brokerage or trading systems over the period 1992–1996. Furthermore, commission rates have come down only very slowly in recent years, in spite of greater electronic competition. U.S. weighted-average agency commission rates fell only 10% from 1994 to 1998, from 6.1 cents per share to 5.5 cents per share (Greenwich Associates 1999), in spite of

---

18. Electronic call markets, rather than operating continuously, hold all submitted orders until a single preset point in time. At that time, a central computer calculates the prices at which trades take place according to a fixed algorithm. In the simplest form of call auction, in which orders are placed in only two dimensions, the computer calculates the price that maximizes the number of shares that change hands. All orders to buy (sell) at that price or higher (lower) will trade at that price. There is no bid-offer spread in a call market.

19. OptiMark, until recently, operated on the Pacific Exchange, uses the trader's "satisfaction" level with various price-size combinations as the third dimension in order specification. Bond Connect, owned by State Street and operated on the Boston Stock Exchange, facilitates "Combined Value Trading" for multiple securities.

trading volumes climbing fourfold over this same period.[20] This compares with nonintermediated electronic trading commissions of 0.25–4 cents per share currently prevailing in the U.S. market.[21] U.S. retail commissions also fell very steeply over this period, from an average rate of about $280 per trade to under $70 per trade (Moszkowski and Gutierrez 1999), with some online brokers currently offering commission-free market orders. Furthermore, studies indicate that paying higher institutional commissions does not actually result in lower implicit execution costs; in fact, there appears to be a positive correlation between the two.[22] What accounts for the persistence of institutional commission rates in the face of growing volumes and competition?

For many institutions, the cost differential with nonintermediated trading is frequently justified on the basis of the need for research and related services from traditional brokers, the price of which is implicitly accounted for in the trading commissions. Electronic brokerage or trading, on the other hand, typically involves an "execution-only" service on the part of the provider.

More than half of U.S. institutional commission payments are not actually controlled by the traders, but rather by a combination of the firm's portfolio managers (40%), analysts (12%), and clients (10%). These figures were remarkably stable over the period 1996–1998. Trader control increases from 40% to 48% for large institutions, paying over $20 million in commissions annually (Greenwich Associates 1999). Fourteen percent of portfolio managers actually specify the broker to be used on the majority of their orders submitted to the trading desk (Schwartz and Steil 2000),[23] and 64% indicate that the trading desk's choice of broker should reward good research on most transactions (Schwartz and Steil 2000).[24]

---

20. The value of shares traded in the United States rose from $3.56 trillion in 1994 to $13.15 trillion in 1998 (Securities Industry Association, 1999).

21. Comprehensive institutional commission data for the European markets are harder to come by. Anecdotal evidence from London institutional traders suggests that commissions have also been falling only very slowly in the United Kingdom.

22. See Berkowitz et al. (1988), who explicitly adjust for trade difficulty. The findings of Domowitz and Steil (1999 and chapter 7 of this book), which compared execution costs between traditional brokers and execution-only electronic trading service providers, are consistent. Keim and Madhavan (1997) find a positive correlation coefficient between explicit and implicit costs of 0.14 for sells and 0.07 for buys.

23. This is consistent with our finding that 16% of traders report that their choice of broker is determined by the portfolio managers on more than half their orders.

24. Slightly fewer traders, 55%, indicate that choice of broker should be driven by research more than half the time.

Table 8.2
Factors Determining How Institutions Choose Brokers

	All Traders	U.S. Traders	Larger Fund Traders	Smaller Fund Traders	All CIOs	U.S. CIOs
Lowest possible execution costs	3.53	3.76	3.70	3.18	3.39	3.61
Fastest possible execution	3.37	3.42	3.67	3.00	3.24	3.22
Rewarding good research	3.39	3.24	3.20	3.61	3.42	3.11
Soft commission obligations	2.45	2.87	2.59	2.21	2.44	2.44
Portfolio manager direction	2.39	2.24	2.37	2.41	N/A	N/A

Scale: 1 ("never") to 5 ("very frequently," or 75–100% of the time).
Source: Schwartz and Steil (2000).

Table 8.2 presents data from Schwartz and Steil (2000) illustrating the factors driving choice of broker. Institutional head equity traders were asked how frequently their choice of broker was driven by the factors indicated, and CIOs were asked how frequently the trader's broker choice *should* be driven by these factors. The scale was 1 ("never") to 5 ("very frequently").[25]

As is apparent from the responses, factors other than minimizing execution cost are significant. "Rewarding good research," which is wholly unrelated to seeking best execution, featured prominently. "Soft commission obligations," which represent a binding prior commitment to paying for research-related services through trading commissions (see below), were not dominant but were nonetheless significant.

Larger institutional traders (over median sample asset size of $6.2 billion) placed considerably more emphasis on both execution cost and speed than did smaller institutional traders, which directed their commissions largely to pay for research services that they could not provide in-house. Traders in general also put slightly more emphasis on the trade-related factors of cost and speed than CIOs.

The study further found that, on average, traders directed 26% of their order flow to specific broker-dealers as a means of payment for

25. 2 = "infrequently," or 1–24% of the time. 3 = "sometimes," or 25–49% of the time. 4 = "regularly," or 50–74% of the time. 5 = "very frequently," or 75–100% of the time.

"research, trading or information systems or third-party services."
U.S. traders directed a considerably larger portion of their orders for
such purposes (32%) than did traders in other major markets (e.g.,
Europe, 18%).

Many institutions have formal "soft commission"—or, in the
United States, "soft dollar"—arrangements with their brokers, which
commit them to paying a minimum annual sum in trading commissions in return for ongoing company research and other services.[26]
The term "research" must, as a practical matter, be understood
broadly to encompass everything from long-term fundamental company and macroeconomic analysis, sometimes purchased from a
third party, to publicly available products such as newspapers, to
immediate buy and sell recommendations.

Over half of all U.S. institutional commissions are targeted in
advance, as an annual minimum commitment, to specific brokers to
pay for a combination of:

• research services from that broker (32% of total commissions)
(Schwartz and Steil 2000);[27]

• third-party research acquired by the broker, and other "soft" services such as trading and analytic technology (12%) (Greenwich
Associates 1999); and

• commitment to providing capital to facilitating trades (16%)
(Greenwich Associates 1999).

The degree to which institutions provide research services internally or subcontract them from broker-dealers should be a matter of
business judgment. A problem of fiduciary accountability arises,
however, when the cost of acquiring research services is embedded
in the cost of individual trade transactions. A fund manager's portfolio management services are contracted by fund holders—either
individual investors or other institutions, such as pension funds. An
explicit management fee schedule is associated with such services.
Yet if the fund manager is dependent on brokers for research and
other services necessary to manage client funds, and the fees for such

---

26. Thirty-two percent in Schwartz and Steil (2000), 30% in Greenwich Associates
(1999). This figure appears to be lower in other markets: 22% in Canada, 12% in Australia, and 18% in Europe (Schwartz and Steil, 2000).
27. Greenwich Associates (1999) cited an almost identical figure of 30%.

services are embedded in future trading commissions, it is exceptionally difficult, if not impossible, for clients to monitor and control such expenditure. The most salient principal-agent problems associated with the practice are as follows:

• The greater the soft dollar business a fund manager does with brokers, the lower his or her explicit expenses will be, as such expenditure comes directly out of client funds. This gives the fund manager a strong incentive to use soft dollars as a means of disguising expenses that should rightfully be reflected in the management fee schedule that is agreed with the client.

• Funds are managed on behalf of clients whose portfolios can require vastly different research inputs. A client contracting index-tracking services, for example, will have no research requirements associated with the management of his or her funds, yet brokerage commissions paid by the fund manager will frequently comprise such services and correspondingly reduce the client's returns. This occurs because trading desks combine orders from both active and index fund portfolio managers, and "soft" the combined orders with brokers to whom they have soft commission obligations. Potentially worse, the research-directed order may be given precedence over the nondirected index fund order, thus auguring an inferior execution for the latter.

• The fund manager frequently has an incentive to engage in excessive trading, otherwise known as "churning," with client funds in order to meet soft commission targets. Such targets may also influence the manager's choice of broker on a given transaction and may conflict with the manager's fiduciary obligations.

• The inherent opacity of soft dollar arrangements makes them open to more egregious abuse. The SEC found that 62% of U.S. broker-dealers that had soft dollar agreements with clients did not have the arrangements in writing.[28] The services being purchased with client soft dollars may not always be research-related, but rather of specific and direct benefit only to the fund management firm or its individual traders. Such practices may be illegal but are also frequently difficult to detect. The SEC found that 35% of U.S. broker-dealers that were

---

28. See the SEC Web site (http://www.sec.gov/news/studies/softdolr.htm). The period examined was November 1996 to April 1997.

examined paid for at least one product or service for their clients that appeared to be unrelated to research or execution.[29]

Individual retail fund holders have no effective way to discipline soft dollar business. Institutional fund holders such as pension funds, however, have established a range of procedures for controlling the practice, or at least internalizing part of the benefits:

• Some institutions manage their own trading, and negotiate execution-only commissions with brokers. Data are scarce, but such commissions appear to average under 4 cents per share in the United States, or approximately two-thirds of standard institutional commissions (Council of Institutional Investors 1999). This is still more than twice the average commission for self-directed electronic brokerage or trading services.

• Some institutions agree **directed brokerage** arrangements with their money managers or investment advisors, whereby the latter are obliged to execute a certain percentage of transactions with a broker designated by the client. The client arranges in advance with the broker to have a portion of the standard institutional commission paid by the money manager—generally around 60%—rebated directly to the client's fund. This procedure is known as **commission recapture**. The practice allows the client to negotiate its own brokerage fees, but does not fully "unbundle" execution and nonexecution costs. The money manager will be obliged to use the designated broker for a portion of the trading in the client's funds, whether or not that particular broker is optimally suited to handle a given trade.

Given the inherent problems of incentive structure and monitoring in soft dollar and directed brokerage arrangements, it is not surprising that studies have documented significant losses in trading performance attributable to them. After adjusting for order characteristics and institution-specific differences, Conrad et al. (1999) calculate that soft dollar trade executions cost the client an average of

---

29. These products and services included, among other things, rent, computer hardware used for administrative or personal use, CFA exam review courses, AIMR membership dues, travel expenses, cable and satellite television for nonresearch areas, telephone service, employees' salaries, messenger services, consulting services, postage, parking fees, office equipment, word processing software, tuition, and tax preparation services.

0.07% more than discretionary executions for buy trades and 0.20% more for sells. Such studies do not attempt to measure or allocate any benefits unrelated to execution efficiency that may accrue to fund holders from soft dollars, but do provide an important indication of the *cost* of such benefits. Wagner and Glass (1998) report that money managers handling directed trades on behalf of plan sponsors frequently execute them after trades in the same stocks on behalf of other fund holders and that such "sequencing" practices can result in higher trading costs attributable to delayed execution. They report findings of a Plexus Group study of a large growth fund manager from 1993 to 1994 that revealed cost savings amounting to 0.03% of principal deriving from lower commissions on directed trades, but trading cost losses of 0.43% deriving from delayed execution on such trades.

Soft commission practices are regulated in various forms by different government agencies and private sector self-regulatory organizations in different countries. In the United States, both the SEC and the Department of Labor have guidelines on the use of soft dollars, focused largely on trying to weed out the practice where it involves nonexecution services not clearly related to "research." The 1975 amendments to the 1934 U.S. Securities and Exchange Act charge the SEC with defining research, and the SEC has changed the list of items comprised by the term numerous times since then. The practice remains controversial, and views on whether and how it should be regulated, reformed, or abolished differ significantly both within the securities industry and among regulatory authorities.

Among fund managers, views on soft commissions are quite diverse, but generally positive. Schwartz and Steil (2000) found that 67% of head institutional traders believe that it is "appropriate for a fund management firm to pay 'soft commissions' on trades as compensation for broker research." Similarly, 61% believe that such payments are also appropriate "as compensation for third-party services, such as computer information or trading systems."

Nonetheless, a substantial 51% believe that it is "desirable" (20%) or "highly desirable" (31%) actually to unbundle payment for external research and brokerage commissions. Only 8.2% consider this "undesirable" (6.6%) or "highly undesirable" (1.6%). However, views are split on the degree to which it is, as a practical matter, *feasible* to unbundle these services and charge for them separately. Thirty-one

Table 8.3
Criteria CIOs Use to Determine Quality of Trades

1. Execution price of order relative to VWAP	3.06
2. Speed of execution	2.76
3. Execution price of each trade relative to contemporaneous market price	2.69
4. Average daily execution price relative to the day's closing price	2.53
5. Commission cost	2.10
6. No evaluation made	1.88

Scale: 1 ("never") to 5 ("very frequently," or 75–100% of the time).
Source: Schwartz and Steil (2000).

percent consider it "feasible" (26%) or "highly feasible" (5%), while an almost identical 29% consider it "infeasible" (21%) or "highly infeasible" (8%).

One existing market solution to this cost-bundling problem is a broker "give-up" function incorporated into electronic brokerage systems.[30] Whereas the institution can maintain its anonymity and control order flow into the market internally, each trade is assigned to a broker designated by the institution, and that broker is compensated according to a fixed commission schedule. Thus the institution can, where it chooses, continue to pay for nonexecution services via execution fees, while at the same time eliminating the broker's role in executing trades. This obviously does not address the fiduciary problems inherent in soft commissions, which we discussed above.

8.4.3   VWAP Trading

The volume-weighted average price (VWAP) for a security over a trading day has taken on an enormous significance as a benchmark for evaluating trading performance. Schwartz and Steil (2000) found that CIOs rank VWAP performance well above other criteria for evaluating how well their traders handle their orders (see table 8.3). The underlying logic is that VWAP provides an objective measure of the entire market's contribution to determining the price of a stock, and should therefore also be an objective criterion against which to measure an individual trader's performance. If the trader buys stock below (above) VWAP, he or she has "outperformed" ("underperformed") the market.

---

30. State Street's Lattice Trading system employs such a function.

As this logic is widespread, it should not be surprising that VWAP has taken on the essential property of "Goodhart's Law." Monetary economist Charles Goodhart famously noted that "any observed statistical regularity will tend to collapse once pressure is placed upon it for control purposes" (1984, p. 96). As a major benchmark for trading performance, VWAP naturally affects the actual behavior of traders, and so significantly affects the determination of VWAP itself.

Wagner and Edwards (1993) estimate that about 40% of U.S. institutional orders exceed the relevant stock's average daily trading volume. If traders fill orders of this size within a single day, their trading performance is likely to appear very poor against a VWAP benchmark. Chan and Lakonishok (1995) find that only about 20% of the value of institutional buy orders is completed within a day, and less than half within four days. Traders generally cannot hope to account for more than about 20% of a day's market volume and not fall awry of VWAP. Traders therefore hold back huge portions of their orders, filling them over several days, and often a week or more, as a means of staying within or near the VWAP benchmark. Each day, they stop buying (selling) when the price moves above (below) VWAP. When a large number of institutional traders in the market behave like this, share prices naturally fail to reflect true levels of demand, thus eliminating the relevance of VWAP as an indicator of such demand. VWAP merely reflects those small portions of each order that are actually brought to the market each day, in the expectation that they are too small to affect the market price significantly. Prices will eventually come to reflect the latent demand in actual orders, but with a time lag. A VWAP trader can therefore "chase a stock" several percentage points up or down over several days, appearing skilful against VWAP while often damaging the fund's performance. Chan and Lakonishok (1995) find that market impact costs are significantly higher when measured for trade *packages* rather than individual trades, underscoring the flaws inherent in VWAP as a trading performance benchmark. American Century Mutual Fund actually discovered that one of its brokers that ranked best under a VWAP methodology ranked *worst* under a methodology that accounted for share price movements the day after trades.

8.5   Trading Costs and Market Structures

8.5.1   *Auction versus Dealer Markets*

Most major studies of institutional trading costs across markets have naturally focused on the United States, where data are plentiful and the traditional existence of distinct market structures on the NYSE and Nasdaq has sustained great interest in cross-market comparisons. The majority of such studies have concluded that execution costs are lower on the NYSE than on Nasdaq.[31] This is consistent with the conclusions of studies comparing spreads and trading costs on the continental European electronic auction markets and the old London Stock Exchange SEAQ-I dealer market system.[32] Taken as a whole, these findings have been widely interpreted as a reflection of the superiority of the auction market structure— whether specialist-based or wholly electronic—with respect to the dealer market structure.

There are a number of reasons why such an interpretation should be treated with caution:

• First, the data used to measure costs in one market are not always comparable to the data used in another. In particular, not all studies have accounted for the fact that trading on the Nasdaq and SEAQ markets is done net of commissions—meaning that the price of the trade effectively incorporates a commission payment to the dealer, rather than being added on by the broker, as it is in the auction markets.

• Second, the characteristics of the stocks being traded in auction and dealer markets may differ systematically, and this will affect trading costs without necessarily impugning one or the other trading structure. Dealer markets have traditionally been implemented where the securities listed, at least initially, are perceived to be relatively illiquid and therefore relatively more difficult and costly to trade.

---

31. See, in particular, Huang and Stoll (1996a), which itself contains a thorough literature review.
32. See Pagano and Röell (1990) on French stocks, Schmidt and Iversen (1992) on German stocks, Impenna et al. (1995) on Italian stocks, and Andersen and Tychon (1993) on Belgian stocks.

• Third, the trading strategies used in auction and dealer markets tend to differ systematically, and accounting for such differences is complicated by the fact that the strategies employed are themselves endogenous to a given market structure. In particular, greater information leakage in dealer markets naturally gives rise to larger trade sizes and faster execution of portfolio manager orders.[33]

• Fourth, the structures of specific markets contain varying amounts of "impurities"; elements of dealer markets exist in most auction markets and vice versa. A trade on the NYSE may be executed on the floor with varying degrees of specialist intervention, or "upstairs" with an exchange member acting as a dealer. Trades on the Nasdaq market are increasingly executed via electronic communications networks (see section 8.5.3), which function as electronic auction markets, rather than via dealers.

Recent studies on the U.S. markets that have attempted to mitigate some of these distortions have found more similar trading costs between the NYSE and Nasdaq markets than most earlier studies. Jones and Lipson (1999) examine trading costs using a sample of institutional orders in shares of firms that have switched exchanges. The study accounts for commission costs, controls for investment style, and isolates the impact of the listing venue by examining the cost of trading shares of the same firm in one market and another. They find no significant difference in trading costs across the three largest U.S. markets: the NYSE, Nasdaq, and AMEX. While controlling for investment style in measuring trading costs, they also document the relevance of market structure to the composition of traders in a stock and the investment and trading strategies that they apply. In particular, Jones and Lipson found a higher incidence of worked orders—defined as orders executed through multiple brokers over multiple days—in the trading of shares switching from Nasdaq to the NYSE, which was absent in AMEX to NYSE switches. This is a logical reflection of differences in information leakage between dealer and auction markets. They also found momentum traders accounting for a greater portion of trading, and value traders accounting for a lesser portion, in shares switching from Nasdaq to the NYSE.

---

33. In an anonymous auction market, on the other hand, traders are more willing to split large orders into small ones and execute them over a longer period of time.

Domowitz and Steil (1999 and chapter 7 of this book) also accounted for commission costs, and were able to isolate the proportion of trading via electronic systems (such as Instinet) in both Nasdaq and NYSE (and regional exchange) stocks. They found nearly identical trading costs for buy trades via the traditional nonelectronic execution mechanisms of the Nasdaq and NYSE markets. However, they found substantially higher trading costs for sell trades in the Nasdaq market—a difference that persisted when comparing electronic Nasdaq executions with electronic NYSE executions. As the authors were working with single-institution time-series data, it would appear that the difference in sell costs is due to different handling of sell orders, particularly between Nasdaq and NYSE stocks, in the specific institution studied. The difference in sell costs would appear to be unrelated to market structure. Keim and Madhavan (1998) also found higher costs for sells than for buys, using trading data from twenty-one institutions. It would appear that traders tend to demand more immediacy when selling than when buying, which is reflected in larger average trade sizes on sells. The cost of immediacy is evidenced in Domowitz and Steil (1999 and chapter 7 of this book) by the finding that electronic call market trading, for which immediacy is impossible, was considerably cheaper than continuous trading, whether electronic or intermediated, for both listed and Nasdaq sells (27% and 43% less, respectively). The difference was insignificant for buys, which appeared to be transacted more patiently.

8.5.2 *Intermediated versus Nonintermediated Markets*

In attempting to gauge the trajectory of market structure evolution, the foregoing discussion suggests that the critical distinction may not be between auction and dealer markets, but rather between intermediated and nonintermediated markets. Our analysis of the impact of technological change on the industrial structure of the trading industry, developed in chapter 7, suggests that human intermediation of trades—whether via market makers in dealer markets or specialists in auction markets—is a significant component of the cost of trading. This is evident in our findings that trading through nonintermediated electronic auction markets generally yields considerable trading cost savings vis-à-vis trading through intermediated floor auction markets.

Advances in trading automation and telecommunications have made it increasingly easy for investors, both institutional and individual, to bypass human intermediaries when they believe it to be in their interests to do so. Such an effect militates against the persistence of both dealer markets and floor auction markets, and favors systems that facilitate the most direct matching of buyer and seller orders. This logic is consistent with the observation that almost all existing or former floor and dealer markets have chosen to convert to or add electronic auction trading over the past five years, and that new markets have all chosen such trading.

Human intermediation of trades, particularly large block and complex portfolio trades, will not disappear. The implication is rather that intermediation that is *built into* trading structures by design, rather than being chosen by the investor, is unlikely to withstand increasing contestability in the market for trading systems.

Survey findings from Schwartz and Steil (2000) are consistent with the logic of increasing disintermediation of trading. When asked about their anticipated level of trading *directly* through exchanges or electronic order-matching systems in three years time, 80% of institutional head equity traders said it would be higher, and 14% said it would be much higher. Only 2% said it would be lower. When asked whether they saw broker-dealers more as *competitors* or more as *agents* than they did five years ago, 43% of institutional traders said "competitors," and 24% said "agents." This indicates a growing perception among institutional traders that conflicts of interest are built into the trade intermediation process.

In the short-term, the transition from more to less intermediated trading environments will have an impact on liquidity at different trade sizes. Widespread anecdotal evidence (firm data are lacking) suggests that dealer capital became more expensive in the United Kingdom—first for foreign and then domestic stocks—after the successful introduction of electronic auction systems on the European continent at the beginning of the 1990s, and after the launch of the SETS auction system in 1996, and in the United States after implementation of the Nasdaq order-handling rules in 1997. Data from the London Stock Exchange in the early 1990s, since discontinued, indicated considerable cross-subsidization of market maker activities by trade size, with large profits on small trades offsetting losses on midsize block trades. Auction systems naturally tend to attract the smaller trades that can be matched without dealer intervention, thus leaving dealers to handle the larger—often loss-making—blocks. The breakdown of cross-subsidies therefore implies lower profits, or losses, for dealers, which in turn implies more expensive liquidity for institutional block transactions.

8.5.3 ECN Trading

8.5.3.1 Alphabet Soup
Over the past decade, numerous acronyms have been created to describe electronic trading systems that are owned, and usually operated, outside the traditional, generally mutualized or government-owned, stock exchanges. The earliest widely used acronym was PTS, for "proprietary trading system." What generally distinguished PTSs from their exchange counterparts, besides their ownership and governance structure, was that they offered trading services directly to institutional investors; there was generally no requirement to channel orders through broker-dealers.

This generic term, applied most frequently to Instinet and Posit, was generally resisted by nonexchange operators, as the perception spread that PTSs were, in essence, "unregulated exchanges." Indeed, they were generally not regulated as exchanges, but rather as brokers. The two major exceptions were the Arizona Stock Exchange (AZX), which is classified as an exchange by the U.S. SEC but exempt from most exchange regulatory requirements as long as its volume remains low, and Tradepoint, which is a Recognized Investment Exchange in the United Kingdom, like the London Stock Exchange. Tradepoint also has a "low-volume exemption" from the SEC to offer European stock trading in the United States.

The SEC subsequently encouraged widespread use of the term ATS, or "alternative trading system," to which it applied a legal meaning and regulatory obligations different from those applied to brokers or exchanges. Regulation ATS, or "Reg ATS," as it is popularly known, detailed such obligations, which came into effect in 1999.

Within the Nasdaq marketplace, ATSs were given the name electronic communications network (ECN). At the time of writing, there were ten such ECNs in operation,[34] the largest of which are Instinet

---

34. Archipelago, Attain, Brass Utility, Instinet, Island, Market XT, Redibook, Strike Technology, NexTrade, and Tradebook.

(16% of Nasdaq dollar volume at the end of 1999) and Island (8%). Currently, Instinet handles primarily institutional and broker-dealer order flow, but it is considering expanding its business into the retail sector, where Island is currently predominant. As ATS trading in the United States is overwhelmingly concentrated in the Nasdaq market, the term "ECN" quickly took on a generic status equivalent to the old PTS and is now widely used as a synonym for ATS in the United States and elsewhere. We will therefore use the term "ECN" in the discussion that follows.

8.5.3.2 Institutional ECN Use

The NASD reported that ECNs handled approximately 30% of Nasdaq trade volume in 1999, up from approximately 20% in 1996.[35] Survey data compiled by Greenwich Associates (1999) indicate an increase in institutions using ECNs from 53% to 63% between 1996 and 1998. Seemingly paradoxically, however, they also identified a year-to-year *decline* in institutional Nasdaq volumes transacted through ECNs from 24% to 15% over the same period. Reported institutional ECN volumes in NYSE and other listed and international stocks remained roughly stable at 6–8%. What accounts for the apparent decline in Nasdaq ECN volumes, relative to total volumes, and the much lower ECN use for listed stocks?

There is no ready way to account scientifically for the Greenwich findings on Nasdaq ECN usage. However, there are logical explanations for the reported decline in relative ECN usage that may help to illuminate the effects of market structure regulation on trading in the U.S. markets.

The most significant exogenous event affecting Nasdaq market structure over this period was a regulatory one: the introduction of the SEC's "order-handling rules" in January 1997.[36] These had two primary effects: First, the new rules obliged Nasdaq market makers to incorporate customer limit orders in their obligatory market quotes. If a customer order was equal to or better than the posted quote of the receiving market maker, that order became the market maker's new quote in the Nasdaq quote display system (the "Level II Montage") for at least the size of the customer order. Second, the

---

35. The NASD counts as ECN trades orders that are executed internally on an ECN and orders that are routed to an ECN for execution. Orders that are routed out from ECNs to other market participants for execution are not counted.
36. Securities Exchange Act Release No. 37619A (September 6, 1996).

new rules likewise obliged Nasdaq to display the best bids and offers from all ECNs.[37]

Prior to implementation of the order-handling rules, Nasdaq market structure was considerably simpler, and certainly less fragmented. The Nasdaq dealer market structure handled approximately 80% of the volume,[38] and Instinet handled almost all of the other 20%. Instinet was effectively the electronic auction market for Nasdaq stocks. Being the earliest market entrant, Instinet had the enormous advantage of long-standing and substantial two-way order flow.[39]

After implementation, ECNs no longer had to rely on their own subscriber base to match orders. ECNs that could not generate sufficient critical mass to match orders internally (as stock exchanges must normally do) could now function instead as order-routing systems, using liquidity generated elsewhere in the Nasdaq market to satisfy their customer orders.

Three major effects were apparent; the first has been lauded by the SEC, the second has become an object of tremendous concern, and the third appears to have gone largely unnoticed.

The first effect was a narrowing of the inside spread for most Nasdaq stocks—approximately 40% between 1997 and 1999. Although the SEC has cited this fact repeatedly in its positive evaluation of the order-handling rules,[40] it is not in itself a meaningful measure of investor benefit. As we explained in section 8.2.2.1, the scholarly literature demonstrates that interdealer competition will naturally produce *quoted* spreads that are wider than the inside spread in an auction market. But quoted spreads are not a valid measure of trading costs, particularly in a dealer market, where trades frequently take place within the spread. By absorbing limit orders into quoted spreads, such spreads will naturally condense toward auction market levels, but with no clear effect on the total cost of trading. As Pagano and Steil (1996) demonstrated, using the

---

37. In 1999, Reg ATS made it *mandatory* for ECNs to display such orders publicly on Nasdaq. Prior to Reg ATS, Instinet, the largest ECN, allowed institutions the *choice* as to whether their order was disclosed to market makers and non-Instinet members.

38. Many commentators observe that the Nasdaq dealer market structure is itself "fragmented," but this is a matter of semantics. A dealer market by its nature relies on competition among intermediaries to ensure liquidity for investor buy and sell orders. A "consolidated" dealer market would not be a dealer market at all, but rather a "specialist" market.

39. See the discussion of network externalities in section 7.1.

40. See, for example, Release No. 34-42450 (February 23, 2000: section IV:B).

example of SEAQ International, limit-order competition to a dealer market will change market maker behavior in ways that tend to reduce their willingness to commit capital to intermediating trades. Indeed, this appears to be the case in the Nasdaq market since implementation of the order-handling rules.

As Moszkowski and Gutierrez of Salomon Smith Barney (SSB) noted, "The combination of narrower spreads and higher overall market volatility has made the risk/return trade-off in the dealer market less favorable and caused many dealers to be disintermediated out of the market" (1999, p. 40). The number of market makers declined about 10%, from 530 to 478, in the year following implementation of the order-handling rules, and SSB estimates a continuing decline to about 350 by 2005. SSB reduced the number of Nasdaq stocks for which it made markets by 22%, from 1706 to 1329, in the year following the order-handling rules. Other securities houses report similar declines. Narrower quoted spreads, consequentially, are also likely to be accompanied by higher costs on dealer-facilitated block transactions (see section 8.5.1). Counterfactuals are obviously impossible to prove, but spreads should logically have come down without regulatory intervention, through either increased usage of Instinet or the eventual introduction of a Nasdaq auction system (see below).

The second effect was to increase "fragmentation" in the Nasdaq market. The order-handling rules operate as a means of redistributing property rights to limit orders and quotations among dealers and ECNs in a manner that greatly facilitates competition from the newer ECNs. ECNs other than Instinet and Island internally match only about 5–10% of customer trades.[41] Before the order-handling rules, this match rate was insufficient to make competition among ECNs viable, as evidenced by Instinet's near-100% market share in ECN trading. Few traders would put orders onto a system that was accessed only by a small group of subscribers. After implementation of order-handling rules, however, the ECNs could simply route their orders to Nasdaq, which was now obliged to display them as if the ECNs were market makers. The result was an uncomfortable halfway house between a dealer market and an auction market. Dealers finding themselves disintermediated by public limit-order display

---

41. See, for example, "Wall Street Fuddy Duddies CLOBber the Future," *Wall Street Journal*, March 8, 2000.

stopped making markets in many stocks. Yet the Nasdaq Montage became only a poor approximation of a limit-order book, as quotes from market makers and ECNs were not consolidated, and only the best bids and offers from each were displayed. Significantly, the ECNs continued to charge for executions against their limit orders, while market makers were still prohibited from doing the same for their quotes.

The predictable result of the order-handling rules was a proliferation of ECNs and a decline in Instinet's market share of order-book trading of about 40%. Separate order books were now scattered throughout the Nasdaq market. The SEC has repeatedly expressed concern over this fragmentation of the Nasdaq market, but appears to interpret it as a result of free competition rather than of regulatory intervention. Market participants widely share the view that were Nasdaq to introduce its own electronic auction system (a consolidated limit-order book, or CLOB, as it is popularly referred to in the United States), trading would naturally coalesce onto such a system. A 1996 NASD proposal to establish such a system failed to obtain the necessary support of either its members or the SEC.[42]

The third effect is a result of the market fragmentation discussed above: Institutions are directing less of their order flow to ECNs as the costs of monitoring the proliferating pools of Nasdaq liquidity increase. The Nasdaq Montage assists institutions only in identifying the best bid or offer in the Nasdaq market, but not the depth of the marketplace. The volume available at the inside spread is very low in comparison to the average institutional order size. Therefore institutions are obliged to search the ECN order books and market maker quotes manually in order to identify buying and selling opportunities. This is a highly labor-intensive, and therefore costly, process that appears to have encouraged institutional traders to subcontract an increasing proportion of their Nasdaq trading to broker-dealers since 1997. These broker-dealers will themselves often execute part or all of an institutional order on ECNs (explaining part of the *overall* rise in relative ECN volumes), but the Greenwich data reflect only those orders that are routed to ECNs directly by institutions. The cost to fund holders of this increase in liquidity search subcontract-

---

42. See, for example, the following on the SEC's Web site: http://www.sec.gov/rules/sros/nd9909n.htm. NASD members argued that Nasdaq, being wholly owned by a self-regulatory organization, had no right to operate a trading system in competition with its members.

ing to broker-dealers is a direct consequence of the order-handling rules.

Reported institutional use of ECNs for listed (mainly NYSE) shares has been relatively low, and relatively stable, since 1996. There are three primary reasons for this:

• ECNs operate auction market structures, as do the NYSE and regional exchanges. While there are considerable differences between the electronic nonintermediated version and the specialist-based floor version, quoted spreads in floor auctions still tend to be narrower than those in dealer markets, for reasons enumerated in section 8.2.2.1. There is therefore less scope for spread narrowing via ECNs.

• NYSE Rule 390 prohibits member firms and their affiliates from transacting in NYSE-listed securities listed as of April 26, 1979,[43] away from a national securities exchange. Under pressure from the SEC, this rule was eliminated in May 2000.

• Owing to the idiosyncratic structure of the U.S. equity markets, soft dollar arrangements generally apply only to listed stocks.[44] Given the enormous scope of institutional soft dollar business, it is clear that the choice of broker or trading venue for much listed business is not actually driven by concern over the cost of execution. Therefore, even if ECN trading is significantly less costly than floor trading, institutions having significant soft dollar obligations to brokers will have a very limited incentive to use it.

8.5.3.3 The Future of ECNs

ECNs are a distinctly American phenomenon and are likely to remain so. The primary benefits they bring to the U.S. markets—anonymity, finer trading increments,[45] disintermediation, low commissions, and faster executions—are achievable with all of the electronic auction systems operated by exchanges outside of the United States. It is

---

43. NYSE Rule 19c-3 amended Rule 390 so as to restrict it to stocks listed on the Exchange as of April 26, 1979.
44. The traditional dealer market structure of Nasdaq has meant that stocks are traded net of commissions, meaning that commissions are implicitly factored into the price paid by the buyer or received by the seller.
45. At the time of writing, U.S. trading was still largely in fractions rather than decimals. The primary exchanges price in $1/16$ increments, whereas ECNs display orders in increments as fine as $1/256$. In the Nasdaq montage, however, this improvement is rounded away. Therefore one must be a subscriber of an ECN posting finer increments to benefit from them.

their corporate and governance structure that sets them apart from most exchanges, although the latter are increasingly abandoning the traditional mutual structure in favor of that which the ECNs have adopted (see section 7.3). Thus the distinction between an ECN and an exchange is becoming increasingly blurred, a phenomenon that is evidenced by the recent takeover of the Pacific Exchange's equity trading arm by Archipelago, a Nasdaq ECN. Outside of regulatory arbitrage opportunities created by legal distinctions between the two forms of organization, we can expect the economic relevance of the distinction to decline rapidly toward zero.

8.6 The Future of Institutional Trading

To extrapolate from our analysis in chapters 7 and 8, our broad expectations for industry trends are the following:

• continued growth in institutional assets and order sizes;[46]

• continued growth in institutional awareness of trading costs;[47]

• continued decline in nontintermediated electronic trading costs, both in absolute terms and relative to traditional floor and dealer intermediation structures;[48]

• increased direct electronic access to foreign trading systems;

• continued regulatory pressure on traditional dealer market practices;

• continued demutualization of securities exchanges and decline in the control of trading intermediaries over trading system development and direct investor access;

---

46. Sixty percent of CIOs report that their average order size increased by over 15% between 1996 and 1998, and 25% said that it had more than doubled (Schwartz and Steil 2000). Only 5% report a decline. When asked what level of trading skill was required for a new trader on his or her trading desk compared with three years prior, 69% of head equity traders said that it was higher (23% indicated "much higher"), and only 1% said that it was lower. Of the possible reasons suggested in the survey, the highest ranked was "larger order sizes."

47. Schwartz and Steil (2000) found that 27% of institutions surveyed used outside consultants to analyze their trading costs.

48. Schwartz and Steil (2000) found that institutional traders generally expected lower trading costs three years after the survey date, although European and Australian traders were more sanguine than their North American counterparts. Overall, 52% expected their total trading costs to stay roughly the same (within 10% either way), while 42% expected them to be at least 11% lower. Thirty percent of U.S. traders expected lower costs, compared to 83% of Europeans and Australians. Only 3% (two Americans) expected higher costs.

• growing pressure on profit margins of trading intermediaries;

• increased public awareness of soft commission abuses; and

• continued blurring of competitive barriers between exchanges and ECNS, exchanges and brokers, and brokers and institutions.

We explain below how we believe such trends will affect specific features of the marketplace.

8.6.1   Trading Systems

In the absence of distortions created by new regulations forcing market linkages, we can expect considerable consolidation of continuous electronic auction systems—the type operated by virtually all European exchanges and ECNs in the United States. This would be in contrast to the recent proliferation of new ECNs in the United States, which is predominantly a regulation-induced phenomenon. Mergers of exchanges (e.g., Eurex, Nasdaq-AMEX, Euronext, virt-x) and trading systems (e.g., Norex, Eurex-CBOT) will accelerate. This will lead to more securities traded on fewer systems, and enhancement of powerful network externalities for those leading the consolidation process. The trend in Europe over the past several years has been for equity-trading platforms to be adapted to accommodate derivatives and, more recently, fixed income products as well. Concerns over fragmentation will give way to concerns over monopolization, which are likely to be kept relatively muted by the effect of increasing contestability of the trading services industry; the cost of bringing new trading systems to market, and to adapting them quickly to handling alternative securitized products, should continue to decline rapidly.

At the same time, new electronic call market systems—consolidating orders for execution at a single point in time—are likely to increase their market share of trading volume. Systems such as OptiMark and BondConnect are just the first generation of systems capable of processing orders in three or more dimensions. Although they are widely seen as excessively complex in comparison with continuous systems, such perceptions are likely to change as trading cost concerns intensify. As the London experience and more recent Nasdaq experience indicate, dealer capital is likely to become more expensive as the less risky and traditionally more profitable trades are increasingly disintermediated. Institutions will therefore increasingly be compelled to utilize call auction systems for block and portfolio trades as their order sizes continue to grow.

In the longer term, the ability to specify complex contingent orders for computer execution without leaking strategic information to the market should lead to some reconsolidation of the portfolio management and trading process. The two have become radically split over the course of the past decade, as the rapid growth in institutional assets has made it imperative for funds to split investment implementation from investment decision making. However logical the division of labor, it has led to a situation in which few portfolio managers have more than a rudimentary understanding of the trading process or the actual costs associated with immediacy relative to patience. Call auctions reward patience by consolidating liquidity that otherwise dissipates through time, and processing orders in three or more dimensions allows, and encourages, the portfolio manager to specify much more precisely what the hierarchy of objectives is, in terms of ranking potentially executable combinations of trade sizes and execution prices. Currently, soft commission dependency and insufficient knowledge of the relationship between trading systems, trading costs, and investment returns significantly limit portfolio manager demand for changes in trading desk practices.

8.6.2   The Major Players

The economics of trading can be expected to have a significant impact on the characteristics of the dominant institutions. The automation-driven trend toward less intermediated trading will continue to drive down the cost of trade execution, thereby exposing a widening gap between pure trade execution cost and soft commission brokerage. The imputed cost of soft commission services—in particular, research—will therefore continue to rise, as it has been doing; otherwise, soft commissions—and therefore brokerage margins—will be forced down significantly. This will be to the distinct advantage of larger institutions, whose trading volumes afford them higher bargaining leverage on transaction fees, and particularly to funds run by large broker-dealer firms themselves. Such firms can allocate the cost of in-house analyst capabilities across a wide range of investment banking activities, thereby allowing them to eschew soft commission payments to other brokers and to take the fullest advantage of nonintermediated electronic trading structures. The trend does, in fact, appear to be moving toward greater dominance of the fund management business by broker-dealers; seven of the ten best-selling new U.S. mutual funds in 1999 were owned by broker-dealers. If it does, it would begin to reverse a decade-long trend that witnessed brokerage's share of U.S. fund assets decline from 21% to 10%.[49]

8.6.3   Trade Intermediation

The brokerage function, intermediating order transmission from an investor to a trading system operator, is a vestige of the era of floor-based exchanges. Floor-based trading structures require limitations on physical access to the place where transactions take place, thereby necessitating the transmission of nonmember orders to the floor by the exchange's members. Such access restrictions, as we explained in chapter 7, are neither necessary nor, it would appear, commercially sensible for trading system operators utilizing electronic routing and order-matching systems. Therefore it would appear inevitable that the traditional brokerage function will be competed away by trading system operators offering electronic access direct to investors, largely on a transaction rather than "membership fee" basis. This reflects the relentless decline in the marginal cost of adding new users to a trading network toward zero. The intermediary function is likely to be relegated to credit risk guarantees to the trading system operator for investor trades, making the brokerage function much more akin to a traditional banking function. Even this function, however, is likely to be limited as larger institutions choose to become direct members of clearinghouses, thereby disintermediating the credit guarantee function of the broker as well. In the longer term, there will be no logical distinction between sell-side and buy-side[50] broker and institution.

8.6.4   Public Policy

There is considerable confusion about the impact of technology on market competition, and hence great potential for inappropriate

---

49. "Big Brokers Try New Tricks as Competition Rises," *Wall Street Journal*, February 2, 2000.
50. The term "sell-side" denotes those in the industry who sell trading services, the brokers; the term "buy-side" denotes those who buy them, namely, institutional investors.

public policy responses. To extrapolate from SEC publications and official statements, the following assumptions would appear to be driving U.S. policy:

• Technological advance causes trading system proliferation and hence damaging fragmentation of liquidity across market centers.

• Market centers linked by obligatory intermarket trading systems reduce fragmentation.

• All executable orders in the market can and should be obliged to interact with all other executable orders.

• Price transparency is a public good, and can and should therefore be mandated by law.

• Rapidly increasing trading volumes require increasing government scrutiny and control over computer processing capacity of trading system operators.

These assumptions are not self-evidently compelling, either in terms of the way markets actually function or in terms of suggesting mechanisms by which governments can make them function more efficiently.

Technological advance has undoubtedly fueled the development of trading systems, both by reducing development and implementation costs and by increasing processing capacity for more advanced order-matching algorithms. But liquidity in a given security split among identical trading architectures, such as continuous electronic auctions, is rare and tends to be very short-lived. Few U.S. ECNs manufacture their own two-way order flow, but rather access liquidity generated elsewhere through market linkages compelled by government regulation. Therefore it is not surprising that, far from integrating the Nasdaq market, the order-handling rules have fragmented it through ECN proliferation. The effect of the Intermarket Trading System (ITS) in the listed market is similar: The consolidation of the U.S. regional exchanges effectively ceased with its implementation two decades ago.

In a market environment defined by full property rights for the generators of marketable orders, network externality effects will be dominant, and fragmentation within a given architecture will be ephemeral. The market linkages cannot themselves "integrate" the market, as they make visible and accessible only a very limited portion of the limit orders in each market center. In the case of both the

Nasdaq Montage and ITS, only the best bid and offer are available. This is invariably for small size, and therefore of limited interest to institutions. ITS orders are further subjected to a delay of up to two minutes with no guarantee of execution.

Compare such an integration approach with a market-driven one. Private commercial systems in Europe are implementing technology to create "virtual" consolidated limit order books, where there are competing ones, by building proprietary order-routing facilities to each and displaying *all* orders in a given security from whatever marketplace is posting them.[51] A single order can be executed almost instantaneously across multiple exchanges. This is clear evidence of market forces driving the integration of isolated pools of liquidity.

This does not mean that all markets can naturally interface one with another. Differentiated architectures will naturally emerge to cater to different trading strategies, such as block and portfolio trading. Call markets will naturally compete with continuous markets. This type of product differentiation is inevitable when traders have different objectives.

Competing trading architectures imply that executable orders in a security will not always interact without regulatory compulsion. But trader behavior is not exogenous to order interaction rules: obliging block and portfolio traders to split or reveal orders as a means of satisfying limit orders in other markets will naturally drive a portion of their business to more accommodating markets,[52] or otherwise change their trading patterns to avoid undesired results.

The effect is the same with government-mandated trade publication rules. Auction market system operators have a natural incentive to publish trades quickly after execution, as they can generate considerable income selling real-time data to private vendors such as Reuters and Bloomberg. The fact that such data typically account for around 10% of exchange revenue in European markets and 15% at the NYSE indicates that they are manifestly not a public good (otherwise they could not successfully be charged for). The incentive structure is entirely different in dealer markets, where securities firms are committing risk capital to intermediating large trans-

---

51. An example is the RoyalBlue Fidessa-EMMA Trading Platform in the United Kingdom.
52. See section 7.2.2 and Pagano and Steil (1996: 14–15) on Paris-London regulatory arbitrage.

actions. Immediate revelation of large dealer purchases indicates to the market that there is excess supply of the stock at the transaction price; the dealer will be looking to offload this position in the near future. Schwartz and Steil (2000) document just how strong the natural incentive to withhold such information from the market can be: A remarkable 41% of North American institutional traders indicated that their dealers "regularly" or "very frequently" delayed publication of risk trades over $5 million in size, in contravention of publication rules.[53] In Europe, where many major national markets have explicit rules to accommodate delayed publication of block trades, the figure was only 8%.

Finally, market regulators are naturally and justifiably concerned with systemic risk. In this vein, SEC officials have focused increasingly on vetting the transaction processing capacity of exchanges. But this presumes that a competitive market would not itself properly discipline the capacity investment choices exchanges make. This is flawed on at least two important grounds: First, exchanges will lose, and indeed have lost, significant trading volumes to competitor exchanges when they suffer computer processing failures. OM Stockholm Exchange became a major competitor to Helsinki Exchanges in Nokia trading only after a one-off Helsinki computer failure forced trading to Stockholm. U.S. online brokers routinely suffer large order flow losses and share price declines when their Internet systems go down. Their executives report system outages as being among their greatest competitive fears.[54] Second, the complex computerized transaction-handling systems necessary to integrate floor exchanges, or dealer markets with ECNs, are inherently much more prone to failure than are simple order-matching systems.[55] They will therefore require massive backup capacity, the optimal level of which is well beyond the ability of regulators to determine. The frequency of Nasdaq system failures is testimony to the dangers of trying to link

---

53. The exact question was as follows: "When you trade a large block of shares (over $5 million) directly with a dealer, how often does the dealer 'stop' ('work' or 'protect') the order—that is, guarantee a price that he or she will try to improve on, but not print the trade until natural counterparties are found—or otherwise deliberately delay publishing the trade to the market?" The response "regularly" is defined as 50–74% of the time; the response "very frequently" is defined as 75–100% of the time.

54. "Survey of Online Brokerage Executives Finds Outages Remain a Top Worry," *Wall Street Journal*, April 4, 2000.

55. The Island ECN, which accounts for about 10% of Nasdaq transactions, runs on PCs.

new competitors to a designated "primary market"—one that is accountable to the government for its infrastructure management, rather than the market.

It is difficult to conclude that regulatory intervention on market structure issues is either necessary or beneficial in the increasingly contestable marketplace that advances in computerization and tele-communications have wrought. The lack of such intervention at a pan-European level has facilitated the enormous improvements in market efficiency and integration that have marked the past decade.

Thorny fiduciary issues in institutional trading remain with regard to explicit and implicit soft commission brokerage. These should be of concern not only in terms of their direct impact on client invest-ment returns, but also in terms of their indirect impact via the dis-tortionary effect on market structure development. Widespread failure to unbundle execution costs from the cost of other brokerage services results in orders being diverted from more to less efficient trading venues, and therefore inflates trading costs across the entire market. As we have discussed, the opacity of these arrangements makes them very difficult to stamp out. Institutional trustees have the means to elicit reasonable levels of disclosure on the soft com-mission activities of their money managers, but individual mutual and pension fund holders are clearly at a major disadvantage in this regard. Beyond robust prosecution of patent soft commission abuses, regulators can best encourage the demise of the practice by facilitat-ing the continued demutualization of exchanges and, with it, con-tinued disintermediation of trading. Direct institutional access to trading systems reduces pure execution costs significantly, and thereby adds pressure on brokers to repackage and price explicitly services that are unrelated to execution.

Glossary

ABO (accumulated benefit obligation): Liability of a defined benefit pension fund if it were to be wound up immediately.

Active management: Discretionary approach that seeks to identify and purchase misvalued securities, with the implicit assumption that the market is inefficient and that not all relevant information is present in securities prices.

Actuarial assumptions: Assumptions made by actuaries in assessing the funding status of a defined benefit pension fund or the solvency of a life insurance company.

Actuarial fairness: Concept in insurance implying that the expected present value of benefits (on a given set of actuarial assumptions) equals the present value of contributions.

Adverse selection: Situation in which a pricing policy induces a low average quality of sellers in a market, while asymmetric information prevents the buyer from distinguishing quality.

Agency costs: Costs arising from the deviation between the agent's and principal's interests in an agency relationship. Includes both the costs to the principal of the behavior of the agent and any expenditures incurred to control the agent, such as monitoring expenditures by the principal and bonding expenditures by the agent.

Agency relationship: Contract under which one or more persons (principals) engage another (the agent) to perform some service on their behalf that involves delegation of some decision-making responsibility to the agent.

AIMR: U.S. Association of Investment Management and Research.

Alternative investments: Assets whose returns are orthogonal/uncorrelated to those of the market and hence improve diversification (art, venture capital, hedge funds, etc.).

Alternative Trading System: See **Electronic communications network**.

Anglo-Saxon countries: English-speaking advanced countries with developed capital markets as well as banks (United States, United Kingdom, Canada, Australia).

Annuity: Form of financial contract, usually offered by insurance companies, which provides a given income at a regular interval from retirement till death; usually backed by long-term bonds; can be flat-rate or inflation-indexed.

Asset allocation: Long-term strategic allocation of an entire portfolio across different instruments such as bonds and equities (see also **Security selection**).

Asset-liability management: A quantitative technique used to help structure asset portfolios in relation to the maturity structure of liabilities. Often employs a **liability-immunizing portfolio**.

Asset management: The process whereby assets collected by institutional investors are actually invested in the capital markets.

ATS: Acronym for alternative trading system. See **Electronic communications network** for definition.

Auction market: Also frequently termed an agency auction market. Term applied to markets in which investor buy and sell orders interact directly. Contrast with a **dealer market**, in which an intermediary buys from one investor and sells to another. Auction markets can be floor-based, with a **specialist** intervening selectively to buy or sell when investor orders are lacking, or wholly automated, with buy and sell orders routed electronically and matched by computer. Auction markets can operate continuously, or periodically (see **Call market**).

Balanced manager: Asset manager who undertakes both asset allocation and stock selection on a discretionary basis.

Bancassurance: Combination of banking and insurance business in a single financial conglomerate.

Basis point: $1/100$ of 1%.

Beta coefficient: Showing the correlation of a security's price with the market index.

Bid-offer or ask spread: Term applied to the gap between the best bid and offer (ask) price for a security.

Block trade: A large trade executed in a single transaction. Blocks are formally defined as trades in excess of 10,000 shares on the New York Stock Exchange.

Book reserve scheme: Form of pension scheme in which the employer guarantees certain retirement benefits and sets up provisions on the company balance sheet to cover them.

Book value accounting: System of accounting that values assets at purchase price.

Broker-dealer: A market intermediary, generally a securities firm or wholesale bank, that facilitates trades on behalf of investors. Formally, brokers match customer buy and sell orders without taking proprietary positions themselves, whereas dealers buy from and sell to investors using their own capital and share inventory.

Buy-side: Term applied to institutional investors, or those who buy trading services from broker-dealers (the **sell-side**). "Buy-side" can also refer to the buyer on a given trade.

Call market: Term applied to **auction markets** in which trading takes place periodically, rather than continuously. At regular announced intervals, all buy and sell orders are compared and matched according to a specified algorithm. Call markets can match orders either at a single clearing price or at different prices depending on the conditions attached to the various orders. Call markets can be fully automated or operated by a human intermediary (such as a **specialist**, at the morning opening of the New York Stock Exchange). Call markets can either determine clearing prices themselves (these are known as call auctions) or simply match buy and sell orders according to a price determined in another market (these are known as **crossing systems** or crossing networks).

CALPERS: California Public Employees Retirement System.

Capital adequacy: Regulatory requirement for banks to maintain a certain ratio of shareholders' funds to assets.

CD (certificate of deposit): A negotiable certificate issued by a bank as evidence of an interest-bearing time deposit.

Closed-end fund: Mutual fund offering liquidity to holders via ability to trade shares on exchanges (U.K.: Investment Trust).

Commission: Fee paid by an investor to an intermediary, such as a **broker-dealer**, for executing a trade on an exchange or other trading system.

Commission recapture: Arrangement between an institutional client and a money manager whereby the former negotiates for a portion of all trading commissions paid by the latter to a specific broker to be rebated by the broker directly to the client's funds. (See also **Directed brokerage**.)

Commitment: Informal, long-term, two-way, largely exclusive relationship between borrower and lender, hence "relationship banking." (Compare **Control**.)

Complete markets: Theoretical construct providing a full set of markets covering all present and future contingencies.

Contestable market: Technically, a market with costless entry and exit as the primary defining conditions. Contestable markets impose competitive pricing discipline on incumbents, even where they operate as monopolists, owing to the potential for quick, profitable entry by new competitors.

Continuation strategy: Approach to active management that attempts to exploit a presumed positive serial correlation in asset prices.

Contrarian strategy: Approach to active management that attempts to profit from a presumed negative serial correlation or mean reversion in asset prices.

Control: Exclusive focus on the formal provisions of the debt contract in any transaction, hence transactions banking (compare **Commitment**).

Core-satellite approach: Method of wholesale asset management whereby the bulk of a portfolio is indexed (the core) while the remainder is invested by a variety of active managers (satellites).

Corporate governance mechanisms: Means whereby providers of external finance to a company (especially equity finance) ensure that management is not acting contrary to their interests.

Corporate governance movement: Describes strategy of institutional investors, notably in the United States, to exert direct leverage on management of firms in which they invest to improve profitability.

Covenant: Restriction on the behavior of the borrower agreed at the time of issue of a debt instrument, breach of which allows the lender to claim default (often called an indenture).

Coverage: Proportion of the working population covered by pension plans.

CP (commercial paper): A short-term unsecured and generally marketable promise to repay a fixed amount (representing borrowed funds plus interest) on a certain future date and at a specific place. Usually issued by financial or nonfinancial companies.

Credit rationing: Process whereby provision of debt to a given borrower is limited.

Credit risk: Risk that the borrower will fail to repay interest or principal on debt at the appointed time. Used interchangeably with "default risk."

Cross-holdings: Corporations holding shares in each other. Usually undertaken to cement business relationships rather than for corporate governance purposes.

Crossing system: A **call market** in which the price at which buyers and sellers trade is determined in another market.

Dealer market: Term applied to markets in which a trading intermediary, a dealer, buys from and sells to investors using its own capital and inventory of securities (as contrasted with an **auction market**).

Default: Failure of the borrower to comply with the terms of the debt contract (breach of covenants, failure to repay principal, failure to pay interest).

Defined benefit pension scheme: Pension scheme in which the benefits are defined in advance by the sponsor, independently of the contributions and asset returns.

Defined contribution pension scheme: Pension scheme in which only contributions are fixed and benefits therefore depend solely on the returns on the assets of the fund.

Demutualization: Term applied to the process of separating ownership of a securities exchange from membership and expanding ownership to non-members.

Dependency ratios: (Old age) ratio of persons over the retirement age to those of working age. (Total) ratio of those over retirement age and below school leaving age to the population of working age.

Deposit insurance: Provision of a guarantee that certain types of bank liability are convertible into cash.

Direct financing: Provision of external finance from saver to end-user via securities markets rather than banks.

Directed brokerage: Arrangement between an institutional client of a money manager or investment advisor whereby the latter is obliged to execute a certain percentage of trading transactions with a broker designated by the client. The client then generally receives a rebate from the broker of a portion of the commissions paid (see **Commission recapture**).

Disintermediation: Diversion of funds that are usually intermediated into direct finance. May be used more narrowly to imply any shift away from banks to other intermediaries.

Duration: Average time to an asset's discounted cash flows.

Dynamic hedging: Investment strategy that aims to replicate the payoff of a call option, thus protecting the value of a portfolio from shortfall risk while maintaining upside potential. Can be performed by using continuous adjustment in long and short exposures.

ECN: See **Electronic communications network**.

Effective spread: A measure of the size of the gap between the best bid and offer (ask) price for a security based on actual transaction prices, thereby accounting for transactions that take place within the **quoted spread**.

Efficient market: A market in which prices continually and instantaneously reflect all available information.

Electronic communications network: Term applied particularly to electronic trading and order-routing systems used in the Nasdaq market, but more widely to electronic systems owned and operated outside the traditional member-based stock exchanges.

Emerging market: Stock market in less developed country.

EPF (employee pension fund): Japanese pension fund for large firms that are able to contract out of earnings-related social security.

ERISA (Employee Retirement Income Security Act): U.S. pension law of 1974 that defined fiduciary responsibilities, set minimum funding standards and vesting rules, and set up benefit insurance scheme.

Euro area (euro zone): Subset of European Union countries that adopted a Single Currency, the euro, on January 1, 1999. The euro area (euro zone) comprises Austria, Belgium, Finland, France, Germany, Ireland, Italy, Luxembourg, the Netherlands, Portugal, and Spain.

EU-11: See **Euro area**.

EU-15: Countries of the European Union, comprising the euro area plus Denmark, Greece, Sweden, and the United Kingdom.

Exchange rate risk: Risk that the domestic currency value of foreign assets will vary as a consequence of exchange rate adjustment.

Execution: Term applied to a completed buy or sell transaction in a security.

Execution cost: Term applied to the cost of trading, which comprises both **explicit cost** (fees and commissions) and **implicit cost** (primarily **market impact**).

Exit: An approach to corporate governance in which shareholders seek to sell underperforming shares in the market or to takeover raiders (compare **Voice**).

Expected return: Gain from holding a financial claim net of expected loss from default risk, etc.

Explicit cost: Term applied to the most visible components of trading cost, specifically trading fees and brokerage commissions.

External finance: Finance that is not generated by the agent itself, which may be either debt or equity.

External management: Fund management conducted by a company other than the institutional investor itself.

Fertility rate: The number of children born to an average woman over her lifetime in a given country at a given time.

Fiduciary: An individual having power, control, management, or disposition with regard to institutional assets, who is responsible to the ultimate beneficiaries for their safekeeping.

Final salary/final average plan: Defined benefit pension plan in which the benefit is based on earnings at or near retirement.

Financial crisis: Major collapse of the financial system, entailing inability to provide payments services or to allocate capital; realization of systemic risk.

Financial fragility: A state of balance sheets that offers heightened vulnerability to default in a wide variety of circumstances. Used to refer largely to difficulties of households, companies, and individual banks as opposed to the financial system as a whole (see systemic risk).

Financial innovation: The invention and marketing of new financial instruments that repackage risk or return streams.

Financial intermediation ratio: Proportion of the total of financial claims in an economy that are held by financial intermediaries.

Floating-rate note: A medium-term security carrying a floating rate of interest that is reset at regular intervals in relation to some predetermined reference rate.

Floor auction: An **auction market** operated on a trading floor, usually with some form of **specialist** responsible for each security.

Flow of funds balance sheets: Statistical tables showing aggregate financial claims in an economy, broken down by sector and instrument.

Forward rate agreement: An agreement between two parties that wish to protect themselves from interest rate risk. They agree on an interest rate for a specified period from a given future settlement date for an agreed principal amount. The parties' exposure is the interest rate difference between the agreed and actual rate at settlement.

401(k) plan: U.S. employer-sponsored defined contribution pension plan that enables employees to make tax-deferred contributions from their salaries to the plan.

FRA: See **Forward rate agreement**.

Free cash flow: Cash that the company does not require for operations or profitable investment.

Free rider problem: Tendency for a party to an agreement or transaction to take advantage of others' compliance, which reduces the incentives for others to comply; for example, in securities markets, disincentive to gather information about a company, owing to the ability of other investors to take advantage of it at no cost to themselves.

FRN: See **Floating-rate note**.

Front-running: Term applied to an intermediary trading ahead of a customer trading order, thereby benefiting the intermediary at the customer's expense. The action is illegal in many markets.

Fund family: Group of mutual funds under the same ownership, between which switches are permitted at low or zero cost.

Fund management: See **Asset management**.

Fund of funds: A mutual fund that invests solely in other mutual funds.

Fund supermarket: Single point of sale for a large number of nonproprietary mutual funds, usually offering discounts on standard commission rates.

Funded pension scheme: A scheme in which pension commitments are covered by real or financial assets.

Futures contract: An exchange-traded contract generally calling for delivery of a specified amount of a particular grade of commodity or financial instrument at a fixed date in the future.

Gearing: Debt as a proportion of balance-sheet totals (used interchangeably with "leverage").

Generic asset management sector: Comprises managers undertaking strictly quantitative and nondiscretionary strategies such as management of index funds, immunization, and annuities.

GIC: See **Guaranteed investment contract**.

GIPS: Global investment performance standard, a global standard for performance measurement.

Global portfolio: Portfolio comprising proportionate holdings of each security market according to its weight in global market capitalization. Minimizes risk for a given return if markets are globally efficient.

Greenmail: Repurchase of stock by a company from a potential takeover raider at an unfavorable price to forestall an actual bid.

Gross capital flows: Flows in one direction only, into or out of a country or market.

Growth strategy: Form of continuation strategy in which investors seek to profit from an overreaction of the market to past performance.

Guaranteed investment contract: A contract offered by an insurance company that guarantees a rate of return on the investment for a given period.

Hedge fund: A form of mutual fund that is usually private and unadvertised, offering high risk and high return investment for wealthy individuals.

Hedging: Taking an offsetting position in one security to reduce risk on another, for example taking a position in futures equal and opposite to a cash position. A perfect hedge removes nondiversifiable/systematic risk.

Herding: Mimetic behavior on the part of asset managers, which may generate market instability.

Holding period return: Return on an asset including capital gains or losses over a given time period (holding period).

Home asset preference: Feature of investment portfolios that hold more assets in the home country than the global portfolio would indicate.

IBO (indexed benefit obligation): Liability of a defined benefit pension fund that indexes retirement pensions to prices or wages.

Illiquidity: Inability to transact rapidly in financial claims at full market value.

Immaturity: An immature pension fund has more workers relative to pensioners than it will in long-run equilibrium.

Immediacy: Term applied to the immediate execution of an investor's trading order, generally involving only a single trade and frequently requiring the intermediary to use its own capital or share inventory to facilitate the trade.

Immunization: Construction and maintenance of a portfolio of assets of the same duration as liabilities so that both are subject to offsetting changes in value.

Implicit cost: Term applied to the less visible components of trading cost, including the **spread, market impact**, and **opportunity cost**.

Incomplete contracts: Debt contracts that do not specify behavior of the borrower in all possible contingencies.

Index fund: Fund that seeks to reproduce or replicate the behavior of a market index.

Indexation: (Inflation) Rule that payments arising from a financial contract be increased in line with prices or wages. (Portfolio) Holding of all the securities in a market in line with their relative capitalization, or a subset whose combined risks and expected returns approximate those of the market index. (Global) Holding of assets in all securities markets proportionate to their global capitalization weights.

Indexed bond: A bond whose return is tied to an index, such as consumer prices.

Information leakage: In securities trading, refers to information regarding an investor's identity, orders, or intentions that leaks into the market via intermediaries and moves prices to the investor's detriment.

Inside spread: The gap between the best publicly quoted bid and offer (ask) price for a security. Contrast with the **effective spread**.

Insider: A party to a transaction having relevant information that is not available to the other party.

Insolvency: The state of a balance sheet in which liabilities exceed assets (compare **Illiquidity**).

Institutional intermediation ratio: The proportion of intermediated claims in an economy that are held by institutional investors.

Institutional investors: Specialized financial intermediaries that manage funds collectively on behalf of small investors toward a specific objective in terms of acceptable risk, return maximization, and maturity. Institutional investors include pension funds, mutual funds, and life insurance companies.

Institutionalization: The process whereby institutional investors become dominant in terms of capital market activity, household saving, and corporate financing.

"Instividualization":   (1) The tendency for institutional saving to increasingly come under the direct control of the household sector in respect of asset allocation and (2) the tendency for investment risk to be borne directly by the household sector rather than by a corporate pension fund sponsor or life insurance company.

Interest-rate risk: Risk arising from changes in value of financial claims caused by variations in the overall level of interest rates.

Intermediation: The process whereby end-providers and end-users of financial claims transact via a financial institution, rather than directly via a market. In securities trading, refers to execution of an investor's trade with the assistance of an intermediary, such as a **broker-dealer**.

Internal finance: Finance generated within the borrower: retentions and depreciation.

Internal management: Fund management conducted under the auspices of the sponsor.

Investment Services Directive (ISD):   European Union directive, transposed into national law in all the member states, concerning the conduct and regulation of cross-border investment business, including securities trading. The ISD assigns primary authority for the regulation of most such business to the state in which the relevant firm or exchange is legally domiciled (the home state).

Investment trust: British name for a closed-end mutual fund.

IRA (Individual Retirement Account):   Form of personal defined contribution pension in the United States.

ISA: Individual Savings Account, a form of personal saving in the United Kingdom whereby asset returns are free of tax.

ISD: See **Investment Services Directive**.

Junk bonds: High-yielding bonds that are below investment grade and are at times used in corporate takeovers and buyouts.

LBO: See **Leveraged buyout**.

LDCs: Less developed countries.

Lender of last resort: An institution, usually the central bank, that has the ability to produce at its discretion liquidity to offset public desires to shift into cash in a crisis, to produce funds to support institutions facing liquidity difficulties, and to delay legal insolvency of an institution, preventing fire sales, and calling of loans.

Leverage: Debt as a proportion of the total balance sheet (used interchangeably with "gearing").

Leveraged buyout: Corporate acquisition through stock purchases financed by the issuance of debt (which may include junk bonds).

Liabilities: Cash outlays made at a specific time to meet the contractual terms of an obligation issued by an institutional investor.

Liability-immunizing portfolio: Asset allocation strategy wherein the assets are selected in such a way that their risk, return, and duration characteristics match those of liabilities. This protects the portfolio against risks of variation in interest rates, real earnings growth, and inflation in the pension liabilities. Often a component of **asset-liability management**.

Life cycle: Pattern of saving, borrowing, and consumption over a person's lifetime; life-cycle hypothesis is of borrowing in young adulthood, repayment and saving in middle age, and dissaving in old age.

Life insurance company: Financial institution specialized in contracts offering guaranteed payments to individuals at the time of death.

Limit order: An order to buy (sell) a security when available at a specified price or lower (higher).

Limited liability: A feature of corporations whereby equity holders cannot be held liable for losses in excess of the value of their investment.

Limit-order book: An electronic listing of orders to buy and sell a given security at different prices.

Liquid assets: Assets that are easily transformed into cash (i.e., having liquidity).

Liquidation: Encashment of a position or claim; in bankruptcy, sale of a defaulting borrower's assets and distribution to creditors.

Liquidity: The liquidity of a market is proxied by a number of variables, in particular by (1) the width of the **bid-offer spread**; (2) the depth of the market, or the volume of securities that can be traded at prevailing bid and offer prices; (3) **immediacy**, or the time required to complete a transaction; and (4) the resiliency of the market, or the time required for prices to return to the level prevailing before a large trade (see **Market impact**).

Liquidity constraint: Limits on borrowing preventing individuals from reaching desired level of consumption; in the context of life cycle, preventing attainment of life cycle optimum.

Liquidity risk: Risk of illiquidity of a claim as defined above.

Listed stocks: In the United States, refers to stocks listed on the officially recognized exchanges (the New York Stock Exchange, the American Stock Exchange, and the regional exchanges—i.e., not Nasdaq).

Managerial approach: An industrial organization concept that addresses the implications of the ability of firms in oligopolistic situations to deviate from short-term profit maximization.

Market impact: Also called **price impact**. Refers to the impact of trading a security on its market price. In general, placing a market order to buy (sell) stock will induce a temporary premium (discount) in the stock's price that is reversed over time—to the detriment of the buyer (seller).

Market liquidity risk: Risk that the liquidity of a market may diminish sharply.

Market maker: A dealer with affirmative trading obligations, generally requiring the dealer to buy and sell a given security, up to a specified maximum amount, at bid and offer prices to which the dealer is precommitted.

Market order: An order to buy or sell a security at the prevailing market price.

Market risk: Risk that the value of marketable securities will change while the investor is holding a position in them. Sometimes used more narrowly to indicate systematic risk that cannot be eliminated by diversification.

Market timing: Attempt on the part of investors to buy at troughs and sell at peaks in market prices.

Market value accounting: A system of accounting that values assets at current market prices.

Matching: A special case of immunization in which the assets are chosen so that their cash flows precisely replicate those of the liabilities.

Maturity: (1) The time between issuance and repayment of principal on a debt instrument. (2) A mature pension fund has a long-term equilibrium ratio of workers to pensioners.

Mean-variance approach: An approach to asset allocation wherein portfolio choices are based solely on the average return of the portfolio and its volatility.

Minimum funding regulations: Rules to ensure that a satisfactory relationship between assets and liabilities is maintained in defined benefit funds or life insurance portfolios.

Momentum strategy: See **Continuation strategy**.

Money market mutual fund: A mutual fund that invests solely in money market instruments (such as CDs, CP, and short-term bonds), which generally seeks to maintain a fixed nominal value of one dollar per unit. Often usable similarly to bank deposits with, for example, checking facilities.

Money markets: Wholesale markets for short-term, low-risk investments.

Monitoring: Close observation of actions of agents by principals after funds have been committed to agents, to ensure that agents are acting in their interests (see **Agency costs**). Applications include both institution-asset manager and lender-borrower relations (compare **Screening**).

Monopolistic competition: Industrial organization concept for a market in which atomistic firms sell somewhat differentiated products but are unable to make monopoly profits.

Moral hazard: Incentive of beneficiary of a fixed-value contract, in the presence of asymmetric information and incomplete contracts, to change their behavior after the contract has been agreed in order to maximize their wealth, to the detriment of the provider of the contract.

Mutual fund: Managed and pooled investment fund whose shares are sold to retail investors (U.K.: unit trust or investment trust).

Net capital flows: Balance of inflows to a country and outflows from it.

Net worth: Assets less debt, also called "net assets."

New paradigm: Anticipated shift of U.S. wholesale asset management toward large firms that offer balanced as well as specialized management.

Noise traders: Transacters in securities markets that do not act on the basis of information about appropriate market prices.

Nonintermediated trading: Trading without the assistance of a **broker-dealer**, generally through the use of an electronic trading system.

OECD (Organization for Economic Cooperation and Development): Club of the richest industrialized countries.

Open-end fund: Mutual fund offering liquidity to holders via direct redemption of holdings (U.K.: unit trust).

Opportunity cost: The cost associated with incompletely filled or delayed trading orders.

Option: The contractual right, but not the obligation, to buy or sell a specified amount of a given financial instrument at a fixed price before or at a designated future date. A *call option* confers on the holder the right to buy the financial instrument. A *put option* involves the right to sell the financial instrument.

Order: An instruction to buy or sell a security.

Order-driven market: See **Auction market**.

Order-matching system: A trading system that automatically executes qualifying buy and sell orders, also called a continuous electronic **auction market**.

Order-routing system: An electronic system that routes orders directly from investors to broker-dealers or a trading mechanism.

OTC: Acronym for "over the counter," referring to Nasdaq stocks in the United States.

Overlay strategy: Transactions in derivatives (such as purchase and sale of index futures) that seek to change a position without any transaction in the underlying, thus avoiding disturbance of long-term portfolios. Such strategies facilitate unbundling of fund management into currency, market, and industry exposure and allow the institution to control risk precisely.

Passive management: Nondiscretionary, rule-based approach to asset management involving holding of securities without seeking to profit from trading them; usually associated with portfolio indexation. It assumes that the market is efficient and hence returns are maximized by holding the market.

Pay-as-you-go: Form of pension scheme wherein contributions of employers and employees are relied on to pay pensions directly.

PBO (projected benefit obligation): Liability of a defined benefit pension fund assuming continuation of the fund and hence allowing for future wage rises for employees that will increase their accrued benefits.

Pension fund: Assets accumulated to pay retirement obligations. For defined contributions, it is the same as the plan (see below), for defined benefits, it is the means to back up or collateralize the employer's promises set out in the plan.

Pension plan: Contract setting out the rights and obligations of members and sponsor in an occupational pension scheme.

PEP: Personal equity plan, a form of personal saving in the United Kingdom in which asset returns are free from tax (now replaced by **ISAs**).

Perfect capital market: Theoretical construct featuring complete contracts (see above), perfect information to all parties, no costs of default and ability of all agents to borrow freely at the going rate against their wealth, including future wage income.

Performance measurement: Evaluation of returns and risks on a portfolio relative to a market, an absolute benchmark or comparable portfolios.

Personal pension: Individual defined contribution pension contract, usually arranged with a life insurance company.

Portfolio effect: Increase in the spread over risk free on a given debt security when issuance increases to induce investors to hold a larger share of their portfolio in this form. May be difficult to distinguish from a credit quality or liquidity effect.

Portfolio indexation: See **Indexation**.

Portfolio insurance: Method of computer-aided trading in equities that seeks to protect the value of a portfolio against declines in the market by means of transactions in stock index futures.

Portfolio management: See **Asset management**.

Portfolio Manager: Professional employed by a fund management firm to select the securities to be held by a given fund or group of funds.

Position: Holdings of financial instruments, whether in positive amounts (long position) or negative amounts (short position). Hence position risk: risks arising from such holdings, which are usually market/interest-rate risk but may also include liquidity risk or credit risk.

Preferencing: The practice of giving a trading order to a preferred dealer, who is then expected to match or improve on the best quoted price in the market.

Price impact: See **Market impact**.

Primary market: Market in which financial claims are issued (compare **Secondary market**).

Principal-agent problem: See **Agency relationship** and **Agency costs**.

Private placement: Issue of securities offered to one or a few investors rather than the public; not registered; usually very illiquid.

Program trading: Term applied to types of computer-aided transaction strategies in securities markets.

Proprietary trading system: See **Electronic communications network**.

Prudent man rule: Obligation of asset managers to invest as a prudent investor would on his own behalf (in particular, with appropriate diversification).

PTS: Acronym for "proprietary trading system," now commonly referred to, particularly in the United States, as **electronic communications network**.

Quote matching: Term applied to a dealer offering to match the best quoted bid or offer price for a given security.

Quoted spread: The gap between the quoted bid and offer (ask) price for a security. Contrast with the **effective spread**.

Rational expectations: Hypothesis that investors and other agents in the economy act in the light of all the available information, including knowledge of underlying patterns of behavior in markets.

Real return: Return on an asset less actual inflation (ex post real return) or expected inflation (ex ante real return).

Realized spread: Also called the realized half-spread, the term refers to the difference between the **effective spread** and decreases in asset value following sells and increases in asset value following buys. The latter measure, sometimes called **market impact** (or price impact), reflects the market's assessment of private information conveyed by the trade. The realized spread may also be interpreted as a measure of the reversal from the trade price to posttrade economic value.

Relationship banking: See **Commitment**.

Remote access: Trading on a given stock exchange via direct electronic off-site connection.

Remote membership: In the European Union, the term refers to membership of a stock exchange in a given member state without having any office or other form of physical presence in that member state. Remote membership necessarily implies **remote access**, but not vice versa.

Replacement ratio: The ratio of pension to earnings at the point of retirement.

Reserve funding: See **Book reserve scheme**.

Retail asset management sector: Comprises institutions managing mutual funds and personal pensions.

Risk: The danger that a certain contingency will occur; often applied to future events that are susceptible to being reduced to objective probabilities (compare **Uncertainty**).

Risk premium: Expected additional return for making a riskier investment.

Risk pricing: The degree to which price of an instrument reflects the risks involved, allowing for diversification.

Run: Rapid withdrawal of short-term funds from a borrower (e.g., a bank), which exhausts its liquidity and leaves some lenders unable to realize their claims.

Screening: Evaluation of the quality of agents by principals before funds have been committed to agents, to ensure that agents will act in their interests (see **Agency costs**). Applications include both institution-asset manager and lender-borrower relations (Compare **Monitoring**).

SEC (Securities and Exchange Commission): The U.S. securities market regulator.

Secondary market: The market in which primary claims can be traded.

Securities investment trust: Japanese name for mutual funds.

Securitization: (1) The process by which traditional intermediated debt instruments, such as loans or mortgages, are converted into negotiable securities. (2) The development of markets for a variety of negotiable instruments, which replace bank loans as a means of borrowing. Used in the latter sense, the term often suggests disintermediation of the banking system, as investors and borrowers bypass banks and transact business directly or via institutional investors.

Security selection: The choice of specific claims within a given instrument category, such as equities of a particular company (see **Asset allocation**).

Sell-side: Term applied to broker-dealers, or those who sell trading services to institutional investors (the **buy-side**). "Sell-side" can also refer to the seller on a given trade.

Shareholder activism: See **Corporate governance movement**.

Short-termism hypothesis: The suggestion that the behavior of shareholders, notably willingness to sell out to takeover raiders, induces a preference for short-run returns on the part of corporate management, which may be contrary to overall profitability and economic efficiency.

Shortfall risk: The risk that assets covering guaranteed claims, as in a defined benefit pension fund or insurance contract, do not cover the liabilities.

Size indicator: The sum of financial claims in an economy as a proportion of GDP.

Soft commissions: Commission payments from institutional investors to **broker-dealers** that comprise compensation for services, generally research-related, that are not associated with the execution of a given trade. Institutions with soft commission arrangements agree to pay a minimum annual sum in trading commissions to a given broker in exchange for ongoing company research and other services.

Soft dollars: See **Soft commissions**.

Specialist manager: A discretionary asset manager who focuses on a single instrument or strategy; undertakes only security selection, not asset allocation.

Specialist: An intermediary assigned to facilitate trading in a given stock, generally with negative and affirmative trading obligations designed to delimit the scope of his or her intervention. New York Stock Exchange specialists participate as buyer or seller in roughly one-quarter of trades.

Spread: The difference between the yields on two securities, such as between risky and risk-free debt. Also used for the difference between bid and offer price offered by a market maker.

Spread: See **Bid-offer spread**.

Stock index arbitrage: The simultaneous purchase and sale of futures and underlying stocks to make a risk-free profit from any differences in pricing between them.

Strategic asset allocation: See **Asset allocation**.

Strategic competition: Industrial organization concept for a form of industrial behavior in which firms carry out policies aimed to induce competitors to make a choice that is more favorable to the strategic mover than would otherwise be the case.

Structure-conduct-performance model: An approach to industrial organization that assumes that the profitability of the industry and its pricing policy can be understood in terms of structural features such as market concentration, product differentiation, ease of entry, and elasticity of demand for the product.

Style analysis: The attempt by active asset managers to define precisely their approach to investment (e.g., type of security and approach to active management) and adhere to it.

Sunk costs: Costs incurred by a new entrant to a product market that cannot be recovered on exit.

Surplus: Excess of assets over guaranteed liabilities in a defined benefit pension fund or life insurance portfolio.

Survival bias: Inaccurate estimation of a financial return or verification of a hypothesis owing to the exclusive focus on the markets, institutions, or instruments that survived throughout the evaluation period, ignoring those that failed or closed down.

Swap: A financial transaction in which two counterparties agree to exchange streams of payments over time according to a predetermined rule; normally used to transform the market exposure associated with a loan or bond from one interest rate base (fixed-term or floating-rate) or currency of denomination to another; hence interest rate swaps and currency swaps.

Systematic risk: Risk that cannot be eliminated by portfolio diversification.

Systemic risk: The danger that disturbances in financial markets and institutions will generalize across the financial system so as to disrupt the provision of payment services and the allocation of capital.

Tactical asset allocation: Short-term adjustment to the asset allocation in response to profit opportunities.

Term policy: A life insurance policy that offers a certain sum in the case of death during the period of the contract and otherwise no return.

Total return: Holding period return.

TQPP (tax-qualified pension plan): Japanese fund for smaller firms that are unable to contract out of social security.

Transaction cost: In securities trading, refers to the costs of execution transactions (see **Execution cost**).

Transactions banking: See **Control**.

Trust: Basis of private pension law and organization of certain mutual funds in the Anglo-Saxon countries. Trustees are appointed to act "in the best interests of beneficiaries" under common law.

UCITS directive: A European Union law that permits mutual fund business to be carried out across the Union under sole regulation by the home authority, except for disclosure and selling, which remain a host country matter.

Uncertainty: A term applied to expectations of a future event to which probability analysis cannot be applied (financial crises, wars, etc.).

Underperformance: A shortfall in asset returns and risks relative to a given benchmark.

Underwriter: An institution that provides a guarantee of a certain price to an issuer of a security; it may also manage and sell the issue, but these functions are separable.

Unit trust: British name for an open-end mutual fund.

Unsystematic risk: Idiosyncratic risk on securities or other financial claims that can be eliminated by appropriate diversification.

Upstairs trading: In an **auction market**, refers to trades—generally large **block trades**—arranged away from the trading floor or central trading system.

Value strategy: A form of contrarian strategy that involves the purchase of securities that have low market prices relative to fundamental measures of value.

Variable life policy: A term life insurance policy that includes a non-guaranteed saving element.

Voice: An approach to corporate governance in which investors seek to influence managers directly (compare **Exit**).

VWAP (volume-weighted average price):   The daily VWAP for a given security is frequently used as benchmark against which to measure trading performance.

Whole-life policy: A term life insurance policy that includes a guaranteed saving element.

Wholesale asset management sector: Comprises managers of company pension funds and other external managers.

Wholesale markets: Financial markets used by professional investors for instruments or transactions that have a large minimum denomination.

Window dressing: Deliberate adjustment of a portfolio at the time of an external evaluation to show performance in a falsely favorable light.

Yield: The current rate of return on a security (for an irredeemable instrument, coupon as a proportion of market price; for a dated security, also takes into account investor's capital gain or loss over the period to maturity).

Yield gap: The difference between yields on securities; generally refers to spread between equities and bonds.

References

Aaron, H. J. 1966. The social insurance paradox. *Canadian Journal of Economic and Political Science*, 32, 371–77.

Ackermann, C., R. McEnally, and D. Ravenscraft. 1999. The performance of hedge funds; risk, return and incentives. *Journal of Finance*, 54, 833–74.

Ackert, L. F., and B. F. Smith. 1993. Stock price volatility, ordinary dividends and other cash flows to shareholders. *Journal of Finance*, 48, 1147–60.

Aitken, B. 1996. *Have institutional investors destabilized emerging markets?* Working Paper WP/96/34. Washington, D.C.: International Monetary Fund.

Allen, F., and D. Gale. 1995. A welfare comparison of the German and U.S. financial systems. *European Economic Review*, 39, 179–209.

Allen, F., and D. Gale. 1997. Financial markets, intermediaries and intertemporal smoothing. *Journal of Political Economy*, 105, 523–46.

Allen, F., and A. M. Santomero. 1999. What do financial intermediaries do? Working Paper No. 99-30-B. Philadelphia: Financial Institutions Center, The Wharton School, University of Pennsylvania.

Ambachtsheer, K. 1988. Integrating business planning with pension fund planning. In *Asset allocation: A handbook*, ed. R. Arnott and F. Fabozzi. Chicago: Probus.

Ambachtsheer, K., and D. Ezra. 1998. Pension fund excellence. New York: Wiley.

Amihud, Y., H. Mendelson, and R. A. Wood. 1990. Liquidity and the 1987 stock market crash. *Journal of Portfolio Management*, 16, 65–69.

Anderson, R. W., and P. Tychon. 1993. *Competition among European financial markets: The case of Belgian cross-listed stocks*. Discussion Paper 9314. Lovain, Belgium: Département des Sciences Economiques, Université Catholique de Louvain.

Arnold, T., P. Hersch, J. H. Mulherin, and J. Netter. 1999. Merging markets. *Journal of Finance*, 54(3), 1083–1107.

Attanasio, O., and T. De Leire. 1994. *IRAs and household savings revisited: some new evidence*. Working Paper No. 4900. Cambridge, Mass.: National Bureau of Economic Research.

AUTIF. 1998. *Unit trust information service market research survey and report*. Association of Unit Trusts and Investment Funds Research Report, January.

Baggiolini, E. 1996. Struttura e competizione nei mercati mobiliari europei: Analisi di efficienza tra i diversi sistemi di trading. Graduate thesis, Università di Pavia, Pavia, Italy.

Bajtelsmit, V. L., and J. L. VanDerhei. 1997. Risk aversion and pension investment choices. In *Positioning pensions for the twenty-first century*, ed. M. S. Gordon, O. S. Mitchell, and M. M. Twinney. Philadelphia: Pension Research Council, University of Pennsylvania Press.

Bank of England. 1999. *Financial Stability Review, November 1999*. London: Bank of England.

Bank of England. 2000. *Financial Stability Review, June 2000*. London: Bank of England.

Banks, J., R. Blundell, and A. Dilnot. 1994. Tax-based savings incentives in the UK. Paper delivered to the conference on International Comparisons of Household Savings, 19 May, OECD, Paris.

Basel Committee. 1999. *Sound practices for banks interactions with highly leveraged institutions*. Basel: Basel Committee on Banking Supervision, Bank for International Settlements.

Bateman, H., and J. Piggott. 1993. *Australia's mandated retirement income scheme: An economic perspective*. Retirement Income Perspectives: two papers prepared for the office of EPAC, July.

Baumol, W. J., C. J. Panzar, and D. R. Willig. 1988. *Contestable markets and the theory of industry structure*. San Diego: Harcourt Brace Jovanovich.

Beckaert, G., and C. R. Harvey. 1995. Time varying world market integration. *Journal of Finance*, 50, 403–44.

Beckers, S. 1999. Investment implications of a single European capital market. *Journal of Portfolio Management*, Spring, 9–17.

Beebower, G., and G. Bergstrom. 1977. A performance analysis of pension and profit sharing portfolios: 1966–75. *Financial Analysts Journal*, 33 (May/June), 31–42.

Benartzi, S., and R. Thaler. 1995. Myopic loss aversion and the equity premium puzzle. *Quarterly Journal of Economics*, 110, 73–92.

Benos, A., and M. Crouhy. 1996. Changes in the structure and dynamics of European securities markets. *Financial Analysts Journal*, May/June, 37–50.

Berger, A., A. K. Kashyap, and J. M. Scalise. 1995. The transformation of the US banking industry: What a long strange trip it's been. *Brookings Papers*, 2, 55–218.

Berger, A., and G. Udell. 1992. *Securitisation, risk and the liquidity problem in banking*. Working Paper S-92-2. New York: Salomon Center, New York University.

Berglöf, E. 1996. Corporate governance. In *The European equity markets: The state of the union and an agenda for the millennium*, ed. B. Steil. London: European Capital Markets Institute and the Royal Institute of International Affairs.

Berkowitz, S. A., D. E. Logue, and E. A. Noser. 1988. The total cost of transactions on the NYSE. *Journal of Finance*, 43, 97–112.

Berlinski, M. R., and S. Western. 1997. *Perspectives on the United States asset management business*. Paris: Organization for Economic Cooperation and Development.

Bernard, V., and J. Thomas. 1990. Evidence that stock prices do not fully reflect the implications of current earnings for future earnings. *Journal of Accounting and Economics*, December, 13, 305–40.

Bernheim, B. D., and J. K. Scholz. 1992. *Private saving and public policy*. Working Paper No. 4213. Cambridge, Mass.: National Bureau of Economic Research.

Bernheim, B. D., and J. B. Shoven. 1988. Pension funding and saving. In *Pensions in the U.S. economy*, ed. Z. Bodie, J. B. Shoven, and D. A. Wise. Chicago: University of Chicago Press.

Beschloss, A. M., and A. S. Muralidhar. 1997. Managing the risks of implementing a currency overlay. *Journal of Pension Plan Investing*, 1, 79–93.

Bessembinder, H., and M. H. Kaufman. 1996. *Quotations and trading costs on the domestic equity exchanges*. Working Paper. Tempe, Ariz.: Department of Finance, Arizona State University.

Bessembinder, H., and M. H. Kaufman. 1997. A cross-exchange comparison of execution costs and information flow for NYSE-listed stocks. *Journal of Financial Economics*, 46 (December), 293–319.

Bikhchandani, S., D. Hirschleifer, and I. Welch. 1992. A theory of fads, fashions and cultural change in informational cascades. *Journal of Political Economy*, 100, 992–1026.

Bikhchandani, S., and S. Sharma. 2000. *Herd behavior in financial markets: A review*. Working paper WP/00/48. Washington, D.C.: International Monetary Fund.

Bingham, T. R. G. 1992. Securities markets and banking, some regulatory issues. In *Financial innovation*, ed. H. Cavanna. London: Routledge.

BIS. 1986. *Recent innovations in international banking (the Cross Report)*. Basel: Bank for International Settlements.

BIS. 1992. *Recent developments in international interbank relations*. Basel: Bank for International Settlements.

BIS. 1995. *Sixty fifth Annual Report*. Basel: Bank for International Settlements.

BIS. 1998. *Sixty eighth Annual Report*, Chapter V: Asset prices and the asset management industry. Basel: Bank for International Settlements.

Bishop, G. 1998. *Securitizing European saving*. New York: Salomon Smith Barney, 1 December.

Bisignano, J. 1991. European financial deregulation, the pressure for change and the cost of achievement. In *The deregulation of financial intermediaries: Proceedings of a conference*. Sydney, Australia: Reserve Bank of Australia.

Bisignano, J. 1993. The internationalization of financial markets: measurement, benefits and unexpected interdependence. Paper presented at the XIIIeme Colloque Banque de France-Université, Paris, November.

Bisignano, J. 1995. Paradigms for understanding changes in financial structure: Instruments, institutions, markets and flows. Paper presented to a conference on Structural Change and Turbulence in International Financial Markets, 9–10 November, Geneva.

Bishop, G. 1999. The euro's fourth quarter: completing a successful first year in the bond market. No. 7 of a series *Delivering the benefits of EMU*. London: Schroder Salomon Smith Barney.

Black, F. 1971. Towards a fully-automated exchange, Part I. *Financial Analysts Journal*, 27, 29–34.

Black, F. 1980. The tax consequences of long-run pension policy. *Financial Analysts Journal*, September–October, 17–23.

Blake, D. 1995. *Pension funds and pension schemes in the United Kingdom*. Oxford, England: Oxford University Press.

Blake, D. 1997. *Pension funds and capital markets*. Discussion Paper PI-9706. London: The Pensions Institute, Birkbeck College.

Blake, D. 1999. Portfolio choice models of pension funds and life assurance companies, similarities and differences. *Geneva Papers on Risk and Insurance*, 24, 327–57.

Blake, D. 2000a. Two decades of pension reform in the UK—What are the implications for occupational pension schemes? *Employee Relations*, 22, 223–45. Discussion Paper PI-2004. London: The Pensions Institute, Birkbeck College.

Blake, D. 2000b. Does it matter what pension scheme you have? *Economic Journal*, 110, F45–F81.

Blake, D., B. Lehmann, and A. Timmermann. 1997. *Performance measurement using multiple asset class portfolio data: A study of UK pension funds*. Discussion Paper PI-9704. London: The Pensions Institute, Birkbeck College.

Blake, D., B. Lehmann, and A. Timmermann. 1998. *Performance clustering and incentives for the UK pension fund industry*. LSE Financial Markets Group Discussion Paper No. 294, London School of Economics.

Blake, D., B. Lehmann, and A. Timmermann. 1999. Asset allocation dynamics and pension fund performance. *Journal of Business*, 72, 1999, 429–62.

Blake, D., and A. Timmermann. 1999. The hazards of mutual fund underperformance: A Cox regression analysis. *Journal of Empirical Finance*, 6, 121–52.

Blanchard, O. J. 1993. The vanishing equity premium. In *Finance and the International Economy* 7, ed. R. O'Brien. Oxford, U.K.: Oxford University Press.

Blommestein, H. J. 1996. Structural changes in financial markets: Overview of trends and prospects. In *The new financial landscape*. Paris: Organization for Economic Cooperation and Development.

Blommestein, H. J., and K. Biltoft. 1996. Trends, structural changes and prospects in OECD capital markets. In *The new financial landscape*. Paris: Organization for Economic Cooperation and Development.

Blommestein, H. J., and M. G. Spencer. 1996. Sound finance and the wealth of nations. *North American Journal of Economics and Finance*, 7, 115–24.

Blume, L., D. Easley, and M. O'Hara. 1994. Market statistics and technical analysis: The role of volume. *Journal of Finance*, 49(1), 153–81.

Blume, M., and M. Goldstein. 1997. Quotes, Order Flow, and Price Discovery. *Journal of Finance*, 52(1), 221–44.

Bodie, Z. 1990a. Pension funds and financial innovation. *Financial Management*, Autumn, 11–21.

Bodie, Z. 1990b. Pensions as retirement income insurance. *Journal of Economic Literature*, 28, 28–49.

Bodie, Z. 1991. Shortfall risk and pension fund asset management. *Financial Analysts Journal*, 48 (May/June).

Bodie, Z, 1995. On the risk of stocks in the long run. *Financial Analysts Journal*, 52 (March/April), 67–68.

Bodie, Z., and D. B. Crane. 1997. Personal investing: Advice, theory and evidence. *Financial Analysts Journal*, November/December, 13–23.

Bodie, Z., and E. P. Davis, eds. 2000. *The foundations of pension finance*. Edward Elgar.

Bodie, Z., A. Kane, and A. J. Marcus. 1999. *Investments*. Homewood, Ill.: Irwin.

Bodie, Z., R. C. Merton, and W. Samuelson. 1992. Labor supply flexibility and portfolio choice in a life cycle model. *Journal of Economic Dynamics and Control*, 16, 403–426.

Bodie, Z., and O. S. Mitchell. 1996. Pension security in an aging world. In *Securing employer-based pensions: An international perspective*, ed. Z. Bodie, O. S. Mitchell, and J. A. Turner. Philadelphia: University of Pennsylvania, Wharton School, Pension Research Council; Philadelphia: University of Pennsylvania Press.

Bodie, Z., J. B. Shoven, and D. A. Wise. (eds.). 1987. *Issues in pension economics*. National Bureau of Economic Research Project Report series. Chicago: University of Chicago Press.

Bogle, J. C. 1992. Selecting equity mutual funds. *Journal of Portfolio Management*, 18, 94–100.

Bogle, J. C. 1998. The implications of style analysis for mutual fund performance evaluation. *Journal of Portfolio Management*, Summer, 34–42.

Bollerslev, T., and I. Domowitz. 1991. Price volatility, spread variability, and the role of alternative market mechanisms. *Review of Futures Markets*, 10, 78–102.

Bolt, W., and M. Peeters. 1998. Corporate governance in the Netherlands. In *Corporate governance, financial markets and global convergence*, ed. M. Balling, E. Hennessy, and R. O'Brien. Dordrecht: Kluwer.

Booth, P. M., and Y. Yakoubov. 2000. Investment policy for defined contribution pension schemes close to retirement: An analysis of the "lifestyle" concept. *North American Actuarial Journal*, 4(2), 1–19.

Booth, T., and J. Wrighton. 1999. Down but not out. *Institutional Investor*, July, 45–50.

Borio, C. V., L. Chincarini, and K. Tsatsaronis. 1997. Institutional investors, asset management and financial markets. Mimeo. Basel: Bank for International Settlements.

Börsch-Supan, A. 1996. The impact of population aging on savings, investment and growth in the OECD area. In *Future global capital shortages—real threat or pure fiction?* Paris: Organization for Economic Cooperation and Development.

Bos, E. 1994. *World population projections 1994–95*. Washington, D.C.: The World Bank.

Boyd, J. H., and M. Gertler. 1994. *Are banks dead? Or are the reports greatly exaggerated?* Working Paper No. 531. Minneapolis: Federal Reserve Bank of Minneapolis.

Brennan, M. J., and B. Solnik. 1989. International risk-sharing and capital mobility. *Journal of International Money and Finance*, 8, 359–73.

Brinson, G. L., L. Randolph Hood, and G. Beebower. 1986. Determinants of portfolio performance. *Financial Analysts Journal*, 43 (August/September), 39–44.

British Invisibles. 1997. *City business series 1997—Fund management*. London: British Invisibles.

British Invisibles. 2000. *City business series 2000–statistical update, fund management*. London: British Invisibles.

Broby, D. 1997. *The changing face of European fund management*. London: FT Financial Publishing.

Brown, K. C., W. V. Harlow, and L. T. Starks. 1996. Of tournaments and temptations: An analysis of managerial incentives in the mutual fund industry. *Journal of Finance*, 51, 85–110.

Brown, S. J., and W. Goetzmann. 1995. Performance persistence. *Journal of Finance*, 50, 678–98.

Brown, S. J., and W. Goetzmann. 1997. Mutual fund styles. *Journal of Financial Economics*.

Brown, S. J., W. Goetzmann, and R. G. Ibbotson. 1997. *Offshore hedge funds, performance and survival 1989–95*. Working Paper No. 5909. Cambridge, Mass.: National Bureau of Economic Research.

Browne, F. X., and J. Fell. 1994. *Inflation: dormant, dying or dead?* Technical Paper No. 6/RT/94. Central Bank of Ireland, Dublin.

Buckberg, E. 1996. *Institutional investors and asset pricing in emerging markets*. Working Paper WP/96/2. Washington, D.C.: International Monetary Fund.

Burt, T. 1999. Daimler switches funds. *Financial Times*, December 15.

Calian, S. 1998. France's MATIF begins to trade contracts on gilts. *Wall Street Journal*, 15 July, C17.

Capel, J. 1995. Major themes within the UK fund management industry. James Capel UK equity research, July 1995.

Caprio, G., and A. Demirgüç-Kunt. 1998. The role of long term finance: theory and evidence. *World Bank Research Observer*, 13, 171–89.

Carey, M. S., S. D. Prowse, and J. D. Rea. 1993. Recent developments in the market for privately placed debt. *Federal Reserve Bulletin*, February, 77–92.

Carhart, M. 1997. On persistence in mutual fund performance. *Journal of Finance*, 52, 57–82.

Cartapanis, A. 1993. Le role déstabilisant des mouvements de capitaux sur le marché des changes: une question de contexte. Paper presented at the XIIIeme Colloque Banque de France-Université, Paris, November.

CFTC. 1977. *Proceedings of the CFTC Conference on Automation in the Futures Industry.* Washington, D.C.: Commodity Futures Trading Commission.

Chan, L. K. C., N. Jagadeesh, and J. Lakonishok. 1996. Momentum strategies. *Journal of Finance*, 51, 1681–1713.

Chan, L. K. C., and J. Lakonishok. 1993. Institutional trades and intraday stock price behavior. *Journal of Financial Economics*, 33, 173–99.

Chan, L. K. C., and J. Lakonishok. 1995. The behavior of stock prices around institutional trades. *Journal of Finance*, 50, 1147–74.

Chan, L. K. C., and J. Lakonishok. 1997. Institutional equity trading costs: NYSE versus Nasdaq. *Journal of Finance*, 52, 713–35.

Cheetham, C. 1990. Using futures in asset management. *The Treasurer*, September, 14–18.

Chevalier, J. A., and G. D. Ellison. 1995. *Risk taking by mutual funds as a response to incentives.* Working Paper No. 5234. Cambridge, Mass.: National Bureau of Economic Research.

Chevalier, J. A., and G. D. Ellison. 1999a. Are some mutual fund managers better than others? Cross sectional patterns of behavior and performance. *Journal of Finance*, 54, 875–99.

Chevalier, J. A., and G. D. Ellison. 1999b. Career concerns of mutual fund managers. *Quarterly Journal of Economics*, 114.

Chordia, T. 1996. The structure of mutual fund charges. *Journal of Financial Economics*, 41, 3–39.

Christie, W., J. Harris, and P. Schultz. 1994. Why did NASDAQ market makers avoid odd-eighth quotes? *Journal of Finance*, 49, 1841–60.

Christie, W. G., and P. H. Schultz. 1994. Why do NASDAQ market makers avoid odd-eighth quotes? *Journal of Finance*, 49(4), 1813–40.

Cifuentes, R., and S. Valdes Prieto. 1997. Pension reforms in the presence of credit constraints. In *The economics of pensions*, ed. S. Valdes-Prieto. Cambridge, England: Cambridge University Press.

Clark, G. L. 2000a. *Pension fund capitalism.* Oxford, England: Oxford University Press.

Clark, G. L. 2000b. *European pensions (Dutch), social solidarity and competition policy.* Working Paper in Geography No. WPG 03-00. Oxford, England: Oxford University.

Clark, R. L. 1994. The impact of market access and investment restrictions on Japanese pension funds. Special Report SR-26. Washington, D.C.: Employee Benefit Research Institute.

Clyde, P. 1997. Do institutional shareholders police management? *Managerial and Decision Economics*, 18, 1–10.

Coffee, J. 1991. Liquidity versus control, the institutional investor as corporate monitor. *Columbia Law Review*, 91, 1277–1368.

Coggin, D., F. Fabozzi, and S. Rahman. 1993. The investment performance of US equity pension fund managers. *Journal of Finance*, 48, 1038–57.

Collins, S., and P. Mack. 1997. The optimal amount of assets under management in the mutual fund industry. *Financial Analysts Journal*, 53 (September/October), 67–73.

Conference Board. 1999. *Institutional investment report, financial assets and equity holdings*. New York: The Conference Board.

Conrad, J. S., K. M. Johnson, and S. Wahal. 1999. Institutional Trading and Soft Dollars. University of North Carolina at Chapel Hill Working Paper, Chapel Hill, N.C.

Cooper, W. 1998. High on junk. *Institutional Investor*, June, 57–62.

Coppejans, M., and I. Domowitz. 1996. *Liquidity-corrected variance ratios and the effect of foreign equity ownership on information in an Emerging Market*. Working Paper. Evanston, Ill.: Economics Department, Northwestern University.

Coppejans, M., and I. Domowitz. 1997. *The performance of an automated trading system in an illiquid environment*. Working Paper. Evanston, Ill.: Economics Department, Northwestern University.

Cornell, B., and R. Roll. 1981. Strategies for pairwise competitions in markets and organisations. *Bell Journal of Economics*, 12, 201–3.

Corsetti, G., and K. Schmidt-Hebbel. 1997. Pension reform and growth. In *The economics of pensions*, ed. S. Valdes-Prieto. Cambridge, England: Cambridge University Press.

Council of Institutional Investors. 1999. *It's your money: What pension fund officials should know about soft dollars, directed brokerage and commission recapture*. Washington, D.C.: Council of Institutional Investors.

Cutler, D., J. Poterba, and L. Summers. 1990a. Speculative dynamics and the role of feedback traders. *American Economic Review*, 80 (Papers and Proceedings), 63–68.

Cutler, D., J. Poterba, L. Sheiner, and L. Summers. 1990b. An aging society, opportunity or challenge? *Brookings Papers on Economic Activity*, 1, 1–56.

Dailey, L., and J. Motala. 1992. Foreign investments of pension funds in six countries. In *Background papers to report on international capital flows*. Washington D.C.: International Monetary Fund.

Daniel, K., M. Grinblatt, S. Titman, and R. Wermers. 1997. Measuring mutual fund performance with characteristic based benchmarks. *Journal of Finance*, 52, 1035–58.

D'Arista, J. W., and T. Schlesinger. 1993. *The parallel banking system*. Briefing Paper. Washington, D.C.: Economic Policy Institute.

Davidson, W. N., and D. Dutia. 1989. A note on the behavior of security returns: a test of stock market overreaction and efficiency. *Journal of Financial Research*, 12, 245–52.

Davis, E. P. 1986. *Portfolio behavior of the non-financial private sectors in the major economies*. Economic Paper No. 17. Basel: Bank for International Settlements.

Davis, E. P. 1988. *Financial market activity of life insurance companies and pension funds*. Economic Paper No. 21, Basel: Bank for International Settlements.

Davis, E. P. 1993a. The development of pension funds, an approaching financial revolution for Continental Europe. In *Finance and the international economy 7 (winners of the*

1993 Amex bank essay competition), ed. R. O'Brien. Oxford, England: Oxford University Press.

Davis, E. P. 1993b. Whither corporate-banking relations? In *The future of UK industrial competitiveness*, ed. K. Hughes. London: Policy Studies Institute.

Davis, E. P. 1993c. The UK fund management industry. *The Business Economist*, 24(2), 36–49.

Davis, E. P. 1994a. Market liquidity risk. In *The competitiveness of financial institutions and centers in Europe*, ed. D. Fair and R. Raymond. Dordrecht, The Netherlands: Kluwer Academic Publishers.

Davis, E. P. 1994b. Banking, corporate finance and monetary policy: an empirical perspective. *Oxford Review of Economic Policy*, 10(4), 49–67.

Davis, E. P. 1995a. *Pension funds, retirement-income security and capital markets—an international perspective*. Oxford, England: Oxford University Press.

Davis, E. P. 1995b. *Debt, financial fragility and systemic risk*, revised and extended version. Oxford, England: Oxford University Press.

Davis, E. P. 1995c. Institutional investors, unstable financial markets and monetary policy. In *Risk management in volatile financial markets*, ed. F. Bruni, D. Fair, and R. O'Brien. Dordrecht, The Netherlands: Kluwer.

Davis, E. P. 1995d. Financial fragility in the early 1990s: What can be learnt from international experience? Special Paper No. 76. LSE Financial Markets Group, London School of Economics.

Davis, E. P. 1995e. An international comparison of the financing of occupational pensions. In *Securing employer provided pensions: an international perspective*, ed. Z. Bodie, O. Mitchell, and J. Turner, Philadelphia: University of Pennsylvania Press (also Special Paper No. 62, Financial Markets Group, LSE).

Davis, E. P. 1996a. The role of institutional investors in the evolution of financial structure and behavior. In *The future of the financial system*, Proceedings of a conference held at the Reserve Bank of Australia, RBA, Sydney, and LSE Financial Markets Group Special Paper No. 89.

Davis, E. P. 1996b. Pension fund investments. In *The European equity markets: The state of the union and an agenda for the millennium*, ed. B. Steil. London: European Capital Markets Institute and the Royal Institute of International Affairs.

Davis, E. P. 1996c. *International experience of pension reform and its application to the Netherlands*. Working Paper No. 11. London: Pensions Institute, Birkbeck College.

Davis, E. P. 1997a. *Public pensions, pension reform and fiscal policy*. Staff Paper No. 5. Frankfurt: European Monetary Institute.

Davis, E. P. 1997b. *Private pensions in OECD countries: the United Kingdom*. Labor Market and Social Policy Occasional Paper No. 21. Paris: Organization for Economic Cooperation and Development.

Davis, E. P. 1997c. Population aging and retirement income provision in the European Union. In *Aging societies, the global dimension*, ed. B. Bosworth and G. Burtless. Washington D.C.: Brookings Institution Press (also Special Paper, Royal Institute of International Affairs, London).

Davis, E. P. 1998a. Regulation of pension fund assets. In *Institutional investors in the new financial landscape*, ed. H. Blommestein and N. Funke. Paris: Organization for Economic Cooperation and Development.

Davis, E. P. 1998b. Policy and implementation issues in reforming pension systems. Working Paper No. 31. London: European Bank for Reconstruction and Development.

Davis, E. P. 1998c. Pensions in the corporate sector. In *Redesigning social security*, ed. H. Siebert, Kiel, Germany: Kiel Institute for World Economics.

Davis, E. P. 1998d. *Pension fund reform and European financial markets—a reappraisal of potential effects in the wake of EMU*. Special Paper No. 107. LSE Financial Markets Group, London School of Economics.

Davis, E. P. 1998e. *Linkages between pension reform and financial sector development*. Discussion Paper No. PI-9909. London: The Pensions Institute, Birkbeck College.

Davis, E. P. 1998f. *Investment of mandatory funded pension schemes*. Discussion Paper No. PI-9908. London: The Pensions Institute, Birkbeck College, and in *Funding of Social Security Pensions*, ed. J. Turner and D. Latulippe. Geneva: International Labor Office.

Davis, E. P. 1998g. European pensions, "fundamental" influences and the role of Economic and Monetary Union. *Journal of Pension Fund Management and Marketing*, 3, 206–37.

Davis, E. P. 1999a. EMU and financial structure. In *Financial Market Trends*. Paris: Organization for Economic Cooperation and Development.

Davis, E. P. 1999b. Institutionalization and EMU: implications for European financial markets. *International Finance*, 2, 33–61.

Davis, E. P. 1999c. *Financial data needs for macroprudential surveillance—What are the key indicators of risk to domestic financial stability?*, Handbooks in Central Banking, Lecture Series No. 2. London: Center for Central Banking Studies, Bank of England.

Davis, E. P. 1999d. Russia/LTCM and market liquidity risk. *The Financial Regulator*, 4(2), 23–28.

Davis, E. P. 2000a. *Pension funds, financial intermediation and the new financial landscape*. Working Paper No. PI-2010. London: The Pensions Institute, Birkbeck College. Forthcoming in *Kredit und Kapital*.

Davis, E. P. 2000b. *Regulation of private pensions: A case study of the UK*. Working Paper No. PI-2009. London: The Pensions Institute, Birkbeck College. Forthcoming in *Revue d'Economic Financiere*.

Davis, E. P. 2000c. Portfolio Regulation of Life Insurance Companies and Pension Funds, paper presented at the XI ASSAL/OECD Conference on Insurance Regulation and Supervision in Latin America, Oaxaca, Mexico, 4–8 September 2000. Discussion Paper No. PI-0101, London: The Pensions Institute, Birkbeck College.

Davis, E. P., and G. Fagan. 1997. Are financial spreads good predictors of growth and inflation in EU countries? *Journal of Applied Econometrics*.

Davis, E. P., and A. R. Latter. 1989. London as an international financial centre. *Bank of England Quarterly Bulletin*, 29, 516–28.

Davis, E. P., and C. P. Mayer. 1991. Corporate finance in the euromarkets and the economics of intermediation. Discussion Paper No. 570. London: Centre for Economic Policy Research.

Davis, E. P., and S. Salo. 1998. *Excess capacity in EU and US banking sectors—Conceptual, measurement and policy issues.* Special Paper No. 105. LSE Financial Markets Group, London School of Economics.

Davis, S. I. 1997. Global institutional fund management: key drivers and trends. In *Institutional investors in the new financial landscape.* Paris: Organization for Economic Cooperation and Development.

Daykin, C. 1995. Occupational pension provision in the United Kingdom. In *Securing employer-based pensions, an international perspective,* Ed. Z. Bodie, O. S. Mitchell, and J. Turner. Philadelphia: University of Pennsylvania Press.

De Bondt, W., and R. Thaler. 1985. Does the stock market overreact? *Journal of Finance,* 40, 793–805.

De Bondt, W., and R. Thaler. 1994. *Financial decision making in markets and firms: A behavioral perspective.* Working Paper No. 4777. Cambridge, Mass.: National Bureau of Economic Research.

De Grauwe, P. 1989. *International money: Postwar trends and theories.* Oxford: Clarendon Press.

Del Guercio, D. 1996. The distorting effects of the prudent-man laws on institutional equity investments. *Journal of Financial Economics,* 40, 31–62.

Del Guercio, D., and J. Hawkins. 1999. The motivation and impact of pension fund activism. *Journal of Financial Economics,* 52, 293–340.

DeLong, J. B., A. Shleifer, L. Summers, and R. Waldman. 1990. Positive feedback investment strategies and destabilizing rational speculation. *Journal of Finance,* 45, 379–95.

Demirgüç-Kunt, A., and R. Levine. 1996. Stock market development and financial intermediaries: stylized facts. *World Bank Economic Review,* 10, 291–321.

Demirgüç-Kunt, A., and V. Maksimovic. 1996. Stock market development and firm financing choices. *World Bank Economic Review,* 10, 341–69.

Dermine, J. 1996. European banking with a single currency. *Financial Markets, Institutions and Instruments,* 5, 63–101.

Dermine, J. 1999. European capital markets: Does the euro matter? In *European capital markets with a single currency,* ed. J. Dermine and P. Hillion. Oxford: Oxford University Press.

Dermine, J., and L. H. Röller. 1992. Economies of scale and scope in French mutual funds. *Journal of Financial Intermediation,* 2, 83–93.

De Ryck, K. 1997. *EMU and pension funds.* Brussels: European Federation for Retirement Provision.

Deutsche Bundesbank. 1996. Financial market volatility and its implications for monetary policy. *Deutsche Bundesbank Monthly Review,* April, 10–20.

Devenow, A., and I. Welch. 1998. Rational herding in financial economics. *European Economic Review*, 40, 603–15.

Diamond, D. 1984. Financial intermediation and delegated monitoring. *Review of Economic Studies*, 51, 393–414.

Diamond, D. 1991. Monitoring and reputation: The choice between bank loans and directly placed debt. *Journal of Political Economy*, 99, 401–19.

Diamond, D., and P. Dybvig. 1983. Bank runs, deposit insurance, and liquidity. *Journal of Political Economy*, June, 401–19.

DiBartolomeo, D., and E. Witkowski. 1997. Mutual fund misclassification: evidence based on style analysis. *Financial Analysts Journal*, September/October, 32–43.

Dickinson, G. M. 1992. Prospects for the ECU and the impact of EMU on private pensions. In *The future of pensions in the European community*, ed. J. Mortensen. Published by Brasseys for the Centre for European Policy Studies.

Dickinson, G. M. 1998. Issues in the effective regulation of the asset allocation of life insurance companies. In *Institutional investors in the new financial landscape*, ed. H. Blommestein and N. Funke. Paris: Organization for Economic Cooperation and Development.

Dilnot, A., and P. Johnson. 1993. *The taxation of private pensions*. London: Institute for Fiscal Studies.

Domowitz, I. 1995. Electronic derivatives exchanges: Implicit mergers, network externalities, and standardization. *Quarterly Review of Economics and Finance*, 35(1), 163–75.

Domowitz, I., J. Glen, and A. Madhavan. 1997. Market segmentation and stock prices: Evidence from an emerging market. *Journal of Finance*, 52(3), 1059–85.

Domowitz, I., J. Glen, and A. Madhavan. 1998. International cross-listing, foreign ownership restrictions, and order flow migration: Evidence from Mexico. *Journal of Finance*, 53(6), 2001–27.

Domowitz, I., J. Glen, and A. Madhavan. 2000. *Liquidity, volatility and equity trading costs across countries and over time*. Working Paper. University Park, Pennsylvania: Pennsylvania State University.

Domowitz, I., and B. Steil. 1999. Automation, trading costs, and the structure of the securities trading industry. *Brookings-Wharton Papers on Financial Services*, 33–92.

Dutto, P. K. 1997. Competition and collusion in dealer markets. *Journal of Finance*, 52, 245–77.

Eaglesham, J. 1998. UK backs single market in funds. *Financial Times*, 14 April.

EBRD. 1996. *Transition report 1996*. London: European Bank for Reconstruction and Development.

Economist. 1997. Europe's fund phobia. *The Economist*, 29 March.

Edey, M., and K. Hviding. 1995. *An assessment of financial reform in OECD countries*. Economics Department Working Paper No. 154. Paris: Organization for Economic Cooperation and Development.

Edey, M., and J. Simon. 1996. *Australia's retirement income system: implications for saving and capital markets*. Working Paper No. 5799. Cambridge, Mass.: National Bureau of Economic Research.

Edwards, F. 1995. *Mutual funds and financial stability*. Working Paper PW-95-31. New York: Columbia Business School.

Edwards, F. 1996. *The new finance*. Washington, D.C.: AEI Press.

Edwards, F., and X. Zhang. 1998. *Mutual funds and stock and bond market stability*. Special Paper No. 101. Financial Markets Group, LSE.

Edwards, J., and Fischer, K. 1991. *Banks, finance and investment in Germany since 1970*. Discussion Paper No. 497. London: Center for Economic Policy Research.

Edwards, J., and K. Fischer. 1994. *Banks, finance and investment in Germany*. Cambridge, U.K.: Cambridge University Press.

Edwards, S. 1995. *Why are saving rates so different across countries?* Working Paper No. 5097. Cambridge, Mass.: National Bureau of Economic Research.

Eichengreen, B., and D. Mathieson. 1998. *Hedge funds and market dynamics*. Occasional Paper No. 166. Washington, D.C.: International Monetary Fund.

Eichengreen, B., J. Tobin, and C. Wyplosz. 1995. Two cases for sand in the wheels of international finance. *Economic Journal*, 105, 162–72.

Eichholz, P. M. A. 1996. Does international diversification work better for real estate than for stocks and bonds? *Financial Analysts Journal*, January–February, 56–62.

Elliehausen, G., and J. Wolken. 1990. *Banking markets and the use of financial services by small and medium-sized businesses*. Staff Study 160. Washington, D.C.: Boards of Governors of the Federal Reserve.

Ellis, C. D. 1992. A new paradigm, the evolution of investment management. *Financial Analysts Journal*, 48 (March/April), 16–18.

Elston, J. A. 1993. Firm ownership structure and investment, theory and evidence from German panel data. Mimeo.

Elton, E. J., M. J. Gruber, S. Das, and C. R. Blake. 1996. The persistence of risk adjusted mutual fund performance. *Journal of Business*, 69, 133–57.

Ely, D. P., and K. J. Robinson. 1997. Are stocks a hedge against inflation? International evidence using a long run approach. *Journal of International Money and Finance*, 16, 147–67.

Ennis, R. M. 1997. The structure of the investment management industry, revisiting the new paradigm. *Financial Analysts Journal*, 53 (July/August), 6–13.

Erb, C. B., C. R. Harvey, and T. E. Viskanta. 1997. Demographics and international investment. *Financial Analysts Journal*, 53 (July/August), 14–28.

Estrella, A., and F. S. Mishkin. 1995. *Predicting US recessions: Financial variables as leading indicators*. Working Paper No. 5379. Cambridge, Mass.: National Bureau of Economic Research.

European Central Bank. 2000a. *EU banks' income structure*. Frankfurt: European Central Bank.

European Central Bank 2000b. *The impact of the euro on money and bond markets.* By J. Santillan, M. Bayle, and C. Thygesen, Occasional Paper No. 1. Frankfurt: European Central Bank.

European Commission. 1999. *Supplementary pension schemes.* Commission Communication (11 May 1999). Brussels: Internal Market Directorate General, European Commission.

European Commission. 2000. *Study on pension schemes of the member states of the European Union.* Document MARKT/2005/99-EN Rev2. Brussels: European Commission, Internal Market Directorate General.

Evans, M., and K. K. Lewis. 1993. Trends in excess returns in currency and bond markets. *European Economic Review.*

Faccio, M., and M. A. Lasfer. 2000. Do occupational pension funds monitor companies in which they hold large stakes? *Journal of Corporate Finance,* 6, 71–85.

Falkenstein, E. G. 1996. Preferences for stock characteristics as revealed by mutual fund portfolio holdings. *Journal of Finance,* 51, 111–35.

Fama, E. 1985. What's different about banks? *Journal of Monetary Economics,* 15, 29–39.

Fama, E. 1991. Efficient capital markets II. *Journal of Finance,* 45, 1575–1618.

Fama, E., and K. French. 1996. Multifactor explanations of asset price anomalies. *Journal of Finance,* 51, 55–84.

Farrell, J., and G. Saloner. 1986. Installed base and compatibility: Product preannouncements and predation. *American Economic Review,* 76(5), 940–55.

Feldman, L., and J. Stephenson. 1988. Stay small or get huge—Lessons from securities trading. *Harvard Business Review,* 663, 116–23.

Feldstein, M. 1974. Social security, induced retirement and aggregate capital accumulation. *Journal of Political Economy,* 82, 902–56.

Feldstein, M. 1977. Social security and private saving: International evidence in an extended life cycle model, In *The economics of public services,* ed. M. Feldstein and R. Inman. Paris: International Economic Association.

Feldstein, M. 1978. Do private pensions increase national savings? *Journal of Public Economics,* 10, 277–93.

Feldstein, M. 1995. *Social security and saving, new time series evidence.* Working Paper No. 5054. Cambridge, Mass.: National Bureau of Economic Research.

Feldstein, M., and A. A. Samwick. 1998. The transition path in privatizing social security. In *Privatizing social security,* ed. M. Feldstein. Chicago: University of Chicago Press.

Fell, J. 1996. *The role of short rates and foreign long rates in the determination of long term interest rates.* Staff Paper No. 4. Frankfurt: European Monetary Institute.

Fernald, J. D., F. Keane, and P. C. Mosser. 1994. Mortgage security hedging and the yield curve. *Federal Reserve Bank of New York Quarterly Review,* Summer-Fall, 92–100.

Ferris, S. P., and D. M. Chance. 1987. The effect of 12b-1 plans on mutual fund expense ratios: A note. *Journal of Finance,* 42, 1077–82.

Ferson, W. E., and C. Harvey. 1992. Seasonality in consumption based asset pricing: An analysis of linear models. *Journal of Finance*, 47, 511–52.

Ferson, W. E., and C. Harvey. 1993. Risk and the predictability of international asset returns. *Review of Financial Studies*, 6, 527–66.

Ferson, W. E., and R. W. Schadt. 1996. Measuring fund strategy and performance in changing economic conditions. *Journal of Finance*, 51, 425–60.

Financial Times. 1998. *Financial Times* survey: Pension fund investment. *Financial Times* 14 May.

Financial Times. 1999. *Financial Times* survey: Pension fund investment. *Financial Times* 21 May.

Financial Times. 2000. *Financial Times* survey: Pension fund investment. *Financial Times* 12 May.

Firth, M. 1995. The impact of institutional stockholders and managerial interests on the capital structure of firms. *Managerial and Decision Economics*, 16, 167–75.

FMA. 1999. *Fund managers survey 1999*. London: Fund Managers Association.

Fontaine, J. A. 1997. Are there good macroeconomic reasons for limiting external investments by pension funds? The Chilean experience. In *The economics of pensions*, ed. S. Valdes-Prieto. Cambridge University Press.

Fortune, P. 1993. Stock market crashes: What have we learned from October 1987? *New England Economic Review*, March/April, 3–24.

Fortune, P. 1997. Mutual funds, part I: reshaping the American financial system. *New England Economic Review*, July/August, 45–72.

Fortune, P. 1998. Mutual funds, part II: fund flows and security returns. *New England Economic Review*, Jan./Feb., 4–22.

Franke, G., and D. Hess. 1995. *Anonymous electronic trading versus floor trading*. Discussion Paper 285. Konstanz, Germany: Fakultat für Wirtschaftswissenschaften und Statistik, University of Konstanz.

Frankel, J. A. 1992. Measuring international capital mobility: A review. *American Economic Review*, 82, 197–202.

Frankel, J. A., and S. L. Schmukler. 1996. Country fund discounts and the Mexico crisis of December 1994: Did local investors turn pessimistic before international investors? *Open Economies Review*, 7, 511–34.

Franks, J., and C. P. Mayer. 1989. *Risk, regulation, and investor protection: The case of investment management*. Oxford: Oxford University Press.

French, K., and J. M. Poterba. 1990. Investor diversification and international equity markets. Mimeo. University of Chicago/MIT.

French, K., W. Schwert, and R. Stambaugh. 1987. Expected stock returns and volatility. *Journal of Financial Economics*, 19, 3–29.

Friedman, B. M. 1996. Economic implications of changing share ownership. *Journal of Portfolio Management*, 22, 59–70.

Frijns, J., R. Kleynen, and F. Quix. 1995. Risk management from the perspective of the economic functions of different financial institutions. Paper presented at the 1995 SUERF conference, Thun, Switzerland.

Froot, K. A. 1993. Currency hedging over long horizons. National Bureau of Economic Research Working Paper No. 4355.

Froot, K. A., P. O'Connell, and M. Seasholes. 1999. *The portfolio flows of international investors*. Working Paper, August. Cambridge, Mass.: Harvard Business School.

Froot, K. A., D. S. Scharfstein, and J. C. Stein. 1992. Herd on the street: Informational inefficiencies in a market with short-term speculation. *The Journal of Finance*, 47, 1461–84.

Frost, A. J., and I. J. S. Henderson. 1983. Implications of modern portfolio theory for life insurance companies. In *Modern portfolio theory and financial institutions*, ed. D. Corner and D. G. Mayes. London: Macmillan.

Gale, W. 1997. *The effect of pension wealth: A re-evaluation of theory and evidence*. Washington, D.C.: Brookings Institution.

Gallo, J., G. Lockwood, and L. Joseph. 1995. Determinants of pension funding and asset allocation decisions. *Journal of Financial Services Research*, 9, 143–58.

GAO. 1989. *Private pensions: Portability and preservation of vested pension benefits*. Washington, D.C.: U.S. General Accounting Office.

Garber, P., and M. P. Taylor. 1995. Sand in the wheels of foreign exchange markets: A skeptical note. *Economic Journal*, 105, 173–80.

Gehrig, T. 1993. An information based explanation for the domestic bias in international equity investment. *Scandinavian Journal of Economics*, 95, 97–109.

Genotte, G., and H. Leland. 1990. Market liquidity, hedging and crashes. *American Economic Review*, 80, 999–1021.

George, T., G. Kaul, and M. Nimalendran. 1991. Estimation of the bid-ask spread and its components: A new approach. *Review of Financial Studies*, 4, 623–56.

Gillan, S. L., and L. T. Starks. 1995. *Relationship investing and shareholder activism by institutional investors*. Working Paper. Austin, Texas: University of Texas.

Gilson, S., J. Kose, and L. Lang. 1990. Troubled debt restructurings, *Journal of Financial Economics*, 27, 315–53.

Glosten, L. R., and P. R. Milgrom. 1985. Bid, ask and transactions prices in a specialist market with heterogeneously informed traders. *Journal of Financial Economics*, 14, 71–100.

Goetzmann, W., B. Greenwald, and G. Hubermann. 1992. *Market response to mutual fund performance*. Working Paper. New York: Columbia University.

Goldman Sachs. 1998. *Hedge funds demystified, their potential role in institutional portfolios*. Goldman Sachs and Financial Risk Management Ltd.

Goldman Sachs and Frank Russell. 1999. Report on alternative investing by tax exempt organizations 1999. New York: Goldman Sachs and Frank Russell.

Goldsmith, R. W. 1985. *Comparative national balance sheets: A study of twenty countries, 1688–1978*. Chicago and London: University of Chicago Press.

Golec, J. 1992. Empirical tests of a principal-agent model of the investor-investment advisor relationship. *Journal of Financial and Quantitative Analysis*, 27, 81–96.

Goodfellow, G. P., and S. J. Schieber. 1997. Investment of assets in self directed retirement plans. In *Positioning pensions for the twenty-first century*, ed. M. S. Gordon, O. S. Mitchell, and M. M. Twinney. Philadelphia: Pension Research Council, University of Pennsylvania Press.

Goodhart, C. 1984. *Monetary theory and practice: The UK experience*. London: Macmillan.

Gooptu, S. 1993. *Portfolio investment flows to emerging markets*. Paper WPS 1117. Washington D.C.: World Bank.

Gorton, G., and G. Pennacchi. 1992. Money market funds and finance companies, are they the banks of the future? In *Structural change in banking*, ed. M. Klausner and L. J. White. Business One. Homewood, Ill.: Irwin.

Gorton, G., and F. A. Schmid. 1996. *Universal banking and the performance of German firms*. NBER Working Paper No. 5453.

Graham, G. 1997. Fund managers: Facing a less rosy future. *Financial Times*, 19/7/97.

Greenwich Associates. 1998. *Technology takes over the catbird seat*. April. Greenwich, Conn.: Greenwich Associates.

Greenwich Associates. 1999a. *How funds are coping with uncertain markets*. April. Greenwich, Conn.: Greenwich Associates.

Greenwich Associates. 1999b. *Advances and anomalies in "nontraditional" trading*. A Report to Institutional Investors in the United States. Greenwich, Conn.: Greenwich Associates.

Grier, P., and E. J. Zychowicz. 1994. Institutional investors, corporate discipline and the role of debt. *Journal of Economics and Business*, 46, 1–11.

Grossman, S., and O. Hart. 1980. Takeover bids, the free rider problem and the theory of the corporation. *Bell Journal of Economics*, 11, 42–64.

Grossman, S., and J. E. Stiglitz. 1980. On the impossibility of informationally efficient markets. *American Economic Review*, 70, 393–408.

Gruber, M. J. 1996. Another puzzle, the growth in actively managed mutual funds. *Journal of Finance* 51, 783–810.

Grunbichler, A., F. A. Longstaff, and E. S. Schwartz. 1994. Electronic screen trading and the transmission of information: An empirical examination. *Journal of Financial Intermediation*, 3(1), 166–87.

Grundfest, J. A. 1990. Internationalization of the world's securities markets: Economic causes and regulatory consequences. *Journal of Financial Services Research*, 4, 349–78.

Halpern, P., N. Clakins, and T. Ruggels. 1996. Does the emperor wear clothes or not? The final word, or almost, on the parable of investment management. *Financial Analysts Journal*, 52 (July/August), 9–15.

Halpern, P., and I. I. Fowler. 1991. Investment management fees and the determinants of pricing structure in the industry. *Journal of Portfolio Management*, 17 (Winter), 74–79.

Handa, P., and R. A. Schwartz. 1996. Limit order trading. *Journal of Finance*, 51, 1835–61.

Hannan, T. H. 1991. Bank commercial loan markets and the role of market structure: evidence from surveys of commercial lending. *Journal of Banking and Finance*, 15, 133–49.

Hansell, S. 1992. The new wave in old age pensions. *Institutional Investor*, November, 57–64.

Hargraves, M., G. J. Schinasi, and S. R. Weisbrod. 1993. *Asset price inflation in the 1980s: A flow of funds perspective*. Working Paper No. WP/93/77. Washington, D.C.: International Monetary Fund.

Harris, E., and E. Gurel. 1986. Price and volume effects associated with changes in the S and P 500: New evidence for the existence of price pressures. *Journal of Finance*, 41, 815–29.

Harris, L. E. 1994. Minimum price variations, discrete bid-ask spreads, and quotation sizes. *Review of Financial Studies*, 7 (Spring), 149–78.

Harris, M., and A. Raviv. 1990. Capital structure and the informational role of debt. *Journal of Finance*, 45, 321–50.

Harrison, D. 1997. *Pension provision and fund management in Europe*. London: Financial Times Financial Publishing.

Harvey, C. 1991. The world price of covariance risk. *Journal of Finance*, 46, 111–57.

Haugen, R. 1995. *The new finance: The case against efficient markets*. Englewood Cliffs, N.J.: Prentice-Hall.

Haugen, R. 1997. *The beast on Wall Street*. Cambridge, Mass.: Harvard University Press.

Heller, P., R. Hemming, and P. W. Kohnert. 1986. *Aging and social expenditures in major industrial countries 1980–2025*. Occasional Paper No. 47. Washington D.C.: International Monetary Fund.

Heller, P., and E. Sidgwick. 1987. *Aging, savings and the sustainability of the fiscal burden in the G-7 countries*. Mimeo. Paris: Organization for Economic Cooperation and Development.

Hellwig, M. 1991. Banking, financial intermediation and corporate finance. In *European financial integration*, ed. A. Giovannini and C. P. Mayer. Cambridge, U.K.: Cambridge University Press.

Hendricks, D., J. Patel, and R. Zeckhauser. 1993. Hot hands in mutual funds: Short term persistence in performance 1974–88. *Journal of Finance*, 48, 93–130.

Hepp, S. 1990. *The Swiss pension funds*. Paul-Haupt.

Hepp, S. 1992. Comparison of investment behaviour of pension plans in Europe: Implications for Europe's capital markets. In *The future of pensions in the European community*, ed. J. Mortensen. Published by Brassey's, London, for the Centre for European Policy Studies, Brussels.

Holzmann, R. 1997a. *Pension reform, financial market development and economic growth, preliminary evidence from Chile*. IMF Staff Papers, 44/2.

Holzmann, R. 1997b. On economic benefits and fiscal requirements of moving from unfunded to funded pensions. *European Economy Reports and Studies*, 4, 121–66.

Hoogduin, L. H., and G. H. Huisman, 1998. *The financial structure in the Netherlands and Germany: Different, harmonious and on the move?* Reprint 547. Amsterdam: De Nederlandsche Bank.

Hoshi, T., A. Kashyap, and D. Scharfstein. 1990. The role of banks in reducing the costs of financial distress in Japan. *Journal of Financial Economics*, 27, 67–88.

Hoshi, T., A. Kashyap, and D. Scharfstein. 1991. Corporate structure, liquidity, and investment: Evidence from Japanese industrial groups. *Quarterly Journal of Economics*, 106, 33–60.

Hoshi, T., A. Kashyap, and D. Scharfstein. 1993. *The choice between public and private debt: An analysis of post deregulation corporate financing in Japan.* Working Paper No. 4211. Cambridge, Mass.: National Bureau of Economic Research.

Howell, M., and A. Cozzini. 1990. *International equity flows, 1990 edition.* London: Salomon Brothers.

Howell, M., and A. Cozzini. 1991. *Games without frontiers: Global equity markets in the 1990s.* London: Salomon Brothers.

Howell, M., and A. Cozzini. 1992. *Baring Brothers' Capital Flows 1991/2 Review.* London: Baring Brothers.

Howell, M., and A. Cozzini. 1995. *The financial silk road: Baring Brothers' capital flows 1995 review.* London: Baring Brothers.

HSBC. 1998. *UK fund management: Major themes.* London: Pan European Research Department, HSBC.

Hu, Z. 1995. *Market volatility and corporate investment.* Working Paper WP/95/102. Washington, D.C.: International Monetary Fund.

Huang, R. D., and H. R. Stoll. 1996a. Dealer versus auction markets: A paired comparison of execution costs on NASDAQ and the NYSE. *Journal of Financial Economics*, 41, 313–57.

Huang, R. D., and H. R. Stoll. 1996b. Competitive trading of NYSE listed stocks: Measurement and interpretation of trading costs. *Financial Markets, Institutions, and Instruments*, 5(2), 1–55.

Hubbard, R. G. 1986. Pension wealth and individual saving: Some new evidence. *Journal of Money, Credit and Banking*, 18, 167–78.

Hubbard, R. G. 1994. *Money, the financial system and the economy.* Reading, Mass.: Addison Wesley.

Huiser, A. P. 1990. Capital market effects of the aging population. *European Economic Review*, 34, 987–1009.

Hurley, M. P., S. I. Meers, B. J. Bornstein, and N. R. Strumingher. 1995. *The coming evolution of the investment management industry, opportunities and strategies.* New York: Investment Management Industry Group, Goldman Sachs.

IFMA. 1996. *Fund managers survey 1996.* London: Institutional Fund Managers Association.

IMF. 1991. *International capital markets report*. Washington, D.C.: International Monetary Fund.

IMF. 1993. *International capital markets, Part I: Exchange rate management and international capital flows*. Washington, D.C.: International Monetary Fund.

IMF. 1994. *International capital markets report*. Washington, D.C.: International Monetary Fund.

IMF. 1996. *World economic outlook, May 1996*. Washington, D.C.: International Monetary Fund.

IMF. 1997. European Monetary Union, institutional framework for financial policies and structural implications. In *International Capital Markets Report 1997*. Washington, D.C.: International Monetary Fund.

IMF. 1998. *World economic outlook and international capital markets, interim assessment December 1998—Financial turbulence and the world economy*. Washington, D.C.: International Monetary Fund.

Impenna, C., P. Maggio, and F. Panetta. 1995. *Innovazioni strutturali nel mercato azionario: Gli effetti della contrattazione continua*. Temi di Discussione del Servizio Studi No. 248. Rome: Banca d'Italia.

Institutional Investor. 1996. In-house afire. *Institutional Investor*, April.

Institutional Investor. 1999. Euro 100 cross border express—Europe's largest money managers. *Institutional Investor*, November.

Intersec. 1995. *European external management survey 1995*. Stamford, Conn.: Intersec Consulting.

Investment and Pensions Europe. 1999a. Global investment group driven by pensions assets growth. *Investment and Pensions Europe*, May, 23.

Investment and Pensions Europe. 1999b. UK pension funds steer clear. *Investment and Pensions Europe*, June, 35.

Investment Company Institute. 1995. Mutual fund shareholder response to market disruptions. *Perspective*, 1(1).

Investment Company Institute. 1996. Mutual fund shareholder activity during US stock market cycles 1944–95. *Perspective*, 2(2).

Investment Company Institute. 1998. US emerging market equity funds and the 1997 crisis in Asian financial markets. *Perspective*, 4(2).

Investment Company Institute. 1999a. Mutual funds and the retirement market. *Fundamentals: ICI Research in Brief*, 8(4).

Investment Company Institute. 1999b. *Mutual fund fact book 1999*. Washington, D.C.: Investment Company Institute.

Investment Company Institute. 1999c. 401(k) plan asset allocation, account balances and loan activity. *Perspective*, 5(1).

Investment Company Institute. 1999d. Mutual fund costs 1980–98. *Perspective*, 5(4).

Investment Company Institute. 1999e. Operating expense ratios, assets and economies of scale in equity mutual funds. *Perspective*, 5(5).

Investment Company Institute. 2000. *Mutual fund fact book 2000*. Washington, D.C.: Investment Company Institute.

Investors Chronicle. 1997. Survey: Pension fund management. *Investors Chronicle*, 3 (October), 41–56.

Investors Chronicle. 1998. Survey: Pension fund management. *Investors Chronicle*, 2 (October), 89–106.

Ippolito, R. A., and J. A. Turner. 1987. Turnover fees and pension plan performance. *Financial Analysts' Journal*, November/December, 16–26.

Jagadeesh, N., and S. Titman. 1993. Returns to buying winners and selling losers: Implications for stock market performance. *Journal of Finance*, 48, 65–91.

James, C. 1987. Some evidence on the uniqueness of bank loans. *Journal of Financial Economics*, 19, 217–36.

James, C., and P. Wier. 1990. Borrowing relationships, intermediation and the cost of issuing public securities. *Journal of Financial Economics*, 28, 149–71.

James, K. R. 2000. *The price of retail investing in the UK*. Occasional Paper Series No. 6. London: Financial Services Authority.

Jarrell, G. A. 1984. Change at the exchange: The causes and effects of deregulation. *Journal of Law and Economics*, 27, 273–312.

Jensen, M. C. 1968. The performance of mutual funds in the period 1945–64. *Journal of Finance*, 23, 389–416.

Jensen, M. C. 1986. Agency costs of free cash flow, corporate finance and takeovers. *American Economic Review*, 76, 323–29.

Jensen, M. C. 1993. The modern industrial revolution, exit, and the failure of internal control mechanisms. *Journal of Finance*, 48, 831–80.

Jensen, M. C., and W. Meckling. 1976. Theory of the firm, managerial behavior, agency costs and ownership structure. *Journal of Financial Economics*, 3, 305–60.

John, O. 1999. *Active investment management charges survey*. London: Towers Perrin.

Joines, D. H., and J. G. Manegold. 1995. *IRAs and saving: Evidence from a panel of tax-payers*. Mimeo. Los Angeles: University of Southern California.

Jones, C. M., and M. L. Lipson. 1999. Execution costs of institutional equity orders. *Journal of Financial Intermediation*, 8, 123–40.

Jorion, P., and W. N. Goetzmann. 1999. Global stock markets in the twentieth century. *Journal of Finance*, 54, 953–80.

Kahn, R. N., and A. Rudd. 1995. Does historical performance predict future performance? *Financial Analysts Journal*, 51 (November/December), 43–52.

Kane, E. 1986. Appearance and reality in deposit insurance; the case for reform. *Journal of Banking and Finance*, 10, 175–88.

Kang, J., and R. Stulz. 1995. *Why is there a home bias? An analysis of foreign portfolio equity ownership in Japan.* Working Paper No. 5166. Cambridge, Mass.: National Bureau of Economic Research.

Kaplan, S. 1994. Top executive rewards and firm performance, a comparison of Japan and the United States. *Journal of Political Economy*, 102, 510–46.

Kaplan, S., and J. Stein. 1993. The evolution of buy-out pricing and financial structure in the 1980s. *Quarterly Journal of Economics*, 108, 313–57.

Karpoff, J. M., P. H. Malatesta, and R. A. Walkling. 1996. Corporate governance and shareholder initiatives, empirical evidence. *Journal of Financial Economics*, 42, 365–95.

Katz, M. L., and C. Shapiro. 1986. Technology adoption in the presence of network externalities. *Journal of Political Economy*, 94(3), 822–41.

Katz, M. L., and C. Shapiro. 1992. Product introduction with network externalities. *Journal of Industrial Economics*, 40(1), 55–84.

Katz, M. L., and C. Shapiro. 1994. Systems competition and network effects. *Journal of Economic Perspectives*, 8(1), 93–115.

Kaufman, G., and L. R. Mote. 1994. Is banking a declining industry: A historical perspective. *Economic Perspectives*, Federal Reserve Bank of Chicago, May/June, 4–21.

Keim, D. B, and A. Madhavan. 1996. *Execution costs and investment performance: An empirical analysis of institutional equity trades.* Working Paper. Philadelphia: Rodney L. White Center, Wharton School, University of Pennsylvania.

Keim, D. B., and A. Madhavan. 1997. Transaction costs and investment style: An interexchange analysis of institutional equity trades. *Journal of Financial Economics*, 46, 265–92.

Keim, D. B., and A. Madhavan. 1998. The cost of institutional equity trades. *Financial Analysts Journal*, 54, 50–69.

Kempf, A., and O. Korn. 1996. *Trading system and market integration.* Working Paper 96-2. Mannheim, Germany: Lehrstuhle für Finanzwirtschaft, University of Mannheim.

Kihn, J. 1996. To load or not to load? A study of marketing and distribution charges of mutual funds. *Financial Analysts Journal*, 52 (May/June), 28–36.

King, M. A., and L. Dicks-Mireaux. 1988. Portfolio composition and pension wealth: An econometric study. In *Pensions in the US economy*, ed. Z. Bodie, J. B. Shoven, and D. A. Wise. Chicago: University of Chicago Press.

Kofman, P., and J. T. Moser. 1997. Spreads, information flows, and transparency across trading systems. *Applied Financial Economics*, 7(2), 281–94.

Kohl, R., and P. O'Brien. 1998. The macroeconomics of aging, pensions and savings; a survey. Economics Department Working Paper No. 200. Paris: Organization for Economic Cooperation and Development.

Kohn, M. 1994. *Financial institutions and markets.* New York: McGraw-Hill.

Kotlikoff, L. J. 1996. Privatizing social security; how it works and why it matters. In *Tax policy and the economy*, ed. J. M. Poterba. Cambridge, Mass.: MIT Press.

Kotlikoff, L. J., K. A. Smetters, and J. Walliser. 1998. *Social security: Privatization and progressivity.* Working Paper No. 6428. Cambridge, Mass.: National Bureau of Economic Research.

Kreps, D. 1990. Corporate culture and economic theory. In *Perspectives on positive political economy*, ed. J. Alt and K. Shepsle. Cambridge, Mass.: Cambridge University Press.

Kumar, A., ed. 1997. *The regulation of non-bank financial institutions, the US, the European Union and other countries.* World Bank Discussion Paper No. 362. Washington, D.C.: International Bank for Reconstruction and Development.

Kyle, A. S. 1985. Continuous auctions and insider trading. *Econometrica*, 53(4), 1315–35.

Lakonishok, J., A. Schleifer, and R. W. Vishny. 1991a. *Do institutional investors destabilize share prices? Evidence on herding and feedback trading.* Working Paper No. 3846. Cambridge, Mass.: National Bureau of Economic Research.

Lakonishok, J., A. Schleifer, and R. W. Vishny. 1991b. Window dressing by pension fund managers. *American Economic Review Papers and Proceedings*, 81, 227–31.

Lakonishok, J., A. Schleifer, and R. W. Vishny. 1992a. The structure and performance of the money management industry. *Brookings Papers: Microeconomics* 1992, 339–91.

Lakonishok, J., A. Schleifer, and R. W. Vishny. 1992b. The impact of institutional trading on stock prices. *Journal of Financial Economics*, 32, 23–43.

Lakonishok, J., A. Schleifer, and R. W. Vishny. 1993a. Contrarian investment, extrapolation and risk. *Journal of Finance*, 49, 1541–78.

Lakonishok, J., A. Schleifer, and R. W. Vishny. 1993b. Institutional trades and intraday stock price volatility. *Journal of Financial Economics*, 33, 173–99.

LaPlante, M., and C. J. Muscarella. 1997. Do institutions receive comparable execution in the NYSE and Nasdaq markets? A transaction study of block trades. *Journal of Financial Economics*, 45, 97–134.

La Porta, R., F. Lopez-Silanes, and A. Schleifer. 1999. Corporate ownership around the world. *Journal of Finance*, 54, 471–517.

Lee, C. 1993. Market integration and price execution for NYSE-listed securities. *Journal of Finance*, 48, 1009–38.

Lee, P. 1994. Overdue for intensive care. *Euromoney*, 1994 (February), 40–46.

Leibowitz, M. L., and S. Kogelman. 1991. Asset allocation under shortfall constraints. *Journal of Portfolio Management*, Winter, 18–23.

Leinweber, D. 1995. Using information from trading in trading and portfolio management. *Journal of Investing*, 4(1), 40–50.

Leroy, S. F., and R. D. Porter. 1981. The present value relation, tests based on implied variance bounds. *Econometrica*, 49, 555–74.

Levine, R., and S. Zervos. 1996. Policy, stock market development and long run growth. *World Bank Economic Review*, 10, 323–39.

Levis, M. 1989. Stock market anomalies; a reassessment based on U.K. data. *Journal of Banking and Finance*, 13, 675–96.

Loeb, T. F. 1983. Trading cost, the critical link between investment information and results. *Financial Analysts Journal*, 39 (May/June), 39–44.

Lohse, D. 1996. Trading firms make markets in fewer issues. *Wall Street Journal*, 14 October, C1.

McCarthy, D. D., and J. A. Turner. 1989. Pension rates of return in large and small plans. In *Trends in Pensions*, ed. J. Turner and D. J. Beller. Washington, D.C.: U.S. Department of Labor.

McCauley, R. N., and W. R. White. 1997. *The euro and European financial markets.* Working Paper No. 41. Basle: Bank for International Settlements.

McConnell, J. J., and C. J. Muscarella. 1985. Corporate capital expenditure decisions and the market value of the firm. *Journal of Financial Economics*, 14, 399–422.

Macey, J., and M. O'Hara. 1996. *The law and economics of best execution.* Working paper. Ithaca, N.Y.: Johnson Graduate School of Management, Cornell University.

Mack, P. R. 1993. Recent developments in the mutual fund industry. *Federal Reserve Bulletin*, November, 1001–12.

Madhavan, A., M. Richardson, and M. Roomans. 1997. Why do security prices fluctuate? A transaction-level analysis of NYSE stocks. *Review of Financial Studies*, 10(4), 1035–64.

Makin, C. 1993. When I'm 64. *Institutional Investor*, October, 52–59.

Malkiel, B. G. 1990. *A random walk down Wall Street.* New York: Norton.

Malkiel, B. G. 1995. Returns from investing in equity mutual funds, 1971 to 1991. *Journal of Finance*, 50, 549–72.

Marsh, P. 1990. *Short-termism on trial.* London: Institutional Fund Managers Association.

Martinson, J. 1998. The ABC of management performance, according to P and D. *Financial Times*, December.

Masson, P., T. Bayoumi, and H. Samiei. 1995. *International evidence on the determinants of private saving.* Working Paper No. W95/51. Washington, D.C.: International Monetary Fund.

Masson, P., and R. W. Tryon. 1990. Macroeconomic effects of projected population aging in industrial countries. *IMF Staff Papers*, 37, 453–85.

Mayer, C. 1996. *Corporate governance, competition and performance.* Economics Department Working Paper No. 164. Paris: Organization for Economic Cooperation and Development.

Mehra, R., and E. C. Prescott. 1985. The equity premium: A puzzle. *Journal of Monetary Economics*, 15, 145–61.

Melamed, L. 1977. The mechanics of a commodity futures exchange: A critique of automation of the transaction process. *Hofstra Law Review*, 6(1), 149–72.

Mercer, W. 1996. *European pension fund managers guide 1996.* London: William M. Mercer.

Mercer, W. 1999. *European pension fund managers guide 1999*. London: William M. Mercer.

Mercer, W. 2000. *European pension fund managers guide 2000*. London: William M. Mercer.

Merrill Lynch. 1997. *Social security—The need for reform*. Corporate and public policy report. New York: Merrill Lynch Co.

Merton, R. C., and Z. Bodie. 1995. A conceptual framework for analyzing the financial environment. In *The global financial system, a functional perspective*, ed. D. B. Crane et al. Cambridge, Mass.: Harvard Business School Press.

Miles, D. 1993. *Testing for short termism in the UK stock market*. Economic Journal, 103, 1379–96.

Miles, D. 1996. *Demographics and saving: Can we reconcile the evidence?* Mimeo. London: Imperial College.

Miles, D., and B. Patel. 1996. *Saving and wealth accumulation in Europe, the outlook into the next century*. New York: Merrill Lynch, Financial Research.

Mitchell, O. S. 1999. *New trends in pension benefit and retirement provisions*. Working Paper No. 7381. Cambridge, Mass.: National Bureau of Economic Research.

Mitchell, O. S., and P. L. Hsin. 1994. *Public pension governance and performance*. Working Paper No. 4632. Cambridge, Mass.: National Bureau of Economic Research.

Monks, R. A. 1997. Corporate governance and pension plans. In *Positioning pensions for the twenty-first century*, ed. M. S. Gordon, O. S. Mitchell, and M. M. Twinney. Philadelphia: Pension Research Council, University of Pennsylvania Press.

Moon, J. J., L. R. Pizante, R. K. Strauss, and J. M. Tukman. 1998. *Asset management in the 21st century, new rules, new game*. New York: Investment Management Industry Group, Goldman Sachs.

Morandé, F. G. 1998. Savings in Chile: What went right? *Journal of Development Economics*, 57, 201–28.

Morck, R., A. Schleifer, and R. Vishny. 1988. Management ownership and market valuation: An empirical analysis. *Journal of Financial Economics*, 20, 293–315.

Morling, S., and R. Subbaraman. 1995. *Superannuation and saving*. Research Discussion Paper No. RDP 9511. Sydney, Australia: Reserve Bank of Australia.

Moszkowski, G., and G. Gutierrez. 1999. *Trading up: The equity markets and the new world of electronic trading*. New York: Salomon Smith Barney US Equity Research.

Munnell, A. H. 1986. Private pensions and saving: New evidence. *Journal of Political Economy*, 84, 1013–31.

Myers, S., and N. Majluf. 1984. Corporation financing and investment when firms have information that investors do not have. *Journal of Financial Economics*, 12, 187–221.

Myners, P. 2000. *The Myners review of institutional investment for HM Treasury*. London: H.M. Treasury.

Nakamae, N. 1999. Recession takes toll of life insurers. *Financial Times*, 10 June.

Nakamae, N., and A. Harney. 1999. Japanese pension chiefs peer into a bottomless pit. *Financial Times*, 16 July.

Neumann, M. 1986. *Moeglichkeiten zur Entlastung der gesetzlichen Rentenversicherung durch kapitalbildende Vorsorgemassnahmen.* Univ. Tuebingen.

Nickell, S., and S. Wadhwani. 1987. *Myopia, the dividend puzzle and share prices.* Working Paper No. 272. LSE Centre for Labour Economics, London School of Economics, London.

O'Barr, W. M., and J. M. Conley. 1992. *Fortune and folly: The wealth and power of institutional investing.* Homewood, Ill.: Irwin.

O'Hara, M. 1995. *Market microstructure theory.* Cambridge, U.K.: Blackwell.

OECD. 1991. *Systemic risks in securities markets.* Paris: Organization for Economic Cooperation and Development.

OECD. 1993. *Policy issues in insurance.* Paris: Organization for Economic Cooperation and Development.

OECD. 1995. Corporate governance in Italy. In *OECD survey of Italy 1995.* Paris: Organization for Economic Cooperation and Development.

OECD. 1996. *Policy issues in insurance—Investment, taxation and insolvency.* Paris: Organization for Economic Cooperation and Development.

OECD. 1997. *Institutional investors statistical yearbook.* Paris: Organization for Economic Cooperation and Development.

OECD. 1998. *Bank profitability, financial statements of banks 1998.* Paris: Organization for Economic Cooperation and Development.

Olsen, R. A. 1996. Implications of herding behavior for earnings estimation, risk assessment and stock returns. *Financial Analysts Journal*, July/August, 37–41.

Pagano, M., and A. Roell. 1990. Trading systems in European stock exchanges: Current performance and policy options. *Economic Policy*, 10(1), 65–115.

Pagano, M., and B. Steil. 1996. Equity trading I: The evolution of European trading systems. In *The European equity markets: The state of the union and an agenda for the millennium*, ed. B. Steil. London: European Capital Markets Institute and the Royal Institute of International Affairs.

Peel, M. 1999. Mega caps win a big vote of confidence. *Financial Times*, 6 July.

Pensions and Investments. 1997. *Japan dumps fund investment restrictions.* April 14, 1997.

Pensions and Investments. 1998. Special report: Money managers. *Pensions and Investments*, 18 May, 23–114.

Perold, A. F. 1988. The implementation shortfall: Paper versus reality. *Journal of Portfolio Management*, 14, 4–9.

Perold, A. F., and R. S. Salomon. 1991. The right amount of assets under management. *Financial Analysts Journal*, 47 (May/June), 31–39.

Perold, A. F., and E. Sirri. 1993. *The cost of international equity trading.* Working paper. Cambridge, Mass.: Harvard University.

Pesando, J. E. 1992. The economic effects of private pensions. In *Private pensions and public policy*. Paris: Organization for Economic Cooperation and Development.

Peskin, M. W. 1997. Asset allocation and funding policy for corporate sponsored defined benefit pension funds. *Journal of Portfolio Management*, Winter, 66–73.

Petersen, M. A., and D. Fialkowski. 1994. Posted versus effective spreads: Good prices or bad quotes? *Journal of Financial Economics*, 35(3), 269–92.

Petersen, M. A., and R. G. Rajan. 1994. The benefits of lending relationships: evidence from small business data. *Journal of Finance*, 49, 3–38.

Pfaff, M., R. Huler, and R. Dennerlein. 1979. Old age security and saving in the Federal Republic of Germany. In *Social security and private saving*, ed. G. M. von Furstemburg. Cambridge, Mass.: Ballinger.

Phillips, B. 1997. Why bigger isn't (necessarily) better. *Institutional Investor*, October, 105–112.

Pirrong, S. C. 1996. Market liquidity and depth on computerized and open-outcry trading systems: A comparison of DTB and LIFFE bund contracts. *Journal of Futures Markets*, 16(3), 519–43.

Plexus Group. 1998. *The official icebergs of transaction costs*. Commentary No. 54. Los Angeles: Plexus Group.

Poterba, J. M., and L. H. Summers. 1992. *Time horizons of American firms: New evidence from a survey of CEOs*. Cambridge, Mass.: Harvard Business School.

Poterba, J. M., S. F. Venti, and D. A. Wise. 1993. *Do 401(K) contributions crowd out other personal saving?* Working Paper No. 4391. Cambridge, Mass.: National Bureau of Economic Research.

Poterba, J. M., S. F. Venti, and D. A. Wise. 1996. *Personal retirement saving programmes and asset accumulation: Reconciling the evidence*. NBER Working Paper No. 5599.

Pozen, R. C. 1998. *The mutual fund business*. Cambridge, Mass.: MIT Press.

Pragma Consulting. 1999. *Rebuilding pensions, security, efficiency, affordability: Recommendations for a European code of best practice for European second pillar pension funds*. Brussels: European Commission.

Rajan, A. 2000. *Fund management: New skills for a new age*. London: Fund Managers' Association.

Ramanlal, P., K. Hargis, and C. G. McDonald. 1997. When do markets consolidate? An analysis of market maker incentives and market characteristics. Working Paper. Columbia: University of South Carolina, Finance Department.

Rappaport, A. M. 1992. Comment on pensions and labour market activity. In *Pensions and the economy*, ed. Z. Bodie and A. H. Munnell. Philadelphia: Pensions Research Council and University of Pennsylvania Press.

Reserve Bank of Australia. 1991. The deregulation of financial intermediaries. *Proceedings of a conference, 20–21 June 1991*. Sydney, Australia: Reserve Bank of Australia.

Revell, J., ed. 1997. *The recent evolution of financial systems*. London: Macmillan.

Riley, B. 2000. Specialist managers look across Atlantic. *Financial Times*, 26 April.

Ritter, J. 1991. The long term performance of IPOs. *Journal of Finance*, 46, 3–27.

Robinson, G. 1998a. SFE in push to go fully electronic. *Financial Times*, 6 April, 25.

Robinson, G. 1998b. Screen test looms. *Financial Times*, 17 July, 6.

Roe, M. J. 1992. Mutual funds in the boardroom. In *Studies in international corporate finance and governance systems: A comparison of the US, Japan and Europe*, ed. D. H. Chew. Oxford, England: Oxford University Press.

Roll, R. 1984a. Orange juice and weather. *American Economic Review*, 861–80.

Roll, R. 1984b. A simple implicit measure of the effective bid-ask spread. *Journal of Finance*, 39, 1127–39.

Roll, R. 1986. The hubris theory of corporate takeovers. *Journal of Business*, 59, 197–216.

Roll, R. 1997. Chapter 5. In *Handbook of equity style analysis*, ed. D. Coggin and F. Fabozzi. New Hope, Pa.: Frank J. Fabozzi Associates.

Rose, P. S. 1994. *Money and capital markets*. Burr Ridge, Ill.: Irwin.

Roseveare, D., W. Leibfritz, D. Fore, and E. Wurzel. 1996. *Aging populations, pension systems and government budgets: simulation for 20 OECD countries*. Economics Department Working Paper No. 168. Paris: Organization for Economic Cooperation and Development.

Rossi, N., and I. Visco. 1995. *National savings and social security in Italy*. Temi di Discussione del Servizio Studi, Rome: Banca d'Italia.

Rybczynski, T. 1995. The development of European capital markets: the main trends and their implications. In *The changing face of European banks and securities markets*, ed. J. Revell. London: Macmillan.

Rybczynski, T. 1997. A new look at the evolution of the financial system. In *The recent evolution of financial systems*, ed. J. Revell. London: Macmillan.

Rydén, B. 1995. *The reform of the Stockholm Stock Exchange*. Stockholm, Sweden: Stockholm Stock Exchange, November.

Sandmann, G., and A. F. Vila. 1996. *Stochastic volatility, error correction, and dual listing in futures markets*. Working Paper. London: London School of Economics, Financial Markets Group.

Sanford, C. S. 1993. *Financial markets in 2020*. Federal Reserve Bank of Kansas City Symposium, August.

Scharfstein, D. S., and J. C. Stein. 1990. Herd behavior and investment. *American Economic Review*, 80, 465–79.

Schleifer, A., and R. W. Vishny. 1990. Equilibrium short term horizons of investors and firms. *American Economic Review*, 80, 148–53.

Schleifer, A., and R. W. Vishny. 1997. A survey of corporate governance. *Journal of Finance*, 52, 737–83.

Schmidt, H., and P. Iversen. 1992. Automating Germany equity trading: Bid-ask spreads on competing systems. *Journal of Financial Services Research*, 6(4), 373–97.

Schulz, B. 1993. Mit britischen Aktionären leben. *Frankfurter Allgemeine Zeitung*, 12 April.

Schwartz, R. A., and B. Steil. 1996. Equity trading III: Institutional investor trading practices and preferences. In *The European equity markets: The state of the Union and an agenda for the millennium*, ed. B. Steil. London: European Capital Markets Institute and the Royal Institute of International Affairs.

Schwartz, R. A., and B. Steil. 2000. Institutional portfolio management and order handling: Results of an international survey of CIOs and head equity traders. Working Paper. New York: Council on Foreign Relations.

SEC. 1963. *Special study of securities markets: Report of the special study of the SEC.* Washington, D.C.: U.S. Securities and Exchange Commission.

SEC. 1996. *Order execution obligations.* Release 34-37619A. Washington, D.C.: U.S. Securities and Exchange Commission.

Securities Industry Association. 1999. *1999 Securities Industry Fact Book.* New York: Securities Industry Association.

Sellon, G. H. 1992. Changes in financial intermediation: The role of pension and mutual funds. *Federal Reserve Bank of Kansas City Economic Review*, Third Quarter, 53–70.

Shah, A., and S. Thomas. 1996. *How competition and automation have changed the Bombay Stock Exchange.* Technical Report. Bombay: Centre for Monitoring the Indian Economy.

Sharpe, W. 1995. *The styles and performance of large seasoned US mutual funds.* Working Paper. Stanford, Calif.: Stanford University Business School.

Shiller, R. J. 1990. *Market volatility.* Cambridge, Mass.: MIT Press.

Shiller, R. J. 2000. *Irrational exuberance.* Princeton, N.J.: Princeton University Press.

Shiller, R. J., and J. Pound. 1989. Survey evidence of diffusion of interest and information among institutional investors. *Journal of Economic Behavior and Organization*, 12, 47–66.

Shyy, G. M., and J. H. Lee. 1995. Price transmission and information in bund futures markets: LIFFE vs. DTB. *Journal of Futures Markets*, 15(1), 87–99.

Sias, R. W. 1996. Volatility and the institutional investor. *Financial Analysts Journal*, March/April, 13–20.

Simon, B. 1993. Investors revolt in sleepy Canada. *Financial Times*, 18 May.

Singh, A. 1995. *Corporate financing patterns in industrializing countries: A comparative international study.* Technical Paper 2, April. Washington, D.C.: World Bank.

Sirri, E. R., and P. Tufano. 1992. *The demand for mutual fund services by individual investors.* Working Paper. Cambridge, Mass.: Harvard University.

Sirri, E. R., and P. Tufano. 1995. The economics of pooling. In *The global financial system: A functional perspective*, ed. D. B. Crane et al. Cambridge, Mass.: Harvard Business School Press.

Sirri, E. R., and P. Tufano. 1998. Costly search and mutual fund flows. *Journal of Finance*, 53, 1589–1622.

Slovin, M. B., M. E. Sushka, and J. A. Polonchek. 1993. The value of bank durability: Borrowers as stakeholders. *Journal of Finance*, 48, 247–66.

Smith, C. 1998. Great expectations. *Institutional Investor*, June, 68–76.

Smith, M. P. 1996. Shareholder activism by institutional investors: Evidence from CALPERS. *Journal of Finance*, 51, 227–52.

Smith, R. S. 1990. Factors affecting saving, policy tools and tax reform. *IMF Staff Papers*, 37, 1–70.

Smyth, K. 1994. The coming investor revolt. *Fortune*, 13, 66–76.

Solnik, B. H. 1988. *International investments*. Reading, Mass.: Addison-Wesley.

Solnik, B. 1998. Global asset management. *Journal of Portfolio Management*, Summer, 43–51.

Solnik, B., C. Boucrelle, and Y. Le Fur. 1996. International market correlation and volatility. *Financial Analysts Journal*, 52(5), 17–35.

Steil, B., ed. 1994. *International Financial Market Regulation*. Chichester, England: John Wiley.

Steil, B. 1996. Equity trading IV: The ISD and the regulation of European market structure. In *The European equity markets: The state of the union and an agenda for the millenium*, ed. B. Steil. London: European Capital Markets Institute and Royal Institute of International Affairs.

Steil, B. 1998. *Regional financial market integration: Learning from the European experience*. Special Paper Series. London: Royal Institute of International Affairs.

Stiglitz, J. E. 1993. *Financial systems for Eastern Europe's emerging economies*. San Francisco: ICS Press.

Stigum, M. 1990. The money market. Homewood, Ill.: Dow-Jones Irwin.

Stoll, H. 1995. The importance of equity trading costs: Evidence from securities firms' revenues. In *Global equity markets: Technological, competitive, and regulatory challenges*, ed. R. A. Schwartz. Chicago: Irwin Professional Publishing.

Strickland, D., K. W. Wiles, and M. Zenner. 1996. A requiem for the USA, is small shareholder monitoring effective? *Journal of Financial Economics*, 40, 319–38.

Tam, P.-W. 1998. Supermarkets worry fund firms. *Wall Street Journal Europe*, 28 December.

Tamura, M. 1992. Improving Japan's employee pension fund system. *Noruma Research Institute Quarterly*, Summer 1992, 66–83.

Targett, S. 1999. Unilever pension fund sues MAM. *Financial Times*, 8 October.

Targett, S. 2000. Pension industry faces closer scrutiny. *Financial Times*, 3 July.

Targett, S., and E. Wine. 2000. Loss of balance, *Financial Times*, 21 January.

Tett, G. 1999. Unwinding of corporate Japan surges. *Financial Times*, 2 July.

Timmins, N. 1999. Risking a scandal. *Financial Times*, 12 July 1999.

Tirole, J. 1989. *The theory of industrial organization*. Cambridge, Mass.: MIT Press.

Treynor, J. 1981. What does it take to win the trading game? *Financial Analysts Journal*, January/February, 37, 55–65.

Treynor, J., and F. Black. 1973. How to use security analysis to improve portfolio selection. *Journal of Business*, 46, 66–86.

Trzcinka, C. 1997. *Institutional investing*. Paris: Organization for Economic Cooperation and Development.

Trzcinka, C. 1998. The conflicting views and management practices of institutional equity investing. *Financial Markets, Institutions and Instruments*, 7, 20–53.

Trzcinka, C., and R. Shukla. 1992. *Performance studies*. New York University Salomon Brothers Center Series. New York: New York University.

Trzcinka, C., and R. Zweig. 1990. *An economic analysis of the costs and benefits of SEC rule 12b-1*. Monograph Series in Finance and Economics 1990-1. New York: Salomon Brothers Center for the Study of Financial Institutions.

Van Loo, P. D. 1988. *Portfolio management of Dutch Pension Funds*. Reprint 197. De Nederlandsche Bank.

Venti, S. F., and D. E. Wise. 1994. RRSPs and savings in Canada. Paper presented at a conference "Public Policies That Affect Private Saving," 19 May, OECD, Paris.

Vila, A. F., and G. Sandmann. 1996. *Floor trading versus electronic screen trading: An empirical analysis of market liquidity in the Nikkei Stock Index futures markets*. Working Paper. London: Financial Markets Group, London School of Economics.

Wagner, W. H., and M. Edwards. 1993. Best execution. *Financial Analysts Journal*, 49(1), 65–71.

Wagner, W. H., and S. Glass. 1998. The dynamics of trading and directed brokerage. *Journal of Pension Plan Investing*, 2(3), 53–72.

Wahal, S. 1994. *Public pension fund activism and firm performance*. Working Paper. Chapel Hill, N.C.: University of North Carolina.

Wahal, S. 1996. Public pension fund activism and firm performance. *Journal of Financial and Quantitative Analysis*, 31, 1–23.

Walkling, R., and M. Long. 1984. Agency theory, managerial welfare and takeover bid resistance. *Rand Journal of Economics*, 15, 54–68.

Walter, I. 1999. The asset management industry in Europe: competitive structure and performance under EMU. In *European capital markets with a single currency*, ed. J. Dermine and P. Hillion. Oxford: Oxford University Press.

Warther, V. A. 1995. Aggregate mutual fund flows and security returns. *Journal of Financial Economics*, 39, 209–35.

Watson Wyatt. 1997. *Benefits Report Europe USA Canada 1997*. Brussels: Watson Wyatt Data Services Europe.

Wermers, R. 1999. Mutual fund herding and the impact on stock prices. *Journal of Finance*, 54, 581–622.

White, W. 1998. The coming transformation of Continental European banking? BIS Working Paper No. 54.

WM. 1995. *WM UK pension fund service annual review, 1995.* Edinburgh, Scotland: The WM Company.

WM. 1999a. *WM UK pension fund annual review, 1998.* Edinburgh, Scotland: The WM Company.

WM. 1999b. Internal managers take the laurels. *Investment and Pensions Europe,* October, 61–4.

WM. 2000. *1999 UK pension fund industry results.* Edinburgh, Scotland: The WM Company.

Wohlever, J. 1993. Excess capacity in the mutual fund industry. In *Studies on excess capacity in the financial sector.* New York: Federal Reserve Bank of New York.

Wojnilower, A. M. 1997. Business cycles in a financially deregulated America. Paper presented at the International Economic Association conference "Monetary theory as a basis for monetary policy," 4–7 September, Trento, Italy.

World Bank. 1992. *Financial deregulation, changing the rules of the game.* EDI Development Studies. Washington, D.C.: International Bank for Reconstruction and Development.

World Bank. 1993. *The East Asian miracle; economic growth and public policies.* Oxford: Oxford University Press.

World Bank. 1994. *Averting the old age crisis.* Washington, D.C.: International Bank for Reconstruction and Development.

World Bank. 1996. *World demographic statistics.* Washington, D.C.: IBRD.

Wrighton, J. 1998. Big, bigger, biggest, Euro 100 asset management. *Institutional Investor,* November, 63–78.

Wrighton, J. 1999. America's largest overseas investors. *Institutional Investor,* July, 85–6.

Wyatt. 1993. *1993 Benefits report Europe USA.* Brussels: The Wyatt Company.

Zheng, L. 1999. Is money smart? A study of mutual fund investors' fund selection ability. *Journal of Finance,* 54, 901–33.

Zingales, L. 1995. What determines the value of corporate votes? *Quarterly Journal of Economics,* 110, 1075–1110.

Name Index

Subject Index